REVIEW OF RESEARCH IN EDUCATION

Review of Research in Education is published annually on behalf of the American Educational Research Association, 1430 K St., NW, Suite 1200, Washington, DC 20005, by SAGE Publications, 2455 Teller Road, Thousand Oaks, CA 91320. Send address changes to AERA Membership Department, 1430 K St., NW, Suite 1200, Washington, DC 20005.

Member Information: American Educational Research Association (AERA) member inquiries, member renewal requests, changes of address, and membership subscription inquiries should be addressed to the AERA Membership Department, 1430 K St., NW, Suite 1200, Washington, DC 20005; fax 202-238-3250; e-mail: members@aera.net. AERA annual membership dues are $150 (Regular and Affiliate Members), $110 (International Affiliates), and $40 (Graduate and Undergraduate Student Affiliates). **Claims:** Claims for undelivered copies must be made no later than six months following month of publication. Beyond six months and at the request of the American Educational Research Association, the publisher will supply missing copies when losses have been sustained in transit and when the reserve stock permits.

Subscription Information: All non-member subscription inquiries, orders, back-issue requests, claims, and renewals should be addressed to SAGE Publications, 2455 Teller Road, Thousand Oaks, CA 91320; telephone (800) 818-SAGE (7243) and (805) 499-0721; fax: (805) 375-1700; e-mail: journals@sagepub.com; http://www.sagepublications.com. **Subscription Price:** Institutions: $291; Individuals: $60. For all customers outside the Americas, please visit http://www.sagepub.co.uk/customercare.nav for information. **Claims:** Claims for undelivered copies must be made no later than six months following month of publication. The publisher will supply missing copies when losses have been sustained in transit and when the reserve stock will permit.

Abstracting and Indexing: Please visit http://rre.aera.net and, under the "More about this journal" menu on the right-hand side, click on the Abstracting/Indexing link to view a full list of databases in which this journal is indexed.

Copyright Permission: Permission requests to photocopy or otherwise reproduce copyrighted material owned by the American Educational Research Association should be submitted by accessing the Copyright Clearance Center's Rightslink® service through the journal's website at http://rre.aera.net. Permission may also be requested by contacting the Copyright Clearance Center via its website at http://www.copyright.com, or via e-mail at info@copyright.com.

Advertising and Reprints: Current advertising rates and specifications may be obtained by contacting the advertising coordinator in the Thousand Oaks office at (805) 410-7763 or by sending an e-mail to advertising@sagepub.com. To order reprints, please e-mail reprint@sagepub.com. Acceptance of advertising in this journal in no way implies endorsement of the advertised product or service by SAGE or the journal's affiliated society(ies). No endorsement is intended or implied. SAGE reserves the right to reject any advertising it deems as inappropriate for this journal.

Change of Address: Six weeks' advance notice must be given when notifying of change of address. Please send old address label along with the new address to ensure proper identification. Please specify name of journal.

International Standard Serial Number ISSN 0091-732X
International Standard Book Number ISBN 978-1-4522-79169 (Vol. 37, 2013, paper)
Manufactured in the United States of America. First printing, March 2013.

Printed on acid-free paper

REVIEW OF RESEARCH IN EDUCATION

Extraordinary Pedagogies
for Working Within
School Settings Serving
Nondominant Students

Volume 37, 2013

Christian Faltis, Editor
Jamal Abedi, Editor
University of California, Davis

AMERICAN
EDUCATIONAL
RESEARCH
ASSOCIATION

Ⓢ SAGE

Review of Research in Education

Extraordinary Pedagogies for Working Within School Settings Serving Nondominant Students

Volume 37

EDITORS

CHRISTIAN FALTIS
University of California, Davis

JAMAL ABEDI
University of California, Davis

AMERICAN EDUCATIONAL RESEARCH ASSOCIATION

Tel: 202-238-3200 Fax: 202-238-3250
http://www.aera.net/pubs

FELICE J. LEVINE
Executive Director

JOHN NEIKIRK
Director of Publications

Contents

Cover image © Digital Vision/Thinkstock

Introduction

Extraordinary Pedagogies for Working Within School Settings Serving Nondominant Students

CHRISTIAN FALTIS
JAMAL ABEDI
University of California, Davis

There are pedagogies used in schools that are extraordinary, in the sense that they intentionally go beyond the ordinary understandings and practices many children and youth experience as individuals in schools on a daily basis, to guide them toward the pursuit of social justice, agency as learners, and constructive action. However, audiences may not have read or learned about these pedagogies unless they appeared in journals as a separate item or a collection of articles in a themed volume. For the past several volumes, *Review of Research in Education* has focused on issues of equity, youth culture, and democracy. In this volume, we continue this pattern to center on extraordinary pedagogies in school settings serving nondominant students. Our intention is to share with you through these reviews some of the exceptional pedagogies that teachers and educators have developed in recent years to address the needs of nondominant students and families served by public schools and institutions of higher learning.

EXTRAORDINARY PEDAGOGIES

Extraordinary pedagogies are not about "best practices" or what might be the most effective method for teaching to the students' learning needs. In this volume, extraordinary pedagogies encompass larger sociocultural issues, bringing attention to how poverty, race, social class, and language interact with local practices in teaching and learning, and in the everyday lives of families, educators, children, and youth. Extraordinary pedagogies examine alternative ways of engaging families and communities; they encourage teachers to become aware of themselves as practitioners and human beings who are mediated by their own sociocultural experiences; they expand

Review of Research in Education
March 2013, Vol. 37, pp. vii-xi
DOI: 10.3102/0091732X12462989
© 2013 AERA. http://rre.aera.net

understandings of narrative inquiry and arts-based learning for posing questions and agency in learning; they draw on the abilities and practices that children and youth of color bring to school; and they point to practices for future generations of children and youth for whom ordinary teaching and learning practices have neither sufficed nor helped in countering the widespread inequities in schooling.

Extraordinary pedagogies begin with the proposition that schools and educators must learn and do more than the ordinary. A prominent theme emerging from these chapters is that teachers and teacher educators must take greater responsibility for understanding the historical, societal complexities that come into play each and every school day. In this volume, the core of all of the extraordinary pedagogies presented seeks to humanize educational practices through the examination of issues of racism, classism, agency, sexism, poverty, community, and language. Finally, this volume provides a vast review of pedagogical practices and frameworks for addressing the needs of diverse children and youth in school.

OVERVIEW OF THE VOLUME

The 10 chapters in this volume speak to the extraordinary pedagogies teachers and educators have found to be noteworthy for working with nondominant students. Whereas many of the authors in the volume review quantitative studies that show significant impact on students' engagement and achievement, others look to qualitative studies as evidence for pedagogies that make a difference in the lives and schooling of nondominant children and youth.

The volume begins with a thorough examination of poverty and schooling. In the United States of America, more than 15 million children live in poverty, and nearly all of these children attend public schools throughout their childhood. Milner offers an extensive review of how poverty has been conceptualized—not an easy task—and using a critical race theory lens, argues that educators who take responsibility for the elimination of inequity in schools—from school funding and resources (libraries, committed teachers, classroom materials, well-kept buildings) to hiring practices—and who continue to learn about culturally relevant pedagogy can go a long way in reducing the impact that poverty has on schooling.

The next chapter by Howard turns attention to Black male youth, perhaps the most academically and socially marginalized group in U.S. schools and universities. Howard acknowledges early in his chapter that Black male identity is complex and diverse, but throughout the literature he reviewed, Black males are unabashedly essentialized as being "at risk" and largely "uneducable." Owing to this deficit portrayal, Howard argues for a multipronged paradigm shift in how Black male youth are viewed and understood in teacher education and local classrooms alike, a shift that includes an array of counternarratives and counterpractices, starting with dispelling myths about Black males and stereotypes about Black males, and ranging from addressing microtransgressions to rethinking content curriculum to make it culturally relevant.

Many readers are likely familiar with the Funds of Knowledge framework developed in the early 1990s; however, little is known about the discourse(s) of Funds of Knowledge concerning the power and agency of teachers and students embedded within and/or emerging from the enactment of Funds of Knowledge. In this chapter, Rodríguez argues that Funds of Knowledge pedagogies need to be clarified and extended by theoretical dialogue with other "anti-cultural-deficit" frameworks, lest they become another way of teaching poor Latino/a children in ways that pay little more than superficial attention to the cultural wealth that children and youth bring to school. Rodríguez presents a strong case, based on her review, for the Community Cultural Wealth framework rooted in Critical Race Theory and Chicana/o Studies as a site of power and agency for teachers and students who wish to address the power imbalances that can result when teachers and students are not involved in the co-construction of knowledge that emerges from using students' Funds of Knowledge.

A recurring theme throughout this volume is that extraordinary pedagogies for working within school settings that serve nondominant students must be humanizing, that is, they must pay attention to communities, families, and youth served by school. In her chapter, Salazar lays out foundational principles and practices for humanizing pedagogy. Drawing on Freire's work, among others, Salazar shows how humanizing pedagogy respects and draws from students' histories, realities, and perspectives not only to validate students' interests and experiences but also to develop critical consciousness in teachers and students alike toward issues of power, privilege, and social injustice in school and society.

The chapter by Baquedano-López, Alexander, and Hernández presents a critical review of parental engagement. The review points to new efforts by teacher educators and teachers to rethink parental engagement by examining the roles of race, class, and immigration in how schools ordinarily conceptualize parents and families of children of color. The authors present a decolonial approach to parental engagement as a way to challenge current thinking about modernity and development and the "crisis of education" at the heart of deficit-based parental involvement models. This decolonial approach calls into question the practices that perpetuate the exclusion of family and community knowledge in the promotion of local and home culture in school activities and parental engagement practices.

Harper reviews the literature on Black students in predominately White institutions of higher education to examine peer pedagogical practices Black students use productively to manage the racist environments they are sure to encounter during their time on campus. Drawing on both historical and current research on this topic, Harper shifts attention to peer pedagogy, specifically how Black peers, along with other minoritized students, teach one another about how to address racism on campus and seek out faculty mentors who help them navigate the racial climates of university settings. This chapter points to new areas of research for gaining insights into how Black students successfully navigate to and through colleges and universities despite the persistence of racist practices and deficit thinking levied toward Black and other minoritized students.

Narrative inquiry is about "thinking narratively" to shape an assortment of stories in which teachers, children, and members of the community tell about what matters most in the classrooms, schools, and universities. Huber, Caine, Huber, and Steeves make a strong case for narrative inquiry as a counternarrative to the prescriptive, transmission-oriented brand of schooling, which seeks to silence the narratives of school, students, and families. Through an extensive review of the literature on narrative inquiry, these authors tell us about the power of personal and community narratives for the development of counternarratives to reclaim the local spaces in which narrators live and experience life in schools. They found that transforming schools from ordinary, therefore, requires at least telling a different story based on the narratives and stories of teachers, students, and members of the community who envision a more socially just place called school.

The chapter by Chappell and Cahnmann-Taylor showcases arts-based scholarship and pedagogy that strives to humanize education by engaging in sustained, local, and critical practices in school and communities. The literature they review supports the inclusion of the arts in and out of schools to expand critical awareness of an increasingly diverse world; to challenge stereotypes, misconceptions, and ignorance; and to promote collaboration among teachers, students, and members of the communities served in schools. They argue forcefully that school, community, and public arts-based activities are a valuable way for disrupting the deficit scripts and for promoting more socially aware and socially just citizens.

Palmer and Martínez discuss teacher agency and the preparation of teachers of emergent bilingual students, especially of Latino/a students, the nation's largest bilingual population. In their review of the literature, Palmer and Martínez acknowledge that although much of what goes on in schools is geared to high-stakes standardized assessment preparation, they find evidence for many potential spaces to promote bilingualism and language development. Their review found that entering these spaces requires a fundamental rethinking of traditional notions of what bilingualism means in communities and schools, of how language positioning works, and of what it means to invest in language practices. Finally, the literature review led them to conclude that teachers and teacher educators need to think beyond language to examine the broader questions of race, poverty, and class to make truly transformative changes in how language-as-a-local-practice happens in schools.

In the final chapter, Bunch reviews the literature on the practices that "mainstream" teachers and teacher educators have been taught to use with English learners and then presents a strong argument for the development of *pedagogical language knowledge* that all teachers need to have and be able to use to engage and support English learners. Bunch reviews an assortment of new approaches to understanding language as a social practice, that build teachers' understandings of language as action, doing and using language in academic contexts for interacting, interpreting, and showing understanding within the content areas.

Overall, the narrative these chapters suggest is that extraordinary pedagogies are not only possible but also necessary to interrupt and challenge the current educational establishment that has attempted to refocus attention on learning outcomes, without taking into accounts the larger issues of race, class, poverty, and language. In this volume, our goal has been to provide readers with an array of efforts that open up possibilities for transforming schooling to make schooling experiences better for all children, regardless of their ethnic, class, and language backgrounds. Doing so, we argue, requires extraordinary pedagogies.

ACKNOWLEDGMENTS

First, we would like to thank the authors for their thoughtful work and insights into what are highly complex issues facing education. We want to thank the consulting editors for their time, efforts, and valuable advice. Thank you to all of the outside reviewers who provided comments and feedback to authors. We extend a special acknowledgement to Kelsey Krausen, our editorial assistant, who kept everyone on track and communicated so gracefully with authors, consulting editors, and reviewers. We wish to thank Todd Reitzel, Felice Levine, and Alana Schwartz of the AERA Publications Committee for their guidance throughout the process. Lastly, we want to acknowledge Sara Sarver, our Project Editor at SAGE publications. Sara is a gem in the publishing world.

Chapter 1

Analyzing Poverty, Learning, and Teaching Through a Critical Race Theory Lens

H. RICHARD MILNER IV

Peabody College of Vanderbilt University

I n this chapter, I explore poverty as an outside-of-school factor and its influence on the inside-of-school experiences and outcome of students. I consider the interconnected space of learning, instructional practices, and poverty. In particular, I use critical race theory as an analytic tool to unpack, shed light on, problematize, disrupt, and analyze how systems of oppression, marginalization, racism, inequity, hegemony, and discrimination are pervasively present and ingrained in the fabric of policies, practices, institutions, and systems in education that have important bearings on students—all students—even though most of the studies reviewed did not address race in this way. I analyze the interrelationship between race and poverty. My point in using race as an analytic site is not to suggest that people are in poverty because of their race but to demonstrate how race can be a salient factor in how people experience and inhabit the world and consequently education. My point is that we (those of us in education and who care about it) should work to eradicate poverty for all students, not just students of color. However, we need to understand and question why a disproportionate number of students of color live in poverty and are from lower socioeconomic backgrounds. We should not ignore this reality: Proportionally, more people/students of color live in poverty than do White people. Why? Carefully examine Table 1.

Adapted from Munin (2012) and Simms, Fortuny, and Henderson (2009), Table 1 demonstrates the disproportionate representation of White, Black, and Hispanic (Brown) low-income families in the United States. In Munin's (2012) words,

In an equitable society, if Whites constitute 65% of the total population, they should also make up 65% of those in the low-income bracket. But this group is actually 23.6 percentage points lower in

Review of Research in Education
March 2013, Vol. 37, pp. 1-53
DOI: 10.3102/0091732X12459720
© 2013 AERA. http://rre.aera.net

1

TABLE 1
Low-Income Families by Race

Race	Percentage of Low-Income Families	Percentage of U.S. Population
White	42	65.6
Black	22	12.2
Hispanic/Brown	30	15.4
Total percentage for Black and Brown	52	27.6

Source. Adapted from Munin (2012) and Simms, Fortuny, and Henderson (2009).

representation in the low-income family category. Conversely, Blacks make up a larger percentage than their overall size in the low-income population by 9.8 percentage points. The same is true for Hispanics, who constitute a greater share of the low-income group compared to their population size by 14.6 percentage points. (pp. 4–5)

But a consistent question throughout this review is: Why? In this sense, studies need to carefully examine, beyond descriptive statistics, the causes, relationships, and reasons so many more children/students of color live in poverty. In the last column of Table 1, I calculate the total percentage of low-income families of color (Black and Brown) in relationship to their population proportion.

Inside of school, there are pedagogical approaches that have important implications for students living in poverty—instructional practices that are responsive to the complex needs of them (Gay, 2010; Howard, 2010; Ladson-Billings, 2009; Moll & Gonzalez, 2004; Nieto, 2000). In the final sections, because this literature focuses more broadly on practices that meet needs of diverse backgrounds of students than solely poverty, I consider instructional practices and learning opportunities that converge on the idea that students should be educated in a way that helps them understand what poverty is, why it exists, and, perhaps most important, how people can speak out against and transcend it. I will review the literature on some of what we know about the intersected space of poverty, learning, and teaching and highlight effective instructional practices that seem to address this intersection because there is not one pedagogical approach that has shown to be exclusively useful for success of students living in poverty. In this sense, I consider how poverty as an outside-of-school variable influences learning and related educational experiences inside of school.

In the pages of many journals, books, monographs, and reports, authors are attempting to measure, explain, describe, and understand disparities that exist between European American (White) students and their African American (Black), Hispanic, and Latino American (Brown) counterparts (Barton & Coley, 2010; Chubb & Loveless, 2002; Jencks & Phillips, 1998; Jenkins, 2006; Pino & Smith, 2004; Rothstein, 2004). Moreover, studies continue examining policies and experiences of students whose

FIGURE 1
2000 and 2010—Annual Salary

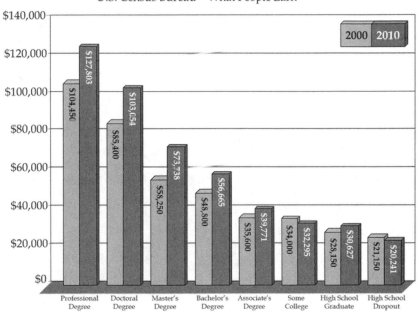

U.S. Census Bureau • What People Earn

	2000	2010
Professional Degree	$104,450	$127,803
Doctoral Degree	$85,400	$103,054
Master's Degree	$58,250	$73,738
Bachelor's Degree	$48,800	$56,665
Associate's Degree	$35,600	$39,771
Some College	$34,000	$32,295
High School Graduate	$28,150	$30,627
High School Dropout	$21,150	$20,241

Source. Adapted from U.S. Census Bureau (2012).

first language is not English (Iddings, Combs, & Moll, 2012; Irizarry & Donaldson, 2012), and students living in poverty—the focus of this review. Poverty is a serious social problem in the United States[1] that has a profound influence on students' experiences in schools. Noguera and Wells (2011) explained that a fundamental reason schools (educational experiences for students) have not improved substantially in the United States is because "federal education policy has not adequately addressed the ways in which poverty and inequality influence student learning and school performance" (p. 11). Many other researchers agree that educational and federal policy is failing to address and ultimately transform schools that do not meet the needs of all students, especially those living in poverty (Anyon, 2005; Darling-Hammond, 2010; Lareau, 2003; C. M. Payne, 2008; Tate, 2008).

Policy is not the only site of criticism and concern in explaining the troubling interconnectedness of poverty, students' experiences in schools, and student performance (often framed as student achievement and outcomes).[2] For instance, parents' educational level and family income appear to be strong outside-of-school predictors of student achievement in schools (Henslin, 2004; Kozol, 1991). Figures 1 and 2 demonstrate the relationship between educational attainment level and earnings, both annually and over a career span.

FIGURE 2
2000 and 2010—Career Salary

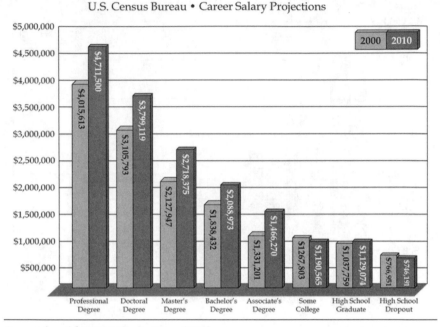

U.S. Census Bureau • Career Salary Projections

Source. Adapted from U.S. Census Bureau (2012).

Educational attainment level matters in terms of the amount of money most people earn and consequently their ability to acquire material possessions. The home and quite frankly school district parents are able to afford for their children, because property taxes fund school systems across the United States, can be correlated with the buyers' (parents) educational level. Resources can be limited in high poverty schools and so might student experiences. Figures 1 and 2 demonstrate variance of earning between those with high and low levels of education. As will be demonstrated throughout this chapter, experiences of students and their families living in poverty outside of school as well as the resources and material conditions afforded to them inside of school may affect students' potential for higher levels of education. In this sense, there are cycles and generations of people living in poverty that the educational system may not be eliminating or at best helping to reduce (Anyon, 1980; Kozol, 1991).

Coleman (1969, 1988) reported that schools played relatively little influence on the achievement of students and consequently students' life chances. He found outside-of-school factors such as poverty as extraordinarily central determinants of student success. Caldas and Bankston (1997) argued that Coleman's research, however, generally "treated inequities in outcome as results of the family resources that individual students bring to school" (p. 270). Caldas and Bankston's research attempted to measure the extent to which in-school variables such as peer pressure shaped students' behavior. Their conclusions countered Coleman's findings in some important ways. They argued for the "importance of taking characteristics of school populations, as well as individual school characteristics, into consideration as significant influences on individual academic achievement" (p. 274).

As a collective body of research mostly aimed at demonstrating and to a lesser degree explaining why some students living in poverty are not as successful in schools as those not living in poverty,[3] research on poverty and education can be framed through three spheres of study, theorizing, and analyses:

- Research focused on out-of-school factors such as unemployment, family income, parental styles, parental educational level, geography, and resources in the home such as the number of books available to children
- Research focused on in-school factors such as instructional practices, resources and the lack thereof in school, administrative practices, school culture, and the nature of relationships between teachers and students as well as between teachers and parents/family members
- Research focused on the effects of out-of-school factors on outcomes and experiences in school

I analyze these bodies of literature through a critical race theory (CRT) analysis, namely, providing raced questions that might assist us in thinking about what is missing from the studies I review. What race-centered questions are missing in the studies/ literature reviewed, and how might critically centering these questions complement, disrupt, and/or change the narratives present in the literature about the intersection of poverty, learning, and teaching to advance the field?

While the first two spheres of inquiry, explained above, are compellingly important, they seem to operate in disjointed and sometimes competing ways (Caldas & Bankston, 1997; Coleman, 1969; Noguera & Wells, 2011). Debates about which sphere matters more, out-of-school or in-school, have not allowed much progress in terms of building effective policies and related practices that bridge both. Although research in the out-of-school line of research is persuasive, relying solely on outside-of-school variables and how they affect what happens to students inside of school can make it difficult to empower practitioners, especially teachers, to believe that they can indeed make a real difference for all students, including those living in poverty. Practitioners may ponder over the following question: How do I meet the needs of students living in poverty in my classroom or school when they have so many challenges at home/outside the classroom? The point here is not that outside-of-school factors are not essential elements to consider; they are important. As I reviewed the masses of literature focused on outside-of-school factors, I kept returning to a root, fundamental and what will become a permeating question throughout this review: But what about the role of schools—specifically counselors and administrators and especially teachers—in being responsive to the outside-of-school realities that influence students who live in poverty? In the final sections of this chapter, my goal is to examine the literature on classroom instructional practice—an inside-of-school factor that takes outside-of-school variables into account.

Evidence has revealed that teachers and teaching can be the most powerful *inside-of-school* predictors of success for students (Barton, 2003; Gay, 2010; Howard, 2010; Ladson-Billings, 2009). To illuminate, Barton (2003) found that curriculum rigor, which is intricately and inextricably connected to teacher expectation, was the strongest inside-of-school predictor of student academic achievement. In short, the literature reviewed provides compelling evidence that both inside-of-school and outside-of-school variables are essential sites of analysis in considering the interrelated nature of poverty, learning, and teaching.

Framing questions of this review are the following: In what ways does poverty influence and intersect with teaching and learning opportunities in schools? How can instructional practices be used to respond to the material conditions of those living in poverty? Proportionately, why are there so many more students of color living in poverty than White students? And what questions related to race are not explored in the research literature that could assist the field in making sense of complex problems in education and beyond, particularly for populations of color? Answers to these questions are not absolute or simple, but I explore them.

Defining Poverty

It is difficult to definitively define what is meant by poverty, and most of the studies I reviewed did not provide clear definitions of or explanations for how they were using it.[4] Cass (2010), in the report titled *Held Captive: Child Poverty in America*, reminded us that "15.5 million children are living in poverty in America— the highest child poverty rate the nation has seen since 1959. And the younger the children are the poorer they are" (p. 3). Although numerous studies demonstrate relationships between poverty and other variables, qualitatively, it is less clear just what it is. Poverty has been found to have lasting effects on peoples' social, economic, and psychological well-being (Pritchard, 1993), and studies of poverty and socioeconomic status (SES) have been linked to school size (Coldarci, 2006), trust (Goddard, Salloum, & Berebitsky, 2009), students' and teachers' sense of community (Battistitch, Solomon, Dong-il, Watson, & Schaps, 1995), classroom and school technology use and integration (Page, 2002), growth trajectories in literacy among English language learners (Kieffer, 2008), public high school outcomes and college attendance rates (Toutkoushian & Curtis, 2005), the ability of young children (ages 5–8) to self-regulate (Howse, Lange, Farran, & Boyles, 2003), and course selection and enrollment in rigorous mathematics (Klopfenstein, 2005).

TABLE 2
2009 Poverty Guidelines for the United States

Persons in Family	Poverty Guidelines, 48 Contiguous	Poverty Guidelines, Alaska	Poverty Guidelines, Hawaii
1	$10,830	$13,530	$12,460
2	$14,570	$18,210	$16,760
3	$18,310	$22,890	$21,060
4	$22,050	$27,570	$25,360
5	$25,790	$32,250	$29,660
6	$29,530	$36,930	$33,960
7	$33,270	$41,610	$38,260
8	$37,010	$46,290	$42,560
For each additional person, add	$3,740	$4,680	$3,740

Source. Federal Register, Vol. 74, No. 14, January 23, 2009, pp. 4199–4201.

TABLE 3
2011 Poverty Guidelines for the United States

Persons in Family	48 Contiguous States and D.C.	Alaska	Hawaii
1	$10,890	$13,600	$12,540
2	$14,710	$18,380	$16,930
3	$18,530	$23,160	$21,320
4	$22,350	$27,940	$25,710
5	$26,170	$32,720	$30,100
6	$29,990	$37,500	$34,490
7	$33,810	$42,280	$38,880
8	$37,630	$47,060	$43,270
For each additional person, add	$3,820	$4,780	$4,390

Source. Federal Register, Vol. 76, No. 13, January 20, 2011, pp. 3637–3638.

Drawing from the U.S. Bureau of the Census (2005), Burney and Beilke (2008) explained that "a family is considered to be poor if its income for a particular year is below the amount deemed necessary to support a family of a certain size" (p. 297). Consider data from 2009 and 2011, respectively, which outline the poverty levels for families and individuals according to the federal government (Tables 2 and 3).[5]

I attempt to demonstrate from these two data points that the poverty line is increasing as defined and classified by the federal government while the economy

TABLE 4
Families Below Poverty Line by Race

Race/Ethnicity	Percentage Below Poverty Line
White	9.4
Black	23.7
Hispanic/Brown	22.3
Asian	10.2
Total Percentage for Black, Brown, and Asian	56.2

Source. Adapted from Munin (2012) and DeNavas-Walt, Proctor, and Smith (2009).

seemed to be worsening. For instance, excluding Hawaii and Alaska, in 2009, a family of four earning less than $25,360 was considered below the poverty line, whereas in 2011 a family of four earning less than $25,710 was considered below it. The increase in light of the significant economic downturn over the course of the 2-year period was $350, although more families struggled with their finances and in spite of inflation. The federal government's classification has significant implications for the kinds of resources available to families such as welfare support, subsidized housing—including section VIII—health care assistance, as well as Head Start opportunities for young children.

Munin (2012), building from DeNavas-Walt, Proctor, and Smith (2009), provided a contemporary picture of families living below the poverty line by race. Table 4 demonstrates that White families represented about 9.4% of those living in poverty, whereas Black and Hispanic families represented 23.7% and 22.3% respectively. Munin shared an important point of clarification of the data in Table 4:

Families of color are much more likely to live in poverty and thereby have less access to societal benefits granted to the economically privileged. However, it is important to point out that this [race and poverty] is not a perfect correlation. Not all people of color are poor, nor are all White people rich. It is very difficult to live in poverty, regardless of one's race. (p. 7)

Tables 2 to 4 provide some quantitative perspective about poverty; however, poverty in many ways is socially constructed because there is diversity in people's experiences living in poverty—below the poverty line. In this way and from a philosophical perspective, I am suggesting that poverty is not an absolute term but a relative one that depends on a wide range of factors beyond the poverty line; this point will be expanded on throughout.

Perhaps the most disturbing reality of living in poverty is the limitations of what low income and related resources allow people to do. For instance, it can be difficult for those in poverty to gain access to high-quality health care, to eat healthily especially fruits and vegetables that may be too expensive or that those living in poverty may have a difficult time acquiring due to the fact that they live in food deserts (often in rural spaces), or gain access and experience to high-quality, effective schools. Thus, it is difficult to concretely define poverty because of the range of people's experiences living in it. Accordingly, studies reviewed in this chapter employed different definitions in their investigations. Students receiving free and reduced lunch were most often used as a marker and identification of poverty, social class, or socioeconomic status in studies on poverty. Thinking seriously about what it means to live and for the purposes of this review learn without necessary resources for success is at the root of this discussion. It matters more, from my perspective, that we think about the causes, outcomes, and consequences for people living in poverty than to settle on a universal definition due to the relative nature of it. For instance, not all students fail because they live in poverty, and some live meaningful and productive lives (McGee & Spencer, 2012), although a popular perspective is that those living in poverty are inferior and need to be understood in order to save or fix them (R. Payne, 1996). On the one hand, it is necessary to allow researchers to construct definitions that appropriately match the social context, idiosyncrasies, and nuances of their particular studies. On the other hand, this inconsistency in the definitional work associated with poverty makes it difficult to build the research literature in the area because of different perspectives researchers use in studying and conceptualizing it. So poverty can be defined (a) based on the federal government's formula of the poverty line, (b) based on free and reduced lunch formulas that vary from state to state, or (c) based on particular characteristics and situations people find themselves in because of the amount of monetary and related material capital that they have or do not have.

REVIEW METHOD

Initially, the databases were searched for peer-reviewed journal articles over the last 10 years (2001–2011) using the following keywords, either individually or in some combination: Poverty, Education, Teaching, Learning, and/or Social Class.[6] I decided to review this 10-year time span because I was much more interested in constructing a thematic review where I determined how various research studies converged and diverged recently than constructing an historical review that would have required that I review several decades of literature. Indeed, the amount of literature over decades on this topic is vast, and it would be difficult with page limitations to thoroughly conduct such an historical review. As I reviewed the articles, I looked for patterns as they emerged across, between, and among them. I focused on micro-level findings and insights as well as macro-level ones to determine themes across the studies. These themes are presented in later sections of this chapter.

Several databases were searched to this end: InfoTrack, Wilson Web, Google Scholar, and Eric. Although my target timeframe for the review was initially limited to 10 years, as I synthesized the literature, I noted the articles and what I came to think about as germinal readings, including books and policy briefs, related to poverty, education, teaching, and learning that many of the articles in my targeted review referenced. These germinal readings also became central to my review and rather than rely on these readings as secondary sources, I read those documents and included them as well to support and help build the established themes. For instance, although Oscar Lewis's (1961, 1966) work was published well before 2001, a discussion of poverty without overt attention to his influence would be incomplete. There were also many important research and conceptual articles that I included before 2001. Again, these readings seemed especially important to include in the review when (a) a theme emerged in the 10-year span but was underdeveloped because there were few studies (in a few cases there was one study) during that period and additional research/literature was needed or when (b) authors in the 10-year span continued to draw from particular readings, pieces of literature prior to 2001, to construct their analyses. In such cases, these documents were reviewed and also included. I also included some literature outside of education on the topic to provide perspective outside of the field and to develop the themes that emerged from the 10-year time frame.

Also, in general, the goal of the review was to synthesize empirically based articles although many conceptual and some commentary articles were included—especially when they shed light on, countered, or expanded on themes that emerged from the empirical papers. The original review yielded a total of 48 articles, with the expanded review resulting in approximately 79 manuscripts, books, and reports analyzed. Additional citations that appear in the reference list are included to help elucidate and substantiate the analytic tools from CRT made throughout this synthesis.[7]

Critical Race Theory Perspectives

My analysis of the literature concerning students living in poverty and their educational experiences draws from CRT to help elucidate the intersected nature of race and poverty. However, my goal is to maintain the integrity of the studies reviewed and simultaneously critique what is available through the posing of race-related questions. In their study of high-poverty urban schools, Slaughter-Defoe and Carlson (1996) explained that

it is important to search for the main effects of race and culture in any study within a society that is as stratified as that of the United States. . . . However, not only are they [race and culture] important to society generally, they are also important to education. (p. 69)

This theoretical body of literature allows me to explain, critique, counter, and analyze what I have read and to perhaps provide a lens for readers to think through, critique, and further expand what we know (theoretically, conceptually, and empirically) and how we know it (ontologically and epistemologically).

From my view, it is difficult and perhaps ineffectual to synthesize the research literature regarding poverty without drawing some explicit connections to race although most studies do not make such connections. Understanding the links between and among race, social class, and/or poverty (Arnold & Doctoroff, 2003; Ladson-Billings, 2006; Lareau, 2003; Ullucci, 2012) is essential because many believe that race is insignificant and they ignore it—especially during a period in history when the United

States has elected an African American president.[8] Practitioners, policymakers, teachers, principals, counselors, theoreticians, researchers, and citizens, writ large, still struggle to understand how race matters in society and consequently in education. Although a large body of research and conceptual arguments is clear that race matters in education and outside of it[9] (Allen, in press; Alridge, 2003; Beachum & McCray, 2011; Boutte, 2012; Carter Andrews, 2009; Gooden, 2012; Kirkland, 2011; Leonardo, 2009; Lynn, 2006; Sealey-Ruiz, 2011; Terrill & Mark, 2000; Tillman, 2002; Toshalis, 2011; Vasquez Heilig, Brown, & Brown, in press; White-Smith, 2012), some deliberately avoid it because they rationalize that issues of disparity and disproportionality in educational outcomes, for instance, are consequences solely of SES rather than race. However, as Ladson-Billings and Tate (1995) explained,

Although both class and gender can and do intersect race, as stand-alone variables they do not explain all of the educational achievement differences apparent between Whites and students of color. Indeed, there is some evidence to suggest that even when we hold constant for class, middle-class African-American students do not achieve at the same level as their White counterparts. (p. 51)

Cooper, Crosnoe, Suizzo, and Pituch (2009), drawing from the 2007 U.S. Census Bureau, wrote, "Although poverty cuts across racial lines, the likelihood of growing up in an impoverished family is much higher for racial-minority children than for White children" (p. 861). Although multiple layers of discourse related to disparities, inequities, and realities in education are racialized, I have learned that many White teachers' discourses in public schools, in particular, demonstrate that they struggle to see the link between poverty and *race* (Milner, 2008, 2010). Teachers I have studied who teach students of color and students living in poverty tended to feel much more comfortable talking about or thinking about poverty or social class than race, and many seemed to struggle to see the relationship between the two. Ironically, strong racial messages and implications are pervasive in many of the challenges we face in education related to outcomes in education such as patterns in special education (Artiles, Klingner, & Tate, 2006; Blanchett, 2006; Noguera, 2003; O'Connor & Fernandez, 2006), under-representation of students in gifted education (Ford, 2010), and office referral rates and patterns of students to the office for misbehavior who are subsequently suspended and expelled (Davis & Jordan, 1994; Skiba, Michael, Nardo, & Peterson, 2002). Yet practicing teachers may ignore or at best minimize race, racism, and discrimination as explanatory rationales for these patterns (Milner, 2010). In their minds and discourses, poverty/social class trumps race as well as the intersecting nature of them. Still, in a policy brief titled *The Color of Poverty: Why Racial and Ethnic Disparities Persist*, Lin and Harris (2009) posed two provocative questions. They wrote, "Given substantial progress in civil rights and anti-discrimination policies—as well as the increased ethnic diversity of the nation—why is poverty still so colored? Why have racial differences in poverty persisted for so long?" (p. 1).

Critical race theorists perceive issues of race and racism as permanent and endemic to the very fabric of the United States, and they begin with the premise that race matters and should thus be investigated and theorized about (Brown-Jeffey & Cooper, 2011; Horsford, 2010; Hughes & Berry, 2012; James, 2012; Jay, 2003; Ladson-Billing & Tate, 1995; Martin, 2009; Parker & Lynn, 2002). In this sense, issues of race are everywhere, and race will continue to be an area of importance in society and consequently education—even in mostly White social contexts or when discussions concern a majority of White people. Developed and conceptualized mostly by scholars of color, CRT emerged from law as a response to critical legal studies and civil rights scholarship. Critical race theorists are concerned with disrupting, exposing, challenging, and changing racist policies that work to subordinate and disenfranchise certain groups of people and that attempt to maintain the status quo (Tate, 1997).

Derrick A. Bell laid the foundation for CRT in two law review articles: "Serving Two Masters: Integration Ideals and Client Interests in School Desegregation Litigation" (1976) and "Brown v. Board of Education and the Interest-Convergence Dilemma" (1980). Tate, Ladson-Billings, & Grant (1993) cited scholarship associated with CRT in their analysis of the history of school desegregation law and related implementation. In an article published in *Urban Education,* Tate (1994) referenced CRT as a school of thought associated with critiquing stock racial narratives while interjecting voice scholarship as a means to build theory and inform practice in the law. Tate argued that this was a sound strategy for education scholarship as he reflected on his educational experiences in a successful urban Catholic school. Ladson-Billings and Tate (1995) advanced CRT as a theoretical project in education research in a *Teachers College Record* publication. They argued that although studies and conceptual discussions examining race existed in the field of education, the field needed further explanatory tools to assist in empirical and conceptual arguments related to race.

Ladson-Billings and Tate (1995) argued that race was undertheorized, not understudied, in education and that although studies existed in the field of education that examined race, the field suffered from a lack of conceptual and analytic tools to discuss race, operationalize it, and move the field forward. Indeed, scholars in education have recognized the promise and utility of CRT in education, and their work has made meaningful contributions to what is known about race in education (Chapman, 2007; Dixson & Rousseau, 2005; Duncan, 2005; Parker & Lynn, 2002; Tate, 1997). Several tenets and ideas frame the work of critical race theorists in education. For instance, Howard (2008) outlined four frames that shape the work of critical race theorists in education. They

(1) . . . theoriz[e] about race along with other forms of subordination and the intersectionality of racism, classism, sexism, and other forms of oppression in school curriculum; (2) . . . challeng[e] dominant ideologies that call for objectivity and neutrality in educational research . . . (3) . . . offer . . . counterstorying as a liberatory and credible methodological tool in examining racial oppression; (4) . . . incorporate[e] transdisciplinary knowledge from women's studies and ethnic studies to better understand various manifestations of discrimination. (pp. 963–964)

In particular, the narrative and counternarrative have been successfully employed as analytic tenets to help make sense of race. Solorzano and Yosso (2001) maintained that CRT "challenges the dominant discourse on race and racism as it relates to education by examining how educational theory and practice are used to subordinate certain racial and ethnic groups" (p. 2). In this way, the questions I pose throughout this analysis are used to provide a more complicated perspective to the storylines available in the discourse about poverty and education. The remainder of this chapter is organized around several themes that emerged from my review. In the next section, I discuss outside-of-school influences of poverty on education.

Outside-of-School Influences of Poverty on Education

Unfortunate outside-of-school realities can be common among students living in poverty that influence their experiences and outcomes inside of school. Students living in poverty may have experienced the following:

- They have suffered physical, psychological, and/or emotional abuse.
- Their family members and sometimes students themselves suffer from harmful addictions such as drug abuse, gambling, or alcoholism.
- They experience health and nutrition problems. Health problems include high rates of "asthma, ear infections, stomach problems, and speech problems" (Duffield, 2001, p. 326). And their eating patterns may be sporadic, not eating well-balanced meals or missing meals altogether.
- They attend school fewer days than other children, are transient, arrive at school late, and have difficulty concentrating on learning and interacting with classmates.
- They (and their families) are more likely than those not living in poverty to be homeless.

From a sociological perspective, B. A. Lee, Tyler, and Wright (2010) found that "homeless children suffer from their parents' poverty, as evidenced by more frequent school mobility, absenteeism, and grade retention; lower achievement test scores; and a greater risk of learning disabilities, behavioral disorders, and related problems" (p. 505).

Student and Family Homelessness

Student and family home structures, particularly homelessness, have been shown to influence students' experiences and outcomes in schools, and student voices can help us understand how they navigate multiple environments as homeless youth (Farrugia, 2011). Duffield (2001) examined the effects of homelessness on students' school attendance, enrollment, and academic success. She described homelessness as "the manifestation of severe poverty and lack of affordable housing; simply put, homeless families are too poor to afford housing" (p. 324). Students become homeless either as individuals or with their families, and homelessness can result from "family problems, economic problems, and residential instability" (p. 325). From an ecological perspective, Nooe and Patterson (2010) conceptualized homelessness in the following way:

Homeless individuals may experience changes in housing status that includes being on the street, shared dwelling, emergency shelter, transitional housing, and permanent . . . hospitalization and incarceration in correctional facilities. (p. 105)

Similar to conceptions of poverty, homelessness is not well defined and categorized both in the literature and in society. Finley and Diversi (2010) stressed this problem and the fuzziness of how homelessness is defined, especially from policymakers' perspectives because homelessness is seen as a much smaller epidemic than it actually is and consequently resources to assist individuals can be limited. They expressed that the numbers have been distorted, leading people into believing the fallacy that the homelessness situation is not as bad as it seems. In their words,

Let us be clear here. Such distortion has profound consequences for actual lives. For instance, families forced into couch surfing with relatives and friends are most often not counted. . . . Nor are the families living in tent cities, vehicles, and parks around the country. As a result, thousands of lives and stories are buried under an ideologically self-serving sensation that things aren't as bad as some claim. Or if the housing crisis is as bad as it seems, it is due solely to irresponsible individual choices. (p. 7)

Finley and Diversi (2010) provided a collection of textual representations of homelessness from different vantage points across the United States. The researchers' goal was to assemble real-life images to contribute to scholarly and public perspectives about the human condition and to provide words and photographic images that are often ignored. Moreover, their point was to extend and problematize scholarly and public discourse that would suggest that homeless people are living in poverty because they have somehow failed as individuals, which may take the pressure and attention away from policies and practices that have not helped much.

Mawhinney-Rhoads and Stahler (2006) observed that

homeless children are particularly at risk for poor educational outcomes, which can have lifelong consequences for their future livelihood and economic independence. If school systems do not provide special educational interventions to address the particular educational barriers that these children face, then it is likely that these children will stay marginalized in the lowest economic rung of society. (p. 289)

In their study, they identified several educational barriers that homeless students experience in schools that should be addressed through policy and practice. One barrier identified was residency—challenges that homeless students and their families face because schools require proof of residency. In essence, Mawhinney-Rhoads and Stahler (2006) found that when students are homeless without a permanent residency or address (or perhaps when they are living out of a car) "the issue of residency can block some students from attending certain schools or maintaining their status in their current school" (p. 291). A second barrier identified by the researchers was what they called "guardianship" (p. 292). The main issue as discussed by these researchers was that "homeless children often reside with a family member who is not a legal guardian" (p. 292) and consequently these children may be denied access to school or be put through turmoil. Another barrier identified for homeless children and their families was the lack of medical records, as students may not have these documents when requested. Students and their families who are transient often lose these types of documents, and this can result in difficulty for their families. Transportation was another issue identified. The authors explained that "because homeless families are so often transient, a homeless child attending school and residing in a temporary shelter within a given school district might move 30 days later to another shelter outside the district boundaries" (p. 292). Such moves can make it complicated to get to school on time or to attend school at all. If the family does not have access to a car or public transportation, homeless students have an added burden to their educational experiences. A final barrier identified was socioemotional challenges where homeless students tend to have difficult times interacting with peers and their teachers. The students may have low self-esteem and may find it difficult to get along with others because they are worried about their home situations or perhaps because they are suffering from lack of sleep or rest. Mawhinney-Rhoads and Stahler (2006) concluded that school reform policies for homeless students need to be responsive and tailored to meet the evolving needs of the students they serve.

It is important to note there are homeless students who "beat the odds," persevere, and succeed in spite of the conditions outlined above. Moreover, there are students who have a roof over their heads but because they are not on the streets, these students and their families do not classify themselves as homeless (Mawhinney-Rhoads & Stahler, 2006). The story of homeless students should not end with the idea that they only experience turmoil because some of them, whether they classify themselves as homeless or not, succeed in the midst of challenging situations. My point in sharing these examples is not to generalize across the population of homeless students but to provide a snapshot of some consequences and realities of those living in poverty.

CRT would ask how race has affected the lives and experiences of homeless children and their families to gauge if policies, for instance, have helped or hindered progress among particular groups of students. Moreover, what are the racial demographic patterns of homeless children and youth? And perhaps most importantly how might racial discrimination and other forms of oppression and marginalization perpetuate homelessness? Mawhinney-Rhoads and Stahler (2006) found that "today, a significant proportion of the homeless population is comprised of minority, single-mother households with multiple children" (p. 290). In particular, these authors surmised that there was an overrepresentation of homeless Black people, representing about 40% of the homeless population, with children being the fastest growing sector in the United States.

Geography and Social Contexts Matter

In addition to homelessness, the locations where students and their families live seem to influence their experiences in education. Because of structural and systemic inequities (Anyon, 2005; Haberman, 1991; Kozol, 1991, 2005; MacLeod, 1995;

Milner, 2010) and what Tate (2008) advanced as geography of opportunity, the topographical landscape can shape where businesses, transportation, housing, and related resources are strategically located. Students and their families are forced to take particular jobs that can be limited by where they live. From a CRT perspective, are Black and Brown people more concentrated in areas where public transportation is scarce, for instance? Moreover, in what other ways can the environment of students and their families contribute to their overall experiences?

Munin (2012) explained how environmental conditions can negatively affect children. He explained that children of color and those living in poverty are much more likely to be exposed to hazardous environmental conditions that can have an influence on their health and consequently their performance in schools:

Families live amid air and water pollution, waste disposal sites, airports, smokestacks, lead paint, car emissions, and countless other environmental hazards. . . . However, exposure to these toxins is not shared equally among our population. Studies show that these environmental conditions disproportionately affect people of color and the poor. (p. 29)

The conditions described above have shown to increase asthma among children, cause mothers to deliver babies prematurely and with low birth weights, increase children's diagnosis with attention deficit hyperactivity disorder, and increase student absenteeism (Munin, 2012). Thus, the outside-of-school location—where children live—and the environmental conditions around them can have a profound impact on students and their families. Most of these environmental situations extend far beyond the control of students and their families.

From a social work developmental perspective, Fram, Miller-Cribbs, and Horn (2007) found it important for social workers to study and address links between poverty, SES, and achievement, particularly in the southern region of the United States (also, see Morris & Monroe, 2009). Similar to Tate (2008), much of the conceptualization of their study emphasized the importance of understanding geography of opportunity. Exceptions to the salience of race, though, exist, especially in the south. Beginning in 1998, in their study from the first two years of the Early Childhood Longitudinal Study of 3,501 kindergarteners, Fram et al. (2007, p. 317) found that "although race looms large in southern understandings of daily life . . . family structure, maternal attributes, peers' skill levels, and rural and nonrural location" were the most salient factors in explaining variation in students' achievement in their particular study.

In addition, the contexts of students living in poverty range from rural to urban. Cass (2010) found that poverty can be more pronounced in rural areas, whereas others see poverty most common in urban environments. In both rural and urban spaces, students living in poverty can experience several disheartening realities: housing instability; hunger; health and nutrition problems; school instability; physical, emotional, and psychological abuse due to stress; family instability; and, perhaps most important for the purposes of this review, inadequate schools and educational

FIGURE 3
Rural Poverty Housing

Source. Photo adapted from H. Richard Milner's (in progress) research project, Studying Places of Poverty.

FIGURE 4
Rural Poverty Housing

Source. Photo adapted from H. Richard Milner's (in progress) research project, Studying Places of Poverty.

experiences. Consider the photos that demonstrate two different types of housing in both rural and urban environments (Figures 3, 4, and 5).

FIGURE 5
City Poverty Housing

Source. Photo adapted from H. Richard Milner's (in progress) research project, Studying Places of Poverty.

The photos in Figures 3 and 4 are homes in the rural south that families actually occupy. Both homes are located on dirt roads and the nearest major supermarket is 10 to 15 miles away. There are no public transportation options in the rural town and very few jobs are available in the town. Citizens typically drive (carpool when possible) 20 to 30 miles to another town for work. The closest Wal-Mart to the rural town is approximately 35 miles away. The nearest hospital is about 25 miles away. Those in the rural community typically rent homes with a reasonable amount of property/land around the home. Neighbors are typically at least 20 to 25 feet away from each other. Although families live below the poverty line, some of them own their homes and the accompanying land because it was passed down to them from family members. Property taxes, though, can be challenging for those who own their houses. The value of the land and homes, though, is extremely low due to the lack of infrastructure, business, and related amenities that attract people and corporations to areas.

Whereas people living in rural poverty tend to have land around them without neighbors too close, those living in city poverty, or those living in large urban, metropolitan areas may reside in apartment-style homes, typically known as housing projects, which may be supported through governmental Section VIII programs, governmental housing (Figure 5). Although those living in rural poverty typically do not experience high levels of crime, for instance, those in the city experience higher rates of it. Those in urban cities also benefit from public transportation and other conveniences that large cities have to offer. In short, while both rural and urban families live in poverty, their experiences (benefits and challenges) can be quite different. Schools in both rural and urban areas have their challenges. With poverty being the constant thread, consider the following challenges that are perhaps consequences of outside-of-school difficulties that schools in both rural and urban contexts experience.

I have adapted many of these examples from Barton's (2003) policy analysis, *Parsing the Achievement Gap: Baseline for Tracking Progress:*

- There is a disproportionate number of new educators in high-poverty schools; students whose teachers have 5 years of experience or more make 3 to 4 months more progress in reading during a school year.
- Teachers are absent from school more often in high-poverty schools in comparison with schools in other locations; as a result, students are taught by substitute teachers, many of whom are not trained in subject matter domains or teaching.
- There is often a lack of commitment and persistence among educators in high-poverty schools. Educators graduate from college/teacher education programs and work in high-poverty schools until another position becomes available in a "more desirable" location.
- There is a disproportionate number of educators teaching outside their field of expertise in high-poverty schools.

In essence, the different geography of those living in poverty results in similarities and differences, depending on the particulars inherent to the location.

Policy and School Funding

At the heart of what seems to be necessary to reform and improve schools with high representation of students living in poverty (both rural and urban) is the need to increase funding and resources. However, researchers have found that increasing funding, without explicit links to how programs, policies, and practices should be altered or transformed, can be unsuccessful in high-poverty schools (Bracey, 1997; Noguera & Wells, 2011; Nyhan & Alkadry, 1999). In their analysis, Noguera and Wells (2011) concluded that several millions of dollars in funds to support schools had virtually done very little to transform and affect the achievement of students in high-poverty schools. They cite opportunity and support grants as well as other financial supports from several donors and programs, including Annenberg, The Bill and Melinda Gates Foundation, and Title 1 as somewhat innocuous in making huge strides for children living in poverty. In their words,

> While it may be unfair to characterize the reform efforts . . . as a total failure, it is accurate to point out that the changes enacted as a result of the grants did not result in the large-scale improvement that was hoped for. It was especially clear that very little progress was made in the poorest communities where school failure was more pervasive. (p. 8)

Even though this and related arguments about the limitations of increased funding and resources provide a view into the complexity of the matter and provide insight into social stratification and the maintenance of the status quo, one might ask: What would the educational experiences for children living in poverty who benefited from the grants and other programs have been like without the increased support? In other words, some gains, as these authors point are, are better it seems than none at all from my perspective. From a CRT perspective, knowing which racial demographic of students benefitted most from the added resources and how the support correlated with attendance rates, test score gains, graduation rates, and other factors would be logical. Teams of researchers, it seems from this critique, need to be committed to thinking about how increased funding and support programs can facilitate the most effective, wide-ranging, scalable benefits for all students. Although poverty transcends race and is prevalent in communities of students across it, analyzing which populations of students received the added support and their levels of resulting performance could provide important information about how we address the overrepresentation and disproportionate representation of children of color living in poverty. Indeed, our goal should be to eliminate poverty for all racial groups, but from a CRT perspective, examining how resources were used, for whom, and the outcomes can advance the field and perhaps help elucidate why proportionately so many more children of color live in poverty.

In addition, there appears to be a misunderstanding of the relationship between equity and equality when analyzing school resource and fund allocation. Money and resources are unequal in different social contexts (Tate, 2008): Numbers of high-need districts where resources are low too often receive the same resources as districts with much greater resources. For instance, some districts distribute

equally funded programs into schools regardless of how many students need them. For example, a district might allocate $100,000 to each school with English-language learners, even though one school might have 200 students with limited English proficiency and another—often a more affluent school—might have only 20 [students]. (Roza, 2006, p. 11)

Secada (1989) pointed to a major difference between equality and equity. He wrote,

There is a history of using terms like equity and equality of education interchangeably. Though these constructs are related, equality is group-based and quantitative. Equity can be applied to groups or to individuals; it is qualitative in that equity is tied to notions of justice. (p. 23)

Equity, according to Secada (1989), is defined as judgments about whether or not a given state of affairs is just. For instance, equity in education may mean that we are attempting to provide students, regardless of their racial, ethnic, cultural, or SES background, with what they need to succeed—not necessarily the exact same goals and visions across different environments. Secada further explained:

The essence of equity lies in our ability to acknowledge that even though our actions are in accord with a set of rules, the results of those actions may still be unjust. Equity goes beyond following the rules . . . equity gauges the results of actions directly against standards of justice. (p. 23)

In this sense, equity and equality do not necessarily have the same meaning; what is necessary for success in one school or district or with one student may be quite different from the next.

Traditional conceptions of equality and equity may be easier to accomplish in educational policy and reform; it is not very complex to provide schools, districts, and states with the same funding, for example, across the board. However, it is quite complex and multifaceted to outline and carry out equality and equity in educational policies with heightened attention on matters of the particular and distinctive needs of students and families living in poverty.

Wiener and Pristoop (2006) wrote, "States need to take a greater share of education funding and target more money to the districts with the biggest challenges" (p. 9) and the greatest needs. Moreover, Roza (2006) declared that "if public schools systems are serious about closing achievement gaps, they must begin to allocate *more* [italics added] resources to the students with the greatest needs" (p. 12). Such positions—where policies allow for and allocate funds on a "need" basis, where they are responsive to schools and districts—may seem antithetical to the very essence of what equity or equality actually means or *should* mean. Critics of such an approach—where funding is distributed across states, districts, and schools with serious attention placed on the financial needs of students—suggest that it is inequitable, in fact, to provide certain communities and certain groups of students with more support than another. Critics may question: How is it equitable to provide one district with something different or more than what another receives? At the core of such a question is the equity and equality debate. From a CRT perspective, careful analyses are needed to determine funding patterns and resource reforms with communities of color. Studying these funding decisions and implementations can help us understand why, proportionately, more people of color live in poverty and perhaps provide yet another explanation for gaps in test scores.

Liu (2006) wrote that "wealthier, high-spending states receive a disproportionate share of Title I funds, thereby exacerbating the profound differences in education spending from state to state. Title I makes rich states richer and leaves poor states behind" (p. 2). In essence, there appears to be instances where richer states receive more funding than states with students from lower SES and poverty. To explain, Liu (2006) stressed that "high-spending states get more Title I money per poor child than low-spending states. The net effect is that Title I does not reduce, but rather reinforces, inequality among states" (p. 2). To illuminate,

Maryland, for example, had fewer poor children than Arkansas but received 51 percent more Title I aid per poor child. Massachusetts had fewer low-income children than Oklahoma but received more than twice as much Title I aid per poor child. Similarly, Minnesota had fewer poor children than New Mexico but received 27 percent more Title I aid per poor child. (Liu, 2006, p. 2)

And according to Liu (2006), wealthier states do not necessarily exert more energy in providing educational support but have "higher per-pupil spending and thus receive higher Title I aid per poor child" (p. 2). Ladson-Billings (2006) concluded that because of the variance in per-pupil expenditure, there is no achievement gap but rather an education debt that our education system owes to so many students, especially those living in poverty, that it has underserved.[10] Ladson-Billings challenged educational researchers to reconceptualize and move beyond the achievement gap discourse. Irvine (2010) explained that a perceived achievement gap is the result of other gaps that seductively coerce people into believing that an achievement gap actually exists. Rather than focusing on a perceived achievement gap, from her analyses, Irvine recommended that attention should be placed on closing other gaps that exist in education, which cause researchers, policymakers, practitioners, and administrators to believe there is an achievement gap. For Irvine, other gaps that shape our belief in an achievement gap include

the teacher quality gap; the teacher training gap; the challenging curriculum gap; the school funding gap; the digital divide gap; the wealth and income gap; the employment opportunity gap; the affordable housing gap; the health care gap; the nutrition gap; the school integration gap; and the quality childcare gap. (p. xii)

From Irvine's perspective, when we address the many other gaps that structurally and systemically exist in educational practice, achievement results can improve. Similarly, Delpit (2012) found in her analyses of infant and early development studies that an achievement gap does not exist at birth between Black students and White ones. Her synthesis suggests and is substantiated by Sleeter (2012) that schools actually can cause and reinforce gaps in achievement.

"Standardized" policies that do not take into account the multiple layers of needs and issues in particular contexts often result in inequities and inequalities that can be difficult to control or reverse (Kozol, 1991). A problem is that "district budget documents report how money is spent by *category* and *program* rather than by *school*" [italics added] (Roza, 2006, p. 9). The categories and programs are uniform, so it is difficult to determine which areas need additional funding. As evident in Liu's (2006) analysis, the reverse should be true. Richer states probably should not receive more funding because they spend more per student. Poorer states conceivably should receive additional funding to help provide additional support for students in need. Districts attempt to provide a "one formula/policy paradigm fits all" approach across the board, and the students (i.e., in states, districts, and schools) who may really need the extra support do not receive it. Roza (2006) wrote,

More often, the patterns are created in response to pressures to equalize services across all schools. Where earmarked categorical funds such as federal Title I money pay for such extra services as full-day kindergarten or reading specialists in high-need schools, more flexible state and local money is often used to fund the same services in the low-need schools. (p. 11)

Indeed, as Ryan (1999) declared from a moral and legalistic perspective, we should be practicing equity in funding because of "basic fairness and decency to innocent children" (p. 315).

School Dependence

Students living in poverty as well as subpopulations of students of color rely and sometimes depend on schools to meet myriad needs that other populations of students may not need (Delpit, 2012). By school dependence, I mean that students living in poverty may depend on the school (teachers, counselors, administrators) to provide resources to assist them in their development that they may not receive out-side of school. This dependence can include breakfast and lunch, academic support in difficult subject areas, as well as exposure to museums and other learning centers through fieldtrips. Whereas breakfast and lunch are necessary for human and aca-demic development for students living in poverty as well as those who do not, those not living in poverty have a greater chance of these needs being met outside of school while those living in poverty have a greater need—that is, they may depend on the school. In essence, research has shown that students from lower SES and who grow up and live in poverty depend more than their more affluent classmates on school to help them understand, navigate, negotiate, and even function in school (Delpit, 1995, 2012; Howard, 2010; Milner, 2010). These students are sometimes classified as school dependent (King, 1993; Klopfenstein, 2005). This means that, although it is important for parents to be involved in the educational experiences of their children, teachers, administrators, counselors, and other school-related personnel play a critical role in the social, emotional, behavioral, and cognitive development of these students because students rely on schools in ways that other students from more affluent com-munities may not have to. The expectations, responsiveness, and influence of teachers for their students become even more powerful for children living in poverty in this sense because students can rely on their teachers and the structure of school to expose them to the culture of power (Delpit, 1995) in order to help them "do" school success-fully. Teachers matter in the overall framework of meeting needs of school-dependent students. Findings from the Konstantopoulous (2009) study revealed that "in early grades, teacher effects in one grade lead to higher academic achievement in the fol-lowing grade. This finding supports the notion that effective teachers [and teaching] can increase achievement significantly for all students" (p. 108). In other words, teachers can be *the* difference maker for school-dependent students.

Factor analyses were used to study 1,000 African American and 260 Latino third graders' perceptions of their school environment (Slaughter-Defoe & Carlson, 1996). The researchers, through their analyses of the 24-item measure, found that African American students viewed their relationships with teachers to be most important in evaluating the school context. These relationships centered not only on schoolwork but also personal problems that the African American students wanted to discuss with their teachers. Latino students stressed that notions of fairness, care, and praise for putting forth effort were most important in their interactions with their teachers. This study suggests that relationship building and sustaining them can have an influ-ence on how welcome students feel in an environment and also demonstrate how school-dependent youth can rely on relationships to help them construct positive attitudes about school and consequently put more effort in their schoolwork.

Parental and Family Involvement

Parental and family involvement crosses the boundary between outside- and inside-of-school. Such involvement can influence how well connected students are to academic and social expectations of schools. Studies related to poverty and what was sometimes referred to as SES focus, to some degree, on the role of parents, families, and their involvement in their children's education.[11]

Focused on parental involvement, in their study of different racial and ethnic groups living in poverty, Cooper et al. (2010) found that African American, Hispanic, and White[12] students experienced more academic problems than students from more affluent families. However, the researchers found no difference between those from low SES and high SES Asian students—a nontrivial finding. Both groups of Asian students (low and high SES) tended to perform well on academic measures. The researchers also found that "poor" and "nonpoor" African American students both participated in organized extracurricular activities. Unfortunately, the researchers determined that this organized activity did not necessarily correlate with higher achievement in schools for these students although research would suggest that organized activities would supplement students' in-school learning and consequently their performance on tests. The point here is that family and parental decisions to include students in out-of-school activities, for example, can have an influence on students, and those living in poverty could potentially benefit. However, this was not the case for African American students in this study. The Cooper et al. study determined that strong values and high expectations of the Asian students' families were common between both the low and high SES students, which resulted in the academic success of students from both groups. From a CRT perspective, analyzing differences within a racial group provides a storyline that complicates generalized notions about particular groups of people. A common story across the literature is the idea that students from higher SES outperform those from lower SES. Moreover, a persistent narrative in the literature is that White students outperform other racial groups of students in both high and low SES groups. For instance, Whiteness is normalized and other racial groups are compared to the constant norm of it (Foster, 1999); even when Asian students outperform other racial/ethnic groups, they are still compared to White students. This study counters those storylines, further supporting the notion that looking at the intersection of race/ethnicity and poverty can provide compelling insight into what we know and what we *think* and *believe* we know.

Brooks-Gunn and Duncan (1997) found we know very little about high achieving students who also live in poverty. Although some (and still not enough) students living in poverty beat the odds and succeed in schools and are classified as gifted and high achievers, it is not clear the percentages of these students, where they attend school, and the sources (outside and inside of school) of their academic success. More research is needed in this area, especially with an eye toward racial patterns.

Exceptions exist as some students do attempt to examine those who are high achievers and living in poverty. For example, in their study of African American families living in poverty, Gutman and McLoyd (2000) examined the management and involvement of parents both out of and in school. In their qualitative study, they learned that parents of high achievers used particular strategies in assisting their students with homework and had supportive conversations with their students at home about their potential. At school, parents of high achievers were involved but had particular reasons for their involvement. Outside of school, parents of high achievers had their children actively involved and engaged in community through extracurricular activities—including religious activities. This storyline might counter discourses that might suggest that (a) students cannot be high achievers and/or (b) parents do not have specific, deliberate practices to keep their children involved, engaged, and successful in and out of school. For instance, do Black parents show up for PTA meetings? Questions about why or why not are necessary. Do these parents work during the meeting times? Are there problems with transportation? Moreover, do these parents feel that their needs and interests are being addressed at the meetings? Teachers sometimes have negative images of parents living in poverty when parents do not "participate" or function in school activities to the degree teachers believe necessarily appropriate (Milner, 2007). Understanding why parents do not participate or underparticipate needs to be of central concern in the research community.

Not only have studies examined parents' expectations and values espoused for their children (see, for instance, Cooper et al., 2009), there has also been an emphasis on parents' expectations of teachers. Whereas parental and family involvement seem to be a critical aspect of students' academic and social success in schools, research has found that parents place value in and have different expectations and demands of their children's teachers. Jacob and Lefgren (2007) discovered that parents in high poverty contexts "strongly" (p. 59) placed value on the effectiveness and ability of teachers to raise their children's test scores. Contrarily, those from higher SES, according to the study, placed more emphasis on teachers' ability to keep their children "happy" (p. 60). The researchers wrote:

> Because academic resources are relatively scarce in higher-poverty schools, parents in these schools seek teachers skilled at improving achievement even if this comes at the cost of student satisfaction. . . . In higher-income schools, parents are likely to oppose measures that increase the focus on standardized test scores at the cost of student satisfaction. (pp. 63–64)

Again, because students living in poverty may be more "school dependent," parents may rely on teachers and the school to increase students' test scores. Those from more affluent backgrounds may have the means to seek home tutoring in order to supplement and complement learning necessary for test score success and thus they are not as dependent on schools.

Milne and Plourde (2006) conducted another study that focused on race, poverty, and families. They provided insights from one of the only studies on poverty and students' academic success. They studied and identified essential elements of success that assisted high achieving students living in poverty. Parents in the qualitative study of six second-grade high poverty and high achievers had educational materials in the home, such as books and other written materials. Parents were deliberate in spending quality time with their children to ensure they (as parents) were aware of student needs and expectations of the school. They had dinner together regularly, talked extensively to their children, and the families served as a strong support system for their children. Through talk in the home, parents also stressed the importance and value of education because they, indeed, valued education themselves. The idea that those in poverty do not value education is countered and disrupted in this study as it is clear that these families living in poverty demonstrated strong beliefs in the importance of it. From a CRT perspective, it is essential that such positive narratives, again, known as counternarratives to negative ones, be told about families of color. The Milne and Plourde narrative helps disrupt and counter conceptions that families living in poverty, Black families in this case, did not value education or that they did not participate and support their children in developing academic and social skills in the home that were transferable to school.

The outside-of-school influences of poverty on education must be understood so that policymakers as well as practitioners understand the complex interplay between outside-of-school situations and what happens inside school. For instance, thinking deeply about how transportation challenges may influence people's ability to work provides a layer of explanation of students' lived experiences that might not be considered when educators (policymakers and practitioners) use their own lenses and frames of references based on their personal experiences. Educators may believe that people in a community do not work because they do not want to rather than because they do not have the transportation means to get to work. When there are transportation avenues (busses, trains, for instance), job opportunities may be hours away from those living in poverty because as Tate explained (2008) corporations set up businesses in locations that benefit them (taxes) and the executives' families such as strong school systems.

Inside-of-School Practices and Poverty

So far, I have emphasized several outside-of-school variables that influence students' inside-of-school experiences and outcomes: student and family homelessness, geography and social contexts, policy and school funding, outside-of-school realities that cause school dependence, and parental/family involvement with their children at home and school. In the next sections of this chapter, I consider the nexus between inside-of-school practices and poverty that have been explored in the literature.

Language and Literacy

Unlike the majority of empirical studies published on poverty, those with a language arts emphasis were more qualitative in their research designs and approaches. Although the studies emphasized nuances that too many of the studies in other areas did not, they too rarely had an explicit focus on race to make sense of what they learned about the participants, the policies they reviewed, the instructional practices explored, the learning opportunities available, or the social contexts they investigated.

Language and literacy researchers would argue that reading is a core competence for transcending and overcoming poverty (Adler & Fisher, 2001; Edmondson & Shannon, 1998).[13] Perhaps this is the reason studies that focused on subject matter learning (such as mathematics or science) and poverty were mostly concentrated in language and literacy. Edmondson and Shannon (1998) surmised that literacy education and learning to read in particular can help people either "prevent or overcome poverty" (p. 104). Similar to other areas of emphases in the research literature, poverty is linked to student test scores and particularly success in reading. Adler and Fisher (2001) stressed that "children who do not learn to read fluently and independently in the early grades have few opportunities to catch up to, and virtually no chance to surpass, their peers who are reading on grade level" (p. 616). In sharing their synthesis of the research literature regarding effective language and literacy instruction for all students, they explained that "instruction that provides opportunities [for students] to master concepts of print, the alphabetic principle, word recognition skills, and phonemic awareness and that affords engagement and interest in reading through a wide range of materials in the context of developmentally appropriate instruction" (p. 616) were essential.

Building on the established literature, these researchers identified several successful literacy qualities and practices exemplified in their case study of a beat the odds high-poverty school, Emerald Elementary School: strong focus on student outcomes, multiple reading programs in every classroom, shared responsibility for student success, strong leadership at school and classroom levels, and veteran, knowledgeable, and committed faculty and staff. However, this study like many others in the area of language arts did not take race into consideration in their analysis. From a CRT perspective, race is a central component to the ways in which researchers should analyze and think through what they find in their studies. The findings in this study would suggest that the instructional practices and strategies identified above are race- or at best culture-neutral. To be clear, CRT would not argue in support of a one-size-fits-all approach to teaching or implementing an instructional or leadership policy based on race. However, because race and racism are still common in society and in schools, students of color experience inequity and other forms of discrimination that informs their experiences (Milner, 2010), and these experiences should be used to anchor instructional practices and related policies and practices. In what ways might the leadership practices espoused in the Adler and Fisher (2001) study be saturated in White, middle-class ideology, for instance? What instructional literacy practices best meet the needs of students of color living in poverty in a particular environment? What evidence supports these instructional approaches?

Emphasizing the importance of literacy and access to reading materials such as books, Pribesh, Gavigan, and Dickinson (2011) examined differences in school library characteristics and resources such as the number of staff members and books included and/or added to the library. They also studied the schedule and number of days that the libraries were closed in schools where there was a large concentration of students living in poverty. The researchers found "alarmingly, . . . that the students in most need—those attending schools with the highest concentrations of students living in poverty—had the fewest school library resources to draw on" (p. 143). Although this study provides an important view of the conditions of and opportunities for students to use library facilities, again, we know very little about the racial and ethnic background of the populations of students living in poverty and where the libraries were zoned considering my earlier point that geography is important to foreground in studies about poverty, learning, and teaching. It is important to note that examining the intersection of race and poverty can provide a lens for researchers and consumers of the findings of research to disentangle the role and salience of race in the educational experiences, opportunities, and outcomes of the libraries for particular students. In other words, from what racial background are students who are being underserved by the library, and how might knowing this shape how we think about student outcomes and disparities such as those that emerge from standardized test scores, which are often discussed from a racialized framework?

Focusing on reading and other in-school variables, Fram et al. (2007) found that students living in poverty tended to be raised in single-parent homes mostly with mothers with "lower" educational levels, and many of these students were born to teenage mothers. The authors classified these conditions as "risk factors" and identified several school-related practices that shaped students' experiences. In their words, "the classroom contexts in which they learn are in some ways different, and perhaps less desirable, than those offered to their peers in other schools" (p. 316). They found that teachers were less credentialed and consequently qualified in many of these schools and that students spent large amounts of time in "achievement groups." Teachers followed general standards without being responsive to the individual needs of students, and their students were tracked into classrooms with classmates who had below grade-level reading skills. Data from their analyses of the first 2 years of the Early Childhood Longitudinal Study Kindergarten Cohort led the researchers to conclude and advocate for "mixed-ability peer groups" (p. 318) in reading to assist in students' learning and development and suggested that teachers needed to be better prepared to understand how to work with children living in poverty. In short, the Fram et al. study investigated school-level influences on student achievement.

Curriculum as Policy

In examining the Language Arts curriculum in a school district, Smagorinsky, Lakly, and Johnson (2002) found that district officials expected teachers across the diverse district to use the same curriculum materials, in the same order, and even at the exact same time of day. These researchers explained that the curriculum

uniformity meant that all students, whether living in an affluent suburb, in the inner city, or on a farm on the fringe of the county would receive the same [curriculum] at the same time. . . . The curriculum further tied to standardized county-wide tests that assessed students after each unit, further pressuring teachers to follow the curriculum guide faithfully. (pp. 198–199)

In this way, scripted curriculum does not allow or at best makes it difficult for teachers to respond to the social context and realities of their work: for instance, what is necessary for success in a suburban district might look qualitatively different from a rural or urban environment. Moreover, following a scripted curriculum can be difficult if teachers are concerned about and committed to developing a curriculum that is responsive to the lived experiences of students, especially those whose life experiences are often on the fringes of teaching and learning.

Furthermore, Smagorinsky et al. (2002) found that selected novels were "unappealing" (p. 199) to students and that the flow and organization of the expected curriculum was incoherent and unresponsive to the particular idiosyncrasies inherent to particular social contexts. Although a scripted curriculum may sound like an ideal approach, especially in populations of students who have been underserved such as those in poverty, Ede (2006) wrote, "The diverse ethnic and cultural makeup of today's classrooms makes it unlikely that one single curriculum will meet the needs and interests of all students" (p. 31).

In a qualitative study of third-grade students, Dutro (2010) investigated the extent to which students from poverty were able to connect with district-mandated reading curriculum. She found that the mandated curriculum portrayed "economic struggle as a temporary condition, located only in historical or national disaster contexts" (p. 255). This researcher also explained that the teacher's edition for the curriculum, which teachers used to guide learning, included language that did not support students' critical thinking regarding the relationship between themselves and poverty. In essence, this study demonstrated how the curriculum can be disconnected from students' lived experiences and how the curriculum can be framed in ways that do not allow them to think about and critique matters in their own communities that might help them understand more deeply how the world works, for whom, and what they can do to transform inequity (Freire, 1998).

From a CRT perspective, documents and policies—if we conceive a teacher's curriculum edition as a policy document—should be examined to disentangle (Howard, 2008; Ladson-Billings & Tate, 1995; Milner, 2008) the ways in which race shapes what is and is not emphasized in the document. In this sense, a curriculum document is a policy document that can be systematically examined to think about the ways in which particular racial groups of students might experience the curriculum in schools. I agree with Dutro (2010) as she found that curriculum materials should "allow children to see themselves, access experiences that differ from their own, and foster talk about issues of equity and social justice" (p. 257). On a micro level, some teachers may believe, however, that focusing on matters of inequity or social justice is disadvantageous or irrelevant to the "real" curriculum (A. E. Lewis, 2001; Milner, 2010). As a result, they avoid such emphases. CRT would demand that the curriculum be seen as a form of property to help students understand and examine the relationships between and among language and literacy, poverty and race, not only poverty and language arts. Such opportunities can allow students to examine their own lives, make connections, draw conjectures about inconsistencies, and think about the direction of their current or future lives as they interact with others.

Class Size

An additional inside-of-school factor that has been investigated to determine the relationship between poverty, learning, and teaching is class size. Conventional wisdom might suggest that smaller class size would almost automatically increase student test scores. However, results are scattered regarding the effectiveness of reduced class size for student achievement among those living in poverty. Some evidence suggests that reducing class size for students living in poverty has little direct impact on student achievement scores (Nyhan & Alkadry, 1999). Over the past 20 years, states and even the federal government have increased attention on the effectiveness of smaller class sizes for students, and researchers have explored the utility and benefits of smaller class sizes for students living in poverty (Reichardt, 2001).

From my view, to suggest that class size does not matter from a broader, more holistic approach, beyond student test scores, is unreasonable. Whereas researchers may not have found powerful links between reduced class size and student test scores, my research has revealed that smaller class size can have a powerful influence on the sociology of the classroom, especially in populations with large percentages of students living in poverty (Milner, 2008, 2010) and large percentages of school-dependent students. In classrooms with fewer students, I found teachers are able to communicate more directly with individual students, address needs both connected to and disconnected from the curriculum, and plan for more innovative curriculum and instructional practices. Sadly, our obsession with test scores (Irvine, 2010; Ladson-Billings, 2006; Milner, 2012) can limit other potentially beneficial aspects to student development.

Jepsen and Rivkin (2009) studied the effects of reduced class size on student achievement (test scores), specifically in mathematics and reading, in the state of California. They contextualized the study in the following way:

In the summer of 1996, California enacted the most expensive state level education reform in U.S. history. The state's class-size-reduction . . . program reduced K-3 class sizes throughout the state by roughly ten students per class, from 30 to 20, at an annual cost that exceeds one billion dollars. (pp. 224–225)

Recognizing the complexities of studying the interplay and effects of reduced class size, teacher quality, and student achievement, the researchers concluded that smaller class sizes did raise math and reading achievement. However, these results were not straightforward. The researchers reported that

although the results show that smaller classes raised mathematics and reading achievement, they also show that the increase in the share of teachers with neither prior experience nor full certification dampened the benefits of smaller classes, particularly in schools with high shares of economically disadvantaged, minority students. (Jepsen & Rivkin, 2009, p. 223)

The researchers also reported little or no evidence of class size reduction on demographic characteristics. It is difficult to examine improvements from different racial demographics of students when results do not attempt to determine how well particular groups of students perform as a result of the reduction of class size. Of course, the authors argued that other competing factors made it difficult to determine the effectiveness of class size reduction because teacher quality (the number of years and experiences of teachers) varied. For instance, were increases in student achievement a result of the quality of the teacher or the reduction in class size? The researchers questioned whether the reduction of class size was worth the amount of money spent.

Graue, Hatch, Rao, and Oen (2007) conducted a qualitative exploratory study with nine high-poverty schools to investigate a statewide class size initiative. The class reduction required changes in staffing, instructional strategies, and space allocations. Pupil–teacher ratios decreased, and the researchers concluded that the results were mixed; researchers determined that reforms were necessary both programmatically as well as instructionally. For instance, reducing the number of students in a classroom may not have lasting influences on their test scores if teachers continue teaching in the same ways they had with larger numbers of students. In this sense, what teachers actually do instructionally, these researchers found, was essential to the success of class size reduction. Thus, the researchers stressed the importance of professional development to assist teachers (both individually and schools in the collective) to transition from larger to smaller classroom sizes. Most of the studies in this area have been in elementary schools.

Instructional Practices and Frameworks That Do and Do Not Work

With a synthesis of research about the intersections of poverty, learning, and teaching established, I turn now to focus specifically on instructional practices. Before moving into depth with instructional practices that work—what I call radical classroom reform pedagogy, I provide a snapshot of what is common in many schools but do not seem effective for many students living in poverty. My point in sharing a view of these ineffective frameworks and instructional practices is to demonstrate and shed light on frameworks and practices that seem to be so widespread in many educational settings with students living in poverty. Perhaps it is because of them (the practices and frameworks presented here) that students living in poverty have not fared well in schools because schools have failed them. In this sense, before identifying what can and should be, I am demonstrating what needs to be transformed and radically reformed.

Frameworks and Practices That Do Not (Necessarily) Work

Haberman (2000) explained that students living in poverty are too often miseducated because they are not trained and empowered to think through complex problems. He observed that some students who drop out of school were more developed and prepared to function in society than others who stay in school for 13 years. From a policy and legal studies perspective, Burch (2001) explained that "citizens residing in affluent districts (overwhelmingly White) are educated to govern, whereas citizens residing in economically disadvantaged districts (overwhelmingly people of color) are educated to be governed" (p. 265). Anyon (1980, 1997), Kozol (1991), and Haberman (1991, 2000) all demonstrated, to an extent, that teachers in high-poverty schools conceived knowledge construction as basic skills that students are taught by a teacher (who is the knower) in order to receive a reward (Haberman, 2000).

To illuminate, Anyon (1980) provided one of the most provocative and compelling examples of social stratification and social reproduction produced in schools. She described four layers of schools where students were stratified and where social and societal privileges were either enabled or suppressed at the expense of students. Students in the low-income schools were taught to build knowledge about how to simply function and obey orders. Moreover, students in these schools were not taught to question authority or to engage in critical thinking about the content of various texts they were engaging. Students were not empowered to think about inequity or how to develop skills to confront or change racist and inequitable policies and practices either in or out of school. Much of the learning centered on completing worksheets and direction following, whereas the more affluent schools allowed students to engage in deeply complex activities where they learned how to problem solve, build and convey their positions and arguments, and engage in critical thinking while building and showcasing their creativity. In this sense, schools were complicit, perhaps unknowingly, in replicating and reinforcing the status quo, and perhaps guaranteeing that society will remain stratified. In Anyon's (1980) words, "Knowledge and skills leading to social power and reward are made available to the advantaged social groups but are withheld from the working classes, to whom a more 'practical' curriculum is offered" (p. 366).

I recall walking down a hallway in an urban, high-poverty, elementary school in the Midwest when a teacher proclaimed: "We are not moving until I see a straight line" (see Milner, 2010). I was stunned as I noticed the third graders desperately trying to figure out how to construct the line straight enough so that they could "move." For approximately 6 minutes, the teacher stood there with a look of disgust on her face because the students apparently could not construct the line straight enough for her satisfaction. I wondered what kinds of learning opportunities the students were missing (or perhaps gaining) during her 6 minutes of "teaching" the students that they would not move until she saw a straight line. This story is not unique. All over the country and especially in urban, high-poverty schools, teachers focus so much on rules that they sometimes forget they are working with human beings who are developing and grappling with a range of matters (Milner, 2010; Noguera, 2003).

Although I have spent a lot of time visiting urban schools (from elementary to high), I have also visited and observed suburban and independent schools. What I have learned is that student behaviors are similar in many ways in these different social contexts (urban/high poverty as well as independent/suburban/wealthy): students talk sometimes without raising their hands, they have conflicts with their classmates, they forget to complete their homework, they sometimes use profanity, and they even struggle sometimes to stand in a straight line (see Milner, 2010). However, there is a stark difference between how the teachers and other adults with power and in charge handle students' mistakes in suburban and independent schools. In many urban schools, students are treated like prisoners (see the important work of Noguera, 2003, for more on this), whereas in suburban and independent schools, students are treated as individuals who are learning and developing. In many urban and high-poverty schools, students are being taught and are learning how to follow rules but are rarely learning how to develop their own academic, social, and political awareness and positions on issues. In this way, schools are preparing students for the kind of jobs they will assume: to follow directions. Urban and high-poverty spaces are preparing their students to take orders. Suburban and independent schools are preparing their students to develop authority, confidence, and privilege and how to give orders (Anyon, 1980; Haberman, 2000; Milner, 2010). It is important to note that I am not suggesting that teachers should not help students understand rules and the consequences in store for them if/when they do not understand and/or follow them. I understand that we must have rules and laws in schools and society to live and function. However, focusing on rules more than helping students develop other important knowledge and skills is problematic yet so pervasive in schools across the United States, especially in schools with high populations of students of color and those living in poverty.

In addition, some researchers, teacher educators, policymakers, teachers, and principals believe that subject matter expertise is the only real important feature to student and teacher success. However, Haberman (1995), building from 40 years of research of teachers of urban and high-poverty students, explained that while it is essential for teachers to know their content/subject matter, this is insufficient for the kind of work necessary to be successful in urban and high-poverty schools. He maintained that many teachers fail in high-poverty environments because they do not have the ability to connect with students and build relationships with them where students are willing to participate in learning. In this way, subject matter knowledge is necessary but is insufficient in meeting the needs of students living in poverty. Yet many teacher education programs focus much of their attention on preparing teachers in the subject matter and miss another important element to their work: preparing teachers to understand students and to connect with them by building meaningful relationships. Although the idea that building relationships with students may seem logical and straightforward, many teachers struggle to develop them (Milner, 2010).

Ruby Payne's Framework

Ruby Payne conducts scores of professional development seminars with school districts across the country about teaching students living in poverty. I was quite reluctant to critique Payne's framework in this research review for many reasons. I decided to include it in this chapter mainly because an important thread of this review concerns instructional practices with students living in poverty and so many school districts across the country draw from and rely extensively on Payne's framework. I believe it is essential to include aspects of the Payne framework in this review to allow practitioners and those who study and educate/train teachers opportunities to critique and think about what the framework provides, what it does not, and perhaps what it should. Payne's self-published book, *A Framework for Understanding Poverty* (1996), outlines her much relied on, underresearched conjectures and assertions for teachers teaching students who live in poverty. According to Payne (1996), the framework is intended to challenge educators—teachers, principals, counselors, and even policymakers—to rethink what they know about the nexus of poverty, learning, and teaching. The book rests on 12 principles:

Poverty is relative. Poverty occurs in all races. Generational and situational poverty are different. This work is based on patterns. All patterns have exceptions. Schools operate from middle-class norms and values. Individuals bring with them the hidden rules of the class in which they were raised. There are cultural differences in poverty. This study is cross-cultural and focusses on economics. We must neither excuse them nor scold them. We must teach them. We must teach them [students] that there are two sets of rules. To move from poverty to middle class, one must give up (for a period of time) relationships for achievement. Two things that help one move out of poverty are: education and relationships. Four Reasons one leaves poverty are: "too painful to stay, vision or goal, key relationship, and special talent/skill." (p. 3)

Criticism of Payne's framework, books, lectures, and overall philosophy are extensive (Bomer, Dworin, May, & Semingson, 2008; Gorski, 2006; Murnane, 2007; Osei-Kofi, 2005). Gorski (2006), for instance, explained that Payne's approach and message fail to critique systemic barriers and inequities in schools and rely on cultural deficit models in explaining the fixed categories she advances. Moreover, Gorski surmised that her work has conservative values embedded throughout the fabric of the texts and messages she sends. An even closer examination of Payne's work reveals that much of her framework rests on and draws from anecdote; research is thin to support her claims, and few critical analyses of racism, discrimination, and oppression are attended to on any substantive level, a critique that is supported from a CRT perspective. Unlike many frameworks and conceptual analyses, however, Payne does at least address in her framework what might be seen as the elephant in the room in her poverty discussions: race. However, the ways in which she addresses race is stereotypic and undernuanced. Accordingly, the framework seems to do more to reinforce stereotypes than to address systemic and structural forms of racism that can prevent many students of color living in poverty from succeeding. In short, the way Payne attends to race, by suggesting that students and families of color do not understand how to operate in the normative White-mainstream "culture," can actually do more harm than good because she operates from a deficit perspective and has a shallow, undertheorized understanding of race and the intersection of race and poverty.

Consistent among the critique of Payne's work and her blaming of students and their families for not understanding how to operate in the normative "middle-class" culture are those outlined in the work of Oscar Lewis (1959, 1961, 1966). From an anthropological perspective (Ladson-Billings, 2009), poverty is not a culture although

Lewis and Payne classify and categorize it as such. From an anthropological perspective, Lewis is credited or perhaps criticized for constructing and conceptualizing what he called a "culture of poverty" to describe, contextualize, and name the practices of families in Mexico and Puerto Rican families in San Juan and New York. Lewis identified several behaviors that painted these families as inferior, deficient, and substandard to mainstream cultural norms, expectations, and behaviors. In this sense, according to Osei-Kofi (2005), Lewis and subsequently Payne pathologized those living in poverty. However, it is important to note that Lewis described behaviors and practices of those in these communities because of the structural consequences and conditions of poverty. Although some have argued that Lewis's work takes a deficit perspective of the communities he studied, a closer examination of his work may demonstrate that in many ways he is describing cultural practices of his research participants that seem to result from material and structural conditions of poverty.

Misunderstanding Meritocracy

Although some educators have a difficult time confronting matters of race and accordingly adopt colorblindness in their work (Lewis, 2001), I have found that they readily identify disparities in students' SES as causes of gaps in their students' experiences (Milner, 2010), although hooks (2000) would argue that educators reject and avoid SES and poverty conversations, too. My research demonstrated that educators appeared to be more at ease, confident, and comfortable reflecting about, reading, and discussing how SES, particularly resources related to wealth and poverty, influence educational disparities, inequities, outcomes, and opportunities. However, although educators appear more comfortable addressing SES and class, they tend to misunderstand the SES nexus.

Based on my research, I have learned that educators may embrace the idea that their own, their parents', and their students' success and status have been earned. They may believe that failure emanates solely as a result of making bad decisions—for example, a student's decision not to put forth effort in a class. However, unearned opportunities and consequences are sometimes passed down from one generation to the next. Yet many educators believe that their own success is merited because they have worked hard, followed the law, had the ability and skill, and made the right choices and decisions. They have little or no conception of how class and socioeconomic privilege and opportunity manifest. For instance, wealthy or middle-class teachers of any racial background can fail to recognize their SES privilege and can fail to understand what opportunities this privilege affords them (Kozol, 2005). Teachers in general can fail to understand that they have gained their status through a wide range of unearned advantages, chances, circumstances, and consequences (Milner, 2010). People who grow up in poverty or those from lower SES generally do not start their educational or life experiences in a fair or equitable position (Ladson-Billings, 2006).

At the center of the meritocracy argument for student success is opportunity. Darling-Hammond (2010) found that we are placing too much emphasis on student test scores in the name of achievement and outcomes and that we actually should be focused on opportunity gaps rather than achievement gaps, and I agree (Milner, 2010). That is, U.S. society is philosophically and ideologically structured such that all people are supposedly created equally with the *same* opportunities for success. In reality, however, educational practices and opportunities are not equal or equitable (Anyon, 1980; Darling-Hammond, 2010; Henslin, 2004). There is enormous variation in students' social, economic, historic, political, and educational opportunities, which is in stark contrast to the "American dream"—one that adopts and supports meritocracy as its creed or philosophy. Still many educators believe that if people, their students in particular, just work hard enough they will be rewarded and will achieve success. They can fail to recognize systemic barriers and institutional structures that prevent opportunity and success, even when students are hard working. If the meritocracy argument were accurate, from a sociological perspective, Henslin (2004) wrote,

> All positions would be awarded on the basis of merit. If so, ability should predict who goes to college. Instead, family income is the best predictor—the more a family earns, the more likely their children are to go to college . . . while some people do get ahead through ability and hard work, others simply inherit wealth and the opportunities that go with it . . . in short, factors far beyond merit give people their positions in society. (p. 174)

Thus, meritocracy seems to be a myth because it maintains that any person living in U.S. society will achieve the "American dream," as long as he or she has the ability, works hard, is effortful, follows the law, and makes good decisions. However, opportunity gaps can

> undermine one of our most powerful and core beliefs that we as Americans cling to: that no matter what circumstances children are born into, all have the opportunity to become educated and, if they work hard, to pursue their dreams. (Randolph-McCree & Pristoop, 2005, p. 2)

This philosophy can reject institutionalized and structural issues and barriers that permeate policies and practices such as racism, sexism, classism, and discrimination both in the classroom and in society. The meritocracy argument does not appropriately take into consideration social reproduction and property that wealthier students often inherit—materially, physically, socially, and culturally—capital and property that have been and continues to be passed down from one generation to the next (Ladson-Billings & Tate, 1995).

A permeating theme of a meritocratic way of seeing the world centers around a we/they binary that some adopt as they position themselves and their "earned" success in opposition to others. Apple (2006) explained that

> the binary opposition of we—they becomes important. . . . For dominant groups, "we" are law-abiding, hardworking, decent, and virtuous. "They"—usually poor people and immigrants—are very different. They are lazy, immoral, and permissive. These binary oppositions act to exclude indigenous people, women, the poor, and others from the community of worthy individuals. (p. 22)

These dichotomous, binary conceptions can allow people to rationalize their successes as those that have been earned through their being law-abiding, hard-working, and virtuous. An important question in this regard is the following: How can we expect students to have the same outcomes on achievement measures when structural inequities place some groups of students in poorly run schools with fewer resources and underqualified teachers while others receive the opposite (Darling-Hammond, 2010; Ladson-Billings, 2006)? Overall, what I have outlined in this section has not seemed to work although the mindsets, practices, and approaches are consistently present in schools serving high populations of those living in poverty.

Instructional Practices That Work

In this section, I conceptualize what seems to work in populations of students living in poverty—who sometimes are underserved in educational settings.

Toward a Radical Classroom Reform Pedagogy

Noguera and Wells (2011) were resolute and unyielding in their critique of what they called a No Excuses Reform Movement where decision makers in support of it proclaim that poverty is not and should not be an obstacle to meeting the needs of students. This movement would suggest that, on a micro-level, "a combination of hard work, good teaching, and accountability are all that are needed to produce a greater degree of educational success" (Noguera & Wells, 2011, p. 11). Although I agree that myriad factors can hinder progress in classrooms when teachers are working with students living in poverty, there is evidence to suggest teachers can be responsive to students' needs although too many are not. Both the ineffective preparation of teachers as well as the lack of support they receive while teaching are reasons for teachers' inability to be responsive to and effective for students living in poverty (Darling-Hammond, 2010). To be clear, I agree that it will take more than a teacher and/or a particular instructional approach to address poverty in learning and teaching at scale. If teachers wait on meso- or macro-level policies and mandates to support their work, however, serious progress may never be made because those in power may operate from ideological positions, many times disconnected from empirical research and also moral consciousness. The political, in this sense, is ideological (Anyon, 2005; Noguera & Wells, 2011), and policymakers may not understand the huge levels of privilege they have when making decisions for students and their families. Thus, similar to "No Excuse Reformers," we should not allow poverty to supersede teachers' and school districts' attempts and documented success to teach in transformative ways with children living in poverty.

Because there is no specified, definitive body of collective literature that addresses effective pedagogical practices to meet the needs of children living in poverty, I draw from an established body of research that has been developed empirically about teaching practices that have proven successful for students whose needs have historically not been met in school. Some of these studies and frameworks were constructed specifically with children living in poverty. In this section, I provide insight for what I will call radical classroom reform pedagogy. The instructional practices (mindsets, policies, approaches) described in this section are radical in the sense that they sound logical to many practitioners, theorists, and researchers but require more than just words for practitioners attempting to implement them in schools with strict, myopic, traditional bureaucracies that can make it difficult for teachers to actualize. They are also radical in that in many instances they are not being implemented for one reason or another in classrooms across the United States because many teachers operate as they always have. They see instructional practices described in this section as inappropriate, too controversial, or something extra or additional that they must learn and enact with particular groups of students. They may become frustrated and believe that parents of their students should prepare them to assimilate into the classroom instructional practices already established—whether they are effective or not for all students.

Several pedagogical frameworks exist and are well established in the research literature that can help educators meet the needs of students living in poverty. Some of the most compelling research in the area of responding to the needs of students whose outside-of-school experiences are complexly difficult is grounded in what Ladson-Billings (2009) conceptualized and called culturally relevant pedagogy, Gay (2010) conceptualized and called culturally responsive teaching, Moll and colleagues conceptualized and called funds of knowledge (Moll & Gonzalez, 2004), and C. D. Lee (2007) conceptualized and called cultural modeling. Although most of the frameworks I review and draw from in this section have culture in their description, I am not suggesting that there is a culture of poverty as O. Lewis (1966) and R. Payne (1996) have conceptualized. Rather, I am suggesting that students and families living in poverty can engage in cultural practices (Gutiérrez & Rogoff, 2003) as a reaction to or in opposition to the material conditions and structural inequities that can be lastingly devastating for them, their families, and communities.

Consistent across these theories about instructional practices (what will be referred to as frameworks throughout this section) is the importance of teacher learning and understanding of the background and lived experiences of students. In particular, teachers are challenged to develop tools to inquire and learn about the outside-of-school aspects of students, their families, and communities. Teachers are learning about their students' assets, evolving understanding and knowledge base in subject matter areas, their preferences, experiences, successes, challenges, and worldviews both inside and outside of the classroom. C. D. Lee (2007) explained that teachers should think about and use this learning about their students as "cultural data sets" (p. 35) from which to build and learn. Similarly, Ladson-Billings (2009) explained that teachers should study their students in deciding what to teach and how. What teachers learn about students should be centralized both in the curriculum[14] (what students have the opportunity to learn) as well as through instruction (how they teach the curriculum).

Moll and Gonzalez's research pointed to the necessity to learn from and with the families of students as important curricula and instructional sites in the classroom.

The funds of knowledge emphasis have a powerful connection to how we might think about working with families, and parents in particular, to develop instructional practices. The framework necessitates that teachers see or perhaps locate expertise of students and their families as assets—even those living in poverty. Moll's framework would recommend that family members of students teach teachers about home practices that can be linked to the subject matter taught and covered inside of school. Lee's cultural modeling framework also challenges teachers to focus on outside-of-school factors that shape learning inside of school. However, her framework is linked more closely to students themselves in everyday practices whereas Moll's framework is broader in scope. The idea here is that students and teachers are actively engaged in knowledge construction and learning about the outside-of-school practices of students and families that can be mirrored and connected to the in-school curriculum in different subject areas for instruction. C. D. Lee (2007), in her important book, *Culture, Literacy, and Learning: Taking Bloom in the Midst of the Whirlwind*, provided explicit examples of how teachers in different subject areas including literacy and mathematics can use students' practices to connect with learning in school. Interestingly, some would argue that mathematics, for instance, does not require attention to students' particular worldviews or outside-of-school cultural practices. They see mathematics curriculum and instruction as neutral. However, both Lee and Ladson-Billings (2009) demonstrated how essential understanding who students really are can be in the teaching and learning exchange across the different subject matter areas.

In short, from a curriculum perspective, Ladson-Billings (2009) explained that teachers should use their learning about students and their families to construct, deconstruct, and reconstruct what is taught in schools and also how the curriculum is taught. Additionally, CRT would recommend that teachers carefully examine the (common core) standards and related policy expectations to ensure students' racial backgrounds and interests are not ignored or overlooked in what is required and expected to be covered.

These instructional approaches would suggest that students in P-12 schools should be actively engaged in learning about poverty in their different subject areas and developing tools that empower them to speak against injustice, inequity, and also to change unfortunate realities. For instance, three interrelated tenets shape Ladson-Billings's conception of culturally relevant pedagogy: academic achievement, sociopolitical consciousness, and cultural competence. I want to draw from her empirical conceptualization of sociopolitical consciousness as a site to explain what teachers can do instructionally to address poverty and race. In explaining the interplay between educational content/subject matter and society, Ladson-Billings (1992) maintained that culturally relevant pedagogy is an approach that empowers students to examine and critique what they are learning to make connections to the real world (outside of school). It emphasizes not only academic success but also social success and helps students maintain important identity characteristics that form aspects of who they are, who they want to be, and who they are becoming.

This instructional framework suggests that students in P-12 classrooms develop a critical consciousness and that they move beyond spaces where they simply or solely consume knowledge without critically examining it. The idea is that teachers create learning environments where they develop voice and perspective and are allowed to participate (more fully) in the multiple discourses available in a learning context by not only consuming information but also through deconstructing and reconstructing it (Freire, 1998). It also encourages teachers to help students identify and think about issues in their community such as unemployment and develop knowledge and skills to determine what unemployment means to them, their families, and communities.

In this sense, students are posing questions like why more people of color live in poverty and how issues of inequality may contribute to this representation. For instance, the idea that the unemployment rate plays a meaningful role in national debates as well as in local contexts for teachers and students would be centralized and incorporated into curricula and instructional opportunities to enable both teachers' and students' levels of critique, positioning, and consciousness. In this way, through exposure to structures that perpetuate and ensure poverty, students are equipped to develop a kind of sociopolitical consciousness that empowers them to want to change how society works both for themselves and for others. Sociopolitical consciousness means that students are not willing to accept situations that place their families, for instance, in situations where they depend on a system to "rescue" them from the realities of poverty. Rather, students become equipped to think about why things are as they are in their localized communities and make connections to broader structures on meso and macro levels. Moreover, students are empowered to move beyond the individual to systemic, collective matters that shape the world. A pressing question, though, from this perspective is age/developmental appropriateness for students to experience such curriculum and teaching.

In this sense, the teacher is not the only or the main arbiter of knowledge (Eisner, 1994; McCutcheon, 2002) and curriculum construction in a classroom. Students are expected and empowered to develop intellectually and socially in order to build skills to make meaningful and transformative contributions to society. Students in poverty are challenged to think about why they are in poverty and to question inequitable circumstances that contribute to these situations. In essence, culturally relevant pedagogy is an approach that helps students "see the contradictions and inequities" (Ladson-Billings, 1992, p. 382) that exist inside and outside of the classroom. Through culturally relevant teaching, teachers prepare students with skills to question inequity and to fight against the many isms and phobias that they encounter while allowing students to build knowledge and to transfer what they have learned through classroom instructional/learning opportunities to other experiences.

Finally, similar to questions about when it is most developmentally appropriate for students to discuss and learn about race in the curriculum (A. E. Lewis, 2001; Milner, 2010), some question the appropriateness of discussions of poverty and SES in the classroom (hooks, 2000). Although teachers may opt not to have discussions or develop curriculum materials and instructional practices about SES or poverty, students do often think about these issues and even at an early age (Chafel, 1997).

Although their ways to communicate may not be as forthcoming or nuanced as older people about poverty, they know that differences exist between and among people (Anyon, 1980). So should we ignore this knowledge that students have because teachers/ adults do not feel comfortable to address it? According to Haberman (1991), students should be engaged in questions like why are some people poor while others are rich? And what is poverty and how do people get out of it?

Indeed, teachers' thinking and beliefs shape their practices with students (Banks, 2001; Gay, 2010). Accordingly, the ways in which teachers think about students in poverty, their situations, and whether they believe it is appropriate for them to include aspects of poverty in their instruction can play a role in what students learn and how they develop (Gay, 2010). Whereas I have provided instructional strategies that seem important in meeting the complex needs of students who have lived or are living in poverty, Gutiérrez and Rogoff (2003) cautioned against essentializing and generalizing practices based on traits of individuals or even groups of people, students, and families. They encouraged researchers, theoreticians, and practitioners alike to understand the complexities—the "importance and benefits of knowing about the histories and valued practices of cultural groups rather than trying to teach prescriptively according to broad, underexamined generalities about groups" (p. 20). In this regard, instructional practices outlined here are meant to help teachers understand and gauge students' experiences and practices and to examine the practices of students (inside and out of school) in order to use them as opportunities to build curriculum and teach students. Thus, I am not suggesting that teachers implement these practices without deeply examining the needs, realities, and practices of their students. All the evidence reviewed in this section of the chapter suggests that the curriculum and instructional practices should be tailored to help students recognize how oppression, discrimination, and marginalization are central to why many people (of color) live in poverty. Students, then, learn how to understand, interpret, and read the *world* and the *word* (Freire, 1998) and work to mobilize themselves and others out of poverty. Students are knowers and teachers construct the learning environment in a way that showcases and honors what students know. Again, students move from a self-motivated perspective where they are only concerned about themselves to a more collective one where they realize that when another person (or people) lives in poverty, we all are at a disadvantage.

In sum, based on my review in this section, P-12 teachers are encouraged to (a) learn about students' outside-of-school situations and realities; (b) learn to recognize and name the assets that students and their families possess; (c) connect outside-of-school experiences to the "real," expected curriculum in school; (d) build meaningful and sustainable relationships with students and their families; (e) use real-world examples and situations about poverty in instructional practices; (f) help students recognize injustice; (g) empower students to change inequitable, unfair policies and practices as they encounter them; and (h) develop what I am calling radical classroom reform pedagogy as an instructional framework for teaching, not an add on to what and how they should be teaching.

Summary of Research Patterns

Several micro-, meso-, and macro-level themes emerged from my review of the research literature that I summarize in a list below. The points are meant to provide a summative perspective for researchers and theoreticians as we work to advance the field:

- The majority of empirical studies examined and available in the literature was quantitative studies where researchers did not critically examine race as a variable even though, proportionately, more people of color live in poverty than White people. Most often, when race was considered and mentioned in these studies they were descriptive and not critiqued, problematized, or nuanced.
- Much of the literature on poverty and SES takes a developmental approach and focuses, to some extent, on the early childhood and elementary years of students' development and learning. One important finding from this research was early childhood education, including Head Start, can have a profound influence on students' future (later) academic and social experiences in school.
- Overwhelmingly, studies reviewed on poverty and education focused on connections between poverty/SES and student test scores, what was classified as student achievement. These studies tended to focus on test scores and did not consider other important aspects of the teaching and learning intersection such as the sociology of the classroom or relationships between teachers and students.
- Fewer qualitative studies are available in the literature that focused on poverty/SES though some conceptual papers are available. Language and literacy studies employed qualitative methods more often than other focus areas.
- There were two qualitative studies that focused exclusively on high achieving students living in poverty, a major shift and divergence from how most studies were designed. Most studies focused on low(er) performance and achievement and essentially rationalized how poverty was the cause for undesirable student outcomes.
- The number of children living in poverty has increased over the last three decades, and although studies still examine poverty, the literature base is somewhat sporadic and disjointed. There is no common understanding or conceptualization of what a collective body of researchers means by poverty, from what I was able to surmise, which is a definitional issue that seems to play a role in the development and advancement of research in the field.
- Poverty and low SES were conceptualized and determined often through school free and reduced lunch programs, rates, and patterns.
- Although students from all racial and ethnic backgrounds experience poverty, students of color are much more likely to live in poverty than are their White counterparts. It is unclear what roles racist and discriminatory policies, practices, structures, and systems play in this disproportion based on the majority of literature available.
- Depressingly negative and deficient language was common in much of the research literature about students and their families living in poverty. Researchers

discussed what they termed "disadvantaged" or "at-risk" students and parents, for instance, in elucidating their research findings from studies.

- Most of the research identified problems with families, students, and communities and offered thin recommendations and interventions to address the problems identified. When recommendations for improvement were offered, most of them focused on macro- and some meso-level recommendations. Few recommendations were made on a classroom, instructional level, which is a reason I drew from literature that had a broader "cultural" scope in the previous section of this chapter.

- The amount of time students are in poverty can have a lasting influence on their academic and social success over subsequent years in schools. The longer a child lives in poverty the more devastating educational experiences can be. In essence, students living in poverty during the early years of life can have negative educational experiences later. Brooks-Gunn and Duncan (1997) found that "children who experience poverty during their preschool and early school years have lower rates of school completion than children and adolescents who experience poverty only in later years" (p. 56).

- Few theoretical, analytic, and conceptual tools are used, especially in empirical quantitative studies, to situate, describe, and discuss findings regarding poverty and SES. In this sense, the literature base is borderline atheoretical.

- Subject–matter specific studies regarding poverty and teaching focused mostly in language and literacy. Although additional studies reviewed focused on other subject matter areas such as mathematics, the studies were much more general in nature and did not focus, in particular, on particular elements of the fabric of the curriculum and instructional practices of the subject matter.

- All the evidence reviewed and synthesized in this chapter suggest that while schools can play a pivotal role in decreasing the poverty rate among students and in meeting their complex needs, schools cannot accomplish success independently. Outside-of-school factors matter, too. In addition, the evidence suggests that teachers can make a difference inside of the classroom but that they must be prepared and supported to develop and enact curriculum and instructional opportunities that meet the needs of students living in poverty.

CONCLUSIONS

I conclude stressing the point that while I am encouraging researchers in particular to critique and center race in their investigations of poverty and education, I do so cautioning them to move forward with integrity, attention, and concern to the populations they study. Stereotyping and positioning populations of color in deficit, "at-risk," and inferior ways can misrepresent the nuances and complexities that manifest in communities. However, although engaging and critiquing the intersection of race and poverty can be nebulous and dangerous (see Milner, 2007), we still need to carefully attend to it, not ignore it, if we are committed to addressing the uneven proportion of people of color living in poverty. Until we pose the tough questions and engage in the analytic and critical work to solve "the race problem," we will continue seeing disparities. Ignoring race in studies of poverty will not advance what we know about why so many more people of color live in poverty than White people. A danger is when race is used but not understood and could cause people to stereotype populations of students and their families based on their membership in particular groups (Gutiérrez & Rogoff, 2003; Milner, 2007) rather than examining structural and systemic processes and systems that have real consequences for people because of race.

Evans (2005) argued (similar to Ladson-Billings, 2006, and Irvine, 2010) that we need to broaden our conceptions of an achievement gap. He suggested that schools and students themselves should not be the only sources of blame in thinking about disparities that exist in education. Rather, he found that the broader social context of students' experiences needs to be examined and interrogated in thinking about what needs to be done to address problems. His conceptual analysis suggestsed that the following were critical elements to consider in understanding student success:

- family structure (whether there are two parents in the home),
- security of students (how safe students feel at home),
- the kinds of intellectual learning opportunities available to students (the extent to which parents read and engage their children cognitively),
- television watching (the extent to which parents limit television watching), and
- parents' monitoring, assistance, and help with homework.

In addition, Evans declared that parents must make sure students show up for school regularly. This line of thinking, which Evans grounds and supports in the Coleman Report, suggests that schools play a very small role in the success of students.

Such a way of thinking limits the role and responsibility of schools (educators, principals, teachers, counselors) who are underprepared to teach and who are not able to develop learning strategies and tools that speak to the needs of all students. Whereas it is logical and evidence supports the argument that outside-of-school factors play a role in the "achievement" of students (Coleman, 1988; Noguera & Wells, 2011), it seems irrational to suggest that those in schools have not and do not play a significant role in the success and learning of students. There are many examples of micro-, meso-, and macro-level policies and practices that demonstrate both small- and large-scale influences and effects that schools play in the success or demise of students (Kozol, 1991; Ladson-Billings, 2009). I am not arguing that Evans is wrong in his assessment that factors and variables beyond school are critical elements to consider in understanding, naming, and explaining what is known in the literature as achievement gaps. Parents and families must take responsibility for the education of their children, too. However, Evans, similar to others, does not begin to penetrate how inequitable funding and resources and other outside-of-school factors such as policy actually perpetuate and sustain disparities in low-income schools and communities. My overall point here is that the research directions on poverty need to focus on building knowledge about the intersected nexus of outside-of-school and inside-of-school factors that shape student success. The evidence is clear that both areas are essential in the overall experiences of students, and arguments in support of one over the other does not seem to advance the field.

Finally, human suffering because of poverty should be unacceptable and frankly embarrassing in a country that is as resource wealthy as the United States. No child, in particular, should have to suffer from the lack of resources necessary for him or her to function well in and out of school. Shame on us for allowing poverty to continue!

ACKNOWLEDGMENTS

I am grateful to Barbara Bales and Pedro Noguera for their careful and helpful feedback on an earlier version of this chapter. I also appreciate the feedback from two anonymous reviewers of this chapter. In addition, I am thankful to Alvin Pearman, Raquel Pointer, and Jay Simpson for helping me gather the resources reviewed in this chapter. Finally, Chris Faltis and his editorial team provided important suggestions and insights that improved this chapter.

NOTES

[1]Although the relationship between poverty and education is a serious concern across the globe, this review focuses on poverty and education in the United States.

[2]Throughout this chapter, I use *student achievement* because it is so commonly used in the literature. Most often, unless otherwise noted, researchers and theorists use *student achievement* synonymously with *student test scores*. Philosophically and empirically, I struggle with the idea that achievement can solely or mostly be measured by test scores. In this sense, student achievement is socially constructed, privileged, prioritized, and classified by a power structure that places value on particular behaviors and outcomes over others. For instance, why are particular kinds of achievement in certain subject matter domains viewed as superior to others?

[3]Throughout this manuscript, I use *students living in poverty* rather than *poor students* or another form of classifying and describing students. I agree with Haberman (2000) as he explained that "language is not an innocent reflection of how we think. The terms we use control our perceptions, shape our understanding, and lead us to particular proposals for improvement" (p. 203). My decision to use particular phrases and terms are in no way meant to minimize or denigrate the people or places analyzed and discussed. The language I use represents my best attempt to maintain coherence and concurrently the integrity of the literature I review and analyze. Mostly, I hope to respect the populations represented in the studies reviewed.

[4]Social class and poverty are linked (Anyon, 1980; Rothstein, 2004; Weis & Dolby, 2012). They are not treated identically in the research literature. For instance, Weis and Dolby (2012) explained that class should be understood as

> practices of living . . . The books we read (or if we read at all); our travel destinations (if we have them and what they look like); the clothes we wear; the foods we eat; where and if our children go to school, how far and with what degree of success, with whom, and under what staff expectations and treatment; where and with whom we feel most comfortable; where we live and the nature of our housing; where and if we attend and complete postsecondary education, and under what expectations for success and imagined or taken for granted financing (parents, public/state/national/federal money, on or off campus job) are all profoundly classed experiences, rooted not only in material realities but also in shared culturally based expectations and understandings. . . . (p. 2)

[5]In defining and "measuring" poverty, the U.S. Census Bureau (2012) used "a set of money income thresholds that vary by family size and composition to determine who is in poverty. If a family's total income is less than the family's threshold, then that family and every individual in it is considered in poverty. The official poverty thresholds do not vary geographically, but they are updated for inflation. . . . The official poverty definition uses money income before taxes and does not include capital gains or noncash benefits (such as public housing, Medicaid, and food stamps)" (http://www.census.gov/hhes/www/poverty/about/overview/measure. html).

[6]Many studies emerged with socioeconomic status and class as keyword, and it was impossible to include them all. I opted to include studies that focused on socioeconomic status and/ or class if they had direct influences on poverty. This means that some studies were not included if there was not an explicit use and operationalizing of the construct poverty in the analysis. For instance, Rothstein's (2004) analyses provided important implications regarding poverty, but the thrust of his argument focused on how social class (not necessarily poverty) affected student outcomes. His work calls for a widening of our conceptions of what an achievement gap is, and he challenged researchers to consider developmental matters that shaped young students' readiness and performance once they begin school. Thus, it is impossible to include every study in such a review and decisions had to be made that best fit into the overall goal of this review.

[7]It is not my goal to critique every study from a critical race theory perspective but to centralize race and its relationship to poverty through the themes presented. My goal is to help readers think about why race and poverty should be studied and analyzed jointly and to pose questions to assist readers in making sense of what is and is not included regarding race in studies on poverty.

[8]The 2008 election of Barack Obama to the presidency led many people in the U.S. and abroad to believe that his election transcended centuries of racism, oppression, marginalization, and discrimination. White Americans, and those from other racial and ethnic groups, including some Black Americans, proclaimed what seemed to be a modern day cliché: that it was "a new day" in U.S. society. Some believed that we as a country had arrived at some postracial, postoppressive, postdiscrimination era because White voters had obviously helped elect an African American president. This position does not allow educators to recognize the pervasiveness (and candidly permanence) of race, racism, and other more general forms of discrimination and prejudice in the U.S. Indeed, some White Americans supported the election of President Obama; many did not. Thus, while individual educators may not (consciously) commit racist acts, broader policies and practices are often rife with racism. Accordingly, educators who do not view themselves as racist individuals can have trouble recognizing how racism works and how it can manifest in broader, systemic and institutionalized structures.

[9]Lareau (2003) demonstrated how race shows up in segregated housing patterns she observed. Moreover, her study revealed that middle-class Black parents monitored the "racial composition of each activity" (p. 121) before enrolling their children so that their children were not the only Black children in particular activities.

[10]The education debt carries several important features according to Ladson-Billings (2006): historical debt, economic debt, sociopolitical debt, and moral debt.

[11]Parental and family involvement goes beyond parents and families showing up to school at Parent Teacher Association (PTA) meetings. For instance, parental and family involvement can mean that parents are engaged in home-based activities such as ensuring that homework is completed, monitoring student progress and improvement through school visits and in the home, talking over the phone (or via email) to teachers and administrators, planning activities for the school, participating in fund-raising activities, attending and assisting with field trips, attending extracurricular activities such as sports and plays, staffing concession stands, volunteering in the classroom, and serving on advisory boards (Hoover-Dempsey & Sandler, 1997).

[12]Some studies conflated ethnic and racial categories.

[13]Although this review is focused on studies in the U.S., it is important to note that studies about poverty and language arts were not exclusive to a U.S. context. For instance, in a Canadian study of students in 10 high poverty schools in grade one, Haughey, Snart, and da Costa (2001) designed three interventions to determine their effectiveness in raising the achievement of students. Using students' test scores as the measure, students in the study made "noteworthy" (p. 301) improvements in the areas of writing and reading. The interventions were designed to focus on reducing class size through literacy instruction, continuous professional development, and intensified focus specifically on literacy instruction.

[14]The curriculum can be defined as what students have the opportunity to learn in schools (Eisner, 1994; McCutcheon, 2002). Eisner (1994) postulated several forms of the curriculum: (a) the explicit curriculum concerns student-learning opportunities that are overtly taught and stated or printed in documents, policies, and guidelines, such as in course syllabi, the common core standards, or on school websites; (b) the implicit curriculum is intended or unintended but is not stated or written down; it is also known as the hidden curriculum; (c) a third form of curriculum, the null curriculum, deals with what students do not have the opportunity to learn. Thus, information and knowledge that are not available for student learning are also forms of the curriculum because *students are actually learning something based on what is not emphasized, covered, or taught.* What students do not experience in the curriculum becomes messages for them. For example, if students are not taught to question, critique, or critically examine power structures, the students are learning something—possibly that it may not be essential or appropriate for them to critique the world in order to improve it. From Eisner's perspective, what is *absent* is essentially *present* in student learning opportunities through the curriculum.

REFERENCES

Adler, M. A., & Fisher, C. W. (2001). Early reading programs in high-poverty schools: A case study of beating the odds. *The Reading Teacher, 54*, 616–619.

Allen, Q. (in press). "They think minority means lesser than": Black middle-class sons and fathers resisting microaggressions in the school. *Urban Education.*

Alridge, D. P. (2003). The dilemmas, challenges, and duality of an African-American educational historian. *Educational Researcher, 32*(9), 25–34.

Anyon, J. (1980). Social class and the hidden curriculum of work. *Journal of Education, 162,* 366–391.

Anyon, J. (1997). *Ghetto schooling: A political economy of urban educational reform.* New York, NY: Teachers College Press.

Anyon, J. (2005). *Radical possibilities: Public policy, urban education, and a new social movement.* New York, NY: Routledge.

Apple, M. W. (2006). Understanding and interrupting neoliberalism and neoconservatism in education. *Pedagogies: An International Journal, 1*(1), 21–26.

Arnold, D. H., & Doctoroff, G. (2003). The early education of socioeconomically disadvantaged children. *Annual Review of Psychology, 54*, 517–545.

Artiles, A. J., Klingner, J. K., & Tate, W. F. (2006). Representation of minority students in special education: Complicating traditional explanations. *Educational Researcher, 35*(6), 3–5.

Banks, J. A. (2001). Citizenship education and diversity: Implications for teacher education. *Journal of Teacher Education, 52*(1), 5–16.

Barton, P. E. (2003). *Parsing the achievement gap: Baseline for tracking progress.* Princeton, NJ: Educational Testing Services.

Barton, P. E., & Coley, R. J. (2010). *The black-white achievement gap: When progress stopped.* Princeton, NJ: Educational Testing Services.

Battistitch, V., Solomon, D., Dong-il, K., Watson, M., & Schaps, E. (1995). Schools as communities, poverty levels of student populations, and students' attitudes, motives, and performance: A multi-level analysis. *American Educational Research Journal, 32*, 627–658.

Beachum, F. D., & McCray, C. R. (2011). *Cultural collision and collusion: Reflections on hip-hop culture, values, and schools.* New York, NY: Peter Lang.

Bell, D. A. (1976). Serving two masters: Integration ideals and client interests in school desegregation litigation. *Yale Law Journal, 85*, 470–516.

Bell, D. A. (1980). Brown v. Board of Education and the interest-convergence dilemma. *Harvard Law Review, 93*, 518–533.

Blanchett, W. J. (2006). Disproportionate representation of African Americans in special education: Acknowledging the role of White privilege and racism. *Educational Researcher, 35*(6), 24–28.

Bomer, R., Dworin, J., May, L., & Semingson, P. (2008). Miseducating teachers about the poor: A critical analysis of Ruby Payne's claims about poverty. *Teachers College Record, 110*, 2497–2531.

Boutte, G. S. (2012). Urban schools: Challenges and possibilities for early childhood and elementary education. *Urban Education, 47*, 515–550.

Bracey, G. W. (1997). Money matters: No it doesn't, yes it does. *Phi Delta Kappan, 79*, 162–164.

Brooks-Gunn, J., & Duncan, G. J. (1997). The effects of poverty on children. *Future of Children, 7*(2), 55–71.

Brown-Jeffey, S., & Cooper, J. E. (2011). Toward a conceptual framework of culturally relevant pedagogy: An overview of the conceptual and theoretical framework. *Teacher Education Quarterly, 38*(1), 65–84.

Burch, K. (2001). A tale of two citizens: Asking the Rodriguez question in the twenty first century. *Education Studies, 32*, 264–278.

Burney, V., & Beilke, J. (2008, April). The constraints of poverty on high achievement. *Journal for the Education of the Gifted, 31*, 295–321.

Caldas, S. J., & Bankston, C., III. (1997). Effect of school population socioeconomic status on individual academic achievement. *Journal of Educational Research, 90*, 269–277.

Carter Andrews, D. J. (2009). The construction of Black high-achiever identities in a predominantly White high school. *Anthropology & Education Quarterly, 40*, 297–317.

Cass, J. (2010). *Held captive: Child poverty in America* (Children's Defense Fund Report). Washington, DC: Children's Defense Fund.

Chafel, J. A. (1997). Children's views of poverty: A review of research and implications for teaching. *Educational Forum, 61*, 360–371.

Chapman, T. K. (2007). Interrogating classroom relationships and events: Using portraiture and critical race theory in educational research. *Educational Researcher, 36*, 156–162.

Chubb, J. E., & Loveless, T. (Eds.). (2002). *Bridging the achievement gap.* Washington, DC: Brookings Institution Press.

Coldarci, T. (2006, October). Do smaller schools really reduce the "power rating" of poverty? *The Rural Educator, 28*(1), 1–8.

Coleman, J. S. (1969). *Equality and achievement in education.* Boulder, CO: Westview Press.

Coleman, J. S. (1988). Social capital in the creation of human capital. *American Journal of Sociology, 94*, 95–120.

Cooper, C. E., Crosnoe, R., Suizzo, M.-A., & Pituch, K. (2009). Poverty, race, and parental involvement during the transition to elementary school. *Journal of Family Issues, 31*, 859–883.

Darling-Hammond, L. (2010). *The flat world and education: How America's commitment to equity will determine our future.* New York, NY: Teachers College Press.

Davis, J. E., & Jordan, W. J. (1994). The effects of school context, structure, and experiences on African American males in middle and high school. *Journal of Negro Education, 63*, 570–587.

Delpit, L. (1995). *Other people's children: Cultural conflict in the classroom.* New York, NY: New Press.

Delpit, L. (2012). *Multiplication is for White people: Raising expectations for other people's children.* New York, NY: New Press.

DeNavas-Walt, C., Proctor, B. D., & Smith, J. C. (2009). *Income, poverty, and health insurance coverage in the United States: 2008.* Washington DC: U.S. Census Bureau. Retrieved from http://www.census.gov/prod/2009pubs/p60-236.pdf

Dixson, A. D., & Rousseau, C. K. (2005). And we are still not saved: Critical race theory in education ten years later. *Race, Ethnicity and Education, 8,* 7–27.

Duffield, B. (2001). The educational rights of homeless children. *Educational Studies, 32,* 323–336.

Duncan, G. A. (2005). Critical race ethnography in education: Narrative, inequality and the problem of epistemology. *Race, Ethnicity and Education, 8,* 93–114.

Dutro, E. (2010). What "hard times" means: Mandated curricula, class-privileged assumptions, and the lives of poor children. *Research in the Teaching of English, 44,* 255–291.

Ede, A. (2006). Scripted curriculum: Is it a prescription for success? *Childhood Education, 83*(1), 29–32.

Edmondson, J., & Shannon, P. (1998). Reading education and poverty: Questioning the reading success equation. *Peabody Journal of Education, 73*(3/4), 104–126.

Eisner, E. W. (1994). *The educational imagination: On the design and evaluation of school programs.* New York, NY: Macmillan.

Evans, R. (2005). A special section on the achievement gap: Reframing the achievement gap. *Phi Delta Kappan, 86,* 594–598.

Farrugia, D. (2011). The symbolic burden of homelessness. *Journal of Sociology, 41,* 71–87.

Finley, S., & Diversi, M. (2010). Critical homelessness: Expanding narratives of inclusive democracy. *Cultural Studies, Critical Methodologies, 10*(1), 4–13.

Ford, D. Y. (2010). *Reversing underachievement among gifted black students.* Waco, TX: Prufrock Press.

Foster, M. (1999). Race, class, and gender in education research: Surveying the political terrain. *Educational Policy, 13,* 77–85.

Fram, M., Miller-Cribbs, J., & Horn, L. (2007). Poverty, race, and the contexts of achievement: Examining educational experiences of children in the U.S. South. *Social Work, 52,* 309–319.

Freire, P. (1998). *Pedagogy of the oppressed.* New York, NY: Continuum.

Gay, G. (2010). *Culturally responsive teaching: Theory, research, and practice* (2nd ed.). New York, NY: Teachers College Press.

Goddard, R. D., Salloum, S. J., & Berebitsky, D. (2009). Trust as a mediator of the relationships between poverty, racial composition, and academic achievement: Evidence from Michigan's public elementary schools. *Educational Administration Quarterly, 45,* 292–311.

Gooden, M. A. (2012). What does racism have to do with leadership? Countering the idea of color-blind leadership: A reflection on race and the growing pressures of the urban principalship. *Journal of Educational Foundations, 26*(1–2), 67–84.

Gorski, P. (2006). The classist underpinnings of Ruby Payne's framework. *Teachers College Record Online.* Retrieved from http://www.tcrecord.org/Content.asp?ContentID=12610

Graue, E., Hatch, K., Rao, K., & Oen, D. (2007). The wisdom of class-size reduction. *American Education Research Journal, 44,* 670–700.

Gutiérrez, K., & Rogoff, B. (2003). Cultural ways of learning: Individual traits and repertoires of practice. *Educational Researcher, 32*(5), 19–25.

Gutman, L., & McLoyd, V. (2000). Parents' management of their children's education within the home, at school, and in the community: An examination of African American families living in poverty. *Urban Review, 32*(1), 1–24.

Haberman, M. (1991). The pedagogy of poverty versus good teaching. *Phi Delta Kappan, 73*, 290–294.

Haberman, M. (1995). *Star teachers of children in poverty.* West Lafayette, IN: Kappa Delta Pi.

Haberman, M. (2000). Urban schools: Day camps or custodial centers? *Phi Delta Kappan, 82*, 203–208.

Haughey, M., Snart, F., & da Costa, J. (2001). Literacy achievement in small grade 1 classes in high-poverty environments. *Canadian Journal of Education, 26*, 301–320.

Henslin, J. M. (2004). *Essentials of sociology: A down-to-earth approach* (5th ed.). Boston, MA: Pearson.

hooks, b. (2000). *Where we stand: Class matters.* New York, NY: Routledge.

Hoover-Dempsey, K. V., & Sandler, H. M. (1997). Why do parents become involved in their children's education? *Review of Educational Research, 67*, 3–42.

Horsford, S. D. (2010). Mixed feelings about mixed schools: Superintendents on the complex legacy of school desegregation. *Educational Administration Quarterly, 46*, 287–321.

Howard, T. C. (2008). "Who really cares?" The disenfranchisement of African American males in PreK-12 schools: A critical race theory perspective. *Teachers College Record, 110*, 954–985.

Howard, T. C. (2010). *Why race and culture matter: Closing the achievement gap in American classrooms.* New York, NY: Teachers College Press.

Howse, R. B., Lange, G., Farran, D. C., & Boyles, C. D. (2003). Motivation and self-regulation as predictors of achievement in economically disadvantaged young children. *Journal of Experimental Education, 71*(2), 151–174.

Hughes, S. A., & Berry, T. (Eds.). (2012). *The evolving significance of race: Living, learning and teaching.* New York, NY: Peter Lang.

Iddings, A., Combs, M. C., & Moll, L. (2012). In the arid zone: Drying out educational resources for English language learners through policy and practice. *Urban Education, 47*, 495–514.

Irizarry, J. G., & Donaldson, M. L. (2012). Teach for América: The Latinization of U.S. schools and the critical shortage of Latina/o teachers. *American Educational Research Journal, 49*, 155–194.

Irvine, J. J. (2010). Foreword. In H. R. Milner's (Ed.), *Culture, curriculum, and identity in education* (p. xi-xii). New York, NY: Palgrave Macmillan.

Jacob, B. A., & Lefgren, L. (2007). In low-income schools, parents want teachers who teach. *Education Next, 7*(3), 59–64.

James, C. E. (2012). Students "at risk": Stereotypes and the schooling of Black boys. *Urban Education, 47*, 464–494.

Jay, M. (2003). Critical race theory, multicultural education, and the hidden curriculum of hegemony. *Multicultural Perspectives, 5*(4), 3–9.

Jencks, C., & Phillips, M. (1998). *The Black-White test score gap.* Washington, DC: Brookings Institution Press.

Jenkins, T. S. (2006). The challenges of educating black males within American society. *Journal of Black Studies, 37*, 127–155.

Jepsen, C., & Rivkin, S. (2009). Class size reduction and student achievement. *Journal of Human Resources, 44*, 223–250.

Kieffer, M. J. (2008). Catching up or falling behind? Initial English proficiency, concentrated poverty, and the reading growth of minority learners in the United States. *Journal of Education Psychology, 100*, 851–868.

King, S. (1993). The limited presence of African-American teachers. *Review of Educational Research, 63*, 115–149.

Kirkland, D. E. (2011). Books like clothes: Engaging young Black men with reading. *Journal of Adolescent & Adult Literacy, 55*, 199–208.

Klopfenstein, K. (2005). Beyond test scores: The impact of black teacher role models on rigorous math taking. *Contemporary Economic Policy, 23*, 416–428.

Konstantopoulous, S. (2009). Effects of teachers on minority and disadvantaged students' achievement in the early grades. *Elementary School Journal, 110*, 92–113.

Kozol, J. (1991). *Savage inequalities: Children in America's schools.* New York, NY: Crown.

Kozol, J. (2005). *The shame of a nation: The return of apartheid schooling in America.* New York, NY: Crown.

Ladson-Billings, G. (1992). Liberatory consequences of literacy: A case of culturally relevant instruction for African American students. *Journal of Negro Education, 61*, 378–391.

Ladson-Billings, G. (2006). From the achievement gap to the education debt: Understanding achievement in U.S. schools. *Educational Researcher, 35*(7), 3–12.

Ladson-Billings, G. (2009). *The dreamkeepers: Successful teachers of African American children* (2nd ed.). San Francisco, CA: Jossey-Bass.

Ladson-Billings, G., & Tate, B. (1995). Toward a critical race theory of education. *Teachers College Record, 97*, 47–67.

Lareau, A. (2003). *Unequal childhoods: Race, class, and family life.* Berkeley: University of California Press.

Lee, B. A., Tyler, K. A., & Wright, J. D. (2010). The new homelessness revisited. *Annual Review of Sociology, 36*, 501–521.

Lee, C. D. (2007). *Culture, literacy, and learning: Taking bloom in the midst of the whirlwind.* New York, NY: Teachers College Press.

Leonardo, Z. (2009). *Race, whiteness, and education.* New York, NY: Routledge.

Lewis, A. E. (2001). There is no "race" in the schoolyard: Colorblind ideology in an (almost) all White school. *American Educational Research Journal, 38*, 781–811.

Lewis, O. (1959). *Five families: Mexican case studies in the culture of poverty.* New York, NY: Basic Books.

Lewis, O. (1961). *The children of Sanchez: Autobiography of a Mexican family.* New York, NY: Random House.

Lewis, O. (1966). The culture of poverty. *Scientific American, 215*, 19–25.

Lin, A. C., & Harris, D. (2009, January). *The color of poverty: Why racial and ethnic disparities persist* (Policy Brief, No. 16). Ann Arbor, MI: National Poverty Center.

Liu, G. (2006). *How the federal government makes rich states richer.* Washington, DC: Education Trust.

Lynn, M. (2006). Education for the community: Exploring the culturally relevant practices of Black male teachers. *Teachers College Record, 108*, 2497–2522.

MacLeod, J. (1995). *Social reproduction in theoretical perspective. Ain't no makin it: Aspirations and attainment in a low-income neighborhood.* San Francisco, CA: Westview Press.

Martin, D. (2009). Researching race in mathematics education. *Teachers College Record, 111*, 295–338.

Mawhinney-Rhoads, L., & Stahler, G. (2006). Educational policy and reform for homeless students: An overview. *Education and Urban Society, 38*, 288–306.

McCutcheon, G. (2002). *Developing the curriculum: Solo and group deliberation.* Troy, NY: Educators' Press International.

McGee, E. O., & Spencer, M. B. (2012). Theoretical analysis of resilience and identity: An African American engineer's life story. In E. Dixon-Román & E. W. Gordon (Eds.), *Thinking comprehensively about education: Spaces of educative possibility and their implications for public policy* (pp. 161–178). New York, NY: Routledge.

Milne, A., & Plourde, L. A. (2006). Factors of a low-SES household: What aids academic achievement? *Journal of Instructional Psychology, 33*, 183–193.

Milner, H. R. (2007). Race, culture, and researcher positionality: Working through dangers seen, unseen, and unforeseen. *Educational Researcher, 36*, 388–400.

Milner, H. R. (2008). Critical race theory and interest convergence as analytic tools in teacher education policies and practices. *Journal of Teacher Education, 59,* 332–346.

Milner, H. R. (2010). *Start where you are, but don't stay there.* Cambridge, MA: Harvard Education Press.

Milner, H. R. (2012). Beyond a test score: Explaining opportunity gaps in educational practice. *Journal of Black Studies, 43,* 643–718.

Moll, L., & Gonzalez, N. (2004). Engaging life: A funds-of-knowledge approach to multicultural education. In J. Banks & C. Banks (Eds.), *Handbook of research on multicultural education* (2nd ed., pp. 699–715). San Francisco, CA: Jossey-Bass.

Morris, J. E., & Monroe, C. R. (2009). Why study the U.S. South? The nexus of race and place in investigating Black student achievement. *Educational Researcher, 38,* 21–36.

Munin, A. (2012). *Color by number: Understanding racism through facts and stats on children.* Sterling, VA: Stylus.

Murnane, R. J. (2007). Improving the education of children living in poverty. *Future of Children, 17,* 161–182.

Nieto, S. (2000). Placing equity front and center: Some thoughts on transforming teacher education for a new century. *Journal of Teacher Education, 51,* 180–187.

Noguera, P. A. (2003). Schools, prisons, and social implications of punishment: Rethinking disciplinary practices. *Theory Into Practice, 42,* 341–350.

Noguera, P. A., & Wells, L. (2011). The politics of school reform: A broader and bolder approach for Newark. *Berkeley Review of Education, 2*(1), 5–25.

Nooe, R. M., & Patterson, D. A. (2010). The ecology of homelessness. *Journal of Human Behavior in the Social Environment, 20,* 105–152.

Nyhan, R. C., & Alkadry, M. G. (1999). The impact of school resources on student achievement test scores. *Journal of Education Finance, 25,* 211–227.

O'Connor, C., & Fernandez, S. D. (2006). Race, class, and disproportionality: Reevaluating the relationship, poverty and special education placement. *Educational Researcher, 35*(6), 6–11.

Osei-Kofi, N. (2005). Pathologizing the poor: A framework for understanding Ruby Payne's work. *Equity & Excellence in Education, 38,* 367–375.

Page, M. S. (2002). Technology-enriched classrooms: Effects on students of low socioeconomic status. *Journal of Research on Technology in Education, 34,* 389–409.

Parker, L., & Lynn, M. (2002). What's race got to do with it? Critical race theory's conflicts with and connections to qualitative research methodology and epistemology. *Qualitative Inquiry, 8*(1), 7–22.

Payne, C. M. (2008). *So much reform, so little change: The persistence of failure in urban schools.* Cambridge, MA: Harvard Education Press.

Payne, R. (1996). *A framework for understanding poverty.* Highlands, TX: Aha! Process.

Pino, N. W., & Smith, W. L. (2004). African American students, the academic ethic, and GPA. *Journal of Black Studies, 35,* 113–131.

Pribesh, S., Gavigan, K., & Gail Dickinson, G. (2011). The access gap: Poverty and characteristics of school library media centers. *Library Quarterly, 81,* 143–160.

Pritchard, A. M. (1993). A common format for poverty: A content analysis of social problems textbooks. *Teaching Sociology, 21*(1), 42–49.

Randolph-McCree, I., & Pristoop, E. (2005). *The funding gap 2005: Low-income and minority students shortchanged by most states* (Special Report). Washington, DC: Education Trust.

Reichardt, R. (2001). *Reducing class size: Choices and consequences* (Policy Brief). Denver, CO: Mid-continent Research for Education and Learning.

Rothstein, R. (2004). *Class and schools: Using social, economic, and educational reform to close the black-white achievement gap.* Washington, DC: Economic Policy Institute.

Roza, M. (2006). *How districts shortchange low-income and minority students.* Washington, DC: Education Trust.

Ryan, J. E. (1999). Schools, race, and money. *Yale Law Journal, 109*, 249–316.

Sealey-Ruiz, Y. (2011). Learning to talk and write about race: Developing racial literacy in a college English classroom. *English Quarterly. The Canadian Council of Teachers of English Language Arts, 42*(1), 24–42.

Secada, W. G. (1989). Agenda setting, enlightened self-interest, and equity in mathematics education. *Peabody Journal of Education, 66*(2), 22–56.

Simms, M. C., Fortuny, K., & Henderson, E. (2009). *Racial and ethnic disparities among low-income families.* New York, NY: Urban Institute.

Skiba, R. J., Michael, R. S., Nardo, A. C., & Peterson, R. L. (2002). The color of discipline: Sources of racial and gender disproportionality in school punishment. *Urban Review, 34*, 317–342.

Slaughter-Defoe, D. T., & Carlson, K. G. (1996). Young African American and Latino children in high-poverty urban schools: How they perceive school climate. *Journal of Negro Education, 65*, 60–70.

Sleeter, C. (2012). Confronting the marginalization of culturally responsive pedagogy. *Urban Education, 47* 562–584.

Smagorinsky, P., Lakly, A., & Johnson, T. S. (2002). Acquiescence, accommodation, and resistance in learning to teach within a prescribed curriculum. *English Education, 34*, 187–211.

Solorzano, D. G., & Yosso, T. J. (2001). From racial stereotyping and deficit discourse toward a critical race theory in teacher education. *Multicultural Education, 9*(1), 2–8.

Tate, W. F. (1994). From inner city to ivory tower: Does my voice matter in the academy? *Urban Education, 29*, 245–269.

Tate, W. F. (1997). Critical race theory and education: History, theory, and implications. In M. Apple (Ed.), *Review of research in education* (Vol. 22, pp. 195–247). Washington, DC: American Educational Research Association.

Tate, W. F. (2008). Geography of opportunity: Poverty, place, and educational outcomes. *Educational Researcher, 37*, 397–411.

Tate, W. F., Ladson-Billings, G., & Grant, C. A. (1993). The Brown decision revisited: Mathematizing social problems. *Educational Policy, 7*, 255–275.

Terrill, M., & Mark, D. (2000). Preservice teachers' expectations for schools with children of color and second-language learners. *Journal of Teacher Education, 51*, 147–153.

Tillman, L. C. (2002). Culturally sensitive research approaches: An African American perspective. *Educational Researcher, 31*(9), 3–12.

Toshalis, E. (2011). The rhetoric of care: Preservice teacher discourses that depoliticize, deflect, and deceive. *Urban Review, 44*, 1–35.

Toutkoushian, R. K., & Curtis, T. (2005). Effects of socioeconomic factors on public high school outcomes and rankings. *Journal of Educational Research, 98*, 259–271.

Ullucci, K. (2012). Learning to see: The development of race and class consciousness in White teachers. *Race, Ethnicity and Education, 14*, 561–577.

U.S. Census Bureau. (2005). *Poverty thresholds 2004.* Retrieved from http://www.census.gov/hhes/www/poverty/thresh04.html

U.S. Census Bureau. (2012). *How the Census Bureau measures poverty.* Retrieved from http://www.census.gov/hhes/www/poverty/about/overview/measure.html

Vasquez Heilig, J., Brown, K., & Brown, A. (in press). The illusion of inclusion: Race and standards. *Harvard Educational Review.*

Weis, L., & Dolby, N. (2012). *Social class and education: Global perspectives.* New York, NY: Routledge.

Wiener, R., & Pristoop, E. (2006). *How states shortchange the districts that need the most help.* Washington, DC. Education Trust.

White-Smith, K. A. (2012). Beyond instructional leadership: The lived experiences of principals in successful urban schools. *Journal of School Leadership, 22*, 6–25. *Source.* Photo adapted from H. Richard Milner's (in progress) research project, Studying Places of Poverty.

Chapter 2

How Does It Feel to Be a Problem?
Black Male Students, Schools, and
Learning in Enhancing the Knowledge Base
to Disrupt Deficit Frameworks

Tyrone C. Howard
University of California, Los Angeles

Despite a multitude of school reform efforts, increased standardization in schools, the influx of charter schools nationwide, the promulgation of high-stakes testing, the supposed promise of educational policies such as No Child Left Behind, the surge of districts being taken over by states, and the growing corporate presence to oversee schools, there still remains a large segment of students attending U.S. schools who fail to gain access to a high-quality education (Darling-Hammond, 2006, 2010; Howard, 2010). These trends are most disturbing at a time when increasing globalization and the need for highly skilled individuals may lead to countless numbers of students who find themselves on the academic margins today and will most certainly be on the economic and social fringes in the near future. Although this academic and social exclusion will undoubtedly affect students across all racial, gender, and socioeconomic groups, there are persistent data that show that certain student groups are more severely and disproportionately affected by school failures than others. One of those groups, African American[1] males, is the focus of this work. African American males will be the focus because they continue to be one of the more academically and socially marginalized students in U.S. schools (Anderson, 2008; Noguera, 2008). The outcomes in school in many ways mirror their condition in the larger society (Polite & Davis, 1999). This work seeks to shed some light on some of the challenges that exist for Black males in their pursuit for academic success.

A close examination of a number of political, social, and economic indicators reveals the ongoing challenges of what it means to be Black and male in the United States.

Review of Research in Education
March 2013, Vol. 37, pp. 54-86
DOI: 10.3102/0091732X12462985
© 2013 AERA. http://rre.aera.net

Many of these challenges begin at birth and persist over time. Disproportionately high infant mortality rates, born and reared into chronic poverty, overrepresented in underfunded schools, Black males, like many other individuals reared in economically depressed areas, face major life challenges from the outset (Anderson, 2008). What is perplexing is the intensity and persistence in which the social ills continue to have a deleterious effect on Black males well into adulthood in ways that it does not affect other populations. This is exhibited when looking at data that reveal the manner in which Black males have chronically high unemployment, are overincarcerated, have disparate health conditions, and ultimately lower life expectations than any of the largest racial/ethnic and gender groups in the United States (U.S. Department of Commerce, 2007, 2009). The complex, yet complicated picture of life for Black males in the United States remains a topic of study and analysis across a multitude of disciplines, and although many have described the depth and breadth of the problem from a research, policy, and practice standpoint, minimal change has occurred on a large-scale level (U.S. Census Bureau, 2011). Needless to say, there is more to be studied, analyzed, and learned. Therefore, the focus of this work is to provide a selected synthesis on the research on, about, or concerned with Black males within the context of education.

The challenges that exist for Black males have been well documented (Anderson, 2008; Balfanz & Legters, 2004; Ferguson, 2003; Gibbs, 1988; E. T. Gordon, Gordon, & Nembhard, 1994; Hopkins, 1997; Howard, 2008; Madhubuti, 1990; Mincy, 2006; Noguera, 2001; Polite & Davis, 1999; Staples, 1982). Frequently labeled as problems, prone to violence, invoking fear in many, and deemed as undesirable in certain circles, the view of Black males is diverse and extreme on many levels. Loathed in various environments, applauded in others, perhaps no other group of people are emulated yet despised simultaneously to the extent that Black men are today. However, the paradoxical perception of Black males within the larger society remains puzzling. There are ongoing elements of mainstream and popular culture that have been developed, sustained, and made into multi–billion dollar industries based on the talents, creative genius, intellect, and identities of Black males. Thus, in many ways, this love-hate affair represents the illogicality of how many Black males are viewed within mainstream society. Ladson-Billings (2011) discusses "the love-hate relationship with Black males" (p. 8). She asserts,

We see African American males as "problems" that our society must find ways to eradicate. We regularly determine them to be the root cause of most problems in school and society. We seem to hate their dress, their language and their effect. We hate that they challenge authority and command so much social power. While the society apparently loves them in narrow niches and specific slots—music, basketball, football, track—we seem less comfortable with them than in places like the national Honor Society, the debate team, or the computer club. (p. 9)

THE LANDSCAPE OF BLACK MALES IN U.S. SCHOOLS

Black males constitute close to 4 million, or 7% of the U.S student population (U.S. Department of Education, 2011). Like any other subgroup, Black males possess a number of overlapping identities and diverse experiences. Thus, to characterize the group in monolithic terms would be problematic for obvious reasons. However, it is not the goal of this work to unpack the complexity and multiple layers of Black male identity. The intersectionality of Black male identity has been examined in other works, and some of it will be discussed in this chapter (Howard & Reynolds, in press; McCready, 2004). This work is an attempt to paint a picture that tends to reflect many of the educational challenges (and the contributing factors) facing this population in a variety of ways that often cuts across the multiple identity markers that Black males possess. It has been well established in the professional literature that Black males face myriad challenges in the nation's schools and colleges (Harper, 2012; Jackson, 2007). The academic achievement of Black males in PreK-12 and postsecondary schools has been the subject of a number of scholarly works over the past three decades (M. C. Brown & Davis, 2000; Davis, 2003; Franklin, 1991; Gibbs, 1988; E. T. Gordon et al., 1994; Hopkins, 1997; Madhubuti, 1990; Noguera, 1996; Polite, 1994; Polite & Davis, 1999; Price, 2000). Much of this work has been concerned with the identification of informative research, effective strategies, and critical concepts that seek to address two areas: (a) reasons that explain the persistent under-achievement of Black males in U.S. schools and society and (b) viable interventions that can help improve the educational aspirations and life chances of Black males. This previous research on Black males has been much needed given the troublesome state of many Black males in P-20 schools and a number of other social indicators. Needless to say, many of the challenges that Black males encounter are not dramatically different from those encountered by other males of color, namely, Latino, Southeast Asian, and Native American males (Conchas & Vigil, 2012; Noguera, 1996, 2008). Educational research has often fallen short in examining race, class, and gender intersections in schools and how they influence the schooling experiences of various populations. Ladson-Billings and Tate (1995) contend that race has been, and continues to be, undertheorized. Although previous works have documented some of the challenges that African American males encounter in schools, there is a pressing need to examine the larger body of research on Black males and develop a comprehensive account of what we know about this population, what general trends exist in the literature about them, identify some of the strengths and problems with the current literature base, and be able to offer some recommendations for future research, theory, and practice on this population.

HOW DOES IT FEEL TO BE A PROBLEM?

In his groundbreaking work, *The Souls of Black Folks*, W. E. B. DuBois (1903) begins his chapter "Of Our Spiritual Strivings" with a provocative question, one that has important relevance for Black males attending U.S. schools today: "How does it feel to be a problem?" DuBois frames this question within the context of how African Americans, striving for social, economic, and political inclusion at the turn of the 20th century, were continuously seen as a "problem" for the country. In the years before and after DuBois's work, a number of works in the professional literature characterized African

Americans in problematic terms, and a litany of works and their titles over the 20th century illustrated how the population was perceived in troublesome ways. A perusal of these works would reveal titles such as *The Negro Problem: Abraham Lincoln's Solution* (Pickett, 1969), *What Shall We Do With the Negro?* (Escott, 2009), *American Dilemma: The Negro Problem* (Myrdal, 1944), *The Negro: The Southerners' Problem* (Page, 1904), and *The White man's Burden* (Riley, 1910), to name a few. In many ways, DuBois's question precisely speaks to the manner in which Black males at the turn of the 21st century may feel if they were to peruse much of the social science literature, popular press, mainstream media, and even within the academic discourse about their academic performance and overall potential. A read through of a majority of the literature on Black males would reveal a number of disturbing classifications. In conducting research for this work, the terms that frequently came up with Black males were phrases such as *at-risk, endangered, remedial, in crisis, ineducable, extinct,* and *left behind.* These terms shed insight into how much of the literature has fallen short in providing a more holistic and affirming account of Black males in schools. In this chapter, I provide a selective review of the research that has documented African American males and their experiences in PreK-12 schools, but the search is done in a way that seeks to highlight those works that disrupt the persistence of deficit-based notions.

A selective literature review was conducted as a way to understand and document research involving African American male students. Using electronic databases and selective citations (Cooper, 1988), scholarly peer-reviewed articles published from 2000 to 2012 were examined. In some selected cases, works published before 2000 were used. These works were included because of the seminal nature they contributed to the knowledge base on Black males. For example, Gibbs (1988) was often cited in many of the more recent works and was seen as one of the more important works in documenting scholarship and practice on Black males. The same can be said for the work of Polite and Davis (1999), Staples (1982), and Franklin (1991). A comprehensive and systematic search of electronic databases was performed using five educational and social science search engines: EBSCO HOST (Academic Search Premier SocINDEX with Full Text), JSTOR, Google Scholar, Wilson Web Social Sciences Full Text, and ERIC. During the searches, I combined the following key words and terms in various combinations until an overlap point was reached, which began to yield similar works: African American males *or* boys, *or* Black males *or* boys. Data-based studies with quantitative, qualitative, or mixed designs were prioritized. A few conceptual works were included only because they were often cited in many of the empirical works. After removing duplicates, excluding studies that only included a female population, I selected studies only conducted within the United States and those studies relevant to Black males. These remaining articles were examined to determine if they included empirical works on African American males. An additional step that was taken was to look at empirical works that examined Black males who were demonstrating some type of school success or academic promise. The step was taken to avoid reifying the discourse of deficit on Black males. Thus, I deliberately excluded works that highlighted or revealed "problems" with

Black males. The final review checked if studies met all six criteria. A study was selected if it

1. was conducted within the United States;
2. used quantitative, qualitative, or mixed methods study designs;
3. was conducted within the last 12 years;
4. reported disaggregated data on or about successful or high achieving African American males, or effective pedagogies with them;
5. was published in a peer-reviewed journal, scholarly book; and
6. specifically addressed African American/Black males (not males of color).

After these works were identified, I narrowed the search down to pay particular attention to works that were concerned with one of four key areas: (a) literacy, (b) mathematics, (c) discipline and/or punishment, and (d) teacher education or teacher practice. These areas were selected because much of the literature on Black males shows the discrepancies that they experience in these areas, so I sought to confine my review to these core areas.

It should be noted that there is a growing number of works that examine the schooling experiences and challenges of boys in general (Gurian, 2001; Skelton, 2001; Weaver-Hightower, 2003) and some specific to boys of color (Conchas & Vigil, 2012; Rios, 2011). These works are important because they recognize the growing data that demonstrate that school outcomes and experiences for boys has gradually declined over the past several decades in P-20 schools. Those works were not included in this review because this work sought to specifically address the issues affecting African American males. This approach was taken due to some of the unique challenges and seeming disproportionate issues that afflict Black males. Although it is clear that boys of color face more harsh penalties in schools (Gregory, Skiba, & Noguera, 2010; Losen & Skiba, 2010), underperform academically (Schott Foundation for Public Education, 2010), and graduate at lower rates than their White male counterparts, closer scrutiny reveals that Black males are most in need of intervention given a paucity of data that document their realities in schools and the wider society. At the risk of engaging in "Oppression Olympics," this step is not taken to determine who suffers most, or who is most severely oppressed and excluded in schools, but to shine the spotlight on a particularly disturbing set of realities affecting one particular group. Finally, it should be noted that this work hopefully contributes to a larger body of important work addressing boys of color (Conchas & Noguera, 2004).

BLACK MALES AND PUBLIC PERCEPTION

The characterizations of Black males undoubtedly influences the manner in which the larger society may frame its perception of the group, and most disturbingly these same characterizations can be internalized by the group itself, and subsequently have an impact on the manner in which they view themselves and become complicit in their own challenges educationally and socially (Howard & Flennaugh, 2011). But DuBois's question "How does it feel to be a problem?" is important to note for Black males: What does it mean when you are viewed as a problem? And I pose several additional education-related questions: How does it affect one's behavior? How does one develop coping strategies? How does it influence teacher behavior? How does it affect placement for special and gifted education? And perhaps, most important, how does it influence one's pursuit of academic success and social inclusion? It is also notable to examine how the deficit-oriented construction of Black males presents major problems, and how even equity-minded[2] researchers who engage in research on Black males may often contribute to the manner in which Black males are viewed.

In this review, four areas will be analyzed and discussed regarding African American males and their educational prospects. Each of these areas has implications for research, theory, policy, and practice for African American males; their educational prospects; and subsequently their life chances. In the first part of this work, I will provide a brief summary on the educational status of African American males. This will include current trends and data on Black males in P-20 schools across the country. These data will be laid out in an attempt to provide a cursory account of where Black males are academically and socially in schools. Following the summary of the educational status of African American males, I will then develop three additional areas, one area will be what I term the *paradigmatic shift analysis*, which is an attempt to make a conceptual and theoretical shift away from viewing African American males as being uneducable and academically inferior, to one where literature is examined on African American males who experience academic success. In this section, I will detail how and why such a shift can occur and what role practitioners and researchers can play in the process. An examination of the research and theory on Black male success will provide a move away from much of the problematic literature that highlights shortcomings and deficiencies with Black males and make a needed contribution toward the development of a more comprehensive and robust picture of the Black male experience in schools, and not one situated in primarily deficit-laden accounts of Black male achievement, but one centered on the complexity, success, and diversity of Black males' experience in U.S. schools. In the third section, I will examine the literature on Black males that addresses explanations and causes for their current state of affairs. A perusal of these data is useful because it offers researchers and practitioners vital frameworks to understand factors affecting Black males and, most important, ways of intervening effectively on their behalf. In the fourth section of the work, I will detail a *micro-level* analysis of Black males in classrooms, which will focus explicitly on research that examines effective instructional practices for African American males *in* the classroom, with a particular focus on literacy, math, and school discipline–related issues. The micro-level analysis will review research on pedagogy that has contributed to increased academic outcomes for African American males such as culturally responsive pedagogy, critical literacy, and other forms of extraordinary or transformative pedagogies (Banks, 1993; Delpit, 1995, 2012; Gay, 2010; Ladson-Billings, 2006). Moreover, this section will seek to identify best practices and useful interventions that improve the teaching and learning relationships between Black males and their teachers. Although this section does not seek to be prescriptive, it does highlight works that can offer important implications for practitioners. This section also seeks to inform practitioners and teacher educators about what the knowledge base tells us about exemplary practice for African American males. Finally, I will conclude this work with recommendations for future research and for interventions that may be best suited to disrupt the disturbing trends experienced by Black males and other disenfranchised student groups.

CURRENT STATE OF AFFAIRS FOR BLACK MALES

The educational status of Black males presents a complex picture, with much to be said about the manner in which schools, community, and homes best meet their needs. The picture, from multiple sources, paints a disturbing account of the overall manner in which many schools are falling woefully short in meeting the needs of Black males. However, what is crucial to note is that the monolithic picture that is often painted is not sufficient to capture the full set of experiences of Black males. As previously stated, the purpose of this work is to offer an antideficit view of Black males' performance in schools. However, there is a need to offer a snapshot of some of the discouraging data that exist on how Black males experience schools. The data that are offered here on Black male performance are not intended to offer the usual account of how *Black males have academic deficiencies*; moreover, in an attempt to redirect explanations for Black males' experiences and outcomes in U.S. schools these data are laid out in a manner that suggests that the deficits may lie in the structures, policies, practices, and programs in schools that Black males attend. Thus, the focus in this work is not centered on how to *fix Black males* rather the suggestion is that these data may lead us to question how we *fix schools* and practices that serve Black males. Therefore, a cursory view of the statistics will be given to reflect the voluminous data that demonstrate how schools thus far have fallen woefully short in engaging Black males academically and providing the appropriate structures to foster their maximum performance. An examination of national data reveals that approximately 47% of Black males graduated within 4 years from U.S. high schools in 2008, compared with 78% for White males (Schott Foundation for Public Education, 2010). Although reading scores of Black males in Grades 4 and 8 have increased over the past decade, they still trail behind White, Latino, and Asian males, and a large majority fall short of grade-level proficiency (U.S. Department of Education, 2009b). In a number of large urban districts across the country, Black males *without disabilities* had lower reading scores in Grades 4, 8, and 12 and lower grade-level proficiency than White males *with disabilities* (U.S. Department of Education, 2009b). In many large urban districts across the country, the reading achievement scores for eighth-grade Black males are consistent with the reading scores for fourth-grade Asian American and White males (U.S. Department of Education, 2009b).

Despite progress over the past decade, math proficiency scores of Black males continue to significantly trail behind their White, Latino, and Asian male counterparts (U.S. Department of Education, 2009a). In 2009, Black males in Grades 4 through 8, *who were not eligible* for free or reduced lunch, had lower math scores than White males *who were eligible* to receive free and reduced lunch (U.S. Department of Education, National Center for Educational Statistics, 2011). At the high school level, Black males are among the subgroups least likely to take and pass AP courses and exams (College Board, 2012). Over the past three decades, the ACT and SAT scores of Black males were significantly lower than their White, Latino, and Asian counterparts (U.S. Department of Education, 2009a). Black males are the subgroup of students most likely to be retained during their K-8 education (Aud, Fox, & Kewal Ramani, 2010) and are three times more likely than Latino and Asian males to be suspended from elementary and secondary schools (Aud et al., 2010; Gregory et al., 2010).

The aforementioned data highlight a breadth of areas where schooling conditions have not adequately served Black males well. It is important to note that the larger body of literature on Black males does present explanations that are tied to historical, community, and home factors, which present a multitude of challenges that Black males encounter before they even enter schools (Anderson, 2008; Coley, 2011; Wilson, 2008). There are extensive data that show that Black children have higher infant mortality rates than Whites (Murphy, Xu, & Kochanek, 2012). Black children are more likely to be born into poverty and have less access to adequate health care compared with White, Asian, and Latino children (Brookings Institute, 2011; U.S. Department of Commerce, 2009). Data on Black males show that they are more likely to live in crime-plagued neighborhoods, become victims of homicide, and become susceptible to many of the challenges that affect low-income communities where many Black males reside (Centers for Disease Control and Prevention, 2011; Truman & Rand, 2010). It is important to note some of these realities, because what they reflect are serious challenges that exist in many communities where Black males may reside. Anderson (2008) uncovers many of these realities and makes a sociological analysis of how and why institutions and public and social policy have fallen short in providing Black males a realistic chance for life success. Some have gone further by stating that the state of affairs for Black males is more of a public health issue than previous research has suggested (Hilfiker, 2002). Because the literature on these variables has been expanded further in other works, they are not given extant attention and analysis here. Undoubtedly, historical, economical, sociological, psychological, and epidemiological factors all influence the manner in which populations of young people enter, experience, and perform in schools (Ladson-Billings, 2006). Thus, the purpose is to not ignore those factors, and explore them further, rather the unit of analysis on this work is deliberately tied to school factors, and more specifically classroom instruction.

One of the problems with the current literature on Black males is an almost exclusive focus on them as being poor and residing in urban communities and the challenges that are present in such environments. Many of the challenges that confront Black males in education goes beyond their communities and their social class status and is directly located in classrooms, the lack of racial awareness and cultural ignorance among school personnel, apathetic teacher attitudes, and poor-quality instruction that they receive, be it in urban, rural, or suburban schools (Howard, 2008; Milner, 2007, 2008). The monolithic portrayal of Black males in poor urban communities fails to consider the increasing social class diversity among Black males. B. Gordon (2012) asserts that today approximately one third of African American families live in suburban communities and send their children to middle-class schools where they still underperform compared with their White peers. Thus, even the so-called privileges that accompany social and economic mobility do not seem to thwart the presence of race and racism when it comes to the schooling experiences of Black males. Therefore, understanding the challenges of race and gender for Black males is crucial to any thorough examination of their schooling experiences. The intersectionality of race, class, and gender and other identity markers are fundamentally critical in research concerned with young Black males as they are in the case of any subgroup (Crenshaw, 1989, 1995). Each marker in its own way profoundly influences identity construction, self-concept, interactions with the world, and meaning making. Again, Black males possess multiple identities that are profoundly shaped by race, socioeconomic status, and gender in all of their complex manifestations.

PARADIGMATIC SHIFT ANALYSIS

One of the goals of this work is to reframe the knowledge base on how Black males experience schools. To that end, a paradigmatic shift analysis suggests casting a new light, or offering a new frame to analyze a group or a phenomenon. Kuhn's (1970) work on scientific knowledge is appropriate here. According to Kuhn, "A paradigm is what members of a scientific community, and they alone, share" (p. 150). The shift in a paradigm therefore seeks to move to a new set of views, understandings, and types of knowledge constructed. A paradigm shift also attempts to change the basic assumptions or norms within the ruling theory of science. It also leads to new understandings of concepts, ideas, and knowledge. Banks (1993) contends that the "knowledge construction process describes the procedure by which social, behavioral, and natural scientists create knowledge and how the implicit cultural assumptions, frames of references, perspectives, and biases within a discipline influence the ways that knowledge is constructed within it" (p. 5). Thus, in constructing new knowledge about Black males, researchers need to be cognizant of the frames used to engage in research about them, the questions that are posed, and the methods used to examine their experiences. Therefore, conceptual and theoretical frames that are centered on a discourse of them being endangered, extinct, or at-risk when discussing Black males lend themselves to identifying problems with them, without any institutional or structural critique. This shift calls for researchers to dismiss deficit-laden frames and to move toward a more asset-based approach, which recognizes the strengths, promise, and potential of students and can lead to opening up research approaches that delve into a more comprehensive, nuanced, complex, and authentic account of them.

What is essential for social scientists concerned with Black male achievement and experiences in schools to do is to engage in a paradigm shift of how Black males are viewed, studied, and understood. Accordingly, the next sections of the chapter attempt to move the unit of analysis from Black male failure to Black male success and to highlight empirical works that have revealed useful findings that highlight and examine the increasing number of works that offer a different portrayal of Black males in schools. Though these works are not as plentiful as many of the deficit-based work on Black males, there are works that demonstrate a level of persistence, resilience, and intellectual giftedness in Black males. It is also noteworthy to mention that this review reveals many more works that were offering successful interventions than in research prior to 2000, so in some ways the paradigm shift may already be occurring. Nonetheless, this work seeks to continue moving the field in this direction if this is truly the direction that work on Black males is moving toward. The reality that is frequently absent from the discourse on Black males is that not all of them are suffering and dropping out of schools, most of them are not imprisoned, many of them do experience varying degrees of academic success and social adjustment in schools, many are hard-working and disciplined, and yet their accounts are frequently absent from the narrative on Black males' educational experiences and realities. In many ways, the normalized depiction of Black males as academic failures has become so enmeshed in the educational fabric of many schools and districts that it almost becomes alarming and inexplicable when Black male success outside the athletic domain occurs (Taylor, 1999). This shift is crucial to uncover how certain school cultures and pedagogical practices are able to engage these young men in the learning process in a manner that many practitioners and researchers do not believe are possible, or are an aberration when it takes place. Furthermore, when discussing best practices, the question must be posed, *best practices for whom?* Not best practices for teachers who engage in a pedagogy of poverty (Haberman, 1991), where they fail to challenge Black males intellectually; the discussion on best practices here centers on ones that enrich their academic experiences, enhance their cognitive capacities, build on their sociocultural knowledge and realities, and ultimately prepare them for postsecondary pursuits, and the development of knowledge, skills, and dispositions that will allow them to fully participate in a democratic society as capable and contributing members to the nation-state and the global community.

Crucial to the paradigmatic shift is to understand the historical portrayal of Black men in the United States. Polite and Davis (1999) uncover the pathological manner in which Black males have often been historically described as brutes, criminals, entertainers, intellectually inferior, and physically superior. Often characterized as docile and hypersexual, the images of Black males have been part of the United States' DNA from the country's outset and has set much of the tone on race in the United States for centuries (Gibbs, 1988). In one of the more illuminating work on Black males, and the narrative that has been weaved over time, A. Brown (2011) offers a historical examination of the manner in which Black males have been portrayed in the social science literature, which raises important questions and concerns about how researchers have played a prominent role in the negative construction of Black males, even as they claim to disrupt some of the troubling accounts of them. Brown suggests that from the 1930s to the present there have been four recursive narratives about Black males that have informed the general populace about Black males. He identifies these four narratives—(a) *absent and wandering*, (b) *castrated and emasculated*, (c) *soulful and adaptive*, and (d) *endangered and in-crisis*—as being staples in the normalized manner in which Black males are seen within popular media and how much of social science research feeds into this characterization of Black males as being in need of intervention, lacking in emotional and social support, and in perpetual need of male mentorship and role modeling. Much of A. Brown's (2011) work is focused on how these narratives can be rewritten, reconceptualized in a manner that is asset-based and see Black males from a position of possibility, and not one that continues to calcify them as directionless, hopeless, and deficient.

From a theoretical and methodological stance, one of the tools that may be used to combat age old and narrow constructions of Black male experiences and can be useful in the paradigm shift is to center them as the author of their experiences. More scholars have made the call for narrative inquiry and counterstorytelling that has the potential to relocate and resituate the experiences of marginalized populations in a more accurate context (Posner, 1997). It can be helpful to acknowledge the permanence of storytelling from the dominant paradigm when it comes to ideas such as meritocracy, democracy, and equality; ideas and concepts that many citizens in this country believe are just that—ideas and concepts, not realized ways of life. Thus, in constructing the new paradigm on Black male experiences and outcomes, new voices must be centered in the analysis, voices that are often overlooked, ignored, or outright dismissed—and that is the voices of Black males themselves. Sleeter & Bernal (2003) state, "At issue is the question of what counts as truth and who gets to decide" (p. 249). bell hooks (1990) talks about the dangers of White interpretations of the Black experience and the mainstream's suspicion of the Black experience as told by Black people. Far too often everyone other than Black males have offered commentary, analysis, and narrative of their experience. The African proverb that is appropriate here is, "Do not let the lion tell the giraffe's story." Black males' accounts of their own school experiences have registered only a minor blip on the radar of social science research because it is assumed that they are unable or unwilling to tell it. Some may question their ability to accurately tell their story. The critics also contest how representative these accounts are of all members of the group, or what Rosen (1996) refers to as "vulgar racial essentialism." In other words, there are those who would challenge the authenticity of these accounts to the point where depictions are represented in grossly overgeneralized ways. While there is an understanding of this viewpoint to avoid essentializing of any group, one must resist the propensity to question the veracity of Black male voices, when so many others have not been questioned in a similar fashion. The need for alternate voices and diverse viewpoints is important, and a paradigmatic shift requires the fluidity and multifaceted nature of identity for all individuals, and does not attempt to create monolithic constructions or experiences of any group. All theoretical frameworks have their shares of strengths and weaknesses, and narrative theorists recognize that the framework is not a panacea for all that ails children of color in U.S. schools, and will be subject to various critiques. However, these critiques should not prevent a much needed examination of student voices and perspectives in education to occur. More important, future research concerned with Black males and their educational experiences can directly address these critiques conceptually and empirically, which will only strengthen the paradigm as it continues to emerge in educational research.

LITERATURE ON BLACK MALES: EXPLANATIONS FOR THE CURRENT CONDITION

The literature of Black male academic performance and experiences, and explanations for it, has been outlined in a number of works over the past three decades. E. T. Gordon et al. (1994) called for scholars to move away from genetic and cultural explanation of Black male underachievement and to examine for structural explanations. Using the lens of institutional racism and discrimination, they suggested that drugs, crime, violence, inferior schooling, and economic instability provided more reliable insights into why Black males struggle to adapt in schools. Some scholars have suggested that explanations of Black male underperformance are a result of oppositional identities to mainstream cultural norms and practices and have resulted in some Black students refusing to become academically engaged because they run the risk of being ostracized by their peers (Fordham & Ogbu, 1986; Ogbu, 1987). Subsequent to this work, Ogbu (2003) further contended that for many middle-class Black students, their failure to engage was due to community forces that inform Black student school success. He defines community forces as "the ways minorities interpret and respond to schooling . . . the beliefs and behaviors within the minority community regarding education that minority students bring to school" (pp. vii-xiii).

Ogbu's (1987) work has often been critiqued for its failure to locate the impact of racism and discrimination on the schooling experiences of African American students, their beliefs and actions, and the manifestation of low expectations and differential teacher–student relations. Other scholars examine the schooling outcomes of Black males and a structuralist perspective, which attributes negative school experiences and outcomes to structural factors such as class structures and arrangements as the genesis of their underperformance and overall disenfranchisement (Massey & Denton, 1993; Wilson, 1978, 1987). Stinson (2010) tested Ogbu's oppositional theory and the concept of "acting White" and examined the "voices" of four academically successful African American male students as they respond, in retrospect, to the theoretical concept burden of "acting White." He found that the concept did not have much of an effect on the way that the young men saw their academic prospects. These young men saw their identities as complex, multilayered, and still evolving. Although they acknowledged some of the stereotypes that existed about them, they did not internalize notions of sacrificing racial or cultural integrity in the pursuit of academic excellence. Stinson states that "(a)lthough each acknowledged that the burden potentially existed, it was not so much understood as a burden of acting White in regards to school . . . but rather as a burden of somehow molding oneself into the (White) hegemonic images of success" (p. 58).

Wilson (2008) reinforces the structural argument when he states that Black males suffer disproportionately from what he terms the "new urban poverty" (p. 56), wherein poor, racially segregated neighborhoods have a substantial majority of its residents either unemployed or completely withdrawn from the labor force. His analysis shows that the unemployment levels of Black males surpass those of every other subgroup and exclude them from active participation in the political economy that continues to be dependent on highly skilled labor force and adequate levels of education, which many Black males are frequently lacking. One can infer from these findings that the trickledown effect it has on Black males in K-12 schools, and in many ways, its genesis may lie here as well.

On the other side of the structuralist debate are those who subscribe to a cultural perspective, which would attribute these same experiences and outcomes to factors such as the moral codes that govern families and communities. Although there are many who strongly support one viewpoint or the other, some scholars are dissatisfied with the determinism of the structuralist viewpoint, which renders individuals as passive objects of larger forces and similarly dissatisfied with the "blame the victim" perspective of the culturalists, which views individuals as hopelessly trapped within a particular social/cultural milieu (Ryan, 1976).

Noguera (2001) contends that there are both structural and cultural factors that play out in detrimental ways for Black males that must be further analyzed and addressed if changes are to disrupt patterns of school underperformance of Black males, and a further investigation of how identity is shaped within school contexts for Black males that takes into consideration race, gender, class, and place are essential for educators to understand if they are to effectively engage them in the learning process. Noguera's work challenges the work of Fordham and Ogbu (1986) by claiming evidence that shows that many Black males deliberately challenge racial stereotypes and redefine their racial identities to demonstrate that it is possible to do well in school and still maintain racial pride and cultural integrity. Works such as Noguera's are critical because it offers a counternarrative to the account that has been repeatedly offered on Black males, wherein they are essentially doomed to academic failure because of oppositional behavior and are unable to overcome the myriad obstacles in their path to academic success. The research on high-achieving African American males consistently shows a level of resilience, persistence, and determination to overcome racialized stereotypes about them (Conchas & Noguera, 2004; Howard, 2008, Price, 2000). Particularly, Noguera (2008) describes how both "subjective and objective dimensions of identity related to race and gender are constructed in schools and how these influence academic performance" (p. 27).

From the perspective of critical race theory (CRT) theorists, the plight of Black males in schools is an expression of racism that is endemic to North American society (Bell, 1992; Crenshaw, Gotanda, Peller, & Thomas, 1995; Delgado, 1995; Howard, 2008; Ladson-Billings & Tate, 1995). CRT theorists argue that because racism is such an integral part of society in the United States, it is embedded in practices, norms, ideologies, and values that have become symptomatic of the more explicit and formal manifestations of racialized power (Crenshaw et al., 1995). Scholars such as Duncan (2002) contend that the discourses about and on Black males are embedded in practices and values that normalize racism in the United States and create "conditions that marginalize adolescent black males, placing them *beyond love* [italics added] in schools and in the broader society" (p. 131). Duncan's work on the manner in which adolescent Black boys experience schools is an example of the type of work that positions their voices at the heart of the analysis, and in it, the participants shed light on how racial discrimination is a staple of their schooling experiences.

Though not as critically focused on racism as CRT scholars are, Claude Steele (1992) has also suggested race plays a role in the educational experiences of African American students in ways that many educators may not realize. He contends that racial stigma is an unrecognized component of underachievement among students of color. He argued,

Doing well in school requires a belief that school achievement can be a promising basis of self-esteem and that belief needs constant reaffirmation even for advantaged students. Tragically, I believe the lives of Black Americans are still haunted by a specter that threatens this belief and the identification that derives from it at every level of schooling. (p. 72)

Although most of Steele's work that has examined the effects of stereotype threat has been with students in higher education, increasing amount of the research has begun to look at the potential effect of the concept on K-12 students. Osborne (1997) tested Steele's hypothesis regarding identity formation and found that as Black males move through high school, the correlation between their academic performance and measures of their self-esteem declined consistently and dramatically, a pattern not observed in other groups. His findings suggest that many Black males believe that their fate has been determined and that failure is inevitable.

An area that has received more attention in the study of Black males has been the expanding definition and conceptualization of masculinity. An attempt has been made to problematize traditional ways that masculinity is defined and played out in society and how these narrow notions affect Black males (Staples, 1982). McCready (2004) suggests that many Black males experience troubling social interactions in schools because of diverse masculinities, which may affect their academic outcomes. He contends that researchers need to take into account multiple categories of difference and forms of oppression to understand and suggest interventions for gay and gender nonconforming Black male students in urban schools. Therefore, a more complete analysis of how Black males experience schools needs to create and sustain a discourse about how masculinity is often narrowly defined within Black cultural contexts, thus making it difficult for many Black males to display alternate forms of masculinity. This work is vital because of hypermasculine and heteronormative ideologies and practices that are pervasive in many Black communities and the larger society, which characterizes what it means to be male and Black in some disturbing ways that are not consistent with the manner that countless numbers of Black males display their own identities.

Whereas some scholars examine cultural, structural, racial, and identity variables in evaluating how Black males see schools, others contend that local-level classroom experiences play a much larger role than what is reflected in the literature, in particular teacher attitudes and perceptions. In a closer examination of how teacher perceptions and attitudes influence Black males' experiences in schools, Rong's (1996) study showed that teachers' perceptions of student social behaviors are a result of complex interactions of students' and teachers' race and gender. The results showed that female teachers perceived female students more positively regardless of teachers' race. However, White female teachers perceived White students more positively the same way that they perceived White male students more positively than Black male students, but Black female teachers made no distinction among race for students. These findings raise important questions about how teacher attitude and perception influence Black male educational outcomes.

Rong's work was not the first to examine the effects of teacher attitudes and perceptions on students and their school experiences and outcomes. Rosenthal and Jacobson's (1968) work was among the first extensive studies to suggest that teacher expectations may influence the academic performance of school-age children. This practice, known as the pygmalion effect, is cited as one of the reasons that many African American students in general, and Black males in particular, are disengaged from schools. Rist's (1970) study further highlighted how the pygmalion effect can happen as early as kindergarten, and subsequently becoming a self-fulfilling prophecy when teachers' attitudes become internalized by students, affecting academic experiences, performances, and outcomes. A number of other scholars have documented the manner in which teacher perceptions tend to have a negative effect on Black males more than any other group (Howard, 2008; Milner, 2007; Reynolds, 2010; Rios, 2011). Much of this work shows that they are often viewed as having characteristics more consistent with academic disengagement (lazy, nonthinkers, hostile in class, discipline problems) than showing behavior congruent with academic success (Hall, 2001; Wood, Kaplan, & McLoyd, 2007).

More recently, empirical work has demonstrated the manner in which teacher expectations can have an important influence on student outcomes. McKown and Weinstein (2008) examined the relationship between child ethnicity and teacher expectations and discovered high levels of teacher preference for White and Asian students over African American and Latino students. Moreover, their findings suggest that the teachers' expectation levels contributed in a major way to the academic disparities that existed among racial groups. What this work continues to reinforce is the salience that race continues to play in schools. Despite claims of being in a postracial era, schools in many instances appear to be a primary location where students, at the most earliest of ages, have significant advantages or disadvantages based on racial/ethnic orientation. Moreover, meaningful efforts directed at improving the outcomes of Black males must pay explicit and careful attention to the intersectionality of race and gender. However, broad characterizations of intersectionality that fail to analyze the manner in which being Black, male, middle class, or poor can profoundly shape educational experiences and outcomes.

Hargrove and Seay (2011) investigated teachers' beliefs and perceptions about the low representation of Black males in gifted education. Their survey research discovered different explanations between teachers of color and White teachers about the under-representation of Black males in gifted education. White teachers were more likely to see nonschool factors as explanations (e.g., home/parents/community) than teachers of color. White teachers also placed little attention on their instruction and beliefs as a reason for why Black males were less likely to be referred to gifted education more than any other group. Furthermore, teachers of color did not see the use of nonstandard English as a barrier to school success in ways that White teachers did. Their research documents the salience that teacher attitudes and beliefs play in the perception of Black males, wherein deficit thinking about Black males' potential and promise was quite prevalent in teacher perceptions. They recommend that there needs to be a more explicit and direct dialogue about reports of the results of engaging public school teachers in the conversation about the underrepresentation of African American males in gifted programs.

Reynolds (2010) examined the role that parenting played in school outcomes for Black males. Using a qualitative case study approach with a CRT and phenom-enological lens for analysis, she interviewed Black middle-class parents about their experiences in public secondary schools. She documented the manner in which Black parents believed that school officials frequently excluded them from access to infor-mation that could aim them and their students. Moreover, the parents discussed how their sons, in particular, were victims of lowered expectations, deficit thinking, and subject to racial microaggressions by teachers and school administrators. She recom-mends that schools move toward seeing Black parents as full partners in a manner that dispels myths about Black males. She suggests that future research should con-tinue to examine the manner in which Black males and their parents are frequently targets of explicit and implicit forms of racism and discrimination.

Lynn, Bacon, Totten, Bridges, and Jennings (2010) examined teachers' and admin-istrators' perspectives and opinions on the persistent failure of African American male high school students in a low-performing, yet affluent area termed Summerfield County. Their focus group and individual interviews revealed persistent apathy among school personnel, a permanence of low expectations in an overall environ-ment that stifled teacher care and creativity, which stifled the academic and personal/social development of Black males.

Lewis, Butler, Bonner, and Jourber (2010) examined the resulting impact of dis-ciplinary patterns and school district responses regarding African American academic achievement. In studying the disciplinary patterns in a Midwest school, there were four key goals in this work: (a) to investigate all behavior occurrences among African American males in comparison to their peers during the 2005–2006 academic school year, (b) to detail the discipline responses recommended by the school district for these offenses, (c) to calculate the total amount of class time missed as a result of school district prescribed resolutions, and (d) to provide a connection to performance on standardized test reporting for the larger African American student population in this urban school district. The findings from their study revealed that African American male students were disciplined at a rate of three-to-one and had the highest level of disciplinary referral over any other student group. Lewis et al. recommend several steps to address these inequities and to reduce the disproportionate number of Black males: (a) implement culturally relevant professional development for classroom management, (b) establish a discipline advisory committee, (c) enforce a three-strike rule for violent offenses, and (d) referral for counseling/therapy.

What these works represent are a consistent stream of ideologies and narratives that dominate many schools about Black male potential. In her work on what she terms the "institutional narrative" on children, intersectionality, and academic outcomes, Ferguson (2003) states,

According to the statistics, the worse-behaved children in the school are black and male, and when they take tests they score way below their grade level. They eat candy, refuse to work, fight, gamble, chase, hit, instigate, cut class, cut school, cut hair. They are defiant, disruptive, disrespectful, and profane. These black males fondle girls, draw obscene pictures, make lewd comments, intimidate others, and call teacher names. They are banished from the classroom to the hall, to the discipline office, to the suspension room, to the streets so that others can learn. (p. 46)

She further states,

In the range of normalizing judgments, there is a group of African American boys identified by school personnel as, in the words of a teacher, "unsalvageable." This term and the condition it speaks to is specifically about masculinity. School personnel argue over whether these unsalvageable boys should be given access even to the special programs designed for those who are failing in school. Should resources defined as scarce, be wasted on these boys for whom there is no hope? (p. 96)

Ferguson's point conveys the pervasive manner in which many Black males, oftentimes at the earliest ages of primary school, are given deleterious labels and are victims of persistent microaggressions (Solorzano, 1998), which suggest that they are not worthy of the very programs deemed to assist those in greatest need. In many ways, the issue of *who really cares* about Black males (Howard, 2008) or that they are *beyond love* (Duncan, 2002) becomes loud, clear, and prevalent through much of their schooling experiences. Furthermore, in many instances, they are viewed, whether justified or not, as the worse behaved, the least talented, and the most dangerous group of students on the school grounds. These realities lead us to question how Black males can experience any degree of academic success or social inclusion when such beliefs and ideologies exist among school personnel and in some cases even among their peers. The next section of this chapter offers some insights into works that reveal how this success occurs even in the most hostile of learning environments.

MICRO-LEVEL ANALYSIS: EXTRAORDINARY PEDAGOGIES AND BLACK MALES

Recent attention has been given to studying in school and classroom contexts to examine practices that may contribute to improved school outcomes for Black males.

For example, one of the areas that has garnered attention recently has been the efficacy of single-sex schools and classrooms for Black males. As more efforts have been placed on the creation of single-sex schools for Black males, few empirical studies have examined if they have improved outcomes, and if so, what strategies and theories are used in these learning environments? In one of the recent studies investigating the effectiveness of single-sex schools for Black and Latino males, Fergus and Noguera (2010) discovered a series of instructional strategies that were used in single-sex schools that had a positive influence on their educational experiences and outcomes. Their 3-year study on seven single-sex schools discovered that they were centered on social/emotional programming, rites of passage programs, community service requirements, culturally responsive instruction, rigorous curriculum, and an emphasis on basic skills. They discovered two theories of change that guided their work: understanding the social and emotional needs of Black and Latino boys and understanding how the academic needs of Black and Latino boys have surfaced and how to target strategies and interventions to address those needs. What is important to note about the findings from Fergus and Noguera are the foci on changing boys' notions of masculinity, helping forge an academic identity that is connected to their social identities, and an explicit and sustained focus on developing and enhancing core basic academic skills.

Camangian (2010) used critical autoethnography with African American high school youth as a means to engage them in literacy, and he discovered that the cultural narratives used in the process were instrumental in building critical social analysis of their lives, their communities, and ultimately putting forth more effort and having better outcomes with course content. He asserted that such approaches can have a dual purpose as they can tap into youth confusion and anger in order to engage them as critical readers, writers, and oral communicators. And he contends that

critical literacy happens as students are guided to interrogate their multiple identities, the social conditions that define their worldviews. . . . And that through these practices, critically caring literacy pedagogies draw from students' cultural frameworks and lived experiences to engage them in learning that nurtures caring relationships, reflecting concern for their lives outside of the classroom while illuminating and disrupting existing power relations. (p. 179)

Baldridge, Hill, and Davis (2011) explored the role of community-based organizations and how they support the academic and personal development of Black males. Their work is important because they shed insight on how Black males make sense of their schooling experiences. Critical to their accounts is the manner in which the young men discussed tolerating school as opposed to immersing themselves in it, the persistence of noncaring teachers, and a host of other social and academic obstacles that exist in schools and how they were often "smart enough to drop out" (p. 130) rather than continue to locate themselves within a space that did not foster their development, affirm their identities, and speak to their realities. However, their involvement with a community-based organization designed to assist young men transition into adulthood proved to be helpful because teachers in the program built positive relationships with them (unlike teachers in school), provided them with relevant skills and knowledge for their community context, and helped them to learn "real-world skills" that schools did not teach.

In an additional work that explores the efficacy of nonschool learning spaces for Black males, Fashola (2003) investigated the salience of after school programs. She discovered that effective programs were specific in the group(s) that they targeted, and provided ongoing professional development to staff and faculty working with African American males. She identified the Boys and Girls Club, Big Brothers/Sisters, and the Coca-Cola VYP as programs that were able to offer support to supplement the academic shortcomings that may exist for African American males. What is important to note about both of the previously mentioned works is the importance that nonschool spaces can provide for African American males. These spaces have certain advantages that schools may not have, namely, fewer restrictions on assessment measures and hiring of staff, which may result in a more fruitful environment for African American males to learn. Each of these studies raises important questions for both researchers and practitioners to consider in the examination and the efficacy of out-of-school learning contexts to see where African American males have thrived.

It is notable to observe the manner in which African American males thrive in afterschool sports activities. Duncan-Andrade (2010) offers insightful data and recommendations as he documents and examines the type of roles and the relationships that athletic coaches have with Black and Brown male youth and how teachers can benefit from observing these relationships. Duncan-Andrade asserts that the difficulty that many teachers experience with some of the most recalcitrant students in the classroom are quite different from the types of relationships that athletic coaches establish with them outside of the classroom. The level of investment, commitment, and overall concern that coaches demonstrate toward young men is instrumental in their development, and that teachers, unlike many coaches, are often unaware or unconcerned about the social and cultural realities that many young men encounter. Thus, a pedagogy consisting of authentic care, concern, and investment is critical to the optimum development of Black males.

Building on the idea that gender and race matches can have a positive influence on the academic outcomes, A. L. Brown (2009) looked at the role that African American male teachers played with African American male students, using a theoretical conception of performance, which understands any social actors' (e.g., teachers, social activists) performative agency as guided and constrained by the beliefs they hold about the individuals they serve. In short, he found that "teachers understood their African American male students to hold particular dispositions to learning, or they thought their teaching style of performance would instill in these students the needed dispositions and attitudes to schooling and life" (p. 425). Brown's analysis found that the teachers placed an emphasis on discipline and responsibility, yet also had a wide range of performance strategies to engage Black male students in a social discourse about their academic potential and performance.

This work builds on some of Lynn's previous work (2002) wherein he used CRT as a analytical lens for examining the pedagogical practices of a Black male teacher working with Black male high school students and discovered how cultural knowledge of Black male epistemologies and knowledge can lead to new theoretical approaches for Black males and subsequently improve their schooling experiences and outcomes.

The importance of teachers and teaching for Black males offers important insights; equally as notable are the ways that these young men make meaning of their schooling experiences. In an examination of how African American males made meaning out of their high school experiences around race, Howard (2008) captured the voices and perspectives of day-to-day occurrences of high school–aged youth. His research discovered that Black males believed that they were frequent targets of racial microaggressions, differential treatment, and negative stereotypes. What was paramount in Howard's work is the manner in which the young men frequently used put downs, lowered expectations, and doubting teachers as a motivation to perform better in schools and prove teachers and peers wrong about their academic potential. Moreover, the critical race, counterstory framework provided the students a well-received opportunity to frankly discuss race and their opportunities to learn. These students from a diverse set of socioeconomic backgrounds offered quite similar accounts of how they are frequently punished harsher than their non-Black peers, held to a different standard, and are expected to excel athletically, but not to do so academically.

In a study that captured the complexity of race, class, gender, and the pursuit of education, Price (2000) described the challenges of six school-aged Black male youth. What is important to note about the participants in Price's work is the diversity among each of the young men in pursuit of a high school diploma. This work helps challenge the unitary notion of Black males and uncovers the myriad obstacles both personally and academically that these young men encounter along their educational journey. The two primary themes that are prevalent among these young men is seeing high school graduation as a symbol of achievement and as a ticket to economic success and highlights their resilience, determination, and discipline to not succumb to the culture of failure created in the schools that they attend.

As schools struggle to find the appropriate approaches in key content areas, there is credible work that helps address this concern. Nasir's (2012) work complicates the nexus of identity, learning, and out-of-school contexts for Black males. Her contention is that when racialized identities are aligned with school or other cultural practices, the manner in which African American students experience and perform in schools can be enhanced. Her work contends that learning and identity are social and cultural processes that influence the manner in which students experience schools. Furthermore, her research contends that in a racially stratified society race matters. Her research explored the identity, learning, and out-of-school context intersection by investigating African American males within the context of their participation in basketball and track. She discovered that adults who had a working knowledge of cultural practices and and personal histories, and could build authentic relationships were able to maximize students' effort and performance. Her call is that similar stances could serve to benefit students in learning contexts. She found similar types of outcomes when Black males engaged in the participation of dominoes as a means to situate mathematics within a culturally mediated framework. She states,

Learning and identities in these practices were supported by the social organization of play, including the presence of clear roles; opportunities for having something of oneself valued and taken up; and the assumption that participants' racialized identities as African American, did not conflict with the dispositions and skills required of players and participants. (p. 58)

Nasir's work brings to bear the manner in which sociocultural realities of students' lives provide a rich platform to understand the intellectual characteristics that help influence their identities as learners and how a firm grasp of these features can inform teaching in a manner that does not require students to sacrifice cultural integrity in the pursuit of academic success.

In his critical ethnographic study of African American male youth in South Los Angeles, Terry (2010) explored the role of community-based knowledge, interests, and inquiry in the reorientation of students to mathematics. In their participatory action research project, the use of mathematical concepts, knowledge, and skill was largely directed by what the students *themselves* wanted to research and know more about. Rather than textbook-determined busywork, then, mathematics became an exciting critical cultural activity that was propelled by students' inherent interests in the research questions. The student-centered nature of this kind of mathematical activity represents an extension of the notion of "care" discussed in this article, beyond teacher–student interaction, into the nature of the curriculum itself. His findings suggest that the instrumental role African American students played in determining the cultural contexts in which mathematics was studied directly affected students' sense of the usefulness of mathematics as a tool that they too can own. Terry argues that this is a crucial step not only toward reversing low performance in mathematics but also, perhaps more important, toward helping students develop a vision of themselves as mathematicians. This is an important foundation from which students can begin to seek out careers in STEM disciplines. His work builds on the work of other scholars such as Martin (2007, 2009), who poses important conceptual, theoretical, and practical recommendations on how to address math disparities between African American students and their peers. Martin's work examined the construction of identities that are at the intersection of being an African American and doing math. His work suggests that the struggle for mathematics and African Americans goes well beyond the school context and is more intimately tied to identity and the participation in the larger opportunity structure. In his work with Black males, he sought to capture firsthand experiences that students had with mathematics literacy and discovered that for the young men, despite their interest in and ability to do math well, they consistently received negative messages about their ability to do mathematics, were not expected to participate in mathematics, and believed that their lower level status in society (as Black and male) influenced the manner in which they were encouraged to participate in mathematical development as learners.

In one of the more underresearched areas of school performance, literacy for African American male adolescents, Tatum (2009) asserts that improving their performance is contingent on "engaging these young males in reading and writing texts that pay attention to their multiple identities—academic, cultural, economic, gendered, personal, and social—becomes a bridge to opportunities" (p. 14). He goes on to provide a number of strategies, texts, and approaches that can be instrumental in improving literacy performance for Black males. One of his contentions is that a wider construction of literacy must be developed that goes beyond merely teaching students how to read and write, but an approach that incorporates what he calls *enabling texts*, situated within an ethic of care from teachers, structured within collaborative learning environments, and mediated by culturally and socially responsive literature.

Tatum's call for rethinking literacy approaches has been echoed by a number of scholars who maintain that traditional methods of literacy instruction are narrow, decontextualized from reality, and socially foreign and is frequently the primary reason why many African American males disengage from the teaching and learning process (Delpit, 1995; Delpit & Dowdy, 2002; Duncan-Andrade & Morrell, 2008). Central to these works has been the notion that the idea of Black males being intellectually defunct and functionally illiterate is terribly misguided and that when a more critical approach to literacy is developed, one that is situated within popular culture, social media, and engaged in a social critique of circumstances and communities that young men are familiar with, their levels of literacy performance are quite robust. Duncan-Andrade and Morrell (2008) offer accounts of how using a critical pedagogy framework they were able to engage young Black and Latino students in an urban English classroom. They also speak to how they incorporated this type of pedagogy without having to give up traditional academic standards in the process:

In no way, shape, or form did our focus on academic literacy compromise our commitment to critical pedagogy and to literacy education for individual freedom and social change. In fact, we felt that it was only within a pedagogy firmly committed to freedom and social change that we were able to motivate students to develop sophisticated academic literacies. (p. 34)

Uwah, McMahon, and Furlow (2008) examined the relationship between perceptions of school belonging, academic self-efficacy, and educational aspirations among a sample of African American male high school students. Using a correlation and multiple regression design, they examined the relationship between perceptions of school belonging, educational aspirations, and academic self-efficacy. The results showed that encouraging Black males to participate and increasing their sense of belonging had a positive influence on schooling experiences and outcomes. They recommend that school counselors play a pivotal role in helping create a sense of community and belongingness for Black males if they want them to have a sense of connectedness to the school culture and climate.

Murrel (1999) examined what he described as responsive teaching for African American male adolescents, and his findings suggested that the social context of learning to be critical and that considerable communication, coordinated action, and common understanding are important in engaging students. More specifically, he also stated that math teachers who were responsive constructed meaningful relationships with students and their subject matter, had a familiarity with discourse routines and speech events used by African American adolescents, and contended that the students in his study showed (a) a preference for question posing, teacher challenge approach; (b) a preference for requesting information; (c) an eagerness to show off the knowledge they possess; (d) a penchant for extended explanation; and (e) a preference for "getting over" rather than admitting ignorance. Murrell's findings are useful because they provide insight into some of the specific approaches that resonate with high levels for effort and engagement with Black males.

In one of the more comprehensive analyses of Black male achievement, Toldson (2008) explored factors that statistically improve their educational outcomes. By analyzing indicators from four national surveys (Health Behavior in School-Age Children, National Crime Victimization Survey: School Crime Supplement, National Survey of American's Families, and National Survey on Drug Use and Health), he uncovered key findings to transform academic outcomes for Black males. In an exhaustive analysis of (a) personal and emotional factors, (b) family factors, (c) social and environmental factors, and (d) school factors, he discovered that students who felt happiest about life was a strong predictor for academic success, and liking school and not feeling bored by it had statistical significance. In addition, having teachers who fostered academic growth and who were interested in them as people and were fair in their interactions with them made a notable difference in school outcomes as well. Toldson's (2008) findings are important because they provide a holistic analysis of the factors that influence school experience and performance for Black males. Whereas many of the findings, such as school safety, stable home life, having financial support, high aspirations for academic success, and parental involvement, which all have a positive correlation for school outcomes for Black males, are not surprising, they are telling, because it reflects the need to provide Black males with many of the same support sources and assets that their peers from different ethnic and gender groups receive. One of the disheartening analyses that are offered from deficit-based frameworks for Black males is that something "different" must be done for them compared with what is done for other students. In contrast, the accounts of many Black males would suggest that the very reason why many do underperform is because they are treated differently than their peers and not given the same level of expectations, support, and feelings of importance as their peers are; thus, the implications then become less on fixing what is wrong with Black males in schools but correcting the approaches and ideologies of those that are purported to serve them.

Using an oppositional culture theory framework, Harper and Davis (2012) conducted a systematic content analysis of essays written by 304 Black male undergraduates attending colleges and universities across the United States, by probing two central questions. "What are your intellectual interests and long-term career aspirations relative to education, and how were they developed?" and "If you had a Ph.D. in education, what would you do in response to the educational problems or social phenomena that concern you most?" Their results offered a counternarrative that African American males place a high value on education despite what they viewed to be as "schools that suck" and were acutely aware of inequalities in their schools. In spite of these challenges, they discovered that most of the undergraduate students still viewed education as the great equalizer and maintained plans to pursue Ph.D.s as a way to disrupt educational inequality. This research situates the perspectives, opinions, and pursuits of Black males in a framework that challenges them as deficit, violent, and indifferent toward education

Zell (2011) investigated the role of mentoring from a peer-based academic and social integration program. This study was part of a larger project in which matriculation, retention, and graduation rates of African American male collegians involved were examined. The findings revealed that the African American males benefitted from the emotional and psychological support received from this space. In particular, the participants spoke that six key tenets—academic motivation, personal presentation, validation of emerging skills, personal growth, ethic of collaboration, and rewards through accountability—were most essential in their persistence to graduation.

What is important to note about the research on Black males is that several key themes emerge in a review of the research. One of the strengths of the literature on Black males is the frequent mentioning of the need to pay attention to the social and emotional development of Black males in various contexts. Much of the recent research and scholarship has contended that environments that are sensitive to the sociocultural context of teaching and learning provide Black males with a much better chance for school success. One of the challenges in disrupting the persistent presence of Black males in special education classrooms is to address some of the misguided perceptions and cultural ignorance that their teachers may possess. However, a second area that cannot be dismissed are some of the real social challenges and emotional obstacles that many Black males are trying to navigate on a daily basis. Research that examines schools or programs that give explicit attention to some of the pressures and challenges young men are encountering are grossly needed.

A second area that emerges, and one that is a limitation of the research, is the need for inquiry on the development of core basic academic skills for Black males. Given the persistent underperformance, many programs that may prove to be effective in educating Black males recognize some of the academic shortcomings that exist for them and commit additional resources, time, and effort to help shore up areas in literacy and numeracy that are pivotal building blocks for academic success. Fergus and Noguera (2010) stressed the utility of single-sex schools that provided sustained support for academic skill development and the usefulness it had on academic outcomes. Additional research on useful strategies, content, and pedagogical approaches will only strengthen our understanding of what is helpful for Black males who are struggling learners. Finally, a third area that seems pervasive in the literature is the salience of identity. Approaches to servicing Black males that recognize the complexity and dynamic nature of Black male identity are most likely to have long-lasting impact. A number of studies have raised issues about notions of masculinity, divergent social class status, cultural orientations, linguistic diversity, and biracial and multiracial classifications that all are part of the Black male identity and experience. The disruption of monolithic accounts of Black males has important theoretical and conceptual implications for future study of the group. A growing number of works have conceptually discussed the role that identity plays in learning; however, studies that seek to peel back the multiple layers of identity for Black males will provide new insights into understanding their realities and subsequently supporting their academic pursuits.

IMPLICATIONS AND CONCLUSIONS

Despite the emergence of research that seeks to disrupt narrow notions of Black male identity, there remains a persistent sense that this group is still a problem. At schools across the country, wherever there is even a minimal presence of Black male youth, disciplinary infractions increase, grade retention is higher, and dropout rates soar. Thus, DuBois's question still rings true, "How does it feel to be a problem?" The final section of the chapter will consider future directions necessary, still grounded in the literature, for research, theory, policy, and practice for educating African American males. I will also discuss what seems necessary to move the field forward and conceptualize a set of broad and specific implications for research, policy, and practice that researchers and practitioners might address to systemically build knowledge and synergy in the education of Black males.

What is painfully evident in the education of Black males is that there are a multitude of factors at work in their schooling experiences. Needless to say issues such as poverty, racism, fatherlessness, and poor-quality teachers and schools undoubtedly influence their social and academic worlds. But what is notably absent in the analysis of Black males' school realities is the unforgiving resilience that many seem to display on an ongoing basis in pursuit of academic excellence. One of the steps that would be vital in helping reconstruct the perception of Black males would be additional inquiry on high-performing Black males. Studies that are focused on Black males navigating difficult terrain, and how they address the life challenges inside and outside of school would be important contributions. In addition, inquiry that is focused on identifying schools that are effective in educating Black males is desperately needed. Although much of the discourse speaks to the challenges that schools have, some schools are disrupting these accounts and creating school environments that lead to their success. The Urban Preparatory High School in Chicago has produced results that many would deem impossible with Black male students, a 100% graduation rate, and with the overwhelming majority of the graduates attending college. Sites such as these need to be further analyzed to determine the characteristics that are used to cultivate success. The literature also informs us that personal relationships matter in the education of Black males. Milner (2008) talks about *other fathering* as a concept that speaks to the role that men can play in Black males' lives and personal development. There is a need to investigate the relationships that Black males have with school personnel to determine how they are formed, sustained, and how they contribute to better academic success. It also seems clear that culture matters (Milner,

2010). Documenting the vast range of cultural knowledge that Black males possess is vital, and more important is studying how educators learn about this knowledge and then tailor their pedagogy accordingly.

Absent from the discourse is the discipline and tenacity that large numbers of Black males play in supportive roles as older siblings at home, working part-time jobs to support caregivers, and playing protective roles for loved ones. And though a disproportionate number of Black males are involved in sports, what is often lost from this dialogue is the hard work, determination, sacrifice, countless hours, discipline, and mental focus that many of them display to excel in the athletic domain and in the classroom. Placing attention on the resolve and creativity that is displayed at home, in the community, and in the athletic domain may also shed light for how to transform classrooms.

To enhance our knowledge base, future research on this population has to look at different ways of describing and conceptualizing Black males. The monolithic portrayal of Black males needs to be disrupted, challenged, and reframed (Howard & Flennaugh, 2011). Issues of identity need to be unpacked and studied with an explicit focus on the intersection of multiple identities—those tied to race, class, gender, sexual orientation, school subject matter, and age. Black males' conceptions of masculinity would be insightful, as well as documenting Black males born outside of the United States and the cultural and social meaning of their experiences, as well as those who have biracial or multiracial designation. Not only does this have implications for those who engage in research and practice on Black males, it also has the potential to transform the image that Black males have of themselves. Milner (2007, 2009) states that "many Black males have been . . . kidnapped into believing that they are inferior and unable to succeed in school. They have been deceived about the possibilities of their lives, especially educationally" (p. 245). Thus, the need to disrupt the notions of Black male inferiority has multiple layers of oppression, which frequently are part of the analysis.

Future research on Black males needs to have a multipronged approach. One of the areas that is frequently overlooked is teacher preparation. Little research in the teacher education literature pays attention to how teachers are prepared to work with Black males, or for that matter with males of color. Given that the overwhelming majority of classroom teachers are White, female, and middle class (Institute of Education Sciences, n.d.), it leaves a lot to be desired about the levels of experiences and exposure that many of these individuals have had working with, teaching, or interacting with Black males. Furthermore, it is conceivable to call into question the fact that the sociocultural norms, practices, and tools that many Black males use to navigate their world are often diametrically at odds with those of the teachers they are most likely to encounter (Gay & Howard, 2001). Thus, it would be critical for teacher preparation programs to give careful consideration to how teachers can build the capacity, skill set, and knowledge to work with males of color in general, but Black males in particular.

An additional area in need of analysis would be curriculum orientation. One of the more common responses from many Black males and other students of color is the persistent exposure to curriculum that is culturally and socially irrelevant and completely disconnected from their realities. Whereas some scholars have raised this issue and called for curriculum to be informed by cultural and social media informed by contemporary issues, events, and topics (Camangian, 2010; Duncan-Andrade & Morrell, 2008), there still seems to be a considerable gap between the types of knowledge most valued in a school context and the types of knowledge possessed by diverse groups of students (Banks, 1993). Some schools have taken more culturally responsive and critical pedagogy approaches, but we need to know more about what influence, if any, these curriculum orientations have had on the school experiences and academic outcomes for Black males.

Another area that requires additional inquiry would be assessment approaches used in schools. Given the pervasiveness of high-stakes testing in suburban, rural, and urban schools, additional research is necessary to help understand how such test-centered environments affect Black males. In addition, there needs to be further scrutiny given to the knowledge that is evaluated in such standards-based tests. This is not to suggest that core areas such as literacy, math, writing, history, and science should not be assessed; however, the high stakes placed on these mechanisms is what needs to be questioned and examined further. Hood (2001) calls for a closer analysis on the role of culture in educational assessment and the need to create, implement, and maintain more culturally responsive approaches in evaluation for diverse populations.

Although the research base on Black males has been informative and expansive over the last several decades, there still remains more to be studied, analyzed, and learned about the diversity of their experiences. The population continues to change and be shaped by a multitude of other variables, just as any group of students. Innovative approaches to examining how they experience schools and those practices and approaches that are contributing to their success continue to be in demand. Hopefully, researchers over the next decade will provide us with new insights and knowledge that can be vital in their transformation. It was not my attempt to provide a simplistic or reductionist account of how to conduct research on Black males. One of the problems with previous research is that it has attempted to do just that—provide a singular account of Black males and offer prescriptive accounts of how to best understand them. It has been my goal to show the rich diversity and complexity in the group along with the growing numbers of works that use a wide range of approaches to examine their school experiences and outcomes.

NOTES

I would like to acknolwedge Justin McClinton for his research support for this manuscript.
[1]African American and Black are used interchangeably throughout this text.

[2]Equity-minded researchers are those whose works are committed to achieving parity and access for underserved and diverse populations. See Oakes, Welner, Yonezawa, and Allen (2005).

REFERENCES

Anderson, E. (2008). *Against the wall: Poor, young, Black, and male*. Philadelphia: University of Pennsylvania Press.

Aud, S., Fox, M., & Kewal Ramani, A. (2010). *Status and trends in the education of racial and ethnic groups* (NCES 2010-015; U.S. Department of Education, National Center for Education Statistics). Washington, DC: Government Printing Office.

Baldridge, B. J., Hill, M. L., & Davis, J. E. (2011). New possibilities: (Re)engaging Black male youth within community-based educational spaces. *Race, Education, and Education, 14*, 121–136.

Balfanz, R., & Legters, N. (2004, September). *Locating the dropout crisis. Which high schools produce the nation's dropouts? Where are they located? Who attends them?* (Report 90). Baltimore, MD: Johns Hopkins University.

Banks, J. A. (1993). Multicultural education: Historical development, dimensions, and practices. *Review of Research in Education, 19*, 3–49.

Bell, D. A. (1992). *Faces at the bottom of the well*. New York, NY: Basic Books.

Brookings Institute. (2011). *The recession's ongoing impact on America's children: Indicators of children's economic well-being through 2011*. Retrieved from http://www.brookings.edu/research/papers/2011/12/20-children-wellbeing-isaacs

Brown, A. (2011). Racialised subjectivities: A critical examination of ethnography on Black males in the USA, 1960s to early 2000s. *Ethnography and Education, 6*, 45–60.

Brown, A. L. (2009). "Brothers gonna work it out": Understanding the pedagogic performance of African American male teachers working with African American male students. *Urban Review, 41*, 416–435.

Brown, M. C., & Davis, J. E. (2000). *Black sons to mothers: Compliments, critiques, and challenges for cultural workers in education*. New York, NY: Peter Lang.

Camangian, P. (2010). Starting with self: Teaching autoethnography to foster critically caring literacies. *Research in the Teaching of English, 45*, 179–204.

Centers for Disease Control and Prevention. (2011). *Leading causes of death in males United States*. Retrieved from http://www.cdc.gov/men/lcod/index.htm

Coley, R. J. (2011, June 4). *A strong start: Positioning young Black boys for educational success: A statistical profile* (ETS's Addressing Achievement Gaps Symposium). Washington, DC: National Press Club.

College Board. (2012, February 8). *The 8th annual AP report to the nation*. Retrieved from http://media.collegeboard.com/digitalServices/public/pdf/ap/rtn/AP-Report-to-the-Nation.pdf

Conchas, G. Q., & Noguera, P. A. (2004). Understanding the exceptions: How small schools support the achievement of academically successful Black boys. In N. Way & J. Chu (Eds.), *Adolescent boys in context* (pp. 317–337). New York: New York University Press.

Conchas, G. Q., & Vigil, J. D. (2012). *Streetsmart, school smart. Urban poverty and the education of adolescent boys*. New York, NY: Teachers College Press.

Cooper, H. (1998). *Synthesizing research* (3rd ed.). Thousand Oaks, CA: Sage.

Crenshaw, K. (1989). Demarginalizing the intersection of race and sex. *University Chicago Legal Files*, pp. 139–167.

Crenshaw, K. (1995). Mapping the margins: Intersectionality, identity politics, and violence against women of colour. In K. Crenshaw, N. Gotanda, G. Pellet, & K. Thomas (Eds.), *Critical race theory: The key writings that formed the movement* (pp. 357–383). New York, NY: New Press.

Crenshaw, K., Gotanda, N., Peller, G., & Thomas, K. (Eds.). (1995). *Critical race theory: The key writings that formed the movement*. New York, NY: New Press.

Darling-Hammond, L. (2006). The flat earth and education: How America's commitment to equity will determine our future. *Educational Researcher, 36*, 318–334.

Darling-Hammond, L. (2010). *The flat world and education: How America's commitment to equity will determine our future*. New York, NY: Teachers College Press.

Davis, J. E. (2003). Early schooling and academic achievement of African American males. *Urban Education, 38*, 515–537.

Delgado, R. (Ed.). (1995). *Critical race theory: The cutting edge.* Philadelphia, PA: Temple University Press.

Delpit, L. (1995). *Other people's children: Cultural conflict in the classroom.* New York, NY: New Press.

Delpit, L. (2012). *Multiplication is for White people: Raising expectations for other people's children.* New York, NY: New Press.

Delpit, L., & Dowdy, J. K. (Eds.). (2002). *The skin that we speak.* New York, NY: New Press.

DuBois, W. E. B. (1903). *The souls of Black folk.* Chicago, IL: A. C. McClurg.

Duncan, G. A. (2002). Beyond love: A critical race ethnography of the schooling of adolescent Black males. *Equity & Excellence in Education, 35*, 131–143.

Duncan-Andrade, J. M. (2010). *What a coach can teach a teacher: Lessons urban schools can learn from a successful sports program.* Washington, DC: Peter Lang.

Duncan-Andrade, J. M., & Morrell, E. (2008). *The art of critical pedagogy: Possibilities for moving from theory to practice in urban schools.* New York, NY: Peter Lang.

Escott, P. D. (2009). *What shall we do with the Negro: Lincoln, White Racism, and Civil War America.* Charlottesville: University of Virginia Press.

Fashola, O. S. (2003). Developing the talents of African American male students during nonschool hours. *Urban Education, 38*, 398–430.

Fergus, E., & Noguera, P. (2010). *Theories of change among single-sex schools for Black and Latino boys: An intervention in search of theory.* New York: New York University, Metropolitan Center for Urban Education.

Ferguson, A. A. (2003). *Bad boys: Public schools in the making of Black masculinity.* Ann Arbor: University of Michigan Press.

Fordham, S., & Ogbu, J. U. (1986). Black students' school success: Coping with the "burden of 'acting white.'" *Urban Review, 18*, 178–206.

Franklin, C. W. (1991). The men's movement and the survival of African American men in the 90s. *Changing Men, 21*, 20–21.

Gay, G. (2010). *Culturally responsive teaching. Theory, research and practice* (2nd ed.). New York, NY: Teachers College Press.

Gay, G., & Howard, T. C. (2001). Multicultural education for the 21st century. *Teacher Educator, 36*, 1–16.

Gibbs, J. T. (1988). *Young, black, and male in America.* New York, NY: Auburn House.

Gordon, B. (2012). "Give a brotha a break!" The experiences and dilemmas of middle-class African American male students in white suburban schools. *Teachers College Record, 114*(4), 1–13. Retrieved from https://www.tcrecord.org/library/abstract.asp?contentid=16416

Gordon, E. T., Gordon, E. W., & Nembhard, J. G. G. (1994). Social science literature concerning African American men. *Journal of Negro Education, 63*, 508–531.

Gregory, A., Skiba, R. J., & Noguera, P. A. (2010). The achievement gap and the discipline gap: Two sides of the same coin? *Educational Researcher, 39*, 59–68.

Gurian, M. (2001). *Boys and girls learn differently! A guide for teachers and parents.* San Francisco, CA: Jossey-Bass.

Haberman, M. (1991, December). The pedagogy of poverty versus good teaching. *Phi Delta Kappan*, 290–294.

Hall, R. E. (2001). The ball curve: Calculated racism and the stereotype of African American men. *Journal of Black Studies, 32*, 104–119.

Hargrove, B. H., & Seay, S. E. (2011). School teacher perceptions of barriers that limit the participation of African American males in public school gifted programs. *Journal for the Education of the Gifted, 34*, 434–467.

Harper, S. R. (2012). *Black male student success in higher education: A report from the National Black Male College Achievement Study.* Philadelphia: University of Pennsylvania Center for the Study of Race and Equity in Education.

Harper, S. R., & Davis, C. H. F. (2012). They (don't) care about education: A counternarrative on Black male students' responses to inequitable schooling. *Educational Foundations*, Winter-Spring, 103–120.

Hilfiker, D. (2002). *Urban injustice. How ghettoes happen.* New York, NY: Seven Stories Press.

Hood, S. (2001). Nobody knows my name: In praise of African American evaluators who were responsive. In J. C. Greene & T. A. Abma (Eds.), *Responsive evaluation* (New Directions for Evaluation, *Vol. 92*, pp. 31–43). San Francisco, CA: Jossey-Bass.

hooks, b. (1990). *Yearning: Race, gender, and cultural politics.* Boston, MA: South End Press.

Hopkins, R. (1997). *Educating black males: Critical lessons in schooling, community, and power.* New York: State University of New York Press.

Howard, T. C. (2008). "Who really cares?" The disenfranchisement of African American males in PreK-12 schools: A critical race theory perspective. *Teachers College Record, 110*, 954–985.

Howard, T. C. (2010). *Why race and culture matters in schools: Closing the achievement gap in America's classrooms.* New York, NY: Teachers College Press.

Howard, T. C., & Flennaugh, T. (2011). Research concerns, cautions & considerations on Black males in a "post racial society". *Race, Ethnicity and Education, 14*, 105–120.

Howard, T. C., & Reynolds, R. E. (in press). Examining Black male identity through a raced, classed, and gendered lens: Critical race theory and the intersectionality of the Black male experience. In M. Lynn and A. Dixson (Eds.), *Handbook of research on critical race theory* New York, Routledge Press.

Institute of Education Sciences. (n.d.). *The condition of education.* Retrieved from http://nces.ed.gov/programs/coe/

Jackson, J. F. L. (2007). *Strengthening the African American educational pipeline: Informing research, policy, and practice.* New York: State University of New York Press.

Kuhn, T. S. (1970). *The structure of scientific revolution* (2nd ed.). Chicago, IL: University of Chicago Press.

Ladson-Billings, G. (2006). From the achievement gap to the education debt: Understanding achievement in U.S. schools. *Educational Researcher, 35*(7), 3–12.

Ladson-Billings, G. (2011). Boyz to men? Teaching to restore Black boys' childhood. *Race, Ethnicity and Education, 14*, 7–15.

Ladson-Billings, G., & Tate, B. (1995). Toward a critical race theory of education. *Teachers College Record, 97*, 47–67.

Lewis, C. W., Butler, B. R., Bonner, F. A., & Jourber, M. (2010, February). African American male discipline patterns and school district responses resulting impact on academic achievement: Implications for urban educators and policy makers. *Journal of African American Males in Education, 1*(1). Retrieved from http://journalofafricanamericanmales.com/wp-content/uploads/downloads/2010/03/African-American-Male-Discipline-Patterns1.pdf

Losen, D. J., & Skiba, R. J. (2010). *Suspended education: Urban middle schools in crisis.* Montgomery, AL: Southern Poverty Law Center.

Lynn, M. (2002). Critical race theory and the perspectives of Black men teachers in the Los Angeles public schools. *Equity & Excellence in Education, 35*, 87–92.

Lynn, M., Bacon, J. N., Totten, T. L., Bridges, T. L., & Jennings, M. E. (2010). Examining teachers' beliefs about African American male students in a low performing high school in an African American school district. *Teachers College Record, 112*, 289–330.

Madhubuti, H. (1990). *Black men: Obsolete, single, dangerous?* Chicago, IL: Third World Press.

Martin, D. B. (2007). Mathematics learning and participation in the African American context: The co-construction of identity in two intersecting realms of experiences. In N. S. Nasir & P. Cobb (Eds.), *Improving access to mathematics* (pp. 146–158). New York, NY: Teachers College Press.

Martin, D. B. (2009). Does race matter? *Teaching Children Mathematics, 16*(3), 134–139.

Massey, D. S., & Denton, N. A. (1993). *American apartheid*. Cambridge, MA: Harvard University Press.

McCready, L. (2004). Understanding the marginalization of gay and gender non-conforming Black male students. *Theory into Practice, 43*, 136–143.

McKown, C., & Weinstein, R. S. (2008). Teacher expectations, classroom context, and the achievement gap. *Journal of School Psychology, 46*, 235–261.

Milner, H. R. (2007). African American males in urban schools: No excuses—Teach and empower. *Theory into Practice, 46*, 239–246.

Milner, H. R. (2008). Disrupting deficit notions of difference: Counter-narratives of teachers and community in urban education. *Teaching and Teacher Education, 24*, 1573–1598.

Milner, H. R. (2010). *Start where you are, but don't stay there*. Cambridge, MA: Harvard Education Press.

Mincy, H. R. (2006). *Black males left behind*. Washington, DC: Urban Institute.

Murphy, S. L., Xu, J. Q., & Kochanek, K. D. (2012). Deaths: Preliminary data for 2010. *National Vital Statistics Reports, 60*(4). Hyattsville, MD: National Center for Health Statistics.

Murrell, P. (1999). Responsive teaching for African American male adolescents. In V. C. Polite & J. E. Davis (Eds.), *African American males in school and society* (pp. 82–96). New York, NY: Teachers College Press.

Myrdal, G. (1944). *The American dilemma: The Negro problem and modern democracy*. New York, NY: Harper.

Nasir, N. S. (2012). *Racialized identities: Race and achievement among African American youth*. Stanford, CA: Stanford University Press.

Noguera, P. (1996). Responding to the crisis of Black youth: Providing support without further marginalization. *Journal of Negro Education, 65*, 37–60.

Noguera, P. (2001). The role and influence of environmental and cultural factors on the academic performance of African American males. *Motion Magazine*. Retrieved from http://www.inmotionmagazine.com/pnaamale1.html

Noguera, P. (2008). *The trouble with Black boys . . . and other reflections on race, equity, and the future of public education*. San Francisco, CA: Jossey-Bass.

Oakes, J., Welner, K., Yonezawa, S., & Allen, R. L. (2005). Norms and politics of equity-minded change: Researching the "zone of mediation." In M. Fullan (Ed.), *Fundamental change: International handbook of educational change* (pp. 282–305). Berlin, Germany: Springer.

Ogbu, J. (1987). Variability in minority school performance: A problem in search of an explanation. *Anthropology and Education Quarterly, 18*, 312–334.

Ogbu, J. (2003). *Black American students in an affluent suburb: A study of academic disengagement*. New York, NY: Erlbaum.

Osborne, J. (1997). Race and academic misidentification. *Journal of Educational Psychology, 89*, 728–735.

Page, T. N. (1904). *The Negro: The southerners' problem*. New York, NY: Scribner.

Pickett, W. P. (1969). *The Negro problem: Abraham Lincoln's solution*. New York, NY: Negro Universities Press.

Polite, V. C. (1994). The method in the madness: African American males, avoidance, schooling, and chaos theory. *Journal of Negro Education, 60*, 345–359.

Polite, V. C., & Davis, J. E. (1999). *African American males in school and society. Practices and policies for effective education*. New York, NY: Teachers College Press.

Posner, R. A. (1997). Narrative and narratology in classroom and courtroom. *Philosophy and Literature, 21*, 292–305.

Price, J. N. (2000). *Against the odds: The meaning of school and relationships in the lives of six African American men*. Greenwich, CT: Ablex.

Reynolds, R. (2010). "They think you're lazy," and other messages Black parents send their Black sons: An exploration of critical race theory in the examination of educational outcomes for Black males. *Journal of African American Males in Education, 1*(1), 143–165.

Riley, B. F. (1910). *The white man's burden: A discussion of the interracial question with special reference to the responsibility of the white race to the Negro problem.* Birmingham, AL.

Rios, V. (2011). *Punished: Policing the lives of Black and Latino boys.* New York: New York University Press.

Rist, R. (1970). Student social class and teacher expectations: The self-fulfilling prophecy in ghetto education. *Harvard Educational Review, 40,* 411–451.

Rong, X. L. (1996). Effects of race and gender on teachers' perceptions of the social behavior of elementary students. *Urban Education, 31,* 261–290.

Rosen, J. (1996, December 9). The bloods and the crits. *The New Republic,* p. 27.

Rosenthal, R., & Jacobson, L. (1968). *Pygmalion effect in the classroom: Teacher expectations and pupils' intellectual development.* New York, NY: Holt, Rhinehart, & Watson.

Ryan, W. (1976). *Blaming the victim.* New York, NY: Vintage.

Schott Foundation for Public Education. (2010). *Yes we can: The Schott 50 state report on public education and Black males.* Cambridge, MA: Author.

Skelton, C. (2001). *Schooling the boys: Masculinities and primary education.* Buckingham, England: Open University Press.

Sleeter, C. E., & Bernal, D. D. (2003). Critical pedagogy, critical race theory, and anti-racist education: Implications for multicultural education. In J. A. Banks & C. A. M. Banks (Eds.), *The handbook of research on multicultural education* (2nd ed., pp. 240–259). San Francisco, CA: Jossey-Bass.

Solorzano, D. (1998). Critical race theory, racial and gender microaggressions, and the experiences of Chicana and Chicano scholars. *International Journal of Qualitative Studies in Education, 11,* 121–136.

Staples, R. (1982). *Black masculinity: The black man's role in American society.* Washington, DC: Black Scholar Press.

Steele, C. M. (1992, April). Race and the schooling of Black Americans. *Atlantic Monthly, 269,* 68–78..

Stinson, D. W. (2010). When the "burden of acting White" is not a burden: School success and African American male students. *Urban Review, 43,* 43–65.

Tatum, A. W. (2009). *Reading for their life: (Re)Building the textual lineages of African American adolescent males.* Portsmouth, NH: Heinemann.

Taylor, E. (1999, April). Bring in "Da Noise": Race, sports, and the role of schools. *Educational Leadership, 56*(7), 75–78.

Terry, C. L. (2010). Prisons, pipelines, and the president: Developing critical math literacy through participatory action research. *Journal of African American Males in Education, 1*(2), 1–33.

Toldson, I. A. (2008). *Breaking barriers: Plotting the path to academic success for school-age African-American males.* Washington, DC: Congressional Black Caucus Foundation.

Truman, J. L., & Rand, M. R. (2010, October). Criminal victimization, 2009 (National Crime Victimization Survey). *Bureau of Justice Statistics Bulletin.* Retrieved from http://bjs.ojp.usdoj.gov/content/pub/pdf/cv09.pdf

U.S. Census Bureau. (2011). *CPS 2011 Annual Social and Economic supplement.* Retrieved from http://www.census.gov/cps/data/cpstablecreator.html

U.S. Department of Commerce, Census Bureau, American Community Survey, 2007. Bureau of Justice Statistics, Prison inmates at Midyear, Current Population Survey, 2009.

U.S. Department of Education, Institute of Education Science, National Center for Education Statistics. (2009a). *National Assessment of Educational Progress (NAEP), 2009 Mathematics.* Washington, DC: Author.

U.S. Department of Education, Institute of Education Science, National Center for Education Statistics. (2009b). *National Assessment of Educational Progress (NAEP), 2009 Reading.* Washington, DC: Author.

U.S. Department of Education, National Center for Education Statistics. (2011, April). *Digest of Education Statistics, 2010* (NCES 2011-015, chap. 1). Washington, DC: Author. Retrieved from http://nces.ed.gov/pubs2011/2011015.pdf

U.S. Department of Education, National Center for Education Statistics. (n.d.). *Common Core of Data. "Public Elementary/Secondary" and "Local Education Agency Universe Survey."* Retrieved from http://nces.ed.gov/ccd/

U.S. Department of Justice, Office of Justice Programs, Bureau of Justice Statistics. (2011). *Jail inmates at Midyear 2010* (NCJ 233431). Washington, DC: Author.

Uwah, C. J., McMahon, H. G., & Furlow, C. F. (2008). School belonging, educational aspirations, and academic self-efficacy among African American high school students: Implications for school counselors. *Professional School Counseling, 11,* 296–305.

Weaver-Hightower, M. (2003). The "Boy Turn" In research on gender and education. *Review of Educational Research, 73,* 471–498.

Wilson, W. J. (1978). *The declining significance of race.* Chicago, IL: University of Chicago Press.

Wilson, W. J. (1987). *The truly disadvantaged.* Chicago, IL: University of Chicago Press.

Wilson, W. J. (2008). *More than just race: Being Black and poor in the inner city.* New York, NY: Norton & Simon.

Wood, D., Kaplan, R., & McLoyd, V. C. (2007). Gender differences in the educational expectation of urban, low-income African American youth: The role of parents and the school. *Journal of Youth and Adolescence, 36,* 417–427.

Zell, M. (2011). I am my brother's keeper: The impact of a Brother2Brother program on African American men in college. *Journal of African American Males in Education, 2,* 214–233.

Chapter 3

Power and Agency in Education: Exploring the Pedagogical Dimensions of Funds of Knowledge

GLORIA M. RODRIGUEZ

University of California, Davis

The purpose of this chapter is to explore the pedagogical dimensions of the Funds of Knowledge (FoK) framework and approach with a focus on the role of power and agency in the sites where such teaching and learning takes place. It is clear that educators continue to find both potential and challenge in developing appropriate methods for engaging increasingly diverse student populations in public school settings. Many educators seek not just to instruct but to inspire, connect with, and engage students in meaningful learning experiences. However, the racial/ethnic, cultural, and socioeconomic differences that continue to exist between student populations and teachers in many educational settings produce an imperative to create teaching-and-learning environments that are characterized by mutual understanding among students and educators. Challenged further by the current meritocratic policy context that privileges conformity and standardization over responsiveness and inclusiveness, educators confront hegemonic forces that continue to shape public education for the majority of students living in poverty or who are ethnically, linguistically, and otherwise diverse. To more fully understand and appreciate the contributions to critical pedagogy offered by the FoK approach, this review takes up notions of power and agency within the pedagogical dimensions as they play out in the variety of settings documented in current literature. The key research questions guiding this review are the following:

Research Question 1: What do we know from the Funds of Knowledge literature about the development and enactment of pedagogies within and beyond the formal classroom?

Review of Research in Education
March 2013, Vol. 37, pp. 87-120
DOI: 10.3102/0091732X12462686
© 2013 AERA. http://rre.aera.net

Research Question 2: What is/are the discourse(s) in the Funds of Knowledge literature relative to the power and agency of teachers and students (and students' variously defined communities) embedded within and/or emerging from the enactment of the associated pedagogies?

Research Question 3: How might Funds of Knowledge pedagogical notions be further clarified and extended by theoretical dialogue with other "anti-cultural-deficit" (i.e., counter-hegemonic) frameworks, particularly the Community Cultural Wealth framework rooted in Critical Race Theory and Chicana/o Studies?

Considerable attention within the literature is paid to naming the content and sources of FoK (Hogg, 2011), so we have growing evidence of the "how" (instructional practice) and "what" (curriculum) of teaching and learning that is guided by this approach. However, somewhat less accessible within this literature is the "why" or pedagogical realm of the FoK approach. Likewise, embedded within the goals of the FoK approach are concerns regarding the power and agency of teachers and communities; yet the power relations and dynamics that must be addressed as an FoK approach is implemented are not always made explicit, much less problematized, in literature that aims to raise awareness of the potential linkages between household and schooling practices. This analysis is undertaken to make the pedagogies and associated power implications of the FoK work more explicit to allow us to consider critically the broader purposes attached to teaching and learning when framed and guided by the FoK approach. By situating the FoK framework within the context of counter-hegemonic movements in educational theory and practice, the endeavor to examine the power and agency elements of FoK is further supported by interaction with the Community Cultural Wealth (CCW) framework, given its focus on recognizing community assets to counter the pervasive cultural deficit characterizations of minoritized populations.

To attend to these analytical pursuits, I begin the chapter by describing and situating the Funds of Knowledge framework and approach as established by Amanti, González, Greenberg, Moll, Vélez-Ibáñez,[1] and other associates, which will provide some initial contextualization of the work reviewed in this analysis. Next, I present the critical review of the FoK literature to discuss the within and beyond school pedagogies revealed in the settings represented in these studies. I follow this up with an examination of the power and agency discourses reflected within this body of literature to further chart the evolution of thought and practice within the FoK work. This leads to my placing FoK and the CCW framework in theoretical dialogue as a means to further expand our understanding of the particular contributions of these frameworks in countering the pervasiveness of cultural deficit models in education. Finally, I offer brief concluding remarks.

FUNDS OF KNOWLEDGE: ORIGINS AND INITIAL THEORETICAL INFLUENCES

To properly contextualize this review, it is necessary to first establish the theoretical origins and traditions embodied—not always made explicit but certainly indicated by the practices enacted in the studies reviewed—in the FoK approach. What we discover in this contextualization are the contributions of a variety of theoretical perspectives that synthesize into a complex foundation for developing classroom practices that facilitate the learning (and teaching) experiences of students. Such experiences reveal a variety of sources of learning and thus imply a variable set of teaching-and-learning practices drawn from within and outside of the formal school setting.

The FoK framework and approach were established in the late 1980s and early 1990s by university researchers Luis Moll, Norma González, James Greenberg, Carlos Vélez-Ibáñez, along with Cathy Amanti, a teacher who served as a collaborative researcher, through their work in educational settings in Tucson, Arizona. From the early literature discussing the FoK framework and approach, one can see that the impetus was twofold: First, the university researchers sought to identify practices that could counteract the negative impact of pervasive cultural deficit views and explanatory models (theorized further in Valencia & Solórzano, 1997) regarding economically, linguistically, and socially diverse students and families. Second, to better inform the instructional practices and enhance the learning experiences of diverse students, they also sought to use an inquiry process with teachers that would enable them to learn more about (and from) their students' home lives as a means to better connect the knowledge production occurring within the school to that occurring beyond the school. In attending to these dual purposes, the aim was to improve students' academic outcomes and their future life prospects.

The notion of Funds of Knowledge, according to Vélez-Ibáñez and Greenberg (1992/2005), has antecedents in discussions of various household funds as conceptualized in the anthropological study by Wolf (1966), titled *Peasants*. In this study, Wolf discussed various internationally situated communities representing the lower economic castes of their respective societies and their production and maintenance of resources or "funds" that were needed to support their households. Vélez-Ibáñez and Greenberg (1992/2005) posited that there existed a range of strategic practices (funds of knowledge) associated with the development of such basic household funds. Their view was that these "funds of knowledge" were not well understood but critical to the well-being of the diverse families represented among school communities in the United States and worthy of attention as potential educational resources to counteract the reductive forms of schooling diverse students were experiencing in most classrooms. Within the educational application of this notion, Funds of Knowledge are defined as the "historically accumulated and culturally developed bodies of knowledge and skills essential for household or individual functioning and well-being" (González, Moll, & Amanti, 2005, p. 72). In a recent review of literature, Hogg (2011) finds that various researchers have adapted the definitions of FoK to include both sources and content of the specified knowledge. The initial FoK definition provided by González, Moll, & Amanti (2005)[2] had resonance with Wolf's original use in that it was a way to better describe forms of knowledge that arise dynamically from a range of everyday experiences among marginalized—and therefore poorly understood—populations who interact with mainstream society via its social structures. However, the use of the notion of "funds" also appears to reflect the FoK initiators' intentionality to address the concerns expressed in early writings regarding the characterizations of particularly low-income, immigrant students and communities as "deficient" in their social and cultural backgrounds.

During my teacher training, I was led to believe that low-income and minority students were more likely to experience failure in school because their home experiences had not provided them with the prerequisite skills for school success in the same way as the home experiences of middle- and upper-class students. The result has been that traditionally low-income and minority students have been offered lessons reduced in complexity to compensate for these perceived deficits. . . . My teaching experience did not validate the expectations I garnered from my teacher preparation studies. In my daily teaching practice I saw high levels of academic engagement and insight in my students who had typically been labeled "at risk" because of their demographic characteristics. I saw they were as capable of academic success as students from any other background. Additionally, most were fluent in two languages! Participating in the Funds of Knowledge project allowed me to delve into this seeming paradox. (Amanti's "teacher view," González, Moll, & Amanti, 2005, pp. 7–8)

That is, rather than allow the assumption of "cultural deficits" to persist in the educational arena, the initiating researchers emphasize the presence of knowledge, skills, and strategies among students that were produced in settings beyond the school—and therefore, beyond the immediate view (and appreciation) of their teachers.

The founding researchers' methods involve teachers taking on the role of ethnographers to seek out deeper understanding of their students and the communities represented in the schools. Teachers are called on in this approach to become learners with their students and to use interview and observation methods to begin to document for themselves the history, forms of knowledge, and skills that are operating within the households visited (González, Moll, & Amanti, 2005). Within this context, it is important to note that González (2005) asserts a distinction between viewing the ethnographic work as a study of "culture," as a construct that it is cohesive, static, and consistent across groups and time, versus a study of "cultural practices," which may reflect certain traditions and historical context but remain dynamic in response to current contexts. It is also important to recognize that González, Moll, and colleagues established a significant shift in anthropological thought and method by pursuing analyses of cultural practices that allowed researchers and educators to move away from notions of "culture" as a unifying construct, which was the reigning paradigm at the time FoK was introduced (González, Wyman, & O'Connor, 2011). Such distinctions in analytical approaches further resisted simplistic, dismissive, and essentialist treatments of the diverse communities (and their household practices) with whom educators work. In turn, the engagement of teachers, specifically, as co-constructors of knowledge versus merely consumers of research knowledge, is not only meant to sensitize teachers to the challenges students and families face outside of school but also to establish meaningful social relations through which knowledge production and exchange can be facilitated and fortified over time (González et al., 2011).

As initially theorized, gathering evidence and examples of students' FoK allows teachers to develop an awareness of the potential resources that could be used within the classroom to better connect with students' existing forms of knowledge (McIntyre, Rosebery, & González, 2001). Although highlighted in a variety of ways in the establishing publications of FoK project findings, the pedagogical and episte-mological practices found in the students' lived experience within their family house-holds appear to be less emphasized among contemporary scholars than the content and curricular potential of students' FoK. This issue arises as a critique in recent literature (e.g., Zipin, 2009; Zipin & Reid, 2008) and is further evidenced in Hogg's (2011) review of the literature to arrive at definitions and meanings associated with the phrase, "funds of knowledge," which likewise do not generally elaborate the mul-tiple ways of knowing as much as the content and forms of knowledge referenced by various researchers.

Within the rationales offered for the FoK research and pedagogical developments initiated in Arizona is a foregrounding of the need to engage in a power analysis of the local communities as a means for establishing a sense of historical context for the school community. For example, Vélez-Ibáñez and Greenberg (1992/2005) detail the migration stories of parents whose children were represented among the students enrolled in the study site schools to identify the strategic uses of home knowledge to keep the family afloat in their new context. They also illuminate the marginal-ization processes to which these families had been subjected due to varying eco-nomic conditions both in their native countries and in the United States. Likewise, in González, Moll, Floyd Tenery, et al.'s (2005) description of the starting and ending points of teachers who engaged in ethnographic research to document the FoK that their students represented, they allow us to see how socioeconomic and cultural dif-ferences—and their associated forms of privilege/disadvantage—might influence the distribution of classroom learning opportunities among students in schools attended by marginalized populations. In these discussions González, Moll, Floyd Tenery, et al. (2005) make more explicit that the pedagogical imperatives implied by the FoK framework and approach are necessarily emancipatory and counter-hegemonic.

The work that Moll (1990) does to connect the FoK work to Vygotsky's theories on psychology, learning, and development has been instructive in properly situating the newest iterations of FoK-informed work being produced in the past 10 years. It is clear from the earliest writings linking FoK to Vygotsky's approaches to the study of teaching and learning that Moll, Greenberg, and colleagues were always interested in the transformative potential of teaching, premised on the belief that learning is a socially mediated set of processes that reflect the influence of social history and con-text within which learners (and teachers) carry out their activities. In addition, there is intentionality in Moll and Greenberg's (1990) explication of the work undertaken in the development of FoK to engage teachers as learners in the same manner that they encouraged the teachers, in turn, to engage their students—by reaching beyond the confines of the classroom to tap into the various resources (FoK) that exist in communities or sites beyond the formal academic setting.

> Our analysis shows that families control their resources through social relations that connect households to each other and facilitate, among other functions, the transmission of knowledge among participants. We have termed these diverse, socially mediated transactions the *exchange of funds of knowledge*. It is how these social systems of knowledge operate—these extended zones of proximal development—that has attracted our attention. . . . These exchanges are also reciprocal. It is this reciprocity that establishes and maintains the necessary trust among participants to keep the system active and useful. . . . Our claim is that by developing social networks that connect classrooms to outside resources, by mobilizing funds of knowledge, we can transform classrooms into more advanced contexts for teaching and learning. . . . We are convinced that teachers can establish, in systemic ways, the necessary social relations outside classrooms that will change and improve what occurs within the classroom walls. (Moll & Greenberg, 1990, pp. 344–345)

As indicated, it is clear that one important purpose espoused by these researchers in seeking to transform the academic learning process is to engage teachers to use resources beyond the classroom to strengthen the learning (and outcomes) of students within the formal academic setting. Although not explicitly a process of student or community empowerment, what results from the approaches used by Amanti, González, Greenberg, Moll, Vélez-Ibáñez, and associates is a purposeful support for teacher empowerment, which leads to the inclusion of community knowledge resources (FoK) that carry the potential for broader forms of empowerment and representation among students, families, and community members.

CRITICAL REVIEW OF FOK LITERATURE: UNPACKING WITHIN- AND BEYOND-CLASSROOM PEDAGOGIES

Identifying Sources and Parameters for Inclusion in This Review

To identify the studies to be reviewed for this analysis, I conducted searches of peer-reviewed literature using the keywords "Funds of Knowledge" and "pedagogy" to begin the process. This approach was intended to cast a wide net from which I could examine abstracts to determine whether the focus of the individual pieces presented detailed, rich analyses and evidence of the pedagogical dimensions of FoK. In total, 64 items were located, which included research that had been published between 1992 and 2011. To further focus the literature to be reviewed, I separated earlier pieces that were written by the researchers who initiated the Funds of Knowledge work, particularly those articles that established the foundations of the approach and rationales for FoK. These articles and books were used in the discussion of the foundational elements of FoK, as a means for introducing the approach here and situating its origins within its various disciplinary influences. I also eliminated articles that were written primarily as "how to" or prescriptive pieces to benefit, for example, novice FoK practitioners. The remaining 45 peer-reviewed sources—predominantly journal articles and a smaller number of books and book chapters—were therefore the focus of the following discussions of the pedagogical dimensions of FoK.

Also important to consider is that this analysis does not seek to ground the discussion in particular content or subject areas, educational levels, or geographical locations. Similar to the approach used by McIntyre et al. (2001), the review includes literature that showcases teaching-and-learning processes using an FoK approach across several subject areas, such as science, mathematics, language arts, and (multi) literacy development. Likewise, there is representation of both PK-12 and postsecondary education–based research included in this analysis. The majority of the research reviewed was carried out in preschool and elementary education contexts, a few in secondary settings, and the higher education pieces dealt most frequently with teacher education issues. Finally, given the international resonance of the FoK work, several of the studies included in this analysis were conducted in contexts outside of the United States; however, a critical linkage among these studies is the dynamic of immigrant, indigenous, or other minoritized populations being educated in either communities of color by predominantly White teachers or, in some cases, being educated as subpopulations within predominantly White institutions.

Analytical/Organizational Approach to Unpacking FoK Pedagogies

It is easy to be impressed by the creativity and responsiveness of teachers—as evidenced by their FoK-informed practices—regarding the needs, aspirations, talent, and potential of their students, including the ability to access the home-life experiences that contribute to the diversity and complexity of the classroom environment. However, we are called on to delve more deeply into this realm to unpack the pedagogies that, while inspired and informed by an attention to the full scope of the students' lived experience, may still reflect a pervasive power relationship that positions the educator as one who can pick and choose those aspects of students' lives that "belong" in the realm of the classroom. Thus, she or he is also positioned to deemphasize those aspects of their students' lives that produce profound lessons but are less enticing to educators as sources of classroom undertakings. (Indeed, Zipin, 2009, makes this argument in the context of a social justice framing of FoK, which will be taken up in more detail in this chapter.) In this sense, the potential exists for a reproduction of teacher-centered pedagogical approaches even within the context of FoK sensibilities and (self) critical engagement with teaching and learning for student, school, and community transformation. This is not to say that this literature represents just another instance of "feel good" education that does not lead to academic outcomes that are meaningful or that carry currency for continued learning and development among students and teachers alike. Rather, it is an attempt to aid in problematizing how and whether—the degree to which—adopting an FoK approach results in pedagogical practices that create the conditions for redefined power relationships that support, in turn, redefined forms of agency within schools, especially among populations that are otherwise commonly viewed in deficit terms as the burdens, victims, or deficient populations of society.

It is difficult to establish a single definition for pedagogy for purposes of examining the FoK literature. Thus, the approach taken in this analysis is more inductive to extract the "lived" pedagogies that are manifested in the classroom and nonclassroom settings in the studies reviewed. At its most rudimentary level, teachers' purview in the classroom involves, in part, three key elements that are most frequently discussed within the literature reviewed: the what (curriculum), the how (instruction), and the why (pedagogy) of teaching and learning. That some of the studies reviewed here reveal a blending—perhaps conflating—of the instructional method with pedagogical approach is understandable because all three elements are so inextricably linked that we may find distinctions at times to be imposed and artificial. Nevertheless, if pedagogy is the "why" or embedded purposes of teaching and learning (Hattam & Zipin, 2009), it implies that its articulation is found in the practical, theoretical, and value-laden choices that teachers make with intentionality (sometimes conscious but often underlying) as they engage with their students. Also, in the attempts by FoK researchers and collaborating educators to bridge school knowledge and students' home knowledge, there exists the potential for identifying the pedagogical practices that emerge from family/community-defined epistemologies. Thus, as the literature review proceeds, the definitions and articulations of pedagogy that emerge from the analysis are organized into within-classroom and beyond-classroom pedagogies. Of course, it is important to clarify that this organizing system is not intended to dichotomize the notions of pedagogy that emerge from the research but simply to present the forms of pedagogy arising from varying social contexts.[3]

Unpacking the Within- and Beyond-Classroom FoK Pedagogies

In the framing of FoK work, researchers typically emphasize a concern for countering the pervasiveness of cultural-deficit characterizations of students who are low income or of color or otherwise marginalized within mainstream educational settings (e.g., Camangian, 2010; González, Andrade, Civil, & Moll, 2001; Longwell-Grice & McIntyre, 2006; Riojas-Cortez, 2001; Riojas-Cortez & Flores Bustos, 2009; Risko & Walker-Dalhouse, 2007; Thomson & Hall, 2008; Upadhyay, 2006). Beyond just improved characterizations, of course, is the concern for embracing the lived experiences of children and youth to identify sources of knowledge and learning that can serve as rich resources for enhanced and expanded learning (and learner identities) within the formal educational setting (e.g., Dworin, 2006; Gutiérrez, 2002; Marquez Kiyama, 2010; Rogers, Light, & Curtis, 2004; Sugarman, 2010). In this sense, the concern is about creating learning environments that are more accepting and inclusive, as well as more effective in producing academic outcomes among students that prepare them for future educational and developmental undertakings (e.g., Basu & Calabrese Barton, 2007; Dantas, 2007; Fisher, 2006; Hattam & Prosser, 2008; Marquez Kiyama, 2010; Zanoni et al., 2011; Zipin, 2009). From the outset, this dual concern/purpose involves the risk of maintaining the externally driven pursuit of certain types of learning of specified forms of knowledge, even as the possibilities for engaged learning are widened within the classroom. These pursuits, in turn, involve the risk of circumscribing the pedagogical possibilities that educators are willing to entertain. Indeed, at the heart of a critique of standardization-driven pedagogical approaches is an associated critique of the very definition of what it is to be *educated*— and how the educational system may fail repeatedly in democratizing the process for gathering meaningful input into the formation of pedagogical practices that help realize the vast potential of increasingly diverse learning communities within and beyond the boundaries of the school setting (Zipin, 2009). It is noted briefly here that Rios-Aguilar, Marquez Kiyama, Gravitt, and Moll (2011) take up similar concerns in recent work, which will be discussed in greater detail later in this review.

Within-Classroom Pedagogies

Three key themes emerge as one examines the research literature representing the application of FoK approaches in a variety of classroom settings. The themes include the following: (a) engaging students in the co-construction of knowledge to deepen or extend academic knowledge through FoK; (b) recognizing and encouraging the utilization within the classroom of multiple FoK among students, including home/family FoK as well as youth and popular culture FoK; and (c) moving beyond solely the connection between student/family/community FoK and academic content and instruction to a process of classroom transformation involving the reorientation of both teachers and students as learners and agents within and beyond the classroom. In addition to the foundational documentation of the application of FoK approaches in the classroom by McIntyre et al. (2001) and the teacher-researchers whose work is examined in González, Moll, and Amanti (2005), which included studies exemplifying all three themes, the following literature review provides additional evidence of the pedagogical themes in a variety of scholarly educational projects. Important to note is that a few studies' pedagogical contributions adhere to more than one theme and will be cited and discussed accordingly.

Five studies (Fraser-Abder, Doria, Yang, & De Jesus, 2010; Henderson & Zipin, 2010; Pirbhai-Illich, 2010; Riojas-Cortez, 2001; Upadhyay, 2006) reflect well the first theme of the co-construction of knowledge with students to enhance their academic preparation and school-valued knowledge. The pedagogies emerging within this theme can be viewed in terms of *pedagogy as perspective and relevance across social/cultural/historical contexts.*

In one example, in the area of literacy development and in the context of the Australia-based *Redesigning Pedagogies in the North (RPiN) Project*, Henderson and Zipin (2010) present evidence of teaching-and-learning processes that position students as actively involved in the co-construction of the curricular focus and learning outcomes in the classroom. Discussing high school (Grades 8 and 9) student work using the medium of clay animation visual arts to tell stories about their lives, the authors describe a "double democracy" (p. 21) approach in curricular and peda-gogical practices that seek to give voice to students' FoK in a manner that positions students and teachers to learn reciprocally in their joint pursuit of knowledge. The pedagogical choices made by the teacher are guided by the direction, inspiration, and interests of the students to present problems of importance to their communities and develop solutions that are likewise relevant to community life, thus requiring an element of mutual trust throughout the teaching/learning process regarding all parties involved. Even as individual students are charged with specific responsibili-ties for cocreating a narrative and presentation of their community-based issues, the sense of interdependence that replaces competition among students further reflects and reinforces the double-democracy principles. In addition, the substantive inputs supporting the clay animation projects require high levels of student engagement and responsibility for developing a range of literacies to be able to prepare for school and public presentations of their problem/solution animations.

As another example, in the area of science education, Upadhyay (2006) presents the use of students' (and teacher's) lived experience to teach "meaningful science" (p. 95) in an urban elementary classroom. The researcher's data collection approach was focused on understanding "why and for what purpose" (p. 98) the teacher engaged with students' lived experiences in the science teaching/learning process. Upadhyay situates the use of FoK for science instruction as an approach that helps promote the integration of lived experiences as a way to connect science to students' everyday lives and thus facilitate learning through relevance and resonance. Although definitely citing and engaging in the use of FoK teaching approaches, the focal teacher in this richly described case study appears to remain in charge of determining which students' FoK are useful in supporting science education in the classroom. The focal teacher, however, engaged with students in an open manner such that one could see how students' input was taken seriously and helped guide the teaching, as well.

A key distinction of the second theme is that students' FoK from multiple sources are used as equally valued (vs. only supplementary) forms of knowledge as the more conventional curricular content in the various subject areas examined. Eleven stud-ies (Calabrese Barton & Tan, 2009; Camangian, 2010; Dworin, 2006; Fraser-Abder et al., 2010; Gupta, 2006; Gutiérrez, 2002; Henderson & Zipin, 2010; Kurtyka, 2010; Marshall & Toohey, 2010; Riojas-Cortez, Huerta, Flores Bustos, Perez, & Riojas Clark, 2008; Thomson & Hall, 2008) provide evidence of these endeavors. The pedagogies reflected in this second theme can also be deemed *pedagogy as resis-tance to schooling hegemonies (particularly to cultural deficit thinking) and as relation-ship and interaction that promote a sense of humanity.*

Camangian (2010), in one U.S. example, takes up the use of autoethnography (which he distinguishes as not just chronological accounts of life events but a criti-cal analysis explaining the implications of such events) to pursue the development of "critically caring literacies" (p. 180) among teachers. He further applies critical lit-eracy pedagogies to draw out high school students' FoK, arguing that the use of such approaches is important in forging caring and authentic relationships between youth of color (described in the variety of ways they are marginalized) and their teachers. Also, the author considers the use of critical literacy pedagogies as a means to use students' autoethnographies as a source for students' critical analysis of the world around them. Camangian frames this work as a method of humanizing pedagogies that work with the "texts" with which students are most resonant—their lived experiences—and link their learning activities to authentic caring between teachers and students. He indicates the need to listen to youth in their accounts of their lived experience: In so doing, he finds the transformation of the classroom space that once silenced them into a space for developing a social analysis of their own experience and that of others.

In a quite different setting, Marshall and Toohey (2010) undertake a study with elementary-level children who are Punjabi Sikh in Canada to understand what happens when their FoK contradict schooling discourses. In this instance, students interviewed their grandparents about their (the grandparents') childhoods and translated their narratives into picture books. The authors discuss through their analysis how the children are drawing on family FoK, as well as popular culture resources (in this study, viewed as a source of youth-defined FoK) to represent their hybrid experience as immigrant children who are growing up in 21st-century North America. For example, they discuss how experiences presented in the children's grandparents' stories are recontextualized for contemporary settings and experiences that the children can identify with, for example, drawings of grandparents in current day attire, as well as the different representations of English and home language text within their story books. Interestingly, Marshall and Toohey note that the project produced discussions among children about why Punjabi was not taught at their school when such a high proportion of them spoke the language (73%), which the authors cite as an instance of the children challenging the dominant culture of the school.

In another example of writing and creative arts that allows us to appreciate the difficulty of embracing the pedagogical stances of the second theme, Thomson and Hall (2008) consider the particular challenges of using an FoK approach in a setting in England in which the national curriculum does not create avenues for incorporating students' home and family knowledge. The authors provide three examples to illustrate both the challenges and possibilities of applying FoK in this restrictive environment. Thomson and Hall are clear in setting out to learn whether a primary school can tap into students' home and family knowledge as either a form of curriculum in its own right or as a scaffold toward the national curriculum. The authors present three projects, the first two conducted at one school and the third conducted at another school seeking to emulate the practices of the first. The three projects include the following: (a) dramatic writing that ended up including some (fictional) storylines that were rejected by school staff for being too adult, yet children were able to engage in developing a piece of "collective writing" (p. 93) that demonstrated their ability to tap into FoK about their own lives and of the "television genres" (p. 93) with which they were familiar; (b) self-portrait project involving sketchbooks that were viewed as notebooks within the original writing project, which the authors discuss as a means for the children to invite family members to contribute their own drawings and otherwise allow them to contribute their FoK at school, thereby potentially changing the curricular focus of their classroom. The authors noted a missed opportunity as the sketchbooks were eliminated in succeeding iterations of the project, and they also describe conditions in which the children's art was overshadowed by a concern for their mastery of certain artistic "skills" (p. 95); and (c) portraiture project, through which the authors note that the strong sense of place-based focus (pp. 97–99) in the self-portraits enabled the teacher to encourage the students' use of their FoK in producing their portraits. According to the authors, there were clear connections also made with local historical context, even as the teacher sought to link this to *national* curriculum.

Eight studies (Basu & Calabrese Barton, 2007; Calabrese Barton & Tan, 2009; Camangian, 2010; Fitts, 2009; Henderson & Zipin, 2010; Marshall & Toohey, 2010; Riojas-Cortez, 2001; Street, 2005) exemplify the third theme of classroom transformation and the reorientation of teachers and students in their roles, identities, and relationships with each other. *Pedagogy as micro- and macro-level consciousness and as conduit for personal, institutional, and societal transformation* best summarizes the pedagogical forms that emerge within this third theme.

In addition to the issues raised by the RPiN project as showcased in Henderson and Zipin's (2010) analysis of the use of FoK for engaging students in a "double democratic" pedagogy and Camangian's (2010) demonstration of youth-to-youth relationships that support rigorous social analysis and personal growth and improvement, Calabrese Barton and associates provide additional compelling evidence of this third theme. For example, in Calabrese Barton and Tan (2009), the authors discuss the shifting discourses in a middle school science classroom that connects strongly with students' FoK and their use in science learning. They pose research questions (paraphrased from p. 51) to explore the standpoint of students: What FoK do students bring to their science classroom, and how do students leverage their FoK for science learning? Also, how did the use of students' FoK transform the discourses and engagement of the sixth-grade learning community and members? In conducting this investigation, Calabrese Barton and Tan seek to understand the emergence of hybrid spaces in which the discourses of students' FoK challenge the discourses of school science. Through a thoroughly detailed case study analysis, the authors show that when providing the conditions for students to engage their FoK and multiple (home, family, popular culture, school) discourses, the science classroom can support both academic achievement and inclusion of a variety of student voices. The researchers further elaborate that when the teacher sanctions this form of participation through assignments designed to link with students' FoK, more students participate, and they also contribute substantively to the science discussions. The authors note in discussing their findings that the power distribution tends to be less top-down (teacher-to-students) in the hybrid spaces than in more traditional approaches to science teaching and learning. Given the gatekeeping practices commonly associated with science education, the resultant transformative classroom relations and substantive content linked to the employment of students' FoK are particularly striking.

Beyond-Classroom Pedagogies

Although the studies reviewed within the category of "beyond-classroom pedagogies" include research activities that had clear connections to classroom practice, the distinction drawn here for analytical purposes is the attempt to document pedagogies that are rooted in community cultural practices and heritage knowledge (e.g., Fisher, 2006; Hammond, 2001; Keis, 2006; Riojas-Cortez et al., 2008; Smythe & Toohey, 2009; Sugarman, 2010). As noted in the discussion regarding classroom-based pedagogies informed by FoK approaches, these studies apply a variety of theoretical perspectives in conjunction with the use of FoK strategies; however, these studies appear to be more explicitly directed at understanding the broader transformative potential of such pedagogical approaches (e.g., Basu & Calabrese Barton, 2007; Moje et al., 2004; Zipin, 2009; Zipin & Reid, 2008; Zipin, Sellar, & Hattam, 2012). Furthermore, these studies help demonstrate the purposes of stepping out of the confines of classroom contexts (and associated disciplinary divisions of knowledge) to address the biases that are reproduced through hegemonic practices carried out by researchers and educators, as they learn what it means to work in alliance with community members and students as experts in community-based knowledge. In this realm, it may serve well to view these approaches and purposes in terms of *pedagogy as reclaiming, recontexualizing, and intercultural sense-making*.

For a greater sense of the ethos of this pedagogical work, Hammond's (2001) detailed account of the multilayered phases of collaborative science learning in a project that takes place in a community setting proves quite useful. Her descriptive case study discusses the collaborative versus hegemonic science education strategies developed via cross-cultural exchanges between teachers and Mien families in Sacramento, California. Within this project, building a field house and establishing a garden are activities central to the development of curricula and learning opportunities for elementary-level schoolchildren, their teachers, and their parents. Parents also engage as experts in science teaching/learning along with children; indeed, the project's focus is on creating avenues for learning various forms of science (not just Western science). Project collaborators use a FoK approach in many aspects, including encouraging teachers to go into the community and interview parents to develop books that document community history, knowledge, and practices. Also, the project contributors use summer program time to test science teaching practices developed from FoK activities and discoveries among teachers. In reciprocal fashion, the project engages parents as experts to bring community science into the classroom to create relevance for immigrant children and families, while also providing students with access to Western, school-learned science. Hammond discusses the role of "cultural conflict" (p. 991) and conflict resolution in working together to build the "Mien-American" garden house (i.e., reflecting a negotiation of characteristics and requirements from both community and school sources, pp. 989–991). Hammond further explains that the teaching and learning evolves as an interaction of multiple ways of knowing rather than as an imposition of one knowledge tradition. Hybridized notions of culture and learning are reflected in various results, including the movement from multicultural science to "multiscience" (pp. 986–987), changing roles of teachers and learners, and utilization of dialogues to promote intercultural understanding.

To illuminate beyond-classroom pedagogies even further—and in many respects as a means for further problematizing the FoK approach as it has been enacted in formal educational settings—it is useful to consider the research that has begun to extend our view of FoK pedagogy through explorations of perhaps more troubling knowledge that students bring to the classroom and school community. Interestingly, in their attempts to remain open to the possibilities and potential of the FoK approach for engaging students' and families' personal and cultural histories and reference points, teachers encounter forms and sources of knowledge that challenge their sensibilities around creating safe learning environments that preserve children's innocence with the intention of preventing them from (re)experiencing the impact of war, conflict, violence, abject poverty, racism, sexism, homophobia, and other forms of bias and oppression. Teachers may be wary to make classroom use of such knowledge, seeing it as emotionally threatening to students and risky for schools. Yet our notions of pedagogy are expanded by considering adversity as a potential source of purposefulness to instructional and curricular development—as demonstrated in the complex epistemological approaches among students, parents, grandparents, and community elders who use accounts of lived experiences that render life lessons, forms of resistance, and connections to contemporary and historical struggles (Camangian, 2010; Fisher, 2006; Johnson, Baker, & Bruer, 2007; Marshall & Toohey, 2010; Sugarman, 2010; Zipin, 2009).

Zipin (2009) provides cogent arguments to address the need for further problematizing the FoK approach in light of the existence of community knowledge and epistemologies that may develop through processes that are troubling, sometimes extremely so, in their impact on the well-being of students and families. He terms these forms of knowledge as "dark FoK" (p. 320) that are distinguished as arising from the adversity that students and families experience in exceedingly difficult circumstances and conditions in their homes and neighborhoods. This includes, for example, the effects of poverty, racism, and violence, which are often avoided by teachers as sources of curriculum and student engagement with classroom-based learning. To address this concern, Zipin argues for an expansion of the FoK framework to include "dark FoK" that speak to the contemporary challenges that many immigrant and otherwise marginalized and displaced students and families experience, such that it calls into question the salience of the term "community," as well as the utility of eliciting students' knowledge about more difficult experiences but stopping short of their use as additional resources for school transformation.

Zipin (2009) articulates a key argument regarding how the use-value of *funds* of knowledge (i.e., community developed/transmitted knowledge) challenges the selective and dominant power of exchange-value knowledge (i.e., cultural capital, which reflects and reproduces capitalist principles and power structures). These assertions are further elaborated via lessons drawn from the RPiN work in Zipin and Reid (2008). According to Zipin (2009), the potential to challenge extant social reproduction processes via schooling is weakened if FoK, drawn from students' lived experiences to build curriculum, selectively omits or overlooks the full spectrum of possibilities for recontextualizing FoK for classroom teaching and learning. Indeed, this would constitute a mechanism of control of knowledge, perhaps more for the protection of teachers than students. Within this analysis, Zipin also interrogates the FoK literature for its seeming lack of attention to community ways of knowing— which he calls "funds of pedagogy" (p. 318)—as an omission that has significant bearing on the possibility of maximizing the transformative impact of the FoK approach. In these arguments, it appears that Zipin is calling for a more comprehensive treatment of critical consciousness among all constituents involved in an FoK approach. This commitment aligns well with the broader social change purposes expressed in the recent formulations of FoK-informed practices (e.g., Calabrese Barton & Tan, 2009; Camangian, 2010; Fisher, 2006; Moje et al., 2004), which reveal the Freirean influences taken up in early FoK work and will be discussed later in the theoretical dialogue with the CCW framework (Yosso, 2005).

FoK-Informed Pedagogies: Embracing Border-Crossing/Hybridity as Legacy

The first research question guiding this review was, "What do we know from the Funds of Knowledge literature about the development and enactment of pedagogies within and beyond the formal classroom? Returning to this question, I conclude this section by highlighting the point that even as more is understood about the promise of FoK, the development of associated pedagogies remains in motion, ever evolving. What is important to consider as we circle back to the intentionality of the initiating FoK researchers is that the newly associated forms of transformative educational practice, while stated in contemporary terms more explicitly as counter-hegemonic praxis, are compatible with the founding researchers' commitments to emancipatory practices that embrace the knowledge and epistemologies that operate in nonacademic contexts. Indeed, it is crucial to fully appreciate that most FoK researchers and practitioners initiated their endeavors not simply to ensure that students broadened their repertoire of knowledge and skills for greater individualistic academic success. Rather, the FoK approach is meant to encompass in our conceptualizations of learning and development a recognition of the critical role of social history and context in mediating what is learned (and taught), thus holding the potential for vast levels of transformation and knowledge production—and shifting definitions of academic success. Part of the evolutionary process, of course, is engaging with the constraints on FoK pedagogical developments emerging from broader power structures, as reflected in social conditions, restrictive educational policies, and the complexities of intercultural understanding. Rather than viewing the legacy of FoK approaches solely in the realm of teacher empowerment for the bridging or blending of students' home and school skills and knowledge for school-based success, what the literature reveals is a push for students' empowerment via their recontextualization of FoK from multiple sources into new, hybrid or "third space" FoK. Indeed, González (2005) foreshadows such a legacy by distinguishing the task and promise of FoK endeavors as theorizing cultural practice to realize the project's greater transformative power in education:

As discourses come to recognize the situated nature of knowledge and the partiality of all knowledge claims, the metaphor of borders and border-crossers has been foregrounded. However, the ultimate border—the border between knowledge and power—can be crossed only when educational institutions no longer reify culture, when lived experiences become validated as a source of knowledge, and when the process of how knowledge is constructed and translated between groups located within nonsymmetrical relations of power is questioned. As minoritized students continue to be subjected to standardized and prescriptive tests, the issue of whose knowledge and whose voice are embedded in these measures can be answered only as we cross the furthest border between knowledge and power. (p. 42)

González's assertions therefore invite a closer examination of the power dynamics, relations, and structures that surround or are embedded within the contexts in which the FoK pedagogical endeavors are carried out. The remaining sections of the chapter proceed with such an analysis of the literature to deepen our understanding of the potential and promise of the FoK framework and approaches to education as contributions to critical pedagogy.

ANALYSIS OF POWER AND AGENCY DISCOURSES IN FOK PEDAGOGIES

Although a complete historical discussion of the concepts of power and agency (such as that undertaken by Hindess, 1996) is beyond the scope of this chapter, it is important to establish an understanding for readers of the perspectives enlisted in this analysis of FoK scholarship and later in the theoretical dialogue with the CCW framework. In this chapter, ideas regarding power and agency are drawn from the work of critical education scholars Michael Apple (see Apple, 1995, 1999, 2004; Apple & Buras, 2006), Paulo Freire (see Freire, 1970/1993), and Henry Giroux (see Giroux, 2005, 2006, 2011), particularly given the power dynamic theorized in various ways by these and the FoK scholars regarding the institutional resistance to community knowledge within educational systems. Contributing also to the conceptualizations of power and agency for this chapter is the work of Chicana feminists Dolores Delgado-Bernal and Sofía Villenas, whose analyses of Mexican origin/ Chicana/o students, families, and communities (see Delgado Bernal, 2006a, 2006b; Delgado Bernal & Elenes, 2011; Delgado Bernal, Elenes, Godinez, & Villenas, 2006; Villenas, 2006), with attention to the various forms of knowledge that are produced in spaces beyond the formal school setting, have revealed forms of agency and leadership that go unrecognized and undertheorized by (predominantly White) critical scholars as the various forms of knowledge that are produced in spaces beyond the formal school setting. Indeed, an understanding of power that is key in developing an analysis of FoK pedagogical contributions is that power and agency exist not only in the ability to act with purpose on one's behalf but also in the acts themselves and in being able to communicate the possibility (or even threat) of action—as in the situation of dominant and dominated groups (Freire, 1970/1993; Hindess, 1996).

Ideally, FoK scholarship and practice seek to foster and generate proactive and emancipatory pedagogy that reflects agency among teachers, students, and families/parents. However, as argued by Apple and Buras (2006), in examining oppressed, silenced groups—whom they refer to as the subaltern—there are often contradictions and complexities involved in "giving voice" to the forms of knowledge and multiple ways of knowing that marginalized communities represent. That is, we may not be able to assume that scholars and educators who embrace an FoK approach in their work are not influenced significantly by the surrounding context and power structures to use their positions (and associated privilege) to reproduce some of the same power relations that led to FoK research endeavors in the first place. Also, an analysis of power and agency requires that we take into account the types of power relations that exist within the interactions between teacher and student (or parent/community member), those that are defined to some degree by the authority and voice that are accorded to variously situated members of society. It is difficult, in other words, to remove all of the elements of dominance within education when schools and communities continue to reflect pervasive, overt and subtle, power imbalances that relate to the economic, political, and social history and context of society at every level. Hence, there is profound importance in raising issues such as those taken up by Zipin and Reid (2008) in "making the community curricular" (p. 536) (with similar concerns regarding notions of community explored by Andrews & Ching Yee, 2006) and by Zipin et al. (2012) in "re-imagining community" (pp. 188-189) to problematize FoK and thereby expand our notions of democracy, good citizenship and community, and also challenge the commodification of FoK that perpetuate asymmetrical power relations within and beyond education.

Analysis of power/agency from "marginalized other" standpoints, in relation to FoK developments, is therefore important to undertake because, as noted by Moll and González (2004) in citing their years of experience with this work, most teachers do not live in the neighborhoods (especially low-income ones) where they teach. As disclosed by authors in several studies reviewed here, research and practical applications of the FoK approach are often carried out by teacher-researchers and university collaborators from middle-class economic backgrounds, often minimally exposed to diverse populations in their nonschool personal lives, working with populations who are predominantly low income or of color, often immigrants. Moll and González explain the distinction of the FoK work as aiming to "theorize practice" (in González, Moll, & Amanti, 2005, pp. 20–22) so as to gain access to the forms of knowledge represented among marginalized communities for purposes of improving the educational experiences of students from those communities. The challenges inherent in such an undertaking provide an important opportunity for getting beneath the scholarship to interrogate the power relations and impact of FoK practices on student/community agency. That is, within the process of understanding the extant power relations that are challenged by the pedagogical contributions of FoK approaches to education, it is instructive to consider the positionality of the researchers and educators who are producing this work, with similar scrutiny as they apply to the marginalized communities with whom they work. To this end, we must appreciate the candor, self-analysis, and investigative integrity that FoK researchers bring to their work—particularly as we seek to discern the impact of the varying identities and stances that can be taken up among them: outsider, professional/expert, bridge-builder, learner, translator, ally.

Societal Power Structures as Reference Points for FoK Research/Researchers

Important reference points that several FoK researchers (e.g., Camangian, 2010; Hammond, 2001; Pirbhai-Illich, 2010; Thomson & Hall, 2008; Zanoni et al., 2010; Zipin & Reid, 2008; Zipin et al., 2012) use to situate their work—or to further challenge the notion of FoK in more recent undertakings—involve the acknowledgment of broader, macro-level power structures that persist despite efforts to change the nature of schooling for marginalized students. More specifically, these empirical and theoretical analyses embrace a discourse that rejects the singular pursuit of improved educational outcomes in only standardized, externally and narrowly defined terms as a goal that is shaped by the economic, political, social, and historical power structures that dictate the manner by which schooling is implicated in social stratification and injustice. In addition, as these authors frame their application of FoK pedagogical approaches using the broader societal power structures as a reference point, the silencing of community knowledge and knowledge production (epistemologies) is revealed as a key feature of socially reproductive practices, which include narratives regarding the cultural and intellectual deficiencies (read: inferiority) of minoritized populations. In other words, using societal power structures as reference points enables FoK researchers to engender a social justice or social change orientation to pedagogy that transcends notions of the classroom as the only relevant site for transformative knowledge production and praxis (reflective practice).

Power Relations Within the Context of FoK Research Sites

There are several examples within the FoK literature reviewed for this chapter that demonstrate the researchers' attention to extant power relations in school and community settings. It is helpful to consider the impetus and critical junctures for many researchers and educators who take on the FoK approach in their collaborative work to better appreciate the challenges of fostering practices that confront and intentionally disrupt the "business as usual" of schooling in terms of the roles of teachers, students, and parents/families. Longwell-Grice and McIntyre (2006), for example, allude to the implicit power relations that may have served as obstacles to a more comprehensive implementation of FoK approaches in their study site. In reflecting on the outcomes of their collaborative work (and especially the pitfalls and unintended consequences of particular programmatic features), they provide a compelling view of the extant power dynamics among teachers, students, and families in navigating the changes in both practice and mindset implied by the attempted FoK-informed approaches and the subtle and overt forms of resistance that they observe among their collaborating constituents. Their candor is instructive, as it raises new questions regarding the appearance in the FoK-informed pedagogical literature of ready acceptance and smooth shifts in perspective, professional stance, and personal beliefs and values relative to the educational inclusion of otherwise marginalized communities.

In documenting the transformative potential of FoK approaches that redefine the roles and identities of teacher and student, it is evident from the studies reviewed in which this phenomenon emerges—either intentionally or rather unexpectedly as a product of the FoK approach—that incisive theoretical framing of the pedagogical challenges is critical to such transformations. From the evidence presented, it appears that the FoK approach, in and of itself, does not always lead the researchers and teachers involved in the studies to be intentional in engaging in counter-hegemonic practice or in dismantling the power imbalances that characterize oppressive, narrowly construed forms of teaching/learning dictated by contemporary accountability or standardization policies. In fact, it seems more often the case that FoK researchers and teachers who aim to redress unequal power relations use the FoK approach in tandem with specific theoretical frameworks that seek to identify and interrupt such oppressive conditions within the schooling environment. This illuminates the need for addressing the power relations that exist among teachers and students, as well as with respect to students' families and home communities. A variety of tandem theories are represented amid these studies, including third space theories that point to the hybridity of knowledge production processes that are neither exclusively school- nor community-based but recontextualized by students as a result of more inclusive learning opportunities provided via the FoK approach (Calabrese Barton & Tan, 2009; Fitts, 2009; Hammond, 2001; Moje et al., 2004; Smythe & Toohey, 2009); critical literacy theories that combine with FoK approaches to increase the consciousness of teachers (and students) toward multiple forms of literacy and facilitate students' ability to "read the world" (Camangian, 2010; Fisher, 2006; Freire, 1970/1993; Keis, 2006; Pirbhai-Illich, 2010; Rogers et al., 2004; Street, 2005); sociocultural theories that are linked to the potency of FoK approaches to bring situated and socially mediated learning into relief, particularly for preservice or novice teachers and parents of preschool-age children (Dantas, 2007; Monzo & Rueda, 2003; Nathenson-Mejia & Escamilla, 2003; Riojas-Cortez, 2001; Riojas-Cortez & Flores Bustos, 2009; Riojas-Cortez et al., 2008; Wang, Bernas, & Eberhard, 2005); and social justice and community empowerment theories that link FoK practices to broader critical consciousness imperatives involving the reformulation of social arrangements and the fostering of interdependence among community members (Henderson & Zipin, 2010; Kurtyka, 2010; Sugarman, 2010; Upadhyay, 2009; Zipin & Reid, 2008; Zipin et al., 2012).

Although one may find it helpful to view the treatment of power and power relations or structures within the FoK pedagogical literature as evolving linearly over time, it is likely more accurate to consider this dimension more iterative in its articulation. Only on rare occasion did power dynamics rise to the surface as a by-product of the FoK approach—meaning, not as an element integrated into the framing of the research endeavor from the beginning (e.g., the candid account provided by Longwell-Grice & McIntyre, 2006). The majority of the studies contained acknowledgments of the role of external (macro) and internal (micro) power structures and relations, either in establishing the impetus for FoK approaches as the need for response to cultural deficit characterizations of students and families, identifying the individual and/or institutional challenges of applying FoK, or in analyzing the unexpected (negative and positive) consequences of using such an FoK approach. To further explore some of the complexity of the investigators' and participants' experiences with power (and empowerment) as they engage in new research and schooling practices, roles, and identities, the following section details the forms of agency (and constraints on it) that are discussed or revealed in the literature reviewed.

Teachers as Agents

From the outset of the FoK work, teachers as agents has been a crucial element in launching efforts to enable school communities to better reflect and understand their students and families. The agency of teachers is often circumscribed by the isolation and autonomy associated with their roles in most conventional schooling environments, as well as by the social distance they may confront between their own lived experience and that of their students. With great intentionality, therefore, the FoK framework and approach rely on teachers to take steps in their practice that are not part of the usual repertoire of skills and activities associated with their professional roles—to engage in collaborative, action-oriented, ethnographic research in the communities surrounding their local school settings. Furthermore, as initiated by the founding researchers, teacher-researchers establish meaningful social relations with students and communities as a means for mediating the knowledge production and exchange that take place through the ethnographic process (González et al., 2011).

As documented in the majority of studies using the FoK framework and/or classroom approaches, teachers' agency in forging relationships, gathering new knowledge, and co-constructing classroom practices reflective of these new understandings of context, role, and relationship is a significant shift from the conventions to which teachers were accustomed prior to these undertakings (González, Moll, & Amanti, 2005; González et al., 2011; Moll & González, 2004). Basu and Calabrese Barton (2007), Calabrese Barton and Tan (2009), Henderson and Zipin (2010), and McIntyre et al. (2001) exemplify the impact of teachers' agency in redefining the classroom environment to be inclusive of student- and parent/family/community-produced knowledge and skills. Moreover, within the context of educational research, the FoK approach also reflects a concerted effort on the part of González, Moll, and associates to redress the power asymmetries between university researchers and teachers that lead to the tendency in academia to treat the latter as merely consumers of knowledge produced by the former (Moll & González, 2004).

Despite these critical developments, teachers' agency is also shown in this literature to be somewhat curtailed in the effort to implement an FoK approach that would not only access students' FoK but also the FoK that diverse teachers themselves represent. The pressures to conform to externally driven forms of accountability and standardization for classroom practice appear to limit the extent to which teachers representing communities of color or otherwise minoritized populations are able to integrate their own community knowledge into their classroom practices, despite commitments to FoK-informed pedagogy. Some studies, for example, identified this phenomenon in the context of discussing the employment of diverse educators (teachers and paraprofessionals) to enhance the positive educational impact of their cultural connections to the community and associated FoK and thus better reflect the diversity of the students served in the affected schools (Gupta, 2006; Reyes & McNabb, 1998; Upadhyay, 2006, 2009). Unfortunately, what Martin-Jones and Saxena (2003) and Thomson and Hall (2008) find is that limited opportunities exist in which these educators are able to use their cultural, linguistic, and other community resources to connect with their students, including those experiencing alienation and difficulty as newly arrived immigrant youth. Through in-depth case study analyses, Monzo and Rueda (2003) point out that the power relations between teachers and paraprofessionals potentially result in limited occasions when the paraprofessionals find the time and latitude needed to establish relationships with students that enable all parties to draw on their home knowledge and skills to bridge the divide with traditional school-valued knowledge.

Parents/Community Members as Agents

An interesting dynamic is revealed in the process of reviewing literature that captures the strengths and challenges of reaching beyond classrooms for sources of knowledge and epistemology that better reflect the diverse constituents of given school communities. On the one hand, the literature identifies as key assets the historical knowledge, strategic skills, and contemporary understandings represented among parents and community members in the implementation of the FoK approach (González, Moll, & Amanti, 2005); however, on the other hand, the literature also raises questions about the extent to which parents/community members are called on to directly contribute their skills and knowledge without the filter of school agents' assessments of their utility (Hattam & Prosser, 2008; Zipin, 2009). In addition, despite early warnings from Moll and González (2004) to view cultural practices as dynamic and responsive mechanisms operating in family contexts, there appears to be a tendency in the manner in which the evidence and findings are presented in these studies to view parent/community knowledge as the background or historical inputs that are then used by teachers to generate future-oriented skills and knowledge of greater use (by virtue of its enhanced, school-defined form) for the students. As a result, the agency of parents/community members is located in most of the studies in sites outside of the school setting (e.g., Fisher, 2006; Keis, 2006; Marquez Kiyama, 2010) and thus it is difficult to fully appreciate how their agency coexists and continues to evolve, along with their children's academic development and hybrid cultural practices.[4]

Students/Youth/Children as Agents

In light of the focus of this chapter, it seems particularly important to point out that most references within the key pieces articulating the initial Funds of Knowledge work, and the literature base that has since been generated, leaves a sense of a gap in time, space, and action—and I would argue, student agency—in that households are described as possessing a range of strategic cultural knowledge that students "bring" to the classroom and that teachers can "tap" for the purposes of developing curriculum and instructional practice. What is left out is the process by which the students themselves engage in the types of transformation processes concomitant to those theorized by Vélez-Ibáñez and Greenberg (1992/2005) relative to how parents' FoK evolve, expand, get discarded, or get recontextualized for a different set of family and societal conditions. It seems that this accounting for the important source and substance of familial/cultural knowledge produces a form of student agency that is still circumscribed by the extent to which adults (parents or educators) allow for students/children/youth to integrate the knowledge(s) for themselves and contribute that knowledge directly in ways that make sense to them as learners within the classroom setting and beyond. The development and transformation of FoK among students is thus mediated (perhaps mitigated) by the family and school roles—and power relations—within which students are learning (and teaching). It is not completely evident what the initiators of the FoK work intended with regard to student agency in the teaching-and-learning process; however, in light of the heavy influence of pedagogical/epistemological sources such as Vygotsky and Freire, it seems rather safe to infer that the intention was that of student empowerment, ongoing development or evolution, and emancipation via education.

Nevertheless, despite the limitations noted here and building from the foundational principles of FoK, one does find in the literature several examples of students as agents. Some of these have been discussed at greater length in the previous sections unpacking the various pedagogies (e.g., Andrews & Ching Yee, 2006; Calabrese Barton & Tan, 2009; Camangian, 2010; Kurtyka, 2010; Marshall & Toohey, 2010). In particular, Henderson and Zipin's (2010) work helps illuminate the potential for student agency within the context of their double-democratic FoK-informed pedagogies. These authors make a crucial statement in pointing out how both students and teachers are challenged by a commitment to co-constructed teaching and learning opportunities, such as those informed by an FoK approach, as they cause each group to question and reject long-established roles in favor of new ways of engaging proactively with critical, voiced involvement at every stage of teaching and learning. This reciprocal pro-action enables both parties to revisit and perhaps replace or discard assumptions about what it means to be either student or teacher in the classroom (or other learning) environment.

Researchers as Agents: Considerations of Positionality

It may appear to be a departure from the examination of the focal participants in the studies comprising the FoK pedagogical literature (namely, teachers and students) to take up concerns regarding researchers as agents. However, given several FoK researchers' articulation of roles and activities akin to Giroux's (2005) view of such scholars as "cultural workers" (p. 12) engaged in social, cultural, political, and scholarly "border crossing" (p. 6), this consideration seems warranted to round out our exploration of power and agency within the context of FoK. In addition, the stances taken by the majority of the researchers contributing to this scholarship are clearly intentional with respect to the transformative potential of education, particularly within the context of classroom and community learning and teaching. However, we are called on by our contemplation of power and agency in the pedagogical dimensions of FoK to also consider the extent to which researcher positionality—meaning the standpoints represented either tacitly or explicitly in the work—plays a role in the methodological, collaborative, and analytical choices and (eventual) theoretical formulations and scholarly findings presented in the FoK literature.

I raise this concern here as an invitation to consider the perspectives represented among the researchers as reflecting an array of potentially uninterrogated language, assumptions, beliefs, and privilege that combine to complicate the conclusions we draw from the analyses of students' and communities' lived experiences, as chronicled in these studies. For example, in revisiting Zipin's (2009) call for problematizing the tendency in FoK work to effectively sanitize out the "darker" range of FoK to elevate more positive or hopeful forms, it is likewise useful to consider the implications of having the power as researchers to name the experiences of marginalized peoples (Apple & Buras, 2006). For example, what is the significance of language use in coupling the term *dark* with that which is deemed troubling or difficult in the lifeworlds of diverse students? Indeed, many of us are regularly exposed to societal associations between being dark-skinned and lacking intelligence or beauty or having violent tendencies. Researcher intentions notwithstanding, such connotations exist and have an impact. What assumptions, therefore, are university researchers obligated to make transparent as part of embracing the transformative potential of the FoK approach to research?

Indeed, as explicated by González (2006) in her presentation of the pre-immigration narratives of two mothers participating in schools applying the FoK approaches, one encounters an outlook on life that is grounded in the survival of experiences that most middle-class, university-trained educators or researchers would consider unthinkable, or as González describes "not for the weak of heart" (p. 208). It is striking to note in these narratives and in González's gender analysis that the women are able to transcend these difficult experiences and use them to fuel their actions on behalf of their children without expending energy on comparing realities with those possessing more resources. Still, González reminds us of the need to interrogate the role of researcher in retelling such personal accounts: "The stories of both women touched raw nerves in me, exposing a side of life that we, as researchers, often keep obscured and silenced. To tell their stories is to name their silenced lives" (p. 211).

Likewise, as suggested by Apple (1999), Apple and Buras, (2006), Delgado Bernal et al. (2006), and Figueroa and Sánchez (2005), we may benefit considerably in our understandings of the transformative potential of FoK pedagogical pursuits by reflecting on the positionality of researchers whose personal, social, and political identities mirror the communities in which they carry out their FoK-informed projects to deepen our understanding of—and actively problematize—notions of representation, methodological rigor, and research integrity. Once again, given the espoused purposes of engaging in such complex and forward-thinking educational endeavors as FoK-informed pedagogies, this invitation to reflect on researcher positionality is likely to be met with comparable commitments to introspection and praxis that have been demonstrated in multiple ways throughout this body of scholarship.

It is also essential to continue to examine the positionality of teachers as coresearchers. It is important to recognize that there is a particular challenge with researcher positionality that intersects with considerations of teachers' agency. As noted in the teachers-as-agents discussion above, power imbalances may persist as educational researchers seek to collaborate with teachers as co-constructors of knowledge rather than solely as consumers of research knowledge. González et al. (2011), in fact, offer a framework for the anthropology of education that illuminates the crucial role of relationships among FoK university and teacher researchers (and community constituents) in redressing these enduring power asymmetries and moving the FoK research arena forward in its pursuit of transformative action.

To circle back, the second research question posed for this chapter is, "What is/are the discourse(s) in the Funds of Knowledge literature relative to the power and agency of teachers and students (and students' variously defined communities) embedded within and/or emerging from the enactment of the associated pedagogies?" One can appreciate the complexity of terrain covered by these studies and how their contributions to our exploration of power and agency in education extend beyond just a focus on teachers and students. From the evidence presented in the literature, it is clear that researchers have found utility in adopting discourses that situate FoK pedagogical work as counter-hegemonic praxis within an educational and societal environment that is shaped by asymmetrical power relations at the micro-levels of school communities and persistent, reproductive power structures at the macro-levels of society. The power imbalances and reproductive forces challenging the FoK work are made further visible in the evidence provided regarding the variable enactments of and constraints on teacher, student, parent/community member, and researcher agency in undertaking these collaborative endeavors.

THEORETICAL DIALOGUE BETWEEN FUNDS OF KNOWLEDGE AND COMMUNITY CULTURAL WEALTH

To further the consideration of power and agency within the context of FoK-informed pedagogies, I next place this framework in theoretical dialogue with the Critical Race Theory (CRT)–informed CCW framework (Yosso, 2005). To the extent that both frameworks are used in an effort to provide a counter-hegemonic response to pervasive forms of cultural deficit thinking, it is useful to examine how and whether these distinct endeavors allow for new or conflicting notions of power and agency in the pedagogical realm of education.

Tara J. Yosso presents the Community Cultural Wealth framework in the 2005 article titled, "Whose Culture Has Capital? A Critical Race Theory Discussion of Community Cultural Wealth." Yosso discusses how cultural capital, as explicated by Bourdieu, reflects and reinforces the norms that are associated with the dominant groups of society. To facilitate success among nondominant groups, schools engage in practices that inculcate in all students a regard for—as having the highest value—the beliefs, values, and cultural practices (i.e., cultural capital) of the dominant group, typically referring to a White, upper- or middle-class population. Consistent with such assessments, as the differences represented by low-income populations and/or communities of color are viewed from the perspective of dominant forms of "cultural capital," the explanatory models often employed are informed by cultural deficit views that attribute things such as educational "failure" to the cultural backgrounds of students and their families/communities (Valencia & Solórzano, 1997).

Yosso sees need to push the concept of "capital" further, to recognize various forms of "wealth" that children of marginalized groups bring to school, from an asset perspective. In doing so, she adapts the concept of "wealth" in the Black community articulated in Oliver and Shapiro's (1995) *Black Wealth/White Wealth* in combination with CRT (Delgado & Stefancic, 2001) to propose that various forms of teaching, learning, and knowing are produced as marginalized individuals and communities negotiate the impact of institutionalized racism and other intersecting forms of bias in their daily lives (Solórzano & Yosso, 2009; Taylor, Gillborn, & Ladson-Billings, 2009). Yosso (2005) further proposes, as a counter-hegemonic option, the CCW framework composed of six forms of capital, which represent the processes and forms of knowledge production attributable to the lived experiences of the marginalized communities: (a) aspirational capital—"the ability to maintain hopes and dreams for the future, even in the face of real and perceived barriers" (p. 77); (b) linguistic capital—"the intellectual and social skills attained through communication experiences in more than one language and/or style" (p. 78); (c) familial capital—"the cultural knowledges nurtured among [families] that carry a sense of community history, memory, and cultural intuition" (p. 79); (d) social capital—"networks of people and community resources . . . [that] can provide both instrumental and emotional support to navigate through society's institutions" (p. 79); (e) navigational capital—"the skills of maneuvering through social institutions [inferred historically as] (bracketed phrase in original) not created for People of Color in mind" (p. 80); and (f) resistance capital—"knowledges and skills fostered through oppositional behavior that challenges inequality . . . [including] maintaining and passing on the multiple dimensions of community cultural wealth" (p. 80).

To launch this dialogue, we can see that the FoK and CCW frameworks are compatible to the extent that they are both recognizing forms of knowledge that are often ignored, especially in the current processes of prescriptive, narrowly construed forms of instruction and curriculum (Yosso, 2006). Where these frameworks further overlap significantly is in the thrust of emancipatory discourse for developing a response to the pervasiveness of cultural deficit model thinking among educators working with marginalized communities. They also both draw from the spirit and values embodied in Paulo Freire's (1993) *Pedagogy of the Oppressed*, particularly in its emphasis on the naming of local conditions by those who live them out daily with the intention of improving social conditions and otherwise transforming the world around them (i.e., engaging in *praxis*), as indicated in Yosso's (2006) book, *Critical Race Counterstories Along the Chicana/Chicano Educational Pipeline*. In the case of FoK, the site for transformation is initially identified as the classroom or school; however, this literature never distances itself theoretically or in practice from the surrounding environments of neighborhoods and society.

Where the frameworks diverge is in the FoK focus on learning processes that are directly linked to particular school-defined content areas and skills, whereas the CCW foregrounds forms of learning and living strategies that reflect broader concerns with the oppressive structures of the contexts within which such learning and strategizing takes place (neighborhoods, schools, economy, society). Although hardships or struggles are clearly a part of the realm of discovery for FoK theorists, one clear distinction with the CCW framework is in the manner in which society's sources of inequality are articulated.

It is significant that the CCW framework is derived from and informed by the tenets of CRT, with deep foundations in legal theory and scholarship (Crenshaw, Gotanda, Peller, & Thomas, 1995; Taylor et al., 2009), as well as influences from the fields of sociology, history, ethnic studies, and women's studies (Solórzano & Yosso, 2009). The tenets make explicit the forms of knowledge that are privileged as an effort to elevate the value of lived experience, particularly among individuals and populations who experience the broad impact of institutionalized racism, classism, sexism, and other forms of oppression and marginalization. In the early establishment of CRT, in fact, legal theorists sought to establish a response to the dehumanization and lack of critical consciousness that had become institutionalized features of the legal system and society more broadly speaking. As noted in their introductory comments, Crenshaw et al. (1995) inform us that CRT scholars were motivated by the following dual purpose:

The first is to understand how a regime of white supremacy and its subordination of people of color have been created and maintained in America, and, in particular, to examine the relationship between that social structure and professed ideals such as "the rule of law" and "equal protection." The second is a desire not merely to understand the vexed bond between law and racial power but to *change* it [italics in original]. (p. xiii)

More specifically, the CRT tenets that have been adapted for analyses in education include, according to Solórzano and Yosso (2009): (a) the intercentricity of race and racism with other forms of subordination (p. 132); (b) the challenge to dominant ideology, particularly such notions as "objectivity, meritocracy, colorblindness, race neutrality, and equal opportunity" (p. 132); (c) the commitment to social justice, particularly in pursuing "the elimination of racism, sexism, and poverty; and the empowering of subordinated minority groups" (p. 133); (d) the centrality of experiential knowledge as "legitimate, appropriate, and critical to understanding, analyzing, and teaching about racial subordination," including a variety of "storytelling" (and counter-storytelling) media and genres (p. 133); and (e) a transdisciplinary perspective to counteract the silencing impact of "ahistorical," "unidisciplinary" conventions for approaching the analysis of race and racism (p. 134). Although the tenets resonate with many of the principles and values espoused by a variety of FoK researchers, it is important to point out that the arguments made for a CRT analysis of educational processes are situated within the context of institutionalized racism (with particular reference to the U.S. social and historical context) and its intersectionality with other forms of bias and oppression within social institutions such as schools (Parker & Lynn, 2009; Solórzano & Yosso, 2009).

Counter-storytelling is a key process to take up in engaging CCW in dialogue with FoK. By reframing and relocating the educational "failure" of marginalized students to more explicitly implicate the practices and processes of schooling and other social institutions shaped by a variety of oppressive biases, CCW seems to push further into the realm of resistance to cultural deficit thinking. In addition, counter-storytelling and the other CRT tenets allow educators and researchers in education to connect with the need for a more comprehensive view of the sources and content of FoK (Hogg, 2011) and also the lived experience of marginalization that serves not just as a backdrop but as an additional premise for the creation and evolution of cultural practice and strategic action.

I would argue that the teachers who are featured in the FoK research are individually and collectively involved in a complex process of counter-storytelling. In particular, one must acknowledge that, in addition to their dedication to develop and expand content knowledge, they are also negotiating their own empowerment and working as allies with students and communities who aspire for and pursue improved living conditions or even the ability to just be (González, 2006; González et al., 2011; Moll & González, 2004). It is striking how FoK research is, in general, relatively silent on the racialization effects of schooling and locates class, race, gender, and other aspects of students' and families' identities as part of the background and context of sources or content of FoK rather than showcasing the utilization of community consciousness about these multiple identities as part of the teachers' (and students') pedagogical processes. Nevertheless, we do find compelling examples, especially from the initiating researchers, that demonstrate how FoK work is also positioned uniquely to draw out the counter-stories of institutional navigation, individual and collective resistance, nimble adaptation, and self-determination that characterize the responses of marginalized communities to hostile treatment and conditions (see González, 2006; Hammond, 2001; Hensley, 2005; Mercado, 2005; Vélez-Ibáñez & Greenberg, 1992/2005). Drawing from the evidence presented in this literature review, some key aspects of community critical consciousness involve surviving loss and displacement, reclaiming some of what is lost through recontextualized knowledge, and redefining the meaning and role of education in the changing social context of the present community environment. Engaging this dialogue further may be useful to prompt our thinking about potential operating assumptions that marginalized communities develop of necessity as they navigate an unwelcoming, racist, classist, sexist, homophobic, and otherwise oppressive environment to "re-narrate deficits" (Hattam & Prosser, 2008, p. 95) in pursuit of educational and social justice.

In addition to the utility of staging this theoretical dialogue to illuminate dimensions of power and agency in the pedagogical realm, new theoretical work is emerging to further specify the potential linkages among forms of capital and FoK. In a recent article, Rios-Aguilar et al. (2011) argue for the *combined* use of FoK with theories of social and cultural capital as a lens on the inequities of educational outcomes among minoritized or underrepresented students. Although they are focused somewhat on higher education outcomes, their key objective is to articulate a framework that allows for a deeper understanding of the processes by which FoK can be converted into the forms of capital needed for students to realize their long-term educational goals. The authors theorize further the agency of students, particularly as they locate the conversion of FoK into social/cultural capital within the realm of students' development and educational pursuits. The work is also useful in underscoring the need for the dialogue between CCW and FoK in that the authors argue for creative linkages among such frameworks to transcend the limitations of work that emphasizes the identification of the sources and content of FoK, with no direct attention paid to the power structures and asymmetries that may prevent the productive conversion of the FoK into capital that students can use to move forward in life.

To bring this section to closure, I revisit the third research question guiding this chapter, "How might Funds of Knowledge pedagogical notions be further clarified and extended by theoretical dialogue with other 'anti-cultural-deficit' (i.e., counter-hegemonic) frameworks, particularly the Community Cultural Wealth framework rooted in Critical Race Theory and Chicana/o Studies?" Perhaps the most direct way to address this question in summarizing the theoretical dialogue's revelations is in acknowledging the need for more proactive employment of community-based critical consciousness in approaching FoK work, meaning that which is held among students, parents, and community members. Returning to the issues of positionality, which CRT researchers likewise incorporate into their analyses (Parker & Lynn, 2009; Solórzano & Yosso, 2009), we are made aware of the limited extent to which researchers and collaborating educators confront and engage with the community's sense-making processes in navigating the oppressive features of their social contexts.

The dialogue also reveals the significance of the complex counter-storytelling processes embodied in the CRT-informed CCW framework that is likewise reflected in the teaching, learning, and recontextualizing processes undertaken within the FoK pedagogical endeavors. Finally, as new work continues to problematize the assumptions made about the conversion or mobilization of FoK to advance the goals of students and their communities, we are reminded that the counter-hegemonic potential of this framework and approach are yet to be fully understood or realized.

CONCLUDING REMARKS

Since the initiation of the Funds of Knowledge work in Arizona (a site presently heated with the contestation of educational and civil rights), many educators and researchers have endeavored to reshape the nature of schooling by embracing the opportunity to learn about and integrate into the academic realm students' out-of-school experience, knowledge, and cultural practices. These pursuits are as compelling in their potential to transform education today as they were envisioned to be by the originating FoK scholars and practitioners—perhaps more—as we find even greater evidence of the alienating effects of schooling on economically, linguistically, racially, and otherwise diverse students and their families (Gándara & Contreras, 2009; González et al., 2011; Rumberger & Rodriguez, 2011). This critical review reveals an evolution of thought and practice that reflects commitments to engage in education as a means to consciousness, empowerment, voice, and agency, and these commitments emanate from the scholarship that originated the FoK work. However, the evidence of pedagogical developments that are informed by broader social change and social justice pursuits is striking in an era that is characterized by pressures to conform to hegemonic norms and practices viewed as efficient means to produce more "equal" educational outcomes. Indeed, the theoretical dialogue staged here between FoK and CCW reveals how limiting an approach it might be to focus singularly on transformative practice within the school environment given the need for proactive strategizing from community-based standpoints to mobilize transformation across multiple domains of power and agency, if efforts toward educational and social justice are to gain momentum and force.

Fortunately, rather than adhere to a surface application or romanticized view of FoK approaches that could reproduce the relations of dominance between educators and their constituents, the scholarship in this review also reveals a continued counter-hegemonic movement, and with it, an interest in embracing the knowledge of students and families in its full spectrum of lived experience. In addition, as a commentary on the extant power relations between critical researchers and their constituents, this literature also makes salient the need for deeper examination of the positionalities of scholars who seek to engage in educational research as allies to marginalized communities. Indeed, combating the persistence of cultural deficit-based explanatory models in education requires this sort of multilayered development of consciousness regarding power and agency to more fully realize the vast potential that counter-hegemonic theory and practice, such as the Funds of Knowledge approach, truly represents.

ACKNOWLEDGMENTS

The author wishes to thank the consulting editor, Dr. Lew Zipin, and the chapter reviewer for their insightful critiques and recommendations, as they no doubt strengthened this chapter in its scope and clarity. Any remaining limitations of this work are entirely attributable to the author.

NOTES

1. The initiating researchers are listed here alphabetically, as over time different configurations of collaborating authors have published the foundational literature supporting the Funds of Knowledge work.
2. Originating publications are reproduced in whole or in part with permission from various scholarly journals in a compilation edited by González, Moll, and Amanti (2005) and thus is cited as a primary source in discussions of the FoK theoretical and empirical foundations.
3. Indeed, notions of "hybridity" in the production of knowledge and contextualization of cultural practices (as resistance to binary treatments of such) among teachers, students, and community members becomes an important theme taken up in summarizing the legacy of FoK research and pedagogical practice.
4. Hammond (2001) and Hensley (2005) provide insightful exceptions to this treatment of parents as agents.

REFERENCES

Andrews, J., & Ching Yee, W. (2006). Children's "funds of knowledge" and their real life activities: Two minority ethnic children learning in out-of-school contexts. *Educational Review, 58,* 435–449.

Apple, M. W. (1995). *Education and power* (2nd ed.). New York, NY: Routledge.

Apple, M. W. (1999). *Power, meaning, and identity: Essays in critical educational studies.* New York, NY: Peter Lang.

Apple, M. W. (2004). *Ideology and curriculum* (3rd ed.). New York, NY: RoutledgeFalmer.

Apple, M. W., & Buras, K. L. (2006). *The subaltern speak: Curriculum, power and educational struggles.* New York, NY: Routledge.

Basu, S. J., & Calabrese Barton, A. (2007). Developing a sustained interest in science among urban minority youth. *Journal of Research in Science Teaching, 44,* 466–489.

Calabrese Barton, A., & Tan, E. (2009). Funds of knowledge and discourses and hybrid space. *Journal of Research in Science Teaching, 46,* 50–73.

Camangian, P. (2010). Starting with self: Teaching autoethnography to foster critically caring literacies. *Research in the Teaching of English, 45,* 179–204.

Crenshaw, K., Gotanda, N., Peller, G., & Thomas, K. (Eds.). (1995). *Critical race theory: The key writings that formed the movement.* New York, NY: New Press.

Dantas, M. L. (2007). Building teacher competency to work with diverse learners in the context of international education. *Teacher Education Quarterly, 34,* 75–94.

Delgado, R., & Stefancic, J. (2001). *Critical race theory: An introduction.* New York: New York University Press.

Delgado Bernal, D. (2006a). Learning and living pedagogies of the home: The mestizo consciousness of Chicana students. In D. Delgado Bernal, C. A. Elenes, & S. Villenas (Eds.), *Chicana/Latina education in everyday life: Feminista perspectives on pedagogy and epistemology* (pp. 113–132). Albany: State University of New York Press.

Delgado Bernal, D. (2006b). Rethinking grassroots activism: Chicana resistance in the 1968 East Los Angeles school blowouts. In M. W. Apple & K. L. Buras (Eds.), *The subaltern speak: Curriculum, power and educational struggles* (pp. 141–162). New York, NY: Routledge.

Delgado Bernal, D., & Elenes, C. A. (2011). Chicana feminist theorizing: Methodologies, pedagogies, and practices. In R. R. Valencia (Ed.), *Chicano school failure and success: Past, present, and future* (3rd ed., pp. 99–119). New York, NY: Routledge.

Delgado Bernal, D., Elenes, C. A., Godinez, F. E., & Villenas, S. (Eds.). (2006). *Chicana/Latina education in everyday life: Feminista perspectives on pedagogy and epistemology*. Albany: State University of New York Press.

Dworin, J. (2006). The family stories project: Using funds of knowledge for writing. *Reading Teacher, 59*, 510–520.

Figueroa, J. L., & Sánchez, P. (2005). Technique, art, or cultural practice? Ethnic epistemology in Latino qualitative studies. In T. Fong (Ed.), *Research methods in ethnic studies* (pp. 143–178). Walnut Creek, CA: AltaMira Press.

Fisher, M. T. (2006). Building a literocracy: Diaspora literacy and heritage knowledge in participatory literacy communities. *Yearbook of the National Society for the Study of Education, 105*, 361–381.

Fitts, S. (2009). Exploring third space in a dual-language setting: Opportunities and challenges. *Journal of Latinos and Education, 8*, 87–104.

Fraser-Abder, P., Doria, J., Yang, J., & De Jesus, A. (2010). Using funds of knowledge in an ethnically concentrated classroom environment to teach nutrition. *Science Activities: Classroom Projects and Curriculum Ideas, 47*, 141–150.

Freire, P. (1993). *Pedagogy of the oppressed.* New York, NY: Continuum. (Original work published 1970)

Gándara, P., & Contreras, F. (2009). *The Latino education crisis: The consequences of failed social policies.* Cambridge, MA: Harvard University Press.

Giroux, H. A. (2005). *Border crossings: Cultural workers and the politics of education* (2nd ed.). New York, NY: Routledge.

Giroux, H. A. (2006). *The Giroux reader* (C. G. Robbins, Ed.). Boulder, CO: Paradigm.

Giroux, H. A. (2011). *On critical pedagogy.* New York, NY: Continuum.

González, N. (2005). Beyond culture: The hybridity of funds of knowledge. In N. González, L. Moll, & C. Amanti (Eds.), *Funds of knowledge: Theorizing practices in households, communities, and classrooms* (pp. 29–46). Mahwah, NJ: Lawrence Erlbaum.

González, N. (2006). Testimonios of border identities: "Una mujer acomedida donde quiera cabe." In D. Delgado Bernal, C. A. Elenes, F. E. Godinez, & S. Villenas (Eds.), *Chicana/Latina education in everyday life: Feminista perspectives on pedagogy and epistemology* (pp. 197–213). Albany: State University of New York Press.

González, N., Andrade, R., Civil, M., & Moll, L. (2001). Bridging funds of distributed knowledge: Creating zones of practices in mathematics. *Journal of Education for Students Placed at Risk, 6*, 115–132.

González, N., Moll, L. C., & Amanti, C. (Eds.). (2005). *Funds of knowledge: Theorizing practices in households, communities, and classrooms.* Mahwah, NJ: Lawrence Erlbaum.

González, N., Moll, L., Floyd Tenery, M., Rivera, A., Rendón, P., Gonzales, R., & Amanti, C. (2005). Funds of knowledge for teaching in Latino households. In N. González, L. C. Moll, & C. Amanti (Eds.), *Funds of knowledge: Theorizing practices in households, communities, and classrooms* (pp. 89–111). Mahwah, NJ: Lawrence Erlbaum.

González, N., Wyman, L., & O'Connor, B. (2011). The past, present, and future of "funds of knowledge." In B. Levinson & M. Pollock (Eds.), *A companion to the anthropology of education* (pp. 481–494). Malden, MA: Wiley-Blackwell.

Gupta, A. (2006). Early experiences and personal funds of knowledge and beliefs of immigrant and minority teacher candidates dialog with theories of child development in a teacher education classroom. *Journal of Early Childhood Teacher Education, 27*, 3–18.

Gutiérrez, P. S. (2002). In search of bedrock: Organizing for success with diverse needs children in the classroom. *Journal of Latinos and Education, 1,* 49–64.

Hammond, L. (2001). Notes from California: An anthropological approach to urban science education for language minority families. *Journal of Research in Science Teaching, 38,* 983–999.

Hattam, R., & Prosser, B. (2008). Unsettling deficit views of students and their communities. *Australian Educational Researcher, 35*(2), 89–106.

Hattam, R., & Zipin, L. (2009). Toward pedagogical justice. *Discourse: Studies in the Cultural Politics of Education, 30,* 297–301.

Henderson, D., & Zipin, L. (2010). Bringing clay to life: Developing student literacy through clay animation artwork to tell life-based stories. In B. Prosser, B. Lucas, & A. Reid (Eds.), *Connecting lives and learning: Renewing pedagogy in the middle years* (pp. 20–39). Adelaide, South Australia: Wakefield Press.

Hensley, M. (2005). Empowering parents of multicultural backgrounds. In N. González, L. C. Moll, & C. Amanti (Eds.), *Funds of knowledge: Theorizing practices in households, communities, and classrooms* (pp. 143–151). Mahwah, NJ: Lawrence Erlbaum.

Hindess, B. (1996). *Discourses of power: From Hobbes to Foucault.* Cambridge, England: Blackwell.

Hogg, L. (2011). Funds of knowledge: An investigation of coherence within the literature. *Teaching and Teacher Education, 27,* 666–677.

Johnson, A. S., Baker, A., & Bruer, L. (2007). Interdependence, garbage dumping, and feral dogs: Exploring three lifeworld resources of young children in a rural school. *Early Childhood Education Journal, 34,* 371–377.

Keis, R. (2006). From principle to practice: Using children's literature to promote dialogue and facilitate the "coming to voice" in a rural Latino community. *Multicultural Perspectives, 8,* 13–19.

Kurtyka, F. (2010). "The expression of wise others": Using students' views of academic discourse to talk about social justice. *Teaching English in the Two-Year College, 38*(1), 47–60.

Longwell-Grice, H., & McIntyre, E. (2006). Addressing goals of school and community: Lessons from a family literacy program. *School Community Journal, 16,* 115–132.

Marquez Kiyama, J. (2010). College aspirations and limitations: The role of educational ideologies and funds of knowledge in Mexican American families. *American Educational Research Journal, 47,* 330–356.

Marshall, E., & Toohey, K. (2010). Representing family: Community funds of knowledge, bilingualism, and multimodality. *Harvard Educational Review, 80,* 221–242.

Martin-Jones, M., & Saxena, M. (2003). Bilingual resources and "funds of knowledge" for teaching and learning in multi-ethnic classrooms in Britain. *International Journal of Bilingual Education and Bilingualism, 6,* 267–282.

McIntyre, E., Rosebery, A., & González, N. (Eds.). (2001). *Classroom diversity: Connecting curriculum to students' lives.* Portsmouth, NH: Heinemann.

Mercado, C. (2005). Reflections on the study of households in New York City and Long Island: A different route, a common destination. In N. González, L. C. Moll, & C. Amanti (Eds.), *Funds of knowledge: Theorizing practices in households, communities, and classrooms* (pp. 199–212). Mahwah, NJ: Lawrence Erlbaum.

Moje, E. B., Ciechanowski, K. M., Kramer, K., Ellis, L., Carrillo, R., & Collazo, T. (2004). Working toward third space in content area literacy: An examination of everyday funds of knowledge and discourse. *Reading Research Quarterly, 39,* 38–70.

Moll, L. C. (Ed.). (1990). *Vygotsky and education: Instructional implications and applications of sociohistorical psychology.* Cambridge, England: Cambridge University Press.

Moll, L. C., & González, N. (2004). Engaging life: A funds of knowledge approach to multicultural education. In J. Banks & C. McGee Banks (Eds.), *Handbook of research on multicultural education* (2nd ed., pp. 699–715). New York, NY: Jossey-Bass.

Moll, L. C., & Greenberg, J. B. (1990). Creating zones of possibilities: Combining social contexts for instruction. In L. C. Moll (Ed.), *Vygotsky and education: Instructional implications and applications of sociohistorical psychology* (pp. 319–348). Cambridge, England: Cambridge University Press.

Monzo, L. D., & Rueda, R. (2003). Shaping education through diverse funds of knowledge: A look at one Latino paraeducator's lived experiences, beliefs, and teaching practice. *Anthropology & Education Quarterly, 34*, 72–95.

Nathenson-Mejia, S., & Escamilla, K. (2003). Connecting with Latino children: Bridging cultural gaps with children's literature. *Bilingual Research Journal, 27*, 101–116.

Oliver, M., & Shapiro, T. (Eds.). (1995). *Black wealth/White wealth*. New York, NY: Routledge.

Parker, L., & Lynn, M. (2009). What's race got to do with it? Critical race theory's conflicts with and connections to qualitative research methodology and epistemology. In E. Taylor, D. Gillborn, & G. Ladson-Billings (Eds.), *Foundations of critical race theory in education* (pp. 148–160). New York, NY: Routledge.

Pirbhai-Illich, F. (2010). Aboriginal students engaging and struggling with critical multiliteracies. *Journal of Adolescent and Adult Literacy, 54*, 257–266.

Reyes, C. R., & McNabb, E. (1998). *Expanding and diversifying the teacher work force: Building on local talent and community funds of knowledge*. San Francisco, CA: WestEd.

Riojas-Cortez, M. (2001). Preschoolers' funds of knowledge displayed through sociodramatic play episodes in a bilingual classroom. *Early Childhood Education Journal, 29*, 35–40.

Riojas-Cortez, M., & Flores Bustos, B. (2009). Supporting preschoolers' social development in school through funds of knowledge. *Journal of Early Childhood Research, 7*, 185–199.

Riojas-Cortez, M., Huerta, M. E., Flores Bustos, B., Perez, B., & Clark, E. R. (2008). Using cultural tools to develop scientific literacy of young Mexican American preschoolers. *Early Child Development and Care, 178*, 527–536.

Rios-Aguilar, C., Marquez Kiyama, J., Gravitt, M., & Moll, L. (2011). Funds of knowledge for the poor and forms of capital for the rich? A capital approach to examining funds of knowledge. *Theory and Research in Education, 9*, 163–184.

Risko, V. J., & Walker-Dalhouse, D. (2007). Tapping students' cultural funds of knowledge to address the achievement gap. *Reading Teacher, 61*, 98–100.

Rogers, R., Light, R., & Curtis, L. (2004). Anyone can be an expert in something: Exploring the complexity of discourse conflict and alignment for two fifth-grade students. *Journal of Literacy Research, 36*, 177–210.

Rumberger, R. W., & Rodriguez, G. M. (2011). Chicano dropouts. In R. R. Valencia (Ed.), *Chicano school failure and success: Past, present, and future* (3rd ed., pp. 76–98). New York, NY: Routledge.

Smythe, S., & Toohey, K. (2009). Investigating sociohistorical contexts and practices through a community scan: A Canadian Punjabi-Sikh example. *Language and Education, 23*, 37–57.

Solórzano, D. G., & Yosso, T. J. (2009). Critical race methodology: Counter-storytelling as an analytical framework for educational research. In E. Taylor, D. Gillborn, & G. Ladson-Billings (Eds.), *Foundations of critical race theory in education* (pp. 131–147). New York, NY: Routledge.

Street, C. (2005). Funds of knowledge at work in the writing classroom. *Multicultural Education, 13*(2), 22–25.

Sugarman, S. (2010). Seeing past the fences: Finding funds of knowledge for ethical teaching. *New Educator, 6*, 96–117.

Taylor, E., Gillborn, D., & Ladson-Billings, G. (Eds.). (2009). *Foundations of critical race theory in education*. New York, NY: Routledge.

Thomson, P., & Hall, C. (2008). Opportunities missed and/or thwarted? "Funds of knowledge" meet the English national curriculum. *Curriculum Journal, 19*, 87–103.

Upadhyay, B. (2009). Teaching science for empowerment in an urban classroom: A case study of a Hmong teacher. *Equity & Excellence in Education, 42*, 217–232.

Upadhyay, B. R. (2006). Using students' lived experiences in an urban science classroom: An elementary school teacher's thinking. *Science Education, 90,* 94–110.

Valencia, R. R., & Solórzano, D. G. (1997). Contemporary deficit thinking. In R. R. Valencia (Ed.), *The evolution of deficit thinking: Educational thought and practice* (pp. 160–210). London, England: Falmer Press.

Vélez-Ibáñez, C. G., & Greenberg, J. B. (1992/2005). Formation and transformation of funds of knowledge among U.S.-Mexican households. *Anthropology and Education Quarterly, 23,* 313–335.

Villenas, S. (2006). Pedagogical moments in the borderlands: Latina mothers teaching and learning. In D. Delgado Bernal, C. A. Elenes, & S. Villenas (Eds.), *Chicana/Latina education in everyday life: Feminista perspectives on pedagogy and epistemology* (pp. 147–159). Albany: State University of New York Press.

Wang, X., Bernas, R., & Eberhard, P. (2005). Maternal teaching strategies in four cultural communities: Implications for early childhood teachers. *Journal of Early Childhood Research, 3,* 269–288.

Wolf, E. R. (1966). *Peasants.* Englewood Cliffs, NJ: Prentice-Hall.

Yosso, T. J. (2005). Whose culture has capital? A critical race theory discussion of community cultural wealth. *Race, Ethnicity, and Education, 8*(2), 69–91.

Yosso, T. J. (2006). *Critical race counterstories along the Chicana/Chicano educational pipeline.* New York, NY: Routledge.

Zanoni, J., Rucinski, D., Flores, J., Perez, I., Gomez, G., Davis, R., & Jones, R. (2011). Latina/o community funds of knowledge for health and curriculum. *Journal of Latinos and Education, 10,* 43–58.

Zipin, L. (2009). Dark funds of knowledge, deep funds of pedagogy: Exploring boundaries between lifeworlds and schools. *Discourse: Studies in the Cultural Politics of Education, 30,* 317–331.

Zipin, L., & Reid, A. (2008). A justice-oriented citizenship education: Making community curricular. In J. Arthur, I. Davies, & C. Hahn (Eds.), *The Sage handbook of education for citizenship and democracy* (pp. 533–544). Thousand Oaks, CA: Sage.

Zipin, L., Sellar, S., & Hattam, R. (2012). Countering and exceeding "capital": A "funds of knowledge" approach to re-imagining community. *Discourse: Studies in the Cultural Politics of Education, 33,* 179–192.

Chapter 4

A Humanizing Pedagogy: Reinventing the Principles and Practice of Education as a Journey Toward Liberation

María del Carmen Salazar

University of Denver

I went to school with all of my treasures, including my Spanish language, Mexican culture, *familia* (family), and ways of knowing. I abandoned my treasures at the classroom door in exchange for English and the U.S. culture; consequently, my assimilation into U.S. society was agonizing. One of my earliest memories is of wishing away my dark skin; I wanted desperately to be White, and I abhorred being *la morena*, the dark-skinned girl. I came to associate whiteness with success and brownness with failure. I was overwhelmed with feelings of shame over the most essential elements of my humanness. As a result, my experience in the U.S. educational system was marked by endless struggles to preserve my humanity.

—María del Carmen Salazar

INTRODUCTION: THE NEED FOR HUMANIZATION IN EDUCATION

The preceding epigraph captures my experience as a hyphenated American navigating the *hybrid space* (Bhabha, 1994; Calabrese Barton, Tan, & Rivet, 2008; Gutiérrez, Baquedano-Lopez, & Tejeda, 1999) between my Mexican and U.S. cultures. My educational experience was marked by a deep sense of isolation that resulted from systematic practices in the U.S. educational system that suppressed vital elements of my humanity, both at home and at school. My experience is not unique; students of color have been compelled for generations to divest themselves of their linguistic, cultural, and familial resources to succeed in U.S. public schools.

Review of Research in Education
March 2013, Vol. 37, pp. 121-148
DOI: 10.3102/0091732X12464032
© 2013 AERA. http://rre.aera.net

Such resources are inclusive of Yosso's (2005) conceptualization of *community cultural wealth*, or "an array of knowledge, skills, abilities and contacts possessed and utilized by Communities of Color to survive and resist macro and micro forms of oppression" (p. 77).

Deficit notions of the resources of Communities of Color have fueled intolerance, bigotry, and assimilation throughout the history of U.S. public education. In 1903, W. E. B. Du Bois published *The Souls of Black Folk* in which he asserts that educators inundate African Americans with notions of inferiority because of their racial peculiarities. Although Du Bois examines deleterious perceptions of African Americans at the turn of the 20th century, in reality, throughout U.S. history, educators have intentionally and unintentionally bombarded students of color with messages of their inferiority through a hidden curriculum (Jackson, 1990). Moreover, educators have compelled and at times coerced these students into whiteness (Sanchez, 1993; Woodson, 2006). Although scholars may describe the experience of students of color with detached and objective prose that attempts to explain the human condition of Communities of Color, narratives can be powerful tools for illuminating and challenging the inhumanity that marks the oppressed (Morrell, 2008; Parker & Lynn, 2002). I inject my narrative throughout this section to give voice to the struggles of students of color and as a means to humanize the lexicon that litters academic spaces, which is often presented through the discourse of whiteness including detached, objectified, and linear modes of expression. Furthermore, I attempt to humanize this review of research by presenting my research through my own voice—a voice that stems from a proud and powerful woman, mother, and scholar of color.

I am filled with endless stories of advertent and inadvertent messages of inferiority that compelled me to crave whiteness as a young child. In the third grade, I desperately wanted to be White. My teachers privileged whiteness through the English language and U.S. culture, and they excluded all that was native to me; hence, I ascertained that White children were smarter, more attractive, and affluent. As a result, I became a connoisseur of whiteness when I was eight years old. I observed my White classmates closely and dissected their behaviors until I discovered a common pattern; every White student in my class was in the highest reading group. Thus, I hypothesized that if I propelled myself into the top reading group, the Red Robins, the color of my skin would change and I would become White and worthy. I achieved my goal and my name was called to join the Red Robins. I ran home that day and examined my complexion in the mirror, to no avail; my skin remained the color of burnt toast. I waited anxiously for days, yet the transformation never ensued, and I became distressed that I would have to live in my dark skin forever as *la morena*, the dark-skinned girl.

In recent times, the educational goals for students of color continue to be those of cultural replacement and assimilation into mainstream values and practices. When students of color experience academic difficulties, their struggles are often attributed to their culture, language, and home environment (Cummins, 2001; Macedo &

Bartolomé, 1999; Nieto, 2002; Salazar, 2010; Solórzano & Yosso, 2002; Valenzuela, 1999, 2004; Wade, Fauske, & Thompson, 2008). As a result, these students are expected to "act, speak, and behave as much as possible like the White middle class" (Warikoo & Carter, 2009, p. 374). Concomitantly, they are stripped of cultural resources needed to survive and thrive in the educational system and in U.S. society (González, Moll, & Amantí, 2005; Nieto, 2010; Pizarro, 1998; Sadowski, 2003; Salazar, 2008; Valenzuela, 1999).

Ladson-Billings (1995) suggests that successful students of color experience academic success "at the expense of their cultural and psychological well-being" (p. 475). These students may demonstrate a "raceless persona" (Fordham, 1988, as cited in Warikoo & Carter, 2009, p. 379) to navigate the educational system, thus sacrificing an essential part of their humanity. They may also *act White* (Fordham & Ogbu, 1986) or *act gringo* (Fránquiz & Salazar, 2004) in an effort to fit into the *whitestream* (Grande, 2000). In my research on a high school ESL program (Salazar, 2010), I found that Mexican immigrant students accuse one another of acting gringo when they adhere to English-only rules in the classroom. Ultimately, students of color experience *subtractive schooling* (Valenzuela, 1999) through the denial of their heritage and assimilation into White America.

Educational scholars have long documented the struggles of students of color to resist assimilation, maintain their cultural roots, and merge their *double selves* (Du Bois, 1903). For example, Du Bois describes the struggle of African Americans as follows: "One ever feels his twoness,—an American, a Negro; two souls, two thoughts, two unreconciled strivings; two warring ideals in one dark body, whose strength alone keeps it from being torn asunder" (p. 46). I experienced this sense of *twoness* as a child of two nations; with one foot on either side of the border, yet neither side would claim me. I was torn from my motherland when I was 2 weeks old, the bond was irrevocably severed; consequently, I grew up in a land where I was considered the *other* or worse, an alien. I lived in *nepantla*, the *Mexica* (Aztec) word for no man's (or woman's) land. My educational experience was marked by my struggles to sustain bicultural ways of being.

Warikoo and Carter (2009) suggest that students of color resist teachers who do not understand students' bicultural and multicultural worlds and reinforce cultural lines of demarcation that are systematically imposed in schools. In my own research with Mexican immigrant high school students (Salazar, 2010), I propose that Mexican American students engage in disruptive behavior such as raised voices, disrespectful comments, gestures of disdain, defiance of classroom expectations, and *huelgas* (strikes) to resist practices that exclude their native language and culture from their learning. Furthermore, my research demonstrates that Mexican immigrant students use *boundary maintaining mechanisms* (Fordham & Ogbu, 1986) to pressure their peers to resist English in an effort to maintain their cultural affiliations and resist the whitestream because blurring the boundary might signal to others a sense of shame in one's heritage, language, and culture. For example, a teacher in my research study described the typical discourse of Mexican immigrant students as follows: "Sometimes students tell other students to speak Spanish because they are with other Mexicans. If they speak English with a group of Mexicans it's like they want to be different—White, not Mexicans" (Salazar, 2010, p. 117). Scholars assert that students of color resist the loss of their resources because they perceive the power of their culture as a safe zone against the onslaught of the dominant culture (Quiroz, 2001; Reyes, 2007).

Although students of color may resist overt tactics that strip them of their cultural resources, in recent times, systemic approaches to assimilation are often masked in the language of measurement and quantification that is rampant in 21st-century educational discourse. The focus on measurement and quantification in U.S. public schools results in pedagogical practices that favor high-stakes test-taking skills (Giroux, 2010; Nichols & Berliner, 2007); foster memorization and conformity (Giroux, 2010); promote reductionistic, decontextualized, and fragmented curriculum (Bahruth, 2000; Darling-Hammond, 2012; Rodriguez & Smith, 2011); advance mechanistic approaches that are disconnected from students' needs (Bartolomé, 1994); and reinforce one-size-fits-all scripted practices (de la Luz Reyes, 1992; Fránquiz & Salazar, 2004; Nieto, 2010). Educational scholars stress that such myopic, technical, and generic practices repress and silence students and lead to a decline in student efficacy (Bartolomé, 1994; Giroux, 2010; Huerta, 2011). Furthermore, a pedagogical focus on materials and delivery methods results in a "detachment from the human beings teachers encounter in the classroom" (Rodriguez & Smith, 2011, p. 91). A superficial and uncritical focus on methods often privileges whitestream approaches aimed at assimilation, ultimately robbing students of their culture, language, history, and values, thus denying students' humanity.

Students and educators are constrained from finding meaning in the current educational system as a result of the tension between educators' pedagogical practices and systemic constraints, such as high-stakes standardized tests and district-mandated instructional curriculum. Such restrictive educational policies limit educators from developing humanistic approaches (Fránquiz & Salazar, 2004; Huerta, 2011). Educational scholars call on schools to move away from one-size-fits-all paradigms and instead focus on humane approaches such a humanizing pedagogy (Fránquiz & Salazar, 2004, Freire, 1970; Huerta, 2011). Educators orienting toward a humanizing pedagogy heed the call of Paulo Freire (1970), who laments the state of dehumanization in education and asserts that "the only effective instrument in the process of re-humanization is humanizing pedagogy" (p. 55). A humanizing pedagogy is crucial for both teacher and student success and critical for the academic and social resiliency of students (Fránquiz & Salazar, 2004; Reyes, 2007).

Given that current U.S. educational policy is dominated by standardized and technical approaches to schooling that reinforce assimilationist notions and dehumanize students of color, this review of literature examines Freire's conceptualization of *humanization, pedagogy*, and *humanizing pedagogy* as a counterpractice to dehumanization in education. Moreover, this chapter synthesizes the conceptual and empirical literature on humanizing pedagogy from Paulo Freire and other humanizing pedagogues across the globe. This literature—when synthesized—suggests that the philosophical, theoretical, and operational foundations of humanizing pedagogy can be delineated into five essential tenets and 10 principles and practices for humanization in education. The chapter concludes with a call for the moral responsibility of educators to humanize pedagogy and an appeal for studies that engage the voices of the oppressed as central to humanization in education.

FREIRE'S VISION OF A HUMANIZING PEDAGOGY

Educational scholars have proposed that Paulo Freire is one of the most influential thinkers of modern times, and perhaps the most important and original educational thinker of the 20th century (Carnoy, 2004; Macedo, 1994; Roberts, 2000; Siddhartha, 1999). Indeed, Darder (2002) advances the notion that "more than any other educator of the twentieth century, Paulo Freire left an indelible mark on the lives of progressive educators" (as cited in Schugurensky, 2011, p. 10).

Humanism Influences Freire's Worldview

Humanism is a central component of Freire's worldview and is essential to understanding Freirean philosophy (Dale & Hyslop-Margison, 2010). Freire's philosophy is guided by the notion that humans are motivated by a need to reason and engage in the process of becoming. Freire's focus on humanism is centered on his curiosity in the cognitive capacity of humans to shape their experiences and achieve personal and collective self-actualization, thus developing their full humanity (Dale & Hyslop-Margison, 2010; Schapiro, 2001).

Freire's humanist approach evolved over time through the influence of an eclectic array of intellectual traditions, including liberalism; Marxism; existentialism; radical Catholicism; phenomenology; progressive education; developmentalism; feminism; and critical race theory (Schugurensky, 2011). Scholars note that Freire was particularly influenced by Christian humanism, an approach that promotes the worth of human beings and asserts that humans strive to become more fully human in unity with others, despite impediments to humanization such as injustice, exploitation, and oppression (Kirylo, 2001; Schugurensky, 2011).

Freire was also influenced by the tenets of Marxist humanism that challenged societal structures and systems responsible for reproducing social inequalities and creating a pedagogy of inhumanity (Keet, Zinn, & Porteus, 2009). Kiros (2006) describes Marxist humanism as merging a "focus on systemic violence and structural inequalities with unlocking the humanistic potential of human beings" (p. 217). Through Marxist humanism, Freire denounces oppressive political, social, and educational structures, and he announces the power of the oppressed in reclaiming their full humanity (Kirylo, 2001).

Freire draws on Christian humanism and Marxist humanism as analytical tools to probe the essence of humanity. Hence, the dialogical space between Christian humanism and Marxist humanism reveals the crux of Freire's philosophy of humanization, liberation, hope, and transformation.

Freire's Conceptualization of Humanization and Pedagogy

Although Freire made numerous contributions to liberatory educational paradigms, Dale and Hyslop-Margison (2010) claim that humanization is the single most important element to Freire's philosophical approach. *Humanization* is the process of becoming more fully human as social, historical, thinking, communicating, transformative, creative persons who participate in and with the world (Freire, 1972, 1984). To become more fully human, men and women must become conscious of their presence in the world as a way to individually and collectively re-envisage their social world (Dale & Hyslop-Margison, 2010; Freire & Betto, 1985; Schapiro, 2001). Humanization is the ontological vocation of human beings and, as such, is the practice of freedom in which the oppressed are liberated through consciousness of their subjugated positions and a desire for self-determination (Freire, 1970, 1994). Humanization cannot be imposed on or imparted to the oppressed; but rather, it can only occur by engaging the oppressed in their liberation. As such, Freire (1970) proposes that the process of humanization fosters transformation and authentic liberation of the oppressed; thus, "to transform the world is to humanize it" (Freire, 1985, p. 70).

Whereas Freire's conceptualization of humanization is key to understanding his educational philosophy (Dale & Hyslop-Margison, 2010), his ideological stance related to the underlying notions of pedagogy is vital to the enactment of humanization. Freire's use of the term *pedagogy* is a "complex philosophy, politics, and practice of education . . . that demands of educators a clear ethical and political commitment to transforming oppressive social conditions" (Roberts, 2000, pp. 13–14). According to Freirean ideals, all pedagogy is political and requires radical reconstruction of teaching and learning (Giroux, 1988); moreover, pedagogy must be meaningful and connected to social change by engaging students with the world so they can transform it (Giroux, 2010). As such, meaningful social change can be triggered by curricular resources that are tied to the needs of marginalized students and locally generated by teachers and communities in order to interrupt patterns of exclusion (Giroux, 2004).

Although Freire's pedagogical assertions flow from ethical and political stances that challenge inequity and promote humanization, critics denounce his inability to provide specific formulas and clear methodological examples of his pedagogical vision (Dale & Hyslop-Margison, 2010).

Freirean scholars, however, interpret his pedagogical vision as a way of living in the world rather than a bundle of technical pedagogical practices. Moreover, these scholars proclaim that Freirean pedagogy cannot be reduced to reproducible technical concepts or universally applicable and decontextualized techniques, skills, or methods (Aronowitz, 1993; Bartolomé, 1994; Brady, 1994; Dale & Hyslop-Margison, 2010; Macedo, 1994; Roberts, 2000). As a result, educators who grapple ineffectively with Freire's pedagogical assertions may engage in technical and reductionistic approaches and ignore the ideological implications of schooling (Dale & Hyslop-Margison, 2010).

In fact, Freire was vehemently opposed to reductionistic and decontextualized interpretations of his educational philosophy that identified predetermined technical practices (Dale & Hyslop-Margison, 2010). Freire and Macedo (1998) establish that generic pedagogical approaches are "static and objectifying, with outcomes antithetical to humanization" (as cited in Dale & Hyslop-Margison, 2010, p. 74). Scholars concur that uncritical approaches to teaching and learning strip teachers and students of their individuality and thus undermine the fundamental principles of humanization (Burke, Adler, & Linker, 2008; Dale & Hyslop-Margison, 2010). Consequently, teachers and students are devalued and dehumanized through mechanical pedagogical approaches that distract them from meaningful learning and silence their collective voices (Balderrama, 2001; Burke et al., 2008; Dale & Hyslop-Margison, 2010).

Freire repeatedly emphasizes that his pedagogy is not transferrable across contexts but rather should be adapted to the unique context of teaching and learning (Roberts, 2000; Weiler, 1991). Dale and Hyslop-Margison (2010) assert that "although there are not precise technical methods emerging from Freire's pedagogy, its potential application is limited only by our creativity and imagination" (p. 74). In fact, Freirean pedagogy necessitates that educators reinvent his philosophy and pedagogy across contexts (Rodriguez & Smith, 2011). Above all, Freire encourages educators to listen to their students and build on their knowledge and experiences in order to engage in contextualized, dynamic, and personalized educational approaches that further the goals of humanization and social transformation.

Freire Envisages a Humanizing Pedagogy

Throughout his many literary works, Freire grapples with the meaning of human existence and the purpose of pedagogy; as a result, he envisages a *humanizing pedagogy*. Various scholars note the concept of humanizing pedagogy as one of Freire's original contributions (Huerta & Brittain, 2010; Keet et al., 2009; Parker-Rees & Willan, 2006; Rodriguez, 2008; Salazar, 2008; Schugurensky, 2011). In *Pedagogy of the Oppressed*, Freire (1970) describes humanizing pedagogy as a revolutionary approach to instruction that "ceases to be an instrument by which teachers can manipulate students, but rather expresses the consciousness of the students themselves" (p. 51). Teachers who enact humanizing pedagogy engage in a quest for "mutual humanization" (p. 56) with their students, a process fostered through problem-posing education where students are coinvestigators in dialogue with their teachers. This dialogic approach to education should be pursued with the goal of developing "conscientizacao" (p. 26) or critical consciousness, which is "learning to perceive social, political, and economic contradictions, and to take action against the oppressive elements of reality" (p. 17). There are limitless possibilities for Freire's pedagogical philosophy, and Freire urged his followers to reinvent his ideas in the context of their local struggles.

REINVENTING HUMANIZING PEDAGOGY

The application of Freire's ideas in the context of education in the United States and other countries has been a challenge for educators. Some critics have charged that Paulo Freire offers an elusive portrayal of humanizing pedagogy that is detached from the context of actual classrooms (Dale & Hyslop-Margison, 2010; Schugurensky, 2011). In response, in 1994, Lilia Bartolomé published, "Beyond the Methods Fetish: Toward a Humanizing Pedagogy." This seminal piece was instrumental in situating humanizing pedagogy as a substantive and tangible educational philosophy and practice (Murillo et al., 2009). Bartolomé promotes the notion that a humanizing pedagogy builds on the sociocultural realities of students' lives, examines the sociohistorical and political dimensions of education, and casts students as critically engaged, active participants in the co-construction of knowledge. Bartolomé was followed by a growing number of humanizing pedagogues who answer Freire's call to reinvent humanizing pedagogy in their own context (Rodriguez, 2008).

In what follows, I provide examples of scholarship from across the globe, including South Africa, Brazil, Jamaica, Canada, the United Kingdom, and the United States. Analysis of the literature reveals the following five key tenets are requisite for the pursuit of one's full humanity through a humanizing pedagogy:

1. The full development of the person is essential for humanization.
2. To deny someone else's humanization is also to deny one's own.
3. The journey for humanization is an individual and collective endeavor toward critical consciousness.
4. Critical reflection and action can transform structures that impede our own and others' humanness, thus facilitating liberation for all.
5. Educators are responsible for promoting a more fully human world through their pedagogical principles and practices.

1: The Full Development of the Person Is Essential for Humanization

A humanizing pedagogy is a process of *becoming* for students and teachers (Freire, 1970; Price & Osborne, 2000; Roberts, 2000). Roberts (2000), a scholar from the United Kingdom, further describes the process of becoming in a humanizing pedagogy, "One can never, on the Freirean view, become fully human—one can, at best, become *more* fully human" (p. 41). Scholars of humanizing pedagogy insist that in schools, the process of becoming more fully human must be tethered to the needs of the whole person (Bell & Schniedewind, 1989; Price & Osborne, 2000). For example, Price and Osborne (2000) describe humanizing pedagogy as "a pedagogy in which the whole person develops and they do so as their relationships with others evolve and enlarge" (p. 29). Moreover, the authors note that the purpose of humanizing education is not only to transfer meaningful academic knowledge but to also promote the overall well-being of all students. Cammarota and Romero (2006) state that educators attend to students overall well-being when they connect with students on an emotional level by (a) providing reciprocal opportunities to share their lives, (b) demonstrating compassion for the dehumanizing experiences students of color encounter, and (c) situating learning in social issues that are relevant to the experiences of marginalized communities. Additionally, Talbert-Johnson (2004) adds that schools should be "places where students of color feel their full humanity is visible and cherished by their teachers" (p. 32). The authors suggest that students' full humanity is honored when educators affirm students' ambitions and assist students in dealing with obstacles to their ambitions. The focus on the whole person in humanizing pedagogy is based on Freirean notions that "education is more than technical training because it involves the full development of the person, it has a humanistic orientation" (Schugurensky, 2011, p. 67).

From South Africa, Keet et al. (2009) explore "humanizing" pedagogy and the dimensions of the human experience, stating, "A humanising pedagogy is a radical pedagogy, not a 'soft' one, and its humanising interest is linked to focusing on both structural and psycho-social dimensions of human suffering, and human liberation" (p. 113). A humanizing pedagogy is inclusive of the psychological and emotional dimensions of the human experience; thus, a humanizing pedagogy is intentionally focused on the affective domain (Bell & Schniedewind, 1989) and requires that educators interact with students on an emotional level (Cammarota & Romero, 2006). For instance, Cammarota and Romero (2006) suggest that students and teachers should share their perspectives about life and educators should express verbally and nonverbally their "faith in students' intellectual capacities and a respect for their concerns about the world" (p. 20).

A humanizing pedagogy correlates with caring literature in education and is inclusive of respect, trust, relations of reciprocity, active listening, mentoring, compassion, high expectations, and interest in students' overall well-being (Bartolomé, 1994; Cammarota & Romero, 2006; Gay, 2010). In fact, in my own research with scholar María Fránquiz (Fránquiz & Salazar, 2004), we found that when Chicano/Mexican students develop positive relationships with supportive adults and peers, they are protected from risk behaviors, alienation, and despair. Furthermore, we discovered that strong relationships with adults and peers that are grounded in students' cultural funds of knowledge influence students' academic resiliency through the construction of a strong academic identity, or scholar ethos. The humanizing pedagogy we describe aligns with research on women educators in Brazil by Jennings and Da Matta (2009), who found that a humanizing pedagogy reflects feminist principles in "consciousness-raising through dialogue, knowledge grounded in personal experience, relationship-building, and a view of students as emotional and social beings, not solely cognitive learners" (p. 225).

Ultimately, a humanizing pedagogy is rooted in the relationships between educators and students and, as such, "respects the human, inter-personal side of teaching, and emphasizes the richness of the teacher-student relationships" (Huerta & Brittain, 2010, pp. 385–386).

2: To Deny Someone Else's Humanization Is Also to Deny One's Own

Freire contends that "to deny someone else's humanization is also to deny one's own" (Roberts, 2000, p. 45). Dehumanization, or the denial of humanness to others (Moller & Deci, 2009), is a by-product of a *banking model of education* (Freire, 1970) that transforms students into receiving objects by perpetuating practices such as rote memorization and skill-and-drill that encourage students to receive, file, and store deposits of knowledge transmitted by educators. In a banking pedagogy, educators "constantly tell them (students) what to do, what to learn, what to think, seldom seeking their input, suggestions, comments, feedback, or thoughts about their education" (Cammarota & Romero, 2006, p. 19). The banking model of education promotes passivity, acceptance, and submissiveness and turns students into objects that must be filled by the teacher. By implication, "to treat humans as objects, thereby lessening their abilities to act to transform their world, is to dehumanize them" (Freire, 1982, p. 5). Scholars insist that dehumanizing approaches silence students, lead to self-denigration, and instill a sense of internalized failure and self-contempt (Quiroz, 2001). In my own research (Salazar, 2010), I found that when Mexican immigrant students are denied access and use of their mother tongue in academic spheres, these students begin to devalue their native language and denigrate their culture. Such students are often faced with the choice of conformity and denial of all that is native, or forms of resistance to English that are detrimental to their educational success. In this research, I found that few students engage in transformational resistance where they learn to navigate the world of the oppressor, yet challenge systemic inequities. Students are disempowered when they resign themselves to the conditions of their existence and believe their circumstances will never change or, more important, that they cannot change the conditions of their schooling (Cammarota & Romero, 2006). As a result, silencing becomes commonplace in the colonized minds of marginalized youth submersed in a banking model of education.

The banking model of education is "well suited to the purposes of the oppressors, whose tranquility rests on how well people fit the world the oppressors have created, and how little they question it" (Freire, 1970, p. 57), thus indoctrinating the oppressed to fit into a world of oppression. The banking method of education is described by scholars as *reductive education* (Bartolomé, 1994) and *backlash pedagogies* (Gutiérrez, Asato, Santos, & Gotanda, 2002); these approaches endorse learning in reductionist, highly scripted, skill-focused, and test-centric terms. Such pedagogies "prohibit the use of students' complete linguistic, sociocultural, and academic repertoire in the service of learning" (Gutiérrez et al., 2002, p. 337). In my own research (Salazar, 2010), I documented reductive pedagogies that emphasize rote memorization and remedial learning through the vehicle of "English or nothing" (p. 116) approaches to educating Mexican immigrant students. Burke et al. (2008) maintain that "when life experiences are ignored dismissed or devalued, students infer that their personal perspectives and world views are nonessential to their learning experiences" (p. 66).

Bartolomé (1994) uses the term *dehumanizing pedagogy* to describe deficit approaches in teaching that result in "discriminatory practices that strip students of the cultural, linguistic, and familial aspects that make them unique, self-possessed individuals" (p. 176). Valenzuela's (1999) research provides an example of deficit approaches that subtract students' culture and language, thus resulting in the "de-Mexicanization" of Mexican immigrant students. Consequently, dehumanization reduces students to the "status of subhumans who need to be rescued from their 'savage' selves" (Bartolomé, 1994, p. 176). Such egregious pathologization of students of color locates the nexus of school failure in students and their language, culture, and family (García & Guerra, 2004; Valencia, 1997, 2010) and blocks real and meaningful change in schooling (Wade et al., 2008). Educators must guard against deficit orientations that strip students of their humanity. Although many educators may explicitly advocate for respect of cultural and linguistic differences, educational systems often perpetuate cultural replacement and assimilation into mainstream values and practices through a focus on high-stakes testing, English-only programming, whitestream curriculum, uncritical pedagogy, and deficit perspectives of parents and families.

Dehumanization affects "not only those whose humanity has been stolen but also (though in a different way) those who have stolen it" (Freire, 1993, p. 26). The construct of dehumanization is best understood as a distortion of the vocation of being more fully human; when human beings are dehumanized, both the oppressed and the oppressor are constricted from the intentionality of consciousness and are thereby stifled in their quest for humanization.

3: The Journey for Humanization Is an Individual and Collective Endeavor Toward Critical Consciousness

The individual and collective development of critical consciousness is paramount to the pursuit of humanization. According to Freire (1970), in a humanizing pedagogy, "the method of instruction ceases to be an instrument by which teachers can manipulate the students, because it expresses the consciousness of the students themselves" (p. 513). Students and teachers engage in a quest for *mutual humanization* (Freire, 1970, p. 56) through the development of *conscientizacao* (p. 17), or critical consciousness. Critical consciousness is the process of "learning to perceive social, political, and economic contradictions, and to take action against the oppressive elements of reality" (p. 17). Moreover, critical consciousness is a process by which students learn to "think actively, and with intentionality and purpose" (Frymer, 2005, p. 6) about their own contributions and the contributions of society to the perpetuation of inequity, injustice, and oppression. As such, in research on emancipatory methodologies and aboriginal peoples in Canada, Alexander (2002) found that a humanizing pedagogy "gives the oppressed access to their consciousness and gives voice to their consciousness" (p. 112).

Educators become humanizing pedagogical agents through critical self-consciousness (Keet et al., 2009). In my own research with Fránquiz (Salazar & Fránquiz, 2008), we describe the transformation of one teacher's pedagogical orientations toward her Mexican immigrant students as she developed critical self-consciousness of her deficit notions of her students, and she subsequently built on her students' funds of knowledge through elements of *respeto* (respect), *confianza* (mutual trust), *consejos* (verbal teachings), and *buen ejemplo* (exemplary role model).

Bell and Schniedewind (1989) promote the notion that "consciousness of self can challenge unconscious oppressive or oppressing behaviors" (p. 211). For instance, as educators develop consciousness of their own role in upholding inequitable structures, they come to act as oppositional intellectuals who engage critically with authority to develop pedagogical principles that link learning, social responsibility, and political agency (Giroux, 2010). Milner (2003) engages teacher candidates in critical self-consciousness through race reflective journaling. Through journaling, teacher candidates realize themselves as racial beings and begin to substantively challenge themselves and the role of educational structures in perpetuating oppression.

Although critical self-consciousness is essential for a humanizing pedagogy, Freire insists that the pursuit of humanization can never be an isolated or individualistic endeavor. As such, from Freire's perspective, "Our being, is a being with" (Roberts, 2000, p. 43). Freire envisaged a humanizing pedagogy as "teaching in relationship with the other" (as cited in Murillo et al., 2009, p. 385). Accordingly, a humanizing pedagogy stems from relationships between educators and students and their collective and dialogic pursuit of humanization for all people (Huerta & Brittain, 2010; Price & Osborne, 2000; Roberts, 2000). As such, in my research with Fránquiz, we found that when Mexican/Chicano students are invited to use their voices as central vehicles for expressing their views of social issues that are relevant to their lives, students and teachers are able to co-construct a network of mutual trust that allows them to identify problems and solutions that are dynamic, contextualized, and inclusive of the needs of local communities (Fránquiz & Salazar, 2004). Ultimately, an individual and collective journey toward humanization allows for spaces where humans can "sculpt real and imaginary corners for peace, solace, communion, and personal and collective identity work" (Fine, Weis, Centrie, & Roberts, 2000, p. 132).

A humanizing pedagogy, thus, results from the individual and collective process of critical consciousness that is provoked through dialogue (Freire, 2000). Freire (1997) claims that

dialogue requires an intense faith in humankind: faith in their power to make and remake, to create and recreate; faith in their vocation to be fully human – which is not the privilege of the elite, but the birthright of all humanity. (as cited in Goduka, 1999, p. 48)

Dialogue for critical consciousness is grounded in one's lived experiences, reflects social and political conditions that reproduce inequity and oppression, and fosters action to interrupt and disrupt oppression (Souto-Manning, 2006). An example of dialogic critical consciousness can be found in my research with Fránquiz. We found that a focus on dialogical education with Mexican/Chicano students contradicts and interrupts students' resistance or silence toward their own cultural resources; thus, new possibilities create permeable boundaries that allow for the development of biculturalism (Fránquiz & Salazar, 2004).

Dialogical education poses problems for students about oppressive conditions, social inequities, and the process of transforming inequities to achieve social justice (Dale & Hyslop-Margison, 2010; Gruenewald, 2003). Scholars assert that "by problematizing their collective experiences, they [teachers and students] employ the uniquely human capacity to be contemplative and have in-depth discussion to encourage reflection and eventual transformation" (Dale & Hyslop-Margison, 2010, p. 99). Problem-posing education engages students and educators in critical inquiry and creative transformation and promotes student engagement with issues of language, literacy, culture, ecology, democracy, and humanity (Bahruth, 2000; Schugurensky, 2011). Problem-posing education in classrooms encourages students to (a) connect their everyday lives to global issues, (b) think critically about actions they can take to make a difference within their own communities, (c) see connections between self and society, and (d) examine and challenge structural forces that inhibit humanization (Bigelow & Peterson, 2002; Schugurensky, 2011). As a case in point, Cammarota and Romero (2006) present research on a social justice course in a high school that provides students with opportunities to identify problems of social justice that are relevant to their lives, trigger self-transformation, and situate students as cocreators of transformative social change. The researchers have students write and present *I am Poems* about their identities in order to help students identify issues and problems that are relevant to their daily lives. Additionally, Bigelow and Peterson (2002) detail the importance of problematizing the social studies curriculum by having students rethink the myth of Christopher Columbus, which is often the first sanitized tale children are told about the encounter, or collision, between diverse cultural groups. Such an approach challenges surface-level approaches to teaching about diversity and places the humanity of those who are marginalized at the heart of social justice.

Freire suggests that developing critical consciousness and engaging in transformative dialogue requires teachers and students to become "subjects," rather than "objects," thereby creating reciprocity of teaching and learning. In Freire's words, "All educational practice requires the existence of 'subjects,' who while teaching, learn. And who in learning also teach" (Freire, 1998, p. 67). As a result, teachers and students are essentially critical beings working together to co-construct knowledge (Shor & Freire, 1987), and students can "feel they are knowledgeable Subjects that guide the educational process" (Cammarota & Romero, 2006, p. 20). Jennings and Da Matta (2009) concur that through a humanizing pedagogy, students become "subjects who actively make meaning of their own lives and the world around them, rather than objects who passively receive content knowledge from teachers" (p. 217). Cammarota and Romero (2006) provide an example of humanizing pedagogy in a high school classroom that allows Latina/o youth to dialogue about their experiences and oppressive language policies in their state that legitimize English and marginalize their native language. As a result of intense and critical dialogue on the issue, the students approached their local school board and presented recommendations to serve Spanish-speaking populations in the school district. In this case, the students were empowered to use their critical voice to challenge the prevailing authorities to reconsider disparate policies that provoke repression and intolerance.

For students to move from objects to subjects, Freire and Macedo (1987) point out that "the successful usage of the students' cultural universe requires respect and legitimization of students' discourses, that is, their own linguistic codes, which are different but never inferior" (p. 127). Legitimizing students' resources sets the groundwork for their ability to relate their own narratives and histories to the content of learning, locate themselves in the realities of their current lives, and critically interrogate and use resources to broaden their knowledge and understanding (Giroux, 2010). Moreover, legitimizing students' resources requires shifting the emphasis from teachers to students and "making visible the relationships among knowledge, authority and power" (Giroux, 2010, para. 8).

Bartolomé (1994) adds that in legitimizing students' resources, a humanizing pedagogy "respects and uses the reality, history, and perspectives of students as an integral part of educational practice" (p. 173). Acknowledging and using students' heritage languages, and accessing their background knowledge, make good pedagogical sense and constitute a humanizing pedagogy for students (Macedo & Bartolomé, 1999). Thus, a humanizing pedagogy validates and values students' interests, experiences, and emotions and localizes curriculum to reflect the realities of students' lives (Dale & Hyslop-Margison, 2010). Concomitantly, a humanizing pedagogy takes into account the cultural identities of all students and "encourages teachers to talk to the students and listen to what the students say and don't say" (Ybarra, 2000, p. 169). In my research, I provide an example of humanizing pedagogy that builds on immigrant students' resources through the creation of a material culture in the classroom that signals to students that their cultural and linguistic resources are welcome in the context of learning, including bilingual texts, posters, communications, and cultural artifacts that represent student diversity (Salazar & Fránquiz, 2008).

Scholars further note that in legitimizing students' resources, a humanizing pedagogy is contextualized to the "funds of knowledge" (Hornberger & McKay, 2010; Moll, Amanti, Neff, & González, 1992) of a specific community. For example, in my research with Fránquiz, we identified a culturally based ethic of care as a humanizing pedagogy that reflects values and interactions in Mexican households as sources of strength students need to survive and thrive (Salazar & Fránquiz, 2008). I extend the idea of a culturally based ethic of care in a case study of one teacher's transformation through a focus on Mexican immigrant students' cultural funds of knowledge as resources for academic success (Salazar & Fránquiz, 2008). Svedman (2007) also contextualizes humanizing aspects of teaching Mexican immigrants in her depiction of lessons learned while she was immersed in a Mexican immigrant community in the United States.

Freire (1997) advocates for teachers to engage in humanizing pedagogy that legitimizes and values students' experiences, but he also insists that teachers understand these experiences in a historical, social, and political context. Freire stresses,

What I have been proposing is a profound respect for the cultural identity of students—a cultural identity that implies respect for the language of the other, the color of the other, the gender of the other, the class of the other, the sexual orientation of the other, the intellectual capacity of the other; that implies the ability to stimulate the creativity of the other. But these things take place in a social and historical context and not in pure air. (pp. 307–308)

A humanizing pedagogy includes an understanding of sociohistorical, sociopolitical, and sociocultural contexts of students' and teachers' lives (Balderrama, 2001;

Bartolomé, 1994; Huerta, 2011; Huerta & Brittain, 2010; Nieto, 2003; Nieto & Rolon, 1997; Salazar & Fránquiz, 2008). Rodriguez and Smith (2011) emphasize that humanizing teachers "interrogate their own histories and roles in oppression before engaging in the co-liberation of others" (p. 95). Moreover, a humanizing pedagogy requires the development of teachers' *political clarity*. Trueba and Bartolomé (2000) define political clarity as follows:

The process by which individuals achieve a deepening awareness of the sociopolitical and economic realities that shape their lives and their capacity to transform them. In addition, it refers to processes whereby individuals come to better understand possible linkages between the macropolitical, economic, and social variables and microclassroom instruction. (pp. 278–279)

By engaging in the development of political clarity, educators interrogate their own power and privilege, recognize how these constructs affect others, reposition their work alongside the other, and remain vigilant to elements that constrain humanization (Renner, Brown, Stiens, & Burton, 2010). In research on humanizing education through intercultural service learning in Jamaica, Renner et al. (2010) immerse participants in experiences that distinguish charity, development, and social justice to make visible power and privilege and thus attempt to decolonize intercultural education and interrupt social and political hierarchies. Thus, the scholars claim to engage participants in a process of "unpacking the layers of injustice, and reorganizing, restructuring and re-humanizing systems of power" (p. 50).

In addition to the development of political clarity, *mutual vulnerability* is a key ingredient of humanizing pedagogy because pedagogical engagement is tied to *meaning-making frames*, or political, socioeconomic, cultural, and normative frames of reference, through which individuals and groups view themselves and their world (Keet et al., 2009). Scholars entreat educators to disrupt normative frames that reproduce hierarchies, asymmetrical power, and oppression (Keet et al., 2009). The implication is that educators need to interrogate their meaning-making frames in order to become vulnerable in questioning the cultural, economic, and political rooting of these frames. By engaging in mutual vulnerability, the oppressor and the oppressed unleash their humanistic potential by disrupting systemic inequalities and recreating new vulnerabilities that foster power from solidarity (Keet et al., 2009).

Scholars propose that teachers who practice a humanizing pedagogy "explicitly teach the school's codes and customs, and/or mainstream knowledge, to enable students to fully participate in the dominant culture" (Huerta, 2011, p. 39). Delpit (2006) refers to school's codes and customs of the rules of the culture of those who have power as *the culture of power*; these include "ways of talking, ways of writing, ways of dressing, and ways of interacting" (p. 25). Preparing students to participate successfully in the dominant culture equips students with the knowledge base and discourse styles privileged in society; however, scholars note that this process must be additive to students' existing cultural and linguistic resources (Bartolomé, 1994; Huerta, 2011).

In summary, a humanizing pedagogy engages students in the following ways: making personal connections to learning (Bell & Schniedewind, 1989), validating selves and others (Bell & Schniedewind, 1989), focusing on what they can do and achieve with the cultural and linguistic resources they bring (Fránquiz & Salazar, 2004), expanding on their repertoire of possible selves (Fránquiz & Salazar, 2004), strengthening cultural awareness and identity (Huerta, 2011; Nieto, 2002; Rumberger & Larson, 1998; Salazar, 2008, 2010; Suárez, 2007), intensifying consciousness of their own contribution and the contributions of society and schools to the hegemonic reproduction of oppressive structures (Allen & Rossatto, 2009; Huerta & Brittain, 2010), and instilling a belief in their own humanity (Cammarota & Romero, 2006).

4: Critical Reflection and Action Can Transform Structures That Impede Our Own and Others' Humanness, Thus Facilitating Liberation for All

Freire defines *praxis* as "reflection and action upon the world in order to transform it" (Freire, 1970, p. 145). It is in the intersection of reflection and action that Freire proposes people become "more fully human" (Freire, 1982) and as a result, power is shared by students and educators and the continuous process of rehumanization occurs (Bartolomé, 1994; Glass, 2001; Gottlieb & La Belle, 1990; Huerta, 2011; Huerta & Brittain, 2010). A humanizing pedagogy is a model that combines the skills of humanistic educators with the perspective of critical theorists for the purpose of personal and collective critical awareness and change-oriented action (Bell & Schniedewind, 1989). Hence, a humanizing pedagogy is critical, dialogical, and praxical (Glass, 2001; Huerta, 2011; Huerta & Brittain, 2010; Jennings & Smith, 2002; Roberts, 2000).

Freire (1970) emphasizes that action and reflection occur simultaneously and can potentially transform structures that impede humanization and facilitate liberation. Furthermore, Freire adds that on engaging in critical reflection of reality, one may find it impossible or inappropriate to take immediate action; as a result, critical reflection can also be considered action.

A humanizing pedagogy is a liberating pedagogy whose aim is to "transform existing power and privilege in the service of greater social justice and human freedom" (McLaren, 1997, p. 46, as cited in Goduka, 1999). The ongoing and permanent task of liberation takes place in the actions of humans to transform existing structures that impede the pursuit of social change, global justice, and humanization (Roberts, 2000). Educators orienting toward a humanizing pedagogy engage in critical reflection of systemic inequities and take action to challenge the role of educational institutions, fellow educators, and themselves in maintaining inequitable systems (Bartolomé, 1994; Freire, 1970; Nieto, 2003; Salazar, 2008). As a case in point, in an interview with scholar Sonia Nieto, Fránquiz (2005) describes Nieto's quest to immerse educators in "profoundly multicultural questions that focus on access, equity, and justice" (p. 168) in order to engage educators in personal and collective actions that interrupt inequities.

Although a humanizing pedagogy promotes liberation for educators and students, educators often face obstacles for promoting a humanizing pedagogy in classrooms. For example, Cho and Lewis (2005) describe how the oppressed may resist humanizing pedagogies because of fear of freedom resulting from the internalized oppression that binds the oppressed to the oppressor. Cho and Lewis state, "Internalization and identification with the oppressive power relations constituted in a banking pedagogy may very well block the efforts of the critical educator to raise the consciousness of the oppressed to a level of revolutionary action" (p. 321). Despite the challenges, Freire (1970) insists that "to exist humanely is to name the world, to change it" (pp. 75–76), and he insists that the oppressed must name their own oppression so that they can disrupt inequity and demand social change. A humanizing pedagogy is intertwined with social change; it challenges students to critically engage with the world so they can act on it (Giroux, 2010). For example, curriculum design that is focused on social justice issues can develop students' consciousness of issues related to power, classism, sexism, racism, heterosexism, and ableism and provoke students to engage in project-based learning that challenges oppression (Adams, Lee, & Griffin, 2010). Additionally, through service learning projects that focus on social justice issues, students are able to differentiate between social service and social change (Warren, 1998).

5: Educators Are Responsible for Promoting a More Fully Human World Through Their Pedagogical Principles and Practices

Given that a humanizing pedagogy is a philosophical approach that fosters critical, dialogical, and praxical education (Glass, 2001; Huerta, 2011; Huerta & Brittain, 2010; Jennings & Smith, 2002; Roberts, 2000), educators may be perplexed about practical inroads to a humanizing pedagogy. Educators searching for pedagogical recipes critique Freire's lack of specific technical methods and describe Freire's concepts as vague, imprecise, generic, and oversimplified and unhelpful for practitioners on the ground (Dale & Hyslop-Margison, 2010; Schugurensky, 2011).

A tension exists in the chasm between the theory and practice of humanizing pedagogy. Gore (1993) summarizes the tension between theory and practice in her analysis of two distinct strands of pedagogy, *pedagogical practice* and *pedagogical project*. Gore describes pedagogical practice as offering concrete suggestions intended to help educators, in contrast to pedagogical projects that promote educational theory through abstract political rhetoric. Gore (1992) expresses the need to support classroom teachers in the application of liberatory ideals, and she challenges pedagogical projects that place "a requirement on teachers to do the work of empowering, to be the agents of empowerment, without providing much in the way of tangible guidance for that work" (p. 66).

Bartolomé (1994) attempts to find a synergy between a teacher's philosophical orientation and their instructional methods, and she asserts that both elements are instrumental in creating a humanizing experience for students. Bartolomé stresses that educators should not reject the use of teaching methods and strategies, but rather, they should disavow uncritical approaches to teaching and learning in favor of reflection and action. This allows educators to "recreate and reinvent teaching methods and materials by always taking into consideration the sociocultural realities that can either limit or expand the possibilities to humanize education" (p. 177).

In heeding Freire's call for a humanizing pedagogy, educational scholars have conducted research over the past four decades to illuminate the application of humanizing pedagogy in an educational setting. The section that follows presents a synthesis of 10 principles and practices of a humanizing pedagogy. The principles and practices of humanizing pedagogy differ from the five aforementioned tenets in that these operationalize the theoretical assertions presented in this review to illuminate the perceptible dispositions, knowledge, and skills that educators need to humanize pedagogy. The principles and practices of humanizing pedagogy include the following:

1. The reality of the learner is crucial.
2. Critical consciousness is imperative for students and educators.
3. Students' sociocultural resources are valued and extended.
4. Content is meaningful and relevant to students' lives.
5. Students' prior knowledge is linked to new learning.
6. Trusting and caring relationships advance the pursuit of humanization.
7. Mainstream knowledge and discourse styles matter.
8. Students will achieve through their academic, intellectual, social abilities.
9. Student empowerment requires the use of learning strategies.
10. Challenging inequity in the educational system can promote transformation.

The Reality of the Learner Is Crucial

The reality of the learner is crucial to the development of a humanizing pedagogy and is inclusive of the sociohistorical, sociocultural, and sociopolitical contexts of students' lives inside and outside of school (Bartolomé, 1994; Huerta, 2011; Roberts, 2000). Educators who enact humanizing pedagogy commit to explore the varied macro- and micro-level elements that affect teaching and learning by interrogating multiple forms of oppression in their students' lives (Fránquiz & Salazar, 2004). Moreover, educators actively inquire into students' identities inside and outside of school to further understand the diversity and multiple identities of their students and the cultural differences that affect teaching and learning (Salazar, 2010).

Critical Consciousness Is Imperative for Students and Educators

Critical consciousness is imperative for a humanizing pedagogy in that the development of critical consciousness provides educators and students with the opportunity to become more fully human (Bartolomé, 1994; Freire, 1970; Huerta, 2011; Salazar, 2008). Educators who orient toward a humanizing pedagogy critically evaluate their own beliefs and engage students in critical dialogue that problematizes reality (Bartolomé,

1994; Huerta, 2011; Schugurensky, 2011; Strobel & Tillberg-Webb, 2006). Students and educators develop critical awareness through the following: critique of oppression, questioning of prevailing values and ideologies, and examination of their own status, power, and choices (Bell & Schniedewind, 1989). In so doing, students and teachers engage in the pursuit of "ontological clarity, the why of becoming human" (Rodriguez & Smith, 2011, p. 98).

Students' Sociocultural Resources Are Valued and Extended

Students' cultural, linguistic, and familial resources are valued in a humanizing pedagogy. Educators who orient toward a humanizing pedagogy build on students' culture, history, perspectives, and life experiences (Fránquiz & Salazar, 2004; Huerta, 2011; Huerta and Brittain, 2010; Macedo & Bartolomé, 1999; Salazar, 2008; Suárez, 2007); incorporate content and curricular resources that reflect students' experiences (Huerta, 2011; Salazar, 2008); build students' oral and written language and literacy skills in their bi- or multilanguage registers (Hornberger & McKay, 2010); and strengthen students' ethnic and linguistic identities to support bilingualism and biculturalism so that students develop pride in the strengths and contributions of their communities (Huerta, 2011; Salazar, 2008).

Content Is Meaningful and Relevant to Students' Lives

A humanizing pedagogy incorporates content that is meaningful to students' lives in that it draws on students' lived experiences (Huerta, 2011; Salazar, 2008). A permeable curriculum is essential for a humanizing pedagogy in that it "allows for inclusion of students' linguistic, cultural, and social resources" (Salazar, 2010, p. 120). Dyson (1993) describes a permeable curriculum as one that allows for an interactional space drawing on official school knowledge and students' cultural, social, and linguistic resources. A permeable curriculum serves as a bridge, bringing the worlds of educators and students together in instructionally powerful ways. Educators orienting toward a humanizing pedagogy foster permeability when they accept code-switching in student discourse, support heritage-language use as a means of fostering student comprehension, facilitate student input into the curriculum, provide opportunities for students to make personal connections to content, and include topics that reflect the diversity of students' lives (Fránquiz & Salazar, 2004; Huerta, 2011; Salazar, 2010).

Students' Prior Knowledge Is Linked to New Learning

A humanizing pedagogy integrates students' prior knowledge and links this knowledge to new learning. By acknowledging students' background knowledge, the teacher legitimizes and communicates the value of students' languages and cultures (Bartolomé, 1994; Fránquiz & Salazar, 2004, Huerta, 2011). Additionally, a humanizing pedagogy is additive in that students are treated as experts of their own background knowledge and they are expected to add new content and skills to amplify their knowledge base (Bartolomé, 1994). Moreover, a humanizing pedagogy creates learning conditions where all students can demonstrate their knowledge and expertise in a way that encourages students to "see themselves, and be seen by others, as capable and confident" (Bartolomé, 1994, p. 178).

Trusting and Caring Relationships Advance the Pursuit of Humanization

Freire's conceptualization of humanizing pedagogy is centered on the student and teacher relationship. Educators orienting toward a humanizing pedagogy build trusting and caring relationships with students (Fránquiz & Salazar, 2004; Huerta, 2011; Salazar, 2008). Educators who care engage in the following: listen to students' interests, needs, and concerns; know students on a personal level and attempt to understand students' home experiences; acknowledge the challenges associated with the development of bilingualism and biculturalism; model kindness, patience, and respect; tend to students' overall well-being, including their emotional, social, and academic needs; create a support network for students inside and outside of school; build on the values and contributions of parents; create a safe learning environment where risk-taking and active engagement are valued; allow for native language support; and facilitate student connections to their communities (Bahruth, 2007; Fránquiz & Salazar, 2004; Huerta, 2011; Rodriguez, 2008; Salazar, 2008). Caring relationships are founded on mutual respect between students, families, and teachers, thus humanizing the context of schooling (Bartolomé, 1994).

Mainstream Knowledge and Discourse Styles Matter

A humanizing pedagogy not only builds on students' lived experiences and background knowledge but also teaches students mainstream or dominant knowledge and discourse styles (Bartolomé, 1994). Bartolomé stresses that teachers should act as cultural mentors to support students in accommodating to the culture of the classroom. This is imperative as the classroom culture is often representative of the dominant culture through the curricula and discourse styles that are privileged and reproduced throughout the educational system. By teaching students mainstream knowledge and discourse styles, a humanizing pedagogy provides students with "insider" knowledge that is needed to successfully navigate the educational system (Bartolomé, 1994); however, this process must be additive and not intended to replace students' prior knowledge and discourse patterns (Bartolomé, 1994; Huerta, 2011).

Students Will Achieve Through Their Academic, Intellectual, Social Abilities

A humanizing pedagogy is focused on what students can do and achieve with the cultural resources they bring to the experience of schooling (Fránquiz & Salazar, 2004). Fránquiz (2003) describes the use of the concept of *capacidad* by Latina scholars Sonia Nieto and Maria Torrez-Gúzman to illustrate the responsibility and capacity of Latina/o students to achieve to their highest potential. Educators who orient toward a humanizing pedagogy believe in students' academic, intellectual, and social capacities; hold high expectations; encourage students to think independently; incorporate a range of learning styles; and engage students in solving real-world problems (Bartolomé, 1994; Huerta, 2011; Salazar, 2008). Furthermore, humanizing educators guard against deficit views that are deeply embedded in educational thought and practice (Arias & Morillo-Cambell, 2008; Brown & Souto-Manning, 2008; Dudley-Marling, 2007; García & Guerra, 2004; Skrla & Scheurich, 2004; Valencia, Valenzuela, Sloan, & Foley, 2001; Wade et al., 2008).

Student Empowerment Requires the Use of Learning Strategies

A humanizing pedagogy is empowering though a focus on learning strategies, defined by Bartolomé (1994) as "an instructional model that explicitly teaches students learning strategies that enable them consciously to monitor their own learning" (p. 186). This model provides students with reflective cognitive monitoring and metacognitive skills that facilitate student independence and enable students to self-monitor their own learning and progress. By assisting students in identifying strategies that increase comprehension and learning, students can understand how to use their own meaning-making strategies with conventional academic strategies (Bartolomé, 1994). A humanizing pedagogy is also inclusive of native language support to extend students' metacognitive strategies in bilingual or multilingual spheres (Salazar, 2010).

Challenging Inequity in the Educational System Can Promote Transformation

A humanizing pedagogy requires educators to assist the oppressed in regaining their own humanity by rejecting internalized oppression and taking action to dismantle oppressive ideologies and systems (Freire, 1970). Concomitantly, humanizing pedagogues challenge the role of educational institutions, fellow educators, and themselves in maintaining social inequities (Bartolomé, 1994). Such educators "teach against the grain" (Cochran-Smith, 2001) of policies and practices that dehumanize students, parents, and communities. Additionally, humanizing pedagogues advocate for transformational and revolutionary approaches to improving the education of culturally and linguistically diverse learners, thereby humanizing the experience of schooling for their students and themselves (Salazar, 2010).

CONCLUSION: HOPE FOR HUMANIZATION

I began this chapter with a personal narrative of my journey to reclaim my humanity as a result of the dehumanization I experienced in U.S. public schools. The cost of an education is too high if students are required to divest themselves of their language, culture, and family in order to succeed in U.S. schools and society. Schools should be spaces where all students feel supported as their multiple identities evolve within a meaningful sense of achievement, purpose, power, and hope. This review of literature on humanizing pedagogy is ultimately a proclamation of hope that as educators we can reinvent the principles and practice of education as a journey toward humanization and liberation. Hope is central to Freirean ideology in that it includes "both the denunciation of oppressive structures and the annunciation of a less oppressive world, and hence . . . not only critical but also hopeful and prophetic" (Schugurensky, 2011, pp. 72–73). Hope is also a "crucial precondition for both a healthy pessimism and a source of revolutionary imagination" (Giroux, 2004, pp. 6–7).

This review advances hope for the moral responsibility of educators to embrace a humanizing pedagogy that respects the dignity and humanity of all students. Macedo and Bartolomé (1999) challenge educators toward a moral conviction for humanization. They write,

> The critical issue is the degree to which we hold the moral conviction that we must humanize the educational experience of students from subordinated populations by eliminating the hostility that often confronts these students. This process would require that we cease to be overly dependent on methods as technical instruments and adopt a pedagogy that seeks to forge a cultural democracy where all students are treated with respect and dignity. (pp. 160–161)

Given the literature reviewed in this chapter, one conclusion that can be reached is that it is the moral duty of educators to understand and enact humanizing pedagogy that is grounded in theory, possible in practice, and shaped by the realities of students' and teachers' lives. The moral duty of educators can begin through the following philosophy: "We find each other where we are in the human experience and go from there" (Rodriguez, 2008, p. 345). From this point on, a humanizing pedagogy must be grounded in the diversity of everyday life and interrogate the human experience in the context of power, privilege, and oppression to provoke action toward humanization and liberation (Freire, 1972; Keet et al., 2009; McLaren & Jaramillo, 2006). The moral duty of educators coalesces in what Simon (1992) describes as a space where educators, students, and their families "envisage versions of a world that is 'not yet'—in order to be able to alter the grounds upon which life is lived" (p. 375). This space that is "not yet" allows us to relentlessly strive for humanization, liberation, and transformation in education and society.

To trigger transformation toward humanization and liberation, it is imperative to explicitly name the beliefs and skills of a humanizing educator to support the development of a humanizing pedagogy that advances the humanity, dignity, and achievement of learners of diverse backgrounds. As such, educator preparation and development can instill the philosophy and practice of humanizing pedagogy in a new generation of revolutionary educators. However, although the role of educators and educator preparation is vital to advancing a humanizing pedagogy, this chapter concludes with an appeal for studies that engage the voices of the oppressed to better understand the need for, and the practice of, humanization in education. Currently, most studies on humanizing pedagogy describe the role of the teacher in creating a humanizing experience for students. Some would argue that scholars continue to privilege the experience of the "oppressor" and negate or exclude the agency of the "oppressed" by strictly focusing on the educator's role in a humanizing pedagogy.

Future research should therefore focus on the active role of students in cocreating a humanizing pedagogy in the classroom and beyond.

REFERENCES

Adams, M., Lee, A., & Griffin, P. (2010). *Teaching for diversity and social justice* (2nd ed.). New York, NY: Taylor & Francis.

Alexander, G. C. (2002). Interactive management: An emancipator methodology. *Systematic Practice and Action Research, 15*, 111–122. doi:10.1023/A:1015288407759

Allen, R. L., & Rossatto, C. A. (2009). Does critical pedagogy work with privileged students? *Teacher Education Quarterly, 36*, 163–180.

Arias, B. M., & Morillo-Cambell, M. (2008). *Promoting ELL parental involvement: Challenges in contested times.* Retrieved from http://www.greatlakescenter.org/docs/Policy_Briefs/Arias_ELL.pdf

Aronowitz, S. (1993). Paulo Freire's radical democratic humanism. In P. McLaren & P. Leonard (Eds.), *Paulo Freire: A critical encounter* (pp. 8–24). New York, NY: Routledge.

Bahruth, R. E. (2000). Changes and challenges in teaching the word and the world for the benefit of all humanity. In J. E. Katchen & L. Yiu-Nam (Eds.), *Selected papers from the ninth international symposium on English teaching* (pp. 1–9). Taipei, Taiwan: Crane Publishing.

Bahruth, R. E. (2007, March 9). *Learning how to speak human* (Keynote). Kaohsiung, Taiwan: I-Shou University.

Balderrama, M. V. (2001). The (mis)preparation of teachers in the Proposition 227 era: Humanizing teacher roles and their practice. *Urban Review, 33*, 255–267.

Bartolomé, L. (1994). Beyond the methods fetish: Toward a humanizing pedagogy. *Harvard Educational Review, 64*, 173–195.

Bell, L., & Schniedewind, N. (1989). Realizing the promise of humanistic education: A reconstructed pedagogy for personal and social change. *Journal of Humanistic Psychology, 29*, 200–223.

Bhabha, H. K. (1994). *The location of culture.* New York, NY: Routledge.

Bigelow, B., & Peterson, B. (Eds.). (2002). *Rethinking globalization: Teaching for justice in an unjust world.* Milwaukee, WI: Rethinking Schools Press.

Brady, J. (1994). Critical literacy, feminism, and a politics of representation. In P. McLaren & C. Lankshear (Eds.), *Politics of liberation: Paths from Freire* (pp. 142–153). London, England: Routledge.

Brown, S., & Souto-Manning, M. (2008). "Culture is the way they live here": Young Latin@s and parents navigate linguistic and cultural borderlands in U.S. schools. *Journal of Latinos and Education, 7*(1), 25–42.

Burke, C., Adler, M. A., & Linker, M. (2008). Resisting erasure: Cultivating opportunities for a humanizing curriculum. *Multicultural Perspectives, 10*(2), 65–72.

Calabrese Barton, A., Tan, E., & Rivet, A. (2008). Creating hybrid spaces for engaging school science among urban middle school girls. *American Educational Research Journal, 45*, 68–103.

Cammarota, J., & Romero, A. (2006). A critically compassionate intellectualism for Latina/o students: Raising voices above the silencing in our schools. *Multicultural Education, 14*(2), 16–23.

Carnoy, M. (2004). Foreword. In P. Freire (Ed.), *Pedagogy of the heart* (pp. 7–20). New York, NY: Continuum.

Cho, D., & Lewis, T. (2005). The persistent life of oppression: The unconscious, power, and subjectivity. *Interchange, 36*, 313–329.

Cochran-Smith, M. (2001). Learning to teach against the (new) grain. *Journal of Teacher Education, 52*(1), 3–4.

Cummins, J. (2001). *Language, power, and pedagogy: Bilingual children in the crossfire.* Tonawanda, NY: Multilingual Matters.

Dale, J., & Hyslop-Margison, E. J. (2010). *Pedagogy of humanism (Explorations of Educational Purpose, Vol. 12,* pp. 71–104). New York, NY: Springer.

Darder, A. (2002). *Reinventing Paulo Freire: A pedagogy of love.* Boulder, CO: Westview Press.

Darling-Hammond, L. (2012). Policy frameworks for new assessments. In P. Griffen, B. McGraw, & E. Care (Eds.), *Assessment and teaching of 21st century skills* (pp. 301–340). New York, NY: Springer.

de la Luz Reyes, M. (1992). Challenging venerable assumptions: Literacy instruction for linguistically different students. *Harvard Educational Review, 62,* 427–446.

Delpit, L. (2006). *Other people's children: Cultural conflict in the classroom.* New York, NY: New Press.

Du Bois, W. E. B. (1903). *The souls of Black folk.* Chicago, IL: McClurg.

Dudley-Marling, C. (2007). Return of the deficit. *Journal of Educational Controversy, 2.* Retrieved from http://www.wce.wwu.edu/Resources/CEP/eJournal/v002n001/a004.shtml

Dyson, A. H. (1993). *Negotiating the permeable curriculum: On literacy, diversity and the interplay of children's and teacher's worlds.* Urbana, IL: National Council of Teachers of English.

Fine, M., Weis, L., Centrie, C., & Roberts, R. (2000). Educating beyond the borders of schooling. *Anthropology and Education Quarterly, 31,* 131–151.

Fordham, S., & Ogbu, J. U. (1986). Black students' school success: Coping with the burden of acting White. *Urban Review, 18,* 176–206.

Fránquiz, M. (2003). Literacy reform for Latina/o students. *Reading Research Quarterly, 38,* 418–430.

Fránquiz, M. (2005). Education as political work: An interview with Sonia Nieto. *Language Arts, 83,* 166–171.

Fránquiz, M., & Salazar, M. (2004). The transformative potential of humanizing pedagogy: Addressing the diverse needs of Chicano/Mexicano students. *High School Journal, 87*(4), 36–53.

Freire, P. (1970). *Pedagogy of the oppressed.* New York, NY: Continuum.

Freire, P. (1972). *Pedagogy of the oppressed.* Harmondsworth, England: Penguin.

Freire, P. (1982). Education as the practice of freedom (M. B. Ramos, Trans.). In *Education for critical consciousness* (pp. 1–84). New York, NY: Continuum.

Freire, P. (1984). *Pedagogy of the oppressed.* New York, NY: Continuum.

Freire, P. (1985). *The politics of education: Culture, power and liberation.* New York, NY: Bergin & Garvey.

Freire, P. (1993). *Pedagogy of the oppressed.* New York, NY: Continuum.

Freire, P. (1994). *Pedagogy of hope: Reliving pedagogy of the oppressed.* New York, NY: Continuum.

Freire, P. (1997). *Education for critical consciousness.* New York, NY: Continuum.

Freire, P. (1998). *Pedagogy of freedom: Ethics, democracy, and civic courage* (P. Clarke, Ed.). Lanham, MD: Rowman & Littlefield.

Freire, P. (2000). *Pedagogy of the oppressed.* New York, NY: Continuum.

Freire, P., & Betto, F. (1985). *Essa escola chamada vida—Depoimentos ao reporter Ricardo Kotscho* [This school called life: Testimonials to Ricardo Kotscho Reporter]. Sao Paulo, Brazil: Atica.

Freire, P., & Macedo, D. (1987). *Literacy: Reading the word and the world.* Westport, CT: Bergin & Garvey.

Freire, A., & Macedo, P. (1998). *The Paulo Freire reader.* New York, NY: Continuum.

Frymer, B. (2005). Freire, alienation, and contemporary youth: Toward a pedagogy of everyday life. *InterActions: UCLA Journal of Education and Information Studies, 1.* Retrieved from http://escholarship.org/uc/item/5wd2w4gs

García, S. B., & Guerra, P. L. (2004). Deconstructing deficit thinking: Working with educators to create more equitable learning environments. *Education and Urban Society, 35*, 150–168.

Gay, G. (2010). *Culturally responsive teaching: Theory, research, and practice* (2nd ed.). New York, NY: Teachers College Press.

Giroux, H. A. (1988). *Teachers as intellectuals: Toward a critical pedagogy of learning*. Westport, CT: Bergin & Garvey.

Giroux, H. A. (2004). *The abandoned generation: Democracy beyond the culture of fear*. New York, NY: Palgrave Macmillan.

Giroux, H. A. (2010, November 23). *Lessons to be learned from Paulo Freire as education is being taken over by the mega rich*. Retrieved from http://archive.truthout.org/lessons-be-learned-from-paulo-freire-education-is-being-taken-over-mega-rich65363

Glass, R. D. (2001). On Paulo Freire's philosophy of praxis and the foundations of liberation education. *Educational Researcher, 30*(2), 15–25.

Goduka, I. N. (1999). Educating for democracy in South America: Lessons from Freire humanizing pedagogy. *Democracy and Education, 13*, 42–48.

González, N., Moll, L., & Amantí, C. (2005). *Funds of knowledge: Theorizing practices in households, communities, and classrooms*. Mahwah, NJ: Lawrence Erlbaum.

Gore, J. (1992). What we can do for you! What can "we" do for "you"? Struggling over empowerment in critical and feminist pedagogy. In C. Luke & J. Gore (Eds.), *Feminisms and critical pedagogy* (pp. 54–73). New York, NY: Routledge.

Gore, J. (1993). *The struggle for pedagogies: Critical and feminist discourses as regimes of truth*. New York, NY: Routledge.

Gottlieb, E. E., & La Belle, T. J. (2009). Ethnographic contextualization of Freire's discourse: Consciousness-raising, theory, and practice. *Anthropology & Education Quarterly, 21*, 3–18.

Grande, S. (2000). American Indian geographies of identity and power: At the crossroads of indigena and mestizaje. *Harvard Educational Review, 70*, 467–499.

Gruenewald, D. A. (2003). The best of both worlds: A critical pedagogy of place. *Educational Researcher, 32*(4), 3–12.

Gutiérrez, K., Asato, J., Santos, M., & Gotanda, N. (2002). Backlash pedagogy: Language and culture and the politics of reform. *Review of Education, Pedagogy, and Cultural Studies, 24*, 335–351.

Gutiérrez, K., Baquedano-Lopez, P., & Tejeda, C. (1999). Rethinking diversity: Hybridity and hybrid language practices in the third space. *Mind, Culture, & Activity, 6*, 286–303.

Hornberger, N. H., & McKay, S. L. (2010). *Sociolinguistics and language education*. Tonawanda, NY: Multilingual Matters.

Huerta, T. M. (2011). Humanizing pedagogy: Beliefs and practices on the teaching of Latino children. *Bilingual Research Journal, 34*(1), 38–57.

Huerta, T. M., & Brittain, C. M. (2010). Effective practices that matter for Latino children. In E. G. Murillo, Jr., S. A. Villenas, R. Trinidad Galvan, J. Sanchez Munoz, C. Martinez, & M. Machado-Casas (Eds.), *Handbook of Latinos and education: Theory, research, and practice* (pp. 382–399). New York, NY: Routledge.

Jackson, P. W. (1990). *Life in classrooms*. New York, NY: Teachers College Press.

Jennings, L. B., & Da Matta, G. B. (2009). Rooted in resistance: Women teachers constructing counter-pedagogics in post-authoritarian Brazil. *Teaching Education, 20*, 215–228.

Jennings, L. B., & Smith, C. (2002). Examining the role of critical inquiry for transformative practices: Two joint case studies of multicultural teacher education. *Teachers College Record, 104*, 456–481.

Keet, A., Zinn, D., & Porteus, K. (2009). Mutual vulnerability: A key principle in a humanizing pedagogy in post-conflict societies. *Perspectives in Education, 27*, 109–119.

Kiros, T. (2006). Frantz Fanon. In K. Wiredu (Ed.), *A companion to African philosophy* (pp. 216–224). Oxford, England: Blackwell.

Kirylo, J. D. (2001). *Paulo Freire: The man from Recife*. New York, NY: Peter Lang.

Ladson-Billings, G. (1995). Toward a theory of culturally relevant pedagogy. *American Educational Research Journal, 32*, 465–491.

Macedo, D. (1994). *Literacies of power: What Americans are allowed to know*. Boulder, CO: Westview Press.

Macedo, D., & Bartolomé, L. (1999). *Dancing with bigotry*. New York, NY: St. Martin's Press.

McLaren, P. (1997). *Revolutionary multiculturalism: Pedagogies of dissent for the new millennium*. Boulder, CO: Westview Press.

McLaren, P., & Jaramillo, N. E. (2006). Critical pedagogy, Latino/a education, and the politics of class struggle. *Critical Methodologies, 6*(1), 73–93.

Milner, R. (2003). Teacher reflection and race in cultural contexts: History, meanings, and methods in teaching. *Theory into Practice, 42*, 173–180.

Moll, L., Amanti, C., Neff, D., & González, N. (1992). Funds of knowledge for teaching: Using a qualitative approach to connect homes and classrooms. *Theory into Practice, 31*, 132–141.

Moller, A. C., & Deci, E. L. (2009). Interpersonal control, dehumanization, and violence: A self-determination theory perspective. *Group Processes & Intergroup Relations, 13*(1), 41–53.

Morrell, E. (2008). *Critical literacy and urban youth. Pedagogies of access, dissent and liberation*. New York, NY: Routledge.

Murillo, E. G., Villenas, S., Galvan, R., Sanchez Munoz, J., Martinez, C., & Machado-Casas, M. (Eds.). (2009). *Handbook of Latinos and education*. New York, NY: Routledge.

Nichols, S. L., & Berliner, D. C. (2007). *Collateral damage: How high-stakes testing corrupts America's schools*. Cambridge, MA: Harvard Education Press.

Nieto, S. (2002). *Language, culture, and teaching: Critical perspectives for a new century*. Mahwah, NJ: Erlbaum.

Nieto, S. (2003). Challenging current notions of "highly qualified teachers" through work in teachers' inquiry group. *Journal of Teacher Education, 54*, 386–398.

Nieto, S. (2010). *The light in their eyes: Creating multicultural learning communities* (10th anniversary edition). New York, NY: Teachers College Press.

Nieto, S., & Rolon, C. (1997). Preparation and professional development of teachers: A perspective from two Latinas. In J. J. Irvine (Ed.), *Critical knowledge of diverse teachers and learners* (pp. 89–123). Washington, DC: American Association of Colleges of Teacher Education.

Parker, L., & Lynn, M. (2002). What's race got to do with it? Critical race theory's conflicts with and connections to qualitative research methodology and epistemology. *Qualitative Inquiry, 8*, 7–22.

Parker-Rees, R., & Willan, J. (2006). *Early years education: Major themes in education*. New York, NY: Routledge.

Pizarro, M. (1998). "Chicano power!" Epistemology and methodology for social justice and empowerment in Chicana/o communities. *International Journal of Qualitative Studies in Education, 11*(1), 57–80.

Price, J. N., & Osborne, M. D. (2000). Challenges of forging a humanizing pedagogy in teacher education. *Curriculum and Teaching, 15*(1), 27–51.

Quiroz, P. A. (2001). The silencing of Latino student "voice": Puerto Rican and Mexican narratives in eighth grade and high school. *Anthropology & Education Quarterly, 32*, 326–349.

Renner, A., Brown, M., Stiens, G., & Burton, S. (2010). A reciprocal global education? Working toward a more humanizing pedagogy and practice. *Intercultural Education, 21*(2), 41–54.

Reyes, R. (2007). Marginalized students in secondary school settings: The pedagogical and theoretical implications of addressing the needs of student sub-populations. *Journal of Border Educational Research, 6*, 3–5.

Roberts, P. (2000). *Education, literacy, and humanization: Exploring the work of Paulo Freire.* Westport, CT: Bergin & Garvey.

Rodriguez, A. (2008). Toward a transformative teaching practice: Criticity, pedagogy and praxis. *International Journal of Learning, 15,* 345–352.

Rodriguez, A., & Smith, M. D. (2011). Reimagining Freirean pedagogy: Sendero for teacher education. *Journal for Critical Education Policy Studies, 9,* 91–103.

Rumberger, R. W., & Larson, K. A. (1998). Student mobility and the increased risk of high school dropout. *American Journal of Education, 107,* 1–35.

Sadowski, M. (2003). *Adolescents at school: Perspectives on youth, identity, and education.* Cambridge, MA: Harvard Education Publishing.

Salazar, M. (2008). English or nothing: The impact of rigid language policies on the inclusion of humanizing practices in a high school ESL program. *Equity & Excellence in Education, 41,* 341–356.

Salazar, M. (2010). Pedagogical stances of high school ESL teachers: "Huelgas" in high school ESL classrooms. *Bilingual Research Journal, 33,* 111–124.

Salazar, M., & Fránquiz, M. (2008). The transformation of Ms. Corazon: Creating humanizing spaces for Mexican immigrant students in secondary ESL classrooms. *Journal of Multicultural Perspectives, 10,* 185–191.

Sanchez, G. J. (1993). *Becoming Mexican American: Ethnicity, culture and identity in Chicano Los Angeles 1900–1945.* New York, NY: Oxford University Press.

Schapiro, S. (2001). *A Freirean approach to anti-sexist education with men: Toward a pedagogy of the "oppressor".* Retrieved from http://www.fielding.edu/research/ar_papers/Schapiro.pdf

Schugurensky, D. (2011). *Paulo Freire.* New York, NY: Continuum.

Shor, I., & Freire, P. (1987). *A pedagogy for liberation.* Westport, CT: Greenwood.

Siddhartha. (1999). *Education as a liberalizing tool.* Retrieved from www.unesco.org/most/freirearticle.htm

Simon, R. (1992). *Teaching against the grain.* New York, NY: Bergin & Garvey.

Skrla, L., & Scheurich, J. J. (2004). *Educational equity and accountability: Paradigms, policies and politics.* London, England: Routledge.

Solórzano, D. G., & Yosso, T. J. (2002). Critical race methodology: Counter-storytelling as an analytical framework for education research. *Qualitative Inquiry, 8*(1), 23–44.

Souto-Manning, M. (2006). A critical look at bilingualism discourse in public schools: Auto/ethnographic reflections of a vulnerable observer. *Bilingual Research Journal, 29,* 439–458.

Strobel, J., & Tillberg-Webb, H. (2006, June). *Applying a critical and humanizing framework of instructional technologies to educational practice.* Paper presented at the AECT Research Symposium, Indiana University, Bloomington. Retrieved from http://www.aect.org/events/symposia/Docs/critical%20and%20humanizing%20framework.pdf

Suárez, D. (2007). Second and third generation heritage language speakers: HL scholarship's relevance to the research needs and future directions of TESOL. *Heritage Language Journal, 5*(1), 27–49.

Svedman, D. (2007). From me to you: Lessons from teaching in Segundo Barrio. *Journal of Border Educational Research, 6,* 145–156.

Talbert-Johnson, C. (2004). Structural inequities and the achievement gap in urban schools. *Education and Urban Society, 37*(1), 22–36.

Trueba, H., & Bartolomé, L. (Eds.). (2000). *Immigrant voices: In search of educational equity.* New York, NY: Rowman & Littlefield.

Valencia, R., Valenzuela, A., Sloan, K., & Foley, D. E. (2001). Let's treat the cause, not the symptoms: Equity and accountability in Texas revisited. *Phi Delta Kappan, 83,* 318–326.

Valencia, R. R. (Ed.). (1997). *The evolution of deficit thinking: Educational thought and practice.* London, England: Falmer Press.

Valencia, R. R. (2010). *Dismantling contemporary deficit thinking.* New York, NY: Routledge.

Valenzuela, A. (1999). *Subtractive schooling: U.S.-Mexican youth and the politics of caring.* Albany: State University of New York Press.

Valenzuela, A. (Ed.). (2004). *Leaving children behind: How "Texas-style" accountability fails Latino youth.* Albany: State University of New York Press.

Wade, S. E., Fauske, J. R., & Thompson, A. (2008). Prospective teachers' problem solving in online peer-led dialogues. *American Educational Research Journal, 45,* 398–442.

Warikoo, N., & Carter, P. (2009). Cultural explanations for racial and ethnic stratification in academic achievement: A call for a new and improved theory. *Review of Educational Research, 79,* 366–394.

Warren, K. (1998). Educating students for social justice in service learning. *Journal of Experiential Education, 21*(3), 134–139.

Weiler, K. (1991). Freire and a feminist pedagogy of difference. *Harvard Educational Review, 61,* 449–474.

Woodson, C. G. (2006). *The miseducation of the Negro.* San Diego, CA: Book Tree.

Ybarra, R. (2000). Latino students and Anglo-mainstream instructors: A study of classroom communication. *Journal of College Student Retention, 2,* 161–171.

Yosso, T. (2005). Whose culture has capital? A critical race theory discussion of community cultural wealth. *Race, Ethnicity and Education, 81,* 69–91.

Chapter 5

Equity Issues in Parental and Community Involvement in Schools: What Teacher Educators Need to Know

Patricia Baquedano-López
Rebecca Anne Alexander
Sera J. Hernandez
University of California, Berkeley

In this chapter, we examine the literature on parental involvement highlighting the equity issues that it raises in educational practice. Like so many educators and researchers, we are concerned with approaches to parental involvement that construct restricted roles for parents in the education of their children. These approaches often miss the multiple ways nondominant parents participate in their children's education because they do not correspond to normative understandings of parental involvement in schools (Barton, Drake, Perez, St. Louis, & George, 2004). Moreover, these framings restrict the ways in which parents from nondominant backgrounds can be productive social actors who can shape and influence schools and other social institutions. A great deal of general educational policy on parent involvement draws on Epstein's (1992, 1995) theory and typologies where a set of overlapping spheres of influence locate the student among three major contexts—the family, the school, and the community—which operate optimally when their goals, missions, and responsibilities overlap. Epstein's (1992) *Six Types of Involvement* framework provides a variety of practices of partnership, including the following strategies for involvement: assisting with parenting, communicating with parents, organizing volunteering activities for parents, involving parents in learning at home activities (such as homework), including parents in decision making, and collaborating with community. This perspective, however, can foster individualistic and school-centric approaches (see Warren, Hong, Rubin, & Uy, 2009). We argue

Review of Research in Education
March 2013, Vol. 37, pp. 149-182
DOI: 10.3102/0091732X12459718
© 2013 AERA. http://rre.aera.net

that this is even more problematic when school goals are largely based on White and middle-class values and expectations. Others question the model's inattention to power relations between educational stakeholders, which often position parents as passive or complacent, and call for an expansion of the notion of involvement (S. Auerbach, 2007; Barton et al., 2004; Fine, 1993; Galindo & Medina, 2009). We argue that although conceptually useful, these typologies still reflect a restricted vision of partnership centered on the school's agenda. We note that these typologies do not engage the intersections of race, class, and immigration, which are relevant to the experiences of many parents from nondominant backgrounds. Our view of parent involvement considers parents as agents who can intervene and advocate on behalf of their children, and who can make adaptations and resist barriers to education (see also Hidalgo, 1998). Our review of the literature indicates that parental participation in schools is strongly shaped by perceptions of parents' background and of the roles expected of them by school administrators and teachers and by the organizations (whether local or federal) that fund family literacy and parent involvement programs (S. Auerbach, 2002; Barton et al., 2004; Vincent, 2001). To be sure, these perceptions affect all parents, but the negative equity outcomes of these beliefs and practices particularly affect parents from nondominant backgrounds. Moreover, deficit approaches about students and families who are not from the dominant majority have constructed them as lacking and in need of support (see Valencia, 1991, 2011), reinforcing a view of dependency on school goals. We hope that the literature we review in this chapter helps expand notions of parent involvement and of parents from nondominant groups as productive and engaged participants in communities and schools.

We begin our chapter with a brief historical overview of approaches to parent involvement and the ways in which *neodeficit* discourses on parents permeate current education reform efforts. Next, we address how inequities related to race, class, and immigration shape and are shaped by parent involvement programs, practices, and ideologies. Finally, we discuss empowerment approaches to parental involvement and how these are situated in a broader decolonial struggle for transformative praxis that reframes deficit approaches to parents from nondominant backgrounds.

THE DISCOURSE ON PARENTS: DEFICIT, PROBLEMS, AND REMEDIES

U.S. policy has continuously regulated the parent–school relationship through a normalizing perspective based on middle-class values backed by a century of developmental science focusing on family settings exemplifying those values (Kainz & Aikens, 2007). This normalized view of family does not take into account the complexity of family arrangements and their economic organization, which often negatively affect parents of color (Collins, 1990). The first policy effort that explicitly considered the need for children to be educated away from the home environment was the Civilization Fund Act of 1819, a policy created to provide opportunities for the "improvement" of Native Americans through education and assimilation into the mainstream of society. This led to the creation of boarding schools in the late 1800s located away from reservations (and from the perceived negative influence of the home) where students were forced to learn English and were discouraged from speaking their home languages (Spring, 2001). Much has also been written on the "Americanization" programs at the turn of the 20th century aimed to inculcate Mexican immigrants with the values of American society (see G. González, 1997). These programs, spurred by perceptions of the "Mexican problem" and the passing of the Home Teacher Act of 1915, placed teachers into the students' homes who could then directly instruct parents, and explicitly mothers, on a wide range of practices, from personal hygiene to principles of American governance and citizenship (G. Sánchez, 1984).

The development of parental involvement as a remedy for "problem" minority populations (and for women in particular) was evident at a much broader scale in President Lyndon B. Johnson's *War on Poverty*. Secretary of Labor D. P. Moynihan's report on the African American family argued that in the face of male job loss, the structure of African American families would disintegrate, leading to unemployment and poverty, a cycle of welfare dependency, and the proliferation of single-mother households (Moynihan, 1965). This report turned national attention to the locus of families, and of families of color more specifically, where the perceived gaps in the country's economic stability were to be found. To remediate this situation, a set of federally funded programs were developed, including the Elementary and Secondary Education Act (ESEA) of 1965, and its provision for Head Start and Title I programs. The establishment of Head Start programs, which led to the transition of young children from poor families into federally sponsored day care centers, like many of these early social programs of the Johnson era, highlighted the earlier message underlying the institution of boarding schools for Native American children and youth; that the home (and by extension the minority parent) was not effective to ensure the well-being of children.

These earlier deficit framings of minority parents, coupled with the documentation of the academic performance of minority children through national testing and achievement reports, contributed to neoconservative discourses of a "crisis" in public education (Berliner & Biddle, 1995). This crisis has been framed as a failure of American schools to prepare students to successfully compete internationally as reported in *A Nation at Risk*, a White House document released in 1983 during the Reagan administration that compared standardized test results to achievement results from previous decades. Although some argued the decline was an indication of our failing schools, the report by Coleman (1991) commissioned by the U.S. Department of Education blamed the loss of parents' interest in the education of their children, which he traced to mothers who were leaving the home and joining the labor force. These yearnings for the imagined golden years of the nation, where merit-based rewards, good schools, and the nuclear family were at the core of American values, have influenced many efforts to homogenize diverse student populations in the late 1980s and 1990s through policies and measures such as the elimination of bilingual education and the perceived unfair advantages of affirmative action programs (Gutiérrez, Baquedano-López, & Alvarez, 2000; see also Gándara & Contreras, 2009). This rhetoric has also shaped the context in which the Title I provisions of the ESEA have been expanded with a new language of partnership between parents and schools (Mapp, 2012); yet these new "partnerships" continue to frame parents as problems.

The 2001 reauthorization of the Elementary and Secondary Education Act under the No Child Left Behind (NCLB) Act of 2001 attempted to bridge homes and schools through a variety of mechanisms that aimed to partner with families and communities. This piece of legislation suggested that schools were not doing enough to outreach and *engage* parents from culturally and linguistically diverse backgrounds. Thus, a core position of federal education policy is that the engagement of parents and families in their children's education has the transformative potential to affect students' academic achievement beyond any other type of education reform. This shift in the policy discourse from parent involvement to family engagement illustrates, at least in its rhetoric, an expanded view of the family's role in education (Mapp, 2012). But when parent involvement is positioned as a necessary condition of academic success, it becomes a "common sense" notion (Kainz & Aikens, 2007) that shifts a critical lens away from the social injustices affecting families of color to the perception that parents are uninvolved and, as such, do not deserve quality schooling (Nakagawa, 2000). Within this frame, the essence of the problem resides not in the structure of schools but in the ways in which parents fail at their responsibility to educate their children.

In what follows we identify and discuss a set of tropes that define schools' relationships to parents and which we think are illustrative of the unresolved tensions created by unequal distribution of resources and structural power relations among educational stakeholders. These tropes construct particular roles that also correspond to a set of educational approaches that advance a tone of deficit, urgency, and remedy when they involve parents of nondominant students. We think that an examination of these tropes could be useful for teachers and other professionals to critically assess the goals of programs and initiatives and the effects that they might have in creating inclusive or dismissive roles for parents. Although "antideficit rhetoric" is commonplace in contemporary parent involvement program models (e.g., the ubiquitous use of a discourse of "strengths"), E. Auerbach (1995) warns that this shift may operate as a neodeficit ideology in which even "strength-based" program models could continue to function within a deficit framework.

Briefly, the trope of "Parents as Problems" can be traced to government policies that aim to protect students and aid teachers in having the most control in the education of young students. The trope of "Parents as First Teachers," while seemingly benign in its recognition of the claim that parents are the preeminent socializing agents in a child's life, presents pedagogical substitutions aimed at deemphasizing parental roles through the expansion of normative practices into the home. The discourse of "Parents as Learners" challenges parents' knowledge base and community wisdom by constructing the image of stultified adults in need of guidance (this is a discourse that appears frequently in discussions of immigrant parents who are speakers of languages other than English). In the wake of the educational reform movements of the late 1990s, the theme of "Parents as Partners" became popular and was reinforced through Title I modifications. We also discuss the "Parents as Choosers and Consumers" trope, which is tied to reform efforts that support school choice. We discuss each of these tropes below and the programs that construct and support them.

Parents as First Teachers: Early Learning Programs for Ages 0–5

The home–school relationship begins when a child enters preschool or kindergarten. The underlying assumption behind the support of the first contact between the home and the school is the need for a strong educational experience to ensue. To support this, federally funded early intervention programs prescribe a set of pedagogical practices that low-income parents are to implement as early as the birth of a child. As their children's "first teachers," parents are expected to prepare their children for academic success from the ages of 0 to 5, a time period that is critical to cognitive growth. In the 1990s, President Clinton signed into law national education goals, *Goals 2000* (U.S. Congress, 1994), which included the goal that "All children in America will start school ready to learn" (Goal 1). Although dismantled by the NCLB Act, the National Education Goals Panel (1993) provided objectives in their early childhood report that have largely influenced early childhood intervention programs today, specifically around school readiness. One key goal stated: "Every parent in the United States will be a child's first teacher and devote time each day to helping his or her preschool child learn. To accomplish this, parents should have access to the training and support they need" (The National Education Goals section, Goal 1, Objective 2). President Bush's early childhood education initiative *Good Start, Grow Smart* (U.S. Department of Education, 2002) targeted early childhood education for low-income families through improving federally funded programs such as Head Start, Title I Preschool, and Early Reading First. More recently, the Obama administration announced a $500 million Race to the Top—Early Learning Challenge as an incentive for states to improve the quality of early childhood learning programs "to reduce crime, strengthen national security, and boost U.S. competitiveness" and to "close the school readiness gap" (U.S. Department of Education, 2011). Consequently, early childhood learning programs dictate parent involvement practices for low-income families based on the expectation that (a) parents need interventions that will assist them in teaching their children in ways aligned with school and (b) education begins at birth. These practices, especially for nondominant families, are not without consequence in that they also introduce a set of cultural practices from the dominant community at the risk of subtractive schooling (Valenzuela, 1999) and reductive literacy practices.

Parents as Learners: Family Literacy Programs

The Workforce Investment Act, ESEA, and the Head Start Act promote family literacy programs that are very popular (although top-down) and which are designed to address the home–school connection for districts and schools with culturally and linguistically diverse populations. In terms of their stated goals, these programs aim to mediate incongruences between home and school literacies (Caspe, 2003; Rodríguez-Brown, 2009). Most of these family literacy models target home literacy practices, such as intergenerational literacy programs (Gadsden, 1994) where parents are encouraged to read to their children or listen to their children read. Family literacy programs differ, however, in their understanding of the social, cultural, and political aspects of language and literacy use. In many cases deficit assumptions about nondominant families and their cultural practices tend to drive the purpose, design, and practices of these interventions (Valdés, 1996; Whitehouse & Colvin, 2001).

Family literacy program models thus appear to be influenced by two dominant views of literacy: (a) The decontextualized perspective that (all) families need help in gaining the necessary tools to assist their children with school and (b) the contextualized perspective that recognizes home and community knowledge and experiences (Gadsden, 1994). The first perspective subscribes to the notion that parents' literacy practices are directly correlated with children's motivation around literacy use, and therefore programs should work toward educating families about best school literacy practices. The second viewpoint acknowledges the power of literacy to liberate and empower children and their parents (Delgado-Gaitan, 1990; Freire, 1973), which aligns with productive, strength-building models of family literacy that we review later in the chapter. This viewpoint considers parents as bearers of knowledge, but the extent to which that knowledge is used in literacy activities or in equalizing power relations in schools is not always clear.

Parents as Partners: Partnerships, Contracts, and Compacts

The language written in the federal guidelines for implementing parent engagement programs, procedures, and practices is centered on the idea of partnering with families. The "Parents as Partners" discourse largely influences the ways in which districts and schools perceive parents and their role in their children's education. Parent involvement provisions of Title I require that schools share information with parents on school programs, academic standards, and assessments in order for parents to be more "knowledgeable partners" (Epstein & Hollifield, 1996). One way schools attempt to partner with families is through the use of School–Family Compacts mandated by Title I to outline how families, school staff, and students will share responsibility for improved student academic achievement (U.S. Department of Education, 1996). This practice, however, still constructs a lack of parent involvement as endemic and as something that schools must address to get parents on board with their agenda, particularly on reform efforts. The notion of partnership does not always clearly communicate the kinds of interactions and relationships with families that would include "meaningful consultation, collaboration, and shared responsibility" (U.S. Department of Education, 1996). Additionally, a federal report revealed that less than one third of the states were in compliance with the use of School–Family Compacts and other Title I program components for parent involvement (Stevenson & Laster, 2008). More troublesome is the general language of the law that relegates parent responsibility to monitoring attendance, homework completion, and TV watching, which limits a parent's role to one of surveillance, or "compliance officer or watchdog of the school system" (Mapp, 2012, p. 17). This misses the policy goal of shared responsibility and partnership. The school compacts function similarly to the Parent–School Contracts used by many charter schools, although one study documented how contracts were more a mechanism for compliance rather than inclusion, promising little beyond monitoring parents or using them as part of family selectivity criteria (Becker, Nakagawa, & Corwin, 1997).

Parents as Choosers and Consumers: School Choice

Whereas "school choice" typically refers to a somewhat marginal movement for specific educational reforms (i.e., vouchers), the notion of "parent choice" and the discourses that frame parents as choosers have been institutionalized into mainstream educational reform efforts, including NCLB (DeBray-Pelot, Lubienski, & Scott, 2007) in the form of the "opt out" option. This option enables parents to transfer their children from low performing schools and use reporting requirements designed to make parents "informed consumers." The discourse of school choice emphasizes parents' market-based choices between schools: public versus private school (Goldring & Phillips, 2008), school locations, choice among public schools (where available), selecting public choice options (such as vouchers/charters/magnets), and NCLB's "opt out" option (Ben-Porath, 2009; J. T. Scott, 2005; Minow, 2010). Parents also often make choices about course placements, special education services, parenting training, language use, testing, family survival, and their own form of engagement with activities to influence their children's school and education. All these choices are constrained by structural inequalities, but the "parent as chooser" discourse narrows the notion of involvement to an individual market-based selection between available options.

Debray-Pelot et al. (2007) identify two primary ideologies of "parent choice" movements—neoconservative and neoliberal. "Choice," they argue, emerged out of conservative think-tanks that retain substantial liberal support through a civil rights framing. Neoconservative models are structured around ideas such as parent control and local control, whereas neoliberal ideologies are grounded in market-based principles and an emphasis on rolling back bureaucracy and creating greater freedom. There have also been progressive choice programs, such as those in Seattle, to desegregate through "controlled choice" aimed at reducing inequality between schools (Fuller & Emore, 1996; J. T. Scott, 2005). These progressive programs, which take race (among other factors) into account in placing students, have been undermined by the colorblind choice discourses espoused in the case of Parents Involved in Community Schools (PICS; Dixson, 2011). As Dixson argues, "choice" discourses primarily give parents of color a *forced* choice in that the mechanisms of choice create a hierarchical system of inequitable distribution that harms nondominant families when that choice does not contest neighborhood segregation, racialized tracking, or inequitable resource/opportunity provisions, and existing systems of power harmful to nondominant peoples (e.g., capitalism, nationalism, patriarchy, coloniality, or Eurocentric rationality). Paradoxically, with the decision in PICS, Minow (2010) notes that the limitation on districts' ability to use race as a means to promote integration constitutes the only restriction on parent choice programs. It is in this way that the "parent as chooser" notion is also based on and enacts a fundamentally colorblind discourse that constrains parent involvement and neglects power relations.

We have presented in this section tropes that frame parental and community involvement in education research and practice. We do so to underscore that while policies and practices of parent involvement may even change in response to educational and community movements that seek a better integration among stakeholders in education, schools and teachers remain largely the uncontested bearers of privileged knowledge. In the next section we draw attention to questions of race, class, and immigration status as a set of equity issues at the core of parent and community involvement discourses and practices. These issues are recursive and interrelated and require engagement in both local and broader social and political contexts of educational practice.

KEY EQUITY ISSUES IN PARENT AND COMMUNITY INVOLVEMENT: RACE, CLASS, AND IMMIGRATION

Despite the creation of policies that have generated varying mechanisms to incorporate nondominant students and their families in our public school system, deep inequities persist that are reflected in educational achievement data of nondominant students. As Ladson-Billings (2006) has reminded us, the achievement gap is not the cause of inequalities in our society; instead, we must recognize the history of our country, which ensured through slavery and policies of exclusion the advancement of some but left far too many students of color and their families in economically disadvantaged positions. As Ladson-Billings notes, to seriously begin to understand today's achievement gap, we must tally the educational debt we owe to those left behind by economic disparities and racial oppression. We must also understand how such inequality is maintained in the present. As we explained in the previous section, policies that carry a deficit approach toward nondominant parents still construct them as unfit for parental roles. Although there are a number of factors that coalesce around the discourse and practice of parental and community involvement in the education of nondominant students in schools, in this chapter we consider race, class, and immigration the three equity issues that have the most impact in constructing relations among educational stakeholders and parents from nondominant groups.[1] First, we address the ways in which race continues to shape inequities in parent involvement. To accomplish this we draw on research that advances critical race perspectives (Darder & Torres, 2004; Goldberg, 2002; Ladson-Billings & Tate, 1995), which elaborate on the idea that race is a social construct and a system of social control of resources, access, and power that has real effects on people and institutions (Bonilla-Silva, 2003; Omi & Winant, 1994).[2] We next discuss class as a major determinant of educational opportunity and social capital. Finally, we examine the ways that the immigration statuses of parents (and students) from nondominant backgrounds influence parent and community involvement in schools.

Race

Much of the literature on parent involvement that explores questions of racial inequality or disparity continues to treat race as a natural or essentialized factor (often explanatory) that attributes to racialized parents and their children negative developmental or moral characteristics (e.g., lack of involvement or caring). Although some authors have argued for separate models to determine differences across racial groups (C. E. Cooper, Crosnoe, Suizzo, & Pituch, 2010; Fan, Williams, & Wolters, 2011), the analysis of the structural and institutional characteristics (i.e., racisms) that shape parents' and students' experiences and involvement with schools can still be further explored. Ryan, Casas, Kelly-Vance, Ryalls, and Nero (2010) critique the tendency of much research to focus on parents as a limited construct that ignores the role of "significant others" such as siblings and the extended community, and thus negates the complexity of families. They also problematize the ways researchers impute differences to ethnicity that imply causal relationships and "operationalize" culture in problematic ways, while still ignoring the characteristics of the dominant culture. The findings of their study measuring White and Latino orientations toward school (notwithstanding the potentially essentializing comparison) contradict many dominant assumptions by asserting that Latino parents place greater value on academic achievement than do White parents. They argue that White parents place greater value on *social* achievement instead. They also emphasize the role of "cultural orientation," indicating that the children of Latino parents who are more oriented toward Latino culture have stronger Spanish-language skills, whereas those who are more oriented toward White culture have stronger English-language skills.[3] They note that a focus on parent involvement as a key factor in the racial achievement gap is misguided and diverts resources and attention away from other important aspects of schools that affect student outcomes and experiences.

Williams and Sanchez (2011) point to the obstacles that poor African American families face in inner-city schools. They identify four critical factors limiting these parents' involvement: (a) time poverty, (b) lack of access, (c) lack of financial resources, and (d) lack of awareness. Time poverty (Newman & Chin, 2003) refers to a family's lack of time due to other commitments; access refers to illness and disability (William & Sanchez, 2011, note that poor parents are twice as likely to have difficulty with physical activity) as well as the timing of school events; finances refer to the very limited resources of some inner-city parents and the burden even seemingly incidental costs can impose; last, awareness may be impeded by traditional school-communication strategies such as sending papers home with children, which may not be effective means of communication between school and home. In this sense, what some parents of color experience as institutional barriers constitute channels of access for many White parents (Burton, Bonilla-Silva, Ray, Buckelew, & Freeman, 2010). Lareau and Horvat (1999) report on a study of school–home relations across class statuses showing how particular forms of social capital used by low-income African American parents were rejected by school personnel who dismissed critique and only accepted praise. In contrast, White parents, who began their relationships with the school from a more trusting stance (given also their less-problematic framings in the history of U.S. education) were welcomed to classrooms. Middle-class African American parents were able to negotiate their relationships with teachers by hiding concerns about racial discrimination while staying actively involved and alert. Howard and Reynolds (2008) urge us to consider the variability within middle-class African American parents; in spite of their economic position, some parents still experience racist attitudes as they advocate for their children and other parents may be reluctant to engage in the already set structures of predominantly White middle-class school settings.

Gartrell-Nadine (1995) found that African American parents were tracked into programs outside of the central operation of the school (such as African American PTAs), but the school's central organizing bodies (the general PTA) remained part of the dominant group at school. White parents may also exert positions of dominance in parent organizing spaces (Posey, 2012). Traditional Parent Involvement Structures (TPIS), such as Back-to-School Night and the Parent Teacher Association, have been criticized as insufficient ways to engage families of color (S. Auerbach, 2009). Although there have been important research efforts to recognize parental agency (Barton et al., 2004) and nontraditional parent involvement practices, they may still fail to problematize White, middle-class behavior norms (C. W. Cooper, 2009) inherent in TPIS. It may be that precisely those forms of parental involvement that are most important to the ability of young people to maintain positive identities and negotiate school life from marginalized positions are those that contrast jarringly with schools' expectations of parents.

Burton et el. (2010) point to literature demonstrating that many African American parents from all class backgrounds are engaged in the work of "racial socialization" (Peters, 1985), psychologically preparing their children for life in a racialized society. They note that research (citing Constantine & Blackmon, 2002; L. D. Scott, 2003, among others) has demonstrated how these practices also have a strong positive influence on students' academic outcomes. Drawing on CRT frameworks, Reynolds (2010) points to the important role African American parents play in identifying, deflecting, clarifying, and teaching strategies to resist racism and racial microaggressions in the classroom (see also Chapman, 2007). Carter (2008) argues that collective critical race work is important for parents of color as their enhanced capacity to positively self-identify and create group attachment will enable them to more effectively contest racism in schools and nurture critical understandings in their children. C. W. Cooper (2009) has also pointed to the ways in which collective responsibility for children's and the community's well being is leveraged through practices of "othermothering" (caring collectively for children) and legacies of protest in African American communities. It is also important to understand the processes through which dominant parents may socialize racially dominant students to enact and/or defend positions of racial domination such as White privilege and supremacy (Doane & Bonilla-Silva, 2003). These perspectives point to the fact that racisms are multiple and complex and that they intersect with other forms of oppressive structures (Burton et al., 2010; Collins, 1990; L. T. Smith, 1999).

Last, we address reports in the literature on the multiple forms of surveillance and discipline to which parents of color are disproportionately subjected both inside and outside of schools (Alexander, 2010; Gilmore, 2007). The impact of state systems from child protective services (CPS; Ong, 2003; Ferguson, 2001; Roberts, 2002), to the prison system (Duncan, 2000; Roberts, 2004; Romero, 2000–2001; Valdez, Fitzhorn, Matsumoto, & Emslie, 2012), to Immigration and Customs Enforcement (ICE; Rogers, Saunders, Terriquez, & Velez, 2008) on the lives of many families of color is substantial and complex. Ferguson (2001) describes an African American mother's despair after seeing her authority undermined when CPS intervened as she was physically disciplining her child for having run away. While not endorsing the form of discipline, Ferguson questions the ways in which schools and other state institutions may undermine parents' discipline while simultaneously criminalizing them and their children. Ong (2003), similarly, examines the complex ways in which multiple state agencies intervene in the lives of Cambodian refugee families in a "complex mix of labeling, disciplining and regulating technologies" (p. 190) that reshapes their relationships with their children and their roles as parents. These multiple service and surveillance industries with which schools might intersect also racially constitute the relationship between parents and schools.

Class

Critical to discussions of parent and community involvement in schools is the impact of class status on academic achievement and opportunity. Anyon (2005) argues that poverty continues to be concentrated in urban centers, affecting primarily urban schools in levels dramatically similar to those in 1959, the time of the nation's War on Poverty. Lareau (2000) details the school experiences of working-class and upper-middle-class parents to highlight the pivotal role of social class in parent involvement. She examines how school structures and practices are aligned with middle-class culture and how precisely through serving the middle-class agenda, schools privilege upper-middle-class parents who draw on their own social assets or cultural capital (Bourdieu, 1977) to secure advantages over other people's children. The continued exclusion of the social and cultural resources of working-class parents magnifies the stratification of parent involvement practices and increases the educational inequities parent involvement policies are purportedly working to neutralize. Brantlinger's (2003) study of middle-class families lends support to the notion that schools are shaped by intentional class dominance. Thus, social class is reproduced through the securing of advantage and privilege for one's own children. By disregarding educational inequities affecting others, many middle-class parents come to understand school success as a consequence of their own superiority or meritocracy.

Lewis and Forman (2002) examine and compare the involvement of mostly White upper-middle-class parents at their neighborhood school to that of low-income African American and Latino parents at an alternative school in a low-income neighborhood. Drawing on their ethnographic work, they argue that social class relationships between parents and teachers were critical in structuring relationships and involvement, but not in the ways the literature would predict. They describe strained relationships between teachers and parents at the upper-middle-class school that included teachers hiding from parents and parents employing strict regulation and decision-making power over micro-details such as teacher supply budgets. They also note that teachers felt a sense of being under surveillance, judged, and disrespected. In contrast, they describe overwhelmingly positive relationships between parents and teachers at the alternative school marked by a sense of mutual interdependence, collective interest in the well-being of the children, and an open, honest, and collaborative relationship among the entire school staff as well as parents. They conclude that mutual respect was facilitated by both strong leadership and class relationships (parents being of similar or lesser social class than the teachers) at the school.

Posey (2009, 2012) examines the shifting politics of race and class as middle-class parents return their children to a neighborhood school previously attended primarily by families of color. She explores how the gentrification of the school created important opportunities including an infusion of economic resources, but also intense feelings of displacement, loss of control, and a not-entirely welcomed cultural shift for families of color. She elaborates on how White parents networked with one another to bring friends and allies into the school under the rubric of investing in the neighborhood and transforming the school—something they felt required a critical mass of (mostly White) middle-class parents. This is an important line of research examining the dynamics involving the return of White middle-class parents to urban schools, a sort of "indispensable parent" who undoes the harm of White flight and whose aim is to "save" the failing poor school. McGrath and Kuriloff's (1999) study of a diverse suburban school district in the U.S. northeast revealed the negative impact White upper-middle-class mothers' school involvement had on the involvement of working-class and middle-class African American mothers in the same schools. Besides differential access to schools due to class mobility, White mothers' passive exclusion of nondominant parents from home and school associations, as well as the promotion of their own self-interests (e.g., tracking), further marginalized the African American community present in the schools. These are lucid examples of how politically powerful parents in public schools expect control over their children's education, even at the expense of a quality education for nondominant students in the same schools. As Wells and Oakes (1996) explain, "Powerful parents demand something in return for their commitment to public education—for keeping their children in public schools, as opposed to fleeing to the private schools that many could afford" (p. 139). Affluent parents of successful students are less concerned that all children have access to a quality education and are more concerned that their own children have access to the best type of instruction, are tracked in Advanced Placement and Gifted and Talented Programs, and are recognized with strong letter grades and awards for their academic success (Kohn, 1998). This demand for differentiation (Wells & Oakes, 1996) or advocacy for tracking (McGrath & Kuriloff, 1999) is a type of parent involvement that can be detrimental to students and schools. As Casanova (1996) warns of "controlling parents," they also deprofessionalize teachers and exacerbate the unequal treatment of all parents in schools further stratifying the involved and uninvolved parent along race and class lines.

Immigration

Despite a "generous" period toward immigrant students and their families during the civil rights period, schools have not always served well the needs of immigrant students and their families (Gándara et al., 2010). They have often demanded adherence to an educational system that ignores the knowledge base that multicultural and multilingual families bring and often fails to recognize the gravity of the decisions made by immigrant parents to border-cross (Villenas & Deyhle, 1999) and, in the case of those who are undocumented, to remain "uninvolved" in the particular ways undocumented parents are forced to remain, in order to secure educational opportunities for their children (Rogers et al., 2008). And although theories of immigration have traditionally focused on integration (Alba & Nee, 1997) and adaptation (Zhou & Banston, 1998) into U.S. society, as we have discussed, immigrants have been either excluded from schooling or forcefully Americanized, raising the social distance between family and school (Moll & Ruiz, 2002). The tendency for federal and state educational policies to stress Anglo-conformity is evident in programs such as family literacy interventions that target Latino immigrant parents (Valdés, 1996). These family literacy efforts work to socialize, if not indoctrinate, immigrant families into new linguistic and cultural ways of being. The rapid shift into mainstream culture has serious intergenerational effects. Portes and Rumbaut (1996, 2001a) report in their Children of Immigrants Longitudinal Study that, although parents held high educational expectations of their children, they had to contend with a widening intergenerational gap brought about by the loss of the home language by the younger generations. Thus, the dynamics of immigration and schooling are complex and potentially subtractive and linguistically and educationally restrictive.

Offering an alternative explanation to linear theories of assimilation, Louie (2006) explores the implications of transnational frames of reference on second-generation Chinese and Dominican students, comparing their perspectives on their own educational trajectories. Her finding that Chinese students do not believe they are faring well in school whereas Dominican students believe that they are faring quite well seems "counterintuitive" in light of their actual social and economic statuses where Asian students fare economically better than Dominican students. But Louie urges us to consider the multiple frames of reference needed to push past linear theories of assimilation, given that transnational and ethnic/panethnic frames inform identity formation, education, and mobility of the immigrant second-generation. In earlier work, Louie (2005) discusses "parental sacrifices" of the first generation as reported in interviews with college students and their parents. Parents pointed out that despite having professional or higher level of education they still needed to take on service jobs to support their children. We note that this work also highlights the differential impact that immigration policies, for example H1B visa permits (those that allow temporary employment in specialty occupations), have on the educational opportunities of 1.5- (those arriving to the United States in their teens) and second-generation immigrant students.

There have been important research efforts to identify knowledge and practices in immigrant communities traditionally left out by school institutions, such as the ways families engage in complex practices of translation (Orellana, Reynolds, Dorner, & Meza, 2003; Valdés, 2003; Zentella, 1997). Notably there has been a wealth of literature addressing and expanding on the notion of engaged social networks in the *funds of knowledge* approach to bridging home and school contexts of immigrant families (N. González, Moll, & Amanti, 2005; Moll, Amanti, Neff, & González, 1992). This literature also reports an increased focus on parental agency in family–school connections (McClain, 2010) that bridges relationships between immigrant families and schools (Dryden-Peterson, 2010; N. González, 2005; Valenzuela, 1999).

Student perspectives of their own parents' involvement in their education are not always found in the literature. One exception is that of Suárez-Orozco et al. (2008), who report on the results of the Longitudinal Immigrant Student Adaptation Study, which indicates that immigrant youth believe that their parents have very high expectations for their academic performance. While these assessments, taken from interviews and survey questionnaires, matched parents' reported expectations of their children's education, the teachers in the Suárez et al. study invariably reported that immigrant parents did not care about or express an interest in their children's education. Students also expressed that they felt that teachers or schools had high educational expectations of them (see also Valenzuela, 1999). Such wide, differing views of expected outcomes of education support the notion that there continue to be negative expectations about immigrant parents' involvement in their children's education, even when the children themselves witness otherwise.

Olsen (2009) considers immigrant education a contemporary battleground for U.S. ideological struggles, which she sees as shaped by concerns of "immigration, language rights, educational equity, and access for racial, cultural, and national minority groups, and also by issues relating to national security and foreign policy" (p. 818). Using as an example California's battle over bilingual education through Proposition 227 in 1998 (a ballot initiative that required instruction to be conducted in English), Olsen (2009) highlights the role of organizing in advocating for the educational access and equity of immigrant education. She examines how a statewide coalition for English Learners (Californians Together) was able to mediate the ramifications of public policies and anti-immigrant campaigns that focus on exclusion and are based on centralized educational control. Language policies remind us of how limited parental choice is for immigrant parents who are often not eligible to vote on measures that impact the education of their own children. In this regard, the situation of undocumented families, and their involvement in schools in particular, is important to continue to emphasize. Martínez-Calderón's (2010) study of AB 540[4] students in higher education provides a nuanced view into the experiences of undocumented students and their families negotiating access to school and postsecondary education. The students in her study indicated strong parental support at home, but they also described many of the burdens placed on their parents and barriers they had to overcome. Such burdens included primarily financial duress, fear of the law (and for general safety), as well as conflicts experienced by parents trying to fit the multiple forms of accountability expected from them.

Mangual Figueroa (2011) examines the role of citizenship status among mixed-status Mexican families as they interact around schoolwork, in particular, homework. Her ethnographic study focuses on parents' and children's perceptions of migratory status and the challenges and opportunities afforded by their varying statuses. She discusses the ways local concerns of schools (that children do their homework and behave properly as a marker of school "citizenship") are read by parents in a broader framework of the politics of legality in this country.[5] In this way Mangual Figueroa warns us of the conflation between the language of the school and the disciplinary power of the state. Moll and Ruiz (2002) have introduced the concept of *educational sovereignty* as an educational stance to counter what they describe as the enduring and disabling pedagogical conditions that immigrant Latino students and their families experience. They propose an educational sovereignty approach that engages the larger historical and unequal social structures underlying public education and aims to make them visible. In this way an integration of existing social and cultural resources across schools, households, and communities can bring about educational and social change that also includes immigrant students and their families as agents of this change.

EMPOWERMENT APPROACHES TO PARENTAL AND COMMUNITY INVOLVEMENT

In this section, we discuss research that addresses the pervasive deficit framings of parental involvement, especially as it concerns the educational experiences of non-dominant students. We include in this section a discussion of three different approaches to empowerment in parent involvement: (a) Freirian (Freire, 1970, 1973) school-based parent organizing, (b) parent community organizing, and (c) home–school connections models based on the funds of knowledge approach. We consider these approaches to be foundational for understanding conceptual shifts in the literature on parental involvement. We also discuss possible limitations of each of these approaches. We hope to advance in this way critical debate on the discourse of empowerment.[6] Finally we examine decolonial approaches to parent and community involvement in education research and practice, and we discuss how we might move closer to new framings of parent involvement.

Freirian School-Based Parent Organizing

Many authors working within a Freirian empowerment framework engage both a critique of mainstream parental involvement and of the notion of *involvement* itself (Borg & Mayo, 2001; Rocha-Schmid, 2010; Torres & Hurtado-Vivas, 2011). These authors problematize at least three aspects of parent "involvement": (a) the school as an authoritative/disciplinary site, (b) deficit perspectives on parents and students, and (c) the divestment of the state in education and public services. The critique of the deficit implications of most "involvement" discourse argues that such programs see "parents and their children as 'objects' for rehabilitation" (Rocha-Schmid, 2010, p. 344; see also Borg & Mayo, 2001). Freirian authors also engage a broader critique that links community "involvement" with neoliberal political practices that attempt to shift state responsibilities onto individuals in ways that reflect the "all pervasive market ideology" in which the parent is in effect the consumer (Borg & Mayo, 2001).

We have been noting the critiques of parent involvement approaches that construct restricted parental roles that do not expand on the knowledge and experience that parents have. Torres and Hurtado-Vivas (2011) critically assess mainstream family literacy programs as, essentially, vehicles for narrow parental roles that include homework production, student surveillance, and the creation of increased burden on parents for the academic failure of their children (and their schools). Drawing on interviews with parents during family literacy projects they conducted in the *colonias*[7] of southern New Mexico and western Texas, they discuss among these burdens the fact that schools do not see parents as parents (but often as schoolteachers), the overburdening of homework, and the privileging of mainstream school literacies and knowledge. They further argue that teachers and administrators often lack the linguistic and cultural literacies to work with parents. In response, the authors propose a move toward political literacy for teachers and school personnel. Furumoto's (2003) discussion of "critical parent involvement" bridges the boundary between family literacy, adult education, and parent organizing. The parents described in this research moved beyond traditional family literacy activities of schoolwork supervision, to include the development of a multicultural institute and brought parents into positions where they were teaching not only one another and their children, but also teachers.

There are a number of researchers concerned with parent organizing and decision making, and prominent among these scholars is Delgado-Gaitan (1993), who reports that relationships among researcher, school personnel, and parents can afford new ways of understanding Latino parent involvement in school. Delgado-Gaitan's (1990) ethnographic study highlights the process of empowerment as experienced by traditionally marginalized families through their collective work. She examines parent participation through school and family literacy practices of 20 focal families and teacher/parent training sessions. The findings from this study, which she shared with families and school personnel, helped organize the Latino parent organization—the Comité de Padres Latinos (COPLA). Delgado-Gaitan argues that parent education programs for Spanish-speaking families need to facilitate understanding of the school system in the United States, done, of course, by regarding Latino parents as producers (and not just consumers) of critical knowledge.

Culturally relevant and empowerment models of family literacy (as opposed to top-down deficit models) strive to affirm diverse family literacy practices and encourage critical consciousness among the participants, families, and educators alike. As Reyes and Torres (2007) report, families can also influence the family literacy curriculum to make it relevant to their lived experiences and to achieve the goal of collective and transformative action that could empower them. Their description of the decolonizing family literacy educator serves as a counternarrative to traditional family literacy models and documents the ideological divide between family literacy programs that colonize families with White middle-class literacy practices and those that use Freirian (Freire, 1973) approaches to literacy that affirm diverse family literacy practices. As they argue, the decolonization of family literacy is thus a step toward reinventing the paradigm and the practices that shape the ways in which ethnically and linguistically diverse families engage with, and transform, notions of public education.

One such approach to family literacy is the *Proyecto de Literatura Infantil*, which is based on the notion that reading is an interactive process for the purpose of human growth (Freire, 1970). Targeting Spanish-speaking families, the program involves monthly evening meetings in which strategically chosen children books are used to prompt dialogue among families. Participants engage in four phases of creative dialogue: (a) descriptive, (b) personal interpretative, (c) critical/multicultural, and (d) creative transformation. Participants produce their own collective books where questions are posed by the parents to further dialogue. Additionally, time is spent reading and responding to stories and poetry created by parents and children in the program. Documented through ethnographic and participatory research (Ada & Zubizarreta, 2001), the premise behind the model is that parents have a wealth of knowledge, including family narratives, to share with their children and which can provide valuable resources for their emotional and social development. This project outlines possibilities for engaged participation of families in schools and does much to set the ground for the types of commitments that can develop into more organized forms of parent action.

Many Frierian approaches also engage families in parent and community organizing. An example of parent organizing is that of the *La Familia* initiative in the San Francisco Bay Area (Jasis & Ordóñez-Jasis, 2004–2005) where parents organized to challenge the way student math and science work were evaluated. These parents were able to influence and create access to upper track classes for historically under-represented Latino students. The authors describe these efforts as both increasing partnership with the school and grassroots democracy. Borg and Mayo (2001) describe a parent-organizing project they codesigned with a middle-class parent at a predominately working-class school in Malta, which offers an interesting perspective on a program not located in the United States. The authors describe a "parent empowerment" project in which, through the use of group dialogue and thematic teaching led by the authors, parents articulated complaints about having little information sent from school to home, having school contained within classroom walls, and experiencing patriarchy (as a school-mom problem), prejudice, and resentment from older teachers who were replaced by parents following a previous teacher strike. The authors expressed some frustration, however, with the limitations of this form of organizing arguing that the school administrators primarily viewed parents as "helpers" and not as the more proactive "adjuncts," and even "subjects" limiting democratic participation. This work points to the fluid nature of collaborative work that even under the best possible conditions, still must respond to local social dynamics as well as historical understandings of the role of parents in education.

Despite their explicit questioning of dominant/mainstream practices and their focus on transformative action, Freirian approaches may also have limitations. One concern is that in the efforts to treat parents as equals, Freirian approaches might elide existing (and real) power dynamics. Rocha-Schmid (2010) argues that despite their best intentions, facilitators (here we add researchers) and teachers engage in relationships of domination with parents, shaping discussions based on their own identities, ideologies, and interests. In her work, she examines the ways teacher-power is articulated through discursive techniques such as requesting attention, prompting, praising, shaping turn taking, framing agreement and disagreement, frequent interruptions, even intonation, and emphasis. While recognizing Freire and Macedo's (1995) insistence that there is no such thing as neutral education and that all educational projects are inherently ideological and invested, Rocha-Schmid (2010) problematizes the role of facilitators in positions of power (the researcher included) that can eventually block transformative action and critique. There is a danger, she cautions, that Freirian-based family literacy programs may do a disservice to parents by deluding them into believing they are actually gaining knowledge that will empower them to engage in advocacy for their children while highly unequal power relations remain in place within the educational system. Similarly, the privileged role of the researcher needs to also be examined in terms of who stands to benefit from the researcher's actions, especially in high-stakes circumstances (Delgado-Gaitan, 1993; Villenas, 1996).

Parent Community Organizing

The role of recent community organizing networks has been a counterbalancing force against federal mandates that place a premium on testing and school performance.

But to change perceptions of parents as leaders who are engaged and concerned with the education of their children offers unique challenges. As Warren et al. (2009) note, "partnership" can become a code word for a one-way approach to supporting schools (their agendas, curricula, and mission). Recognizing the social and cultural distance between homes and schools within many low-income urban school districts, new proposals for a relational approach to parent involvement include identifying community-based organizations to serve as intermediaries between the schools and local families. Warren and colleagues examine community organizing, community development, and community service models that push past traditional involvement paradigms to develop meaningful collaborations between educational stakeholders and to bring about a shift in the culture of schools so that they are better aligned with the families they serve. While each model foregrounds the needs of the community, each has a unique focus: a community service model works to provide full-service schools that offer health services and programs outside of the school day to meet families' most basic needs; a community development model strives to open community-based schools where the focus is on economic revitalization in the community; and a community organizing approach focuses on building parent power to push for social change in schools. In this way, schools can profit from the social capital expertise of community-based organizations and can collaborate with such organizations to develop parent leadership that is authentic and meaningful for the particular community served. One such collaborative, the Texas Industrial Areas Foundation, with a number of Alliance schools affiliated with it, represents one of the country's largest community organizing network/collaborative today (Warren, 2011).

Hong (2011) introduces Chicago's Logan Square Neighborhood Association (LSNA) as an example of parent involvement and community organizing. This collaborative develops parent leaders and works toward transforming neighborhood schools. LSNA offers a variety of educational programs, including the Parent Mentor Program, which strives to build parent power and leadership by offering nondominant parents the opportunity to learn about how schools operate and develop multiple ways of participating in schools. The Association is a grassroots effort to change school culture and schools conditions (e.g., overcrowded schools). Drawing on the work on ecologies of parental engagement (Barton et al., 2004), Hong proposes a three-phase framework that includes (a) induction, (b) integration, and (c) investment to explain parent participation in schools, where parent leaders become well positioned to make positive changes for the community's schools. Hong identifies the dynamic process of parental engagement across settings, contexts, relationships, and levels, with the goals of mutual engagement, relationship building, and shared leadership and power. Hong suggests that by working on broad-based community issues (e.g., affordable housing, immigration reform, health care), community organizing groups facilitate positive home–school interactions and bring a holistic view to educational issues. Although sensitive to the ecological approach to educational transformation, it is important for us to note that there could also be limitations posed by the discourse of equal partners in what is a deeply structured system based on relations of power. We further note that organizing work is an additional burden for all families, but especially for those who are already overextended due to their marginalization in other spheres of society.

Home–School Connections: Funds of Knowledge

The funds of knowledge theoretical and pedagogical paradigm is often invoked and used by educators as a transformative practice in connecting home and school (N. González et al., 1993). In its beginnings, this participatory pedagogy project partnered teachers with a local university to study household knowledge in a largely Mexican working-class community in the U.S. Southwest in efforts to counter deficit perspectives of families and low expectations of nondominant students (Moll et al., 1992). The project's premise rested on an understanding that only through the study of the sociopolitical, historical, and economic context of households could a static view of students' and families' culture be avoided, and as a consequence, the social and intellectual knowledge present in homes be recognized as viable resources to be leveraged in the classroom (Moll et al., 1992). From this perspective, families could be better positioned to have their needs addressed by the school rather than continue to subscribe to the traditional home–school paradigms that strive to quickly assimilate families into the structure and culture of schools while simultaneously stifling or subtracting student social development and academic success. We look to scholars expanding the notion of what constitutes funds of knowledge, such as Mangual Figueroa (2011), who encourages educators to validate students' funds of knowledge beyond carpentry or farming, for example, to include other complex practices, such as border crossing or acquiring documentation papers for immigration status.

The empowerment-based approaches discussed here counteract deficit perspectives by leveraging a powerful critique of educational institutions and articulating the "power of parents" (Olivos, 2006) to become active agents, critics, and transformers of education and schools. We note, however, that these approaches are invariably mediated exchanges with a researcher, a parent trainer/leader, a facilitator, or some other institutional agent that "empowers" parents in order for them to be able to produce change. While clearly different from the historically deficit approaches outlined above, these approaches may unintentionally lend to a different deficit understanding of parents as deficient in empowerment or critical consciousness. This understanding can sometimes detract attention from the structural constraints and institutional forms that constrain parent power and shape educational inequality. It is also possible for these approaches to constitute parents as subjects within an educational system that is still dependent on both their subjugation and their labor (see also Larner, 2003). As Anna Tsing (2004) warns, while the aspiration for universalisms (such as social justice, equality, human rights) serves the needs of those who resist oppression and seek empowerment, they can also serve the needs of those in power. It is thus that this *friction* is a double-bind that "extends the reach of the forms of power [people] protest, even as it gives voice to their anger and hope" (Tsing, 2004, p. 9).

TOWARD DECOLONIZING PRACTICE IN PARENT INVOLVEMENT

We have been referring to change that is brought about when there are explicit actions, whether by researchers, teachers, or parents, to engage a decolonial approach in the relationship between school administrators, teachers, and parents. A decolonial approach seeks to challenge the foundations of Eurocentric thinking that support an agenda of modernity and development (Mignolo, 2010)[8] as this implies that nondominant communities cannot be autonomous or sovereign. As we have been pointing out, educational practices are not free of dominant, White, Eurocentric thinking. Our educational system has been built on a European legacy that to this date returns to a history that redeems colonial practices and promotes success through notions of excellence based on Western values such as individually earned merit, which assumes a level playing field. As we discussed at the start of this chapter, our educational system also reflects a neoliberal approach to education that is built on a "crisis of education" that is still attributed to communities of color. The educational system is thus complicit in resisting change that would destabilize a relation that endorses a "civilizing function" (Césaire, 1956/2010; Spring, 2001). This civilizing function reinforces ideologies of what is considered best for nondominant students and their families and delivers an education that fits them. This approach denies other forms of knowledge and above all, parents' and students' autonomy in decision making. This is precisely what a decolonial approach to education seeks to redefine as education researchers have been arguing (see Cruz, 2001; Delgado Bernal, 1998; Grande, 2004; Spring, 2001; Tuck, 2009; Villenas, 1996, among others). It seeks to redress imbalances and exclusionary actions toward students and parents from nondominant communities.

Fundamentally, a decolonial approach to parent involvement recognizes the need for a change in the economic structures that limit parents' participation and decision making on behalf of their children (see also Lareau, 2000). As such, educational reform efforts operating from a decolonial perspective must also seek to identify the location and redistribution of economic wealth. Above all, decolonizing approaches to parental inclusion in schools by necessity must point out and end all forms of epistemic, psychological, and physical violence as are experienced through silencing, linguicisms, segregation, tracking, and the dehumanizing effects of the stunted academic potentials of youth of color. This work needs to identify and address deeply seated inequities that require social change processes rather than simply trust unilateral policy. This approach also brings forth, importantly, a humanizing project in the creation of new thinking and of knowledgeable subjects (Fanon, 1963). For educators, researchers, and practitioners alike, decolonization involves an open questioning of practices that are complicit in the perpetuation of a state of *ghettoization* and colonization (Paperson, 2010), which works to homogenize through the imposition of dominant knowledge (with its corollaries of exclusion) on curricula and commonsense pedagogical practice (see also Apple & King, 1983; Dewey, 1916/1944; Freire, 1970).

In the remainder of this section, we take as one example of how decolonizing practices might work—a set of Latino parent interventions that promote local or home culture in school activities as part of a project of recentering Latino cultural practices in schools. These interventions may take place within school-based parental programs, such as the one documented by Galindo and Medina (2009). In this study, the authors report on the ways a group of Mexican mothers in a parent education and involvement program appropriated the program's developmental assets to outreach to other members of the school and community (and particularly other Latino parents) through what the authors called the performance of a collective self that centered on cultural expression including translation activities for and by parents and the establishment of a program of art and dance that embodied important historical legacies of the community. The authors explain such actions as the "invisible strategies" that parents mobilize and which can be understood as counternarratives to the discourse on disinterest and disengagement of Latino parents. Similarly, Espinoza-Herold (2007) writes about local knowledge and the cultural legacy of linguistic repertoires effectively used as cultural resources of the home that enrich school-based knowledge (see also C. Sánchez, Plata, Grosso, & Leird, 2010). Examples of cultural appropriation are also evident in learning outside of schools such as those described in Baquedano-López (1997, 2004), who documents Spanish-based religious education classes for primarily Mexican immigrant children and English mainstream classes at Catholic parishes in California. In addition to holding instruction in the home language, teachers, who were in their majority also parents or relatives of children attending these classes, consistently influenced and changed the standard Roman-mandated curriculum. They engaged a liberation theology approach that incorporated Mexican secular events and historical facts of sociopolitical circumstance. These parent-teachers also organized with other religious and community groups for improving their children's access to education especially around bilingual education in public schools.

In an example of parents and families fighting cultural exclusion, Dyrness (2009, 2011) draws on her 3-year participatory research project to discuss the ways in which a group of parents established a new school with a social justice focus during the recent small-school reform movement in northern California. Dyrness describes parents' responses to silencing practices from school officials as key curricular and enrollment decisions began to take place. As she explains, cultural exclusion carried out by teachers against parents and families can rest on notions such as race, class, sex, language, immigrant status, country of origin, and neighborhood of residence. Couched in discourses of social justice and equity in policymaking, school administrators failed to realize that their actions were enacting agendas that were racist and exclusionary. Although at first parents began to be vocal about decision making, they realized that this further marginalized some parents, even through concrete actions such as not including their children in the school they had helped establish. It was not until a participatory research group was formed (which included Dyrness) that a research-based critique of the school administration generated a repositioning of parents as key stakeholders at the school. In addition to a change in roles that parents effectively achieved, the research-based knowledge generated by parents served to counter the established primacy of school-based knowledge and decision making. Dyrness notes that the marginalizing actions by progressive White teachers and administrators are prevalent in an "era of good intentions."

There have also been efforts to recognize parents, families, and communities as having knowledge that can offset the traditional school–home relationship. These efforts include the work on funds of knowledge that identifies and engages knowledge sustained by community networks (Moll et al., 1992), which we have discussed in previous sections of this chapter; the implementation of culturally relevant approaches to education (Gay, 2000; Ladson-Billings, 1994, 1995; C. D. Lee, 1995, 2001); and culturally-based approaches to curricular content, for example, in science learning in the early grades (García & Baquedano-López, 2007; O. Lee & Fradd, 1998). There have also been as well important proactive ways of redefining immigrant students and their families' linguistic and cultural legacies as well as the intellectual labor and cultural brokering they do across social institutions (Farr, 2004, 2006; Guerra, 1998; Orellana, 2009; Valdés, 2003; Zentella, 1997). Such work advances a transformational shift that is necessary to reconceive the location of knowledge and of thinking as heterogeneous and multiple (Tlostanova & Mignolo, 2009).

While this chapter has focused primarily on parental involvement in school, we recognize that this is not the only site where decolonization processes can take place. There are other sectors in society that are already engaging decolonizing practices and which overlap with schools. Rogers and Terriquez (2009) remind us of the role of organized labor in creating organized power for educational reform, and more important, to counter disabling discourses about parents. They identify these discourses as the *cultural logics* that shape how people make sense of schooling. Drawing on focus groups interviews with residents and on interviews with labor and civic leaders in Los Angeles, the authors discuss the logic of scarcity, the logic of merit, and the logic of deficits. The three perspectives make it difficult to understand the ways inequality has more to do with policies and social/economic structures rather than with the characteristics of individual children and their families (especially immigrant families). In other words, these "logics" preclude the possibility of collective reframing of the issues at the bottom of educational opportunity, that is, its political economy. As the authors note, while enough support exists among union members, especially those with young children and those living near major schools, some of the challenges considered in engaging the low-wage service sector unions in educational reform are related to prioritizing educational issues when there are a myriad of competing interests, including those of teacher unions.

Efforts at grassroots mobilization have done much to counter negative perception of parents in schools. The case of the Oakland Small Schools movement is an example of reform oriented, parent-driven actions that challenged the district and state interventions and reorganized them (Lashaw, 2008; Yang, 2004). Fuentes (2009/2010) writes about parent mobilization across racial lines. In the study she carried out, such mobilization first began with individuals organizing within their separate communities and then extending efforts to the large community through three organizing efforts: Parents of Children of African Descent, Berkeley Organizing Congregations for Action, and the Coalition for Equity and Excellence in our Schools. Fuentes examines how the three parent groups, all from nondominant communities, put into practice the notion of learning power in their quest for educational justice. In this way they became more effective organizers by acting on and building their understanding of the social, political, and economic factors underlying school conditions. She reports on four main lessons learned from the parent-initiated community organizing: (a) the importance of positionality, (b) the role of adult allies in youth-led projects, (c) the creation of safe spaces, and (d) the building of trust and relationships. Fuentes (2005) has also noted that a key step in parent organizing around schools is the need for parents and organizations to partner with each other first, before they can partner with schools. She describes how parents had to contend, and in effect, tactically strategize with, the perceptions and discourses around each of the organizations and their members. These perceptions framed one group of parents as angry and too political and another as church-going and nice. These stood in opposition to White parents who were, in a dynamic of *racial triangulation*, considered nonpolitical and neutral concerned parents. By publicly diffusing their actions as coming from "just parents," the parent organizers were able to co-opt a passive term and come together to work toward transformation.

CONCLUDING THOUGHTS

We began this chapter with a brief historical synopsis of approaches to parent involvement. We discussed the ways in which neodeficit discourses on parents permeate current education reform efforts and generally construct parents as problems. We argued that the tropes of Parents as First Teachers, Parents as Learners, Parents as Partners, and Parents as Choosers and Consumers find their counterpart in government policies on education and reflect deeply held beliefs about parental roles; these roles are restrictive for parents from nondominant groups but may provide an advantage to White middle-class parents. In this regard, there is a need to broaden the nuclear family model to include communities of support that include family members and community resources. We also discussed the ways in which inequities in parent involvement programs and practices in schools are related to race, class, and immigration. Typical parental involvement practices often marginalize lower-income and racial minority parents while creating pathways of access for White and middle-class parents. The important forms of education, socialization, and advocacy that nondominant parents do engage in are often not only disregarded but sometimes met with hostility by school leaders who interpret them as threatening or too critical. Families' lives are deeply shaped by racial, class, and migrant inequality but schools often fail to acknowledge or understand this, and thus participate in these inequities, embracing deficit perspectives instead.

In the final sections of our chapter, we examined empowerment approaches to parental involvement that are addressing more directly the question of power between school leadership and parent involvement. We discussed the ways in which community involvement efforts counterbalance federal mandates that disadvantage nondominant students, such as testing and school performance indices. These approaches rearticulate the agency of parents as critics and transformers of education to redress economic and other power imbalances that continue to exclude them and their families. We hope that teacher educators find our critique of neoliberal practices useful as they work to elevate the educational achievement of students from nondominant backgrounds. Teachers in particular need to understand the limits of policy efforts to foster parent involvement in school. They also need to be aware of the intersecting dimensions of race, class, and immigration, which are relevant to the educational experiences of many nondominant students. Last, teachers need to be aware of the limits and possibilities of empowerment approaches to parental education. Teachers can make visible and use the knowledge (and power) that parents bring to their interactions with school personnel. They can make imagined possibilities of equity a reality, but they can only do so with a different understanding of the power relationships between parents and schools.

We turn to Motha (2010) as we close this chapter and reintroduce the concept of sovereignty. In an insightful analysis of White South African writer Antjie Krog's (2010) book, *Begging to be Black*, Motha examines one of the book's central themes: Is it possible for Whites to become something other than White in post-apartheid times? In a complex work of literary nonfiction, Krog writes about the possibility of White South Africans decentering the dominant stance to stop seeing with the eyes of colonial legacy and thus engage the necessary processes of un-homing and re-homing and to seek interconnectedness with others. Motha calls for the need to disrupt the sovereign "I" (whether from imperial rule or indigenous right) as a move away from anticolonial longing and toward a postcolonial becoming that enacts not only a postcolonial voice but also a postcolonial listening. To extend Motha's and Krog's ideas to the topic that concerns us here, given that many parental involvement approaches in U.S. schools continue to operate from a sovereign "I," what would it take to correct this stance and adjust to the pressing demands of decolonization? We hope that the work that we reviewed here points us toward trajectories of change as we redefine the parameters of engagement with parents and communities in our schools.

ACKNOWLEDGMENTS

We would like to thank Irenka D. Pareto, Linn Posey-Maddox, Susan Woolley, and members of the Laboratory for the Study of Interaction and Discourse in Educational Research (L-SIDER) at UC Berkeley's Graduate School of Education for helpful comments and intellectual exchange. We thank Mark Warren, Christian Faltis, and an anonymous *RRE* reviewer for their insights and suggestions. Any errors remaining are our own.

NOTES

[1]We are mindful of the intersecting dimension of gender and sexuality in the experience of students and parents from nondominant groups. The review of this work is beyond the scope of this chapter, but the reader is directed to Cruz (2001), McCready (2004), and Woolley (2010). Similarly, disability studies address the persistent barriers that families with children with disabilities experience in social institutions, including schools (Artiles, 2011; R. Smith & Erevelles, 2004; Trainor, 2010).

[2]See also Delgado and Stefancic (2001) for an introductory text to Critical Race Theory (CRT).

[3]Of interest, longitudinal studies of immigrant families to the United States note similar language trends; see Portes and Rumbaut (2001b) and Suárez-Orozco, Suárez-Orozco, and Todorova (2008).

[4]California Assembly Bill 540 allows students who can prove they were residents in California during their high school education to pay in-state college tuition costs.

[5]We also note Bloemraad and Trost's (2008) study of political mobilization of mixed-status families that highlights the ways different generations within the home use multiple symbolic and material resources for making sense of social institutions.

[6]For an excellent discussion of empowerment, the reader is directed to Wright (2010). In particular chapter 6, titled "Real Utopias I: Social Empowerment and the State."

[7]The term refers to rural, unincorporated settlements.

[8]Also of interest is Maldonado-Torres's (2011) introduction to the special issue on the decolonial turn in *Transmodernities: Journal of the Peripheral Cultural Production of the Luso-Hispanic World.*

REFERENCES

Ada, A. F., & Zubizarreta, R. (2001). Parent narratives: The cultural bridge between Latino parents and their children. In M. L. Reyes & J. J. Halcón (Eds.), *The best for our children: Critical perspectives on literacy for Latino students* (pp. 229–244). New York, NY: Teachers College Press.

Alba, R., & Nee, V. (1997). Rethinking assimilation theory for a new era of immigration. *International Migration Review, 31,* 826–874. Retrieved from http://www.jstor.org/stable/2547416

Alexander, M. (2010). *The new Jim Crow: Mass incarceration in the age of colorblindness.* New York, NY: New Press.

Anyon, J. (2005). *Radical possibilities: Public policy, urban education, and a new social movement.* New York, NY: Routledge.

Apple, M., & King, N. (1983). What do schools teach? In H. Giroux & D. Purpel (Eds.), *The hidden curriculum and moral education* (pp. 82–99). Berkeley, CA: McCutchan.

Artiles, A. (2011). Toward an interdisciplinary understanding of educational equity and difference: The case of the racialization of ability. *Educational Researcher, 40,* 431–445. doi:10.3102/0013189X11429391

Auerbach, E. (1995). Deconstructing the discourse of strengths in family literacy. *Journal of Reading Behavior, 27,* 643–661. doi:10.1080/10862969509547903

Auerbach, S. (2002). "Why do they give the good classes to some and not to others?" Latino parent narratives of struggle in a college access program. *Teachers College Record, 104,* 1369–1392. Retrieved from http://www.tcrecord.org/library/Abstract.asp?ContentId=10990

Auerbach, S. (2007). From moral supporters to struggling advocates: Reconceptualizing parent roles in education through the experience of working-class families of color. *Urban Education, 42,* 250–283. doi:10.1177/0042085907300433

Auerbach, S. (2009). Walking the walk: Portraits in leadership for family engagement in urban schools. *School Community Journal, 19*(1), 9–31. Retrieved from http://www.adi.org/journal/ss09/AuerbachSpring2009.pdf

Baquedano-López, P. (1997). Creating social identities through doctrina narratives. *Issues in Applied Linguistics, 8*(1), 27–45.

Baquedano-López, P. (2004). Traversing the center: The politics of language use in a Catholic religious education program for immigrant Mexican children. *Anthropology & Education Quarterly, 35*, 212–232.

Barton, A. C., Drake, C., Perez, J. G., St. Louis, K., & George, M. (2004). Ecologies of parental engagement in urban education. *Educational Researcher, 33*, 3–12. doi:10.3102/0013189X033004003

Becker, H. J., Nakagawa, K., & Corwin, R. G. (1997). Parent involvement contracts in California's charter schools: Strategy for educational improvement or method of exclusion? *Teachers College Record, 98*, 511–536.

Ben-Porath, S. R. (2009). School choice as a bounded ideal. *Journal of Philosophy of Education, 43*, 527–544. doi:10.1111/j.1467-9752.2009.00726.x

Berliner, D. C., & Biddle, B. J. (1995). *The manufactured crisis: Myths, frauds, and the attack on America's public schools*. Redding, MA: Addison-Wesley.

Bloemraad, I., & Trost, C. (2008). It's a family affair: Inter-generational mobilization in the Spring 2006 protests. *American Behavioral Scientist, 52*, 507–532.

Bonilla-Silva, E. (2003). *Racism without racists: Color blind racism and the persistence of racial inequality*. Boulder, CO: Rowman & Littlefield.

Borg, C., & Mayo, P. (2001). From "adjuncts" to "subjects": Parental involvement in a working-class community. *British Journal of Sociology of Education, 22*, 245–266. Retrieved from http://www.jstor.org/stable/1393204

Bourdieu, P. (1977). *Outline of a theory of practice*. Cambridge, England: Cambridge University Press.

Brantlinger, E. (2003). *Dividing classes: How the middle class negotiates and rationalizes school advantage*. New York, NY: Routledge/Falmer.

Burton, L. M., Bonilla-Silva, E., Ray, V., Buckelew, R., & Freeman, E. H. (2010). Critical race theories, colorism, and the decade's research on families of color. *Journal of Marriage and Family, 72*, 440–459.

Carter, D. J. (2008, Winter-Spring). Cultivating a critical race consciousness for African American school success. *Educational Foundations*, 11–28.

Casanova, U. (1996). Parent involvement: A call for prudence. *Educational Researcher, 25*(8), 30–32, 46. doi:10.3102/0013189X025008030

Caspe, M. (2003). *Family literacy: A review of programs and critical perspectives* (Family Involvement Network of Educators and Harvard Family Research Project). Retrieved from http://www.hfrp.org/publications-resources/browse-our-publications/family-literacy-a-review-of-programs-and-critical-perspectives

Césaire, A. (2010). Culture and colonization. *Social Text, 28*, 127–144. [Reprinted Duke University Press] (Original work published 1956)

Chapman, T. K. (2007). The power of contexts: Teaching and learning in recently desegregated schools. *Anthropology & Education Quarterly, 38*, 297–315. doi:10.1525/aeq.2007.38.3.297

Coleman, J. (1991). *Parental involvement in education* (Policy Perspectives Series). Washington, DC: U.S. Department of Education, U.S. Government Printing Office.

Collins, P. H. (1990). *Black feminist thought: Knowledge, consciousness, and the politics of empowerment*. New York, NY: Routledge.

Constantine, M. G., & Blackmon, S. M. (2002). Black adolescents' racial socialization experiences: Their relations to home, school and peer self-esteem. *Journal of African American Studies, 32*, 322–335.

Cooper, C. E., Crosnoe, R., Suizzo, A. M., & Pituch, K. A. (2010). Poverty, race and parental involvement during the transition to elementary school. *Journal of Family Issues, 31,* 859–883. doi:10.1177/0192513X09351515

Cooper, C. W. (2009). Parent involvement, African American mothers, and the politics of educational care. *Equity & Excellence in Education, 42,* 379–394. doi:10.1080/10665680903228389

Cruz, C. (2001). Toward an epistemology of a brown body. *International Journal of Qualitative Studies in Education, 14,* 657–669. doi:10.1080/09518390110059874

Darder, A., & Torres, R. D. (2004). Latinos and society: Culture, politics and class. In A. Darder & R. D. Torres (Eds.), *The Latino studies reader: Culture, economy and society* (pp. 3–28). Malden, MA: Blackwell. (Original work published 1998)

DeBray-Pelot, E., Lubienski, C., & Scott, J. (2007). The institutional landscape of interest group politics and school choice. *Peabody Journal of Education, 82,* 204–230. doi:10.1080/01619560701312947

Delgado, R., & Stefancic, J. (2001). *Critical race theory: An introduction.* New York: New York University Press.

Delgado Bernal, D. (1998). Using a Chicana feminist epistemology in educational research. *Harvard Educational Review, 68,* 555–579.

Delgado-Gaitan, C. (1990). *Literacy for empowerment: The role of parents in children's education.* New York, NY: Falmer Press.

Delgado-Gaitan, C. (1993). Researching change and changing the researcher. *Harvard Educational Review, 63,* 389–412. Retrieved from http://her.hepg.org/content/b336053463h71081/fulltext.pdf

Dewey, J. (1944). *Democracy and education.* New York, NY: Free Press. (Original work published 1916)

Dixson, A. (2011). Democracy now? Race, education, and Black self-determination. *Teachers College Record, 13,* 811–830.

Doane, A. W., & Bonilla-Silva, E. (Eds.). (2003). *White out: The continuing significance of racism.* New York, NY: Routledge.

Dryden-Peterson, S. (2010). Bridging home: Building relationships between immigrant and long-time resident youth. *Teachers College Record, 112,* 2320–2351.

Duncan, G. A. (2000). Urban pedagogies and the celling of adolescents of color. *Social Justice, 27*(3), 29–42.

Dyrness, A. (2009). Cultural exclusion and critique in the era of good intentions: Using participatory research to transform parent roles in urban school reform. *Social Justice, 36*(4), 36–53.

Dyrness, A. (2011). *Mothers united: An immigrant struggle for socially just education.* Minneapolis: University of Minnesota Press.

Epstein, J. L. (1992). School and family partnerships. In M. Alkin (Ed.), *Encyclopedia of educational research* (pp. 1139–1151). New York, NY: Macmillan.

Epstein, J. L. (1995). School/family/community partnerships: Caring for the children we share. *Phi Delta Kappan, 76,* 701–712. Retrieved from http://www.jstor.org/stable/20405436

Epstein, J. L., & Hollifield, J. H. (1996). Title I and school-family-community partnerships: Using research to realize the potential. *Journal of Education for Students Placed at Risk, 1,* 263–278.

Espinoza-Herold, M. (2007). Stepping beyond Sí se puede: Dichos as a cultural resource in mother-daughter interaction in a Latino family. *Anthropology & Education Quarterly, 38,* 260–227.

Fan, W., Williams, C. M., & Wolters, C. (2011). Parental involvement in predicting school motivation: Similar and different effects across ethnic groups. *Journal of Educational Research, 105*(1), 21–35. doi:10.1080/00220671.2010.515625

Fanon, F. (1963). *The wretched of the earth* (C. Farrington, Trans.) New York, NY: Grove Press.

Farr, M. (2004). *Ethnolinguistic Chicago: Language and literacy in the city's neighborhoods.* Hillsdale, NJ: Erlbaum.

Farr, M. (2006). *Rancheros in Chicagoacán: Language and identity in a transnational community.* Austin: University of Texas Press.

Ferguson, A. A. (2001). *Bad boys: Public schools in the making of Black masculinity.* Ann Arbor: University of Michigan Press.

Fine, M. (1993). (Ap)parent involvement: Reflections on parents, power, and urban public schools. *Teachers College Record, 94,* 682–729.

Freire, P. (1970). *Pedagogy of the oppressed.* New York, NY: Continuum.

Freire, P. (1973). *Education for critical consciousness.* New York, NY: Seabury Press.

Freire, P., & Macedo, D. (1995). A dialogue: Culture, language, and race. *Harvard Educational Review, 65,* 377–402.

Fuentes, E. H. (2005). *Just parents: The politics and practices of community organizing for school change* (Doctoral dissertation). Retrieved from Dissertations and Theses @ University of California (AAT 3187035).

Fuentes, E. H. (2009/2010). Learning power and building community: Parent-initiated participatory action. *Social Justice, 36*(4), 69–83.

Fuller, B., & Elmore, R. F. (with Orfield, G.) (Eds.). (1996). *Who chooses, who loses? Culture, institutions, and the unequal effects of school choice.* New York, NY: Teachers College Press.

Furumoto, R. (2003). The roots of resistance: Cultivating critical parental involvement. *Amerasia Journal, 29*(2), 120–138. Retrieved from http://aascpress.metapress.com/content/m17x5x77pg222063/fulltext.pdf

Gadsden, V. L. (1994). *Understanding family literacy: Conceptual issues facing the field* (National Center on Adult Literacy Technical Report TR94-02). Retrieved from http://www.eric.ed.gov/PDFS/ED374339.pdf

Galindo, R., & Medina, C. (2009). Cultural appropriation, performance, and agency in Mexicana parent involvement. *Journal of Latinos in Education, 8,* 312–331. doi:10.1080/15348430902973450

Gándara, P., & Contreras, F. (2009). *The Latino education crisis: The consequences of failed social policies.* Cambridge, MA: Harvard University Press.

Gándara, P., Losen, D., August, D., Uriarte, M., Gómez, M. C., & Hopkins, M. (2010). Forbidden language: A brief history of U.S. language policy. In P. Gándara & M. Hopkins (Eds.), *Forbidden language: English learners and restrictive language policies* (pp. 20–33). New York, NY: Teachers College Press.

García, E. E., & Baquedano-López, P. (2007). Science instruction for all: An approach to equity and access in science education. *Language Magazine, 6*(5), 24–31.

Gartrell-Nadine, P. (1995). *Race and parent involvement in school: Re-structuring contested terrain* (Unpublished doctoral dissertation). University of California, Berkeley.

Gay, G. (2000). *Culturally responsive teaching: Theory, practice, and research.* New York, NY: Teachers College Press.

Gilmore, R. W. (2007). *Golden gulag: Prisons, surplus, crisis and opposition in globalizing California.* Berkeley: University of California Press.

Goldberg, D. T. (2002). *The racial state.* Malden, MA: Blackwell.

Goldring, E. B., & Phillips, K. J. R. (2008). Parent preferences and parent choices: The public-private decisions about parent choice. *Journal of Educational Policy, 23,* 209–230. doi:10.1080/02680930801987844

González, G. G. (1997). Culture, language, and the Americanization of Mexican children. In A. Darder, R. D. Torres, & H. Gutiérrez (Eds.), *Latinos and education: A critical reader* (pp. 158–173). New York, NY: Routledge.

González, N. (2005). *"I am my language": Discourses of women and children in the borderlands.* Tucson: University of Arizona Press.

González, N., Moll, L., & Amanti, C. (2005). *Funds of knowledge: Theorizing practices in households and classrooms.* Mahwah, NJ: Lawrence Erlbaum.

González, N., Moll, L., Floyd-Tennery, M., Rivera, A., Rendón, P., Gonzales, R., & Amanti, C. (1993). *Learning from households: Teacher research on funds of knowledge* (Educational Practice Series). Santa Cruz, CA: National Center for Research on Cultural Diversity and Second Language Learning.

Grande, S. (2004). *Red pedagogy: Native American social and political thought.* Lanham, MD: Rowman & Littlefield.

Guerra, J. (1998). *Close to home: Oral and literate practices in a transnational Mexicano community.* New York, NY: Teachers College Press.

Gutiérrez, K., Baquedano-López, P., & Alvarez, H. (2000). The crisis in Latino education: The norming of America. In C. Tejeda, C. Martínez, & Z. Leonardo (Eds.), *Charting new terrains in Chicano(a) and Latina(o) education* (pp. 213–232). Cresskill, NJ: Hampton Press.

Hidalgo, N. M. (1998). Toward a definition of a Latino family research paradigm. *International Journal of Qualitative Studies in Education, 11*, 103–120. doi:10.1080/095183998236917

Hong, S. (2011). *A cord of three strands: A new approach to parent engagement in schools.* Cambridge, MA: Harvard Education Press.

Howard, T. C., & Reynolds, R. (2008, Winter-Spring). Examining parent involvement in reversing the underachievement of African American students in middle class schools. *Educational Foundations,* 79–98.

Jasis, P., & Ordóñez-Jasis, R. (2004–2005). Convivencia to empowerment: Latino parent organizing at La Familia. *High School Journal, 88*(2), 32–42. Retrieved from http://www.jstor.org/stable/40364269

Kainz, K., & Aikens, N. L. (2007). Governing the family through education: A genealogy on the home/school relation. *Equity & Excellence in Education, 40*, 301–310. doi:10.1080/10665680701610721

Kohn, A. (1998). Only for my kid: How privileged parents undermine school reform. *Phi Delta Kappan, 79*, 568–577. Retrieved from http://www.jstor.org/stable/20439278

Krog, A. (2010). *Begging to be Black.* Cape Town, South Africa: Random House Struik.

Ladson-Billings, G. (1994). *The dreamkeepers: Successful teachers of African American children.* San Francisco, CA: Jossey-Bass.

Ladson-Billings, G. (1995). That's just good teaching! The case for culturally relevant pedagogy. *Theory into Practice, 34*(3), 159–165.

Ladson-Billings, G. (2006). From the achievement gap to the education debt: Understanding achievement in U.S. schools. *Educational Researcher, 35*(7), 3–12. doi:10.3102/0013189X035007003

Ladson-Billings, G., & Tate, W. F., IV. (1995). Towards a critical race theory of education. *Teachers College Record, 1*, 47–69.

Lareau, A. (2000). *Home advantage.* Lanham, MD: Rowman & Littlefield.

Lareau, A., & Horvat, E. M. (1999). Moments of social inclusion and exclusion: Race, class and cultural capital in family-school relationships. *Sociology of Education, 72*, 37–53.

Larner, W. (2003). Guest editorial: Neoliberalism? *Environment and Planning D: Society and Space, 21*, 509–512.

Lashaw, A. (2008). Experiencing imminent justice: The presence of hope in a movement for equitable schooling. *Space and Culture, 11*, 109–124. doi:10.1177/1206331208315931

Lee, C. D. (1995). A culturally based cognitive apprenticeship: Teaching African American high school students skills in literary interpretation. *Reading Research Quarterly, 30*, 608–631.

Lee, C. D. (2001). Is October Brown Chinese? A cultural modeling activity system for under-achieving students. *American Educational Research Journal, 38*, 97–141.

Lee, O., & Fradd, S. (1998). Science for all, including students from non-English-language backgrounds. *Educational Researcher, 27*(12), 12–21.

Lewis, A. E., & Forman, T. A. (2002). Contestation or collaboration? A comparative study of home-school relations. *Anthropology & Education Quarterly, 33*, 1–30.

Louie, V. (2005). *Compelled to excel: Immigration, education, and opportunity among Chinese Americans.* Palo Alto, CA: Stanford University Press.

Louie, V. (2006). Second-generation pessimism and optimism: How Chinese and Dominicans understand education and mobility through ethnic and transnational orientations. *International Migration Review, 40*, 537–572.

Maldonado-Torres, N. (2011). Thinking through the decolonial turn: Post-continental inter-ventions in theory, philosophy, and critique—An introduction. *Transmodernities: Journal of the Peripheral Cultural Production of the Luso-Hispanic World, 1*(2), 1–15.

Mangual Figueroa, A. (2011). Citizenship and education in the homework completion routine. *Anthropology & Education Quarterly, 42*, 263–280. doi:10.1111/j.1548-1492.2011.01131.x

Mapp, K. L. (2012). *Title I and parent involvement: Lessons from the past, recommendations for the future.* Retrieved from http://www.americanprogress.org/issues/issues/2012/03/pdf/titleI_parental_invovlement.pdf

Martínez-Calderón, M. C. (2010). *Out of the shadows: An inquiry into the lives of undocu-mented Latino AB54 students* (Unpublished doctoral dissertation). University of California, Berkeley.

McClain, M. (2010). Parental agency in educational decision making: A Mexican American example. *Teachers College Record, 112*, 3074–3101.

McCready, L. (2004). Understanding the marginalization of gay and gender non-conforming African American male students. *Theory into Practice, 43*, 136–143.

McGrath, D. J., & Kuriloff, P. J. (1999). "They're going to tear the doors off this place": Upper-middle-class parent school involvement and the educational opportunities of other people's children. *Educational Policy, 13*, 603–629. doi:10.1177/0895904899013005001

Mignolo, W. (2010). *The darker side of the renaissance: Literacy, territoriality, and colonization* (2nd ed.). Ann Arbor: Michigan University Press.

Minow, M. (2010). Confronting the seduction of choice: Law, education and American pluralism. *Yale Law Journal, 120*, 814–848.

Moll, L., & Ruiz, R. (2002). The schooling of Latino children. In M. Suárez-Orozco & M. Páez (Eds.), *Latinos: Remaking America* (pp. 362–374). Berkeley: University of California Press.

Moll, L., Amanti, C., Neff, D., & González, N. (1992). Funds of knowledge for teaching: Using a qualitative approach to connect homes and classrooms. *Theory into Practice, 3*, 132–141.

Motha, S. (2010). "Begging to be Black": Liminality and critique in post-apartheid South Africa. *Theory, Culture & Society, 27*, 285–305.

Moynihan, P. (1965). *The Moynihan report.* Retrieved from http://www.blackpast.org/?q=primary/moynihan-report-1965

Nakagawa, K. (2000). Unthreading the ties that bind: Questioning the discourse of parent involvement. *Educational Policy, 14*, 443–472. doi:10.1177/0895904800144001

National Education Goals Panel. (1993, September). *The National Education Goals Report: Building a nation of learners.* Retrieved from http://www2.ed.gov/pubs/goals/report/goalsrpt.txt

Newman, K. S., & Chin, M. M. (2003). High stakes: Time poverty, testing, and the children of the working poor. *Qualitative Sociology, 26*(1), 3–34. doi:10.1023/A:1021487219440

Olivos, E. M. (2006). *The power of parents: A critical perspective of bicultural parent involvement in public schools.* New York, NY: Peter Lang.

Olsen, L. (2009). The role of advocacy in shaping immigrant education: A California case study. *Teachers College Record, 111,* 817–850.

Omi, M., & Winant, H. (1994). *Racial formation in the United States: From the 1960s to the 1990s.* New York, NY: Routledge.

Ong, A. (2003). *Buddah is hiding: Refugees, citizenship and the new America.* Berkeley: University of California Press.

Orellana, M. F. (2009). *Translating childhoods: Immigrant youth, language, and culture.* New Brunswick, NJ: Rutgers University Press.

Orellana, M. F., Reynolds, J., Dorner, L., & Meza, M. (2003). In other words: Translating or "para-phrasing" as a family literacy practice in immigrant households. *Reading Research Quarterly, 38*(1), 12–34. doi:10.1598/RRQ.38.1.2

Paperson, L. (2010). The postcolonial ghetto: Seeing her shape and his hand. *Berkeley Review of Education, 1*(1), 5–34.

Peters, M. F. (1985). Racial socialization of young Black children. In H. P. McAdoo & J. L. McAdoo (Eds.), *Black children: Social, educational and parental environments* (pp. 159–173). Beverly Hills, CA: Sage.

Portes, A., & Rumbaut, R. (1996). *Immigrant America: A portrait* (2nd ed.). Berkeley: University of California Press.

Portes, A., & Rumbaut, R. (Eds.). (2001a). *Ethnicities: Children of immigrants in America.* Berkeley: University of California Press.

Portes, A., & Rumbaut, R. (2001b). *Legacies: The story of the immigrant second generation.* Berkeley: University of California Press.

Posey, L. (2009). *The fine line between integration and gentrification: The politics of middle-class parental engagement in a city public school* (Doctoral dissertation). Retrieved from Dissertations & Theses @ University of California. (ATT 3411172)

Posey, L. (2012). Middle- and upper middle-class parent action for urban public schools: Promise or paradox? *Teachers College Record, 114,* 1–43.

Reyes, L. V., & Torres, M. N. (2007). Decolonizing family literacy in a culture circle: Reinventing the family literacy educator's role. *Journal of Early Childhood Literacy, 7,* 73–94.

Reynolds, R. (2010, April/May). "They think you're lazy," and other messages Black parents send their Black sons: An exploration of critical race theory in the examination of educational outcomes for Black males. *Journal of African American Males in Education, 1*(2), 144–163.

Roberts, D. (2002). *Shattered bonds: The color of child welfare.* New York, NY: Basic Civitas Books.

Roberts, D. E. (2004). The social and moral costs of mass incarceration in African American communities. *Stanford Law Review, 56,* 1271–1305.

Rocha-Schmid, E. (2010). Participatory pedagogy for empowerment: A critical discourse analysis of teacher-parents' interactions in a family literacy course in London. *International Journal of Lifelong Education, 29,* 343–358. doi:10.1080/02601371003700659

Rodríguez-Brown, F. V. (2009). *Home-school connection: Lessons learned in a culturally and linguistically diverse community.* New York, NY: Routledge.

Rogers, J., Saunders, M., Terriquez, V., & Velez, V. (2008). Civic lessons: Public schools and the civic development of undocumented students and parents. *Northwestern Journal of Law and Social Policy, 3,* 201–218.

Rogers, J., & Terriquez, V. (2009). "More justice": The role of organized labor in educational reform. *Educational Policy, 23,* 216–241.

Romero, M. (2000–2001). State violence, and the social and legal construction of Latino criminality: From el bandido to gang member. *Denver University Law Review, 78,* 1081–1118.

Ryan, C. S., Casas, J. F., Kelly-Vance, L., Ryalls, B. O., & Nero, C. (2010). Parent involvement and views of school success: The role of parents' Latino and White American cultural orientations. *Psychology in the Schools, 47,* 391–405. doi:10.1002/pits.20477

Sánchez, C., Plata, V., Grosso, L., & Leird, B. (2010). Encouraging Spanish-speaking families' involvement through dichos. *Journal of Latinos and Education, 3,* 239–248.

Sánchez, G. (1984). *"Go after the women": Americanization and the Mexican immigrant woman 1915–1929* (Working Papers Series No. 6). Stanford, CA: Stanford Center for Chicano Research.

Scott, J. T. (Ed.). (2005). *School choice and diversity: What the evidence says.* New York, NY: Teachers College Press.

Scott, L. D. (2003). The relation of racial identity and racial socialization to coping with discrimination among African American adolescents. *Journal of African American Studies, 33,* 520–537.

Smith, L. T. (1999). *Decolonizing methodologies: Research and indigenous peoples.* London, England: Zed Books.

Smith, R., & Erevelles, N. (2004). Towards an enabling education: The difference that disability makes. *Educational Researcher, 33*(8), 31–36. doi:10.3102/0013189X033008031

Spring, J. (2001). *Deculturalization and the struggle for equality: A brief history of the education of dominated cultures in the United States* (3rd ed.). Boston, MA: McGraw Hill.

Stevenson, Z., & Laster, C. (2008). *2003–2006 Monitoring cycle report.* Washington, DC: U.S. Department of Education: Office of Elementary and Secondary Education, Student Achievement and School Accountability Programs. Retrieved from http://www2.ed.gov/admins/lead/account/monitoring/monitoringcyclerpt1008.pdf

Suárez-Orozco, C., Suárez-Orozco, M. M., & Todorova, I. (2008). *Learning a new land: Immigrant students in American Society.* Cambridge, MA: Harvard University Press.

Tlostanova, M., & Mignolo, W. (2009). Global coloniality and the decolonial option. *Kult, 6,* 130–147.

Torres, M. N., & Hurtado-Vivas, R. (2011). Playing fair with Latino parents as parents, not teachers: Beyond family literacy as assisting homework. *Journal of Latinos and Education, 10,* 223–244. doi:10.1080/15348431.2011.581108

Trainor, A. (2010). Re-examining the promise of parent participation in special education: An analysis of social and cultural capital. *Anthropology & Education Quarterly, 41,* 245–263. doi:10.1111/j.1548-1492.2010.01086.x

Tsing, A. L. (2004). *Friction.* Princeton, NJ: Princeton University Press.

Tuck, E. (2009). Re-visioning action: Participatory action research and indigenous theories of change. *Urban Review, 41*(1), 47–65.

U.S. Congress. (1994). *Goals 2000: Educate America Act. H.R. 1804.* Retrieved from http://www2.ed.gov/legislation/GOALS2000/TheAct/index.html

U.S. Department of Education. (1996). *Policy guidance for Title I, Part A: Improving basic programs operated by local educational agencies.* Retrieved from http://www2.ed.gov/legislation/ESEA/Title_I/parinv2.html

U.S. Department of Education. (2002). *Good Start, Grow Smart: The Bush administration's early childhood initiative: Executive summary.* Retrieved from http://georgewbush-whitehouse.archives.gov/infocus/earlychildhood/earlychildhood.html

U.S. Department of Education. (2011). *Obama administration announces $500 million for Race to the Top-Early Learning Challenge: New state competition to establish and expand high quality early learning programs.* Washington, DC: Press Office, U.S. Department of Education. Retrieved from http://www.ed.gov/news/press-releases/obama-administration-announces-500-million-race-top-early-learning-challenge

Valdés, G. (1996). *Con respeto: Bridging the distances between culturally diverse families and school: An ethnographic portrait.* New York, NY: Teachers College Press.

Valdés, G. (2003). *Expanding definitions of giftedness: The case of young interpreters from immigrant communities.* Mahwah, NJ: Erlbaum.

Valdez, N., Fitzhorn, M., Matsumoto, C., & Emslie, T. (2012). Police in schools: The struggle for student and parental rights. *Denver University Law Review, 78,* 1063–1079.

Valencia, R. (1991). *Chicano school failure and success: Research and policy agendas for the 1990s.* New York, NY: Falmer Press.

Valencia, R. (2011). *Chicano school failure and success: Past, present, and future* (3rd ed.). London, England: Routledge.

Valenzuela, A. (1999). *Subtractive schooling: U.S.-Mexican youth and the politics of caring.* Albany: State University of New York Press.

Villenas, S. (1996). The colonizer/colonized Chicana ethnographer: Identity, marginalization, and co-optation in the field. *Harvard Educational Review, 66,* 711–731. Retrieved from http://her.hepg.org/content/3483672630865482/fulltext.pdf

Villenas, S., & Deyhle, D. (1999). Critical race theory and ethnographies challenging the stereotypes: Latino families, schooling, resilience and resistance. *Curriculum Inquiry, 29,* 413–445. doi:10.1111/0362-6784.00140

Vincent, C. (2001). Social class and parental agency. *Journal of Education Policy, 16,* 347–364. doi:10.1080/0268093011-54344

Warren, M. R. (2011). Building a political constituency for urban school reform. *Urban Education, 46,* 484–512. doi:10.1177/0042085910377441

Warren, M. R., Hong, S., Rubin, C. L., & Uy, P. S. (2009). Beyond the bake sale: A community-based relational approach to parent engagement in schools. *Teachers College Record, 111,* 2209–2254.

Wells, A. S., & Oakes, J. (1996). Potential pitfalls of systemic reform: Early lessons from research on detracking. *Sociology of Education, 69,* 135–143. Retrieved from http://www.jstor.org/discover/10.2307/3108461?uid=3738256&uid=2&uid=4&sid=21100987656323

Whitehouse, M., & Colvin, C. (2001). "Reading" families: Deficit discourse and family literacy. *Theory into Practice, 40,* 212–219. Retrieved from http://www.jstor.org/stable/1477478

Williams, T. T., & Sanchez, B. (2011). Identifying and decreasing barriers to parent involvement for inner-city parents. *Youth Society, 45,* 54–74. doi:10.1177/0044118X11

Woolley, S. W. (2010). *"The silence is enough of a statement": Unintended consequences of silence as awareness-raising strategy* (ISSI Fellows Working Papers). Berkeley: Institute for the Study of Social Issues, University of California, Berkeley.

Wright, E. O. (2010). *Envisioning real utopias.* New York, NY: Verso.

Yang, K. W. (2004). *Taking over: The struggle to transform an urban school system* (Unpublished doctoral dissertation). University of California, Berkeley.

Zentella, A. C. (1997). *Growing up bilingual: Puerto Rican children in New York.* Malden, MA: Blackwell.

Zhou, M., & Baston, C. (1998). *Growing up American: How Vietnamese children adapt to life in the United States.* New York, NY: Russell Sage Foundation.

Chapter 6

Am I My Brother's Teacher? Black Undergraduates, Racial Socialization, and Peer Pedagogies in Predominantly White Postsecondary Contexts

SHAUN R. HARPER

University of Pennsylvania

Much has been written over the past five decades about the experiences of Black students on predominantly White college and university campuses. Willie and Cunnigen (1981) synthesized 130 studies published between 1965 and 1980, many focused on students' confrontations with exclusion, racism, racial stereotypes, and toxic campus racial climates. Sedlacek (1987) found similar themes in his review of 20 years of literature on Black undergraduates at postsecondary institutions at which they were minoritized.[1] Shown in Figure 1 are increases in undergraduate enrollments over a 30-year period; as Black enrollments increased, so too did the number of undergraduates overall. Despite modest gains in access and attainment, contemporary cohorts of Black collegians still encounter campus environments with racial dynamics akin to those described in studies from decades prior. Contemporary scholars continue to document many of the same themes reported in Willie and Cunnigen's (1981) review more than 30 years ago.

The aims of this chapter are twofold: (a) to review an extensive body of research that focuses almost exclusively on racial problems Black students face at predominantly White institutions (PWIs) and (b) to provide insights into how Black students manage to productively navigate racist college and university environments. Hardly anything has been published about the latter. In the next section, I present a conceptual framework that was used to organize the literature and generate new research questions concerning student success in racially alienating and hostile spaces. Next, Black students' experiences on predominantly White campuses are placed in a historical context, followed by a review of several recently published studies on how

Review of Research in Education
March 2013, Vol. 37, pp. 183-211
DOI: 10.3102/0091732X12471300
© 2013 AERA. http://rre.aera.net

FIGURE 1
Black Students' Share of Undergraduate Enrollments, 1980–2010

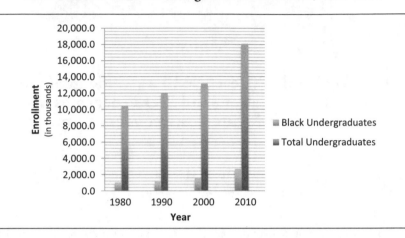

Black students respond to and are affected by campus environments in which they routinely encounter racial stress and stereotypes. I then use data from a national study to showcase pedagogies Black undergraduates employ in teaching their same-race peers and other minoritized students about navigating the racial climate at PWIs, as well as the sites in which such instruction occurs.

ANTI-DEFICIT ACHIEVEMENT FRAMEWORK

Harper's (2012a) anti-deficit achievement framework was constructed for the National Black Male College Achievement Study (details about this 42-campus research project are provided in a later section of this chapter). The framework is informed by three decades of literature on Black men in education and society, as well as theories from sociology, psychology, gender studies, and education. It inverts questions that are commonly asked about educational disadvantage, underrepresentation, insufficient preparation, academic underperformance, disengagement, and Black male student attrition. For example, instead of asking a popular question such as "why are so few Black men enrolled in college," the framework is useful for understanding how aspirations for postsecondary education were cultivated and actualized among those who are enrolled.

It includes *some* questions that researchers *could* explore to better understand how Black undergraduate men successfully navigate their way to and through higher education and onward to rewarding postcollege options (see Figure 2). Insights into these questions shed light on three pipeline points (precollege socialization and readiness, college achievement, and postcollege success) as well as eight researchable dimensions of achievement (familial factors, K–12 school forces, out-of-school college prep resources, classroom experiences, out-of-class engagement, enriching educational experiences, graduate school enrollment, and career readiness).

FIGURE 2
Anti-Deficit Achievement Framework

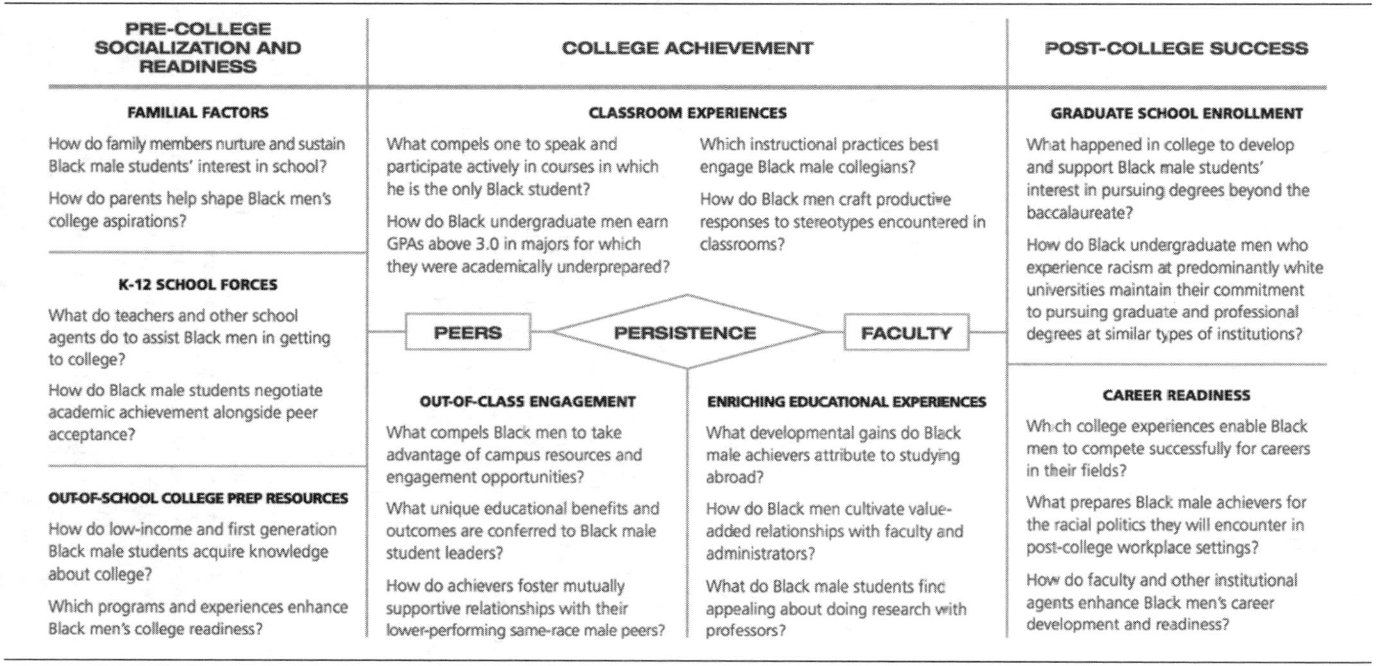

PRE-COLLEGE SOCIALIZATION AND READINESS

FAMILIAL FACTORS

How do family members nurture and sustain Black male students' interest in school?

How do parents help shape Black men's college aspirations?

K-12 SCHOOL FORCES

What do teachers and other school agents do to assist Black men in getting to college?

How do Black male students negotiate academic achievement alongside peer acceptance?

OUT-OF-SCHOOL COLLEGE PREP RESOURCES

How do low-income and first generation Black male students acquire knowledge about college?

Which programs and experiences enhance Black men's college readiness?

COLLEGE ACHIEVEMENT

CLASSROOM EXPERIENCES

What compels one to speak and participate actively in courses in which he is the only Black student?

How do Black undergraduate men earn GPAs above 3.0 in majors for which they were academically underprepared?

Which instructional practices best engage Black male collegians?

How do Black men craft productive responses to stereotypes encountered in classrooms?

PEERS — PERSISTENCE — FACULTY

OUT-OF-CLASS ENGAGEMENT

What compels Black men to take advantage of campus resources and engagement opportunities?

What unique educational benefits and outcomes are conferred to Black male student leaders?

How do achievers foster mutually supportive relationships with their lower-performing same-race male peers?

ENRICHING EDUCATIONAL EXPERIENCES

What developmental gains do Black male achievers attribute to studying abroad?

How do Black men cultivate value-added relationships with faculty and administrators?

What do Black male students find appealing about doing research with professors?

POST-COLLEGE SUCCESS

GRADUATE SCHOOL ENROLLMENT

What happened in college to develop and support Black male students' interest in pursuing degrees beyond the baccalaureate?

How do Black undergraduate men who experience racism at predominantly white universities maintain their commitment to pursuing graduate and professional degrees at similar types of institutions?

CAREER READINESS

Which college experiences enable Black men to compete successfully for careers in their fields?

What prepares Black male achievers for the racial politics they will encounter in post-college workplace settings?

How do faculty and other institutional agents enhance Black men's career development and readiness?

185

This chapter is situated within the college achievement pipeline point. Specifically, I review in subsequent sections decades of research that amplify Black students' struggles in and negative responses to racist postsecondary institutional environments. Nearly everything published about Black undergraduates at PWIs focuses on factors (including toxic campus racial climates) that undermine academic success and sense of belonging—in other words, a one-sided research focus on deficits and negative forces instead of enablers of achievement. Below, I show the durability of these foci in the literature. The anti-deficit achievement framework is then used to explore this inverted version of a commonly pursued research question: How do Black undergraduates learn to excel and productively navigate campus racial climates that historically (and in many instances, contemporarily) have been characterized as racist?

CAMPUS RACIAL CLIMATE IN HISTORICAL CONTEXT

At many predominantly White colleges and universities, Black students have been excluded longer than they have been afforded opportunities to matriculate (Harper, Patton, & Wooden, 2009). For example, in 1870 Richard T. Greener was the first Black student ever to graduate from Harvard, 234 years after the College was founded (Sollors, Titcomb, & Underwood, 1993). Blacks at many other PWIs were not permitted to enter classrooms but instead were forced to listen to lectures in the hallway. Furthermore, the few Black students who were allowed to attend could not live in dormitories, eat in campus dining halls, or interact socially with their White peers. Several institutional histories describe how White students, faculty, alumni, legislators, and other stakeholders resisted (sometimes violently) the admission of Black students (e.g., Goldstone, 2006; Kammen, 2009; McCormick, 1990; Trillin, 1964; Williams, 2001; Williamson, 2003). For example, White protesters at the University of Mississippi attempted desperately to block the admission of James Meredith, its first Black student (Lambert, 2010). Also, Alabama Governor George Wallace stood in the doorway of a building on the University of Alabama campus in 1963 to block the entry of two Black students; with orders from U.S. President John F. Kennedy, the Alabama National Guard was summoned to remove Wallace and escort Vivian Malone and James Hood into the building to register for classes (Clark, 1993).

Six Black students enrolled at Cornell University during the 1904–1905 academic school year; none returned the following fall term. Consequently, seven Black undergraduate men created Alpha Phi Alpha Fraternity as a study and support group for themselves on the predominantly White campus (Ross, 2000). Likewise, in the wake of racial hostility, 10 Black undergraduate men at Indiana University started a social fraternity as a support system for each other. In 1911, Kappa Alpha Psi was founded on the predominantly White campus. Crump (1991) wrote,

Black men were almost completely ignored by White students. To make matters worse, one Black student might be on campus for weeks without seeing another. Under these circumstances, assimilation into the life of the school was impossible. The administration maintained an attitude of indifference as Blacks were slowly matriculated and swiftly forgotten . . . the members of [Kappa Alpha Psi] sought one another's company between classes and dropped by one another's lodging place to discuss a new approach to an old problem. The depressing isolation earlier experienced was relieved as new friendships solidified. (p. 3)

An outgrowth of the Civil Rights Movement, various legislative mandates to desegregate schools and postsecondary institutions (e.g., the Civil Rights Act of 1964) incrementally increased Black student representation in higher education. Notwithstanding, little was done to ensure that students who had been previously excluded would encounter campuses that suddenly felt more inclusive and responsive to their cultural and educational needs. Hence, Black undergraduates at many PWIs found themselves in protest for more professors of color, cultural centers, and Black/ethnic studies programs. Glasker (2002) provides a chronology of what he terms "The African American Student Movement" at the University of Pennsylvania. His timeline includes eight sit-ins and various Black student demonstrations between 1967 and 1978, including one in April 1972 that led to the creation of the W. E. B. Du Bois College House.[2] Glasker goes on to furnish historical evidence of Black students' tireless quests for a sense of belonging at Penn through the 1980s. For decades, minoritized students elsewhere have been similarly striving for equity and inclusion.

Published nearly 30 years ago, Jacqueline Fleming's (1984) groundbreaking book *Blacks in College* remains one of the most widely cited studies on this population. Fleming analyzed students' experiences at eight PWIs and seven Historically Black Colleges and Universities (HBCUs). The comprehensive design of Fleming's study (which included academic records, experiments, blood pressure checks, illness reports, and numerous surveys of racial stress, career interests, and racial identity)—as well as her disaggregated analysis of race, sex, and institutional context—distinguishes it from other research studies on Black students. She found that Black undergraduates at PWIs experienced considerably higher levels of racial stress and intellectual isolation than did their same-race peers on HBCU campuses. Fleming also observed the following at one particular institution her sample:

Black students at Georgia Tech suffer from some of the worst intellectual deterioration found in a white college in this study. Their academic energies are apparently frustrated by classroom incidents and then withdrawn from the classroom into extracurricular pursuits that afford no intellectual benefit. These trends in no way describe the educational experience for White students. (p. 130)

Similar to Fleming, scholars such as Allen (1992); Berger and Milem (2000); Chavous, Harris, Rivas, Helaire, and Green (2004); J. E. Davis (1994); DeSousa and Kuh (1996); Flowers (2002); and Fries-Britt and Turner (2002) have found that Black undergraduates at HBCUs have stronger academic self-concepts and are more satisfied, engaged at higher levels, and less likely to be harmed by racial stress than are their same-race peers at PWIs. These researchers concluded that PWIs are comparatively less affirming educational spaces for Black undergraduates than are historically black institutions.

Campus climate frameworks (e.g., Chang, Milem, & Antonio, 2011; Hurtado, Alvarez, Guillermo-Wann, Cuellar, & Arellano, 2012; Hurtado, Milem, Clayton-Pedersen, & Allen, 1998) emphasize the importance of taking into account an institution's historical legacy. That is, making sense of contemporary problems pertaining to race, stratification, and durable patterns of racial underrepresentation in higher education necessarily entails understanding ways in which various groups of people were excluded, the conditions under which they were eventually granted access, and myriad ways in which generations of them have been numerically and experientially minoritized. The institutional histories cited in this section make clear that several colleges and universities in the United States were created without any attention to Black students' needs and interests; White stakeholders (students, faculty, trustees, alumni, etc.) have established cultural norms that have governed these campuses for decades, in some cases centuries. Hence, it should come as no surprise that many Black undergraduates share certain experiential realities in contexts at which their history of representation is fewer than 50 years.

Researchers posit that Black undergraduates and other minoritized students in predominantly White contexts perform better academically and persist through baccalaureate degree attainment at higher rates when educators and administrators validate their intellectual competence (Bensimon, 2007; Rendón Linares & Muñoz, 2011), deal responsibly with long-standing campus racial climate issues (Chang et al., 2011; Harper & Hurtado, 2007; Hurtado, 1992; Hurtado et al., 2012; Hurtado et al., 1998), and construct environments that engender feelings of belongingness (Gurin, Dey, Hurtado, & Gurin, 2002; Hurtado & Carter, 1997; Patton, 2006, 2010; Strayhorn, 2008a, 2012). But what happens to Black collegians in the absence of these conditions?

CONTEMPORARY BLACK UNDERGRADUATES AND TOXIC CAMPUS CLIMATES

Most contemporary institutions of higher education espouse in their mission statements commitments to diversity, equity, inclusion, cross-cultural learning, and appreciating differences (Morphew & Hartley, 2006); these values are also communicated on websites, in admissions brochures, presidential speeches, and elsewhere. Notwithstanding, Harper and Hurtado's (2007) study of campus racial climates confirms that Black undergraduates continue to feel excluded at many PWIs. Of the 278 undergraduates they interviewed (which included Asian Americans, Blacks, Latinos, Native Americans, and Whites), Black students were most dissatisfied with the campus climate. "One logical explanation for Black student displeasure was the bad reputations that preceded the universities they attended. Some entered their institutions expecting to experience racism" (p. 17). Participants noted that family members and others in their home communities forewarned them of what they would likely experience. Other scholars have written about shared experiences among generations of Black students at PWIs that fall within three categories: (a) "Onlyness," (b) "Niggering" and racial microaggressions, and (c) the shortage of same-race faculty role models. I elaborate on these experiential realities in this section and conclude with an illustrative case that succinctly integrates them.

Onlyness

Harper et al. (2009) report that approximately one quarter of Black undergraduates in 1972 were enrolled at PWIs—in 2010, 83.7% of Black bachelor's degree recipients graduated from PWIs (Snyder & Dillow, 2012). Despite a shift in enrollments from HBCUs to predominantly White campuses, Black undergraduates at PWIs remain underrepresented relative to White students and relative to their own representation of traditional-age college goers (18–24 year olds) in the U.S. population. Perna et al. (2006) used data from the U.S. Department of Education's Integrated Postsecondary Education Data System to examine trends in Black students' enrollment and degree attainment rates at public postsecondary institutions across 19 states (U.S. Department of Education, 2012). Comparative analyses of two time periods (1991 and 2001) showed sluggish growth patterns for Black undergraduates at 4-year institutions generally (with the exception of HBCUs) and at flagship state universities in particular. Noteworthy is that public flagship universities are usually among the largest postsecondary institutions in the country. University of Wisconsin–Madison, UNC Chapel Hill, and Penn State were among the flagships included in Newman, Mmeje, and Allen's (2012) analysis of postsecondary institutions ranked in the Top 50 by *U.S. News & World Report*; White students comprised more than two thirds of undergraduate enrollments on these campuses. Hurtado (1992) found that students at larger universities—Whites and minoritized students alike—are more likely than are their peers at other institution types to perceive considerable racial conflict in the campus environment.

Shown in Table 1 are Black students' enrollments at the 20 largest public colleges and universities in the United States. On average, they comprised 5.3% of full-time, degree-seeking undergraduates in fall 2010. Given the size of these institutions (meaning, the thousands of people and the actual square footage of the campus grounds), it is not uncommon for Black students to be in classrooms and assorted campus spaces where no other member of their racial group is present. One participant in M. Davis et al.'s (2004) study likened this to being "a fly in the buttermilk" (p. 438). Fries-Britt, Younger, and Hall (2010) note this is particularly commonplace in science, technology, engineering, and mathematics (STEM) courses. High achievers in Fries-Britt's (1998) study said they were usually lone representatives of their race in honors courses.

Extreme underrepresentation is usually accompanied by a set of experiences that undermine espoused institutional commitments to fostering inclusive campus climates; these are challenges from which White students at PWIs are almost always exempt. Harper et al. (2011) introduced the term *Onlyness*, which we defined as "the psychoemotional burden of having to strategically navigate a racially politicized space occupied by few peers, role models, and guardians from one's same racial or ethnic group" (p. 190). Black male student leaders in our study discussed the burden they often felt to be exceptional because so few of their same-race peers had been chosen for such prominent campus leadership roles; there was a fear that falling short of perfection would foreclose possibilities for future cohorts of aspiring Black leaders.

TABLE 1
Undergraduate Enrollments at the 20 Largest Public Universities, Fall 2010

University	Total Undergraduates[a] N	Black Undergraduates[a] N	%
Arizona State University	46,894	2,271	4.8
Ohio State University–Main Campus	38,300	2,372	6.2
Pennsylvania State University–University Park	36,954	1,440	3.9
University of Central Florida	35,917	3,373	9.4
Texas A&M University–College Station	35,812	1,079	3.0
University of Texas at Austin	35,267	1,654	4.7
Michigan State University	32,720	2,401	7.3
Indiana University–Bloomington	30,888	1,389	4.5
University of Illinois at Urbana-Champaign	30,292	1,743	5.8
University of Florida	30,210	2,864	9.5
Purdue University–Main Campus	30,118	1,064	3.5
Rutgers University–New Brunswick	28,829	2,196	7.6
University of Minnesota–Twin Cities	28,211	1,251	4.4
Florida State University	28,006	2,881	10.3
University of Wisconsin–Madison	27,374	645	2.4
University of Arizona	26,853	838	3.1
University of Michigan–Ann Arbor	26,096	1,166	4.5
University of Washington	25,564	875	3.4
University of California–Los Angeles	25,434	937	3.7
University of California–Berkeley	24,929	741	3.0

a.Full-time, degree-seeking undergraduate students.
Source. U.S. Department of Education, Integrated Postsecondary Education Data System (IPEDS).

Men on the six campuses were also expected by White peers and administrators to be spokespersons for Black issues and minoritized populations in meetings.

Similarly, M. Davis et al. (2004), Fries-Britt (1998), Fries-Britt and Turner (2002), and Winkle-Wagner (2009) report that professors and peers at PWIs impose this same burden on Black students in classrooms. That is, whenever a topic about race, poverty, or people of color emerges in classroom conversations, Black students are usually expected to speak—even those from rural and suburban areas are presumed to possess expertise on Black affairs in urban contexts. Participants at the PWI in Fries-Britt and Turner's (2002) study had to spend time educating White peers and professors and disrupting flawed assumptions about minoritized persons. These energies could have been invested into academics and outcomes-productive out-of-class experiences, they maintained.

Feagin, Vera, and Imani (1996) describe how Black undergraduates, especially in situations where they are the only one, are affected by the spokesperson expectation:

> Being the unwanted center of attention is stressful and serves to remind Black students of the racial position that they are often assigned in predominantly white classroom settings. The pressure reported by Black students does not come from one isolated act, but from a recurrence of similar situations over several years. (p. 92)

Participants in other qualitative studies (e.g., M. Davis et al., 2004) have expressed similar feelings of tokenization and spotlighting. These and other manifestations of onlyness make Black collegians especially susceptible to what Steele (1997) termed *stereotype threat*, an internalized fear of confirming negative stereotypes about one's racial group, which consequently engenders anxiety and results in academic underperformance. I write more about stereotype threat in the next section.

"Niggering" and Racial Microaggressions

In "Niggers No More: A Critical Race Counternarrative on Black Male Student Achievement at Predominantly White Colleges and Universities," I argue that the near exclusive focus in media, popular discourse, and published research on Black male underperformance, disengagement, and maladaptive behaviors cyclically reinforces a caricature of them that is best described by one of the most racially derogatory terms in American history: *Niggers* (Harper, 2009). I go on to operationalize a definition for "niggering" as the process by which stereotypes about Black boys and men shape people's low expectations for their success in schools and society. It is a repetitive activity through which Black women and men are constantly reminded of their long-standing subordinate standing in the U.S. economy, political systems, and myriad social structures (including schools and colleges). Hearing only negative statistics and pathological narratives about oneself, for example, is a way through which this population is persistently niggered. Black men and women on predominantly White campuses experience this process and the stereotypes embedded in it in myriad ways.

Affirmative action is one of the most contested practices and policy issues in U.S. higher education, especially at elite institutions (Charles, Fischer, Mooney, & Massey, 2009; Espenshade & Radford, 2009; Harper & Griffin, 2011; Harper et al., 2009). Consequently, minoritized students are often presumed to have been otherwise unqualified for admission. That is, many of their White peers and professors presuppose that were it not for affirmative action, those students would not have been afforded undue access to an elite institution (Feagin et al., 1996; Solórzano, Ceja, & Yosso, 2000). Even Black undergraduates who were high achievers in K–12 schools and perform exceptionally in college are accused of having been afforded access because of their race, not academic merit (Charles et al., 2009; Fries-Britt, 1998; Fries-Britt & Griffin, 2007; Fries-Britt & Turner, 2001; Harper, 2012a). Doubts concerning their deservingness of admission are related more generally to questions about Black students' intellectual competence.

In their analysis of data collected over four decades from 214,951 respondents to the UCLA Cooperative Institutional Research Program survey, Griffin, Jayakumar, Jones, and Allen (2010) observed that Black undergraduates in 2004 came from more affluent family backgrounds, had better academic records, and possessed higher levels of confidence in their skills and abilities than did their same-race peers who entered college in prior decades. Despite this, many Whites still believe the overwhelming majority of these students come from low-income families and K–12 schooling experiences that insufficiently prepared them for the rigors of college-level work, especially at highly selective institutions. Given their comparatively lower high school graduation and college enrollment rates, Black men are especially vulnerable to one particular presumption: they do not care about education (Harper & Davis, 2012). This stereotype is exacerbated by their overrepresentation in college athletics. Concerning the image of Black male student-athletes, "One could easily summarize their status as Niggers with balls who enroll to advance their sports careers and generate considerable revenue for the institution without learning much or seriously endeavoring to earn their college degrees" (Harper, 2009, p. 701).

Suspicions concerning Black students' intellectual competence and seriousness about education extend beyond men and student-athletes. Cokley (2003) describes the "anti-intellectual myth," a presupposition that Blacks are not very smart, well read, or serious learners, but instead are lazy and therefore undeserving of opportunities to attend postsecondary institutions of a certain caliber. This myth shows up in a variety of ways on predominantly White campuses, both inside and outside the classroom. For example, White students are often reluctant to select Black classmates to work with them on group projects, especially assignments that will be factored into their grades (Charles et al., 2009; Feagin et al., 1996; Fries-Britt & Griffin, 2007; Fries-Britt & Turner, 2001; Solórzano et al., 2000). Also, Black students are among the least likely to be invited by professors to collaborate on research projects (Harper, 2009, 2012b). Reportedly, some White faculty members are surprised when these students speak well in class and are skeptical when they perform exceptionally on papers (Harper, 2012a).

Outside the classroom, Black student leaders in Harper et al.'s (2011) study who were serving as resident assistants (a paid leadership position on residential campuses) indicated their White supervisors often doubted their competence to effectively perform the job duties. This resulted in hypersurveillance and particular forms of scrutiny from which their White peers seemed exempt. M. Davis et al. (2004) found that Black undergraduates often wrestled with dichotomous feelings of invisibility and hypervisibility. On the one hand, participants in their study felt invisible because the southern university they attended was so large and their encounters with onlyness were so frequent. But, on the other hand, they, like the resident assistants at the six PWIs in Harper et al.'s (2011) study, felt all eyes were often on them because they stood out racially from the majority—similar to a black fly floating in a glass of milk. If the one Black student in the course happens to miss a class session, his or her absence is much likelier than is a White classmate's to be noticed by the professor. When the Black student is present, he or she is considerably more likely than his or her majority peers to experience anxiety about being stereotyped as anti-intellectual and tokenized as the sole voice for all persons from his or her race.

Strayhorn (2008a) found that Black male students' sense of belonging at PWIs hinges in large part on interacting with peers from different racial/ethnic groups. Despite this, I have observed the following:

Their individual and collective belongingness at PWIs is threatened by the constant reinforcement of racist stereotypes that stigmatize them as dumb jocks, Black male criminals from the local community who do not belong on campus, affirmative action beneficiaries who were undeserving of admission, and underprepared "at-risk" students who all emerged from low-income families and urban ghettos. (Harper, 2009, p. 700)

Whereas Strayhorn and others (e.g., Chang et al., 2011; Hurtado et al., 1998; Hurtado et al., 2012) have found that interacting with peers who are racially different produces a range of educational benefits for undergraduates (including Blacks, but especially Whites), it is important to acknowledge that these interactions occasionally involve stereotyping and assorted forms of racial injury. That is, White students—the biggest beneficiaries of cross-racial interactions—oftentimes profit educationally at the expense of minoritized students who are put in the position to teach them and disrupt their racist assumptions (Harper, 2012b).

Despite the well-documented benefits of interactional diversity (Harper & Hurtado, 2007; Hurtado et al., 1998; Hurtado et al., 2012), Espenshade and Radford's (2009) analyses of data from 9,085 respondents to the National Survey of College Experience revealed far fewer than expected patterns of cross-racial interactions. Fifty-six percent of Black students in their sample reported substantive forms of interaction (frequent socialization outside of class, living together, dating, and close friendships) with White peers; only 19% of White respondents reported having had these forms of engagement with Black students. Similarly, participants in qualitative studies (e.g., Feagin et al., 2006; Harper & Hurtado, 2007) have reported persistent segregation trends on predominantly White campuses, despite espoused institutional values concerning student learning through interactions with diverse others (Morphew & Hartley, 2006).

When cross-racial interactions do occur at PWIs, Black students often find themselves on the receiving end of racial stereotypes. In fact, participants across the five PWIs (Harvard, Michigan State, UC Berkeley, University of Illinois, and University of Michigan) in Smith, Allen, and Danley's (2007) study unanimously characterized their campuses as comparatively more hostile toward Black students than Whites. Swim, Hyers, Cohen, Fitzgerald, and Bylsma (2003) termed what these students experience *everyday racism*. Their study included 51 participants at a large predominantly White research university who kept diaries of daily encounters with acts of discrimination, racism, and differential treatment they believed were attributable to their race. Incidents that students reported in their diaries were clustered into four major categories: (a) stares from White onlookers who appeared to be suspicious of or threatened by Blacks; (b) assorted verbal expressions of prejudice, including racial epithets (e.g., Nigger); (c) bad service in university offices and assorted campus establishments (i.e., dining facilities), and (d) miscellaneous interpersonal offenses, including being mistaken for the other Black student in a course, or White students deliberately choosing to not take the empty seat next to a Black person. All but one perpetrator of these incidents were White, and 58% were men.

Participants in numerous other studies (e.g., Feagin et al., 1996; Patton, 2006; Patton & McClure, 2009; Solórzano et al., 2000; Winkle-Wagner, 2009) have reported experiences consistent with Swim et al.'s (2003) study. Researchers have also found that White campus safety officials often require Black students to prove they belong on campus at rates higher than they do others (Smith et al., 2007); White students erroneously presume their Black male peers know where to buy marijuana and other drugs (Harper, 2012a); and assorted White others (including faculty and alumni) presuppose Black undergraduates are student-athletes, great dancers, and expert connoisseurs of rap/hip-hop music (Harper, 2009; Harper et al., 2011; Solórzano et al., 2000; Smith et al., 2007).

Sue et al. (2007) define racial microaggressions as "commonplace daily verbal, behavioral, or environmental indignities, whether intentional or unintentional, that communicate hostile, derogatory, or negative racial slights and insults toward people of color" (p. 271). These occurrences are different from overtly racist acts in that they are subtle and sometimes innocuous; in many instances, the aggressor is not even aware that she or he has behaved in a manner that could be experienced as racist. One example of a microaggression is asking an Asian American student who says she is from California where she is *really* from, which suggests she is not *really* an American. Other examples include telling a Black student he is "so articulate" or he is "not like those other Blacks," both of which convey to him that people from his racial group are not usually viewed as smart, thoughtful, trustworthy, and so on. Sue et al., as well as Harper et al. (2011) and Solórzano et al. (2000) make clear that individual microaggressions in isolation do not inflict much harm. However, the cumulative sum of them and constant exposure to everyday racism negatively affects minoritized students' academic outcomes, psychological wellness, and sense of belonging at PWIs.

Harper and Griffin (2011) note the threat of racial microaggressions and stereotypes is exacerbated at more selective postsecondary institutions, those at which affirmative action access policies and practices are most fiercely contested. Using data from the National Longitudinal Study of Freshmen, Charles et al. (2009) found that male students of color from affluent families, as well as those who had few same-race friends, were most vulnerable to the internalization of negative stereotypes. Moreover, students with strong academic identities—or those whom Steele (1997) would characterize as "highly domain identified"—are also especially susceptible to the negative effects of stereotype threat. Regarding the brightest and most academically capable students, Taylor and Antony (2000) posit,

> Their high degree of self-identification with this domain creates added internal pressure to be perceived in a positive light and to be successful. Thus, stereotype threat has the greatest effect on students who represent the academic vanguard of their group. (p. 187)

One by-product of stereotype threat is what Moore, Madison-Colmore, and Smith (2003) call the "prove-them-wrong syndrome." Undergraduate engineering students in their sample, much like Black participants in other research studies (e.g., Fries-Britt, 1998; Fries-Britt & Griffin, 2007; Fries-Britt & Turner, 2001, 2002; Harper et al., 2011), felt the need to disconfirm negative stereotypes about minoritized students. They often did this by assuming enormous pressure to prove their intellectual competence and right to admission. Interestingly, Cokley (2003) and Griffin (2006) found that some Black students were actually motivated by the proving process and therefore invested more serious effort into their academic pursuits. But Cokley (2001) reports these experiences oblige many Black male students to become "detached from academics and increasingly associated with activities where there are more Black male role models and perceived opportunities" (p. 485). He notes that most of these activities reside outside the classroom, a finding that also emerged in Fleming's (1984) study.

Having to constantly prove themselves and respond to racial stereotypes engendered psychological stress and other symptoms of "racial battle fatigue" (e.g., frustration, shock, anger, disappointment, resentment, anxiety, helplessness, hopelessness, and fear) among the Black collegians that Smith et al. (2007) interviewed. Scholars argue that encounters with racism also lead to troubling behavioral responses and resistant posturing (Harris, Palmer, & Struve, 2011), lowered self-concept (Griffin, Jayakumar, et al., 2010), disengagement inside and outside the classroom (Harper et al., 2011), overengagement in nonacademic clubs and organizations (Cokley, 2003; Fleming, 1984), and reliance on spirituality as a coping and restorative resource (Patton & McClure, 2009). Hurtado and Carter (1997) as well as Strayhorn (2008a, 2012) have linked persistence to sense of belonging in college. That is, undergraduates who feel like they belong and are valued and respected by faculty and peers are more likely to persist through baccalaureate degree attainment than are students who negatively experience their campus environments. The sense of belonging thesis in combination with experiences reported in this section helps explain (at least partially) why two thirds of Black men who start college do not graduate (Harper, 2012a). Not seeing others like them in positions of influence and authority at PWIs could also hamper Black students' motivation to excel, persist, and pursue higher levels of postsecondary education beyond the baccalaureate.

Shortage of Same-Race Faculty Role Models

Several higher education researchers (e.g., Astin, 1993; Bensimon, 2007; Harper, 2012a; Pascarella & Terenzini, 2005; Rendón Linares & Muñoz, 2011; Strayhorn, 2008b, 2012) have noted the important role that institutional agents, especially faculty, play in fostering campus environments that engender a sense of belonging for college students. Given their severe underrepresentation and encounters with "everyday racism" and microaggressions at PWIs, minoritized students need advocates who can validate their competence, belongingness, and racialized experiences. Professors of color most often play these roles at PWIs (Griffin, 2012; Griffin & Reddick, 2011; Turner, González, & Wood, 2008). But what happens on large campuses where minoritized students largely outnumber minoritized professors? Shown in Table 2 are student–faculty ratios at the 20 largest public universities in the United States. On average, there were 32 Black undergraduates to every one Black tenure track faculty member in fall 2010.

In their synthesis of 20 years of literature, Turner et al. (2008) found consistent reports of minoritized faculty being disproportionately affected by heavy service expectations on predominantly White campuses. Their work often includes serving as advisors, mentors, advocates, and problem solvers for students of color at rates that far exceed the engagement of their White faculty counterparts in similar activities. Put differently, students of color seek out White professors (those who are sometimes the perpetuators of low expectations and racial stereotypes in the classroom) less often than they do minoritized faculty role models who can offer restorative care, validation, culturally interesting research opportunities, and helpful advice on how best to navigate a racially alienating or hostile campus environment. Griffin and Reddick (2011) found that Black female faculty, in comparison to their Black male counterparts, carry a heavier burden of mentoring students. "This trend is especially problematic in that there is some indication that Black women may be expected to engage with students in close familial ways, regardless of their desire to do so and despite the personal costs" (p. 1051).

In addition to being sought out, many minoritized faculty members proactively establish relationships with minoritized students. They do so for a range of reasons, including feeling a sense of responsibility for protecting these students from racial injury in their academic programs and departments, elsewhere on campus, and in their future careers. In a qualitative study of Black professors in STEM fields at two PWIs, Griffin, Pérez, Holmes, and Mayo (2010) found the following:

TABLE 2
Black Undergraduates to Black Tenure Track Faculty Ratios at the 20 Largest Public Universities, Fall 2010

University	Undergraduates[a], N	Faculty[b], N	Ratio
Arizona State University	2,271	40	57:1
The Ohio State University–Main Campus	2,372	100	24:1
Pennsylvania State University–University Park	1,440	73	20:1
University of Central Florida	3,373	37	91:1
Texas A&M University–College Station	1,079	67	16:1
University of Texas at Austin	1,654	74	22:1
Michigan State University	2,401	71	34:1
Indiana University–Bloomington	1,389	54	26:1
University of Illinois at Urbana-Champaign	1,743	79	22:1
University of Florida	2,864	74	39:1
Purdue University–Main Campus	1,064	46	23:1
Rutgers University–New Brunswick	2,196	46	48:1
University of Minnesota–Twin Cities	1,251	54	23:1
Florida State University	2,881	45	64:1
University of Wisconsin–Madison	645	43	15:1
University of Arizona	838	19	44:1
University of Michigan–Ann Arbor	1,166	119	10:1
University of Washington	875	36	24:1
University of California–Los Angeles	937	56	17:1
University of California–Berkeley	741	37	20:1

a. Full-time, degree-seeking undergraduate students.
b. Tenured professors and associate professors; tenure track (untenured) assistant professors.
Source. U.S. Department of Education, Integrated Postsecondary Education Data System (IPEDS).

Experiences with mentors affected how professors engaged their mentees around issues of race and racism. A realization of the alienating climate for people of color in STEM played an important role in shaping how participants reached out to and mentored racial minority students. . . . Acknowledging the impact that race could have on their students' careers also pushed the faculty we interviewed to be proactive in their efforts to mentor. (p. 99)

Using social exchange theory, Griffin (2012) acknowledges that Black faculty benefit from the relationships they establish with students. For example, many minoritized professors grapple with similar feelings of onlyness that were described earlier in this chapter. It is not uncommon for a Black professor to be the only faculty member from her or his racial group in an academic program or department at a PWI. Thus, establishing relationships with Black students—even if they are from other academic disciplines on campus—affords these professors opportunities to at least interact with someone else from their same racial/ethnic group. Moreover, Griffin found that Black faculty also profit from working collaboratively with students who are interested in and familiar with their research topics.

Despite the mutually beneficial value of these same-race interactions, they occur irregularly at PWIs, especially in fields where faculty of color are grossly underrepresented (e.g., STEM and economics). Noteworthy is that Black faculty have other responsibilities, including teaching and service to their departments, universities, and academic fields of study. They also must interact with students from racial groups beyond their own, including Whites. Tierney and Bensimon (1996) posit that the more time faculty members spend interacting with students, the less time they have to commit to conducting and publishing research, which is focal in tenure and promotion processes at research universities. Exactly 30% of the Black faculty members at institutions listed in Table 2 were untenured assistant professors; 36.7% were associate professors who had not yet been promoted to the highest faculty rank. Thus, Black faculty at these institutions cannot afford to commit large quantities of time to teaching Black students about responding productively to racist stereotypes and addressing other campus climate problems. In addition to the underrepresentation of minoritized professors, participants in Harper et al.'s (2011) study reported a severe shortage of administrators of color. Those who had staff supervisors of color cited several corresponding benefits, including advice on how to best anticipate and negotiate complex racial politics of the six predominantly White campuses.

Integrating Black Students' Experiences at PWIs

I end this section with a short case example that integrates some of the experiential realities reported in the literature on Black undergraduates at PWIs. I recently gave a pair of lectures at a large, predominantly White university at which I met Damien, a pseudonym for a Black male student who shared with me a disturbing account. Damien was the only Black person—student or otherwise—in a large lecture-style course, an experience he had come to view as normal. At the beginning of one class session, his professor told the seven students who received perfect scores on a previous exam that they were excused from class and exempt from the next test. As the seven students gathered their belongings and paraded out the classroom, the professor stopped only one of them—Damien. "You got a 100%," the professor asked in a tone that simultaneously conveyed confusion and shock. He did not confront the six White students to confirm their perfect performance on the test—only the Black student was singled out. I asked Damien if the professor had perhaps formed a negative opinion of him based on prior interactions. He explained that the lecture hall was huge (more than 200 students) and it was therefore highly unlikely that the professor even knew him or anyone else by name.

In my view, Damien's story is a clear demonstration of niggering, as it was deemed surprising that the only non-White person in the course was one of very few students to earn a perfect score on the exam. This professor's doubt about Damien's intellectual competence is an example of a racial microaggression with which many minoritized students are often confronted. The message was that he surely was not smart or hard working enough to perform so well on a difficult academic activity. This encounter was just one layer of the onlyness Damien experienced from week-to-week as the only Black person in the large lecture hall. There were fewer than 10 Black tenure track faculty members at the university; none were in Damien's academic department. In fact, he had never taken a course taught by an instructor of color. Thus, his options for seeking advice from experienced same-race professors were extremely limited. What the literature on Black undergraduates has not yet made clear is where and how students like Damien learn to navigate the racist features of PWIs in the absence of more faculty of color to teach them.

PEER PEDAGOGIES ON PREDOMINANTLY WHITE CAMPUSES

Astin (1993) as well as Pascarella and Terenzini (2005) assert that peers exert the most influence on how undergraduates experience college. In this section, I summarize findings from the National Black Male College Achievement Study to provide insights into the role Black students play in teaching their same-race peers about responding productively to onlyness, racism, and racial stereotypes on campus. Most of what has been written on Black students at PWIs focuses on the challenges they face and a range of understandable, yet problematic responses to racism (e.g., withdrawal, lowered self-confidence, and aspiration reduction). As mentioned earlier, two thirds of Black undergraduate men who start college do not graduate, which is the lowest college completion rate among both sexes and all racial groups in U.S. higher education. A portion of these high attrition rates can be explained by debilitating encounters with racist stereotypes and an insufficient sense of belonging on predominantly White campuses (Harper, 2012a, 2012b; Strayhorn, 2008a). But one third persists through baccalaureate degree attainment. How do they learn to do so in light of racial realities that have been described in decades of literature on Black students at PWIs? Questions such as this were pursued in the National Black Male College Achievement Study, the largest qualitative research project on Black undergraduate men.

Data for this study were collected from 219 Black male undergraduates at 42 colleges and universities in 20 states across the nation. Four different types of

PWIs were represented in the national study (see Table 3); in addition, interviews were conducted with Black male achievers in HBCUs.[3] On average, the ratio of Black undergraduates to Black faculty at the 30 predominantly White colleges and universities was 43:1; these ratios varied by institution type (see Table 4). Administrators (provosts, deans of students, directors of multicultural affairs, etc.) nominated Black male undergraduates who had earned cumulative GPAs above 3.0, established lengthy records of leadership and engagement in multiple student organizations, developed meaningful relationships with campus administrators and faculty outside the classroom, participated in enriching educational experiences (e.g., summer research programs, internships, and study abroad programs), and earned numerous merit-based scholarships and honors in recognition of their undergraduate achievements. Each student participated in a 2 to 3 hour face-to-face individual interview on his campus and some follow-up interviews were conducted via telephone.

The national study moves beyond deficit perspectives on Black students by highlighting institutional agents, policies, programs, and resources that helped them achieve desired educational outcomes across a range of different institution types. An anti-deficit achievement framework was constructed for the study that inverts commonly asked research questions. For example, instead of adding to the now exhaustive body of literature that highlight all the negative effects of racist encounters on Black male student success in college, emphasis was placed on understanding how these students manage to craft productive responses to racism and factors that enable them to excel academically despite their encounters with racial microaggressions, stereotypes, and low expectations. Additional details about the framework and research methods are provided in Harper (2007, 2012a).

Analyses of data collected from the 30 PWIs in the national study revealed how Black students become institutional agents who assume responsibility for the instruction of their same-race peers at PWIs, specifically pertaining to navigating the campus racial climate. I introduce *peer pedagogies*[4] in this chapter, a term to characterize these practices. Below, I summarize these pedagogical practices, the sites in which such instruction routinely occurs, and how participants in the study assessed the effectiveness of their peer instructors.

Peers Teaching Peers About Race

"It started as soon as I arrived on campus: Black students made sure I knew what it was going to be like to be Black at Harvard." This student, like many others in the study, described a process through which their minoritized peers immediately assumed responsibility for socializing them to racial realities of their respective campus environments. Reportedly, students of color within the first few weeks of the school year engaged in what was characterized by some as a "campaign" to reach newcomers. Older students sometimes searched for same-race others in residence halls; and if they found themselves in courses with first-year students or unfamiliar faces, they would deliberately initiate conversations after class meetings early in the fall term. The structure of

TABLE 3
Predominantly White Institutions in the National Black Male College Achievement Study

Institution Type	College/University
Public research universities	University of Illinois at Urbana-Champaign
	Indiana University–Bloomington
	University of Michigan–Ann Arbor
	Michigan State University
	The Ohio State University–Main Campus
	Purdue University–Main Campus
Highly selective private research universities	Brown University
	Columbia University
	Harvard University
	University of Pennsylvania
	Princeton University
	Stanford University
Liberal arts colleges	Amherst College
	Claremont McKenna College
	DePauw University
	Haverford College
	Lafayette College
	Occidental College
	Pomona College
	Saint John's University (MN)
	Swarthmore College
	Vassar College
	Wabash College
	Williams College
Comprehensive state universities	Brooklyn College, City University of New York
	California State Polytechnic University, Pomona
	California State University, Long Beach
	Lock Haven University
	Towson University
	Valdosta State University

TABLE 4
Black Undergraduates[a] to Black Tenure Track Faculty[b] Ratios by Institution Type in the National Black Male College Achievement Study, Fall 2010

Institution Type	Mean Ratio
Public research universities	23:1
Highly selective private research universities	15:1
Liberal arts colleges	21:1
Comprehensive state universities	62:1

a. Full-time, degree-seeking undergraduate students.
b. Tenured professors and associate professors; tenure track (untenured) assistant professors.
Source. U.S. Department of Education, Integrated Postsecondary Education Data System (IPEDS).

these conversations were often threefold: (a) to introduce oneself to the only other or one of few minoritized students in the class or on the residence hall floor, (b) to invite the new student to contact her or him if ever she or he needed anything, and (c) to forewarn the new student of future feelings and experiences (e.g., onlyness and racial stereotyping) she or he will likely have. This initial exchange often compelled the new student to ask for specific details concerning the realities of race on campus. "He was talking about racism this and racism that—I needed examples. He gave them to me. It scared me," one participant at Lock Haven recalled.

In addition to targeting peers of color in classrooms and campus residential facilities, older students also coupled racial socialization efforts with recruitment for Black/ethnic student organizations. Each institution in the study hosted an annual fall semester student organization recruitment event, which usually included tables staffed by student leaders who distributed promotional materials and talked with peers about joining their respective clubs. Part of the pitch to join groups such as Black Student Union, NAACP, and the National Society of Black Engineers (NSBE), to name a few, was a conversation about why such organizations were essential on a predominantly White campus. An Ohio State student said someone told him, "You're gonna need NSBE because you're gonna be the only Black person in your engineering classes. NSBE will allow you to see other Black students." Others reported the sharing of similar perspectives from peers who were in other academic-related ethnic student organizations (e.g., the Black Wharton Undergraduate Association at Penn). "He asked me if I was in a class where I was the only Black student. I said yes. And he said, 'See that's why you need to join this group.'"

A participant from Occidental remembered an older Black female student assuring him he would need Black Student Alliance. "She said you may not fully recognize why now, but trust me, you will eventually understand." She went on to clarify that the organization served as a safe haven from the toxicity of the campus racial climate. He joined. Others elsewhere indicated that they were intrigued enough to attend at least one meeting of these organizations to see if they were as necessary as the ambassadors and group leaders claimed. A Cal Poly participant shared the following: "I hadn't experienced any type of racism yet. I actually never really even expected to. But I went to the meeting to see what these other minorities were saying about their experiences." Although ethnic student organization leaders articulated a range of seductive aims and purposes associated with membership, participants said they almost always used racial underrepresentation (and the corresponding consequences of onlyness), as well as racial problems on campus, to simultaneously teach and recruit.

Michigan State and a few other universities in the study offered bridge programs to help undergraduates transition from high school to higher education. These programs usually took place over 6 to 8 weeks in the summer preceding students' first semester/quarter on campus. Reportedly, upperclassmen that either volunteered or were paid to work for these programs used their positions as platforms through which to teach students about the realities of race on campus. Formally through structured panels and informally via small group conversations over meals, these older students shared insights into their prior encounters with onlyness and racial microaggressions as well as with racist experiences that were more overt. Beyond storytelling, they also advised program participants on how best to respond to racial issues that would inevitably emerge; shared lists of faculty and staff advocates they should seek out when confronted with racism; insisted that these incoming students use resources in campus counseling centers, as well as in Black/multicultural centers; touted the benefits of membership in ethnic student organizations; explained the necessity of solidarity among minoritized students; and volunteered to engage in longer-term success partnerships with program participants that included but extended beyond racial problem-solving.

Sites of Peer Instruction

Beyond summer bridge programs, minoritized undergraduates used their pedagogies and racial socialization methods in several other venues on the predominantly White campuses. As previously mentioned, leaders of ethnic student organizations often engaged in the simultaneous process of teaching and recruiting. Most participants in the national study were members of at least one predominantly Black campus club. Meetings focused mostly on planning events and other activities aligned with foundational purposes of the groups. Notwithstanding, participants noted that time in these meetings was spent, oftentimes unintentionally, processing racist encounters, validating members' individual and collective experiences, and brainstorming effective ways to respond to and disrupt racism.

I remember one meeting . . . one minute we were trying to decide who was going to the national conference, then suddenly the conversation turned to folks venting about all the racist shit that had happened to them that week.

When I asked how often this occurred, this Indiana University participant laughingly responded, "every single meeting." He was clear that student organization meeting agendas were not devoted entirely to sharing stories but were adaptable enough to afford members much-needed opportunities to vent and exchange navigational strategies that had proven effective.

Based on 2 years of ethnographic fieldwork, Jackson (2012) offers a detailed account of how Black undergraduate men were united through a gender-specific student organization that fostered among them a bond of brotherhood, which, in turn, helped them collectively navigate the challenges of a predominantly White campus. Similar groups existed on several campuses in my national study—H.E.A.D.S. at University of Michigan, Brothers Keeper at Indiana University, Harvard Black Men's Forum, the Princeton Black Men's Awareness Group, and a chapter of Student African American Brotherhood at Cal State Long Beach, to name a few. Though not a formal student organization, undergraduate men of color gathered regularly for "Cold Cuts" at DePauw University, a space in which they fellowshipped, engaged in substantive conversations with same-race others, and received low-cost haircuts (finding a Black barbershop in Greencastle, Indiana, was reportedly difficult).

These groups and spaces served as more than sites for Black men to gather socially. They were also instructional venues for teaching and learning about the racial realities of the PWIs in my project. For example, Black Men United (BMU) is a group at the University of Pennsylvania that brings together students once every 3 weeks for food and structured conversations about Black experiences on campus, politics and social issues, and other topics pertinent to communities of color. That space and others like it elsewhere allow Black male undergraduates to be themselves without the threat of stereotypes. It also enables them to share stories of racial encounters and devise both individual and collective responses. "BMU has taught me how to not only survive, but thrive at Penn," one participant in the national study remarked. Achievers elsewhere said they learned actual strategies from peers in groups such as BMU who had figured out how to deal productively with onlyness, stereotypes and racial insults, and other potentially harmful encounters with White faculty and peers. Furthermore, these were settings in which the participants' intellectual competence and sense of belonging were affirmed. In some ways, merely being in the presence of other talented Black male student leaders taught participants that there were others like them who were smart, validation that was often missing in classrooms where they were lone representatives of their racial group.

Whereas men's groups were cited often as instructional spaces, it is worth noting that participants benefited from having male and female peer instructors on their campuses. Because Black women outnumbered Black men at every institution in the national study (sometimes by more than 2:1), they often had a greater numerical presence and assumed leadership in black/ethnic student organizations at much higher rates. "Sistas hold it down for all of us here. We learn so much from them," a Swarthmore student acknowledged. These women employed pedagogical strategies not only in summer bridge programs and student organizations but also in campus activities sponsored by the Black or multicultural center. Many consciousness-raising dialogues were hosted at the PWIs; technique and resource sharing usually followed awareness, processing, and validation at these events. Resources sometimes included recommendations for people to see on campus who could be helpful, virtual communities on Facebook and blogs, and instructive things to read.

Pedagogies were not always employed in public spaces. Many participants shared stories of individualized instruction they had received from their peers, which sometimes included assigned readings about Blacks and other minoritized students at PWIs. One senior talked about a book his RA gave him 2 years prior:

It was on the stuff African American students go through on white campuses like Purdue. Reading that made me feel normal; I didn't feel crazy anymore. Reading that made me realize that I am not the only one who feels this way. If he hadn't given me that book, I don't think I would have made it here. I remember talking to him after I read the book. We processed the whole thing and he let me know how he has coped with these experiences. He was a graduating senior, so I took notes and benefited from his wisdom. Now I am graduating from Purdue, thanks in part to him and that book he made me read.

Others reflected on critical peer interactions that sounded like one-on-one tutoring on the subject of race. These discussions between minoritized students occurred in residence hall rooms, dining facilities on and off campus, in culture centers, and sometimes immediately after a class session in which assorted racial microaggressions had been committed. These strategy discussions were mainly initiated and facilitated by Black women and men who held some type of leadership role on campus (including, but not limited to, positions in ethnic student organizations).

Attribution and Assessment of Peer Education

Like the graduating senior who predicted he would not have "made it" at Purdue, several others asserted that persisting from year-to-year would have been difficult (in some instances, impossible) had it not been for the instruction they received from other minoritized students. Similar statements were made about ethnic student organizations, especially the groups created expressly for Black undergraduate men. Most participants credited same-race peers for awakening their understandings of what it takes to productively respond to racism at PWIs. Accordingly, they learned the most about race neither in courses nor from professors but from peers in a multitude of spaces. "If there weren't any Black students at Saint John's, I don't know who else would've taught me about myself. I guess it would've been all on me."

In many instances, the achievers actually named other minoritized peers from whom they had learned much about negotiating the realities of race on campus. For example, here is a verbatim exchange between a participant and me in response to an interview question he misunderstood:

Me: Tell me about an extraordinary teacher you have had here.
Participant: Her name is Brandy. She is truly extraordinary.
Me: What classes have you taken with her?
Participant: Classes? Oh, my bad. I didn't realize you were asking about an actual
    professor . . .

Me: Oh, well who is Brandy?

Participant: She's a leader in the Black student community here. She's the person who taught me and a whole lot of other students of color on this campus how to succeed academically, given that the environment is so unfriendly to us. She is our best teacher.

My question was situated in a section of the interview protocol that aimed to identify effective educational practices employed by faculty members. Admittedly, I expected this student to name a professor. Although no one else misunderstood this question, numerous participants at other points in their interviews reflected in similar ways about the powerful impact same-race peers had on their success in general and the shaping of their racial response strategies in particular.

Finally, men I interviewed overwhelmingly attributed their own leadership and engagement on campus to the example set by peers who had been their teachers. That is, they felt a sense of responsibility to become teachers of others because of the instruction they had received. They became resident assistants and leaders in other spaces who reached out to students of color in ways similar to how they had been targeted in prior years. They used similar instructional approaches that had enticed them to join Black/ethnic student organizations. And they ensured that agendas for student organizations, especially Black male groups, included time for the strategic sharing of stories, resources, and strategies that would help minoritized students succeed at higher rates. A Wabash student shared the following: "Many people of color took the time to school me on how to survive this campus. I am taking what I learned and teaching it to other African American students. It would have been selfish of me not to." Considering the reciprocal responsibility of peer instruction, one participant asked, "Am I my brother's teacher?" He responded immediately to his own question with "yes, if not me, then who?"

CONCLUSION

Over 40 years of published research consistently documents troubling racial realities for Black undergraduates and other minoritized students on predominantly White campuses. In the 1960s and 1970s, these experiences ignited student activism and aggressive demands for institutional responsiveness. Scholarship from that era focuses much on student agency. But more recent studies pertaining to race in higher education have been almost entirely concerned with the effects of alienating and debilitating campus racial climates on sense of belonging, as well as a range of academic, social, and psychological outcomes for Black students. These have been important contributions.

Necessary is the publication of new scholarship that unmasks the personal and institutional enablers of achievement, including more sophisticated examinations of how minoritized students manage to persist through baccalaureate degree attainment despite what is known to be the realities of race at many PWIs. Much more remains to be understood about contemporary forms of Black student agency—specifically, how they socialize their same-race peers to racially problematic campus environments, co-create protective and instructional spaces, pass on effective pedagogical practices from one cohort to another, and help each other productively navigate PWIs. Findings from the National Black Male College Achievement Study extend what has long been known about Black students in higher education. More instructive insights into how Black students productively navigate racist spaces are needed, as opposed to studies that focus exclusively on the harmful effects of onlyness, niggering, and stereotyping, and limited access to supportive same-race faculty role models.

The powerful influence of peers on college student outcomes has been well documented in the higher education literature (Astin, 1993; Bensimon, 2007; Pascarella & Terenzini, 2005). Nuances concerning what minoritized undergraduates do to positively affect learning, developmental change, and persistence among their same-race peers and other students of color are lacking in the literature. For example, several arguments have been made in defense of diversifying the student body on college and university campuses. One rationale has been that students (especially White undergraduates) learn much from the cultural knowledge that racially diverse peers bring with them to postsecondary learning environments (Hurtado et al., 1998; Hurtado et al., 2012). Details concerning pedagogical strategies undergraduates employ within and across their racial groups, as well as the content of what students teach each other about race, would advance the study of peer influences in college.

Deeper explanations of organizational resistance and the durability of toxicity in predominantly White campus contexts are also worthy of further study. Given the consistent themes documented in research on racial climates and minoritized student experiences at PWIs, why has institutional change been so slow? Why are onlyness, niggering, and racial microaggressions still so pervasive? Why is the representation of minoritized faculty so low, and Black student to Black faculty ratios so incongruent? In light of espoused institutional commitments to inclusion and diversity (Morphew & Hartley, 2006), why does it remain necessary for undergraduates such as those from PWIs in the National Black Male College Achievement Study to assume the responsibility (or burden) of teaching their same-race peers how to productively navigate campus environments that are contaminated by racism? Studies that explore these and other institution-focused questions would add much to the body of knowledge on racial climates at predominantly White colleges and universities.

NOTES

[1]"Minoritized" is used instead of "minority" throughout this chapter to signify the social construction of underrepresentation and subordination in U.S. social institutions, including colleges and universities. Persons are not born into a minority status nor are they minoritized in every social milieu (e.g., their families, racially homogeneous friendship groups, or places of religious worship). Instead, they are rendered minorities in particular situations and institutional environments that sustain an overrepresentation of whiteness.

[2]The Du Bois College House was created for "any undergraduate student of any race who wishes to study and foster Afro-American culture" at the University of Pennsylvania (Glasker, 2002, p. xvi).

[3]The national study also included 12 Historically Black Colleges and Universities.

[4]Peer pedagogies have not been introduced elsewhere and are being defined herein as the methods minoritized students use to teach each other about the racial realities of predominantly White colleges and universities, as well as how to respond most effectively to racism, racial stereotypes, and microaggressions they are likely to encounter in classrooms and elsewhere on campus.

REFERENCES

Allen, W. R. (1992). The color of success: African American college student outcomes at predominantly White and historically Black public colleges and universities. *Harvard Educational Review, 62*(1), 26–44.

Astin, A. W. (1993). *What matters in college: Four critical years revisited.* San Francisco, CA: Jossey-Bass.

Bensimon, E. M. (2007). The underestimated significance of practitioner knowledge in the scholarship on student success. *Review of Higher Education, 30,* 441–469.

Berger, J. B., & Milem, J. F. (2000). Exploring the impact of historically Black colleges in promoting the development of undergraduates' self-concept. *Journal of College Student Development, 41,* 381–394.

Chang, M. J., Milem, J. F., & Antonio, A. L. (2011). Campus climate and diversity. In J. H. Schuh, S. R. Jones, & S. R. Harper (Eds.), *Student services: A handbook for the profession* (5th ed., pp. 43–58). San Francisco, CA: Jossey-Bass.

Charles, C. Z., Fischer, M. J., Mooney, M. A., & Massey, D. S. (2009). *Taming the river: Negotiating the academic, financial, and social currents in selective colleges and universities.* Princeton, NJ: Princeton University Press.

Chavous, T. M., Harris, A., Rivas, D., Helaire, L., & Green, L. (2004). Racial stereotypes and gender in context: African Americans at predominantly black and predominantly white colleges. *Sex Roles, 51*(1), 1–16.

Clark, E. C. (1993). *The schoolhouse door: Segregation's last stand at the University of Alabama.* New York, NY: Oxford University Press.

Cokley, K. (2001). Gender differences among African American students in the impact of racial identity on academic psychosocial development. *Journal of College Student Development, 42,* 480–487.

Cokley, K. O. (2003). What do we know about the academic motivation of African American college students? Challenging the "anti-intellectual myth." *Harvard Educational Review, 73,* 524–558.

Crump, W. L. (1991). *The story of Kappa Alpha Psi: A history of the beginning and development of a college Greek letter organization* (4th ed.). Philadelphia, PA: Kappa Alpha Psi Fraternity International Headquarters.

Davis, J. E. (1994). College in black and white: Campus environment and academic achievement of African American males. *Journal of Negro Education, 63,* 620–633.

Davis, M., Dias-Bowie, Y., Greenberg, K., Klukken, G., Pollio, H. R., Thomas, S. P., & Thompson, C. L. (2004). A fly in the buttermilk: Descriptions of university life by successful undergraduate students at a predominately White Southeastern university. *Journal of Higher Education, 74,* 420–445.

DeSousa, D. J., & Kuh, G. D. (1996). Does institutional racial composition make a difference in what Black students gain from college? *Journal of College Student Development, 37,* 257–267.

Espenshade, T. J., & Radford, A. W. (2009). *No longer separate, not yet equal: Race and class in elite college admission and campus life.* Princeton, NJ: Princeton University Press.

Feagin, J. R., Vera, H., & Imani, N. (1996). *The agony of education: Black students at White colleges and universities.* New York, NY: Routledge.

Fleming, J. (1984). *Blacks in college: A comparative study of students' success in Black and in White institutions.* San Francisco, CA: Jossey-Bass.

Flowers, F. A. (2002). The impact of college racial composition on African American students' academic and social gains: Additional evidence. *Journal of College Student Development*, 43, 403–410.

Fries-Britt, S. L. (1998). Moving beyond Black achiever isolation: Experiences of gifted Black collegians. *Journal of Higher Education*, 69, 556–576.

Fries-Britt, S., & Griffin, K. A. (2007). The black box: How high-achieving Blacks resist stereotypes about Black Americans. *Journal of College Student Development*, 48, 509–524.

Fries-Britt, S. L., & Turner, B. (2001). Facing stereotypes: A case study of Black students on a White campus. *Journal of College Student Development*, 42, 420–429.

Fries-Britt, S., & Turner, B. (2002). Uneven stories: Successful Black collegians at a Black and a White campus. *Review of Higher Education*, 25, 315–330.

Fries-Britt, S., Younger, T. K., & Hall, W. D. (2010). Lessons from high-achieving students of color in physics. In S. R. Harper & C. B. Newman (Eds.), *Students of color in STEM* (pp. 75–83). San Francisco, CA: Jossey-Bass.

Glasker, W. (2002). *Black students in the ivory tower: African American student activism at the University of Pennsylvania, 1967–1990.* Amherst: University of Massachusetts Press.

Goldstone, D. (2006). *Integrating the 40 acres: The fifty-year struggle for racial equality at the University of Texas.* Athens: University of Georgia Press.

Griffin, K. A. (2006). Striving for success: A qualitative exploration of competing theories of high achieving Black college students' academic motivation. *Journal of College Student Development*, 47, 384–400.

Griffin, K. A. (2012). Black professors managing mentorship: Implications of applying social exchange frameworks to analyses of student interactions and their influence on scholarly productivity. *Teachers College Record*, 114(5), 1–37.

Griffin, K. A., Jayakumar, U. M., Jones, M. M., & Allen, W. R. (2010). Ebony in the ivory tower: Examining trends in the socioeconomic status, achievement, and self-concept of Black male freshmen. *Equity & Excellence in Education*, 43, 232–248.

Griffin, K. A., Pérez, D., II, Holmes, A. P. E., & Mayo, C. E. P. (2010). Investing in the future: The importance of faculty mentoring in the development of students of color in STEM. In S. R. Harper & C. B. Newman (Eds.), *Students of color in STEM* (pp. 95–103). San Francisco, CA: Jossey-Bass.

Griffin, K. A., & Reddick, R. J. (2011). Surveillance and sacrifice: Gender differences in the mentoring patterns of Black professors at predominantly White research universities. *American Educational Research Journal*, 48, 1032–1057.

Gurin, P., Dey, E. L., Hurtado, S., & Gurin, G. (2002). Diversity and higher education: Theory and impact on educational outcomes. *Harvard Educational Review*, 72, 330–367.

Harper, S. R. (2007). Using qualitative methods to assess student trajectories and college impact. In S. R. Harper & S. D. Museus (Eds.), *Using qualitative methods in institutional assessment* (pp. 55–68). San Francisco, CA: Jossey-Bass.

Harper, S. R. (2009). Niggers no more: A critical race counternarrative on Black male student achievement at predominantly White colleges and universities. *International Journal of Qualitative Studies in Education*, 22, 697–712.

Harper, S. R. (2012a). *Black male student success in higher education: A report from the National Black Male College Achievement Study.* Philadelphia: University of Pennsylvania, Center for the Study of Race and Equity in Education.

Harper, S. R. (2012b). Race without racism: How higher education researchers minimize racist institutional norms. *Review of Higher Education*, 36, 9–29.

Harper, S. R., & Davis, C. H. F., III. (2012). They (don't) care about education: A counternarrative on Black male students' responses to inequitable schooling. *Educational Foundations*, 26(1), 103–120.

Harper, S. R., Davis, R. J., Jones, D. E., McGowan, B. L., Ingram, T. N., & Platt, C. S. (2011). Race and racism in the experiences of Black male resident assistants at predominantly White universities. *Journal of College Student Development, 52,* 180–200.

Harper, S. R., & Griffin, K. A. (2011). Opportunity beyond affirmative action: How low-income and working-class Black male achievers access highly selective, high-cost colleges and universities. *Harvard Journal of African American Public Policy, 17*(1), 43–60.

Harper, S. R., & Hurtado, S. (2007). Nine themes in campus racial climates and implications for institutional transformation. In S. R. Harper & L. D. Patton (Eds.), *Responding to the realities of race on campus* (pp. 7–24). San Francisco, CA: Jossey-Bass.

Harper, S. R., Patton, L. D., & Wooden, O. S. (2009). Access and equity for African American students in higher education: A critical race historical analysis of policy efforts. *Journal of Higher Education, 80,* 389–414.

Harris, F., III, Palmer, R. T., & Struve, L. E. (2011). "Cool posing" on campus: A qualitative study of masculinities and gender expression among Black men at a private research institution. *Journal of Negro Education, 80,* 47–62.

Hurtado, S. (1992). The campus racial climate: Contexts of conflict. *Journal of Higher Education, 63,* 539–569.

Hurtado, S., Alvarez, C. L., Guillermo-Wann, C., Cuellar, M., & Arellano, L. (2012). A model for diverse learning environments: The scholarship on creating and assessing conditions for student success. In J. C. Smart & M. B. Paulsen (Eds.), *Higher education: Handbook of theory and research* (Vol. 27, pp. 41–122). New York, NY: Springer.

Hurtado, S., & Carter, D. F. (1997). Effects of college transition and perceptions of the campus racial climate on Latino students' sense of belonging. *Sociology of Education, 70,* 324–345.

Hurtado, S., Milem, J. F., Clayton-Pedersen, A. R., & Allen, W. R. (1998). Enhancing campus climates for racial/ethnic diversity: Educational policy and practice. *Review of Higher Education, 21,* 279–302.

Jackson, B. A. (2012). Bonds of brotherhood: Emotional and social support among college Black men. *Annals of the Academy of Political and Social Science, 642*(1), 61–71.

Kammen, C. (2009). *Part and apart: The black experience at Cornell, 1865–1945.* Ithaca, NY: Cornell University Libraries.

Lambert, F. (2010). *The battle of Ole Miss: Civil rights v. states' rights.* New York, NY: Oxford University Press.

McCormick, R. P. (1990). *Black student protest movement at Rutgers.* Piscataway, NJ: Rutgers University Press.

Moore, J. L., III, Madison-Colmore, O., & Smith, D. M. (2003). The prove-them-wrong syndrome: Voices from unheard African American males in engineering disciplines. *Journal of Men's Studies, 12*(1), 61–73.

Morphew, C. C., & Hartley, M. (2006). Mission statements: A thematic analysis of rhetoric across institutional type. *Journal of Higher Education, 77,* 456–471.

Newman, C. B., Mmeje, K., & Allen, W. R. (2012). Historical legacy, ongoing reality: African American men at predominantly white institutions of higher education. In A. A. Hilton, J. L. Wood, & C. W. Lewis (Eds.), *Black males in postsecondary education: Examining their experiences in diverse institutional contexts* (pp. 87–104). Charlotte, NC: Information Age.

Pascarella, E. T., & Terenzini, P. T. (2005). *How college affects students. Volume 2: A third decade of research.* San Francisco, CA: Jossey-Bass.

Patton, L. D. (2006). The voice of reason: A qualitative examination of Black student perceptions of Black culture centers. *Journal of College Student Development, 47,* 628–646.

Patton, L. D. (Ed.). (2010). *Culture centers in higher education: Perspectives on identity, theory, and practice.* Sterling, VA: Stylus.

Patton, L. D., & McClure, M. L. (2009). Strength in the spirit: A qualitative examination of African American college women and the role of spirituality during college. *Journal of Negro Education, 78,* 42–54.

Perna, L. W., Milem, J., Gerald, D., Baum, E., Rowan, H., & Hutchens, N. (2006). The status of equity for Black undergraduates in public higher education in the south: Still separate and unequal. *Research in Higher Education, 47*, 197–228.

Rendón Linares, L. I., & Muñoz, S. M. (2011). Revisiting validation theory: Theoretical foundations, applications, and extensions. *Enrollment Management Journal, 2*(1), 12–33.

Ross, L. C. (2000). *The divine nine: The history of African American fraternities and sororities.* New York, NY: Kensington.

Sedlacek, W. E. (1987). Black students on White campuses: 20 years of research. *Journal of College Student Personnel, 28*, 484–495.

Smith, W. A., Allen, W. R., & Danley, L. L. (2007). Assume the position . . . you fit the description: Psychosocial experiences and racial battle fatigue among African American male college students. *American Behavioral Scientist, 51*, 551–578.

Snyder, T. D., & Dillow, S. A. (2012). *Digest of education statistics, 2011.* Washington, DC: National Center for Education Statistics, Institute of Education Sciences.

Sollors, W., Titcomb, C., & Underwood, T. A. (Eds.). (1993). *Blacks at Harvard: A documentary history of African-American experience at Harvard and Radcliffe.* New York: New York University Press.

Solórzano, D. G., Ceja, M., & Yosso, T. J. (2000). Critical race theory, racial microaggressions, and campus racial climate: The experiences of African American college students. *Journal of Negro Education, 69*, 60–73.

Steele, C. M. (1997). A threat in the air: How stereotypes shape intellectual identity and performance. *American Psychologist, 52*, 613–629.

Strayhorn, T. L. (2008a). Fittin' in: Do diverse interactions with peers affect sense of belonging for Black men at predominantly White institutions? *Journal of Student Affairs Research & Practice, 45*, 501–527.

Strayhorn, T. L. (2008b). The role of supportive relationships in facilitating African American males' success in college. *Journal of Student Affairs Research & Practice, 45*, 26–48.

Strayhorn, T. L. (2012). *College students' sense of belonging: A key to educational success for all students.* New York, NY: Routledge.

Sue, D. W., Capodilupo, C. M., Torino, G. C., Bucceri, J. M., Holder, A. M. B., Nadal, K. L., & Esquilin, M. (2007). Racial microaggressions in everyday life: Implications for clinical practice. *American Psychologist, 62*, 271–286.

Swim, J. K., Hyers, L. L., Cohen, L. L., Fitzgerald, D. C., & Bylsma, W. H. (2003). African American college students' experiences with everyday racism: Characteristics of and responses to these incidents. *Journal of Black Psychology, 29*, 38–67.

Taylor, E., & Antony, J. S. (2000). Stereotype threat reduction and wise schooling: Towards the successful socialization of African American doctoral students in education. *Journal of Negro Education, 69*, 184–198.

Tierney, W. G., & Bensimon, E. M. (1996). *Promotion and tenure: Community and socialization in academe.* Albany: State University of New York Press.

Trillin, C. (1964). *An education in Georgia: Charlayne Hunter, Hamilton Holmes, and the integration of the University of Georgia.* New York, NY: Viking.

Turner, C. S. V., González, J. C., & Wood, J. L. (2008). Faculty of color in academe: What 20 years of literature tell us. *Journal of Diversity in Higher Education, 1*, 139–168.

U.S. Department of Education. (2012). *The Integrated Postsecondary Education Data System.* Washington, DC: National Center for Education Statistics, Institute of Education Sciences.

Williams, C. G. (2001). *Technology and the dream: Reflections on the black experience at MIT, 1941–1999.* Cambridge: MIT Press.

Williamson, J. A. (2003). *Black power on campus: The University of Illinois, 1965–75.* Champaign: University of Illinois Press.

Willie, C. V., & Cunnigen, D. (1981). Black students in higher education: A review of studies, 1965–1980. *Annual Review of Sociology, 7*, 177–198.

Winkle-Wagner, R. (2009). *The unchosen me: Race, gender, and identity among Black women in college.* Baltimore: Johns Hopkins University Press.

Chapter 7

Narrative Inquiry as Pedagogy in Education: The Extraordinary Potential of Living, Telling, Retelling, and Reliving Stories of Experience

JANICE HUBER
University of Regina

VERA CAINE
University of Alberta

MARILYN HUBER
Independent Scholar

PAM STEEVES
University of Alberta

In the last chapter of *The Truth About Stories: A Native Narrative* (2003), as Thomas King continues to show that "the truth about stories is that that's all we are" (p. 153), he draws close Ben Okri's (1997) thoughts:

In a fractured age, when cynicism is god, here is a possible heresy: we live by stories, we also live in them. One way or another we are living the stories planted in us early or—knowingly or unknowingly—in ourselves. We live stories that either give our lives meaning or negate it with meaningless. If we change the stories we live by, quite possibly we change our lives. (Okri, 1997, as cited in King, 2003, p. 153)

Central in King's puzzle over ways in which changing the stories we live by might change our lives is his story of experiences he lived in relation with a family he once knew, a family with whom he gradually fell out of relation. As he puzzles over why he lived out a story of disconnecting himself from this family, King wonders about dominant narratives shaping North America, dominant narratives that, as described by Okri, we knowingly or unknowingly live by. In particular, King (2003) wonders about the ethics woven into dominant North American narratives: "It's not that we

Review of Research in Education
March 2013, Vol. 37, pp. 212-242
DOI: 10.3102/0091732X12458885
© 2013 AERA. http://rre.aera.net

don't care about ethics or ethical behavior" (p. 163). "Perhaps we shouldn't be displeased with the . . . ethics . . . or any myriad of other codes of conduct suggested by our actions. After all, we've created them. We've created the stories that allow them to exist and flourish" (p. 164). King then concludes: "Want a different ethic? Tell a different story" (p. 164).

As coauthors of this chapter and as educators who compose our lives as narrative inquirers yearning for dominant narratives in classrooms, schools, universities, and the broader places where people interact to be shifted through attention to relationships and lives in the making, understandings of telling, and of living, a different story if we want a different future, keep us hopeful. As we wrote this chapter attentive to the focus of this volume of *Review of Research in Education* on "extraordinary pedagogies for working within school settings serving nondominant students" (C. Faltis & J. Abedi, 2011, personal communication), we held close understandings of ways in which narrative inquiry embodies potential for shaping extraordinary pedagogy in education. We see this potential of narrative inquiry to remake life in classrooms, schools, and beyond as centrally situated in Clandinin and Connelly's (1998) understanding that it is education that lives at the core of narrative inquiry "and not merely the telling of stories" (p. 246). They write,

> We see living an educated life as an ongoing process. People's lives are composed over time: biographies or life stories are lived and told, retold and relived. For us, education is interwoven with living and with the possibility of retelling our life stories. As we think about our own lives and the lives of teachers and children with whom we engage, we see possibilities for growth and change. As we learn to tell, to listen and to respond to teachers' and children's stories, we imagine significant educational consequences for children and teachers in schools and for faculty members in universities through more mutual relations between schools and universities. No one, and no institution, would leave this imagined future unchanged. (pp. 246–247)

This understanding of narrative inquiry, that is, as attending to and acting on experience by co-inquiring with people who interact in and with classrooms, schools, or in other contexts into living, telling, retelling, and reliving stories of experience, lives at the heart of our chapter. We stay attentive to this understanding in each of the four upcoming parts: *The Transcendent Power of Story, Turning Toward the Study of Narrative in Academia, Diverse Methodological Understandings of Narrative in Education Research,* and *Narrative Inquiry, Education Pedagogy, and the Composing of Lives.* Our attentiveness to this central aspect of ways in which narrative inquiry opens possibilities for shifting stories, and therefore, lives, connects us with the knowing of many people whose thinking in relation with story, narrative, experience, and lives shapes our thinking and living as narrative inquirers. In this way, too, our chapter draws readers toward the voices of people who share a vision of the centrality of attending to lives, and the making and remaking of lives, as vitally important work in classrooms, schools, and communities.

PART 1: THE TRANSCENDENT POWER OF STORY

As we begin our chapter with a focus on the transcendent, enduring nature of story, we explore briefly the ancient yet timeless ways in which we human beings have and continue to draw on stories as a way to share, and to understand, who we are, who we have been, and who we are becoming. We also draw on an understanding of the responsibilities and obligations that come with the telling and retelling of experiences. As Lopez (1990) describes,

The stories people tell have a way of taking care of them. If stories come to you, care for them. And learn to give them away where they are needed. Sometimes a person needs a story more than food to stay alive. That is why we put stories into each other's memory. This is how people care for themselves. One day you will be good storytellers. Never forget these obligations. (p. 60)

Throughout the ages and across cultures story continues to express the fundamental nature of humanity. Stories are not to be treated lightly as they both carry, and inspire, significant obligations and responsibilities: stories must be cared for as they are at the heart of how we make meaning of our experiences of the world. Indeed, "storytelling is about survival" (Ross, 2008, p. 65).

The intergenerational aspects of the interwoven nature of human existence and story are made visible by Trinh Minh-ha (1989) when she puts into writing her understanding of *Grandmas' story* as the world's earliest archives carried in the memories of women. *Grandmas' story* "depends on everyone of us coming into being. It needs us all, needs our remembering, understanding, and creating what we have heard together to keep on coming into being. The story of a people. Of us, peoples" (p. 119). Our very identities as human beings are inextricably linked to the stories we tell of ourselves, both to ourselves and with one another.

Similarly, Le Guin (1980) speaks of the ageless nature of storytelling as she reminds us of the enduring draw of the campfire. As generation after generation circle round the fire, stories flow endlessly, gathering us together. Le Guin writes that as we "huddle closer," the stories we tell one another bear witness to our lives, and in this way, she wonders, if perhaps, one of the shortest stories told was an ancient one chiseled in runes on a stone in Northern England translated as "Tolfink carved these runes in this stone." Like Tolfink, Le Guin believes we story ourselves into being, "unwilling to dissolve into darkness" (p. 194). For Le Guin, it is in these ways that we plant our stories in the lives of future generations: we remind them through our stories and the visible remains of the traces our lives leave behind.

Writer and storyteller Marmon Silko (1996) draws further attention to ways stories connect us, allowing us to be present to and with one another and all things, continuing through generations. In her writing, Marmon Silko paints images of the communal process of storytelling in the Pueblo tradition, which is inclusive of all experiences, even difficult ones, so that a person need never separate from the group or feel alone. Everyone, from the youngest to the oldest in the family, is expected to be a part of the listening, the telling, and the remembering. An intergenerational community is brought into being through the sharing of ancestors' stories and stories of ancestors. We learn this understanding as Marmon Silko remembers her Aunt Susie telling her as a child, "They are out there. Let them come in. They're here, they're here with us, *within* the stories" (p. 59). Likening communal storytelling to a journey on an inner landscape, Marmon Silko writes of imagination and growing awareness and that being human is both different from, yet connected to, all things living. As she learned from her ancestors, stories are teachings of the heart: "If you can remember the stories you will be all right. Just remember the stories" (p. 58).

Additionally, as she writes about the distinction of her people learning how to live *with* the land rather than *on* the land, Marmon Silko (1996) shows that in the Pueblo tradition "human identity, imagination and storytelling were inextricably linked to the land" (p. 21). Places on the landscape, she writes, serve as reminders of the events of stories and show ways to survive physically and spiritually, on both inner and outer landscapes. Being on the land calls forth stories embedded within the land and, too, within our bones. Living in the midst of these stories, and our interactions with them, they become part of who we are and who we are becoming. These embodied, lived stories, however, as Crites (1971) describes, may never "be fully and directly told, because they live, so to speak, in the arms and legs and bellies" (p. 295) of people.

As someone who extensively travelled in and interacted with northern Alaska, Lopez (1989) explores his relation with the land through the evocative power of stories. Describing these interactions, Lopez highlights how it was through stories that he became more connected with the lives of animals and the landscape itself, thus deepening his experience and his understanding. As he crossed open ground, Lopez heard stories of the wolverine. Listening to these stories shared by trappers evoked something within Lopez, drawing him closer to what it might mean to be a wolverine and deepening his understanding of fierceness. Lopez believes that this kind of encounter with the wolverine, through story, shaped his inner landscape and, in this way, afforded him a richer experience of wild animals and a more responsive engagement. Indeed, Lopez writes that "the landscape seemed alive because of the stories" (p. 63).

Cruikshank, a researcher who spent years with Elders in the Yukon, a northern territory of Canada, articulates her awakening to ways in which the Elders spoke in stories about their lives—stories of people, animals, and the land intermingling. Of cultural value, and as a way to gain wisdom, the people travelled with narratives providing a kind of map containing pragmatic information as well as offering diverse ways to be in the world. The stories were from long ago and of the present. Angela Sidney, one of the Elders, told Cruikshank (1990): "You people talk from paper, me, I want to talk from grandpa" (p. 356). For Angela Sidney, story is education in its most holistic form, a kind of education that honors the knowledge of previous generations. Reflecting back, Angela Sidney shared that she has "tried to live her life right, just like a story" (p. 340).

As Cruikshank came to know and to understand something of this centrality of stories in the lives of Yukon Elders, she wondered at the persistence of stories through tumultuous times. These wonders, in part, drew Cruikshank (2005) back to the Yukon and into continued relationships, both of which she depended on in her more recent work. In *Do Glaciers Listen? Local Knowledge, Colonial Encounters, and Social Imagination*, she explores how "orally narrated stories do indeed provide empirical observations about geophysical changes and their consequences. But they also demonstrate how glaciers provide substantive material for evaluating changes wrought by colonial histories" (p. 12). Additionally, Cruikshank became "especially intrigued by . . . the potential of stories to make us re-evaluate situations we think we understand" (p. 79).

In compelling and differing ways, each of these writers reveals how narrative transcends temporal, contextual, cultural, and social boundaries. Indeed, Marmon Silko (1996) speaks of human communities as living beings that continually change and, as a result, while the stories change with time, they never end. As well, Trinh Minh-ha (1989) emphasizes that a story, once told, cannot be taken back, but instead perpetually finds ways into other stories: a story is never ending, but changing. Expressing this deeply transcendent, enduring nature of story, Trinh Minh-ha writes that "the story is beautiful, because or therefore it unwinds like a thread. A long thread, for there is no end in sight. Or the end she reaches leads actually to another end, another opening, another 'residual deposit of duration'" (p. 149).

Reading and thinking with the works of the writers made visible above, our living as narrative inquirers has grown increasingly layered, contextualized, alive, and moving. We see their ideas as foreshadowing tremendous potential for pedagogy in classrooms, schools, universities, and communities. Imagining pedagogy through the transcendent power of story, we see how much difference, openness, and place matter. As we are quieted by these thoughts, wonders emerge. We wonder, for example, about possibilities for storying and restorying ourselves and one another into being; we wonder about new kinds of, or maybe forgotten or written over, obligations and ways of interacting and responding to and with one another.

PART 2: TURNING TOWARD THE STUDY OF NARRATIVE IN ACADEMIA

Although numerous writers, as shown above, focus on some of the earliest understandings of story, other writers study narrative from diverse perspectives. As Clandinin and Rosiek (2007) describe, although "narrative inquiry is an old practice that may feel new to us for a variety of reasons" (p. 35), indeed

human beings have lived out and told stories about that living for as long as we could talk. And then we have talked about the stories we tell for almost as long. These lived and told stories and the talk about the stories are one of the ways . . . we fill our world with meaning and enlist one another's assistance in building lives and communities. What feels new is the emergence of narrative methodologies in the field of social science research. With this emergence has come intensified talk about our stories, their function in our lives, and their place in composing our collective affairs. (pp. 35–36)

There has, for example, been a long history of narrative within the traditions of narratology, the study and theory of narrative. The term *narratology* is often used in relation to literary theory and literary criticism. In the 1960s and 1970s, the French structuralists were preoccupied with an overriding concern about linguistic structures (e.g., Levi Strauss's [1963] work on universal structures relevant to different cultural examinations of myth and Labov's [1966] inquiries into sociolinguistic studies of oral stories). These ideas about narrative structures remain traceable in the widespread work of narrative theorists who continue to focus on the literary aspects of narrative in research. We say more about this form of narrative research in Part 3, *Diverse Methodological Understandings of Narrative in Education Research*.

The study of narrative also became increasingly prevalent for theologians, philosophers, psychotherapists, historians, linguists, and literary figures (e.g., Bruner, 1986; Carr, 1986; Crites, 1971; Heilbrun, 1988; Kerby, 1991; MacIntyre, 1981). Indeed, as Mitchell (1981) describes, "To raise the question of the nature of narrative is to invite reflection on the very nature of culture and, possibly, even on the nature of humanity itself" (p. 1). Similarly, Bruner (1986) suggests that narrative knowing is a primary act of mind.[1] Writing that "the formal quality of experience through time is inherently narrative" (p. 291) theologian Crites (1971) argues that experience is storied phenomena. As well, Carr (1986) calls for particular attention to the temporal nature of experience as lives unfold. Both Carr (1986) and Kerby (1991) speak about narrative identity as dependent on the degree of coherence and continuity that can be construed as lives are composed.

In linking this early focus on narrative with the ancient, timeless draw of stories foregrounded in Part 1, we now shift our focus toward the already well-documented "turn to narrative" in social science research.

The Emergence of Narrative in the Social Sciences

Pinnegar and Daynes (2007) describe the turn to narrative in social science research as a time when "the academy opened up in a way that made a space for narrative inquiry" (p. 3). They highlight four thematic turns in this movement. Of the four, the most significant for narrative inquiry was the change of relationship between the researcher and "the researched." In this turn, *subjects* in human research are no longer treated as fixed in place, that is, as static, atemporal, and decontextualized. When drawing on the methodology of narrative inquiry, which explores stories, narratives of experience, as the phenomenon of interest, narrative inquirers "embrace a relational understanding of the roles and interactions of the researcher and the researched" (p. 15). Other shifts, according to Pinnegar and Daynes, include turns toward understanding stories as *data*, moving toward the particular from the universal, and an acknowledgement of blurred, tentative, and multiple ways of knowing. Pinnegar and Daynes describe all of these movements as stemming from a fundamental shift in which attention to people's experiences became central. In this shift toward understanding experience, experience is understood as "the stories people live. People live stories and in the telling of them reaffirm them, modify them, and create new ones" (Clandinin & Connelly, 1994, p. 415).

Understandings such as those highlighted by Pinnegar and Daynes (2007) and Clandinin and Connelly (1994) are both shaped by and continue to reverberate within and across numerous fields of study, including anthropology, education, medicine, nursing, psychology, and sociology. Although narrative either as a method used within a research study or as a research methodology continues to evolve, when attending to the four narrative turns described by Pinnegar and Daynes (2007), we see ways in which landscapes for narrative research in the social sciences began to take shape. In this way, too, we see the interlapping of ideas across fields of study as narrative terms from one discipline were picked up by researchers working within other disciplines.

In the field of anthropology, for instance, story shaped ways for researchers to interrupt the way people of Indigenous cultures were traditionally studied. An example of this interruption is shown in Sarris's (1993) book where he tells the story of Mabel McKay from Mabel's perspective and not from the perspective of an academic with primary commitments to the academy. Basso (1996), too, is respectful of the non-Western ways of knowing of the Western Apache and of their relation to the land and storytelling, which they recollect as "wisdom sits in places" (p. 53).

Also within the field of anthropology, Geertz (1983) highlights the value of the particular through his notion of "local knowledge." In his memoir, Geertz (1995) looks back on the changes he experienced over time and in so doing brings attention to the temporal and that everything is continually changing. He writes,

The problem is that more has changed and more disjointly than one first imagines. The two towns of course have altered, in many ways superficially, in a few ways profoundly. But so and likewise has the anthropologist. So has the discipline within which he works, the intellectual setting within which that discipline exists, and the moral basis on which it rests. (p. 2)

In the field of psychiatry, Coles (1989) writes of his turn toward narrative as shaped early in his career through his interactions with Dr. Ludwig, one of his supervisors: "What ought to be interesting, Dr Ludwig kept insisting, is the unfolding of a lived life rather than the confirmation such a chronicle provides for some theory" (p. 22). In this way, Coles draws attention to the ethical responsibility involved in narrative, noting that "their story, yours, mine—it's what we all carry with us on this trip we take, and we owe it to each other to respect our stories and learn from them" (p. 31).

Within the broad field of psychology, Bruner (1986) is a pioneer in the establishment of the idea that narrative is a primary way of knowing and that we construct worlds from our own perspectives, living by story. Similarly, as Polkinghorne (1988) highlights the need for research approaches that are "especially sensitive to the unique characteristics of human existence," he turns toward "narrative knowledge" (p. x), which he gradually describes as two narrative forms of inquiry, "analysis of narrative" and "narrative analysis" (Polkinghorne, 1995).

Also within the field of psychology, Freeman (2010) and Sarbin (2004) highlight processes of imagination in narrative work. Sarbin writes of imaginings as embodied and perceptual knowing that is constructed narratively such that we draw on our rememberings and enable our *as if* stories. Without imagining there is no possibility of becoming. Additionally, Freeman (2010) considers autobiographical inquiry as a reconfiguring of the past in an evolving narrative that makes sense in present circumstances, thereby shaping more responsive and responsible living in the future. Describing this understanding, Freeman writes that autobiographical inquiry, "Thus emerges as a fundamental tool for ethical and moral recollection, taken here is the classical sense of 'gathering together' that which would otherwise be lost owing to our pervasive tendency toward forgetfulness" (p. 26).

As feminist orientations began to arise in many disciplines within the academy, people working within diverse fields were drawn toward considerations of alternative ways of thinking and working, ways that continued to shape openings for the increasing acceptability of narrative as, or within, research (Pinnegar & Daynes 2007). One groundbreaking example of this intersection between narrative and feminist theories took shape within the field of psychology as research on voice in relation with women's knowledge and identity was pursued collaboratively by psychologists Belenky, Clinchy, Goldberger, and Tarule (1986). Along with the provocative idea of researching and writing collaboratively, Belenky et al. write of women's development in terms of "a narrative sense of self—past and future" (p. 136).

Similar intersections between feminist understandings and narrative can be seen in the work of cultural anthropologist Bateson (1989), who writes of women "composing lives" in improvisatory and relational ways, always making sense of transitions through inventing new stories. Educators Hollingsworth, Dybdahl, and Turner Minarik (1993) also worked in collaborative ways with one another and with groups of teachers as they developed the notion of "relational knowing," knowing that evolves over time through sustained conversation and relationships. As well, lived knowledge and understandings of complex and pluralistic identities permeates the work of Lugones (1987) as she explores how "we inhabit 'worlds' and travel across them and keep all the memories" (p. 14). Playing with the idea that as our lives unfold, as we move into and between multiple worlds, Lugones shows that as we "*world*"-*travel* across *worlds* we construct images of who we are and what we are about, as well as images of who others are and what they are about. Carrying forward these images from across *worlds*, we gain deeper understandings of ourselves, of others, and of the contexts in which we live.

In the reverberations shaped in these intersections between narrative and feminist orientations within and across multiple disciplines, the publication of books such as *This Bridge Called My Back: Writings by Radical Women of Color* (Moraga & Anzaldúa, 1984); *Borderlands/La Frontera: The New Mestiza* (Anzaldúa, 1987); *Making Face, Making Soul/Haciendo Caras: Creative and Critical Perspectives by Feminists of Color* (Anzaldúa, 1995); *Zami: A New Spelling of My Name* (Lorde, 1983); *Sister Outsider: Essays and Speeches* (Lorde, 1984); and *Ain't I a Woman? Black Women and Feminism* (hooks, 1981) shaped awareness of what Adichie more presently names as "the danger of a single story" (Adichie, 2009, TEDGlobal, posted October 2009).

The Emergence of Story, of Narrative Inquiry as Research

Shaping a homeplace for narrative inquiry within this emerging narrative landscape, while at the same time keeping experience as a foremost consideration in their understanding of life in classrooms, Clandinin and Connelly's development of narrative inquiry as a research methodology is deeply shaped by their well-documented turn, and returns, to the works of the paramount philosopher in education in the 20th century, John Dewey (1925, 1934, 1938). For Dewey, education, life, and experience are one and the same. Education is life and life is education, and to study life, to study education, is to study experience. As a philosopher of experience, Dewey theorizes the key terms *personal, social, temporal,* and *situation* to describe characteristics of experience based on his principles of interaction and continuity. Considering the quality of interaction and the quality of continuity in any given situation, Dewey highlights the possibility of understanding experience as educative or mis-educative.[2] Dewey's conceptualization of the nature of experience engendered a way to explore experience, and for Clandinin and Connelly (2000) his ideas shaped an "imaginative backdrop" (p. 2) for the development of narrative inquiry.

Engaged in teacher education, with a particular interest in teacher knowledge, Connelly and Clandinin (1988) grew increasingly attentive to additional education scholars for whom understanding experience is central. In particular, two educational philosophers, Johnson (1990), whose work focuses on embodied knowing, and MacIntyre (1981), whose work focuses on narrative unity, further shaped the development of Clandinin and Connelly's (1994) early conceptualization of narrative inquiry as both phenomenon and method.[3] They write,

It is equally as correct to say inquiry into narrative as it is to say narrative inquiry. By this we mean that narrative is both phenomenon and method. Narrative names the structured quality of experience to be studied and it names the patterns of inquiry for its study. (p. 416)

As we show in later chapter parts, Clandinin and Connelly (2000; Connelly & Clandinin, 2006) now argue they no longer see narrative inquiry as method but as methodology and, even more so, as a way of composing a life, of living (Connelly & Clandinin, 2006). Such understandings shift attention away from narrative inquiry as only focusing on the telling or representation of stories to understandings that "relationship is key to what it is that narrative inquirers do" (Clandinin & Connelly, 2000, p. 189).

As narrative inquirers draw on these understandings of narrative inquiry they note, as highlighted by Elbaz-Luwisch (2010, drawing on Griffiths & MacLeod, 2007), that narrative inquiry is increasingly written about as not only a research methodology but as relationships that can "provide a hearing for the stories of people on the margins, whose experience is generally not heard" (p. 274).

Indeed, narrative inquiry resides in the relationship of researcher and participant(s) who may also become co-researchers as the relationship evolves. It is through relationship that the co-composing of new lives for both becomes possible. Experience as in continual motion and as in continuous co-composition, which shaped narrative inquiry terms such as "being in the midst" (Clandinin & Connelly, 2000, p. 63), are now quite commonly understood as critically important in methodological and pedagogical understandings of narrative inquiry. Woven within these understandings are additional understandings of the messy, uncertain, and nonlinear nature of living out narrative inquiries.

PART 3: DIVERSE METHODOLOGICAL
UNDERSTANDINGS OF NARRATIVE IN EDUCATION RESEARCH

In this part of our chapter, we turn toward a focus on some of the diverse and ever-emergent understandings of narrative research methodology. Within the field of education, the possibilities of including perspectives from authors who engage with narrative on diverse academic or disciplinary landscapes supported a broader and deeper knowing of engaging in inquiries, as well as increasingly textured and richly nuanced descriptions of these engagements. As we highlighted earlier in relation with Marmon Silko's (1996) understandings of story and place, particular stories begin to grow out of particular landscapes.

In 1993, for example, Carter highlights that story and narrative were beginning to be used in the field of education, particularly in relation with understanding teacher knowledge. Considering what it means to be human through studying experience narratively allowed for much more expansive and compelling entry points into educational studies than did a traditionally narrow, technical approach. Drawing on Noddings's (1991) sense that "stories have the power to direct and change our lives" (p. 157), Carter (1993) expresses the excitement of bringing teachers' storied knowledge to bear on research in teaching and teacher education. At the same time, however, Carter points out that in acknowledging teachers' voices a different world for teacher educators might need to take shape, perhaps a world shaped by "helping teachers come to know their own stories" (p. 8).

Also in 1993, Greene brought into the conversation in education stories of "not yet" as she argues for the centrality of the arts and story in a "curriculum for human beings" (p. 211). Greene's notions of *wide-awakeness* and of stories of "not yet" intertwined most notably with narrative inquiry in the possibility and promise of retelling and reliving experience in new and more attentive ways. Additionally, Greene (1995) writes of the necessity of teachers revisiting childhood landscapes to discern multiplicity in the "shapes of childhood" narratives. This notion of multiple selves gave rise to awakening to the idea that there could be other ways of being and living in the world. These ideas became particularly important for narrative inquirers focused on the continual motion of experience and of the potential of retelling stories of our lives through attending across time, place, and situations.

In this same era, Paley's work in education supported attention to the wholeness of children's lives, that is, to ways in which children make sense of their experiences through story and play. Paley (1997) considers schools as places "where children are broken into pieces in order that adults may observe, label and classify them" (p. 54). Indeed, Paley wonders, "And having been so dissected, how does the child become whole again" (p. 54). Significant for narrative inquirers who come to these ideas are the links with living stories, that is, that we are always in a process of becoming.

Although Polakow's (1994) work echoes similar concerns, she positions her research into the lives, and silences, of single mothers and children as both situated within, yet also shaped beyond, dominant institutional (school) narratives to include broader social, cultural narratives at work in America. As she reflects on how the "language of democracy muffles the voices of poor women and their children that echo in the invisibility of the spaces *we* have constructed for *them*," Polakow describes that she has "chosen to tell the story of one vulnerable and growing group of people, for I too am a mother" (p. 3). However, in coming to know and to tell the mothers' stories, Polakow reveals that she has been profoundly affected by the experience, that is, that as she engaged in the inquiry she gradually awakened to the understanding that she cannot know the stories of the mothers and children without reflecting on herself and ways in which the lives of the mothers are considerably different from her life as a mother.[4]

This focus in Polakow's (1994) work on the need to know, the need to understand stories still silent is highlighted in Casey's (1995) review of narrative in education when she writes that "the repertoire of stories still waiting to be told (and studied) is practically limitless. What better way to grapple with making sense of our rapidly changing world than through the study of stories?" (p. 240).

Similarly, as Delpit (1995) writes from within her experiences as a Black mother of a child "who has struggled through nine schools from first to eleventh grade in our attempt to find a school that makes sense" (p. xiii), she highlights that "students of color are doubly disadvantaged in trying to get their voices heard, particularly in the university classroom" (p. 109). Matters of voice and narrative intersect again in Delpit's work as she stories the experiences of non-White educators who feel left out of the dialogue and silenced in matters around educating children from diverse backgrounds. Delpit urges attentiveness to these margins and to the silencing that lives in these places. She simultaneously calls forward questions of whether or not educators are really hearing the stories of so many children and youth in schools. Similar concerns about the "need for story" in classrooms and schools are raised by Dyson and Genishi (1994) when they write that in the midst of then "current concerns about our increasingly diverse student population and about the school's effectiveness in serving those students, we collectively declare . . . the need for story" (p. 6).

One of the ways this growing awareness of the "need for story" in education research was taken up can be traced through Barone's (2001) scholarship, seminal work in shaping a "literary turn in human studies" that opened up possibilities for research embodying "characteristics of imaginative literature, including expressive, evocative language and an aesthetic form" (p. 2). The reverberations from this scholarship continue as, for example, Coulter and Smith (2009, drawing on Barone, 2007) recently drew on Barone's earlier notion of "narrative constructions" as a "recasting of data into a storied form" (p. 577) to argue that "the purposes of research are not antithetical to the purposes of narrative, which include keeping the reader reading to the last page, and that the use of literary elements helps the process" (p. 587).

Rose's (1989) work, which traces his own earlier lived experience as he simultaneously attends to the experiences of youth presently marginalized in schools as a result of dominant institutional narratives that perpetually position youth from "working class backgrounds" as low achieving, is a strong example of the kind of scholarship that marked this turn toward the literary aspects of telling stories as research. In the work of each of these writers it is the wholeness of lives, and the play of contexts on those lives, which directs where attention needs to be turned. Similarly, Vinz (1996, 1997) highlights a teaching life as always in motion, as always composing. Her notions of *dispositioning* to *un know* and *not know* open up understandings of the importance of seeing teachers as in processes of continual growth and change. Phillion, He, and Connelly (2005) further engaged with teachers from diverse backgrounds to bring less often heard narratives to the fore.[5] So, too, did hooks (1994) as she inquires into experiences in her life, experiences both as she was growing up and as she teaches adult students. Miller (1998), reflecting on Greene's (1995, 1997) thoughts about the necessity of incompleteness in teachers' stories, similarly highlights that "incompleteness certainly points to forms of autobiographical inquiry that challenge any fixed or predetermined notions of who one 'is' or 'could be'" (p. 153). The importance of tentative knowing resonates as a tenet of narrative inquiry. Tentative knowing embraces a multiplicity of perspectives over time and place, preserving a sense that the story could be told otherwise. It calls forth that the story is for now; it is unfinished.

As these ideas in relation with narrative and education became significant, so, too, did the ideas of Clandinin and Connelly (1986), which express a similar sense that

the narrative study of schooling has potential for freeing education from a language of the technical, for ensuring that understandings link with fundamental qualities of human experience; and for establishing bonds in method and meaning between education and other fields of endeavor. (p. 385)

Clandinin and Connelly (1986) connect their fundamental premise about narrative to their interest in the "becoming" of teachers. With respect to narrative they write that "it is the study of how humans make meaning by endlessly telling and retelling stories about themselves that both refigure the past and create purpose in the future" (1986, p. 385). They link the development of teacher knowledge not to the development of specialized techniques and terminology but to "providing (teachers) opportunities for reflection upon their practice particularly at moments of contradiction and discontinuity to allow novice teachers to begin to reconstruct their narratives of experience" (p. 386).

For Connelly and Clandinin (1988), one aspect opened up through these experiential, narrative understandings of the enduring influence of teachers' life experiences in shaping classrooms and schools is that curriculum is a life course, a journey that continuously emerges, taking shape along the way. Understanding curriculum in this experiential way requires that "all teaching and learning questions—all curriculum matters—be looked at from the point of view of the involved persons" (p. 4). Connelly and Clandinin see that the people most centrally involved in curriculum are teachers and children.

Key in this experiential, multidimensional, and relational understanding of curriculum as something co-shaped by teachers and children interacting in school situations is that

> situations are . . . composed of persons, in an immediate environment of things, interacting according to certain processes. . . . At any point in time there is a dynamic interaction among persons, things, and processes. . . . Every classroom situation grows out of some preceding classroom situation. . . . Situations have a future. . . . Situations are directional. (Connelly & Clandinin, 1988, pp. 6–9)

These situations and experiences are shaped and shared by children and teachers as they each draw forth and rely on their personal knowledge. It is this knowledge that children and teachers carry forward and that gets called forth in situations; thus, each enters situations as knowing beings. This narrative understanding of teachers' personal knowledge is described by Connelly and Clandinin as "personal practical knowledge." They write that this experiential, narrative understanding of teacher's knowledge

> is a term designed to capture the idea of experience in a way that allows us to talk about teachers as knowledgeable and knowing persons. . . . [Personal practical knowledge is found] in the person's past experience, in the person's present mind and body, and in the person's future plans and actions. Knowledge is not only "in the mind." It is "in the body." And it is seen and found "in our practices." [Personal practical knowledge] is a particular way of reconstructing the past and the intentions for the future to deal with the exigencies of a present situation. (Connelly & Clandinin, 1988, p. 25)

In this way, then, "a narrative, curricular understanding of the person is an understanding that is flexible and fluid" (Connelly & Clandinin, 1988, p. 25), it is an understanding that

> recognizes that people say and do different things in different circumstances and, conversely, that different circumstances bring forward different aspects of their experience to bear on the situation. According to this view, a person's personal practical knowledge depends in important measure on the situation. . . . A narrative understanding of who we are and what we know, therefore, is a study of our whole life, but it does not presume a kind of syrupy "Hollywood" unity. It acknowledges the tensions and differences within each of us. We are, in important ways, what the situation "pulls out" of us. (Connelly & Clandinin, 1988, pp. 25–26)

These similar and differing ideas in relation with narrative and education, each traceable to questions of experience and of the place of experience in composing lives, continue to unfurl in shaping narrative inquiry as a research methodology in education. So, too, do questions about the different ways in which narrative is methodologically understood within education research. Here we are reminded of the works of authors foregrounded in Part 2 and the range of ways in which narrative is understood and taken up, which includes structural linguistic understandings, understandings of plot lines, literary analysis, the composition of literary texts as research, and so on.

In exploring the borderlands between narrative inquiry and postpositivist, Marxist, and poststructuralist forms of inquiry, Clandinin and Rosiek (2007) highlight "borderlands *within* the community of narrative inquirers" (p. 68, italics in original). They offer the following explanation as a way to show these borderlands:

Some narrative inquirers are more interested in the structure of professional identity narratives. Others are more interested in the difficulty some individuals have in addressing the big picture social justice issues in our world. Others are more interested in working with people to aesthetically craft new narrative representations of experience. Some find themselves working to combine these interests and others. (p. 68)

Exploring these internal borderlands, Clandinin and Rosiek (2007) make clear that just as borderlands with narrative inquiry and postpositivist, Marxist, and poststructuralist forms of inquiry can be spaces of tension, struggle, and possibility so, too, can the borderlands within the growing field of narrative inquiry.

Additionally, Clandinin and Murphy (2009) explore ways in which borderlands within narrative inquiry can be shaped by differing ontological and epistemological assumptions. Woven into and among Clandinin and Murphy's wonders is their understanding of narrative inquiry as relational research. They write,

First, and most important, we speak to our participants and ourselves to fulfil the relational responsibilities of representing our co-constructed experiences. The priority in composing research texts is not, first and foremost, to tell a good story; the priority is to compose research texts in relation with the lives of our participants and ourselves. (p. 600)

Clandinin and Murphy (2009) outline three additional concerns about ways in which not privileging the relational in narrative research texts could cause misunderstandings, particularly among readers new to narrative research. They wonder, for example, if less of a focus on the relational aspects might displace, and subsequently result in readers overlooking, the ontological commitment to the relational that "locates ethical relationships at the heart of narrative inquiry" (p. 600). They also revisit ways in which the research texts composed by narrative inquirers need "to [stay open to] invit[ing] meaning making on the part of the reader," in part, "because of the nature of storied experience itself" (p. 600). Their final concern is about ways narrative research texts could be read, that is, as the narrative inquirer being positioned as an "omniscient researcher as someone 'possessing all of the facts'" (p. 601) instead of making visible ways in which narrative inquirers are also part of the phenomena under study. Similarly, as Munro (2007) reflects on "the future of narrative," she writes that "research is still seen as representation. We invest our trust in methods not in our relationships" (p. 493).

In this chapter section, as well as in earlier parts, we have travelled to, within, and across differing times, places, situations, and relationships. In so doing we showed some of the similar as well as different ways in which story and narrative in and as research methodology in and outside of education are understood across cultures, places, and times. We also showed some of the similarities and differences between understandings of narrative in research in diverse fields, including within the field of education (see also Barrett & Stauffer, 2009; Conle, 2003; 2010; Coulter, Michael, & Poynor, 2007; Murray Orr & Olson, 2007). As readers are likely sensing, our living and thinking as narrative inquirers is grounded within Clandinin and Connelly's (2000) understandings of experience as the central aspect of narrative inquiry. They write that

as we tell our stories as inquirers, it is experience, not narrative, that is the driving impulse. We came to narrative inquiry as a way to study experience. For us, narrative is the closest we can come to experience. Because experience is our concern, we find ourselves trying to avoid strategies, tactics, rules, and techniques that flow out of theoretical considerations of narrative. Our guiding principle in an inquiry is to focus on experience and to follow where it leads. (p. 188)

Although these experiential understandings of narrative inquiry are central in the living and telling of our research, we also see their potential reverberations in education pedagogy, reverberations filled with the promise of seeing and living anew.

PART 4: NARRATIVE INQUIRY, EDUCATION PEDAGOGY, AND THE COMPOSING OF LIVES

In bringing these methodological understandings to an understanding of pedagogy in education, we see that who a teacher is and who a teacher is becoming is indelibly connected with the processes, strategies, or style(s) of instruction lived out by a teacher. This too is lived out as teachers are profoundly connected with their students, families, and communities. Thinking in this narrative way about pedagogy we draw on Clandinin and Connelly's (2000) description of narrative inquiry as an ongoing process of "thinking narratively" (p. 21). Becoming increasingly interested in the possibilities opened up by thinking narratively, Clandinin and Connelly draw on Dewey's (1938) theory of experience and his notions of situation, continuity, and interaction to encourage attention to three inquiry terms or "commonplaces of narrative inquiry" (Connelly & Clandinin, 2006, p. 479). These terms are *temporality* (which draws attention to the past, present, and future), *sociality* (which draws attention to interaction between the personal and the social), and *place* (which draws attention to the place or places where stories of experience are lived and told). Furthermore, Downey and Clandinin (2010) highlight that "stories are not just about experience but experience itself; we live and learn in, and through, the living, telling, retelling, and reliving of our stories" (p. 387).

Clandinin, Huber, Steeves, and Li (2011) echo these ideas, that is, that thinking narratively as narrative inquirers is "much more than telling or analyzing stories" (p. 34). They draw on Morris's (2002) distinction between thinking about stories and thinking with stories:

The concept of thinking with stories is meant to oppose and modify (not replace) the institutionalized Western practice of thinking about stories. Thinking about stories conceives of narrative as an object. Thinking with stories is a process in which we as thinkers do not so much work on narrative . . . [but allow] narrative to work on us. (p. 196)

When thinking narratively with stories as pedagogy, that is, attending to the meeting of the diverse lives of teachers, children, families, and communities in school and university classrooms, we need to stay wakeful to the three-dimensional narrative inquiry space. Staying wakeful in this way entails that we are simultaneously attentive to the temporal, social, and place dimensions and interactions within and among all of the stories, all of the personal, social, institutional, cultural, familial, and linguistic experiences lived out and told. We more fully illuminate these ideas in the upcoming section, *Thinking with Counterstories*.

It follows then, that in understanding pedagogy in education by thinking narratively we need to understand teachers, children, families, and community members, individually and socially, as composing storied lives, inside and outside of schools. We also need to understand teachers, children, families, and community members as continuously living out the moments of their days by stories of who they are and who they are becoming. These individual stories entangle with, become shaped by, and shape one another. Similarly, the stories lived and told by children, families, teachers, and community members entangle with and become shaped by, while at times also shape social, cultural, institutional, linguistic, and familial narratives.

Thinking narratively about pedagogy is a complex undertaking. This complexity, in part, is shaped by understanding that all of the stories are always in the midst (Clandinin & Connelly, 2000). Each story, whether personal, social, institutional, cultural, familial, or linguistic, is alive, unfinished, and always in the making; stories continue to be composed with and without our presence. Another complexity that emerges when thinking narratively about pedagogy is that doing so entails the asking of hard questions about what is educative (Dewey, 1938) in the composing of lives. In this way, schooling becomes more than a didactic effort, more than a mere telling of facts, or stories. Education in our lives as narrative inquirers is an ongoing process that sees education as unfolding over time, through interactions, across generations, and embedded within place or places. In thinking narratively we sense responsibilities and obligations to children, families, and communities. Seeing schools in these ways means that we need to imagine the significance and possibilities that our work as educators holds. As we engage with children, youth, families, and also with students in university classrooms, we need to imagine future possibilities and retellings of our encounters.

Here, we are reminded of Lyons and LaBoskey's (2002) work, which looks at teaching practices as scholarship and makes narrative teaching practice public as various scholars across North America story their pedagogy. Lyons, in later work (2010), examines reflective practices and sees some of the key components as having a perspective on knowing, making investigations into one's own practice, taking on an inquiry stance to interrogate the contexts of learning, and adopting attitudes necessary for acquiring the methods of inquiry. Downey and Clandinin (2010) add to this conversation as they explore the tensions and possibilities of understanding narrative inquiry as a form of reflective practice.

Although outside the field of education, yet significant when attending to the importance of thinking narratively in practice, Clandinin and Cave (2008; Clandinin, Cave, & Cave 2011) worked with medical practitioners to develop narrative life histories and identities, in which they see as intertwined practitioners' personal and practical knowledge. They develop the concept of narrative reflective practice with the intent to make visible the knowledge that is often expressed in physicians' practices; a reflective process that allows for the telling, retelling, and reliving of the experiences and tacit knowing; in the long term they focus on shaping opportunities to shift practices (Clandinin, Cave, et al., 2011).

As highlighted throughout this and other sections, thinking narratively about the meeting of lives in classrooms, schools, and universities is indelibly connected with the understanding that "education is interwoven with living and with the possibility of retelling our life stories" (Clandinin & Connelly, 1998, p. 246). In this way, we understand that we meet on storied landscapes with a sense of wonder about who students and teachers are, and are becoming.

The Potential of Thinking Narratively in the Meeting of Lives in Classrooms and Schools

Craig (2011) describes Clandinin and Connelly's ongoing development of thinking narratively as moving from "narratively accounting for teacher knowledge" as personal practical knowledge, to a focus on "narratively accounting for the context in which teachers come to know—their professional knowledge landscapes—to narratively accounting for teachers' identities—that is, teachers' 'stories to live by'" (p. 25). What Craig highlights is both years of sustained inquiry with children and teachers in schools and with pre- and in-service teachers in university classrooms. She also highlights two additional narrative conceptualizations, teachers' professional knowledge landscapes and teachers' stories to live by, each of which continued the growth of thinking narratively about pedagogy and pedagogical possibilities. For Clandinin and Connelly (1995), the metaphor of a professional knowledge landscape enabled attention to

space, place, and time. Furthermore, it has a sense of expansiveness and the possibility of being filled with diverse people, things, and events in different relationships. Understanding professional knowledge as comprising a landscape calls for a notion of professional knowledge as composed of a wide variety of components and influenced by a wide variety of people, places, and things. Because we see the professional knowledge landscape as composed of relationships among people, places, and things, we see it as both an intellectual and a moral landscape. (pp. 4–5)

In addition, Connelly and Clandinin's (1999) conceptualization of teachers' stories to live by weaves together their earlier understandings of teachers' personal practical knowledge and teachers' professional knowledge landscapes (Clandinin & Connelly, 1995). Clandinin et al. (2006) write that when thinking narratively with the narrative conceptualization of stories to live by

> Teacher identity is understood as a unique embodiment of each teacher's stories to live by, stories shaped by knowledge composed on landscapes past and present in which a teacher lives and works. Stories to live by are multiple, fluid, and shifting, continuously composed and recomposed in the moment to moment living alongside children, families, administrators and others both on and off the school landscape. . . . Teachers' stories to live by offer possibilities for change through retelling and reliving stories. This retelling and reliving is a restorying that changes their stories to live by. (p. 9)

Although, as Craig (2011) describes, thinking narratively may "run against the grain of the dominant perception" (p. 22), she, and we, see thinking narratively as central in shaping counterstories (Lindemann Nelson, 1995). These counterstories push against the dominant social, cultural, linguistic, familial, and institutional narratives that currently define, often in narrow and technical ways, that what matters most in classrooms, schools, and universities are not lives in the making but compliance, silence, and test scores. These dominant narratives press down on the lives and dreams of children and youth, as well as the lives and dreams of teachers and families. Thinking narratively creates possibilities for imagining counterstories; stories that hold tremendous potential for educative reverberations in lives, in and outside of schools.

Caine and Steeves (2009) link imagination with playfulness. They see play and imagination as deeply intertwined with the relationships they hold. Imagining counterstories in this way makes the composition of counterstories a relational and active process, a process allowing us to think with relationships. As Xu and Connelly (2010) point out that thinking narratively in practical school-based research draws forth the imagination of an inquirer, they support understandings of ways imagination shapes the complex interactions between teachers, children, families, and narrative inquirers as their lives meet in schools.

Thinking With Counterstories

Lindemann Nelson (1995) describes a counterstory as a narrative told within a chosen community that allows the teller the ability to reenter and reclaim full citizenship within the found community of place in which the teller lives. She further argues that a chosen community offers moral space for self-reflection, as well as offering space for reflection on the dominant community in which the teller finds herself/himself participating.

Piecing together fragments of counterstories made visible in the work of various narrative inquirers, we want to highlight key aspects of thinking narratively, which for us, include notions of co-composing, relational ethics, multiple perspectives, tensions, not fixing and replacing but evolving and shaping, slowing down, and careful, deep attending. As readers will experience, these aspects of thinking narratively in narrative inquiry are entangled in the living, they do not stand separate from one another.

Co-Shaping Narrative Inquiry Spaces on the In-Classroom Place

One way narrative inquiry became lived out within a number of classrooms in western Canada was through the creation of narrative inquiry spaces co-shaped by children and teachers as they gathered to share, to listen, and to respond to one another's life stories in the making. For example, in an urban, culturally diverse Year 1–2[6] classroom we learn of ways a *support circle space* shifted from teachers prefacing the topics to be attended to in the circle, to children sharing stories of feeling left out and not belonging in the classroom and school, to the expression of concerns about practices and structures on the out-of-classroom place, to the sharing of "very personal, real issues and concerns" such as death, divorce, unemployment, and family difficulties (J. I. Huber, 1999, p. 19).

In the accounts of two additional in-classroom narrative inquiry spaces known as *peace candle spaces*, one in an inner-city Year 3–4 classroom and another in a rural Grade 1 classroom, we learn of the educative ways in which the liminality within these spaces shaped opportunities to "step away from the scripted stories of school" to "negotiate[ing] a curriculum of diversity, a curriculum that fit the moment and the lives being lived" (J. Huber, Murphy, & Clandinin, 2003, p. 359). Subsequent inquiry into these *peace candle spaces* foregrounds the tensions present in this meeting of diverse lives, tensions not to be smoothed over if our intentions are to live in ways attentive to lives. Across these accounts of the *support circle* and the *peace candle spaces* we learn of their shifting, evolving nature as a result of the contexts that shape the lives of the children and teachers. These spaces remind us of Marmon Silko's (1996) thinking of the importance of including all of the stories of the people, even stories that differ from those commonly told, as well as stories that are troubling. Although readers are cautioned about the difficulty of engaging in this uncertain, and often uncomfortable, work given the dominant institutional narratives shaping classrooms and schools, liminality is highlighted as "an urgent burden" (J. Huber et al., 2003, p. 360) if lives of diversity are to be respected.

Additional understandings of negotiating narrative inquiry spaces as pedagogy are visible as M. Huber, Huber, and Clandinin (2004) "map out an alternative understanding of resistance on school landscapes" (p. 193). Their inquiry draws on two moments of tension when children's and teacher researchers' stories to live by bumped against stories of school and ways in which the teacher researchers respond in a way that could be interpreted as resisting the story of school. Huber, Huber, and Clandinin[7] provide insights into Jean's and Janice's negotiation of their professional knowledge landscapes in relation with the meeting of their and children's stories to live by. Through their explorations, practices of narrative inquiry pedagogy become visible. For example, through narrative inquiry into rhythms and practices that Jean and Corina lived with one another the bumping of their stories to live by with a school story of discipline becomes visible. In the moment of living, not fully awake to this bumping, Jean enacts "her preferred story of school as a place of inclusion, of belonging" instead of "the part teachers . . . [are] supposed to play in . . . [the school] story of [discipline]" (p. 187). Narratively inquiring into Jean's response awakens Huber, Huber, and Clandinin to how Jean's resistance of the school story of discipline is not, for Jean, an act of defiance or of undermining a dominant story of school. Rather, it emerges as Jean searches for coherence with memories of herself as a child in school, her stories to live by as a teacher researcher, and Corina's and Jean's "shared narrative of living stories of belonging" (p. 188).

In the current push on the educational landscape to live out narratives of the technical and of standardization, it is common to not fully understand the complexity teachers are negotiating in the meeting of these dominant narratives with their lives and in the meeting of these narratives, their lives, and the lives of children and families. We want to emphasize here how important it is to for teachers to have spaces where they can attend to their narrative histories and to all that is at work in the meeting of their and children's diverse lives. For us, M. Huber et al. (2004) highlight that to live pedagogy as narrative inquiry requires understanding that "we cannot understand a moment where [an educators'] . . . and a child's [youths', family members', or colleagues'] stor[ies] to live by bump up against each other without trying to understand how this moment of bumping reverberates back through the stories of each person" (p. 194). Being wakeful to these reverberations is an important aspect of living narrative inquiry as pedagogy.

Co-Shaping Narrative Inquiry Spaces That Interconnect In- and Out-of-Classroom Places

Steeves's work (2000) invites the possibility of considering narrative inquiry relationships as embodying pedagogical purposes in co-composing responsive communities in a time of transition on school landscapes. Steeves lived alongside both a principal in her "out-of-classroom place" and a teacher in her "in-classroom-place"[8] during a time when both of them, each from their own positioning on the school landscape, were experiencing the school landscape as in transition, as shifting and changing. Living on this shifting landscape the evolving stories to live by of both participants became vulnerable. Attending to both the principal's, Jeanette's, life and the teacher's, Karin's, life as they came into relationships with Pam, a narrative inquirer, and together with one another, shaped the beginnings of a responsive community in the school. In this work we learn of ways this narrative inquiry relationship shaped a safe space for the opening of imagination and the broadening and deepening of attention through the three-dimensional narrative inquiry space. In this way, Karin, Jeanette, and Pam co-shaped a space seldom experienced on school landscapes, a narrative inquiry space that supported their stories to live by to continue to compose, often through improvisatory ways during a period of transition at the school. Attending to the life composing of diverse people on school landscapes, including teachers and administrators, enacts an educative life-making place.

Co-Shaping Narrative Inquiry Spaces in Postsecondary Education

Desrochers (2006) provokes wondering about narrative inquiry as creating pedagogical spaces both for learning about, and experiencing, diversity in teacher education. Through participation in a drop-in youth club located in an ethnically diverse low-income community, a space was created whereby preservice teachers began to inquire into their shifting understandings of who they were and, then, who they were in relation with children whose lives were different from their own. Desrochers began by inquiring with the preservice teacher participants into their stories to live by and then continued to inquire into their evolving understandings as their stories to live by bumped against unfamiliar stories told and lived by children they met in the youth club. In this multilayered narrative inquiry, Desrochers creates an intentional narrative inquiry space of "in between" where, as the preservice teachers experienced dispositioning moments of interruption in their stories to live by, they were able to inquire into these moments with Desrochers and one another.[9] Inquiring into these interrupting moments through sustained conversation in relationships attentive to the three-dimensional narrative inquiry space (attentive to temporality, sociality, and place) offered new insights that supported the preservice teachers to recompose and to begin to relive their retold stories. Once more, narrative inquiry is shown to hold extraordinary potential for envisioning new pedagogical ways of considering teacher education for diversity. This re-envisioning holds tremendous potential for who preservice teachers may become in classrooms and schools alongside children, youth, families, and communities. Iftody (2012), too, offers ways to think of agency and provocation in narrative inquiry spaces in teacher education; Schaefer (2012) writes of narrative inquiry as physical education pedagogy.

Steeves et al. (2009) provide further imaginings of a pedagogical counterstory in teacher education. As they write of "The Research Issues Table: A Place of Possibilities for the Education of Teacher Educators," they show ways in which narrative inquiry as pedagogy is embodied in this place. The research issues table is pedagogically shaped as a table of life and education in the way Dewey (1938) would espouse. For this to happen, the "table" is a voluntarily filled, but a deliberately created space (Greene, 1993) that brings together educators from across multiple generations, disciplines, and local, national, and international contexts. In this postsecondary place people have the opportunity to live out their lives as continuously becoming. Such learning to become educators is evoked as they attend carefully to one another round the table through relational knowing, respectful listening, response, continuous inquiry, world traveling, attending tensions, and learning to think narratively. The research issues table is a chosen community within the larger university landscape; one that creates a counterstory to the often prescribed agendas of fixing and replacing "what is wrong in education." Through narrative inquiry a pedagogical space is shaped for counterstories in teacher education, stories that evolve, stories of reconstruction and of recomposing lives.

What we want to highlight here are the threads that connect each of the above retellings of narrative inquiry as pedagogy. Although the dominant narrative in education, including postsecondary education, is that of being an educator, we understand that becoming an educator is always in process, it is a life continuously composed and recomposed in relation with the lives of the people and communities with whom we engage. In thinking about becoming as an open process we are, as highlighted by Lindemann Nelson (1995), in a process of forbearing, of not shutting down what might be; we are in a process of continuous inquiry into the meeting of, and through this meeting, the potential remaking of lives.

Reimagining Schools

In *Composing Diverse Identities: Narrative Inquiries Into the Interwoven Lives of Children and Teachers*, as Clandinin et al. (2006) inquire into and learn from their and participants' experiences at City Heights and Ravine schools they call for a counterstory of school reform,[10] a story "composed to shift the taken-for-granted institutional narrative" (p. 171). The counterstory they imagine is "a story of school composed around the plotline of negotiating a curriculum of lives, a curriculum . . . attentive to the lives of teachers, children, families, and administrators who live on the school landscape at particular times" (p. 172). To understand the negotiation of a curriculum of lives, Clandinin et al. highlight that each of the curriculum commonplaces, that is, learner, teacher, subject matter, and milieu, need to be attended to in shifting, relational ways. They write that

to understand teachers, we need to understand each teacher's personal practical knowledge, his/her embodied, narrative, moral, emotional, and relational knowledge as it is expressed in practice. . . . To understand children, we need to understand children's knowledge as nested knowledge, nested in the relational knowledge between teachers and children (Lyons, 1990; Murphy, 2004). . . . We also need to attend to the nested milieus, in-classroom places, out-of-classroom places, stories of school, school stories, stories of families, and families' stories. . . . And of course, diverse subject matters are also part of the interaction within a negotiation of a curriculum of lives. (pp. 172–173)

Negotiating a curriculum of lives that continuously seeks to hear and to learn from the tensions experienced by children, families, teachers, and administrators as their lives meet, and bump against each other's storied lives and with school stories and stories of school, is described as "complex, tension-filled, and challenging" (Clandinin et al., 2006, p. 173). However, it is within this counterstory, a story that holds within it a place for the negotiation of a curriculum of lives, that lives can become central in schools. In making lives central in school, Clandinin et al. (2006) imagine "compos[ing] stories of school that are respectful, meaningful, and educative for all participants" (p. 174).

For example, Clandinin et al. (2006) make visible the pedagogical promise of thinking narratively in their storying of a principal, Jeanette, a teacher, Lian, a narrative inquirer, Shaun, and an Aboriginal boy, Dylan, who was 12 years old. Together, as they opened a space to listen and inquire into the stories Dylan lived out, including ones of continual and jumbled interruptions/disruptions to his schooling, a fuller picture of Dylan's life was emerging, and Dylan's stories began to "work on them" (Morris, 2002). Attending narratively to Dylan's stories, which began as they attended to the temporal, social, and place dimensions of his experiences, to trace forward and backward looking stories, to personal and social feelings and emotions, as well as to places, held the pedagogical potential of revealing many resonances between stories. We see this as Jeanette, as principal, thinks about her own child, Robbee, and ways he might feel. Lian, as teacher, remembers her beginning teacher years when she learned in many conversations with Jeanette about attending to the whole lives of young children. Shaun, as narrative inquirer, wonders about the "story of school," a dominant institutional narrative in which full attendance is not questioned but normalized to equate with success in school. In these ways and with Dylan, Jeanette, Lian, and Shaun came to see that Dylan was trying to have agency over some aspects of his life at school, to continue to compose stories that were meaningful to him and the familial and cultural stories within which he was embedded. As they, Jeanette, Lian, and Shaun, gradually awakened to Dylan's life, to his hopes and dreams, they improvised an attendance counterstory with Dylan, which supported him, for example, to excuse himself from his music class when he thought he might get into a fight. Dylan was further able to choose what he did with his time in Jeanette's office, an out of classroom place on the school landscape where the rules and regulations of the conduit often dominate over people's lives. Dylan's decision to draw and paint further fit with his image of himself as a member of his family who was good at, and loved, painting. Careful attending to Dylan's stories over time and on and off the school landscape created a more responsive co-composed curriculum for Dylan, one that was respectful of Dylan's shifting stories to live by.

Another narrative inquiry that supported our reimagining schools is M. Huber's (2008) work. In this narrative inquiry, Huber engaged with teenaged youth and their parents and shows how youths' experiences in school are shaping not only their identities, their stories to live by and life curricula, but also their parents' stories to live by and life curricula. As she considers ways this narrative inquiry deepened her understandings of a curriculum of lives, Huber writes: "I came . . . to my research . . . recognizing that parents' stories to live by shaped their children's school experiences and, as well, stories teachers lived by," but the stories of experience shared by the youth participants and their parents have "awakened me to how parents' stories to live by can be shaped as their children's lives intersect, and bump against, other children's and youths' lives, teacher stories, milieu and subject matter" (p. 186).

Another of a number of narrative inquiries that grew out of these earlier multiperspectival narrative inquiries attentive to the composition of a curriculum of lives (Clandinin et al., 2006; J. Huber & Clandinin, 2005) in classrooms and schools began with a focus on the "experiences of children, families, and teachers in an era of growing standardization and achievement testing at a time when the lives of children, families, and teachers are increasingly diverse" (J. Huber, Murphy, & Clandinin, 2011, p. 1).[11] J. Huber et al. (2011) write that as they engaged in narrative inquiries simultaneously attentive to the experiences of diverse children, families, and teachers alongside questions of standardization and diversity, they "somewhat abruptly, began to realize that, to this point, we had understood curriculum making as occurring only in schools" (p. 2). They write that as they attended closely to one child co-researcher, Loyla, and to "the relationships of Loyla's life, we saw multiple instances of ways she engaged in relation with others in curriculum making at home and in the community" (p. 2). *Places of Curriculum Making: Narrative Inquiries into Children's Lives in Motion* illustrates the shifts experienced by Huber, Murphy, and Clandinin in their coming to understand a curriculum of lives as necessarily inclusive of "children engaged in curriculum making not only in school places alongside teachers and children but also engaged in curriculum making alongside members of their families and communities in home and community places" (p. 2). In telling of their awakenings to the worlds of curriculum making beyond the school curriculum making world, Huber, Murphy, and Clandinin highlight multiple tensions, tensions that require children to *world travel* as they simultaneously navigate and compose their lives in these often quite different places.

As we traced in this section some of the ways narrative inquiry has shaped our understanding of the in- and out-of-classroom places within schools, we wanted to continue to make visible the importance of attending to the intersections, to the bumping up places, and to tensions experienced in multiple places and relationships in which life curriculum is made and lived. Attending to these diverse places and relationships allows us to understand narrative inquiry as holding extraordinary potential for shaping pedagogy, that is, for shaping how we might live alongside one another, in classrooms, schools, universities, and communities.

CONTINUING TO IMAGINE . . . TO IMPROVISE
FORWARD LOOKING COUNTERSTORIES

As we continue to imagine and improvise possible forward looking counterstories, we remind ourselves that we situate our knowing in the living, telling, retelling, and reliving of experience and relationships. The transcendent and enduring nature of story shapes our understandings of our need to walk with extreme care as we interact with children, families, and communities. Understanding the transcendent nature of stories requires attentiveness to the resonances and dissonances shaped in the meeting of lives, to the gaps and silences created and opened up. In this meeting of lives the transcendence of dominant social, cultural, and institutional narratives also become visible (Andrews, 2007; Young, 2005).

As we look backward, we see an evolving body of scholarly contributions that speak to the telling and retelling of narrative inquiry as a way to engage with people in relational ways. We, too, see the possibilities to live and relive narrative inquiry as both methodology and phenomena in classroom spaces and in pedagogical ways. It is the attentiveness and ethics embedded within narrative inquiry that calls us to live, to tell, and to retell and relive stories of experience. It continues to be significant for the emerging field of narrative inquiry to attend to personal experience over time, in social contexts, and in place(s), particularly the experiences of people and communities whose experiences are most often invisible, silent, composed, and lived on the margins. Understanding silent, or silenced, lives as holding enormous possibility to shape and to live out counterstories creates awareness of the potential for humbleness and curiosity in our interactions, in school and university classrooms as well as within communities.

As we see the present unfolding we begin to imagine the future, and we see that through seeing narrative inquiry as holding potential for shaping extraordinary pedagogy we can shift the practices and pedagogies within education, within teachers, but most importantly in the relationships we encounter as educators, citizens, and strangers. As we attend to people's experiences through narrative inquiry, a new language, a language of landscapes, of stories to live by, of lives in the midst, develops. Perhaps, as we begin to speak and live different experiences we start to change the stories. Perhaps, it is in these ways that we might move closer to what King (2003) imagines when he writes: "Want a different ethic? Tell a different story" (p. 164).

ACKNOWLEDGMENTS

We wish to acknowledge the contributions of D. Jean Clandinin who served as our consulting author on this chapter. Jean's response along the way was significant to shaping our chapter. We wish also to acknowledge the two people who were anonymous reviewers of earlier drafts of this chapter. Their comments were both insightful and important.

NOTES

[1]While Bruner (1986) sees narrative knowing as more cognitively situated, our understandings of narrative inquiry are more shaped by those of Johnson (1990) who saw the "body in the mind," the mind in the body.

[2]Dewey (1938) believed that experience is educative only when it continues to move a person forward on "the experiential continuum" (p. 38) while miseducative experiences, those that are disconnected from one another, have the "effect of arresting or distorting the growth of further experience" (p. 25).

[3]Johnson (1990) suggests that in order to understand teachers' world views and how they know and interact in their classrooms it is necessary to acknowledge the role the body plays in knowing. He understands teachers' personal practical knowledge as inclusive of the embodied action patterns lived out, for example, in the experiencing and structuring of routines in the classroom. McIntyre's (1981) sense of narrative unity reflects the sense of a unity embedded in a single life. A narrative unity signals one's ability to give a narrative account of one's life that reflects and links birth to death.

[4]As Polakow awakens to this autobiographical aspect of her research she writes that while she gradually realized "how little existential distance separates my life as a mother from that of the mothers and children whose lives are chronicled here," she also stories her awakening to the understanding that "the geography of privilege is all-encompassing—and living on the

other side of privilege in the first America puts one in a world apart from the grim contingency of life on the edges in the other America" (p. 3).

[5]In earlier work Phillion (2002) uses the term *narrative multiculturalism* to highlight the indelible connections between narrative and cultural diversity not only in teachers' autobiographies but also as an important aspect of life in classrooms and schools. In earlier work He (2003) traces the cross-cultural aspects of three women of Chinese ancestry as they recompose their identities, their lives, on a new cultural landscape.

[6]Year 1-2 differs from a graded structure in school in that children of multiple ages are intentionally grouped together in a classroom so as to value, and benefit, from living and learning alongside children of differing ages.

[7]D. Jean Clandinin (co-author of the paper) is the teacher researcher in one moment; Janice Huber (another co-author of the paper) is the teacher researcher in the other moment and Corina is a child in the classroom.

[8]Clandinin and Connelly (1995) describe two epistemologically different places on the professional knowledge landscape of schools. "In-classroom places" are described as mostly safe places where teachers feel secure to live out their personal practical knowledge as teachers alongside children and youth with whom they work. "Out-of-classroom places" are described as professional, communal places filled with imposed prescriptions delivered "down the conduit" (p. 9) in such places as staff meetings, lunchrooms, parent meetings, and so on.

[9]In shaping this kind of intentional space, Desrochers draws on Anzaldúa's (1987) living in the borderland which she describes as a liminal space, a space that is both a site of struggle and of possibility.

[10]Clandinin et al (2006) provide a sense of the "taken-for-granted institutional narrative" of school reform as they write that

policies and practices around high stakes testing were implemented, in part, because of poor achievement scores, high dropout rates and achievement disparities across racial and socio-economic groups. These policies and practices are designed to set in place strict outcomes, powerful surveillance and monitoring mechanisms, and punitive measures if outcomes are not met. . . . The policies and practices were shaped by seeing through the lenses of a system with a vantage point of power. (p. 170)

Throughout their book, Clandinin et al. show how the taken-for-granted institutional narrative of school is one where policy makers and administrators funnelled down prescriptive knowledge and expectations onto school landscapes and into classrooms (the conduit). These narratives silence, cover over, or make invisible the particular lives of people living on school landscapes and, as well, of the meeting of their diverse lives.

[11]See also Chung (2009), whose work shows ways in which school curriculum making reverberates into the lives of families, and, too, ways in which families' lives might be invited to reverberate into school curriculum making.

REFERENCES

Adichie, C. (2009). *The danger of a single story*. New York, NY: TEDGlobal. Retrieved from http://www.ted.com/talks/chimamanda_adichie_the_danger_of_a_single_story.html

Andrews, M. (2007). Exploring cross-cultural boundaries. In D. J. Clandinin (Ed.), *Handbook of narrative inquiry: Mapping a methodology* (pp. 489–511). London, England: Sage.

Anzaldúa, G. (1987). *Borderlands/La Frontera: The New Mestiza*. San Francisco, CA: Aunt Lute Books.

Anzaldúa, G. (Ed.). (1995). *Making face, making soul/Haciendo Caras: Creative and critical perspectives by feminists of color*. San Francisco, CA: Aunt Lute Books.

Aristotle. (1908–1952). *The works of Aristotle* (W. D. Ross, Ed., 12 vols). Oxford, England: Clarendon Press.

Barone, T. (2001). *Touching eternity: The enduring outcomes of teaching.* New York, NY: Teachers College Press.

Barone, T. (2007). A return to the gold standard? Questioning the future of narrative construction as educational research. *Qualitative Inquiry, 13,* 454–470.

Barrett, M., & Stauffer, S. L. (2009). Narrative inquiry: From story to method. In M. S. Barrett & S. L. Stauffer (Eds.), *Narrative inquiry in music education: Troubling certainty* (pp. 7–17). New York, NY: Springer.

Basso, K. (1996). *Wisdom sits in places. Landscape and language among the western Apache.* Albuquerque: University of New Mexico Press.

Bateson, M. C. (1989). *Composing a life.* New York, NY: HarperCollins.

Belenky, M. F., Clinchy, B. M., Goldberger, N. R., & Tarule, J. M. (1986). *Women's ways of knowing: The development of self, voice, and mind.* New York, NY: Basic Books.

Bruner, J. (1986). *Actual minds, possible worlds.* Cambridge, MA: Harvard University Press.

Caine, V., & Steeves, P. (2009). Imagining and playfulness in narrative inquiry. *International Journal of Education and the Arts, 10*(25), 1–14.

Carr, D. (1986). *Time, narrative, and history.* Bloomington: Indiana University Press.

Carter, K. (1993). The place of story in the study of teaching and teacher education. *Educational Researcher, 22*(1), 5–12.

Casey, K. (1995). The new narrative research in education. *Review of Research in Education, 21,* 211–253.

Chung, S. (2009). *Composing a curriculum of lives: A narrative inquiry into the interwoven intergenerational stories of teachers, children, and families* (Unpublished master's thesis). University of Alberta, Edmonton, Alberta, Canada.

Clandinin, D. J., & Cave, M. (2008). Creating pedagogical spaces for developing doctor professional identity. *Medical Education, 42,* 765–770.

Clandinin, D. J., Cave, M., & Cave, A. (2011). Narrative reflective practice in medical education for residents: Composing shifting identities. *Advances in Medical Education and Practice, 2,* 1–7.

Clandinin, D. J., & Connelly, F. M. (1986). Rhythms in teaching: The narrative study of teachers' personal practical knowledge in classrooms. *Teaching and Teacher Education, 2,* 377–387.

Clandinin, D. J., & Connelly, F. M. (1994). Personal experience methods. In N. Denzin & Y. Lincoln (Eds.), *Collecting and interpreting qualitative materials* (pp. 413–427). London, England: Sage.

Clandinin, D. J., & Connelly, F. M. (1995). *Teachers' professional knowledge landscapes.* New York, NY: Teachers College Press.

Clandinin, D. J., & Connelly, F. M. (1998). Asking questions about telling stories. In C. Kridel (Ed.), *Writing educational biography: Explorations in qualitative research* (pp. 245–253). New York, NY: Garland Publishing.

Clandinin, D. J., & Connelly, F. M. (2000). *Narrative inquiry: Experience and story in qualitative research.* San Francisco, CA: Jossey-Bass.

Clandinin, D. J., Huber, J., Huber, M., Murphy, M. S., Murray Orr, A., Pearce, M., & Steeves, P. (2006). *Composing diverse identities: Narrative inquiries into the interwoven lives of children and teachers.* New York, NY: Routledge.

Clandinin, D. J., Huber, J., Steeves, P., & Li, Y. (2011). Becoming a narrative inquirer: Learning to attend within the three-dimensional narrative inquiry space. In S. Trahar (Ed.), *Learning and teaching narrative inquiry: Travelling in the borderlands* (pp. 33–51). Amsterdam, Netherlands: John Benjamins.

Clandinin, D. J., & Murphy, M. S. (2009). Relational ontological commitments in narrative research. *Educational Researcher, 38,* 598–602.

Clandinin, D. J., & Rosiek, J. (2007). Mapping a landscape of narrative inquiry: Borderland spaces and tensions. In D. J. Clandinin (Ed.), *Handbook of narrative inquiry: Mapping a methodology* (pp. 35–75). Thousand Oaks, CA: Sage.

Coles, R. (1989). *The call of stories: Teaching and the moral imagination.* Boston, MA: Houghton Mifflin.

Conle, C. (2003). An anatomy of narrative curricula. *Educational Researcher, 32*(3), 3–15.

Conle, C. (2010). Narrative inquiry: Research tool and medium for professional development. *European Journal of Teacher Education, 23*(1), 49–63.

Connelly, F. M., & Clandinin, D. J. (1988). *Teachers as curriculum planners: Narratives of experience.* New York, NY: Teachers College Press.

Connelly, F. M., & Clandinin, D. J. (1999). *Shaping a professional identity: Stories of educational practice.* New York, NY: Teachers College Press.

Connelly, F. M., & Clandinin, D. J. (2006). Narrative inquiry. In J. Green, G. Camili, & P. Elmore (Eds.), *Handbook of complementary methods in education research* (pp. 477–487). Mahwah, NJ: Lawrence Erlbaum.

Coulter, C. A., & Smith, M. L. (2009). The construction zone: Literary elements in narrative research. *Educational Researcher, 38*, 577–590.

Coulter, C., Michael, C., & Poynor, L. (2007). Storytelling as pedagogy: An unexpected outcome of narrative inquiry. *Curriculum Inquiry, 37*(20), 103–122.

Craig, C. (2011). Narrative inquiry in teaching and teacher education. In J. Kitchen, D. Ciuffetelli Parker, & D. Pushor (Eds.), *Narrative inquiries into curriculum making in teacher education* (Advances in Research on Teaching, Vol. 13, pp. 19–42). Bingley, England: Emerald.

Crites, S. (1971). The narrative quality of experience. *American Academy of Religion, 39*, 291–311.

Cruikshank, J. (1990). *Life lived like a story: Life stories of three Yukon native elders.* Lincoln: University of Nebraska Press.

Cruikshank, J. (2005). *Do glaciers listen? Local knowledge, colonial encounters, and social imagination.* Vancouver, British Columbia, Canada: UBC Press.

Delpit, L. D. (1995). *Other people's children: Cultural conflict in the classroom.* New York, NY: New Press.

Desrochers, C. (2006). *Towards a new borderland in teacher education for diversity: A narrative inquiry into pre-service teachers' shifting identities through service learning* (Unpublished doctoral dissertation). University of Alberta, Edmonton, Alberta, Canada.

Dewey, J. (1925). *Experience and nature.* Mineola, NY: Dover.

Dewey, J. (1934). *Art as experience.* New York, NY: Berkley.

Dewey, J. (1938). *Experience and education.* New York, NY: Collier.

Downey, C. A., & Clandinin, D. J. (2010). Narrative inquiry as reflective practice: Tensions and possibilities. In N. Lyons (Ed.), *Handbook of reflection and reflective inquiry: Mapping a way of knowing for professional reflective inquiry* (pp. 383–397). New York, NY: Springer.

Dyson, A. H., & Genishi, C. (1994). *The need for story: Cultural diversity in classroom and community.* Urbana, IL: National Council of Teachers of English.

Elbaz-Luwisch, F. E. (2010). Narrative inquiry: Wakeful engagement with educational experience. *Curriculum Inquiry, 40*, 263–279.

Freeman, M. (2010). *Hindsight: The promise and peril of looking backward.* New York, NY: Oxford University Press.

Greene, M. (1993). Diversity and inclusion: Toward a curriculum of human beings. *Teachers' College Record, 95*, 211–221.

Greene, M. (1995). *Releasing the imagination: Essays on education, the arts, and social change.* San Francisco, CA: Jossey-Bass.

Greene, M. (1997). *The power of incompleteness. Variations on a blue guitar: The Lincoln Centre Institute lectures on aesthetic education* (pp. 154–160). New York, NY: Teachers College Press.

Geertz, C. (1983). *Local knowledge: Further essays in interpretive anthropology.* New York, NY: Basic Books.

Geertz, C. (1995). *After the fact: Two countries, four decades, one anthropologist.* Cambridge, MA: Harvard University Press.

Griffiths, M., & MacLeod, G. (2007, September). *Personal narratives and policy: Never the twain?* Paper presented at ECER annual meeting, Ghent, Belgium.

He, M. F. (2003). *A river forever flowing: Cross-cultural lives and identities in the multicultural landscape.* Charlotte, NC: Information Age.

Heilbrun, C. G. (1988). *Writing a woman's life.* New York, NY: Ballantine Books.

Hollingsworth, S., Dybdahl, M., & Turner Minarik, L. (1993). By chart and chance and passion: The importance of relational knowing in learning to teach. *Curriculum Inquiry, 23*(1), 5–35.

hooks, b. (1981). *Ain't I a woman? Black women and feminism.* Cambridge, MA: South End Press.

hooks, b. (1994). *Teaching to transgress: Education as the practice of freedom.* New York, NY: Routledge.

Huber, J. I. (1999). Listening to children on the landscape. In F. M. Connelly & D. J. Clandinin (Eds.), *Shaping a professional identity: Stories of educational practice* (pp. 9–19). New York, NY: Teachers College Press.

Huber, J., & Clandinin, D. J. (2005). Living in tension: Negotiating a curriculum of lives on the professional knowledge landscape. In J. Brophy & S. Pinnegar (Eds.), *Learning from research on teaching: Perspective, methodology, and representation* (Advances in Research on Teaching, Vol. 11, pp. 313–336). Oxford, England: Elsevier.

Huber, J., Murphy, S., & Clandinin, D. J. (2003). Creating communities of cultural imagination: Negotiating a curriculum of diversity. *Curriculum Inquiry, 33*, 343–362.

Huber, J., Murphy, M. S., & Clandinin, D. J. (2011). *Places of curriculum making: Narrative inquiries into children's lives in motion* (Advances in Research on Teaching, Vol. 14). Bingley, England: Emerald.

Huber, M. (2008). *Narrative curriculum making as identity making: Intersecting family, cultural and school landscapes* (Unpublished doctoral dissertation). University of Alberta, Edmonton, Alberta, Canada.

Huber, M., Huber, J., & Clandinin, D. J. (2004). Moments of tension: Resistance as expressions of narrative coherence in stories to live by. *Reflective Practice, 5*, 181–198.

Iftody, T. (2012). *On the occasion of provocative pedagogical narrative inquiry: Author(izing) agency in the hybrid spaces of teacher education.* Manuscript in preparation.

Johnson, M. (1990). *The body in the mind: The bodily basis of meaning, imagination, and reason.* Chicago, IL: University of Chicago Press.

Kerby, A. P. (1991). *In narrative and the self: Studies in continental thought.* Bloomington: Indiana University Press.

King, T. (2003). *The truth about stories: A native narrative.* Toronto, Ontario, Canada: House of Anansi Press.

Labov, W. (1966). *The social stratification of English in New York City.* Arlington, VA: Center for Applied Linguistics.

Le Guin, U. K. (1980). It was a dark and stormy night; or why are we huddling about the campfire? In W. J. T. Michell (Ed.), *On narrative* (pp. 187–195). Chicago, IL: University of Chicago Press.

Levi Strauss, C. (1963). *Structural anthropology.* New York, NY: Basic Books.

Lindemann Nelson, H. (1995). Resistance and insubordination. *Hypatia, 10*(2), 23–43.

Lopez, B. (1989). *Crossing open ground.* New York, NY: Vintage Books.

Lopez, B. (1990). *Crow and weasel.* Berkeley, CA: North Point.

Lorde, A. (1983). *Zami: A new spelling of my name—A biomythography.* Freedom, CA: Crossing Press.

Lorde, A. (1984). *Sister outsider: Essays and speeches.* Freedom, CA: Crossing Press.

Lugones, M. (1987). Playfulness, "world"-travelling, and loving perception. *Hypatia, 2*(2), 3–19.

Lyons, N. (Ed.). (2010). *Handbook of reflection and reflective inquiry.* New York, NY: Springer.

Lyons, N., & LaBoskey, V. K. (Eds.). (2002). *Narrative inquiry in practice: Advancing the knowledge of teaching.* New York, NY: Teachers College Press.

MacIntyre, A. (1981). *After virtue: A study in moral theory.* Notre Dame, IM: University of Notre Dame Press.

Marmon Silko, L. (1996). *Yellow woman and a beauty of the spirit: Essays on Native American life today.* New York, NY: Touchstone.

Miller, J. L. (1998). Autobiography and the necessary incompleteness of teacher's stories. In W. C. Ayers & J. L. Miller (Eds.), *A light in dark times: Maxine Greene and the unfinished conversation* (pp. 145–154). New York, NY: Teachers College Press.

Mitchell, W. J. T. (Ed.). (1981). *On narrative.* Chicago, IL: University of Chicago Press.

Moraga, C., & Anzaldúa, G. (Eds.). (1984). *This bridge called my back: Writings by radical women of color.* Boston, MA: Women of Color Press.

Morris, D. B. (2002). Narrative, ethics, and pain: Thinking with stories. In R. Charon & M. Montello (Eds.), *Stories matter: The role of narrative in medical ethics* (pp. 196–218). New York, NY: Routledge.

Munro, P. H. (2007). The future of narrative. *Qualitative Inquiry, 13,* 487–498.

Murray Orr, A., & Olson, M. (2007). Transforming narrative encounters. *Canadian Journal of Education, 30,* 819–838.

Noddings, N. (1991). Stories in dialogue: Caring and interpersonal reasoning. In C. Witherell & N. Noddings (Eds.), *Stories lives tell: Narrative and dialogue in education* (pp. 157–170). New York, NY: Teachers College Press.

Okri, B. (1997). *A way of being free.* London, England: Phoenix House.

Paley, V. G. (1997). *The girl with the brown crayon: How children use stories to shape their lives.* Cambridge, MA: Harvard University Press.

Phillion, J. (2002). *Narrative inquiry in a multicultural landscape: Multicultural teaching and learning.* Charlotte, NC: Information Age.

Phillion, J., He, M. F., & Connelly, F. M. (2005). *Multicultural education: Narrative and experiential approaches.* Thousand Oaks, CA: Sage.

Pinnegar, S., & Daynes, J. (2007). Locating narrative inquiry historically. In D. J. Clandinin (Ed.), *Handbook of narrative inquiry: Mapping a methodology* (pp. 1–34). Thousand Oaks, CA: Sage.

Polakow, V. (1994). *Lives on the edge: Single mothers and their children in the other America.* Chicago, IL: University of Chicago Press.

Polkinghorne, D. (1988). *Narrative knowing and the human sciences.* Albany: State University of New York Press.

Polkinghorne, D. (1995). Narrative configuration as qualitative analysis. In J. A. Hatch & R. Wisniewski (Eds.), *Life history and narrative* (pp. 5–25). London, England: Falmer Press.

Rose, M. (1989). *Lives on the boundary.* New York, NY: Free Press/Simon & Schuster.

Ross, L. J. (2008). Storytelling in sistersong and the voices of feminism project. In R. Solinger, M. Fox, & K. Irani (Eds.), *Telling stories to change the world: Global voices on the power of narrative to build community and make social justice claims* (pp. 65–71). New York, NY: Routledge.

Sarbin, T. R. (2004). The role of imagination in narrative construction. In C. Daiute & C. Lightfoot (Eds.), *Narrative analysis: Studying the development of individuals in society* (pp. 5–20). Thousand Oaks, CA: Sage.

Sarris, G. (1993). *Keeping slug woman alive: A holistic approach to American Indian texts.* Los Angeles: University of California Press.

Schaefer, L. (2012). *Narrative inquiry as physical education pedagogy.* Manuscript submitted for publication.

Steeves, P. (2000). *Crazy quilt: Continuity, identity and a storied school landscape in transition— A teacher's and a principal's works in progress* (Unpublished doctoral dissertation). University of Alberta, Edmonton, Alberta, Canada.

Steeves, P., Yeom, J., Pushor, D., Nelson, C., Mwebi, B., Murray Orr, A., . . . Clandinin, D. J. (2009). The research issues table: A place of possibilities for the education of teacher educators. In C. Craig & L. Deretchin (Eds.), *Teacher education yearbook XVII* (pp. 303–320). Lanham, MD: Rowman & Littlefield Education.

Trinh Minh-ha, T. (1989). *Woman, native, other: Writing postcoloniality and feminism.* Bloomington: Indiana University Press.

Vinz, R. (1996). *Composing a teaching life.* Portsmouth, NH: Heinemann.

Vinz, R. (1997). Capturing a moving form: "Becoming" as teachers. *English Education, 29,* 137–146.

Xu, S., & Connelly, M. (2010). Narrative inquiry for school-based research. *Narrative Inquiry, 20,* 349–370.

Young, M. (2005). *Pimatisiwin: Walking in a good way: A narrative inquiry into language as identity.* Winnipeg, Manitoba, Canada: Pemmican.

Chapter 8

No Child Left With Crayons: The Imperative of Arts-Based Education and Research With Language "Minority" and Other Minoritized Communities

SHARON VERNER CHAPPELL
California State University Fullerton

MELISA CAHNMANN-TAYLOR
University of Georgia

Since the implementation of the No Child Left Behind Act in 2001, public discourse on "failing schools" as measured by high-stakes standardized tests has disproportionately affected students from minoritized communities (such as language, race, class, dis/ability), emphasizing climates of assessment at the expense of broader, more democratic, and creative visions of education (e.g., Jordan, 2010; Krashen, 2008). As advocates of the arts in education and multicultural–multilingual learning for all, we join a chorus of concern about the ways in which the "crayons" (synecdoche for all the "arts") have started to disappear from public school learning and/or are solely included as handmaidens to improved academic achievement. Likewise, we are concerned about the ways diversity education has been strictly targeted at those "Other" students who "lack" the cultural capital expected for academic success in schools (O. Garcia & Kleifgen, 2010; Garda, 2011; Howard, 2006; Nurenberg, 2011).

In this review, we examine the literature on arts education with minoritized youth within landscapes of structural inequity, scientific rationalization, and a resurgence of the racialization of non-White communities and curricula in schools. We identify strong practices in arts education that aim to achieve social justice with both minoritized and majoritized populations. By minoritized youth, we refer to any and all who identify in contextually situated, nondominant communities such as race, class, sexual orientation, language, dis/ability, religion, and gender. As we identify such contexts, we are aware that minority/majority status is unstable and contingent. Despite variations and flexibility, we use this term to identify youth who turn to the arts to navigate their status as "outside" the norm in a variety of ways.

Review of Research in Education
March 2013, Vol. 37, pp. 243-268
DOI: 10.3102/0091732X12461615
© 2013 AERA. http://rre.aera.net

We review scholarship, empiricism, and pedagogy that showcase the possibilities to humanize education through the arts with minoritized youth and their families by engaging in sustained, integrated critical practices in school and community settings. We highlight extraordinary, arts-based pedagogies that challenge current conceptualizations of discrete skills, discipline-based learning, and neutralized curricula. We question the narrow interpretation of standards and the existent empiricism that illuminates the impact of arts education programs as tools for "improving" the academic success of minoritized youth defined by these parameters. In particular, we propose that school-based practitioners learn from research conducted in out-of-school youth participatory and community-based contexts that emphasize linguistic and cultural diversity as essential curricula for all, as realized in part through the arts (Cammarota & Fine, 2008; Hull & Schultz, 2002; Noguera, Cammarota, & Ginwright, 2006; Pacheco, 2012; Soep & Chávez, 2010).

Projects addressing all forms of minoritization as well as responses to injustice, inequity, and discrimination are beyond the scope of this chapter. As scholars in bilingual, bicultural education, we focus primarily on practices with youth in contexts of linguistic and cultural minoritization, while suggesting how these practices might also provide possibilities for youth in other minoritized contexts. We work to understand how the arts facilitate a "culturally sustaining pedagogy" (Paris, 2012), one that engages the cultural and linguistic dexterity and plurality of young people's cultural connectedness across seemingly discrete forms of minoritization.

Finally, we review scholarly turns toward arts-based approaches to research in education, documenting arts education in ways that increase public attention toward complexity, feeling, and new ways of seeing that make the ordinary seem strange and that decenter schooling as usual (Barone, 2000; Eisner, 1997). We examine the nuances of arts-based research—the hopeful possibilities as well as tensions and uncertainties regarding authorship, quality, literal utility (e.g., the value of answers vs. more questions or Barone's [2008] "conspiratorial conversations"), validity, and generalizability (see Eisner, 2008). Just as scientific rationality and a competition-driven economy threaten arts education in schools, so too do they threaten alternative, postmodern empirical approaches that convey qualitative impact. We present some of the finest examples of arts-based research among minoritized communities that point toward scholarship that embraces the arts and showcases their possibilities.

Drawing a relationship across these three contexts—arts education, diversity education, and arts-based research—creates a dynamic possibility for transformative, humanistic school reform for, with, and about minoritized communities. Each area offers a unique and complementary set of practices that can engage academic knowledge, identity development, and social change in locally specific and relevant ways (Pennycook, 2010).

ARTS EDUCATION "AT RISK" IN CLIMATES OF HIGH-STAKES STANDARDIZED TESTING

Driven by the priorities and evaluation indicators of the Elementary and Secondary Education Act of 2001, coined "No Child Left Behind" or NCLB, education reform leaders are currently concerned with the "achievement gap" related to race/ethnicity, gender, language, school location, and other characteristics. These achievement gaps are determined by standardized test results and encourage reformers to use technical, short-term interventions for those groups identified as "at risk" (National Center for Education Statistics, 2011; Trimble, 2005). The arts and minoritized education are positioned currently within a landscape of reform that emphasizes accountability and test score gains for those "at risk," pushing toward budget cuts to educational programming considered not core.

This reform movement has created a bleak picture for arts education. Woodworth et al. (2007) studied California's arts programming, finding that 89% of K-12 schools failed to offer a standard course of study with consistent scope and sequence based on California Standards in the four arts disciplines. Arts facilities and materials were lacking in most schools because of inadequate state funding and reliance on outside monies that create unequal access in schools. Current contexts for youth participation in the school-based arts are also bleak. Generally, youth engagement in arts education has dropped since the 1980s. Only 26% of African American youth and 28% of Hispanic youth report participating in the arts in schools, as compared with 58% of White youth (Rabkin & Hedberg, 2011). Limited access to arts in schools tends to have the greatest impact on minoritized youth, who tend to be hypersegregated in schools with more limited budgets, less culturally and linguistically responsive practices, and highly controlled curriculum based on discrete skill development (Gándara, 2012; Ladson-Billings, 2009; Martinez-Wenzl, Pérez, & Gándara, 2011).

Partnerships with community organizations and grant funders rarely result in sustainable capacity to provide arts-based instruction (such as the enrichment programs of the federal grant programs for the 21st Century Learning Centers in the early 2000s; see Chappell, 2006). Furthermore, much grant funding requires the demonstration of statistical achievement gains as measured through high-stakes tests, tests that are seldom valid tools of measurement for minoritized populations such as English language learners (Abedi, 2004; MacSwan & Rolstad, 2006) and that often erase structural inequities that place minoritized populations "at risk" in the first place (see critiques from, e.g., Underriner & Woodson, 2011, who studied the effects of drama education on obesity with indigenous youth in Arizona). In this way, granting agencies and arts education advocates often use discursive arguments that further marginalize the populations they hope to support.

Furthermore, there has been scant mainstream reform advocating for root cause analysis of general inequity in schools across different communities, let alone to reframe "achievement gap" discourse in terms of the racialization of intellect and tracking of students of color, historic segregation policies and current de facto segregation in schools, and the abandonment of urban centers, among others (Anyon, 2005; Oakes, 2005). Currently, some educational theorists suggest reconceptualizing the achievement gap as an opportunity gap (Darden & Cavendish, 2011; DeShano da Silva, Huguley, Kakli, & Rao, 2007; Flores-Gonzalez, 2005). This term shifts the responsibility from individual improvement in test scores to an analysis of the practices in social, political, and economic institutions that deny equitable access to opportunities for minoritized youth resulting in lower achievement (among other effects) at the local level of classrooms. According to Darden and Cavendish (2011), such opportunity gaps include less experienced teachers assigned to high-poverty schools; schools treated as units within a district rather than considering differences within those units and reallocating funds according to need, resulting in decisions to treat students "the same" versus equitably; schools with larger numbers of "disadvantaged students" receiving less of the general education fund; a lack of culturally and linguistically responsive curriculum, instruction, and family partnerships; and higher facility maintenance in poorer neighborhoods without the money available to address those needs.

Yet despite such opportunity gaps in formal schooling, we have found substantially promising practices and products in the arts (as education and research) that address the question: What makes schools just, equitable, and inclusive for all children? Not that these arts-based experiences necessarily *close* the opportunity gap for minoritized communities, but they serve to illuminate visions of better futures, coming from the perspectives of minoritized youth themselves and their allies. Furthermore, these experiences are underscored by a growing criticism that schools reconsider the social outcomes of literacy learning with an expanded multiliteracies approach (Cope & Kalantzis, 2000; Vasquez, 2008). How can mainstream school reform advocates learn from these exemplars to complicate their visions for arts education and diversity education as a mode of "literacy and justice for all" (Edelsky, 2006) in schools?

WHY MINORITIZED AND MAJORITIZED YOUTH NEED THE ARTS

In arts education advocacy, there is often a temptation to justify the inclusion of the arts (visual, dramatic, and performance art) in schools based on arguments for increased academic achievement in the tested content areas. In her book, *Why Our Schools Need the Arts*, Davis (2008) responds to seven common "objections" taxpayers and policymakers have against including arts education in public schooling, including constraints on curricular time, finances, challenges to valid assessment of learning, the artistic preparedness of all teachers, and the assumption that the arts remain available in community settings regardless of whether they are available in schools. On the defensive and to safeguard arts programs in schools, many well-intended advocates, past and present, turn to arguments that justify the arts in education in terms of other disciplines: for example, the arts raise CRCT, SAT, and other scores and increase students' creative problem-solving abilities that transfer to other (*read: more important*) disciplinary knowledge in literacy, math, and science (Baker, 2011; Bauerlin, 2010; Catterall, Dumais, & Hampden-Thompson, 2012; Deasy, 2002; Fiske, 1999).

Yet these justifications can truncate the dynamic, holistic qualities of arts learning beyond quantifiable skill acquisition. Davis (2008) astutely observes, "You are not asked to transfer something that has sufficient value in itself" (p. 46). She identifies the unique features of learning in and through the arts: tangible products created through imagination and agency, a focus on emotion through expression and empathy, an emphasis on ambiguity through interpretation and respect for multiple points of view, an orientation toward process through inquiry and reflection, and human connections developed through social engagement and responsibility. Research by Harvard's Project Zero complements Davis's observations about art-making, in their work on "studio habits of mind" (Hetland, Veenema, Palmer, Sheridan, & Winner, 2005). When students engage in arts processes, they develop distinct and complementary social practices: developing craft, engaging and persisting, envisioning, expressing, observing, reflecting, stretching and exploring, and understanding art worlds. These findings expand on Ecker's (1963) work that frames art-making as qualitative problem solving, a process with distinct phases of reflective practice. These phases include encountering the big picture of a phenomenon and engaging in preproduction sense-making activities, building tentative relationships through seeing fragments of patterns, identifying emergent themes from these fragments that lead to controlling insights about the phenomenon, using themes to select elements to include in the final art work, and finally, judging the work as complete based on discerning its impact on others, including raising questions about the phenomenon.

Such rationales point to humanizing, integrated purposes for arts education in schools that examine the very heart of learning: Why do people create, question, desire, interact, and make meaning in the world? In letting go of a defensive posture, some arts educators and researchers have refused to translate what the arts "do" in the language of other disciplines and instead celebrate the unique tools that the arts offer "to make and provide meaning through aesthetic symbols" (Davis, 2008, p. 48). The arts and social imagination are intertwined (Greene, 2000), and in shifting the conversation from apology and justification to validation and value, arts education is more likely to serve its transformative, emancipatory, and aesthetic purposes.

During this downturn in arts funding, one significant and popular argument is that "the arts will survive in the community without school support" (Davis, 2008, p. 41). Youth have and will continue to respond to the circumstances of their lives through creative production with or without school support. In these community-based contexts, youth and their adult mentors build multiliteracy communities of practice that negotiate multiple linguistic and cultural differences in their public and private lives (New London Group, 1996; Wenger, 1999). These youth-centered projects regularly negotiate cross-cultural tensions, employ new technologies of communication, and teach through immersive pedagogies that result in explicit skill acquisition expressed in a plurality of texts (New London Group, 1996). Approaches include hip-hop media production (Alim, 2011; E. Wang, 2010), digital storytelling and other digital media texts (Bennett, 2008; Hull & Katz, 2006; Montgomery, 2000), critical literacy analysis and creative writing (Cahnmann-Taylor & Preston,

2008; Fisher, 2007; Haddix, 2011), community history murals (Wallace-DiGarbo & Hill, 2006), devised or applied theatre (Conrad, 2004; Woodson, 2007), and investigative journalism and photography (Gavin, 2003; C. Wang, 2006).

Schools would benefit from drawing on the successes of these out-of-school initiatives, led by artists, researchers, and youth themselves (Walker & Romero, 2012). In this way, the arts can become a tool of minoritized school reform that centers its processes in human dilemmas and agency and that speaks from the perspectives of those communities most affected by policies and cultures of oppression. These arts practices specifically relate to the lives of minoritized youth, use their primary languages and dialects as well as other funds of knowledge, and develop personal and academic knowledge, social critique, and local, direct action (Marshall & Toohey, 2010; Moll, Amanti, Neff, & Gonzalez, 1992; Noguera et al., 2006; Pacheco, 2012; Paris, 2012). Furthermore, the arts in education can assist majoritized student populations in decentering their privileged positionality, in seeing the world from different perspectives including the impact of social dominance and structural inequities on minoritized communities, and their own relationships to those systems of power as majoritized people (Goodman, 2011; Howard, 2006; Souto-Manning, 2011).

WHY ALL STUDENTS/SCHOOLS NEED MINORITIZED EDUCATION

As we question the constructed marginalization of the arts in education, we also wish to deconstruct perspectives on the term *minority* and programs that were developed to serve so-called minority needs. The term *minority* often conflates population size with issues of status and power in society. According to the most recent Census data, minoritized citizens make up 33% of the U.S. population. By 2025, they will constitute 42%, and by 2042, the nation will be a majority-"minority" at 54% (Garda, 2011).

There are many parallels between the marginalized and devalued positioning of the arts in schools and the disenfranchised placement of curriculum and services for minoritized youth (e.g., language services such as bilingual education, American Sign Language interpretation, Black English Vernacular programs, culturally and linguistically enhanced curriculum design for indigenous populations). About the marginalization and omission of the arts, Davis (2008) asks, "When was it decided that academic subjects were by definition non-arts courses? When was it decided that over here are academics and way over there are the arts?" (p. 80). So too might we as advocates of minoritized programming that consider linguistic and cultural differences ask, "When was it decided that programs that are sensitive to differences in race, class, and culture were by definition a remediation or an unnecessary luxury for minority students rather than an opportunity for all?" and "When since civil rights activism did it become acceptable to decide that over *here* are the minoritized youth and way over *there* are those that are not?" Just as the arts can develop problem-solving and perspective taking with both minoritized and majoritized young people, so too can critical diversity education (Cahnmann-Taylor & Souto-Manning, 2010; Kincheloe & McLaren, 2007).

Grinberg and Saavedra (2000) relate the marginalization of bilingual/ESOL education to Bourdieu and Passeron's (1977) theories of institutional labeling that translate social distinctions into academic evaluations and classifications. Grinberg and Saavedra argue,

> The constitution of the field was immersed in discourses that contradicted the emancipatory intention of bilingual education because of the hierarchical nature implied in the construct of cultural disadvantage. . . . Schools were immersed in the discourse that "real" learning and the development of knowledge, skill, and potential, do not occur until students can begin to function and produce in English. (p. 430)

Bilingual and multicultural educators and scholars have often been defined (by themselves and others) as strictly in service to minoritized communities, acting as "bridges" to the "mainstream" as if the goal were to slip invisibly into an Anglo-centric current while maintaining cultural ties if they complement traditional schooling structures. Such programs include the Language Development Program for African American Students in Los Angeles that integrated Black English Vernacular into language arts and the Kamehameha Early Education Program program that addressed distinctive features of Hawaiian discourse into school learning (Au, 1993; Au & Mason, 1981, 1983). Other programs serve to recover heritage language during after school hours as in the Khmer Emerging Education Program in Fresno, California, using visual ethnographic methods to explore themes of language, community, assimilation, and acculturation.

Yet "minority" programs are often targeted politically and sometimes dismantled, particularly when embedded in the regular structures of schooling and problematizing the norms of current educational discourses and ideologies, such as the Mexican American studies in the Tucson Unified School District in Arizona (Teacher Activist Groups, 2012). Critical education (through problem posing and analysis of social inequities) remains marginalized as a specialty program for a marginalized group while "real learning" takes place in mainstream classes, all too often sterilized of controversial issues that promote dialogue across differences. In this way, diversity education, bilingual education, and critical social inquiry have held fragile, tentative positions in school curricula, often locating the voices of participating young people as reactive when their programs are cut—at protest rallies, walk outs, and school board meetings. This reinforces a kind of plague tent mentality—isolating "those kids" and "their needs" until "they" are ready to be a healthy one of "us" and function on majority culture and language terms (Fettes, 1997; Fishman, 1991).

We are not arguing against the importance and often necessity of programs that focus support to minoritized communities and their specific needs (in terms of language, culture, class experience, citizenship status, dis/ability status, and otherwise). What we are suggesting is that when explaining or rationalizing services that target the varying needs of minoritized youth, we should resist the temptation to package these programs as in-service to the majority, allowing the "mainstream" teacher and classroom to go undisrupted and unchanged. By marginalizing all services that appear irrelevant to the majoritized group, we undermine opportunities for transformative and emancipatory practices for all. Garda (2011) argues, "Multiracial schools will never be created and sustained unless whites understand and appreciate the advantages of such schools to *their* children" (p. 599, italics added).

In light of our rapidly changing demographics, which will include increasing numbers of minority leaders in business, social services, government, and other leadership, the questions ought to be how to more equitably share the ability to communicate across linguistic, racial, and cultural competences and social experiences to succeed in an ever more diverse world. Fortunately, we believe arts education provides just such a context for rich and expansive understanding of diversity (Paris, 2012). As Davis (2008) articulates,

The arts provide ways for children to create and communicate their own individual cultures, to experience the differences and similarities among the cultures of family or nationality that are imprinted on different forms of art, and to discover the common features of expression that attest to a human connection contained in and beyond difference. (pp. 22–23)

Cahnmann and Varghese (2006) wrote of the need for bilingual education researchers to step out of bilingual education safehouses, collaborate with others, and more widely disseminate findings from language education research. We believe there is much untapped potential for moving both diversity and arts education from the periphery to the center, allowing the next generation of learners to create something new of their own invention that has never before existed. We believe arts education with and for minoritized youth must also be an education that questions and contextualizes "minority status," where students are encouraged to imagine "what if" and know that what happens next—a paintbrush across paper, a leap across the stage, a handshake with a next door neighbor—will make a difference and may effect real, social change. Thus, arts education has the potential to help children see that one person's Siamese cat is another person's Chihuahua (as in Schachner's [2007] *Skippyjon Jones* books), that perspective is contingent, and that ambiguity and uncertainty are requisite dispositions in a post-multicultural, post-multilingual world.

RESEARCH, MINORITIZED YOUTH, AND THE ARTS

There are three interrelated themes in arts education with minoritized communities: the arts for academic development, the arts for personal and community identity development, and the arts for social change/justice. Across these themes, projects use aesthetic languages of the arts disciplines—visual art, theatre, music, dance, creative writing, and media arts—as meaning-making tools toward particular educational goals.

Arts for academic development projects work to enhance the achievement of students in traditional core content areas. These studies stress the need for breadth and depth in the arts disciplines as well as increased teacher education and teaching artist partnerships (Catterall & Waldorf, 1999; Lukes & Zwicky, in press; Meban, 2002). Other studies address how the arts can be integrated with other subject areas to increase competencies in both the arts and the other discipline (such as literacy, language, social studies, and science; Appel, 2006; Brouillette & Burns, 2005; Burnaford, Aprill, & Weiss, 2001; Burnaford, Brown, Doherty, & McLaughlin, 2007; Mishook & Kornhaber, 2006; Sicre, in press). For example, Dabach (2010) demonstrates the strategy of pairing an aesthetic tool or process with a content area skill, in particular using visual imagery to develop writing skills with English language learners. Older studies, such as Burton, Horowitz, and Abeles (1999) and Oreck, Baum, and McCartney (1999), document how discipline-based arts education develop student competencies within the arts disciplines particularly through apprenticeship and technical job experience in the arts. Recently, however, this focus on the arts and academic development has included using the arts to develop 21st-century "knowledge economies," such as qualitative problem-solving skills (Thomson & Sefton-Green, 2010).

Cultural and linguistic responsiveness is important to the discussion of arts education with minoritized youth (Gay, 2010; Ladson-Billings, 2009), and many projects position this responsiveness at the heart of their pedagogical design. Such pedagogy includes developing an interrelationship between formal written literacy practices and art forms, such as connecting graphic, musical, and theatrical narratives to students' lives. Examples include political cartooning about social justice (Rolling, 2008), analyzing concepts of Americanization and America through writing and drama (Kelin, in press) and visual arts (Landay, Meehan, Newman, Wootton, & King, 2001), and collaborative music mapping (Blair, 2007). These approaches tend to conceptualize the cultural capital of schools as central to student success and the use of the arts as a tool or conduit toward developing such knowledge. The cultural capital of home is often brought into school, such as through the use of family funds of knowledge (Moll et al., 1992) as the curricular content of the arts and literacy experience.

Some researchers, however, articulate the limitations of working within the institutional structure of school to realize critical visions for arts-based academic development with minoritized communities. Chappell (2008) reflects on the ways White privilege affected her ability to connect with minoritized communities both in and out of school, as a student herself and as an arts and language teacher. She uses a border metaphor to reflect on the struggles to move across borders and the potential of the arts to facilitate that reflexive pedagogical movement. These borders are often not easy for arts educators to navigate, due to school's hierarchical power structure and rigidly controlled, neutralized curricula, as examined in the work of Meban (2002) and Picower (2011). Meban (2002) observes an explicit disconnect between the technical drawing skills she was expected as a teaching artist to develop and the social function of art that she hoped to engage. Schools often resist or, at the least, are ignorant of the knowledge-plus-position stance (Boyle-Baise & Zevin, 2009) that the arts as a sociocultural practice demand. Meban (2002) expresses concern about the pressure to self-censor her selection of themes and issues that minoritized communities could benefit from. This concern parallels those of new teachers attempting to navigate social justice teaching in a neoliberal school system of high-stakes testing and mandated curriculum (Picower, 2011). The context of teacher pressure to omit ideology from their curriculum, as it relates in particular to the impacts of social dominance on minoritized communities, often constrains arts education in schools.

Many researchers, however, have documented innovative alternative visions of schooling through the arts with minoritized communities that redefine the cultural capital of schools through community-based approaches. Some teachers have found ways to navigate the school system, aligning social-justice-based pedagogy with standards-based expectations for language and literacy. For example, Saavedra (2011) used the Latin American literary genre of *testimonios* to center her third-grade students' experiences in writing. Through this genre she asked her students to tell their individual stories in relation to group histories of oppression. Dickson (2005, 2007) uses ethnographic interviewing to inspire his Alabama high schoolers' creative writing about intergenerational experiences with racial discrimination and visions of equality. Other teachers have used new media literacies to center their students' lives in the classroom. As part of the San Diego State-Imperial Valley Migrant Education Program Summer Academy, migrant youth created The Comic Book Project (2010), drawing and writing about their experiences being migrant youth and ultimately publishing a collective graphic novel. Schultz (2008) shares the video documentary, Project Citizen 405, created by his fifth-grade classroom to document their efforts to repair their school, repairs promised by the school district years ago. This documentary demonstrates the young people's abilities to draw connections between their personal experiences and the public policies that have minoritized them. These problem-posing inquiry projects are becoming increasingly of interest in teacher education classrooms as pedagogy that links the personal, the institutional, and "real world" applications, oftentimes designed through creative and arts-based processes and products (Bell, 2010; Boyle-Baise & Zevin, 2009; Ponder, Vander Veldt, & Lewis-Ferrell, 2011).

In addition to emerging school-based research in the arts with minoritized youth, ample community-based studies provide a complementary vision to alternative school practices that minoritize particular youth. These studies articulate successful academic development through identity and social change approaches. Similar to the school-based projects mentioned above, research on the arts for personal and community identity explores how the arts open opportunities for minoritized students to voice their experiences, particularly through personal narratives and testimonies of struggle. In community-based settings, these narratives come out of local cultural life, including the self/community as curriculum and the self/community as research study.

For example, Moriarty (2004) studied immigrant participatory arts in the Silicon Valley, California, finding that community cultural arts create social capital built through bonding and bridging: bonding among community members and bridging relationships with other communities. In this way, art is about family, linking art forms to local community themes, and sharing spaces, all of which produce a "shared civic identification" across wider groups. She suggests that participatory arts become the "ultimate venue for public expression in a democracy" (p. 35), with the potential to harness reciprocal relationships toward diversity as a bonding opportunity for learning across difference without requiring a loss of ethnic identity or language. Cahnmann-Taylor and Preston (2008) described a bilingual–bidialectal poetry writing program in an after-school, multi-age, community library setting. They explored the use of bilingual poetry in a bilingual setting to embrace the multifaceted and overlapping dimensions of the "continua of biliteracy (Hornberger & Skilton-Sylvester, 2000) which include standard and vernacular language, approved and taboo subjects, and an emphasis on the poet's portfolio as process and product" (Cahnmann-Taylor & Preston, 2008, p. 249).

Much research focuses on individual minoritized youth perspectives in dialectical relationship to their transnational cultural communities. These young people's counternarratives insist on breaking silences about injustice and oppression against immigrant cultural groups, as well as testifying to the strength of individuals/communities to endure against these circumstances (Aggabao Thelen, 2008; Breunlin, Himelstein, & Nelson, 2008; Glisson, 2008; Pacheco, 2012; Salas, 2008). In his storytelling project with a Hudson River immigrant community, for example, Salas (2008) speaks to the theme of border-crossing, in which participant identities are developed through their telling about physical, psychological, and cultural borders. Such borders are also emphasized in terms of the places that young people traverse in their lives as children of migrant workers, from the fields to the classroom through graffiti art and creative writing (Lewis, in press; Rodríguez-Valls, Kofford, Apodaca, & Samaniego, in press; see Figure 1). Being defined and seen as an undocumented immigrant is another theme that young people explore through problem-based conceptual art and performance in the classroom and on the street (L. Garcia, in press; Harman, Varga-Dobai, Bivins, & Forker, in press; see Figure 2). Other themes include documenting and celebrating the ignored and disappearing histories of indigenous peoples in the United States through oral storytelling and visual art forms (Castagno & Brayboy, 2008; Kelin, 2005).

Minoritized young people are well aware of how the world sees them, with an emerging sense of how they want to be seen, as well as how they want to see themselves. This struggle to articulate developing critical self and world awareness is at the center of many arts education projects (Adams, in press; Chappell, 2009; Lamont Hill, 2009; Schultz, 2008). Mainstream cultural perceptions, often rooted in stereotypes, misconceptions, and ignorance about minoritized populations, often lead to less effective school curricula and relationships with peers and authority figures. Projects such as the one by Reyes (in press) insist on young people analyzing these circumstances rooted in power and social domination rather than being inured to the everyday circumstances they abhor (violence, death, drugs, an unresponsive school and welfare system, the news media portrayal of Black and Brown people, of people in poverty). Reyes and the young people in Youth Roots, Oakland, undertake this

FIGURE 1
To Be Migrant, Created by Students From the Summer Academy of the Migrant Education Program in the ICOE (Imperial Valley County Office of Education)

Source. Photo by Sharon Chappell Image. Artwork used with permission.

FIGURE 2
Students at the May Day March in Downtown Los Angeles

Source. Photo by Luis Genaro Garcia. Reprinted with permission.

analysis both for individual testimony and social critique by composing, recording, and publicly performing hip-hop songs. They demand, "It is NOT what it is"—that young people can and should be in charge of changing the circumstances of their lives, with creative production at the heart of this process.

This relationship between the individual and community, between the self and the social, cultural, and institutional worlds is also a theme that runs through overall school reform efforts and teacher education (Jeffers, 2005; Marron, 2003; McDermott, 2005; Stevenson & Deasy, 2005; Werner, 2002), as well as teacher professional development and alternative school design for minoritized young people. Picower (2011) developed a critical inquiry community for first-year teachers interested in teaching social justice without administrative support. Cahnmann-Taylor and Souto-Manning (2010) designed professional development multicultural learning communities with teachers through Boalian theatre for social change pedagogy. They found an essential element for equity-focused professional development involved ensemble rehearsals of pedagogical struggle, expanding the menu of options teachers had at their disposal for performing bilingual advocacy. Mitsumura (in press) uses ethnodrama techniques with preservice teacher candidates to take on the perspectives of English learner young people and their families. Bond and Etwaroo (2005) document the experiences of an undergraduate course titled "Dance, Movement and Pluralism" to explore the relationship between personal and group questions of identity. Damm (2006) documents a project between college students and Native American youth using cultural heritage music, art, and dance. Rabkin and Redmond (2004) highlight arts integration projects at the center of school reforms that respond to localized contexts and funds of knowledge of low-income communities. Each of these studies shares the goal of supporting teachers and students in developing their identities as artists, in building creative communities of practice that explore cultural questions and problems, and produce public art works that address equity concerns for minoritized communities.

CLIMATES OF SCIENTIFICALLY BASED RESEARCH: HOW CAN WE EVER KNOW IF THE ARTS MAKE A DIFFERENCE

Cahnmann-Taylor (2008) writes, "With the acceptance of post-modern approaches to educational research in the last few decades including feminism, post-structuralism, critical theory, and semiotics, assumptions about what counts as knowledge and the nature of research have dramatically changed" (p. 3). Not only have multiple qualitative research methodologies gained more widespread acceptance but also the tools researchers use to collect data and display findings have been diversified to include artistic as well as traditionally scientific methods. Using arts-based methods to document arts-based educational opportunities has been critical for exploring varied and creative ways to engage in empirical processes and to share questions and findings in more penetrating and widely accessible ways. Rendering the outcomes of arts-based learning through regression analysis of test scores, retention rates, and other quantitative measures of performance fails to illuminate the qualities of experience during arts-based learning.

Researchers of arts-based education often turn to arts-based qualitative inquiry to achieve a variety of empirical goals including social activism (Barone, 2000; Finley & Finley, 1999), critical friends (Weinstein, 2010), making connections between research and lived experience (Garoian, 1999), making meaning through multiple senses and sensibilities (Norris, 2000), provoking thought and questioning long-standing beliefs (Barone, 2001; Finley, 2003), and extending the influence of scholarship to policymakers and the public (Barone, 2000). Weinstein (2010) explains that studies of the arts must also necessarily call into question the researcher's focus and attention:

An arts education orientation encourages us to look for evidence of student success outside of narrowly defined outcomes and more through what young people actually *do* inside and outside the classroom, and what that *doing* reveals about the development of their abilities to choose, negotiate, and accomplish to their own satisfaction complex, multi-modal activities. (p. 5)

Using the arts as research can help us understand more pointedly the experiences of the young people in classrooms, particularly as researchers use multimodality and new literacy approaches similar to those students are using daily in classroom life (Albers & Harste, 2007; Chappell & Faltis, in press). For example, Romero and Walker (2010) describe how youth media productions provided insights into young people's meaning making, while also raising ethical questions about doing educational ethnography in the new media era, as well as presenting new media findings in traditional scholarly publications. By redefining the purposes and roles of research through arts-based practices, we can "walk the talk"—redefining literacies and their values in K-12 classrooms, as well as envisioning new modes of arts-based research and spaces for public interaction.

Arts-based research emerged from a drive to employ the aesthetic dimensions of an experience in both its inquiry and representational phase, by affecting the public's understanding of a social phenomenon epistemologically (Barone & Eisner, 2012). For Barone and Eisner (2012), arts-based research should be active, disrupting equilibrium and certainty—a strategy that the arts can employ through many aesthetic languages to affect dislocation, "through the obviation and undercutting of a prevailing worldview [which] may also mean a useful sort of emancipation of readers and viewers" (p. 16). This strategy is imperative in problematizing the majority/minority dichotomy in diversity education, in advocating for social justice purposes in arts education, and in building spaces for counternarrative practices in education and research.

To document dichotomies and nuances in classroom practice, Eisner (1998) advocated a theory of educational connoisseurship and criticism, calling for the development of researchers as "educational connoisseurs," those so intimately attuned to the art of learning that they are able to put aside things of little consequence, discern what is important, and capture the intricacies and complexities of educational settings. Erickson and Shultz's (1982) study of counselor and student interactions illustrated an early example of such connoisseurship as they used musical notation in analysis to understand why so few counselor–student relationships were successful across interlocutors' cultural differences. These connoisseurs discovered that distorted rhythms in communication were heavily associated with abbreviated and disconnected communication, linking what was said between counselors and students to how it was said and by whom. Erickson, who has experience in music composition and theory, used his creativity to enhance his ability to hear and make sense of discordance and harmony in everyday talk. Similarly, Foster's (1989) study analyzed the musical qualities of an African American teacher's classroom discourse to shed light on the qualities of her success in an urban community college classroom. In particular, Foster focused on the teacher's use of Church-influenced discourse patterns such as vowel elongation, cadence manipulation, and repetition. For these researchers music provided useful tools for analysis and interpretation of educational interactions including minoritized youth.

For Cahnmann-Taylor, Souto-Manning, Wooten, and Dice (2009), theatre was useful in decisions about what constituted "data" as well as how to analyze and repre sent the data. Their research with novice bilingual teachers in the Southeast replaced the traditional "focus group" with theatre activities and collective performances based on Boal's (1979, 1995) theatre of the oppressed techniques. To interpret and repre-sent the emotional qualities of performance data, they responded "artfully," crafting what they refer to as *tran/scripts*, compressed renderings of original transcripts that use techniques from poetry and the dramatic arts to highlight emotional "hot points" and heightened language from the original discourse. They used traditional qualita tive data analysis techniques to identify patterns and tran/scripts to revisit the data as researchers and teacher educators.

In anthropology and education scholarship, poetry and memoir have become powerful opportunities for researchers to document ethnographic empiricism. Several scholars have turned inward toward their home disciplines for theoretical and empirical foundations as well as outward to study the craft of creative writing in order to enliven their various ethnographic narratives of minoritized experience—sharing a variety of creative, self-other ethnographic work about the complexities of charity and adolescent Sudanese refugee identity in the Northeastern United States (Kusserow, 2008); a White teacher's reflections on practice with urban, African American youth (Thorne, 2012); or documenting minoritized communities abroad such as the expe-riences of the few remaining Jews in Tunisia (Stone, 2008) and indigenous medicine in Cameroon (Maynard, 2001). These scholars approach the writing of ethnography as a craft that requires just as much attention to theory and data analysis as to narra-tive, character, image, metaphor, and dialogue. Narayan (2007) argues that creative nonfiction (personal essay, memoir, "faction" [p. 130]) offers the genre space and craft strategies to embrace both creative and academic voices conveying rich, multi-faceted documentation of experience.

All phases of social science research—from deciding what constitutes data to approaches to analysis and forms of representation—can benefit from the researcher's own artistic sensibilities. We agree with Tsao (2011) that researchers need to focus on forms of representation that are "legible and intelligible to the authors on the front lines of those [social justice] movements" (p. 184). Frequently, arts-based research on arts education is written auto-ethnographically, both by and for those on the front lines—researchers who are intimately involved in arts education with minoritized youth. A distinguishing feature of effective auto-ethnographic forms of arts-based research are the renderings of the details of one's own life/sphere with such a depth of craft that the particulars of one's experience resonate at the universal level of capital

"T" truth (Cahnmann, 2003, p. 33). Auto-ethnography in research at times runs parallel to the *testimonio* genre of school-based literacy connecting to students' lives and institutional oppressions that we mentioned earlier.

For example, Johnny Saldaña's (2008) one man show, "Second Chair," is about one adult's memories of playing "second" in high school band, but through the particularities of the performance of a gay, Latino youth, the audience can feel the repercussions of the unfair distribution of status and privilege and the anxiety felt by both young people as well as adults in a competitive, heteronormative, White-dominant society. Nilaja Sun's (2009) one-woman performance of "No Child" portrays a whole cast of characters at a low-income, low-performing school in Bronx—converting herself into various characters including the visiting performance artist-teacher, the many voices of students, revolving teachers, parents, an administrator, a custodian, and even the artist-teacher's Brooklyn landlord. Although the impetus for this work may have been her own very personal experience as a visiting artist in New York City schools, Sun renders and complicates that epiphanic moment of personal trauma into a work of lyric importance for wide audiences (Orr, 2002). Saldaña's and Sun's performances extend the scholar-performer's own experiences in music and theatre education to illuminate both the ecstatic possibilities and immense challenges of working with minoritized youth through the arts.

Similarly, auto-ethnography is a technique employed in community-based, applied theatre settings with minoritized youth populations, such as Q-Speak (2006 and 2007) in Phoenix, Arizona, in which personal reflection, group dialog, and focused interviews result in a collaboratively devised script with auto-ethnographic testimonies and collective narratives. The Albany Park Theatre Project in Chicago is another community-based group that develops and produces ethnographic stories with youth such as *Feast, Remember Me Like This, Aquí Estoy*, and *Saffron*. These shows delve into the themes of these youth's lives, such as multilingualism and multiculturalism, gentrification, immigration, and sexual abuse. What makes one researcher's story (whether expert or novice, individual or collaborative) into high-quality arts-based research is their humble and technically skillful experiences to render what is personal so that it attains universal truths about the human condition.

Varieties of teacher research and action research also constitute forms of arts-based research where, for example, two Latinas reflect on their growing relationship as teacher and student as well as other emerging senses of self (Grúllon & Marín, 2007); where a White, middle-class educator uses narrative portraits to document her own literacy practices with African American youth living and learning in high-poverty contexts (e.g., Hankins, 2003); or where a White American researcher-administrator auto-ethnographically documents her process to begin the first public bilingual, dual-immersion charter school against many social, emotional, and political challenges, in a 95% minority and high-poverty region of Georgia (Giles, 2010). In visual arts research, Irwin and de Cosson (2004) published *A/r/tography*, a collection of work that explores curriculum as aesthetic text through visual renderings as well as prose interpretations. Faltis (2010) reflects on the ways his oil painting about the effects of restrictive immigration and language policies on Mexican communities informs his written scholarship and teaching. Researchers using a range of literary, visual, and performing arts through all stages of the empirical process have contributed to a collective portrait of how the arts make a difference in rich and varied ways in the lives of minoritized youth. Although such artistic portraiture (Lawrence-Lightfoot & Hoffmann-Davis, 1997) often moves audiences' educators and researchers toward empathy and deep feeling, their impact on policy and practice may be limited within the context of larger, scientifically based ideologies about what counts as "valid" and "generalizable" research (Shavelson & Towne, 2002). This limitation should be further analyzed and critiqued while considering the potential of equity-focused arts-based education and research to create productive, humanizing problem-solving communities where positivist and postpositivist social science paradigms have struggled and failed.

IMPLICATIONS AND POSSIBILITIES

How do these areas of arts education/diversity education and research with majoritized/minoritized communities intersect in visions for pre-K-12 teacher preparation and professional development, the education of teaching artists as arts educators in schools and community organizations, and the influence of funding on these structures? Who is responsible for ensuring access to the arts and engagement with the arts as social change tools for minoritized populations, under what circumstances, through what means, and toward what ends? Davis (2008) identified "expertise" as one of the primary objections to arts education: To be taught well, the arts require specialists. She points to the irony that most teachers of young children are expected to have sufficient knowledge of math, science, reading, writing, and social studies but are exempt from the arts.

Beyond the ability to sing "Happy Birthday," direct an acrostic poetry exercise, or color a portrait of Thomas Jefferson, all teachers require the courage, caring, and professional training to explore the arts as active learners and to explore diversity education as a critical, reflective journey alongside our students. We need to disallow statements such as "I don't sing" and "I don't dance," just as we disallow any K-12 teacher to state "I don't read" and "I don't do math." We need to question the assumption of only needing to consider the experiences of bilingual youth if we have them in our classes or those of kids in poverty if they do not bring a lunch to our school. The studies addressed in this article demonstrate that being creative, critical, and publicly engaged are skills we all share and experiences we all crave. We ask of ourselves as educational researchers and teacher educators: How can we better prepare adults to develop these experiences if we do not also reform university pedagogy in teacher and artist education?

Similarly, we need to prepare generations of educators to consider themselves "emergent bilinguals" (O. Garcia & Kleifgen, 2010) and multicultural world citizens, modeling an openness and ability to learn about one or more of the community languages and cultures around them. Whereas preparation in cultural pluralism occurs throughout teacher education, we need to better teach the debate about what it means to be "American," to be a diverse society, to be the same and different at once. This education occurs through teacher-based inquiry projects related to historical and contemporary research on educational quality: *What is good education for a pluralist classroom? For students of specific ethnic, linguistic, gender, and class backgrounds? For developing young citizens of the world?* As teachers and researchers reflect on their own inquiry, about the histories of schooling in the families they teach, about their own qualitative methods, we must also ask questions about empirical quality: *What does good research look like when equity is at the center of its purpose? Who should represent or be represented in the research? Who decides empirical priorities and what counts as valid, vital, and fundable research?*

As to pedagogy, we are not espousing that full artistic competencies or multilingual–multicultural proficiencies are possible for every educator in every school setting, but leaving the arts to "experts only" and isolating multicultural education as exclusively relevant to minority community learning robs teachers and students of significant opportunities for critical, creative, cross-cultural engagement. Scholarship and schooling practices need to build critical, dialogic processes with minoritized *and* majoritized youth. More public display of these processes and their impacts will compel school reformers to see the power of the arts as research, curriculum, and pedagogy for and with minoritized youth. Yet these practices cannot be contained easily into a packaged or scripted curriculum. They are dynamic, emergent methodologies that respond to the local challenges of each community while attending to documented, historical trajectories of oppression that affect all people in the United States and the world. When we commit to a broader application of diversity and arts education with questions of equity, power, and the impact of social dominance at the core, then we must begin again to ask, what and who constitute the "minority"? Such a commitment serves as an invitation into ambiguity and complexity, questioning and challenging dichotomous thinking as far as such dualities (e.g., majority–minority, creative–scientific, academic–arts) undermine aesthetic and equity objectives that lead to more hopeful futures for all.

REFERENCES

Abedi, J. (2004). The No Child Left Behind Act and English language learners: Assessment and accountability issues. *Educational Researcher, 33*(1), 4–14.

Adams, S. (in press). Having our say: English language learners talk back to teachers. In S. Chappell & C. Faltis (Eds.), *The arts and emerging bilingual youth: Building responsive, critical and creative education in school and community contexts.* New York, NY: Taylor & Francis.

Aggabao Thelen, C. (2008). "Our ancestors danced like this": Maya youth respond to genocide through ancestral arts. In R. Solinger, M. Fox, & K. Irani (Eds.), *Telling stories to change the world: Global voices on the power of narrative to build community and make social justice claims* (pp. 39–54). New York, NY: Routledge.

Albers, P., & Harste, J. (2007). The arts, new literacies, and multimodality. *English Education, 40*(1), 6–20.

Alim, H. S. (2011). Hip hop and the politics of ill-literacy. In B. A. U. Levinson & M. Pollock (Eds.), *A companion to the anthropology of education* (pp. 232–246). Oxford, England: Wiley-Blackwell.

Anyon, J. (2005). *Radical possibilities: Public policy, urban education, and a new social movement.* New York, NY: Routledge.

Appel, M. P. (2006). Arts integration across the curriculum. *Leadership, 36*(2), 14–17.

Au, K. (1993). *Literacy instruction in multicultural settings.* Orlando, FL: Harcourt Brace.

Au, K., & Mason, J. (1981). Social organization factors in learning to read: The balance of rights hypothesis. *Reading Research Quarterly, 17,* 115–152.

Au, K., & Mason, J. (1983). Cultural congruence in classroom participation structures: Achieving a balance of rights. *Discourse Processes, 6,* 145–167.

Baker, R. A. (2011). *The relationship between music and visual arts formal study and academic achievement on the eighth-grade Louisiana Educational Assessment Program (LEAP) test* (Dissertation). Louisiana State University, Baton Rouge.

Barone, T. (2000). *Aesthetics, politics and educational inquiry.* New York, NY: Peter Lang.

Barone, T. (2001). Science, art, and the predispositions of educational researchers. *Educational Researcher, 30*(7), 24–28.

Barone, T. (2008). How arts-based research can change minds. In M. Cahnmann & R. Siegesmund (Eds.), *Arts-based inquiry in diverse learning communities: Foundations for practice* (pp. 29–50). London, England: Routledge.

Barone, T., & Eisner, E. (2012). *Arts-based research.* Thousand Oaks, CA: Sage.

Bauerlin, M. (2010). Advocating for arts in the classroom. *Education Next, 10*(4), 42–48.

Bell, L. A. (2010). *Storytelling for social justice: Connecting narrative and the arts in antiracist teaching.* New York, NY: Routledge.

Bennett, W. L. (2008). *Civic life online: Learning how digital media can engage youth.* Massachusetts Institute of Technology. Retrieved from http://www.mitpressjournals.org/doi/pdf/10.1162/dmal.9780262524827.001

Blair, D. V. (2007, October 8). Musical maps as narrative inquiry. *International Journal of Education & the Arts, 8*(15). Retrieved from http://www.ijea.org/v8n15/

Boal, A. (1979). *Theatre of the oppressed.* New York, NY: Urizen Books.

Boal, A. (1995). *The rainbow of desire: The Boal method of theatre and therapy.* London, England: Routledge.

Bond, K. E., & Etwaroo, I. (2005). "If I really see you . . . ": Experiences of identity and difference in a higher education setting. In M. C. Powell & V. M. Speiser (Eds.), *The arts, education, and social change: Little signs of hope* (pp. 87–100). New York, NY: Peter Lang.

Bourdieu, P., & Passeron, J. (1977). *Reproduction in education, society, and culture.* London, England: Sage.

Boyle-Baise, M., & Zevin, J. (2009). *Young citizens of the world: Teaching elementary social studies through civic engagement.* New York, NY: Routledge.

Breunlin, R., Himelstein, A., & Nelson, A. (2008). "Our stories, told by us": The neighborhood story project in New Orleans. In R. Solinger, M. Fox, & K. Irani (Eds.), *Telling stories to change the world: Global voices on the power of narrative to build community and make social justice claims* (pp. 75–90). New York, NY: Routledge.

Brouillette, L. R., & Burns, M. A. (2005). ArtsBridge America: Bringing the arts back to school. *Journal for Learning through the Arts, 1*(1), 46–78.

Burnaford, G., Aprill, A., & Weiss, C. (2001). *Renaissance in the classroom: Arts integration and meaningful learning.* New York, NY: Routledge.

Burnaford, G., Brown, S., Doherty, J., & McLaughlin, J. (2007). *Arts integration: Frameworks, research & practice. A literature review.* Washington, DC: Arts Education Partnership.

Burton, J., Horowitz, R., & Abeles, H. (1999). Learning in and through the arts: Curriculum implications. In E. Fiske (Ed.), *Champions of change: The impact of the arts on learning* (pp. 35–46). Washington, DC: Arts Education Partnership.

Cahnmann, M. (2003). The craft, practice, and possibility of poetry in educational research. *Educational Researcher, 32*(3), 29–36.

Cahnmann, M., & Varghese, M. (2006). Critical advocacy and bilingual education in the United States. *Linguistics and Education, 16*(1), 59–73.

Cahnmann-Taylor, M. (2008). Arts-based research: Histories and new directions. In M. Cahnmann-Taylor & R. Siegesmund (Eds.), *Arts-based research in education: Foundations for practice* (pp. 3–15). London, England: Routledge.

Cahnmann-Taylor, M., & Preston, D. (2008). What bilingual poets can do: Re-visioning English education for biliteracy. *English in Education, 42*, 234–252.

Cahnmann-Taylor, M., & Souto-Manning, M. (2010). *Teachers act up! Creating multicultural learning communities through theatre.* New York, NY: Teachers College Press.

Cahnmann-Taylor, M., Souto-Manning, M., Wooten, J., & Dice, J. (2009). The art & science of educational inquiry: Analysis of performance-based focus groups with novice bilingual teachers. *Teachers College Record, 111*, 2535–2559.

Cammarota, J., & Fine, M. (2008). *Revolutionizing education: Youth participatory actions research in motion.* New York, NY: Routledge.

Castagno, A., & Brayboy, B. (2008). Culturally responsive schooling for indigenous youth: A review of literature. *Review of Educational Research, 78*, 941–993.

Catterall, J., Dumais, S., & Hampden-Thompson, G. (2012). *The arts and academic achievement in at-risk youth: Findings from four longitudinal studies.* Washington, DC: National Endowment for the Arts.

Catterall, J., & Waldorf, L. (1999). Chicago arts partnership in education. In E. Fiske (Ed.), *Champions of change: The impact of the arts on learning* (pp. 47–62). Washington, DC: Arts Education Partnership.

Chappell, S. (2006). Children "at risk": Constructions of childhood in the community learning centers federal after-school programs. *Arts Education Policy Review, 108*(2), 9–15.

Chappell, S. (2008). A rough handshake or an illness: Teaching and learning on the border as felt through art-making. *Journal of Curriculum and Pedagogy, 5*(2), 10–21.

Chappell, S. (2009). Young people talk back: Community arts as a public pedagogy of social justice. In J. Sandlin, B. Schultz, & J. Burdick (Eds.), *Handbook of public pedagogy: Education and learning beyond schooling* (pp. 318–326). New York, NY: Routledge.

Chappell, S., & Faltis, C. (Eds.). (in press). *The arts and emergent bilingual youth: Building responsive, critical and creative education in school and community contexts.* New York, NY: Routledge.

The Comic Book Project. (2010). *I am migrant: The life stories of migrant youth.* San Diego, CA: Center for Educational Pathways, San Diego State University-Imperial Valley Migrant Education Program Summer Academy.

Conrad, D. (2004). Exploring risky youth experiences: Popular theatre as a participatory, performative research method. *International Journal of Qualitative Methods, 3*(1), 12–25.

Cope, B., & Kalantzis, M. (2000). *Multiliteracies: Literacy, learning and the design of social futures.* New York, NY: Routlege.

Dabach, D. (2010). Visual prompts in writing instruction: Working with middle school English language learners. In J. Donahue & J. Stuart (Eds.), *Artful teaching: Integrating the arts for understanding across the curriculum, K-8* (pp. 103–110). New York, NY: Teachers College Press.

Damm, R. J. (2006). Education through collaboration: Learning the arts while celebrating culture. *Music Educators Journal, 93*(2), 54–58.

Darden, E., & Cavendish, E. (2011). Achieving resource equity within a single school district: Erasing the opportunity gap by examining school board decisions. *Education and Urban Society, 44*(1), 61–82.

Davis, J. H. (2008). *Why our schools need the arts.* New York, NY: Teachers College Press.

Deasy, R. (Ed.). (2002). *Critical links: Learning in the arts and student academic and social development.* Washington, DC: Arts Education Partnership.

DeShano da Silva, C., Huguley, J. P., Kakli, Z., & Rao, R. (Eds.). (2007). *The opportunity gap: Achievement and inequality in education.* Cambridge, MA: Harvard Education Press.

Dickson, F. (Ed.). (2005). *Taking the time: Young writers, old stories.* Montgomery, AL: Booker T. Washington Magnet High School.

Dickson, F. (Ed.). (2007). *Our hope: Writings and photographs by teenagers on tolerance and equality.* Montgomery, AL: Booker T. Washington Magnet High School.

Ecker, D. W. (1963). The artistic process of qualitative problem solving. *Journal of Aesthetics and Art Criticism, 21,* 283–290.

Edelsky, C. (2006). *With literacy and justice for all: Rethinking the social in language and education* (3rd ed.). Mahwah, NJ: Lawrence Erlbaum.

Eisner, E. (1997). The promise and perils of alternative forms of data representation. *Educational Researcher, 26*(6), 4–10.

Eisner, E. (1998). *The enlightened eye: Qualitative inquiry and the enhancement of educational practice.* Columbus, OH: Prentice-Hall.

Eisner, E. W. (2008). Persistent tensions in arts-based research. In M. Cahnmann & R. Siegesmund (Eds.), *Arts-based inquiry in diverse learning communities: Foundations for practice* (pp. 29–45). London, England: Routledge.

Erickson, F., & Schultz, J. (1982). *The counselor as gatekeeper: Social interaction in interviews.* Waltham, MA: Academic Press.

Faltis, C. (2010, July 13). Artists and counter-narratives in the new era of anti-immigration. *Teachers College Record.* Retrieved from http://www.tcrecord.org/Content.asp?ContentID=16066

Fettes, M. (1997, May). *Stabilizing what? An ecological approach to language renewal.* Paper presented at the Fourth Stabilizing Indigenous Languages Symposium, Flagstaff, AZ.

Finley, S. (2003). Arts-informed inquiry in QI: Seven years from crisis to guerilla warfare. *Qualitative Inquiry, 9,* 281–296.

Finley, S., & Finley, M. (1999). Sp'ange: A research story. *Qualitative Inquiry, 5,* 313–337.

Fisher, M. T. (2007). *Writing in rhythm: Spoken word poetry in urban classrooms.* New York, NY: Teachers College Press.

Fishman, J. (1991). *Reversing language shift: Theoretical and empirical foundations of assistance to threatened languages.* Avon, England: Multilingual Matters.

Fiske, E. (Ed.). (1999). *Champions of change: The impact of the arts on learning.* Washington, DC: Arts Education Partnership.

Flores-Gonzalez, N. (2005). Popularity versus respect: School structure, peer groups and Latino academic achievement. *International Journal of Qualitative Studies in Education, 18,* 625–642.

Foster, M. (1989). It's cookin' now: A performance analysis of the speech events of a Black teacher in an urban community college. *Language in Society, 18,* 1–29.

Gándara, P. (2012). From González to Flores: A return to the Mexican room? In O. Santa Ana & C. Bustamante (Eds.), *Arizona firestorm* (p. 121–144). Lanham, MD: Roman & Littlefield.

Garcia, L. (in press). Thomas Jefferson High School: May Day service learning project from alumni to future alum. In S. Chappell & C. Faltis (Ed.), *The arts and emergent bilingual youth: Building responsive, critical and creative education in school and community contexts.* New York, NY: Taylor & Francis.

Garcia, O., & Kleifgen, J. (2010). *Educating emergent bilinguals: Policies, programs and practices for English language learners.* New York, NY: Teachers College Press.

Garda, R. A. (2011). The white interest in school integration. *Florida Law Review, 63,* 599–655.

Garoian, C. R. (1999). *Performing pedagogy.* Albany: State University of New York Press.

Gavin, M. (2003). Developing positive negatives: Youth on the edge capture images of their lives with the help from PhotoVoice. *Children, Youth and Environments, 13*(2). Retrieved from http://www.colorado.edu/journals/cye/13_2/FieldReports/PhotoVoice.htm

Gay, G. (2010). *Culturally responsive teaching: Theory, research and practice* (2nd ed.). New York, NY: Teachers College Press.

Giles, D. P. (2010). *"Unchartered" territory: An autoethnographic perspective on establishing Georgia's first public two-way immersion school* (Unpublished dissertation). University of Georgia, Athens.

Glisson, S. (2008). Telling the truth: How breaking silence brought redemption to one Mississippi town. In R. Solinger, M. Fox, & K. Irani (Eds.), *Telling stories to change the world: Global voices on the power of narrative to build community and make social justice claims* (pp. 31–38). New York, NY: Routledge.

Goodman, D. (2011). *Promoting diversity and social justice: Educating people from privileged groups* (2nd ed.). New York, NY: Routledge.

Greene, M. (2000). *Releasing the imagination: Essays on education, the arts and social change.* San Francisco, CA: Jossey Bass.

Grinberg, J., & Saavedra, E. R. (2000). The constitution of bilingual/ESL education as a disciplinary practice: Genealogical exploration. *Review of Educational Research, 70,* 419–442.

Grúllon, G., & Marín, M. (2007). For Latinas who have considered dropping out/when Checkhov is not enuf: Tres generaciones (three generations). *Stage of the Art, 18*(1), 7–9.

Haddix, M. (2011). Black boys can write: Challenging dominant framings of African American adolescent males in literacy research. *Journal of Adolescent & Adult Literacy, 53,* 341–343.

Hankins, K. H. (2003). *Teaching through the storm.* New York, NY: Teachers College Press.

Harman, R., Varga-Dobai, K., Bivins, K., & Forker, D. (in press). Critical performative literacy in a middle school ESOL classroom: Voices for undocumented Latino communities. In S. Chappell & C. Faltis (Eds.), *The arts and emergent bilingual youth: Building responsive, critical and creative education in school and community contexts.* New York, NY: Taylor & Francis.

Hetland, L., Veenema, S., Palmer, P., Sheridan, K., & Winner, E. (2005). *Studio thinking: How visual arts teaching can promote disciplined habits of mind.* Cambridge, MA: Harvard University Graduate School of Education.

Howard, G. (2006). *We can't teach what we don't know: White teachers, multiracial schools.* New York, NY: Teachers College Press.

Hull, G., & Katz, M. L. (2006). Crafting an agentive self: Case studies of digital storytelling. *Research in the Teaching of English, 41*(1), 43–81.

Hull, G., & Schultz, K. (2002). *School's out! Bridging out of school literacies with classroom practice.* New York, NY: Teachers College Press.

Irwin, R. L., & de Cosson, A. F. (Eds.). (2004). *A/r/tography: Rendering self through arts-based living inquiry.* Vancouver, British Columbia, Canada: Pacific Educational Press.

Jeffers, C. S. (2005). Transformative connections: Linking service-learning and pre-service art education. In M. C. Powell & V. M. Speiser (Eds.), *The arts, education, and social change: Little signs of hope* (pp. 149–158). New York, NY: Peter Lang.

Jordan, W. (2010). Defining equity: Multiple perspectives to analyzing the performance of diverse learners. *Review of Research in Education, 34,* 142–178.

Kelin, D., II. (2005). *To feel as our ancestors did: Collecting and performing oral histories.* Portsmouth, NH: Heinemann.

Kelin, D., II. (in press). Which "A" will be? Acculturation, assimilation, Americanization. In S. Chappell & C. Faltis (Eds.), *The arts and emergent bilingual youth: Building responsive, critical and creative education in school and community contexts.* New York, NY: Taylor & Francis.

Kincheloe, J., & McLaren, P. (2007). *Critical pedagogy: Where are we now?* New York, NY: Peter Lang.

Krashen, S. (2008). A fundamental principle: No unnecessary testing (NUT). *Colorado Communicator, 32*(1), 7.

Kusserow, A. (2008). Lost boy. In M. Cahnmann & R. Siegesmund (Eds.), *Arts-based inquiry in diverse learning communities: Foundations for practice* (pp. 109–119). London, England: Routledge.

Ladson-Billings, G. (2009). *The dreamkeepers: Successful teachers of African American children.* San Francisco, CA: Jossey Bass.

Lamont Hill, M. (2009). *Beats, rhymes, and classroom life: Hip-hop pedagogy and the politics of identity.* New York, NY: Teachers College Press.

Landay, E., Meehan, M. B., Newman, A. L., Wootton, K., & King, D. W. (2001). "Postcards from America": Linking classrooms and community in an ESL class. *English Journal, 90*(5), 66–74.

Lawrence-Lightfoot, S., & Hoffmann-Davis, J. (1997). *The art and science of portraiture.* San Francisco, CA: Jossey-Bass.

Lewis, E. (in press). Young writers program for migrant youth. In S. Chappell & C. Faltis (Eds.), *The arts and emergent bilingual youth: Building responsive, critical and creative education in school and community contexts.* New York, NY: Taylor & Francis.

Lukes, M., & Zwicky, C. (in press). Seeing art, seeing the world: Modern art and literacy development with English learners K-12. In S. Chappell & C. Faltis (Eds.), *The arts and emergent bilingual youth: Building responsive, critical and creative education in school and community contexts.* New York, NY: Taylor & Francis.

MacSwan, J., & Rolstad, K. (2006). How language proficiency tests mislead us about ability: Implications for English language learner placement in special education. *Teachers College Record, 108,* 2304–2328.

Marron, V. (2003). The A+ schools program: Establishing and integrating the arts as four languages of learning. *Journal for Learning through Music, 4,* 91–97.

Marshall, E., & Toohey, K. (2010). Representing family: Community funds of knowledge, bilingualism, and multimodality. *Harvard Educational Review, 80,* 221–242.

Martinez-Wenzl, M., Pérez, K., & Gándara, P. (2011). *Is Arizona's approach to educating its English learners superior to other forms of instruction?* (The Civil Rights Project: Proyecto Derechos Civiles). Retrieved from http://civilrightsproject.ucla.edu/research/k-12-education/language-minority-students/is-arizonas-approach-to-educating-its-els-superior-to-other-forms-of-instruction

Maynard, K. (2001). *Sunk like God behind the house* [Poetry]. Kent, OH: Kent State.

McDermott, M. (2005). Torn to pieces: Collage art, social change, and pre-service teachers education. In M. C. Powell & V. M. Speiser (Eds.), *The arts, education, and social change: Little signs of hope* (pp. 49–60). New York, NY: Peter Lang.

Meban, M. (2002, January 25). The postmodern artist in the school: Implications for arts partnership programs. *International Journal of the Arts and Education, 3*(1). Retrieved from http://www.ijea.org/v3n1/index.html

Mishook, J., & Kornhaber, M. (2006). Arts integration in an era of accountability. *Arts Education Policy Review, 107*(4), 3–11.

Mitsumura, M. (in press). Ethnodrama: Transformative learning in multicultural teacher education. In S. Chappell & C. Faltis (Eds.), *The arts and emergent bilingual youth: Building responsive, critical and creative education in school and community contexts.* New York, NY: Taylor & Francis.

Moll, L., Amanti, C., Neff, D., & Gonzalez, N. (1992). Funds of knowledge for teaching: Using a qualitative approach to connect homes and classrooms. *Theory Into Practice,* XXXI(2), 132–141.

Montgomery, K. (2000). Youth and digital media: A policy research agenda. *Journal of Adolescent Health,* 27(2), 61–68.

Moriarty, P. (2004). *Immigrant participatory arts: An insight into community-building in Silicon Valley.* San Jose, CA: Cultural Initiatives in Silicon Valley.

Narayan, K. (2007). Tools to shape texts: What creative nonfiction can offer ethnography. *Anthropology and Humanism,* 32, 130–144.

National Center for Education Statistics. (2011). *The nation's report card: Findings in brief: Reading and Mathematics 2011. National assessment of educational progress at Grades 4 and 8.* Retrieved from nces.ed.gov/nationsreportcard/pdf/main2011/2012459.pdf

New London Group. (1996). A pedagogy of multiliteracies: Designing social futures. *Harvard Educational Review,* 66(1). Retrieved from http://www.hepg.org/her/abstract/290

Noguera, P., Cammarota, J., & Ginwright, S. (2006). *Beyond resistance: Youth activism and community change: New democratic possibilities for practice and policy for America's youth.* New York, NY: Routledge.

Norris, J. (2000). Drama as research: Realizing the potential of drama in education as a research methodology. *Youth Theatre Journal,* 14, 40–51.

Nurenberg, D. (2011). What does injustice have to do with me? A pedagogy of the privileged. *Harvard Educational Review,* 81, 50–63.

Oakes, J. (2005). *Keeping track: How schools structure inequality.* New Haven, CT: Yale University Press.

Oreck, B., Baum, S., & McCartney, H. (1999). Artistic talent development for urban youth: The promise and the challenge. In E. Fiske, (Ed.), *Champions of change: The impact of the arts on learning* (pp. 63–78). Washington, DC: Arts Education Partnership.

Orr, G. (2002). *Poetry as survival.* Athens: University of Georgia Press.

Pacheco, M. (2012). Learning in/through everyday resistance: A cultural-historical perspective on community resources and curriculum. *Educational Researcher,* 41(4), 121–132.

Paris, D. (2012). Culturally sustaining pedagogy: A needed change in stance, terminology, and practice. *Educational Researcher,* 41(3), 93–97.

Pennycook, A. (2010). *Language as local practice.* New York, NY: Routledge.

Picower, B. (2011). Resisting compliance: Learning to teach for social justice in a neoliberal contest. *Teachers College Record,* 113, 1105–1134.

Ponder, J., Vander Veldt, M., & Lewis-Ferrell, G. (2011). Lessons from the journey: Exploring citizenship through active civic involvement. In B. Schultz (Ed.), *Listening to and learning from students: Possibilities for teaching, learning and curriculum* (pp. 115–130). Charlotte, NC: Information Age.

Rabkin, N., & Hedberg, E. C. (2011). *Arts education in America: What the declines mean for arts participation.* Washington, DC: National Endowment for the Arts.

Rabkin, N., & Redmond, R. (Eds.). (2004). *Putting the arts in the picture: Reframing education in the 21st century.* Chicago, IL: Columbia College.

Reyes, G. (in press). It is not what it is: A multidisciplinary approach to critical pedagogy, cultural production, and youth development in the Youth Roots program. In S. Chappell & C. Faltis (Eds.), *The arts and emergent bilingual youth: Building responsive, critical and creative education in school and community contexts.* New York, NY: Taylor & Francis.

Rodríguez-Valls, F., Kofford, K., Apodaca, A., & Samaniego, L. (in press). Migrant students vignette their lives: Languages and cultures cross the fields into the classrooms. In S. Chappell & C. Faltis (Eds.), *The arts and emergent bilingual youth: Building responsive, critical and creative education in school and community contexts.* New York, NY: Taylor & Francis.

Rolling, J. H. (2008, June 10). Sites of contention and critical thinking in the elementary art classroom: A political cartooning project. *International Journal of Education & the Arts,* 9(7). Retrieved from http://www.ijea.org/v9n7/

Romero, D., & Walker, D. (2010). Ethical dilemmas in representation: Engaging participative youth. *Ethnography and Education,* 5, 209–227.

Saavedra, C. (2011). Language and literacy in the borderlands: Acting upon the world through testimonios. *Language Arts,* 88, 261–269.

Salas, J. (2008). Immigrant stories in the Hudson Valley. In R. Solinger, M. Fox, & K. Irani (Eds.), *Telling stories to change the world: Global voices on the power of narrative to build community and make social justice claims* (pp. 109–118). New York, NY: Routledge.

Saldaña, J. (2008). Second chair: An autoethnodrama. *Research Studies in Music Education,* 30, 177–191.

Scachner, J. (2007). *Skippyjon Jones.* New York, NY: Dutton Juvenile.

Schultz, B. (2008). *Spectacular things happen along the way: Lessons from an urban classroom.* New York, NY: Teachers College Press.

Shavelson, R. J., & Towne, L. (Eds.). (2002). *Scientific research in education.* Washington, DC: National Academies Press.

Sicre, D. (in press). ¿Y el caballito de mar, donde vive? Exploring science and literacy through bilingual storytelling and shadow puppetry with Head Start children. In S. Chappell & C. Faltis (Eds.), *The arts and emergent bilingual youth: Building responsive, critical and creative education in school and community contexts.* New York, NY: Taylor & Francis.

Soep, L., & Chávez, V. (2010). *Drop that knowledge: Youth radio stories.* Berkeley: University of California Press.

Souto-Manning, M. (2011). Playing with power and privilege: Theatre games in teacher education. *Teaching and Teacher Education,* 27, 997–1007.

Stevenson, L. M., & Deasy, R. J. (2005). *Third space: When learning matters.* Washington, DC: Arts Education Partnership.

Stone, N. (2008). *Stranger's notebook.* Evanston, IL: Northwestern University Press.

Sun, N. (2009). *No child.* Performance presented at the American Education Research Association Annual Meeting, San Diego, CA. Retrieved from http://www.youtube.com/watch?v=RR5v4xUE2Tw

Teacher Activist Groups. (2012). *No history is illegal: A campaign to save our stories.* Retrieved from http://www.teacheractivistgroups.org/tucson/

Thomson, P., & Sefton-Green, J. (2010). *Researching creative learning: Methods and issues.* New York, NY: Routledge.

Thorne, M. M. (2012, April 5). The Destinee Project: Shaping meaning through narratives. *International Journal of Education & the Arts,* 13(3). Retrieved from http://www.ijea.org/v13n3/

Trimble, S. (2005). *NMSA research summary #20: What works to improve student achievement.* Westerville, OH: National Middle School Association.

Tsao, E. (2011). Walking the walk: On the epistemological merits of literary ethnography. *Anthropology & Humanism,* 36, 178–192.

Underriner, T., & Woodson, S. E. (2011). *(Im)movable paradigms or food fights: Applied theatre meets the health sciences* (Working paper). Toronto, Ontario, Canada: American Society for Theatre Research Conference.

Vasquez, V. M. (2008). *Negotiating critical literacies with young children.* New York, NY: Routledge.

Walker, D., & Romero, D. (2012). *Multiliteracies in urban classrooms and out-of-school contexts professional development workshop.* Toronto, Ontario, Canada: American Educational Research Association Annual Meeting.

Wallace-DiGarbo, A., & Hill, D. (2006). Art as agency: Exploring empowerment of at-risk youth. *Art Therapy: The Journal of the American Art Therapy Association, 23*(3), 119–125.

Wang, C. (2006). Youth participation in PhotoVoice as a strategy for community change. *Journal of Community Practice, 14,* 147–161.

Wang, E. (2010). The beat of Boyle Street: Empowering aboriginal youth through music making. *New Directions for Youth Development, 125,* 61–70.

Weinstein, S. (2010, February 6). A unified poet alliance: The personal and social outcomes of youth spoken word poetry programming. *International Journal of Education & the Arts, 11*(2). Retrieved from http://www.ijea.org/v11n2/

Wenger, E. (1999). *Communities of practice: Learning, meaning and identity.* Cambridge, England: Cambridge University Press.

Werner, L. R. (2002). *Artist, teacher, and school change through arts for academic achievement: Artists reflect on long-term partnering as a means of achieving change.* Minneapolis, MN: Center for Applied Research and Educational Improvement.

Woodson, S. (2007). Performing youth: Youth agency and the production of knowledge in community-based theatre. In A. Best (Ed.), *Representing youth: Methodological issues in critical youth studies* (pp. 284–303). New York: New York University Press.

Woodworth, K. R., Gallagher, H. A., Guha, R., Campbell, A. Z., Lopez-Torkos, A. M., & Kim, D. (2007). *An unfinished canvas: Arts education in California: Taking stock on policies and practices.* Menlo Park, CA: SRI International.

Chapter 9

Teacher Agency in Bilingual Spaces: A Fresh Look at Preparing Teachers to Educate Latina/o Bilingual Children

DEBORAH PALMER
RAMÓN ANTONIO MARTÍNEZ
The University of Texas at Austin

This review poses an increasingly common—and increasingly urgent—question in the field of teacher education: How can teachers best be prepared to educate Latina/o bilingual learners? The answers that we offer here challenge some of the prevailing assumptions about language and bilingualism that inform current approaches to teacher preparation. To work effectively with bilingual learners, we argue, teachers need to develop a robust understanding of bilingualism and of the interactional dynamics of bilingual classroom contexts. Unfortunately, the conceptions of language and bilingualism portrayed in much of the teacher-directed literature fall short of offering teachers access to such understandings. In this review, we will make the case for developing materials for teachers that reflect both more up-to-date theoretical understandings of language practices in bilingual communities and a more critically contextualized understanding of the power dynamics that operate in bilingual classroom contexts. We recognize that helping teachers come to these more robust understandings of bilingual language practices and the interactional dynamics of bilingual contexts implies an ideological shift for educators—and teacher educators—in the United States.

Having made the case for rethinking how we talk to teachers about bilingualism in classroom contexts, we will venture to explore why this matters: What will teachers be better positioned to do once equipped with these understandings? It is our contention that such understandings will better position teachers to manage their classrooms for equity and learning for all students. Indeed, these more robust understandings of language and interaction are necessary if teachers are to capitalize on the flexibility and intelligence displayed by bilingual students as they engage in hybrid

Review of Research in Education
March 2013, Vol. 37, pp. 269-297
DOI: 10.3102/0091732X12463556
© 2013 AERA. http://rre.aera.net

language practices in order to guide them in the development of bilingual/bicultural academic identities that would support their continuing success in school. In fact, we believe that teachers are the professionals best positioned to capitalize on such understandings. As arbiters of their own classrooms' language policies (Menken & Garcia, 2010; Palmer, 2011), they hold one of the most important keys to educational opportunity for bilingual children.

In what follows, we will explore the power and limitations of teacher agency in opening up spaces for rich, authentic learning for bilingual children in school. It has been argued that no matter how intense the constraints placed on us, human beings seem to manage to find spaces in which to assert agency (Holland, Lachicotte, Skinner, & Cain, 1998). However, within the very real constraints of today's public schools, those spaces might be quite restricted (Mills & Gale, 2007). Indeed, teachers in many school contexts are under intense scrutiny, must follow highly scripted curricula and regimented schedules, and must dedicate a great deal of time and effort to preparing children for what are often educationally inappropriate high-stakes standardized assessments. Thus, in exploring the spaces in which teachers can assert agency on behalf of bilingual children, we acknowledge these constraints and honor the tremendous efforts sometimes required of teachers to provide authentic learning opportunities to bilingual children in school.

A Word About Terminology

Throughout this review, we will refer to "bilingual" children and "bilingual" classrooms. Occasionally, when referring specifically to students who are actively engaged in learning a second/additional language, we will use the term *emergent bilingual* (García, 2009; García & Kleifgen, 2010). Following Hopper (1998) and García (2009), we emphasize the emergent nature of bilingualism among these students to highlight both the ongoing process of language acquisition and the tremendous potential of this group of students. It is difficult to locate appropriate terms for the specific community of learners we are discussing; terms, in general, are slippery and value-laden. So we think it is appropriate to take a moment now to explain the terms that we have chosen.

For the past 40 years, there has been a category of children in the education policy documents of the United States called "Limited English Proficient." Defined mainly through their scores on standardized language proficiency assessments, these are often children whose initial proficiency in English is significantly less developed than monolingual "mainstream" English-speaking children, and who at least in some aspect of their lives speak a language other than English.

More recently, educators have begun to favor the terms *English Language Learner* or *English Learner* in an effort to frame these children in a more positive light (i.e., to focus on them as "learners" rather than as "limited" individuals). Unfortunately, these terms are ambiguous: Are we not all learners of the English language throughout our lives, given that language accompanies us as we learn about new ideas and engage with new people? Like Limited English Proficient, English (Language) Learner also assumes a monolingual English-speaking norm, implying that the children who are more competent in another language than they are in English are problematic to their schools (García & Kleifgen, 2010). Moreover, referring to bilingual children as "English (Language) Learners," or as "Limited English Proficient," overlooks the children's primary language skills and their academic learning goals, framing them entirely based on their capacities in English. A child could be a competent speaker of another language, a strong mathematics and science student, a curious reader, a caring older sibling, a leader, yet in so much of the teaching literature, she is framed exclusively as a learner of English. This, in turn, has a profound impact on the ways in which she will experience school, because so often the labels placed on us in school serve to delimit the types of opportunities for which we are considered eligible (Varenne & McDermott, 1998).

According to Garcia (2005, p. 4), "The one attribute of these students that distinguishes them from others is bilingualism." In our effort to both clearly delineate the community of learners that we are referring to and emphasize the kinds of conceptions of language and language practices about which we are writing, we have chosen to refer to "bilingual" or "emergent bilingual" children (García & Kleifgen, 2010). Although we acknowledge the imperfection of these terms, we believe they come closest to reflecting the population we are most concerned with for this review: children along the continua of biliteracy (Hornberger, 2003), engaging in at least two languages in their home, school, and/or community.

We will also generally limit our discussion to the Latina/o community, partly because we need to set reasonable limits, partly because Latino/a bilinguals make up the vast majority of bilinguals in the United States, and partly because our own work has centered on this particular community. Of course, not all Latina/o children are bilingual. Some are monolingual speakers of a language other than English (such as Spanish or Portuguese) who are living in the United States, most likely just about to begin on their path toward bilingualism. Others speak mainly or exclusively English, perhaps with bilingual parents, grandparents, or great grandparents. A great many are "emergent" bilinguals (García & Kleifgen, 2010) who are learning their second language (be it English or Spanish or some other language) as they engage in schooling. Still other children are multilingual—speakers of several languages, perhaps including an indigenous language from their community of origin—and their capacities in all their languages may vary considerably. Although it is beyond the scope of this review to focus on students outside the Latina/o community, we wish to point out that a more robust understanding of language, bilingualism, and classroom interaction can help teachers better meet the needs of *all* bilingual and multidialectal students.

In any event, if a child is a Latina/o student in the United States, anywhere on the continuum of biliteracy (Hornberger, 2003), she is likely to experience marginalization and her language resources are likely to be underutilized and misunderstood in school. As Rosa (2010) observes, Latina/o bilingual students are all too often "expected to speak two languages but understood to speak neither correctly" (p. 38). Dominant ideologies of "monoglot standard" (Silverstein, 1996) and "languagelessness" (Rosa, 2010) inform teachers' perceptions of these students, obscuring potentially fruitful opportunities for leveraging their dynamic and varied linguistic repertoires.

Finally, bilingual and emergent bilingual students axiomatically populate classrooms in which more than one language comes into contact, thus creating bilingual classrooms. These are the students and classrooms about whom this review is concerned. There is also ambiguity with regard to terminology in referring to these classrooms. Whereas some researchers refer to "multilingual" classrooms, in which speakers of multiple languages are present regardless of systematic use of multiple languages in instruction, we will refer primarily to Spanish/English "bilingual" classrooms as those that intentionally serve the needs of Spanish-speaking Latina/o bilingual learners (García & Sylvan, 2011; Martin-Jones, 2000).

THE CURRENT STATE OF TEACHER-ORIENTED LITERATURE

Much of the literature aimed at monolingual English-speaking teachers about educating bilingual students focuses on the particular "needs" of these learners and seeks to offer teachers the methods and strategies necessary to "deal with" these needs. A perusal of recent titles reveals the needs-and-strategies orientation of much of the material: *Fifty Strategies for Teaching English Language Learners* (Herrell & Jordan, 2000), *Meeting the Needs of Second Language Learners: An Educator's Guide* (Lessow-Hurley, 2003), and "Closing the Gap: Addressing the Vocabulary Needs of English-Language Learners in Bilingual and Mainstream Classrooms" (Carlo et al., 2004). These materials have, by and large, been thoughtfully produced by engaged teacher educators concerned about the large number of teachers who are underprepared to teach bilingual students. We acknowledge the general need for materials that will appeal to monolingual teachers, help them open up to the new challenges of reaching and teaching bilingual children, and engage them in the difficult work of learning new skills. We also acknowledge the value of many of the strategies and ideas presented in these materials, designed to help teachers "look *at* rather than *through* the language demands of the classroom" and begin to include second language development in their curriculum, pedagogy, and assessment practices (de Jong & Harper, 2011, p. 87; see also Gibbons, 2002).

However, to a great extent, this literature continues to suffer from what Bartolomé (1994) described as "the methods fetish." Offering a monoglossic perspective on language (García & Sylvan, 2011), this body of literature generally does not ask teachers to question the common American assumption that monolingualism is the norm and that bilingual students must be accommodated until they can achieve a level of English comparable to their monolingual peers. The premise of most of these materials is that teachers can modify their instruction with specific "strategies" and thereby smoothly facilitate learning of both content and language for "English Language

Learners" in the "regular" classroom alongside monolingual peers who presumably do not suffer the lack of English that they suffer. Learning is often equated with learning in English; primary language and literacy skills are rarely acknowledged and even more rarely used to facilitate learning; and teachers' monolingualism is not generally problematized, only students' bilingualism. The language of schooling is often narrowly defined as *academic English*, a term that is far too often left undefined or defined in divergent (Valdés, 2004) or monoglossic (Scarcella, 2003) ways. This allows little space for "academic" registers of other world languages in the classroom and even less space for the often low-status registers or dialects children bring from home or the rich hybrid language practices that emerge in bilingual contexts.

One widely used example is the Sheltered Instruction Observation Protocol (SIOP; Echevarria, Vogt, & Short, 2008), produced by the Center for Applied Linguistics. School districts can purchase SIOP as a professional development package that can include teacher trainings, videos, and follow-up classroom visits. It is a comprehensive protocol for ensuring that teachers have incorporated into their instruction a range of important strategies for effective teaching of "English Language Learners." SIOP has been shown to improve bilingual students' academic performance (Echevarria, Short, & Powers, 2006), and teachers who embrace the systematic set of strategies they provide express feeling improved efficacy with bilingual students. Yet SIOP does not adequately characterize bilingual students' everyday language practices and makes no effort to encourage teachers to find ways to develop students' primary language skills. Furthermore, aside from encouraging teachers to engage bilingual students in frequent opportunities to talk and work together, SIOP spends no time helping teachers unpack the dynamics of interaction in bilingual classrooms. As such, it is ultimately limited in its ability to accomplish the stated goal of "closing achievement gaps" between bilingual and "mainstream" (middle-class) English speaking students.

It is our contention that an exclusive focus on bilingual students' needs (and related methods and strategies for addressing them) normalizes monolingualism and diverts attention from some of the more pressing challenges in educating these learners— challenges that lie not in the learners themselves but in the language ideologies and normative discourses that permeate classrooms, schools, and the surrounding society. Overall, bilingual learners have much the same needs and strengths as monolingual learners; they simply have a greater potential to work and learn in two (or more) languages—a situation that, although still the exception in the United States—is far closer to the norm worldwide. Developing more robust understandings of bilingualism and the interactional dynamics of bilingual contexts will help teachers learn to better engage bilingual learners.

It has been argued by many that teachers need specialized knowledge about language and the language acquisition process to effectively teach children who are learning English in school (August & Hakuta, 1997; Cummins, 1979; Echevarria et al., 2008; Harper & de Jong, 2004; Lucas, 2011; Lucas & Grinberg, 2008; Scarcella, 2003; Valdés, 2001; Valdés, Bunch, Snow, Lee, & Matos, 2005; Wong Fillmore & Snow, 2000). Although we agree that such knowledge is necessary for teachers to work effectively with bilingual students, we contend that it is not enough. Teachers need to rethink their notions of language and bilingualism. Our arguments build on others in teacher education for bilingual students who have attempted to encourage a more critical orientation toward the challenge of educating bilingual students in the United States (Aukerman, 2007; Bartolomé, 2004; Cummins, 2000; Harper & de Jong, 2004; Lucas & Grinberg, 2008; Nieto, 2002; Pavlenko, 2003; Trueba, Bartolomé, & Macedo, 2000). Cummins (2000), for example, suggests that teachers must move beyond specific language features to consider students' identities, to interrogate structures of power, and to build more sophisticated notions of language acquisition. Bartolomé (2004) similarly argues that teachers working in multilingual and multicultural contexts need "political and ideological clarity" so that they can be prepared to "aggressively name and interrogate potentially harmful ideologies and practices in the schools and classrooms where they work" (p. 98). Nieto (2002), too, calls for teacher educators to engage preservice teachers in critical conversations to help them confront the inequities of multicultural and multilingual classrooms. Lucas and Grinberg (2008), in their very thorough review of the literature on preparing all teachers to teach bilingual students, argue that teachers specifically need to experience—or at least dabble in—multilingualism, by studying a language other than English and by having contact with people who speak languages other than English, in order to be better prepared to work with bilingual students. They argue that such an experience can serve as a foundation for teachers' development of "affirming views of linguistic diversity" and "an awareness of the sociopolitical dimension of language use and language education," both of which are fundamental to support bilingual students in their classrooms (Lucas & Grinberg, 2008, pp. 612–613). We wish to take these critical arguments even further, pushing teachers to reenvision bilingualism as a normal process and to view children's actual classroom language practices as tools for social and academic learning and worthy of attention and promotion.

A recent trend in U.S. bilingual education to encourage "dual language education" appears to break from the monolingual norm, pushing teachers to work within a framework of bilingualism and biliteracy (Cloud, Genesee, & Hamayan, 2000; Howard & Sugarman, 2007; Howard, Sugarman, & Christian, 2003; Lindholm-Leary, 2001). The growth of dual language programs throughout the United States represents the potential for an exciting shift in language ideologies from "language as a problem" toward "language as a resource" (Ruiz, 1984), from "subtractive" toward "additive" bilingualism (Lambert, 1975).[1] More and more teachers are pushed to consider bilingualism as an asset to be developed in school. Yet even among dual language educators, the practice of bilingualism and the complexity of interaction in bilingual spaces are in some ways underestimated. Almost without exception, the materials produced for teachers within the dual language contexts encourage teachers to build students' bilingualism and biliteracy through language *separation*, focusing separately (either by using two separate teachers or classrooms or separate segments of the school day/week) on academic registers of "both" of their students' languages and "balancing" language populations such that classrooms have approximately equal numbers of "English-dominant" and "Spanish-dominant" speakers (Y. S. Freeman, Freeman, & Mercuri, 2005; Gomez, Freeman, & Freeman, 2005; Howard & Sugarman, 2007; Lindholm-Leary, 2005). García and Sylvan (2011) describe this shift—and it is indeed a shift in U.S. language ideology in schools—as one from monolingualism to linear bilingualism. This model for bilingual instruction is perhaps best termed *dual monolingualism* (Fitts, 2006) or *parallel monolingualism* (Heller, 1999). Within dual language teacher preparation, there appears to be a goal of producing students who function similarly to monolingual speakers of two distinct languages. In fact, teachers in dual language programs have sometimes proven quite invested in academic registers of their two languages of instruction, leaving little room for the dynamic everyday language practices of bilingual students (Fitts, 2006; McCollum, 1999).

Some have critiqued the strict policies of language separation that characterize most dual language programs, arguing that such separation is artificial and does not allow for the natural development of bilingualism (Lee, Hill-Bonnet, & Gillespie, 2008; M. Reyes, 2001), or that it has unintended consequences and, if examined honestly, does not carry out the intended purpose (Fitts, 2006; Palmer, 2009b). Yet the practice is still widely accepted and defended as necessary to protect "minority" languages (Cloud et al., 2000; Gomez et al., 2005).

We acknowledge the need for protected spaces for languages other than English in U.S. classrooms. Dual language programs certainly make a more concerted and articulated effort at creating these spaces than do other program models, such as transitional bilingual education, where students' primary language is used only until their English develops sufficiently for academic use, or multilingual ESL classrooms, where languages other than English are rarely heard. However, strict language separation, grounded in a linear model of bilingualism, will not achieve the goal of protected spaces for bilingualism in the United States. We need more sophisticated ways to manage interactional dynamics in bilingual classrooms to interrupt English dominance—ways that take into account not only academic language registers but the everyday language practices of bilingual children. What would it look like for teachers in schools to embrace "dynamic bilingualism," whether they are working in a classroom or program that incorporates only one or multiple languages of instruction (García & Sylvan, 2011)? How can we help teachers build a more robust understanding of bilingualism and the power struggles frequently involved in classroom interaction to better prepare them to work with bilingual students?

RETHINKING LANGUAGE: HOW BILINGUAL CHILDREN *DO BEING BILINGUAL*

This section reviews literature that can help teachers better understand the everyday language practices of bilingual children—in other words, how bilingual children *do being bilingual* (Auer, 1984). We begin with the premise that teachers need to develop an understanding of bilingualism that is grounded in actual bilingual *talk* and that what bilingual children actually do in their everyday talk is not necessarily reflective of the abstract notions of bilingualism that underlie many current approaches to teaching emergent bilinguals. We focus here on two critical insights that have emerged from recent theory and research on language and bilingualism: (a) an understanding of language as *practice* and (b) an understanding of *hybridity* as a normal expression of bilingualism.

Language as *Practice*

As mentioned above, much of the literature on preparing teachers to work with bilingual students is grounded in monolingual views of language development that emphasize the systematicity of linguistic *structure*. Here we argue for a different perspective on language—one that normalizes bilingualism and that frames language as a social and cultural practice. Recent scholarship in applied linguistics and related fields has challenged the view that languages are bounded systems of communication, reframing language as *practice*—in other words, as a form of action that emerges within particular social and cultural contexts (García, 2009; Gutiérrez & Rogoff, 2003; Makoni & Pennycook, 2005; Pennycook, 2010). Calling into question the prevailing perspective within mainstream linguistics since de Saussure, this growing body of scholarship has shifted attention "away from language as a system and towards language as something we do" (Pennycook, 2010, p. 8). Pennycook (2010) situates this scholarly trend within what has been called the "practice turn" (Schatzki, 2001) in contemporary social theory. Over the past 40 years, scholars across multiple disciplines have drawn attention to the role of practice in constituting social structures and formations (Bourdieu, 1977; de Certeau, 1984; Giddens, 1979). This emphasis on practice as a theoretical construct is not new to the study of language. Almost three decades ago, for example, Urciuoli (1985) argued against privileging the systematicity of linguistic structure, suggesting that we might better understand language as practice—or *social action* within meaningful local contexts. In recent years, language scholars have increasingly echoed this perspective, fundamentally rethinking the notion of language as a preexisting entity (Blommaert, 2010; Blommaert & Backus, 2012; Jorgensen, Karrebaek, Madsen, & Moller, 2011; Makoni & Pennycook, 2005; Pennycook, 2010). As Pennycook (2010) asserts, framing language as practice "moves the focus from language as an autonomous system that preexists its use . . . towards an understanding of language as the product of the embodied social practices that bring it about" (p. 9).

This radical reframing of language has important implications for understanding bilingualism. Foremost among these implications is the need to view bilingualism as more than simply the "pluralization of monolingualism" (Makoni & Pennycook, 2005, p. 147). As mentioned above, one of the prevailing assumptions in earlier scholarship on bilingualism was that a bilingual speaker's two languages functioned as two autonomous systems. Cummins (2008) refers to this as the "two solitudes" assumption, whereas Heller (1999) calls it the notion of "parallel monolingualism."

More recent scholarship on bi/multilingualism has moved away from this perspective (Franceschini, 2011; García, 2009; García & Sylvan, 2011). If languages themselves are not bounded entities, these scholars argue, it follows that bilingualism is more than simply the combination of two separate linguistic systems. In contrast to monolingual frameworks for understanding bilingualism, García and Kleifgen (2010) propose the notion of *dynamic bilingualism* as a way of highlighting "the development of different language practices to varying degrees in order to interact with increasingly multilingual communities" (p. 42). Rather than view bilingualism as the combination of two separate, bounded languages, she argues, it is more profitably understood as a repertoire of related language practices. Similarly, Gutiérrez and Rogoff (2003) introduce the notion of *repertoires of practice*, which they define as "ways of engaging in activities stemming from observing and otherwise participating in cultural practices" (p. 22). Included in this definition are ways of using language within particular sociocultural contexts. This focus on repertoires of practice extends Gumperz's (1972) foundational notion of *linguistic repertoires* by emphasizing the dynamic nature of the language practices that comprise such repertoires. The notion of repertoires of practice thus opens up possibilities for recognizing the multiplicity of varied and dynamic ways in which bilingual children practice language on a daily basis both in and out of school. Moving away from a focus on languages as bounded systems and toward language in action allows us to better explore everyday language practices such as *translating* or *interpreting* (Orellana, 2009; Orellana & Reynolds, 2008; Valdés, 2002), *crossing* (Rampton, 1995, 2009), *language sharing* (Paris, 2009), and *hybrid language practices* such as Spanish-English code-switching.

Hybridity as a Normal Expression of Bilingualism

In classrooms throughout the nation, bilingual Latina/o students use language in complex and dynamic ways to communicate and make meaning, often switching from one language to another and/or mixing languages within a single interaction or utterance. In linguistics and related fields, this phenomenon has historically been referred to as *code-switching* or, less frequently, *code-mixing* (Alvarez-Cáccamo, 1998; Auer, 1998; Gumperz, 1970; Heller, 1988; Lipski, 1978; Muysken, 1995; Sankoff & Poplack, 1981). Much of the research on code-switching has focused specifically on the Spanish–English variety (Gumperz, 1982; Lance, 1975; Poplack, 1980; Valdés, 1981; Zentella, 1997), including some studies that have focused on classroom settings (Genishi, 1981; Valdés, 1981). Over the past four decades, this body of scholarship has helped us understand code-switching as a normal, intelligent, and socially meaningful linguistic phenomenon (Blom & Gumperz, 1972; Jaffe, 1999, 2007; MacSwan, 1999, 2000; Poplack, 1980; Woolard, 2004; Zentella, 1997). Nonetheless, in some research and in most popular representations, this everyday language practice continues to be framed primarily from a monolingual perspective—in other words, as the combination of two distinct codes. As García (2009, 2010) has argued, such a framing misrepresents how bilinguals actually use language in everyday communicative interactions. As part of a broader paradigmatic shift associated with the *practice turn* discussed above, scholarship on Spanish–English code-switching has moved away from this monolingual perspective and embraced a view that normalizes hybridity.

Again, this paradigm shift is not new to the study of language, dating at least as far back as Urciuoli's (1985) ethnographic work in a New York Puerto Rican community. Urciuoli proposed abandoning the word *code* in favor of the word *practice*, noting that English and Spanish were "pragmatically unified" (Urciuoli, 1985, p. 383) in the bilingual speech of her participants. Gutiérrez, Baquedano-López, and Tejeda (1999) used the term *hybrid language practices* to describe the use of multiple language varieties in a single setting. Building on earlier theoretical discussions of hybridity (Anzaldúa, 1987; Bhabha, 1994), they studied an urban elementary school classroom in which "no single language or register is privileged, and the larger linguistic repertoires of participants become tools for participating and making meaning" (p. 293). Following Gutiérrez et al. (1999), we use the term *hybrid language practices* to include the combination of English and Spanish in conversation. We recognize, however, that there is little consensus about how to label this practice—even among scholars who agree on framing code-switching as a unified language practice rather than as a combination of two separate codes. Recently, García (2009, 2010)has used the term *translanguaging* to refer to bilingual students' hybrid language practices. Extending a term originally used by Williams (1996), she uses translanguaging to refer to the "complex languaging practices of bilinguals in actual communicative settings" (García, 2009, p. 45). Some scholars have begun to adopt this term to explore hybrid language practices in classroom settings (Canagarajah, 2011; Creese & Blackledge, 2010; Hornberger & Link, 2012; Li, 2011). At the same time, language scholars have used various other terms to attempt to capture linguistic hybridity in its spoken and written forms (Canagarajah, 2011), including *transidiomatic practices* (Jacquemet, 2005), *polylingual languaging* (Jorgensen, 2008), *polylanguaging* (Jorgensen et al., 2011), and *code-meshing* (Canagarajah, 2006). Referring specifically to Spanish–English code-switching, Zentella (1997) has highlighted the use of the term *Spanglish*. She notes that, although the term has historically had a pejorative connotation, bilinguals are increasingly using the term to describe their everyday mixture of Spanish and English in a positive light. Some linguists vehemently reject the term *Spanglish* because it is often used to refer inaccurately and pejoratively to the varieties of Spanish spoken by Latinos in the United States (Lipski, 2008; Otheguy & Stern, 2010). They argue convincingly that such a use of the term mischaracterizes local dialects of Spanish and thus perpetuates deficit views of Latina/o bilinguals. These concerns notwithstanding, some researchers studying hybrid language practices in school settings have begun to use *Spanglish* to refer to Spanish–English code-switching and related linguistic phenomena in ways that challenge deficit perspectives (Martínez, 2010; Martínez-Roldán & Sayer, 2006; Rosa, 2010; Sayer, 2008).

Although there is little consensus on what to call the hybrid combination of Spanish and English in conversation, there is almost universal consensus among language scholars that this everyday language practice is a normal and intelligent expression of bilingualism (Lance, 1975; MacSwan, 1999; Poplack, 1981; Woolard, 2004; Zentella, 1997). Indeed, in language contact situations across the globe, translanguaging/hybrid language practices/code-switching/language mixing is the norm (Auer, 1998; Menken & Garcia, 2010; Milroy & Muysken, 1995; Zentella, 1997). What does it mean, then, for educators to understand hybridity as a normative expression of bilingualism—as a legitimate and acceptable way of *doing being bilingual?* What pedagogical implications stem from this understanding that might help inform how we organize teaching and learning for bilingual Latina/o students in today's schools?

In recent years, scholars in education and related fields have helped us begin to explore these questions, highlighting the complexity of bilingual students' hybrid language practices and suggesting some related pedagogical implications (Fránquiz & de la Luz Reyes, 1998; García, 2011; García, Flores, & Chu, 2011; Gort, 2006, 2012; Gutiérrez et al., 1999; Martínez, 2010; Martínez-Roldán & Sayer, 2006; Zentella, 1997, 2005). Zentella (1997), for example, identified multiple functions of Spanish–English code-switching among bilingual children in a New York Puerto Rican community. Debunking deficit views that frame *Spanglish* as resulting from a lack of linguistic competence, she illustrated how bilingual children mixed languages to make meaning, establish social identity, and affirm ties with their local community. In later work, Zentella (2005) has argued that teachers can and should build on students' bilingualism as a resource for language and literacy learning in schools. Similarly, García and Kleifgen (2010) note that teachers "meaningfully educate when they draw upon the full linguistic repertoire of all students, including language practices that are multiple and hybrid" (p. 43). Other scholars have documented bilingual students engaging in hybrid language practices within school contexts, including bilingual and dual language classrooms (Fitts, 2009; García, 2011; Gort, 2006, 2012; Martínez-Roldán & Sayer, 2006; I. Reyes, 2004; Sayer, 2008), as well as "English-only" classrooms that more explicitly discourage Spanish and language mixing (Heller & Martin-Jones, 2001; Martínez, 2010). Martínez-Roldán and Sayer (2006), for example, describe how bilingual students at an elementary school in Arizona mixed English and Spanish during classroom reading activities. Defining *Spanglish* as inclusive of code-switching, the authors illustrate how these students used *Spanglish* as a tool to mediate their interactions with texts. García (2011) describes a case study of a dual language elementary school program in New York where Latina/o kindergartners engaged in dynamic translanguaging practices despite administrative mandates aimed at strictly separating languages. Similarly, Gort (2012) explores code-switching patterns in the writing-related talk of bilingual first-graders at a school in the northeastern United States. Her findings reveal how these students mixed Spanish and English during writing workshop in a two-way immersion program, underscoring the potential of code-switching to serve as a resource for writing. In a similar vein,

Martínez (2010) documents how bilingual middle school students in a Los Angeles classroom used *Spanglish* as a semiotic tool to make meaning in social interaction and to mediate their engagement in academic literacy tasks. Identifying specific ways in which these students' uses of *Spanglish* overlapped with skills articulated in the California English Language Arts Standards, Martínez argues that students' hybrid language practices could be effectively leveraged as resources for cultivating both academic and critical literacies. Across these and other contexts, researchers have highlighted the potential for drawing on bilingual students' hybrid language practices as resources for teaching and learning. Commenting on this pedagogical potential, Hornberger (2003) asserts that bilingual students' learning is "maximized when they are allowed and enabled to draw from across all their existing language skills (in two+ languages), rather than being constrained and inhibited from doing so by monolingual instructional assumptions and practices" (p. 607).

Although bilingual students' hybrid language practices have largely gone untapped as pedagogical resources, some researchers have documented powerful examples of teachers recognizing and leveraging these practices as tools for teaching and learning in the classroom. Gutiérrez et al. (1999), for example, described how one teacher's purposeful use of hybrid language practices helped transform classroom activities into "robust contexts of development" (p. 287). Focusing on a dual immersion classroom in Southern California, the authors illustrated how the teacher "facilitated movement across languages and registers toward particular learning goals" (p. 301). More recently, Gutiérrez (2008) has drawn on empirical data from a case study of the Migrant Student Leadership Institute at UCLA to highlight the role of hybrid language practices in helping nondominant youth cultivate what she calls *sociocritical literacy*. Gutiérrez notes that instructors in this summer program for youth from migrant farmworker backgrounds deliberately privileged the unmarked use of hybrid language practices in their instructional interactions as part of a broader effort to "incite, support, and extend students' repertoires of practice" (Gutiérrez, 2008, p. 160). Describing research on the informal learning context of an innovative after-school program, Gutiérrez, Bien, Selland, and Pierce (2011) highlight the affordances of "polylingual and polycultural learning ecologies" (p. 232) that are deliberately designed to leverage hybridity as a pedagogical resource. They advocate *syncretic* approaches to literacy that "challenge the divide between everyday and school-based literacies and instead exploit the ways school-based and everyday knowledge can grow into one another" (Gutiérrez et al., 2011, p. 258). García and Sylvan (2011) describe a network of high schools for newcomer immigrant students located in New York and California. One of the distinguishing features of these schools, they suggest, is how students' multilingual abilities are cultivated through "plurilingual" instructional practices—incorporating students' full linguistic repertoires as resources for teaching. In related work, García et al. (2011) report on case studies of two high schools in New York City that successfully incorporated students' hybrid language practices as part of their efforts at promoting bilingualism and biliteracy. Michael-Luna and Canagarajah (2007) present results from an ethnographic study of language use in a first-grade bilingual classroom in the Midwestern United States. They document how a first-grade teacher actively supported their students' *code-meshing*, suggesting that his pedagogical approach might serve as a model for practitioners and researchers in higher education who seek to support students' multilingual development.

This growing body of scholarship suggests that researchers in education and related fields are becoming increasingly attentive to the tremendous potential for leveraging linguistic hybridity as a pedagogical resource. Further research in this direction can illuminate this pedagogical potential by documenting additional cases of such leveraging and by exploring connections across multiple contexts. It is our contention, however, that the potential for building on bilingual students' everyday language practices is not simply contingent on rethinking prevailing assumptions about language. To create rich and equitable learning contexts for Latina/o bilingual learners, we argue, teachers need to think beyond language and develop an understanding of the interactional dynamics in bilingual classrooms.

THINKING *BEYOND* LANGUAGE: INTERACTIONAL DYNAMICS IN BILINGUAL CONTEXTS

The classroom contexts in which Latina/o bilingual students practice bilingualism are contested spaces. Pratt (1999) referred to them as "contact zones," places for creativity, agency, and resistance. These contexts are also spaces where social relations of power are reflected and reproduced given the status differential between the languages and cultures involved (Bourdieu, 1977). Across multiple educational contexts, Latina/o bilingual students and their everyday language practices are racialized and stigmatized (Martínez, 2009; Pimentel, 2011; Rosa, 2010). In English-only classrooms, racist and xenophobic ideologies of monglot purism are explicitly embodied in restrictive language policies and their attendant instructional practices (Martínez, 2009). In transitional bilingual education classrooms, teachers' and students' ideologies of English dominance have a tendency to invade the spaces for bilingualism and eliminate Spanish from classroom interaction over time (Palmer, 2011). Even in dual language classrooms, however, these same dominant language ideologies have been documented to inform teachers' and students' perceptions of Latina/o bilingual students, contributing to often unequal interactional dynamics. What can we learn, then, from the interactional dynamics of bilingual spaces that might help teachers create more equitable learning contexts and support the achievement of Latina/o bilingual learners?

The study of bilingual classroom interaction draws guidance from classroom discourse analysis work (Cazden, 2001; Erickson, 2004; Mehan, 1982), exploring patterns inherent in classroom linguistic exchanges, efforts to break away from these deeply ingrained patterns, and their relationship to learning experiences. Martin-Jones (2000), in a review of the literature on bilingual classroom interaction, argued that future research would move in two broad directions.

Some research would "perhaps throw more light on the way in which codeswitching contributes to the scaffolding of joint knowledge construction," whereas other research would

take a more critical turn, grounding micro-analyses of bilingual discourse practices within wider social and historical accounts . . . aiming to reveal links between bilingual discourse practices, ideologies about legitimate forms of bilingualism or monolingualism and the reproduction of asymmetrical relations of power between groups with different languages and different forms of cultural capital. (p. 7)

To a great extent, Martin-Jones's predictions are coming true, although these "two broad directions" are far from separate. On the contrary, they have proven to be integrally related. As we reviewed above, research has begun to explore the role of hybrid language practices in the collaborative construction of knowledge and selves. But this has further reinforced the need for attention to issues of power and ideology in discourse and has informed and enhanced work in classroom discourse analysis. Much of the classroom discourse research taking place in bilingual settings has begun to build a more critical and contextualized account of the micro-analysis of discourse, drawing on aspects of ethnography of communication (Gumperz & Hymes, 1972) and linguistic anthropology (Wortham, 2008) to conduct what some have termed ethnographic discourse analysis (Heller & Martin-Jones, 2001), ethnography and discourse analysis (Palmer, 2008), or multilevel analysis (Saxena, 2009). Links have been formed and interrogated between discourse practices and language ideologies, particularly in terms of the reproduction of asymmetrical relations of power.

Classroom interactional studies in bilingual settings, particularly in intentionally diverse and enrichment-oriented two-way bilingual settings, have in recent years clearly established and reinforced what social theory has been asserting about classrooms for decades (Apple, 1990; Bernstein, 1964; Bowles & Gintis, 2002; Oakes, 1982; Willis, 1977): that they are sites where society's inequities are reproduced daily through classroom discourse (Fitts, 2006; R. Freeman, 1998; Hadi-Tabassum, 2006; Heller & Martin-Jones, 2001; Juarez, 2008; Lowther Pereira, 2010; McCollum, 1999; Palmer, 2009a). Yet because children and teachers always have agency (Holland et al., 1998), albeit within the constraints of structure (Mills & Gale, 2007), it is possible for them to actively recognize and disrupt inequitable relations of power in classroom interaction and create spaces for at least momentary equity, spaces where bilingual students can have a fair shot at learning. Some have characterized these spaces in terms of their hybridity as "contact zones" (Palmer, 2007; Pratt, 1999) or "Third Space" (Hadi-Tabassum, 2006). The following two sections will review this research and then propose two types of moves, two tools, teachers and students can (and appear to) use to defend their hybrid learning selves as they disrupt the status quo, drawing on "positioning theory" and the construct of "investment" in bilingual identities.

Asymmetries of Power in Bilingual Classroom Interaction:
The Case of Two-Way Bilingual Education

As Heller and Martin-Jones (2001) point out, "Education is a key site of struggle over social inequality" (p. 5). Their volume demonstrates this with a collection of cases from around the world that examines educational inequality in the interactional discourse of multilingual school settings. They assert that close analysis of educational interactions in an ethnographic context "allows us to see ways in which social boundaries in local community contexts intersect with institutional categorization processes and ways in which social structure is articulated with human agency" (p. 5). Similarly, we will present a number of examples of research that together make the case for an ongoing tension between the inevitable presence of inequity in children's classroom interaction and the powerful interventions available to teachers and children to counteract inequity. For this purpose, we will specifically look at research that has been conducted in elementary two-way bilingual programs in the United States.

Two-way bilingual programs are a relatively recent phenomenon in American bilingual education in which English-dominant children are intentionally integrated with speakers of another language (usually Spanish) in bilingual classrooms with the goal of bilingualism and biliteracy for all children. Children from both language groups are integrated for at least 50% of the school day, with language and content taught together (Center for Applied Linguistics, 2008). We choose to examine the research in this particular context because among their stated goals, two-way bilingual programs aim to develop students' cross-cultural awareness and to enhance the status of the minority language and its speakers within their programs in order to offer empowering academic achievement for all (Collier & Thomas, 2004; Howard et al., 2003; Lindholm-Leary, 2001). In other words, these are settings that not only inherently produce "contact zones" through intentional integration but are also designed intentionally to disrupt the status quo and to offer "extraordinary pedagogies" to bilingual children in U.S. schools. As Fitts (2006) explains, two-way bilingual programs

provide students with spaces within which to explore the power and efficacy of their multiple languages and dialects, as well as test the sociopolitical boundaries associated with particular linguistic forms. As such, it is important to examine the opportunities that DL programs may offer students to re-structure, or at the very least, to question inequitable social relations. (p. 338)

These settings have much to teach us about the challenges we face even in the best of circumstances; at the same time, they can show us what is possible when teachers and students are working together explicitly toward equitable learning opportunities.

Although dual language programs aim to promote equitable educational outcomes, some research suggests that these contexts may benefit White and English-dominant students more than they benefit Latina/o bilingual students (López & Fránquiz, 2009; Pimentel, Soto, Pimentel, & Urrieta, 2008). An increasing body of research calls for two-way bilingual settings to acknowledge the complexity of interaction in linguistically diverse classroom communities in order to more honestly promote the equity they promise (R. Freeman, 1998; Juarez, 2008; Palmer, 2009a; Valdés, 1997). A number of empirical studies have drawn on a mix of ethnography and discourse analysis to specifically demonstrate and strive to understand the reification of larger societal discourses of inequity within these classrooms (Delgado-Larocco, 1998; DePalma, 2010; Fitts, 2006; R. Freeman, 1998; Hadi-Tabassum, 2006; Lee, Hill-Bonnet, & Raley, 2011; McCollum, 1999; Palmer, 2009a; Pérez, 2004; Potowski, 2004). By closely examining the mechanisms at work in these classrooms, these studies also offer a window into possible strategies for overcoming inequitable discourses in all kinds of linguistically diverse classroom settings.

R. Freeman's (1998) ethnographic discourse analysis of Oyster Bilingual School in Washington, D.C. drew on both classroom interaction data and interview data with teachers to describe the ways that critically aware and engaged teachers appeared to employ "surface linguistic features (e.g. story structure, metaphor, lexical choice, participant role, modality, etc.)" to disrupt negative positionings of bilingual students (p. 101). She characterized their collective efforts as an "alternative educational discourse," arguing that over time, this type of deliberate disruption of hegemony could have powerful implications for equity (p. 101).

R. Freeman's (1998) descriptions of teachers' struggles in the classroom to counter prevailing hegemonic discourses are noted elsewhere as well. Discourses of English dominance are particularly noted in several studies (Delgado-Larocco, 1998; DePalma, 2010; Palmer, 2009a; Potowski, 2004). Delgado-Larocco (1998) revealed, for instance, that although both English- and Spanish-speaking children participated equally in teacher-led lessons, English-speaking children (and with them the English language) dominated playtime in a two-way bilingual kindergarten. DePalma (2010) noted similar patterns, asserting that even the teacher's strong efforts at enforcing Spanish use during "Spanish time" resulted in little movement from her kindergartners, who insisted on engaging mainly in English—particularly for open-ended centers and playtime.

Palmer (2009a) examined the role of English-dominant middle-class students in two-way dual language classrooms, arguing that their very presence, and the cultural and linguistic capital they wield, asserts symbolic dominance in the classroom and turns the classroom into a "site of struggle." Palmer was able to demonstrate the power of teachers' critical awareness of these power dynamics in counteracting their negative impact on equity. She argued, "If a teacher is aware and proactive in confronting English dominance head-on and teaching children to interact appropriately in diverse multilingual multicultural academic settings, this can help tip the balance toward more positive and less negative impacts" (Palmer, 2009a, p. 199).

As she tracked and explored children's language choices in a fifth-grade two-way bilingual classroom, Potowski (2004) demonstrated that children chose English for nearly all social interaction and used English in a wider range of functions, mostly reserving Spanish merely for "on-task topics" related to their schoolwork. Analyzing both extensive recording of their classroom interactions and interviews of children, parents, and teachers, she argued that the context engendered less investment in

Spanish-speaking identities than in English-speaking identities. Pressures from larger district and state assessment policies (which were only in English), accompanied by a lack of opportunities beyond school in which to use Spanish, led to what Potowski refers to as "'leakage' (R. Freeman, 1998) into the classroom of the dominant language patterns in the larger community" (p. 96). Potowski concluded, "True L2 acquisition undoubtedly involves some degree of second identity acquisition" (p. 96), suggesting perhaps that if teachers can be made aware of the power of investment in language and literacy acquisition, they might learn to exploit this power in deliberate ways for powerful language learning for their students. Palmer (2009b) concluded similarly that investment in bilingual identities rather than often-ineffective enforcement of a language separation policy was the key to helping children develop bilingualism.

A language purism focused on standard registers of Spanish and English and a rejection of children's home registers and/or hybrid language practices were noted in several studies (Fitts, 2006; Lee et al., 2011; McCollum, 1999; Palmer, 2010; Pérez, 2004). Fitts (2006) described an "ideology of equality" in the two-way dual language program she studied, in which teachers and children invoked a kind of color-blindness, asserting that all languages and cultures are "basically the same" and thereby "implicitly reinforcing ethnocentrism and assimilation" by "denying important sociohistorical differences" (Fitts, 2006, p. 356). This ideology came through not only in interviews but also in classroom discourse, where in an effort to enforce language equality and "protect" Spanish practice time, children's natural mixing of English words in their Spanish (i.e., their vernacular Spanish) was discouraged in the classroom. Lee et al. (2011) similarly concluded that a two-way bilingual program's policy of language separation led young students to engage in language brokering, trading their own language skills with others in order to succeed across the curriculum and school day. Young children's interactions, according to Lee et al., appeared to support emergent bilingual students' language learning needs, but at the same time to position language brokers as more "able" than students receiving brokering services. Access to "able" student identities, according to Lee et al., was frequently restricted.

Pérez (2004) tracked the implementation of two-way bilingual programs at two elementary schools in San Antonio, Texas, over several years. Teachers in this borderlands context almost universally chose to make spaces for the hybrid language practices that were most natural to the children they served. Although they also intentionally maintained language separation in certain spaces and times, they negotiated these boundaries intentionally and reflectively.

McCollum (1999), applying Bourdieu's construct of linguistic capital to the exchanges in a dual language middle school classroom, found that students of Mexican background learned to value English over Spanish when "Spanish language arts became a battleground where political confrontations regarding the value of a vernacular versus a 'high' academic variety of Spanish regularly occurred" (p. 120). Similarly, looking at teachers' discourses regarding nonstandard registers of English, Palmer (2010) identified the powerful role of racism in teachers' rejection of African American Vernacular English in two-way bilingual contexts.

As she explored the ways that fifth-grade students in a two-way bilingual class-room negotiate language, gender, and race in metalinguistic discussions, Hadi-Tabassum (2006) investigated when, how, and in what ways the children reach a "transgressive third space" where they "arrive at a transcendental understanding of the two languages that subsequently allows for hybridization and fluidity" (p. 3). She concluded that this was a constant, ongoing, tension-ridden process; in several con-texts, Hadi-Tabassum depicted students "tapp[ing] into their student agency in order to confront, speak about and interactively redefine the relationship between the two languages" represented in the dual language program (p. 272).

It seems clear throughout these studies that even in a context such as two-way bilingual education in which equity is explicitly one of the goals of the program, teachers struggle to engage students in equitable learning opportunities in spite of powerful hegemonic discourses. Yet this body of research also suggests that teacher and student agency can have tremendous positive influence on this process. We will next elaborate on two constructs that appear to have proven fruitful to teachers and students in the above studies.

Teachers and Students Disrupting Inequity: Agency and Identity in Bilingual Classroom Interaction

The nexus of language and identity has garnered tremendous attention, and it is beyond the scope of this review to fully elucidate it (Cortazzi & Jin, 2002; Holland et al., 1998; Lee & Anderson, 2009; Norton, 1997). However, the two-way bilingual studies described above suggest that there are some powerful constructs that have been theorized and scrutinized under the broad umbrella of identity and language learning that, if teachers could embrace them, might help them develop better aware-ness of inequity and stronger skills in creating equitable learning spaces. More specifi-cally, we wish to propose that teachers would do well to understand how *positioning* works, and what *investment* is, and to begin to intentionally embrace the potential of these ideas as pedagogical tools.

According to Davies and Harré (1990), positioning is "the discursive process whereby selves are located in conversations as observably and subjectively coherent participants in jointly produced story lines" (p. 48). People are positioned both inter-actively and reflexively (i.e., by oneself). Davies and Harré make clear that position-ing is not necessarily intentional or conscious but that it is ongoing and powerful in terms of the way it can shape our lives and choices. Students and teachers are positioned and assert their own positions through the narrative of classroom talk (Wortham, 2006). Positioning has the potential to marginalize students, for exam-ple, by identifying them as incapable of performing certain academic tasks or as an inadequate speaker of the language of instruction. Similarly, positioning can move initially marginalized individuals such as emergent bilingual Latina/o students into empowering spaces where they are invited to create for themselves academic bicul-tural identities (Palmer, 2008), to serve as "language brokers" to learners of their primary language (Lee et al., 2011), or to model for others the narrative forms and ways of talking and knowing that they know best (Fitts, 2009). Although Davies and Harré (1990) describe positioning as largely occurring in the background as we communicate, that is, as something of which we are largely unaware, we ignore the power of negative positioning at our peril in classrooms. It would behoove us, rather, as teacher educators to bring this powerful dynamic to teachers' attention. Lee et al. (2011) assert that teachers need to

strategically construct opportunities for different students to take up the role of brokers because these repeated positionings have the potential to lead to restricted opportunities for brokees to display and take up an "able" student identity. (p. 323)

It should be noted that although several have asserted the need for teachers to develop awareness of the dynamics of positioning (Fitts, 2009; Lee et al., 2011; Palmer, 2008; Wortham, 2006), none has yet elaborated on how to help teachers develop this awareness. There is certainly a need for further research exploring the ways that teacher educators might develop current and future teachers' awareness of positioning dynamics and examining how such awareness might ultimately influence their practice.

Informed by Bourdieu's (1977) notion of cultural capital, Norton (2000) developed her conception of *investment* in response to phenomena she was noticing in her research with immigrant women that were not accounted for in Second Language Acquisition theory. In contrast to the long-standing concept of *motivation*, which does not account for learners' sociopolitical contexts, *investment* allows for a language learner to have a complex social identity and multiple desires, and it takes into account the power inequities inherent in social contexts. Learners will *invest* in things (including the learning of languages) that they feel will give them an adequate return on their efforts, but there are many other factors that could intervene, and learners are constantly engaged in the process of negotiating these different factors to maximize return. Norton (2000) explains, "A learner's motivation to speak is mediated by other investments that may conflict with the desire to speak—investments that are intimately connected to the ongoing production of the learners' identities and their desires for the future" (p. 120). Potowski (2004) applies this construct to the choices of fifth-grade students in a two-way bilingual context, explaining that it "takes into account the factors influencing a learner's decisions to speak—or to remain silent— and in which language" (p. 77). Potowski's work demonstrates the explanatory power of the concept of investment for helping us understand why some children are able to become highly bilingual and biliterate in two-way dual language education programs whereas others are not.

Learners' choices are clearly complex, and choices about language learning implicate power and identity. If teachers understand that multiple and sometimes conflicting factors enter into learners' decisions about whether and how to invest in learning to speak, read, write, or understand a new language, they can first of all approach these learners with greater patience and sympathy. They can learn to notice and reverse their own negative judgments toward learners' marginalized language practices. Even more important, it is possible that they could develop strategies to support learners in negotiating positive outcomes for themselves. Where students can be convinced to invest in specific bilingual and academic identities, they can learn to make claims for themselves to join multiple communities of practice (Fitts, 2009; Palmer, 2008). Again, as with positioning theory, there is a need for further research that explores ways to help teachers understand investment and works with teachers to begin to translate these understandings into actual classroom practices with potential to positively impact student learning and engagement.

CONCLUSION

Our discussion of teaching in bilingual contexts shifts the focus away from methods and strategies and draws attention to the need for "extraordinary pedagogies" that are informed by robust understandings of language and bilingualism. We have argued that many of the current approaches to teaching bilingual Latina/o students are inadequate because they are informed by monolingual perspectives on language that overemphasize linguistic structure. By making this point, we do not mean to imply that it is unimportant for teachers to cultivate a basic understanding of linguistic structure. Rather, we argue that teachers—and the teacher educators who prepare them to work with Latina/o bilingual students—need to *rethink* prevailing assumptions about language that reify linguistic structure and that normalize monolingualism. Following a growing trend among language researchers and theorists, we argue that linguistic structure is best understood as the emergent *product* of the everyday practice of language (Blommaert & Backus, 2012; Pennycook, 2010; Urciuoli, 1985). Such an understanding of language, we suggest, leads to a more complex and dynamic view of bilingualism, one that normalizes hybridity and that acknowledges the creativity, flexibility, and skill embedded in bilingual students' everyday language practices. Viewing language as practice and hybridity as a normal dimension of bilingualism will enable educators to cultivate a more robust understanding of how bilingual students practice language, better equipping them to leverage students' full linguistic repertoires as resources for teaching and learning. As we have noted, research in this area has documented some promising examples of how teachers can do this. Further research in this direction can also inform how teacher educators help current and prospective teachers learn to maximize the potential embedded in Latina/o bilingual students' everyday language practices.

It is also our contention, however, that even this more robust understanding of language is inadequate without an understanding of the broader contexts of bilingual classrooms as sites of discursive and ideological contestation. Not only do teachers and teacher educators need to rethink language, they also need to *think beyond language* to account for the interactional dynamics of bilingual classrooms in relation to broader social relations of power. As we have discussed above, bilingual classrooms both reflect and reproduce asymmetrical power relations that obtain between Spanish-dominant students and English-dominant students, between students of color and White students, between formal/academic registers and everyday language practices. Absent an understanding of how power manifests itself in the interactional dynamics of bilingual classrooms, teachers risk contributing to the reproduction of broader social inequalities. In contrast, if teachers develop an understanding of how power operates at the interactional level, they will be better equipped to disrupt the hegemonic discourses and ideologies embodied in classroom interaction. Understanding the force of English-only discourses and ideologies within classroom settings will help teachers attend to the ways that bilingual Latina/o students construct bilingual identities in relation to broader issues of power and inequality. This is not to say, of course, that such understandings will necessarily translate directly into effective pedagogical practices for working with bilingual Latina/o students in these contexts. To be sure, we have much to learn still about how to best help current and prospective teachers build on their understandings to inform generative teaching practices (Grossman, McDonald, Hammerness, & Ronfeldt, 2008; Lucas, 2011). Nonetheless, we maintain that such understandings are a necessary starting point for efforts to build on students' linguistic repertoires in ways that promote equity in bilingual settings.

All of this matters for teachers, we argue, because they are uniquely situated as powerful social actors within bilingual classroom contexts. As some of the research has shown, teachers can and do assert their agency despite structural constraints, embracing bilingualism and hybridity as resources for learning while also disrupting dominant discourses and ideologies that discourage dynamic bilingualism. A more conscious identification of opportunities for such disruption, combined with an understanding of some of the mechanisms by which identities are constructed, would offer teachers powerful tools for promoting dynamic bilingualism, biculturalism, and academic achievement in classrooms. This type of informed teacher agency is sorely needed in today's climate of restrictive language policies and reductive literacy practices. Even in dual language programs, where bilingualism is the stated goal, much work still needs to be done in this regard, as Latina/o bilingual students' full linguistic repertoires are often constrained by ideologies and practices of strict language separation. Teachers in such contexts need to actively and deliberately build *syncretic* (Gutiérrez, 2008) spaces where students' hybrid language practices are incorporated, privileged, and leveraged to promote learning. Indeed, by deliberately promoting students' everyday *translanguaging* (García, 2009) practices, teachers can intervene to actively disrupt the inequitable interactional patterns that often characterize dual language settings. Again, the necessary starting point for this type of pedagogical shift is a revised understanding of the practice of bilingualism in bilingual contexts. If teachers first *rethink* language and then *think beyond* language, they can begin to develop the kinds of robust understandings of language and bilingualism that will better position them to construct rich and equitable learning spaces for Latina/o bilingual students.

NOTE

[1]Although Lambert's conception of "additive bilingualism" and Ruiz's conception of "language as a resource" continue to ground teacher preparation in the dual language education field, it must be pointed out that these ideas—as powerful as they are—depend on a conception of language as an object rather than a set of practices, and as such they are not able to help teachers conceptualize "dynamic bilingualism" as we argue they must.

REFERENCES

Alvarez-Cáccamo, C. (1998). From "switching code" to "code-switching": Towards a reconceptualisation of communicative codes. In P. Auer (Ed.), *Code-switching in conversation: Language, interaction and identity* (pp. 29–48). New York, NY: Routledge.

Anzaldúa, G. (1987). *Borderlands/La Frontera*. San Francisco, CA: Spinsters/Aunt Lute Press.

Apple, M. (1990). *Ideology and curriculum*. New York, NY: Routledge/Chapman & Hall.

Auer, P. (1984). *Bilingual conversation*. Amsterdam, Netherlands: John Benjamins.

Auer, P. (1998). Introduction: Bilingual conversation revisited. In P. Auer (Ed.), *Code-switching in conversation: Language, interaction and identity* (pp. 1–24). New York, NY: Routledge.

August, D., & Hakuta, K. (1997). *Improving schooling for language minority-children: A research agenda*. Washington, DC: National Academies Press.

Aukerman, M. (2007). A culpable CALP: Rethinking the conversational/academic language proficiency distinction in early literacy instruction. *The Reading Teacher, 60,* 626–635.

Bartolomé, L. (1994). Beyond the methods fetish: Toward a humanizing pedagogy. *Harvard Educational Review, 64,* 173–194.

Bartolomé, L. I. (2004). Critical pedagogy and teacher education: Radicalizing prospective teachers. *Teacher Education Quarterly, 31,* 97–122.

Bernstein, B. (1964). Elaborated and restricted codes: Their social origins and some consequences. *American Anthropologist, 66*(6, Part 2), 55–69. doi:10.1525/aa.1964.66. suppl_3.02a00030

Bhabha, H. K. (1994). *The location of culture*. New York, NY: Routledge.

Blom, J. P., & Gumperz, J. J. (1972). Social meaning in linguistic structures: Code-switching in Norway. In J. J. Gumperz & D. Hymes (Eds.), *Directions in sociolinguistics* (pp. 407–434). New York, NY: Holt, Rinehart & Winston.

Blommaert, J. (2010). *The sociolinguistics of globalization*. Cambridge, England: Cambridge University Press.

Blommaert, J., & Backus, A. (2012). Superdiverse repertoires and the individual. *Tilburg Papers in Culture Studies, 24.* Tilburg University, Netherlands.

Bourdieu, P. (1977). *Outline of a theory of practice*. Cambridge, England: Cambridge University Press.

Bowles, S., & Gintis, H. (2002). Schooling in capitalist America revisited. *Sociology of Education, 75*(1), 1–18. doi:10.2307/3090251

Canagarajah, S. (2006). The place of world Englishes in composition: Pluralization continued. *College Composition and Communication, 57,* 586–619.

Canagarajah, S. (2011). Codemeshing in academic writing: Identifying teachable strategies of translanguaging. *Modern Language Journal, 95,* 401–417.

Carlo, M., August, D., McLaughlin, B., Snow, C., Dressler, C., Lippman, D., & White, C. E. (2004). Closing the gap: Addressing the vocabulary needs of English-language learners in bilingual and mainstream classrooms. *Reading Research Quarterly, 39,* 188–215.

Cazden, C. (2001). *Classroom discourse: The language of teaching and learning* (Vol. 2). Portsmouth, NH: Heinemann.

Center for Applied Linguistics. (2008). *Directory of two-way bilingual immersion programs in the U.S.* Retrieved from http://www.cal.org/twi/directory/

Cloud, N., Genesee, F., & Hamayan, E. (2000). *Dual language instruction: A handbook for enriched education.* Boston, MA: Heinle & Heinle.

Collier, V. P., & Thomas, W. P. (2004). The astounding effectiveness of dual language education for all. *NABE Journal of Research and Practice, 2*(1), 1–20.

Cortazzi, M., & Jin, L. (2002). Cultures of learning: The social construction of educational identities. In D. Li (Ed.), *Discourses in search of members* (pp. 49–77). New York, NY: University Press of America.

Creese, A., & Blackledge, A. (2010). Translanguaging in the bilingual classroom: A pedagogy for learning and teaching? *Modern Language Journal, 93*, 103–115.

Cummins, J. (1979). Linguistic interdependence and the educational development of bilingual children. *Review of Educational Research, 49*, 222–251.

Cummins, J. (2000). *Language, power and pedagogy: Bilingual children in the crossfire.* Clevedon, England: Multilingual Matters.

Cummins, J. (2008). Teaching for transfer: Challenging the two solitudes assumption in bilingual education. *Encyclopedia of Language and Education, 5*, 1528–1538.

Davies, B., & Harré, R. (1990). Positioning: The discursive production of selves. *Journal for the Theory of Social Behaviour, 20*(1), 43–63.

de Certeau, M. (1984). *The practice of everyday life.* Berkeley: University of California Press.

de Jong, E. J., & Harper, C. (2011). "Accommodating diversity": Pre-service teachers' views on effective practices for English language learners. In T. Lucas (Ed.), *Teacher preparation for linguistically diverse classroom: A resource for teacher educators* (pp. 73–90). New York, NY: Routledge.

Delgado-Larocco, E. L. (1998). *Classroom processes in a two-way immersion kindergarten classroom.* Berkeley: University of California, Berkeley.

DePalma, R. (2010). *Language use in the two-way classroom: Lessons from a Spanish-English bilingual kindergarten.* Bristol, England: Multilingual Matters.

Echevarria, J., Short, D., & Powers, K. (2006). School reform and standards-based education: A model for English-language learners. *Journal of Educational Research, 99*, 195–210.

Echevarria, J., Vogt, M., & Short, D. J. (2008). *Making content comprehensible for English learners: The SIOP model* (3rd ed.). Boston, MA: Pearson.

Erickson, F. (2004). *Talk and social theory: Ecologies of speaking and listening in everyday life.* Cambridge, England: Polity Press.

Fitts, S. (2006). Reconstructing the status quo: Linguistic interaction in a dual-language school. *Bilingual Research Journal, 30*, 337–365.

Fitts, S. (2009). Exploring third space in a dual-language setting: Opportunities and challenges. *Journal of Latinos and Education, 8*(2), 87–104.

Franceschini, R. (2011). Multilingualism and multicompetence: A conceptual view. *Modern Language Journal, 95*, 344–355.

Fránquiz, M., & de la Luz Reyes, M. (1998). Creating inclusive learning communities through English language arts: From chanclas to canicas. *Language Arts, 75*, 211–220.

Freeman, R. (1998). *Bilingual education and social change.* Clevedon, England: Multilingual Matters.

Freeman, Y. S., Freeman, D. E., & Mercuri, S. P. (2005). *Dual language essentials for teachers and administrators.* Portsmouth, NH: Heinemann.

Garcia, E. (2005). *Teaching and learning in two languages: Bilingualism and schooling in the United States* (J. A. Banks, Ed.). New York, NY: Teachers College Press.

García, O. (2009). *Bilingual education in the 21st century: A global perspective.* Malden, MA: Wiley/Blackwell.

García, O. (2010). *Educating emergent bilinguals: Policies, programs, and practices for English Language Learners.* New York: Teachers College Press.

García, O. (with Makar, C., Starcevic, M., & Terry, A.). (2011). Translanguaging of Latino kindergarteners. In K. Potowski & J. Rothman (Eds.), *Bilingual youth: Spanish in English speaking societies* (pp. 33–55). Amsterdam, Netherlands: John Benjamins.

García, O., Flores, N., & Chu, H. (2011). Extending bilingualism in US secondary education: New variations. *International Multilingual Research Journal, 5*(1), 1–18.

García, O., & Kleifgen, J. A. (2010). *Educating emergent bilinguals: Policies, programs, and practices for English language learners.* New York, NY: Teachers College Press.

García, O., & Sylvan, C. E. (2011). Pedagogies and practices in classrooms: Singularities in pluralities. *Modern Language Journal, 95*, 385–400.

Genishi, C. (1981). Codeswitching in Chicano six-year-olds. In R. P. Durán (Ed.), *Latino language and communicative behavior* (pp. 133–152). Norwood, NJ: Ablex.

Gibbons, P. (2002). *Scaffolding language, scaffolding learning: Teaching second language learners in the mainstream classroom.* Westport, CT: Heinemann.

Giddens, A. (1979). *Central problems in social theory: Action, structure and contradiction in social analysis.* Berkeley: University of California Press.

Gomez, L., Freeman, D., & Freeman, Y. (2005). Dual language education: A promising 50–50 model. *Bilingual Research Journal, 29*, 145–163.

Gort, M. (2006). Strategic code switching, interliteracy, and other phenomena of emergent bilingual writing: Lessons from first-grade dual language classrooms. *Journal of Early Childhood Literacy, 6*, 323–354.

Gort, M. (2012). Code-switching patterns in the writing-related talk of young emergent bilinguals. *Journal of Literacy Research, 44*(1), 45–75.

Grossman, P., McDonald, M., Hammerness, K., & Ronfeldt, M. (2008). Dismantling dichotomies in teacher education. In M. Cochran-Smith, S. Feiman-Nemser, D. John McIntyre, & K. E. Dermers (Eds.), *Handbook of research on teacher education: Enduring questions in changing contexts* (3rd ed., pp. 243–248). New York, NY: Routledge & The Association of Teacher Educators.

Gumperz, J. J. (1970). Verbal strategies in multilingual communication. In J. E. Alatis (Ed.), *Report of the twenty-first annual round-table meeting on linguistics and language studies* (pp. 129–147). Washington, DC: Georgetown University School of Languages and Linguistics.

Gumperz, J. J. (1972). Introduction. In J. J. Gumperz & D. Hymes (Eds.), *Directions in sociolinguistics: The ethnography of communication* (pp. 1–25). Oxford, England: Basil Blackwell.

Gumperz, J. J. (1982). Conversational code-switching. In J. J. Gumperz (Ed.), *Discourse strategies* (pp. 59–99). Cambridge, England: Cambridge University Press.

Gumperz, J., & Hymes, D. (1972). *Directions in sociolinguistics: The ethnography of communication.* New York, NY: Holt, Rinehard, & Winston.

Gutiérrez, K. D. (2008). Developing a sociocritical literacy in the third space. *Reading Research Quarterly, 43*, 148–164.

Gutiérrez, K. D., Baquedano-López, P., & Tejeda, C. (1999). Rethinking diversity: Hybridity and hybrid language practices in the third space. *Mind, Culture, and Activity, 6*, 286–303.

Gutiérrez, K. D., Bien, A. C., Selland, M. K., & Pierce, D. M. (2011). Polylingual and poly-cultural learning ecologies: Mediating emergent academic literacies for dual language learners. *Journal of Early Childhood Literacy, 11*, 232–261.

Gutiérrez, K. D., & Rogoff, B. (2003). Cultural ways of learning: Individual traits or repertoires of practice. *Educational Researcher, 32*(5), 19–25.

Hadi-Tabassum, S. (2006). *Language, space and power: A critical look at bilingual education.* Clevedon, England: Multilingual Matters.

Harper, C., & de Jong, E. (2004). Misconceptions about teaching English-language learners. *Journal of Adolescent & Adult Literacy, 48*, 152–162.

Heller, M. (1988). *Codeswitching: Anthropological and sociolinguistic perspectives.* Berlin, Germany: Mouton de Gruyter.

Heller, M. (1999). *Linguistic minorities and modernity: A sociolinguistic ethnography.* London, England: Longman.

Heller, M., & Martin-Jones, M. (2001). *Voices of authority: Education and linguistic difference.* Westport, CT: Ablex.

Herrell, A., & Jordan, M. (2000). *Fifty strategies for teaching English language learners.* Upper Saddle River, NJ: Pearson.

Holland, D., Lachicotte, W., Skinner, D., & Cain, C. (1998). *Identity and agency in cultural worlds.* Cambridge, MA: Harvard University Press.

Hopper, P. (1998). Emergent grammar. In M. Tomasello (Ed.), *The new psychology of language: Cognitive and functional approaches to language study* (pp. 155–175). Mahwah, NJ: Lawrence Erlbaum.

Hornberger, N. H. (2003). *Continua of biliteracy: An ecological framework for educational policy, research, and practice in multilingual settings.* Clevedon, England: Multilingual Matters.

Hornberger, N. H., & Link, H. (2012). Translanguaging and transnational literacies in multilingual classrooms: A biliteracy lens. *International Journal of Bilingual Education and Bilingualism, 15,* 261–278.

Howard, E., & Sugarman, J. (2007). *Realizing the vision of two-way immersion: Fostering effective programs and classrooms.* Washington, DC: Center for Applied Linguistics.

Howard, E., Sugarman, J., & Christian, D. (2003). *Trends in two-way immersion education: A review of the research* (No. 63). Baltimore, MD: Center for Research on the Education of Students Placed at Risk.

Jacquemet, M. (2005). Transidiomatic practices: Language and power in the age of globalization. *Language and Communication, 25,* 257–277.

Jaffe, A. (1999). *Ideologies in action: Language politics on Corsica.* Berlin, Germany: Mouton de Gruyter.

Jaffe, A. (2007). Codeswitching and stance: Issues in interpretation. *Journal of Language, Identity, and Education, 6*(1), 53–77.

Jorgensen, J. N. (2008). Polylingual languaging around and among children and adolescents. *International Journal of Multilingualism, 5,* 161–176.

Jorgensen, J. N., Karrebaek, M. S., Madsen, L. M., & Moller, J. S. (2011). Polylanguaging in superdiversity. *Diversities, 13*(2), 23–37.

Juarez, B. G. (2008). The politics of race in two languages: An empirical qualitative study. *Race, Ethnicity and Education, 11,* 231–249.

Lambert, W. E. (1975). Culture and language as factors in learning and education. In A. Wolfgang (Ed.), *Education of immigrant students: Issues and answers* (pp. 55–83). Toronto, Ontario, Canada: Ontario Institute for Studies in Education.

Lance, D. M. (1975). Spanish-English code-switching. In E. Hernández-Chávez, A. Cohen, & A. Beltramo (Eds.), *El lenguaje de los Chicanos* [The language of Chinanos] (pp. 138–153). Arlington, VA: Center for Applied Linguistics.

Lee, J. S., & Anderson, K. T. (2009). Negotiating linguistic and cultural identities: Theorizing and constructing opportunities and risks in education. *Review of Research in Education, 33,* 181–211. doi:10.3102/0091732X08327090

Lee, J. S., Hill-Bonnet, L., & Gillespie, J. (2008). Learning in two languages: Interactional spaces for becoming bilingual speakers. *International Journal of Bilingual Education and Bilingualism, 11*(1), 75–94.

Lee, J. S., Hill-Bonnet, L., & Raley, J. (2011). Examining the effects of language brokering on student identities and learning opportunities in dual immersion classrooms. *Journal of Language, Identity, and Education, 10,* 306–326.

Lessow-Hurley, J. (2003). *Meeting the needs of second language learners: An educator's guide.* Alexandria, VA: Association for Supervision and Curriculum Development.

Li, W. (2011). Moment analysis and translanguaging space. *Journal of Pragmatics, 43*, 1222–1235.

Lindholm-Leary, K. (2001). *Dual language education.* Clevedon, England: Multilingual Matters.

Lindholm-Leary, K. (2005). *Review of research and best practices on effective features of dual language education programs.* Washington, DC: Center for Applied Linguistics. Retrieved from http://www.lindholm-leary.com/resources/review_research.pdf

Lipski, J. (1978). Code-switching and the problem of bilingual competence. In M. Paradis (Ed.), *Aspects of bilingualism* (pp. 250–264). Columbia, SC: Hornbeam Press.

Lipski, J. M. (2008). *Varieties of Spanish in the United States.* Washington, DC: Georgetown University Press.

López, M. M., & Fránquiz, M. E. (2009). We teach reading this way because it is the model we've adopted: Asymmetries in language and literacy policies in a Two-Way Immersion programme. *Research Papers in Education, 24*, 175–200.

Lowther Pereira, K. A. (2010). *Identity and language ideology in the intermediate Spanish heritage language classroom.* Retrieved from http://arizona.openrepository.com/arizona/bitstream/10150/193890/1/azu_etd_11020_sip1_m.pdf

Lucas, T. (2011). *Teacher preparation for linguistically diverse classrooms: A resource for teacher educators.* New York, NY: Routledge.

Lucas, T., & Grinberg, J. (2008). Responding to the linguistic reality of mainstream classrooms: Preparing all teachers to teach English language learners. In M. Cochran-Smith, S. Feiman-Nemser, D. John McIntyre, & K. E. Demers (Eds.), *Handbook of research on teacher education: Enduring questions in changing contexts* (3rd ed., pp. 606–636). New York, NY: Routledge & The Association of Teacher Educators.

MacSwan, J. (1999). *A minimalist approach to intrasentential code switching.* New York, NY: Garland Press.

MacSwan, J. (2000). The architecture of the bilingual language faculty: Evidence from intra-sentential code switching. *Bilingualism: Language and Cognition, 3*(1), 37–54.

Makoni, S., & Pennycook, A. (2005). Disinventing and (re)constituting languages. *Critical Inquiry in Language Studies: An International Journal, 2*(3), 137–156.

Martin-Jones, M. (2000). Bilingual classroom interaction: A review of recent research. *Language Teaching, 33*(1), 1–9.

Martínez, R. A. (2009). *Spanglish is spoken here: Making sense of Spanish-English code-switching and language ideologies in a sixth-grade English language arts classroom* (Unpublished doctoral dissertation). University of California, Los Angeles.

Martínez, R. A. (2010). Spanglish as literacy tool: Toward an understanding of the potential role of Spanish-English code-switching in the development of academic literacy. *Research in the Teaching of English, 45*(2), 124–149.

Martínez-Roldán, C., & Sayer, P. (2006). Reading through linguistic borderlands: Latino students' transactions with narrative texts. *Journal of Early Childhood Literacy, 6*, 293–322.

McCollum, P. (1999). Learning to value English: Cultural capital in a two-way bilingual program. *Bilingual Research Journal, 23*, 113–133.

Mehan, H. (1982). The structure of classroom events and their consequences for students. In P. Gilmore & A. A. Glatthorn (Eds.), *Children in and out of school* (pp. 59–87). Washington, DC: Center for Applied Linguistics.

Menken, K., & Garcia, O. (2010). *Negotiating language policies in schools: Educators as policy-makers.* New York, NY: Routledge.

Michael-Luna, S., & Canagarajah, A. S. (2007). Multilingual academic literacies: Pedagogical foundations for code meshing in primary and higher education. *Journal of Applied Linguistics, 4*(1), 55–77.

Mills, C., & Gale, T. (2007). Researching social inequalities in education: Towards a Bourdieuian methodology. *International Journal of Qualitative Studies in Education, 20,* 433–447.

Milroy, L., & Muysken, P. (1995). Introduction: Code-switching and bilingualism research. In L. Milroy & P. Muysken (Eds.), *One speaker, two languages: Cross-disciplinary perspectives on code-switching* (pp. 1–14). Cambridge, England: Cambridge University Press.

Muysken, P. (1995). Code-switching and grammatical theory. In L. Milroy & P. Muysken (Eds.), *One speaker, two languages: Cross-disciplinary perspectives on code-switching* (pp. 177–198). Cambridge, England: Cambridge University Press.

Nieto, S. (2002). *Language, culture, and teaching: Critical perspectives for a new century.* Mahwah, NJ: Lawrence Erlbaum.

Norton, B. (1997). Language, identity, and the ownership of English. *TESOL Quarterly, 31,* 409–429.

Norton, B. (2000). *Identity and language learning: Gender, ethnicity and educational change* (Language in Social Life Series). Harlow, England: Longman.

Oakes, J. (1982). The reproduction of inequity: The content of secondary school tracking. *Urban Review, 14,* 107–120.

Orellana, M. F. (2009). *Translating childhoods: Immigrant youth, language, and culture.* New Brunswick, NJ: Rutgers University Press.

Orellana, M. F., & Reynolds, J. (2008). Cultural modeling: Leveraging bilingual skills for school paraphrasing tasks. *Reading Research Quarterly, 43*(1), 48–65.

Otheguy, R., & Stern, N. (2010). On so-called Spanglish. *International Journal of Bilingualism, 15,* 85–100.

Palmer, D. (2007). A dual immersion strand programme in California: Carrying out the promise of dual language education in an English-dominant context. *International Journal of Bilingual Education and Bilingualism, 10,* 752–768.

Palmer, D. (2008). Diversity up close: Building alternative discourses in the dual immersion classroom. In T. Fortune & D. Tedick (Eds.), *Pathways to multilingualism: Evolving perspectives on immersion education* (pp. 97–116). London, England: Multilingual Matters.

Palmer, D. (2009a). Middle-class English speakers in a two-way immersion bilingual classroom: "Everybody should be listening to Jonathan right now . . ." *TESOL Quarterly, 43,* 177–202.

Palmer, D. (2009b). Code switching and symbolic power in a second grade two-way classroom: A teacher's motivation system gone awry. *Bilingual Research Journal, 32,* 42–59.

Palmer, D. (2010). Race, power, and equity in a multiethnic urban elementary school with a dual-language "strand" program. *Anthropology and Education Quarterly, 41,* 94–114.

Palmer, D. (2011). The discourse of transition: Teachers' language ideologies within transitional bilingual education programs. *International Multilingual Research Journal, 5,* 103–122.

Paris, D. (2009). "They're in my culture, they speak the same way": African American language in multiethnic high schools. *Harvard Educational Review, 79,* 428–447.

Pavlenko, A. (2003). "I never knew I was a bilingual": Reimagining teacher identities in TESOL. *Journal of Language, Identity & Education, 2,* 251–268.

Pennycook, A. (2010). *Language as a local practice.* New York, NY: Routledge.

Pérez, B. (2004). *Becoming biliterate: A study of two-way bilingual immersion education.* Mahwah, NJ: Lawrence Erlbaum.

Pimentel, C. (2011). The color of language: The racialized educational trajectory of an emerging bilingual student. *Journal of Latinos and Education, 10,* 335–353.

Pimentel, C., Soto, L. D., Pimentel, O., & Urrieta, L. (2008). The dual language dualism: ¿Quiénes ganan? *Texas Association for Bilingual Education Journal, 10,* 200–223.

Poplack, S. (1980). Sometimes I'll start a sentence in English y termino en español: Toward a typology of code-switching. *Linguistics, 18,* 581–618.

Poplack, S. (1981). Syntactic structure and social function of code-switching. In R. P. Durán (Ed.), *Latino language and communicative behavior* (pp. 169–184). Norwood, NJ: Ablex.

Potowski, K. (2004). Student Spanish use and investment in a dual immersion classroom: Implications for second language acquisition and heritage language maintenance. *Modern Language Journal, 88,* 75–101.

Pratt, M. L. (1999). Arts of the contact zone. In D. Bartholomae & A. Petrosky (Eds.), *Ways of reading* (pp. 581–600). Bedford, MA: St. Martin's.

Rampton, B. (1995). *Crossing: Language and ethnicity among adolescents.* London, England: Longman.

Rampton, B. (2009). Interaction ritual and not just artful performance in crossing and stylization. *Language in Society, 38,* 149–176.

Reyes, I. (2004). Functions of code switching in schoolchildren's conversations. *Bilingual Research Journal, 28*(1), 77–98.

Reyes, M. (2001). Unleashing possibilities: Biliteracy in the primary grades. In M. Reyes & J. Halcon (Eds.), *The best for our children* (pp. 96–121). New York, NY: Teachers College Press.

Rosa, J. D. (2010). *Looking like a language, sounding like a race: Making Latin@ panethnicity and managing American anxieties* (Unpublished doctoral dissertation). University of Chicago, IL.

Ruiz, R. (1984). Orientations in language planning. *National Association for Bilingual Education Journal, 8*(2), 15–34.

Sankoff, D., & Poplack, S. (1981). A formal grammar for code-switching. *Papers in Linguistics, 14,* 3–45.

Saxena, M. (2009). Construction & deconstruction of linguistic otherness: Conflict & cooperative code-switching in (English/) bilingual classrooms. *English Teaching: Practice and Critique, 8,* 167–187.

Sayer, P. (2008). Demystifying language mixing: Spanglish in school. *Journal of Latinos and Education, 7,* 94–112.

Scarcella, R. (2003). *Accelerating academic English: A focus on the English learner.* Oakland: Regents of the University of California.

Schatzki, T. (2001). Introduction: Practice theory. In T. Schatzki, K. Knorr Cetina, & E. von Savigny (Eds.), *The practice turn in contemporary theory* (pp. 1–14). London, England: Routledge.

Silverstein, M. (1996). Monoglot "Standard" in America: Standardization and metaphors of linguistic hegemony. In D. L. Brenneis & R. K. S. Macaulay (Eds.), *The matrix of language: Contemporary linguistic anthropology* (pp. 284–306). Boulder, CO: Westview Press.

Trueba, E. T., Bartolomé, L. I., & Macedo, D. (2000). *Immigrant voices: In search of educational equity* (D. Macedo, Ed.; Critical Perspectives Series). Lanham, MD: Rowman & Littlefield.

Urciuoli, B. (1985). Bilingualism as code and bilingualism as practice. *Anthropological Linguistics, 27,* 363–386.

Valdés, G. (1981). Code-switching as deliberate verbal strategy: A microanalysis of direct and indirect requests among bilingual Chicano speakers. In R. P. Durán (Ed.), *Latino language and communicative behavior* (pp. 98–108). Norwood, NJ: Ablex.

Valdés, G. (1997). Dual language immersion programs: A cautionary note concerning the education of language-minority students. *Harvard Educational Review, 67,* 391–429.

Valdés, G. (2001). *Learning and not learning English: Latino students in American schools* (Multicultural Education Series). New York, NY: Teachers College Press.

Valdés, G. (2002). *Expanding definitions of giftedness: The case of young interpreters from immigrant communities.* Mahwah, NJ: Erlbaum.

Valdés, G. (2004). Between support and marginalisation: The development of academic language in linguistic minority children. *International Journal of Bilingual Education and Bilingualism, 7,* 102–132.

Valdés, G., Bunch, G., Snow, C., Lee, C., & Matos, L. (2005). Enhancing the development of students' language(s). In L. Darling-Hammond & J. Bransford (Eds.), *Preparing teachers for a changing world: What teachers should learn and be able to do* (pp. 126–168). San Francisco, CA: Jossey-Bass.

Varenne, H., & McDermott, R. (1998). *Successful failure: The school America builds.* Boulder, CO: Westview Press.

Williams, C. (1996). Secondary education: Teaching in the bilingual situation. In C. Williams, G. Lewis, & C. Baker (Eds.), *The language policy: Taking stock* (pp.193–211). Llangefni, Wales: CAI.

Willis, P. E. (1977). *Learning to labor: How working class kids get working class jobs.* New York, NY: Columbia University Press.

Wong Fillmore, L., & Snow, C. E. (2000). *What teachers need to know about language.* Washington, DC: US Department of Education Center for Applied Linguistics.

Woolard, K. (2004). Codeswitching. In A. Duranti (Ed.), *A companion to linguistic anthropology* (pp. 73–94). Malden, MA: Blackwell.

Wortham, S. (2006). *Learning identity: The joint emergence of social identification and academic learning.* Cambridge, England: Cambridge University Press.

Wortham, S. (2008). Linguistic anthropology of education. *Annual Review of Anthropology, 37*(1), 37–51.

Zentella, A. C. (1997). *Growing up bilingual: Puerto Rican children in New York.* Oxford, England: Blackwell.

Zentella, A. C. (2005). Introduction: Perspectives on language and literacy in Latino families and communities. In A. C. Zentella (Ed.), *Building on strength: Language and literacy in Latino families and communities* (pp. 1–12). New York, NY: Teachers College Press.

Chapter 10

Pedagogical Language Knowledge: Preparing Mainstream Teachers for English Learners in the New Standards Era

GEORGE C. BUNCH

University of California, Santa Cruz

Sooner or later, as schools move to implement the new Common Core and other forthcoming standards, almost every teacher in the United States will face the challenge of how to support students from homes where English is not the dominant language in meeting subject-matter academic expectations that require increasingly demanding uses of language and literacy in English. In this chapter, I review research that provides potential insights on how "mainstream" teachers might be prepared for responding to this challenge, both in preservice teacher preparation programs and throughout their careers. I argue that efforts to prepare teachers for working with English learners (ELs)[1] to engage with increasing language and literacy expectations across the curriculum requires development of *pedagogical language knowledge* (Galguera, 2011)—not to "teach English" in the way that most mainstream teachers may initially conceive of (and resist) the notion, but rather to purposefully enact opportunities for the development of language and literacy in and through teaching the core curricular content, understandings, and activities that teachers are responsible for (and, hopefully, excited about) teaching in the first place. I review recent literature that presents various approaches to what this knowledge might entail and how teacher preparation and development initiatives might go about fostering it. I conclude by proposing that, in an age of increasing linguistic demands associated with new academic expectations, building teachers' understanding of language as *action* (van Lier & Walqui, 2012) could serve as the foundation for preparing them to engage—and support—ELs in both challenging and meaningful academic tasks.

As educators begin to navigate a new era of policy reform with new common standards at its heart, there are many uncertainties. As I write, teachers, school

Review of Research in Education
March 2013, Vol. 37, pp. 298-341
DOI: 10.3102/0091732X12461772
© 2013 AERA. http://rre.aera.net

administrators, district personnel, state policymakers, and others are scrambling to prepare to implement the new standards, at a time when the science standards have not yet been finalized, high-stakes assessments that will measure students' achievement on the Common Core standards in English language arts and mathematics are still under development, and states are only beginning to revise English language proficiency standards and assessments to correspond to the new standards.

At the same time, as I discuss in the first part of this chapter, there are a number of things that we do know: that the new standards will involve language and literacy demands that are challenging for all students, but especially challenging for ELs; that these challenges call for shifts in the way that instruction for ELs has typically been conceived; that preparing teachers to implement these shifts must become a "mainstream" concern; that ELs represent a heterogeneous population; and that one of the implications of all of the above is that teachers need to know something about language. It is less clear, however, *what* knowledge about language mainstream teachers need in order to engage and support ELs in meeting the kinds of language and literacy demands associated with the new standards, and how teachers might best be prepared to develop this knowledge. After discussing several possible approaches, I argue that what mainstream teachers need is not pedagogical content knowledge about language as might be expected of second language teachers, but rather *pedagogical language knowledge* that is integrally tied to the teaching of the core subject area(s) for which they are responsible. The bulk of the remainder of the chapter is then devoted to exploring how different teacher education and professional development initiatives have envisioned this pedagogical language knowledge and enacted it in their programs.

WHAT WE KNOW

Meeting the New Academic Expectations Will Involve Language and Literacy Demands That Will Be Challenging for All Students, but Especially for English Learners

Language has long been understood to play a central role—perhaps *the* central role—in teaching and learning (see Cazden, 2001; Halliday, 1993; Halliday & Martin, 1993; Mehan, 1979; Schleppegrell, 2004; Vygotsky, 1987b; Wells, 1999). The kinds of learning activities and outcomes privileged by the new standards have emphasized this role by calling for levels of engagement in, and production of, language and literacy that go well beyond the focus on "basic skills" and often scripted curriculum that was at the heart of much of the accountability and testing regime during the No Child Left Behind era (Cummins, 2009; see also Carbone & Orellana, 2010; Dyson, 2008; Enright & Gilliland, 2011; Hillocks, 2002; Pease-Alvarez, Samway, & Cifka-Herrera, 2010). The language and literacy demands that undergird the new standards clearly present challenges for all students, but particularly for students who are still in the process of learning the language of instruction.

The precise nature of the language demands and challenges facing ELs presented by the new standards are only beginning to be unpacked (see Bunch, Kibler, & Pimentel, 2012; Council of Chief State School Officers [CCSSO], 2012; Fillmore & Fillmore,

2012; Hull & Moje, 2012; Moschkovich, 2012; Quinn, Lee, & Valdés, 2012; van Lier & Walqui, 2012; Walqui & Heritage, 2012). But even a cursory look at the standards and frameworks reveal the centrality of language and literacy inherent in the new content-area expectations. For example, the Common Core State Standards for Mathematics (National Governors Association Center for Best Practices and Council of Chief State School Officers, 2010b) emphasize the development of mathematical *practices* as well as content, calling on students to "*explain* correspondences between equations, verbal descriptions, tables, and graphs"; "*justify* their conclusions, *communicate* them to others, and *respond* to the arguments of others"; "*listen or read* the arguments of others, decide whether they make sense, and *ask useful questions* to clarify or improve the arguments" (pp. 6–7, italics added). Similarly, a central component of the Framework for K–12 Science Education (Committee on Conceptual Framework for the New K–12 Science Education Standards [Committee], 2012) is a set of "Scientific and Engineering Practices" that individually and collectively emphasize the role of language in scientific "sense-making" (see also Quinn et al., 2012):

1. Asking questions (for science) and defining problems (for engineering)
2. Developing and using models
3. Planning and carrying out investigations
4. Analyzing and interpreting data
5. Using mathematics and computational thinking
6. Constructing explanations (for science) and designing solutions (for engineering)
7. Engaging in argument from evidence
8. Obtaining, evaluating, and communicating information (Committee, 2012)

Meanwhile, and perhaps least surprisingly, the Common Core State Standards for English Language Arts (which include disciplinary literacy standards as well) call for expanding and raising expectations for students' language and literacy practices. These standards call on students to engage with a variety of sources, including complex informational texts; to use evidence in both writing and oral discourse to inform, argue, and analyze; to demonstrate an awareness of different text types for different audiences and purposes; and to use speaking and listening skills to collaborate, understand multiple perspectives, and present ideas. To do all of the above, the ELA standards require students to concurrently "gain a firm control over the conventions of standard English" and "come to appreciate that language is at least as much a matter of craft as of rules" (National Governors Association Center for Best Practices and Council of Chief State School Officers, 2010a, p. 51).

Supporting ELs' Engagement and Success With the Standards Calls for Shifts in the Kind of Instruction Available for ELs

The language and literacy demands prefaced above clearly call for a shift in the kind of instruction that has typically been available for ELs. For example, writing instruction in secondary English as a Second Language (ESL) classes has often been dominated by grammar and mechanics, "controlled composition," and "copying individual sentences" (Leki, Cumming, & Silva, 2008, p. 23; see also Gebhard & Harman, 2011; Ortmeier-Hooper & Enright, 2011; Valdés, 1998, 2001). Students who have exited ESL classes, whether they are still classified as EL or not, usually transition into low-track, non-college-preparatory regular English classrooms, where the conditions may be equally problematic (Leki et al., 2008). Such courses

make fewer cognitive demands, require little extended prose, expose students to only a few genres, focusing on ones that are supposedly the most practical but are least academic, and so make it even more difficult for the students to develop the kinds of fluency with academic genres and registers that might be required in college. (Leki et al., 2008, p. 24)

Overall, the teaching of writing in the United States has often focused on "skills" such as the teaching and learning of "rules" concerning spelling, punctuation, the structure of sentences or paragraphs, and features of writing such as transition words, often in isolation from the social and meaning-making functions associated with these features (Ivanič, 2004). As Gebhard and Harman (2011) point out, K–12 classroom practices for ELs are still often influenced by behaviorist perspectives on second language acquisition, centering on "drill and practice in language forms with a curricular progression that typically focuses on mastering sound, word, sentence, paragraph, and textual patterns, in that order" (p. 47). It is doubtful that such instructional approaches will prepare ELs for the language and literacy demands associated with the deep engagement in and interaction around the kinds of disciplinary practices called for at the heart of the new standards.

Preparing Teachers to Support ELs in Meeting the New Demands Must Become a "Mainstream" Concern

Just as the Common Core standards envision the development of literacy to be a shared responsibility between language arts teachers and teachers in other disciplines (Bunch et al., 2012), the preparation of ELs for the kinds of language, literature, and learning demands called for by the new standards can no longer be seen as the sole responsibility of a small cadre of language specialists teaching ESL courses (see Bunch, 2010; Fillmore & Snow, 2002; Lucas & Grinberg, 2008; Lucas & Villegas, 2011; Santos, Darling-Hammond, & Cheuk, 2012; Valdés, Bunch, Snow, & Lee, 2005). Students currently classified as ELs represent more than 10% of the total student population in the United States, significantly larger proportions in the country's most populous states (e.g., California, New York, Florida, Texas), and dramatically growing numbers in other states, particularly in the South and Midwest (see Valdés & Castellón, 2011). As mentioned earlier, in addition to those students currently designated as ELs, large numbers of former ELs reclassified as "fluent English proficient" are still in the process of acquiring the English language and literacy necessary to succeed in increasingly challenging academic settings (Olsen, 2010). These reclassified students, along with many ELs who are placed into regular content-area instruction, now form a significant part of what Enright (2011) has called the "new mainstream," which also includes fully functional speakers of English who speak languages other than English at home and students who are monolingual, native speakers of stigmatized varieties of English, such as African American Vernacular English or Chicano English (Godley, Sweetland, Wheeler, Minnici, & Carpenter, 2006). This is not to say that ESL teachers and curriculum specialists will no longer be needed, but rather that the education of ELs must be seen as a shared responsibility by *all* teachers and that the knowledge and skill base for all teachers must be reconceptualized accordingly.

Centralizing—and normalizing—a focus on ELs clearly presents challenges in the United States, where the teaching force is predominantly White,[2] presumably monolingual, and undoubtedly influenced by long-dominant societal ideologies privileging monolingualism and linguistic homogeneity (Crawford, 1992, 1999; O. Garcia, 2009). The challenges are compounded by the fact that most mainstream teachers have received little or no preparation for working with ELs (Lucas, 2011). For this reason, over the past decade or so, an increasing number of publications have addressed the preparation of mainstream teachers for working with ELs, either focusing exclusively on this population (for reviews, see August & Calderón, 2006; August & Shanahan, 2008; Bunch, 2010; E. García, Arias, Harris Murri, & Serna, 2010; Goldenberg & Coleman, 2010; Lucas & Grinberg, 2008) or addressing ELs as part of efforts to prepare teachers for students from a range of linguistically diverse backgrounds (e.g., Fillmore & Snow, 2002; Trumbull & Farr, 2005; Valdés et al., 2005).

Such literature has addressed several different aspects of teacher preparation for ELs. Conceptual overviews have drawn on the literature to analyze and often advocate for particular approaches to the preparation of teachers for linguistic diversity (e.g., Bunch, 2010; Commins & Miramontes, 2006; Fillmore & Snow, 2002; E. García et al., 2010; Harper & de Jong, 2004; Lucas & Grinberg, 2008; Lucas & Villegas, 2011; Lucas, Villegas, & Freedson-Gonzalez, 2008; Trumbull & Farr, 2005; Valdés et al., 2005). Studies, and reviews of studies, have also addressed teachers' knowledge, beliefs, and attitudes related to teaching current and former ELs (e.g., de Jong & Harper, 2011; Faltis, Arias, & Ramírez-Marín, 2010; Gándara, Maxwell-Jolly, & Driscoll, 2005; Pawan & Craig, 2011; Pettit, 2011; Stoddart, Pinal, Latzke, & Canaday, 2002). Existing programs, initiatives, or practices designed to foster the preparation of preservice and in-service teachers for linguistic diversity have been profiled and studied, often by those involved in the intervention (e.g., Athanases & de Oliveira, 2011; Brisk, 2008; Brisk & Zisselsberger, 2011; Echevarria, Short, & Powers, 2006; Galguera, 2011; Gebhard, Demers, & Castillo-Rosenthal, 2008; Hutchinson & Hadjioannou, 2011; Levine & Howard, 2010; Meskill, 2005; Sakash & Rodriguez-Brown, 2011; Short, Fidelman, & Louguit, 2012; Walker, Ranney, & Fortune, 2005; Walker & Stone, 2011). Other literature has addressed efforts to prepare preservice *teacher educators* and those responsible for the professional development of in-service teachers with the knowledge and skills necessary to prepare teachers for working with ELs (e.g., Brisk, 2008; Costa, McPhail, Smith, & Brisk, 2005; Gort, Glenn, & Settlage, 2011; Nevárez-La Torre, Sanford-DeShields, Soundy, Leonard, & Woyshner, 2008; Walqui, 2011). Finally, literature has addressed policy issues relevant to the preparation of teachers for ELs, including teacher assessment, and how teachers respond to different policy and assessment contexts (e.g., Bunch, Aguirre, & Téllez, 2009; Gándara & Maxwell-Jolly, 2006; Pease-Alvarez & Samway, 2012; Pease-Alvarez et al., 2010; Téllez & Waxman, 2006; Varghese & Stritikus, 2005; Villegas & Lucas, 2011).

The predominant message of the literature in all of these areas is that mainstream teachers need "special knowledge and skills" (Lucas, 2011, p. 6) to work with ELs. As I will explore later in this chapter, however, there are a variety of approaches to conceptualizing the nature of that knowledge and those skills, the role of language that undergirds the preparation of teachers for ELs, and how teacher development programs and interventions might best help teachers develop the relevant understandings and expertise.

ELs Represent a Diverse Population

Students designated by their schools and districts as EL include students who are diverse in terms of language and literacy backgrounds, socioeconomic status (both in the United States and, for those born abroad, in their countries of origin), and levels and quality and prior formal schooling (Walqui, 2005). For example, ELs include those who have arrived very recently in the United States and who may speak and understand little or no English, students who have developed enough oral proficiency and literacy in English to engage in some kinds of academic and social tasks but who have difficulty with other kinds, and students who are quite fluent in English but whose non-native-like features of oral or written English, along with underdeveloped academic literacy skills, may have prevented them from exiting the EL designation. Valdés et al. (2005) have used the terms *incipient* bilinguals, *ascendant* bilinguals, and *fully functional* bilinguals to highlight the differences among students often considered ELs. At the same time, ELs at every level of English language proficiency have a range of experiences with literacy in their home languages, from students who have had limited opportunities to develop home-language reading and writing due to substandard or interrupted formal education to students who arrive in the United States with strong academic literacy skills in their first languages.[3] Once students are redesignated as fluent English proficient, they may struggle to succeed in mainstream classes but continue to use and develop each of their languages as circumstances allow and require, exhibiting normal and healthy features of bilingualism that will, by definition, contrast with the language practices of monolingual speakers of English (Grosjean, 1982; Gutiérrez & Orellana, 2006; Orellana & Gutiérrez, 2006; Valdés, 2003, Valdés, Capitelli, & Alvarez, 2011).

ELs also vary in terms of the varieties of English that they will acquire and use. All native speakers of English speak one or more dialect(s), defined by linguists as variations of a language developed by speakers as they grow up and interact with communities based on geography, race, class, ethnicity, or other markers of identity (Finegan & Rickford, 2004; Hudley & Mallinson, 2011; Valdés et al., 2005). In U.S. schools, as in schools worldwide, not all varieties of English carry the same levels of prestige and power, and therefore children from some linguistic communities begin school as native speakers of nondominant, stigmatized dialects of English, such as African American English (AAE), Chicano English, Hawaiian Creole, and dialects used by working-class Anglo-American families (Baugh, 1999; Fought, 2003; Godley et al., 2006; Lippi-Green, 1997; Nero, 2006; Perry & Delpit, 1998; Zentella, 1997). Many ELs live and attend schools in communities where such "nondominant" dialects are widely used, and therefore even the fully developed English of former ELs is likely to be marked with features of often-stigmatized varieties of English such as Chicano English and AAE. In fact, it may be impossible for educators to know whether a particular "non-native-like" feature of students' oral or written language is due to still-developing second language proficiency, fossilized acquisition by more proficient users of the language, or stable features of "contact-varieties" of the target language itself (Valdés, 1992). The point is not that teachers necessarily need to be able to make these particular judgments, but rather that they understand that there are a range of reasons that their students' language might deviate from "native-like" or "standard" English and that this "flawed" language can be used to engage productively in the practices called for by the new standards.

Teachers Need to Know Something About Language

Given the central role of language and literacy in the new common standards, the linguistic needs represented by ELs of different backgrounds, and the lack of current preparation most teachers have received for this population, there is clearly a need to bolster mainstream teachers' knowledge about language. The questions revolve around *what* teachers need to know about this most complex psychological, sociological, and ideological phenomena in order to support ELs, what to prioritize given all the other demands facing teachers as they prepare for and develop their practice throughout their careers, and how teacher preparation programs and professional development initiatives can best support the development of this knowledge. In many cases, it has been unclear what conceptions of language, language development, and language use in academic settings underlie current efforts to prepare teachers for ELs. Perhaps as a result of this lack of clarity, a wide—almost overwhelming—array of language-related knowledge and skills have been proposed as essential for mainstream teachers of ELs. In the next section, I discuss several options for conceiving of the language-related knowledge base necessary for mainstream teachers to create the instructional conditions necessary for ELs to succeed in engaging in the language and literacy expectations associated with the new standards, ultimately arguing that what teachers need is pedagogical *language* knowledge that must be conceived of differently from either the pedagogical content knowledge about language needed by teachers specializing in second language teaching or the pedagogical content knowledge mainstream teachers need in the core subject matters.

CONSIDERING THE LANGUAGE-RELATED KNOWLEDGE BASE FOR MAINSTREAM TEACHERS OF ELS

Perhaps not surprisingly, foundational knowledge in linguistics and second language acquisition (SLA) is often at the center of proposals for what all teachers need to know in order to work effectively with ELs. Fillmore and Snow (2002) have argued that all teachers need a foundation in "educational linguistics." Specifically, they highlight the need for teachers to have knowledge about the basic units of language, regular and irregular forms and how they relate to each other, sociolinguistic variation in language use, historical linguistics to understand why English spelling is so complicated; the "linguistic proficiencies" needed for subject-matter learning (p. 27); and the importance of both interaction with native speakers of English as well as "explicit teaching" of English in academic settings (p. 36). More recently, Lucas and Villegas (2011) have argued that building the expertise of what they call "linguistically responsive teachers" requires, among other areas, a focus on SLA principles, including the distinction between conversational and academic language proficiency; comprehensible input; social interaction for authentic communicative purpose; transfer from L1 to L2; and how anxiety about L2 can interfere with learning (see also Lucas et al., 2008). Valdés et al. (2005) focus on the sociolinguistic knowledge that teachers need to understand that all speakers of English use the dialects, registers, and styles with which they are familiar and come to school as "competent speakers" of their home languages and varieties of language, and the knowledge of disciplinary literacy necessary to support their students in expanding their "linguistic repertoires" to "discuss ideas, to understand texts, and to demonstrate . . . learning" across the curriculum (p. 160).

It is, of course, logical to conceive of fields such as linguistics and SLA as foundational for what teachers need to know in order to support the content and language development of ELs. However, questions have been raised about the breadth and scope of topics that can reasonably be "covered" in teacher preparation and professional development endeavors, which areas should be prioritized, and how language-related knowledge can most effectively be developed by teachers.

First, there is the practical question of the time it takes to provide an adequate introduction to these topics and where in the course of teachers' professional development such instruction should occur. For example, responding to the number of preservice educational linguistics courses proposed by Fillmore and Snow (2002), teacher educators have raised questions about the space and place for such courses in already-intensive teacher education programs (Baca & Escamilla, 2002; Gollnick, 2002; Richardson, 2002). Alternatives have been suggested for including a focus on language and literacy throughout the preservice teacher education curriculum and through professional development opportunities throughout teachers' careers (Baca & Escamilla, 2002; Gollnick, 2002; Valdés et al., 2005).

Second, as Richardson (2002) points out, it is important to consider the relationship between teachers' "formal" or "foundational" knowledge, such as in linguistics and SLA, and the "practical" knowledge necessary to teach effectively. These questions, of course, are among those that have been addressed in the literature on the education of teachers in general (Feiman-Nemser, 2008; Hammerness, Darling-Hammond, & Bransford, 2005; Korthagen & Kessels, 1999) as well as for culturally and linguistically diverse students in particular (A. F. Ball, 2009; Faltis et al., 2010; Walqui, 2008).

Interestingly, the field of second language teaching itself has begun to raise similar questions about the appropriate knowledge base for language teaching. As Johnson (2009) argues, second language teacher educators have historically "positioned disciplinary knowledge about the formal properties of language and theories of SLA as foundational knowledge for the professional preparation of L2 teachers" (p. 11), and they have envisioned language teaching "as a matter of translating theories of SLA into effective instructional practices" (p. 11). Thus, most second language teacher preparation programs "operate under the assumption that it is necessary to provide teachers with discrete amounts of disciplinary knowledge, usually in the form of general theories and methods that are assumed to be applicable to any teaching context" (p. 12). Drawing on Shulman (e.g., 1987) and others (D. L. Ball, 2000), Johnson (2009) has raised questions about the pedagogical content knowledge necessary in that field. Lively discussions have considered what kinds of awareness of language should be at the core of the knowledge base of language teachers (see Andrews, 1999, 2003; Freeman & Johnson, 1998, 2005; Johnson, 2009; Tarone & Allwright, 2005; Trappes-Lomax & Ferguson, 2002).

A third concern relates to which aspects of linguistics, SLA, and related fields are most appropriate for mainstream teacher preparation programs to focus on. Historically, a few concepts from these areas, some of them under significant challenge by scholars in the fields, are privileged and sometimes reified in teacher education programs and professional development endeavors, often without teachers having any idea that they are controversial. For example, multiple theories of second language development have been advanced in the field of SLA (see Atkinson, 2011; Block, 2003; Lightbown & Spada, 2006; van Lier, 2004; van Patten & Williams, 2007; Valdés et al., 2011). Yet a single theory, Krashen's monitor theory (e.g., Krashen, 2003), has long dominated discussions of SLA in teacher preparation texts and curricula, sometimes without any mention of alternative perspectives or the considerable critiques that the theory has generated (see Lightbown & Spada, 2006; van Patten & Williams, 2007). Likewise, Cummins's threshold hypothesis and the distinction between "basic interpersonal communication skills" (BICS) and "conversational academic language proficiency" (CALP) language (e.g., Cummins, 1981, 2000) have dominated teacher preparation programs' approach to academic language, despite critiques of the constructs since their inception (see Bunch, 2006, 2010; Cummins, 2000; Hawkins, 2004; MacSwan, 2000; MacSwan & Rolstad, 2003; Rivera, 1984).

Finally, the question must be raised as to whether SLA is the most appropriate foundational knowledge base for mainstream teachers in the first place (Hawkins, 2004). Teachers, and some teacher educators, might be surprised to learn, as Valdés et al. (2011) point out, that the field of SLA itself has been dominated by a focus not on pedagogical practice but on development of theories of language acquisition, that very little SLA research has focused on children and adolescents, that few longitudinal studies have been conducted, and that there is little evidence that the explicit teaching of language forms leads to productive use of those forms beyond discrete assessments that test for learners' knowledge of them.

Perhaps even more important is the fact that language is not considered by most mainstream teachers to be the principle core content of their professional practice. It is here that it is helpful to distinguish between the notion of pedagogical *content* knowledge, either for second language teachers or for mainstream teachers in their principle subject area(s), and pedagogical *language* knowledge for mainstream teachers in preparing to work with ELs. As Shulman (1987) originally described it, pedagogical content knowledge is "the blending of content and pedagogy into an understanding of how particular topics, problems, or issues are organized, represented, and adapted to the diverse interests and abilities of learners, and presented for instruction" (p. 8). The sources of such knowledge, according to Shulman, include scholarship in the content area itself, educational materials such as curricula and textbooks, findings from formal educational scholarship, and the "wisdom of practice" (p. 11). As mentioned earlier, the notion of pedagogical content knowledge for language teachers has, with some adaptation, been applied to language teaching. In that case, one source of pedagogical content knowledge is knowledge about the target language, linguistics, second language acquisition, bilingualism, and so on. In contrast, the pedagogical content knowledge for mainstream teachers naturally centers on the particular content area or areas they teach (most often, a single content for secondary teachers and multiple content areas for elementary school teachers).[4] Therefore, the knowledge about language necessary for mainstream teachers to teach ELs across the curriculum seems to require a different conceptional foundation than that of pedagogical content knowledge.

Inspired by Galguera (2011), I argue that the pedagogical *language* knowledge of mainstream teachers can be construed as knowledge of language *directly related to disciplinary teaching and learning and situated in the particular (and multiple) contexts in which teaching and learning take place.* To be sure, such an approach draws on insights from linguistics, SLA, and other related fields. Indeed, as Galguera points out, "critical language awareness" (Alim, 2005; Fairclough, 1999, van Lier, 1995) should be at the heart of pedagogical language knowledge, and there is clearly the need for attention to linguistics, SLA, bilingualism, and other language-related knowledge bases as part of teacher education endeavors (Valdés et al., 2005). But the notion of pedagogical language knowledge positions both the knowledge itself and how it might be addressed with teachers in direct relation to teaching and learning at the heart of the curriculum. As Galguera (2011) proposes, it may be through providing teachers with

opportunities to examine specific functions of language in academic contexts and experience ways in which language is used to represent knowledge in classrooms as well as the power and status differences encoded in language [that teachers] begin to construct deep understandings of language. (p. 90)

Therefore, providing teachers with new *experiences*, along with analysis, reflection, and discussion about those experiences, is crucial for the development of pedagogical language knowledge (Galguera, 2011). In the remainder of this chapter, I review literature on teacher preparation practices for ELs that approach the development of what I am conceiving of as pedagogical language knowledge in a variety of ways.

DEVELOPING PEDAGOGICAL LANGUAGE KNOWLEDGE: VARYING APPROACHES IN PRACTICE

In the sections that follow, I draw from recent literature to review examples of current or recent initiatives that can be viewed as addressing the pedagogical language knowledge of mainstream teachers. Selection of these examples, which come from both the research literature and descriptions of recent initiatives in publications geared toward teacher education practitioners, were chosen based on a number of criteria. First, given the focus on *language* in this review, only initiatives that revealed the conception of language, language development, or the role of language in academic instruction grounding the approach were included. Second, to be included, the particular conception of language had to be linked in some direct way to the texts, activities, or practices at the center of mainstream academic instruction, either in specific subject areas or with regard to practices that could cross disciplinary boundaries. Third, the initiative had to explicitly address the preparation of teachers for working with ELs, either as the primary focus or at least with the EL population explicitly mentioned among the students whose needs the program was designed to address. Fourth, the initiative described had to be one that had been implemented in practice, at least in a pilot stage, as opposed to simply recommended or proposed. Finally, some sort of teacher or student outcomes had to be discussed. In order to expand the range of examples I was able to profile and for other reasons I will address below, I admittedly took a lenient approach to the comprehensiveness and rigor with which such outcomes had to be reported to be included in this review. In the final section, I abandon the criteria completely to briefly introduce other potentially promising approaches to pedagogical language knowledge represented in the literature that would have otherwise been excluded.

Before proceeding, it is necessary to emphasize that research on teacher preparation initiatives for linguistic diversity is in its infancy, with few studies systematically measuring outcomes on teachers and even fewer measuring student outcomes (Lucas & Grinberg, 2008). Most reports, including many of the ones that I discuss here, are descriptive in nature. Although most at least briefly mention outcomes on teachers or their students, only a few present data on those outcomes and describe how those data were analyzed. As has been typical of research in this area (see Lucas & Grinberg, 2008), most pieces were authored by those who created and administered the initiatives, providing helpful depth of context but also presenting obvious limitations. Clearly, potential claims regarding the efficacy of each initiative are limited by the available data. Nonetheless, it is important to keep in mind that my rationale in highlighting these particular programs is not to make such claims. Rather, it is to illustrate a variety of approaches to conceiving of and working to develop the pedagogical language knowledge for mainstream teachers to support ELs in the kinds of language and literacy demands associated with the new standards. Further exploration and investigation will clearly be needed for all of the approaches highlighted, as well as for other existing practices endeavoring to support teachers' development of pedagogical language knowledge that have not yet been published.

As a further point of clarification, my intention is not to provide an exhaustive review of the literature on the preparation of teachers for ELs. To allow space to discuss both the approach to language used in each case as well as the initiative itself, I have chosen a relatively small number of approaches to highlight in some depth, privileging those that articulate a coherent conception of language, or at least of the role of language in instruction and learning for ELs. The initiatives profiled represent a range of approaches and contexts, from large-scale, multiyear studies funded by the federal government to one study by a single teacher educator conducting inquiry on his own practice. The practices cut across grade levels and content areas. Included are reports on efforts to prepare teachers, teacher educators, and professional development providers. Target grades include those at the elementary, middle school, and high school levels, although I did not attempt to review literature on the preparation of teachers for teaching initial reading and writing in the early grades, obviously an important area but one beyond the scope of this chapter. Each approach is either targeted toward teachers of a particular content area or, especially in the elementary examples, highlights approaches to help mainstream classroom teachers focus on language-related aspects of instruction in more than one subject area.

Focusing on Linguistic Features of Texts and Tasks Using Systemic Functional Linguistics

One approach to envisioning the pedagogical language knowledge necessary for mainstream teachers has focused on knowledge of the grammatical features of content-area texts and tasks and how teachers can support ELs by introducing them to this knowledge in the context of their disciplinary instruction. Initiatives using systemic functional linguistics (SFL; Halliday, 1994) have provided teachers with tools to analyze the language features central to academic work in different content areas, especially with regard to written texts (e.g., Schleppegrell, 2004; Schleppegrell & Achugar, 2003; Schleppegrell, Achugar, & Oteíza, 2004; Schleppegrell & de Oliveira, 2006). Unlike traditional approaches to grammar instruction, SFL considers the relationship between linguistic form and social context in school settings, focusing on specific linguistic choices that influence and are influenced by different purposes and audiences (see Johns, 2002; Halliday & Martin, 1993; Schleppegrell, 2004; Schleppegrell & Colombi, 2002; Unsworth, 2000; Veel, 1997). Used widely in Australia, SFL has begun to be used in the United States as a means to enable teachers, and students, to understand how the linguistic features of spoken and written texts simultaneously realize and are realized by the social contexts of the production of those texts, including the disciplinary content traditions in which they are embedded (Gebhard, 2010; Schleppegrell, 2004). In the United States, SFL has been described as a response to the concern that the focus on "sheltered instruction" and "comprehensible input" that has traditionally been provided to mainstream teachers when they do have some preparation for working with ELs often does not include enough focus on the "linguistic structures that characterize academic language" (Aguirre-Muñoz, Park, Amabisca, & Boscardin, 2008, p. 298).

Analyzing Linguistic Features of Secondary History Texts

Achugar, Schleppegrell, and Oteíza (2007, p. 11) describe two teacher preparation initiatives designed to help mainstream history teachers develop a *"metalanguage* for talking about how knowledge is constructed in language" in their subject area and how to incorporate that knowledge into their teaching. As part of the California History Project, a teacher development initiative designed to foster content-area knowledge among secondary history teachers, the authors developed "Literacy in History" workshops to support mainstream teachers in working with their increasing numbers of ELs. The workshops were guided by the notions

that students need to develop literacy in important and authentic curriculum contexts, that genre is a way of highlighting patterns in the way language is used to write history, and that focusing on grammar is a means of discussing and critiquing texts. (p. 14)

According to Achugar et al. (2007), a focus on genre helped teachers understand the mismatch between the kinds of texts students are expected to write in history classrooms and those they are assigned to read. Subsequently, in-depth training to deconstruct texts at the sentence level allowed teachers to analyze textbook passages and primary source documents and to incorporate this kind of language analysis with ELs. An external evaluation, according to the authors, showed that ELs and other students of teachers participating in the summer institute had greater gains on a standardized social studies test than did students of nonparticipating teachers. At the same time, teachers reported that learning how to use the language-focused strategies represented a major commitment on their part but that the time and effort necessary diminished as the teachers gained experience. According to the authors, teachers reported that the effort they did expend represented time well-spent because it fostered enhanced critical thinking in their students, more in-depth discussions, and deeper historical understanding.

In a second project, SFL specialists worked with the Institute for Learning initiative at the University of Pittsburgh, as part of its "disciplinary literacy" courses targeted for teachers and administrators with the goal of developing schools' capacity to foster "thoughtful, cognitively demanding engagement with complex written texts, difficult problems, and challenging inquiries," especially for struggling students (Achugar et al., 2007, p. 16). The linguists worked collaboratively with historians to develop guiding questions to help educators connect content and language through the analysis of texts. Teachers and administrators from schools around the United

States participated in 3-week-long professional development sessions that included activities that allowed them to experience, as learners, the opportunity to examine historical texts from a linguistics perspective. The SFL approach is exemplified by the guiding questions used by the initiative to focus teachers on the linguistic and rhetorical features used to construct historical meaning in particular texts (Achugar et al., 2007, p. 17):

1. What is the social purpose of the text?
2. What is going on? (What are the events, who are the participants, and what are the circumstances?)
3. What is the orientation of the writer to the information?
4. What is the relationship between reader and writer?
5. How is the information organized?

To address each of these questions, teachers were directed to identify how the structure and linguistic features of a text provide information. For example, teachers learned that the particular positions taken by an author in relation to an addressed topic can be understood both by identifying modals (such as *will, must, have to, usually*) and through evaluative vocabulary expressing attitudes, emotions, judgments, and appreciation. Likewise, they were taught that how an author constructs a relationship with her intended audience can be revealed both by the use of particular types of clauses (declarative, interrogative, imperative) and by pronouns and "terms of address" (Achugar et al., 2007, p. 17). According to the authors, participants in the institute reported that the linguistic tools and text-exploration strategies featured in the institute increased their confidence in working with ELs, helped their students produce better writing, and fostered more in-depth historical thinking.

Promoting "Functional" Feedback in Secondary English Language Arts

In an example of the use of SFL in secondary English language arts, Aguirre-Muñoz et al. (2008) developed four training modules to familiarize in-service middle school English/language arts teachers with SFL and a genre-based approach to writing instruction. Middle school teachers were encouraged to help their students respond to literature by focusing on the linguistic features authors use to signify protagonists and antagonists, key events, how "qualities and characters are ascribed and evaluated," and how overall cohesion is manifested in the text (p. 300). In addition to reading overviews of SFL theory, teachers were presented with guidance in analyzing examples of texts generated by ELs, the opportunity to role-play "minilessons" designed to teach writing, and joint lesson planning activities. Throughout the sessions, teachers were presented with a set of strategies to incorporate into their discussions of literature and writing instruction and feedback. Aguirre et al. report high satisfaction with the course expressed by teachers and a statistically significant shift in how participants provided feedback, planned for instruction, and incorporated the training into their instruction. Teachers decreased the amount of "traditional" feedback related to writing style and errors and increased their "functional" feedback related to the audiences and purposes students were aiming to address. Furthermore, the authors report, the majority of teachers incorporated the content of the training into their writing instruction.

Using SFL to Enhance Elementary Writing Instruction

At the elementary level, Brisk and Zisselsberger (2011) describe a professional development project that introduced in-service elementary teachers to an SFL approach to the teaching of writing. The authors position the power of SFL in terms of its ability to help teachers focus on how particular syntactic forms are important not because they represent the "correct rules" but rather because they "are essential for certain contexts" (p. 112). Brisk and Zisselsberger argue that SFL-based pedagogy "makes the linguistic, lexical, grammatical, and schematic structure of texts within genres explicit," providing greater access for all learners to be able to understand and produce them (p. 114). The authors designed, implemented, and researched a university-based professional development initiative participated in by participants (eight mainstream K–5 teachers, one K–2 science teacher, one ESL teacher, and a literacy coach) from three elementary schools. The participants attended professional development sessions before and during the school year. In these sessions, the facilitator (Brisk) presented a foundation of SFL and its application to teaching writing and shared materials that included selected target genres found in elementary school texts, explanations of each genre's structural organization and language demands, and strategies for teaching each genre.

According to Brisk and Zisselsberger (2011), interviews and other discussions with teachers revealed that teachers found the materials useful for planning classes and the professional development helpful for complementing their current curricula. All participants tried new ways of teaching writing as a result of the professional development, such as focusing their students' journal writing on a variety of audiences and purposes instead of simply writing for themselves. About two thirds of the teachers "carried out well-planned writing units integrated with their literacy and content area lessons" (p. 117). The majority of participants felt that the most direct impact on their teaching, and by extension on their students' learning, stemmed from the one-to-one coaching provided by the researchers. Teachers found this coaching helpful for incorporating a focus on textual and linguistic features into their existing writing lessons; for planning, enacting, and writing new lessons with these features in mind; and for analyzing student work. Some teachers reported that their change in instructional practices as a result of the initiative had affected their students. These teachers reported that their students' writing had improved because students had been "let in on the secret" of how texts are created in the context of U.S. schooling. Teachers also pointed out that students moved beyond recounts and narratives to experiment with genres such as procedures, reports, and expositions. According to the authors, teachers also associated their own ability to provide better coaching, direction, and feedback with students' ability to write longer, more coherent pieces about a wider variety of topics, and with students' greater enthusiasm toward writing.

Brisk and Zisselsberger (2011) are also forthright about the challenges they faced in introducing teachers to SFL. In response to participants' dissatisfaction with not being able to make connections during the workshops between the professional development's focus on *what* to teach and their desire to learn *how* to teach it, the facilitators devoted the last two sessions to instructional practices, along with guiding steps for teachers to follow. Believing that teachers were struggling with the amount of new information they were encountering, the facilitators themselves analyzed the linguistic features both of commercial texts and sample student texts. The authors point out that the new time and focus devoted to practical guidelines for organizing lessons and units was helpful to teachers but took away time needed to help them gain a better understanding of the functional linguistics approach to use in their future instruction.

Reflecting on potential applications to the preparation of teachers to support ELs for the language and literacy demands presented by new standards, the pedagogical language knowledge offered by the SFL initiatives profiled above centers on awareness of the linguistic features of school texts, the particular ways that language is used to realize meaning in those texts (in particular disciplines), and how teachers can focus students' attention on those features in support of students' engagement with and production of such texts. As mentioned in each of the profiles discussed above, considerable time and effort are needed to prepare teachers with the technical linguistic knowledge necessary to incorporate an SFL approach in their classrooms, which of course implies that teacher educators themselves must have this knowledge as well. The technical demands of SFL have been the source of criticism of the approach (for a discussion of and response to these and other critiques, see Gebhard, 2010; Gebhard & Harman, 2011). Another critique has been the potential for SFL pedagogy to lead to the "static representation of text types rather than a critical analysis of disciplinary discourse" (Gebhard, 2010, p. 801, citing Luke, 1996). Addressing this last critique, at least one teacher preparation initiative for ELs, discussed next, has integrated SFL with critical language awareness in an effort to focus teachers' and students' attention on the roles of power and identity in using language to engage with different audiences for different purposes.

Integrating Genre-Based Pedagogies With Critical Language Awareness

Gebhard and Willett (2008) and their colleagues (Gebhard et al., 2008; Gebhard, Willett, Jiménez Caicedo, & Piedra, 2011) have augmented SFL with insights and commitments from critical language scholars (e.g., Cope & Kalantzis, 1993, 2000; Fairclough, 1989, 1992; Luke, 1996; New London Group, 1996) in teacher preparation initiatives based on "critical instantiation of genre theory and genre-based pedagogies." Such an approach positions SFL as one set of tools in larger efforts to apprentice teachers into becoming "critical text analysts and action-researchers who are able to analyze the linguistic features of their students' emergent academic literacy practices and to implement responsive pedagogical practices" (Gebhard et al., 2008, p. 275). The focus of pedagogical language knowledge in this approach integrates a focus on the linguistic features of disciplinary texts with attention paid to the role of language in the interests, commitments, and power dynamics inherent in texts inside and outside of the classroom.

Gebhard and Willett (2008) describe their initiative as combining insights from SFL (Schleppegrell et al., 2004; Schleppegrell & Go, 2007) and multiliteracies (Cope & Kalantzis, 1993) as part of a master's degree and ESL certificate for preservice and in-service teachers at the University of Massachusetts, Amherst. The ACCELA Alliance (Access to Critical Content and English Language Acquisition), a federally funded partnership between the university and two urban school districts, was designed to prepare mainstream teachers to support ELs academic language development. The project was guided by four principles:

1. Language is a dynamic system of linguistic choices
2. Academic language differs from everyday language in significant ways
3. Teaching academic language means more than teaching vocabulary
4. The goal of academic language instruction is not to replace home and peer ways of using language. (Gebhard & Willett, 2008, p. 43)

Courses in the ACCELA program were organized around local issues, teachers' interests, and national standards in Teaching English to Speakers of Other Languages (Teachers of English to Speakers of Other Languages, 2006). The program introduced teachers to a model for planning curriculum that called for them to identify a project that integrated students' interests, their and their schools' curricular goals, and state standards. Teachers then identified authentic audiences and purposes they wanted their students to address, targeting an academic genre "well-suited to students achieving their purposes in reading and writing about this topic for this audience" (Gebhard & Willett, 2008, p. 43). Examples included letters to policymakers about a salient current issue and "action-oriented" research papers (Gebhard & Willett, 2008, p. 43). After selecting a target genre, teachers were asked to analyze the specialized vocabulary, sentence structures, and organizational conventions relevant to that genre and to provide students with models and instruction to help students understand the associated linguistic features. Teachers then designed supportive material (e.g., graphic organizers and assessment rubrics) and provided students with opportunities to collaborate with other students and the teacher to complete the writing process, including planning, drafting, revising, and editing. Finally, teachers tracked changes in their students' use of academic language and reflected with students on their use of academic language to work toward particular goals in their school and community.

Although Gebhard and Willett (2008) did not discuss outcomes of the program in detail, they reported that the success of the teachers' projects varied. They argue that "most ACCELA teachers developed a deeper understanding of subject matter and the specific language practices used to construct subject-matter knowledge" (p. 45). In an ethnographic case study, Gebhard et al. (2011) investigated the literacy practices of one fourth-grade teacher participating in the ACCELA program and one of that teacher's students over the course of an academic year. According to Gebhard et al. (2011), at the beginning of the year the teacher (a coauthor of the study) was not optimistic about her ability to integrate "ACCELA ideas" in the context of mandated textbooks and standardized expectations that she felt did not represent her students or their interests. Nor did the mandated unit's approach to narrative align with insights on the genre from SFL presented in the ACCELA course. As a result, as she taught the first unit, the teacher ignored both her ACCELA coursework's approach to the features of narrative and her students' inclinations to highlight those same features. Instead, "driven by the teacher's manual," she attempted to shoehorn students' perceptions of narrative into the textbook-prescribed list of features, leading to interactions that "discounted or did not take up other responses that were both valid and provocative" (p. 98). Given her dissatisfaction with her and her students' experiences during the first unit, for the next two units the teacher drew on research on the use of multicultural children's literature as well as SFL-based pedagogies. According to the authors, the focal student's work and comments demonstrated that, over the course of the school year, the student developed an understanding of the features of narrative as a genre, the differences between oral and written registers, and the role of punctuation in instantiating those differences.

Gebhard et al. (2011) are careful to point out that not all ACCELA teachers were as successful as the one profiled in this study in integrating SFL into their classrooms and that several "resisted it entirely." Nonetheless, they argue that the case study demonstrates that, although time-consuming and challenging, engaging in a "three-pronged" approach to professional development, one that addresses standards-based instruction, SFL approaches toward developing academic literacy, and a focus on multicultural literacy, can ultimately be productive. For the purposes of this review, the ACCELA initiative in general, and the teachers' experiences discussed by Gebhard et al. (2011) in particular, represents the potential to augment a focus on pedagogical language knowledge derived from the grammatical focus of SFL with other insights, such as those from critical literacy and critical language studies. Such a combination would clearly represent one approach to preparing teachers for the language and literacy demands that ELs will face in the new standards.

Sociocultural Approaches: Apprenticing ELs Into Academic Practices

Other approaches that can be considered in the service of the development of pedagogical language knowledge for mainstream teachers have focused less on the discrete linguistic features of individual texts and more on the role of language in *participation* in academic *practices*. That is, the "structures" focused on in these approaches often begin not with linguistic structures but rather with structures of participation. The focus is on language as a resource for participation in the structures and activity at the heart of academic work, not primarily through focusing on the ways that participation is embodied in the grammar of language, but rather by looking at multiple layers of language as activity. As such, although the three approaches outlined in this section vary from each other in their approach to language in preparing mainstream teachers for ELs, the pedagogical language knowledge at the heart of each of them can be situated broadly in sociolinguistic and sociocultural approaches to language, learning, and the development of language and literacy (see Block, 2003; Hull & Moje, 2012; Johnson, 2009; van Lier, 2004). Johnson (2009, p. 1) describes the core of a sociocultural perspective as one that "defines human learning as a dynamic, social activity that is situated in physical and social contexts, and is distributed across persons, tools, and activities" (see Rogoff, 2003; Vygotsky, 1978; Wertsch, 1991). In this view, as Johnson (2009) puts it, language "gains its meaning from concrete communicative activity in specific sociocultural contexts" (p. 3), or put differently, "meaning resides not in the grammar of the language, or in its vocabulary, or in the head of an individual, but in the everyday activities that individuals engage in" (p. 44). As Hawkins (2004) has pointed out, such approaches focus on classrooms as "complex social systems" (p. 15), and ELs' language and literacy development, as well as their learning in other areas, as products of social interaction within and outside of those classrooms. Hawkins enumerates a number of concepts relevant to such a view, which for the purposes of this review would also be relevant to the pedagogical language knowledge of mainstream teachers for working with ELs in light of the new standards. Among these are the notions that understanding involves mediation through the use of a variety of linguistic and nonlinguistic tools (Wertsch, 1991) and that learning happens through apprenticeship (B. Rogoff, 1990; Vygotsky, 1987a) in communities of practice (Lave, 1996; Lave & Wenger, 1991). Each of the following initiatives also focuses teachers' attention on the related notion of *scaffolding* for ELs (Walqui, 2006; Walqui & van Lier, 2010).

Participant Structures as Professional Learning Tasks

Galguera (2011), studying the results of his own practice as a teacher educator, focuses on the development of pedagogical language knowledge through preservice teachers' engagement in varying participant structures designed to apprentice teachers' future students into academic discourse communities. The specific participant structures modeled, such as pair-shares, round-robins, and jigsaws, were chosen to highlight for teachers ways to promote the connection between oral language proficiency and reading comprehension, as part of efforts to prepare all students for "language use for academic purposes" (p. 85). The participant structures served as Professional Learning Tasks (PLTs) designed to ground teacher preparation pedagogy "in the tasks, questions, and problems of practice" (D. L. Ball & Cohen, 1999, p. 27, as quoted in Galguera, 2011, p. 91). In this case, the purpose of the PLTs was to provide teachers with examples of language development scaffolds (Walqui, 2006) and opportunities to discuss larger issues of pedagogy and curriculum to promote language development.

The participant structures were also designed to present teachers with a "functional view of academic language," one that focuses on students' ability to use language to do things such as describe complexity and abstractions, use figurative expressions, be appropriately explicit for different audiences, and use evidence for arguments that are "nuanced, qualified, and objective (Zwiers, 2008)" (Galguera, 2011, p. 90, citation in original). Galguera contrasts this approach with those that envision broad distinctions between "academic language" and "social" or "conversational" language (e.g., Cummins, 2008). Drawing on Barnes (1992) and Bunch (2006), Galguera argues that such distinctions are misleading because it is "expected and actually desirable" for students to use vernacular varieties or even their home languages in group work or while preparing for presentational tasks that will require more formal language use in English (Galguera, 2011, p. 89; see also Bunch, 2010).

Galguera (2011) reports on written reflections by and interviews with elementary and secondary teacher candidates in two of his courses regarding the use of two of the targeted participant structures. These included an Extended Anticipation Guide that supported candidates in activities requiring them to read in Spanish, a language that few of the them spoke fluently, and an Oral Language Development Jigsaw requiring students to engage in a series of group configurations to describe "somewhat ambiguous" illustrations to classmates and create a narrative using the illustrations (p. 94; see also Walqui, 2006). Written responses indicated that students were "generally appreciative" of both participant structures, and most students indicated that they would use them in their future placements (p. 95). In interviews, students said that engagement in the participant structures helped them understand and contextualize class readings and discussions more than traditional lectures or class discussions had done. Students particularly highlighted their experiences engaging in the reading task in Spanish, both in terms of the challenges involved in working in a language they had limited proficiency in as well as their feelings of accomplishment regarding what they were able to do with support during the activity. In follow-up interviews reflecting on what lessons about "teaching for language development" remained most salient more than a month after the course, students focused on the role of the target participant structures in scaffolding students' reading development. According to Galguera, both written reflections and interviews also demonstrated evidence of preservice teachers' use of the participant structures to make connections to theories and constructs discussed elsewhere in his course or in other courses in the program.

Preparing Elementary Teachers to Integrate Language and Science Instruction

Stoddart and her colleagues (Stoddart, Bravo, Solis, Mosqueda, & Rodriguez, 2011; Stoddart, Solis, Tolbert, & Bravo, 2010; see also Bravo, Solís, & Mosqueda, 2011; Bravo, Solís, Mosqueda, Collett, & Mckinney De Royston, 2011; Solís, Bravo, Mosqueda, Collett, & Mckinney De Royston, 2011) drew on sociocultural theory to develop a preservice teacher education intervention designed to integrate a focus on inquiry-based science instruction with language and literacy for ELs for preservice elementary teachers of science. The NSF-funded Effective Science Teaching for English

Learners (ESTELL) is designed to prepare novice elementary school teachers to engage with their students in five central practices that manifest the "reciprocal and synergistic" relationship between science learning and language and literacy development (Stoddart et al., 2010, p. 157): *integrating science, language, and literacy development; engaging students in scientific discourse; developing scientific understanding; collaborative inquiry in science learning;* and *contextualized science instruction.*[5] The practices are based on sociocultural theory (e.g., A. S. Rogoff & Wertsch, 1984; Tharp & Gallimore, 1988) positing that students learn through social activity in contexts that are "culturally, linguistically, and cognitively meaningful and relevant" (Stoddart et al., 2010, p. 153), as well as empirical research on effective instruction for ELs emanating from this perspective (see, e.g., Stoddart et al., 2002; Stoddart et al., 2011).

The five practices were incorporated into four science methods courses developed collaboratively between the researchers and teacher educators in three state universities preparing elementary teachers in California (Stoddart et al., 2011). Three courses were designed for candidates preparing to deliver instruction in English and one for candidates pursuing a credential authorizing them to deliver instruction in Spanish. Each course revolved around preparation to teach state-standards-based instructional units designed to illustrate the practices, with methods instructors focusing particularly on one or two of the practices during each unit. In addition, cooperating teachers in student teaching practicum sites participated in 2-day professional development workshops that included an introduction to ESTELL pedagogy, review of lesson plans that exemplify ESTELL practices, observation guides and other mentoring resources, and readings on effective mentoring and science instruction for ELs.

Preliminary results of the first year of the intervention showed statistically significant differences between teacher candidates participating in the intervention compared with a control group for several categories on a classroom observation protocol designed to measure teachers' implementation of the ESTELL principles in their student teaching sites (Stoddart et al., 2011). This positive impact was most pronounced for candidates in the bilingual program, who, compared with the "business as usual" control group (also in a bilingual program), used instructional formats that promoted greater interaction among students and between teacher and students, were more likely to model "science discourse patterns" such as "providing evidence, making scientific explanations, or even proposing methods for conducting inquiry activities," and were more likely to use "the kind of investigatory and epistemic types of questions and commentary that are highly restricted for ELs in classrooms where yes and no, closed type of questions dominate classroom talk" (p. 14). Two additional studies have investigated different aspects of the same intervention. Solís et al. (2011) found that, according to classroom observations conducted during student teaching and again 1 year after earning the credential, treatment group participants outperformed teachers in the control group on two domains (*language and literacy* and *contextualization*). Bravo, Solís, Mosqueda, Collett, et al. (2011) found that the achievement of students on a science writing prompt after a month-long unit taught by ESTELL-trained teachers outperformed students in a control condition.

Preparing Teachers to Scaffold English Learners' Language
Development and Academic Success

Walqui (2011), through WestEd's Quality Teaching for English Learners (QTEL) initiative, has enacted a vision of pedagogical language knowledge for mainstream teachers—and for those who work to prepare them—that integrates sociolinguistic approaches to language and sociocultural approaches to learning (see also Walqui & van Lier, 2010). Drawing on Vygotsky (1978, 1987a) and others, the initiative was based on a view of learning as "joint activity that focuses on academic concepts and skills, and provides opportunities for learning through interaction" (Walqui, 2011, p. 162). As described by Walqui, because "all learning is mediated through language," and because, from a sociocultural perspective, development occurs when learners encounter tasks beyond their present ability to carry out independently, the teacher's role is to offer "deliberate, well-constructed" instruction to foster such development. Joint activity ultimately fosters students' ability to progress "from apprenticeship to appropriation, from the social to the individual plane" (p. 163). Concurrently, QTEL is based on sociolinguistic principles that privilege students' ability to use language to communicate "purposely and appropriately within specific contexts" over their accuracy, correctness, or lexical or grammatical complexity (p. 164). In secondary disciplinary contexts, successful communication is inherently linked to the joint activity required for learning, requiring that "participants in an interaction understand each other's ideas and intentions, respond to them by accepting them, building on what has been stated, or countering arguments in order to accomplish their social purposes" (p. 164).

Sociocultural theory is also the basis for QTEL's conception of how *teachers* learn. QTEL participants are invited to work in their own zones of proximal development, to participate in joint activity that requires them to use relevant concepts and appropriate language (e.g., by participating in and analyzing lessons developed for ELs), and to progress from apprenticeship to appropriation over time (by eventually developing their own lessons based on the models and possibly coming up with their own innovations as their own theory and practice develops).

Walqui (2011) describes this process in a collaboration between WestEd and the New York City Department of Education (NYCDOE) designed to prepare both instructional support specialists (those responsible for the professional development of teachers) and in-service teachers for educating adolescent ELs with "high levels of academic engagement, rigor, and depth." The initiative was designed to help educators learn how to "scaffold the students' development of conceptual, academic, and linguistic subject matter skills" in the middle and high school grades (see also Walqui, 2006). Using an apprenticeship model grounded in the principles discussed above, QTEL's work with NYCDOE involved several phases of professional development designed to allow instructional support specialists to appropriate the "tools, resources, language, and understandings" to support teachers in developing their expertise to teach ELs. Phase 1 included three intensive, week-long institutes for the instructional specialists. These sessions were designed to build a "firm base" in theoretical understandings and instructional practices and included opportunities for the specialists to read and critique professional articles, design lessons, and reflect on the relationship between their prior notions of appropriate instruction for ELs and their emerging understandings based on the institute. In Phase 2, the specialists did participant observation as WestEd staff engaged in professional development with teachers from around the city. In this phase, specialists had the opportunity to observe, participate in, reflect on, and discuss the kind of professional development with teachers that they would ultimately facilitate themselves. In Phase 3, focused on enactment, the instructional specialists, after meeting several prerequisites to demonstrate their ability to do so, led QTEL professional development for New York teachers for five consecutive days, assisted by WestEd "coaches" who provided support throughout the process. During Phase 4, designed to foster appropriation, the specialists designed and conducted a minimum of 3 hours of professional development of their own, with WestEd staff serving as consultants but not active coaches. The specialists videotaped their own sessions and had opportunities to reflect upon sections of the videos afterwards.

Walqui (2011) argues that the kind of learning around which QTEL is centered is only visible when measured, both quantitatively and qualitatively, as changes in engagement in participation over time. Although outcomes of the NYC initiative are not reported in detail, Walqui (2011) relates that evaluations of the initial building the base institutes (Phase 1) were "unanimously superlative" (p. 169). In Phase 3, Walqui argues that the number of specialists who passed the prerequisites and successfully conducted their own sessions is indicative of the power of the apprenticeship model to induce both "handover" of responsibility from project leaders to participating educators and the concurrent "take over" of roles by these same educators.

Two randomized experimental studies (Bos et al., 2012; Rockman et al., n.d.) of other QTEL initiatives found no evidence of improvement of school-level standardized test scores for students in schools where some teachers had participated in QTEL, yet neither study was able to isolate student outcomes for students taught by participating teachers, so the meaning of those findings is unclear. Furthermore, fidelity of QTEL implementation was significantly compromised in both studies, and important limitations were associated with available instruments. These factors may account for other disappointing results, including lack of evidence of change in teacher attitudes, beliefs, and practices. Nevertheless, there were some positive outcomes reported in both studies. Using a measure of classroom quality developed specifically to capture practices aligned with QTEL, Bos et al. (2012) found a statistically significant impact of student-to-student interaction on overall scores on this measure in QTEL classrooms compared with the control. Rockman et al. (n.d.) found beneficial impacts for teachers in the treatment group on assessments measuring teachers' pedagogical content knowledge and on surveys indicating a reduction in teachers' reliance on teacher-directed instruction (i.e., short, known-answer questions) and a decrease in teachers' simplification of communication (consistent with QTEL's promotion of opportunities for the elaborated use of English by both teachers and students). Meanwhile, qualitative data analyzed by Rockman et al. indicate that teachers who participated in QTEL professional development were positive about the program, that qualitative classroom observations revealed increased instances of engagement of students in higher order thinking and reciprocal talk, that teachers reported changes in their own classroom practice, and that teachers and administrators indicated that they observed positive changes in students' learning behaviors and attitudes when they implemented QTEL tasks.

In all three of the initiatives described in this section (focusing on pedagogical language knowledge through professional learning tasks; preparing teachers with sociocultural tools to integrate a focus on language, science education, and ELs; and preparing teachers to scaffold ELs' language development and content learning by means of the QTEL initiative), further qualitative and quantitative research would be helpful to understand the precise nature of the pedagogical language knowledge that the teachers were engaged in developing, the role of the various aspects of the intervention in the development of that knowledge, and the relationship between different aspects of that knowledge and change in classroom practice. All three, however, point to how such knowledge can be treated as related to, and developed in, the kinds of practices that will be central to teaching and learning in the era of new standards.

Other Potential Directions

The initiatives profiled above represent only some of the potential approaches for conceiving of and promoting pedagogical language knowledge for mainstream teachers of ELs in an era of common standards. In this section, I veer from the criteria listed earlier to briefly consider literature that did not meet one or more of the criteria but that suggest other approaches worth further study.

Promoting Students' Home and Community Language, Literacy, and Cultural Practices as Resources for Learning in Mainstream Classrooms

The importance of conceiving of students' home language, literacy, and cultural practices as a resource for both learning and language development in English has long been highlighted as an essential aspect of teacher preparation for ELs. In light of increasing globalization, transnational migration, and linguistic heterogeneity in the 21st century, Garcia and colleagues (O. Garcia, 2009; O. Garcia, Flores, & Haiwen, 2011; Garcia & Kleifgen, 2010) have discussed the need for a "dynamic theoretical framework of bilingualism" that "allows the simultaneous coexistence of different languages in communication . . . and supports the development of multiple linguistic identities" (O. Garcia, 2009, p. 119). Even in the midst of increasing racial and socioeconomic segregation, O. Garcia et al. (2011) assert that linguistic heterogeneity within classrooms is on the rise, as Latinos, Black, and Asian speakers of languages other than English often study in the same, non-White classrooms. O. Garcia (2009) and O. Garcia et al. (2011) describe two schools that promote the home language use of students from a wide variety of linguistic backgrounds within classes where the main medium of instruction is English. In a similar vein, Moschkovich (2007, 2012) has highlighted the necessity of teachers understanding the importance of both students' home languages and their developing English in mathematics classrooms as they demonstrate what they are learning and develop the various "mathematical discourses" relevant to the discipline. Such instructional arrangements are promising for supporting access for ELs to instruction that will prepare them for meeting the new standards, but only if the pedagogical language knowledge of their teachers includes an understanding of the nature of bilingualism, even if those teachers are monolingual speakers of English.

The literature on grounding instruction in the linguistic and cultural practices of nondominant student populations more generally is also relevant for conceptualizing the pedagogical language knowledge for mainstream teachers of ELs. Focusing explicitly on preparing teachers for speakers of stigmatized varieties of English, Godley et al. (2006) focus on sociolinguistic issues, especially those emanating from "negative beliefs about the grammaticality, logic, and even morality of stigmatized dialects" that are "widespread in U.S. society and difficult to change" (p. 30). According to Godley et al., teachers need to learn that "standard" varieties of a language—those valued in schools, businesses, government, and the media—are no better than any other variety by any objective linguistic measures and are preferred only because they represent the varieties used by those in power. The authors point out that substantial research evidence demonstrates "strong connections between teachers' negative attitudes about stigmatized dialects, lower teacher expectations for students who speak them, and thus lower academic achievement on the part of students" (p. 31). They, therefore, conclude that any efforts to diminish the achievement gap between dominant and nondominant students must include a focus on preparing teachers for working with speakers of stigmatized varieties of English (Alim, 2005; Baugh, 1999). The authors, focusing on efforts that research has shown to have positive results (e.g., A. F. Ball & Muhammad, 2003; Okawa, 2003), propose three themes for foundational teacher education courses and programs to address dialect diversity for future and practicing teachers. First, they advocate for anticipating and overcoming resistance based on negative attitudes toward stigmatized dialects (p. 31). Second, they focus on the need to address issues of language, power, and identity, including the need for teachers to become willing to "teach for social change" because "the very act of affirming vernacular language runs counter to mainstream language ideologies" (p. 33). This includes viewing the teaching of standard English as a move designed to increase students' linguistic repertoires as opposed to a more correct substitute for the language varieties students already use. The third focus advocated by Godley et al. involves highlighting pedagogical applications of research on language variation for improving students' academic success and development of literacy by emphasizing dialect diversity as a resource, using contrastive analysis to distinguish dialect patters from errors, and building on rather than replacing students' "robust language competence" (p. 35).

Focusing specifically on secondary content-area instruction for students from linguistically and culturally nondominant groups, Lee (2007) highlights the "crucial importance of understanding cultural displays of knowledge constructed in the everyday routine practices of children and adolescents and the relationship of such displays to targets of academic knowledge" (p. 25). Highlighting work done to understand and focus on the relationship between the home and school practices of linguistically and culturally diverse students in mathematics (e.g., Nasir & Saxe, 2003) and science (e.g., Rosebery, Warren, & Conant, 1992), and her own work on African American students in English literature classrooms, Lee describes "Cultural Modeling" as "a framework for the design of learning environments that examines what youth know from everyday settings to support specific subject matter learning" (p. 15). Lee presents classroom examples of one teacher's use of what she calls "culturally responsive instructional discourse"—designed to maximize the ways in which students' use of "African American Vernacular English and its rhetorical features can serve as a resource for communicating complex discipline specific reasoning, in this case in the study of literature" (p. 107). Lee argues that a wide range of considerations need to be made in order to negotiate differences between community-based and school-based norms (p. 25), several of which are directly related to language and literacy: "linguistic differences, such as differences in norms for verbal interactions, in basic syntactic structures and lexicon, and in assumptions about appropriate gestural language; or other arenas such as in epistemological orientations" (p. 25). To manage such negotiation, Lee (2007) emphasizes the need for teachers to have a deep and broad knowledge of the nature of the target discipline and the role of culture not only in issues such as motivation, topic relevance, and classroom management but also in what she calls the "innards of subject matter learning" (p. 111). Lee argues that while foundational classes during preservice teacher education programs can help, the "pedagogical toolkit" necessary for Cultural Modeling consists of "knowledge-in-practice" that can only be developed in teachers' own classrooms.

Focusing on Informational Density in Content-Area Texts

Recently, Fillmore and Fillmore (2012) have pointed out that to become proficient in reading the kind of complex texts called for by the ELA standards, ELs must have opportunities to engage with such texts. This is because no one, including native speakers of English, is likely to find conversational partners, even teachers, to interact with them in the kind of language used in complex written texts. Furthermore, the authors argue, academic language cannot be "taught" in separate classes in the way that language teaching has usually been conceived. For ELs, the problem is that they have often only encountered simplified texts. As Fillmore and Fillmore put it, such texts, "given prophylactically as a safeguard against failure—actually prevent [ELs] from discovering how language works in academic discourse" (p. 2). According to the authors, much of the challenge in reading complex texts stems from their informational density, because the linguistic means used to embed such density are often unfamiliar to ELs and inexperienced readers. Therefore, according to Fillmore and Fillmore, ELs need instructional support from teachers to "discover how to gain access to the ideas, concepts, and information that are encoded in the text" (p. 6). The authors are clear to point out that they are not arguing that students need to learn the grammatical terms that linguists might use to describe the complexity of a text but rather need support in accessing meaning in such texts. The authors describe efforts developed by Lily Wong Fillmore in several cities to support students in accessing complex texts in science, social studies, and English literature at various grade levels, K–12. A key component of the strategy is having teachers spend a part of each instructional day focusing on a single sentence chosen from the disciplinary text that students were working on. The goal is to help students unpack language that exhibited informational density in order to "gradually internalize an awareness of the relation between specific linguistic patterns and the functions they serve in texts" (p. 6). Fillmore and Fillmore do not address the preparation of teachers for what they would need to know to help students unpack these "juicy sentences" (p. 8), but it is clear that such preparation would require a particular type of pedagogical language knowledge to help students analyze informational density to unpack meaning in the ways advocated for by the authors.

Talk as a Tool for Learning

Although they do not discuss implications for ELs, Michaels and O'Connor (2011) outline an approach they have found successful in getting teachers to foster productive classroom talk conducive to learning. I discuss the approach here because of its potential implications for ELs and the kind of pedagogical language knowledge that would underlie such an approach. Drawing on sociocultural and sociohistorical theory and research on talk as "mediational means," Michaels and O'Connor advocate for working with teachers to understand language as a *tool*, and more specifically, what they call *talk moves* as a tool teachers can employ to foster learning in "any content area, at any grade level, and often at any point in a discussion" (p. 12). The authors describe working with teachers to understand four "necessary and foundational steps" to create the conditions necessary for discussions that enhance students' reasoning and understanding: (a) help students share, expand, and clarify their own thoughts; (b) help students listen carefully to each other; (c) help students "deepen" their reasoning; and (d) help students engage with the reasoning of others. Teachers are then provided with 10 explicit "productive talk tools" (see also Chapin, Anderson, & O'Connor, 2003; Michaels, O'Connor, Hall, & Resnick, 2002). For example, to help students share, expand, and clarify their thinking, teachers provide students with *time to think* through partnering, writing, or wait time; encourage students to *say more*; and verify or clarify students' thinking by *revoicing* what they have said. To help students listen carefully to one another, teachers ask *Who can rephrase or repeat?* and *What did your partner say?* Tools designed to meet the goals of helping students deepen their own and others' reasoning include *Asking for Evidence or Reasoning*, eliciting a *Challenge or Counterexample*, and asking students to *Add On* to their classmates' arguments. Important questions, not addressed by Michaels and O'Connor (2011), must be considered in thinking about the pedagogical language knowledge that would be required for teachers to create the conditions under which students at various stages of learning English could participate in and benefit from the kinds of talk centered classrooms advocated. At the same time, a focus on "talk as tools" is clearly one way to get teachers to think about language in a way that can get them to move beyond a focus on "native-like" or "standard" English and instead focus on the role of language as a resource for learning. Simultaneously, with proper support, it is possible that classrooms featuring the kinds of talk moves advocated for by Michaels and O'Connor could serve as productive sites for promoting the kind of interaction productive for the development of English by ELs.

Supporting the Development of Language Functions Corresponding to the New Standards

Finally, another way to think about the pedagogical language knowledge necessary for mainstream teachers to work with ELs can be extrapolated from a new comprehensive framework developed by the Council of Chief State School Officers for the development of English Language Proficiency standards corresponding to the Common Core State Standards and the Next Generation Science Standards (CCSSO, 2012). The framework itself, along with sample English language proficiency standards meeting the framework's guidelines, suggests that the language demands associated with the standards can only be understood by first looking at the "key practices" associated with each set of standards. For example, key practices in the Common Core standards for mathematics include, among others, making sense of problems and persevering in solving them, reasoning abstractly and qualitatively, constructing viable arguments and critiquing the reasoning of others, and modeling with mathematics. In turn, for each of those practices, the CCSSO framework identifies relevant analytical tasks and productive and receptive language functions.

For example, the analytical tasks behind the practice of constructing viable arguments and critiquing the reasoning of others in mathematics include the following: understanding and using the stated assumptions, definitions, and previously established results; making conjectures and building a logical progression of statements to explore the truth of those conjectures; justifying conclusions, communicating them to others, and responding to counterarguments; and so on (CCSSO, 2012). For that same key practice, the framework identifies relevant receptive language functions, in this case related to comprehending oral and written concepts, procedures, or strategies used in arguments and reasoning: *questions and critiques using words or other representations, explanations offered using words or other representations by others (peers or teachers)*, and *explanations offered by written texts using words or other representations*. Productive language functions for that same practice include those used to communicate using words (orally and in writing) about concepts, procedures, strategies, claims, arguments, and other information related to constructing arguments and critiquing reasoning: *provide written or verbal explanation of argument, justify conclusions and respond to counterarguments, recognize and use counterexamples,* and so on.

As reproduced in Table 1, the framework then provides a matrix conceptualizing the different types of communicative activities that would characterize students' and teachers' language use in classrooms engaged in learning the key disciplinary practices at the heart of each set of common standards. The matrix includes teachers' and students' receptive and productive language tasks, modality (referring to whether communication is "one-to-many," "many-to-many," "one-to-group," or "one-to-one"), and examples of the types of colloquial, classroom, and disciplinary registers that would be relevant for learning in that particular discipline. Although the document was intended to be used by state agencies in their development of English language proficiency standards, it can also be read as an articulation of what would need to be addressed by any attempt to define the pedagogical language knowledge that would serve teachers well in designing classrooms in which ELs could both simultaneously engage with the practices at the heart of the new standards and continue to develop the linguistic resources relevant for doing so.

CONCLUSION

In introducing the framework discussed in the previous section, the authors describe the "double challenge" faced by ELs in light of the new common standards: "They must simultaneously learn how to acquire enough of a second language to participate and learn in academic settings while gaining an understanding of the knowledge and skills in multiple disciplines through that second language" (CCSSO, 2012). In this chapter, I have explored various ways to conceive of, and help teachers develop, the *pedagogical language knowledge* necessary to support ELs in meeting this double challenge. I have argued that the knowledge needed is fundamentally of a different sort than the pedagogical *content* knowledge used either by second language teachers or by mainstream teachers in their target disciplines.

The approaches toward the development of pedagogical language knowledge in the initiatives profiled in this chapter range from using SFL to develop teachers' understandings about the linguistic features of disciplinary texts in order to make these features more transparent to ELs, to sociocultural approaches that engage teachers in participant structures to model the scaffolding necessary to apprentice ELs into the language and literacy practices of different disciplines. In addition to different approaches toward pedagogical language knowledge and its development, the initiatives profiled above also vary in terms of the educators for whom they are targeted (in-service or preservice teachers, elementary or secondary, target subject areas), the size and scope of the intervention, and the depth and type of research that has been conducted on them.

As I have attempted to make clear throughout this chapter, the research claims that can be made regarding student or even teacher outcomes as a result of the initiatives discussed here vary but are mostly quite limited. As pointed out by Lucas and Grinberg

TABLE 1

Discipline-Specific Language in the K–12 Mathematics Classroom

Features of Classroom Language	Teachers' Receptive and Productive Language Use and Associated Language Tasks	Students' Language Use and Associated Language Tasks		
		Oral: Receptive and Productive	Written	
			Receptive	Productive
Modality	Explanations and presentations (one-to-many, many-to-many) Communication with small groups (one-to-group) Communication with individual students (one-to-one) Communication with parents (one-to-one)	Whole-class participation (one-to-many) Small group participation (one-to-group) Interaction with individual peers (one-to-one) Interaction with adults within school contexts (one-to-one)	Comprehension of classroom-based and school-based formal and informal written and multimodal communication	Production of classroom-based and school-based formal and informal written communication, such as • Explanations of word problems • Descriptions of one's own reasoning, solutions, or strategies • Descriptions of others' reasoning, solutions, or strategies
Registers	Colloquial + classroom registers + discipline-specific language and terminology	Colloquial + classroom registers + discipline-specific language and terminology	Math-learner written registers + discipline-specific language and terminology + disciplinary discourse conventions	
Examples of registers	Classroom registers used by teachers for several goals or purposes • Giving directions • Guiding processes • Checking for understanding • Facilitating discussions • Exploring concepts • Presenting	Classroom registers used by students for several goals or purposes • Comprehending oral directions • Asking for clarification • Participating in discussions • Participating in exploratory talk • Participating in presentational talk	Classroom, school, science-learner written texts are of multiple types (and expressed through language in certain registers) • Grade-level texts and textbooks • Teacher handouts/worksheets • Labeling of items in diagrams and other visuals • Writing by other students • Internet materials	

(continued)

TABLE 1 (continued)

Features of Classroom Language	Teachers' Receptive and Productive Language Use and Associated Language Tasks	Students' Language Use and Associated Language Tasks		
		Oral: Receptive and Productive	Written	
			Receptive	Productive
Examples of registers (cont.)	Math discourse registers used by teachers for several goals or purposes • Describing models, patterns, and structures • Explaining relationships between quantities and representations • Explaining reasoning • Constructing and defending arguments	Learner-appropriate math discourse registers and conventions used by students for several goals or purposes • Describing models, patterns, and structures • Explaining relationships between quantities and representations • Explaining solutions and strategies • Explaining one's own or others' reasoning • Constructing, defending, and critiquing arguments, reasoning, and solutions	• Math press articles • Syllabi • School announcements • Formal documents (e.g., grades, assignments, and assessment results)	

Note. Reproduced with permission from the *Framework for English Language Proficiency Development Standards Corresponding to the Common Core State Standards and the Next Generation Science Standards*, Council of Chief State School Officers, 2012, Washington, DC. Copyright 2012 by the Council of Chief State School Officers.

(2008) in an earlier review, empirical research on the preparation of teachers for ELs is strikingly thin (see also August & Calderón, 2006; August & Shanahan, 2008; Goldenberg & Coleman, 2010). Certainly, research measuring teacher and student outcomes stemming from various approaches to preparing teachers for ELs will be necessary as common standards are implemented in the coming years. The shifts will be large in terms of how teachers will need to approach the instruction of ELs in order to support students' engagement in and development of the kind of language and literacy practices called for by the standards. In many cases, there will be strong purchase by teachers on what are likely to be long-held personal and societal beliefs about language and language learning. Therefore, any research agenda must take a long-term view. Areas important to study will be mainstream teachers' current conceptions of language, literacy, and ELs; how those conceptions change over the course of time; what affects this development; how teachers' practices change as a result of interventions based on various notions of pedagogical language knowledge; and, of course, the relationship of all of the above to teachers' classroom practice and student outcomes of various sorts. As these topics are explored, it is important to keep in mind that, as August & Calderón (2006) point out, the relationship between teachers' change in beliefs and change in practice is a complex one (see Ruiz, Rueda, Figueroa, & Boothroyd, 1995). The path of change may not always be "unidirectional" (August & Calderón, 2006, p. 563), and the opportunity to engage in new practices leading to better student outcomes can itself be a catalyst for change in beliefs (see Calderón & Marsh, 1988).

Those responsible for teacher preparation and development, of course, cannot wait until such research is conducted to make decisions regarding what directions to move in to prepare mainstream teachers for ELs, especially given the speed with which implementation of the new common standards is moving. This chapter has pointed to the importance of considering questions about the pedagogical language knowledge that underlies any potential approach to preparing teachers for working with ELs, the degree of correspondence between that knowledge and the language demands ELs will encounter in engaging in the kind of instruction called for by the common standards, and the expertise needed to be developed among teacher educators in order to implement the approach. Ultimately, the question facing decision makers will undoubtedly be what is *absolutely essential* for mainstream teachers to know and be able to do in order to create the instructional conditions in which ELs can productively engage in the key practices called for by the common standards?

That question would most likely be answered differently by proponents of the different approaches discussed here, and one of my arguments in this chapter has been that it is important to understand the differences. At the same time, the initiatives share some important commonalities, and these too are important to consider. Perhaps most important, each envisions language as an essential mediator of teaching and learning rather than as either a discrete curricular target (as has often been the case in ESL instruction) or solely a means to communicate the content one has already learned (often the view held by mainstream teachers, especially at the secondary level).[6] The assumption underlying each of the approaches focused on in this chapter is that ELs develop language and literacy in and through engagement with the kinds of texts and practices called for by the common standards, rather than as a prerequisite to such engagement. The initiatives all also prepare teachers to provide various sorts of support for that engagement, depending on the background of the learner and the demands of the tasks at hand. Although there is room for explicit instruction in each of the approaches, none of them call for the "curricularizing" of language into individual components that must be taught before ELs begin to engage in the types of texts and practices central to the new standards (Valdés et al., 2011).

Another important similarity in all the approaches to pedagogical language knowledge discussed in this chapter is that the focus is not on the extent to which ELs' English can be made to be more "native-like" or "standard" for its own sake but rather on fostering ELs' use and development of linguistic resources for learning and demonstrating learning across the curriculum. Each approach, in one way or another, helps teachers focus on how language is used differently for different audiences and purposes, both within and across different academic and nonacademic settings. Such a focus on audience and purpose helps complicate the overly simplistic contrasts between "everyday" and "academic" language that teachers are often presented when learning about instruction for ELs (Valdes, 2004). Instead, these approaches highlight the wide variety of home and community language and literacy practices that can effectively be employed to do high level academic work, along with the perhaps-unfamiliar (to students, but maybe also to teachers) linguistic and discursive expectations of communicating with various academic audiences for various purposes.

I close by suggesting that as efforts move forward to envision, develop, and study the pedagogical language knowledge necessary for mainstream teachers of ELs, the notion of language as *action* (van Lier & Walqui, 2012) might serve as an overarching principle. As van Lier and Walqui (2012) have pointed out, language is "an inseparable part of all human action," connected to other forms of action, and "an expression of agency, embodied and embedded in the environment" (p. 4). Such an approach, which recognizes that language form and function are "subservient" to action, challenges traditional conceptions of language and language instruction and "requires a different way of thinking about what language *is* and what it *does*" (p. 5). In terms of instruction for ELs, an action-based perspective might look like the following:

> ELs engage in meaningful activities (projects, presentations, investigations) that engage their interest and that encourage language growth through perception, interaction, planning, research, discussion, and co-construction of academic products of various kinds. During such action-based work, language development occurs when it is carefully scaffolded by the teacher, as well as by the students working together. The goals and outcomes specify academic and linguistic criteria for success, and the road to success requires a range of focused cognitive and linguistic work, while at the same time allowing for individual and group choices and creativity. (van Lier & Walqui, 2012, p. 4)

The question at the heart of this review is one that I argue must be central to efforts to prepare teachers for ELs in an era of new common standards: What would teachers need to know about language to enact instruction such as that envisioned in the excerpt above, and how can they best be supported in developing that knowledge, both as they prepare to enter the profession and throughout their careers?

ACKNOWLEDGMENTS

I wish to thank Guadalupe Valdés, Chris Faltis, and two anonymous reviewers for helpful feedback on earlier drafts and Harriet Dang and Nancy Yue for invaluable reference assistance.

NOTES

[1]In this chapter, I use the term *ELs* to refer both to students who are currently designated by their school as in need of language-related support in order to engage in the mainstream curriculum, as well as students who were once designated as such but who have recently been reclassified as "fluent English proficient" or other such institutional designations for students schools deem to no longer be in need of special support. In broadening my use of the term *EL* to include those both currently and formerly classified as such, I attempt to shift the focus to the range of language proficiency levels and literacy development exhibited by students in the process of learning English as an additional language rather than on classification decisions based on assessments and policies that have been the source of considerable debate. I am sympathetic to recent calls to replace the term *EL* with other terms, such as *emergent bilingual*, that better reflect the wide range of linguistic resources that these students use and are developing. Nonetheless, in an effort to communicate effectively with as wide an audience as possible, in this chapter I have decided to use the more widely recognized term *EL*.

[2]Nationwide, according to recent data, 83% of U.S. public school teachers are identified as non–Hispanic White, 7% Black, 7% Hispanic, and 1% Asian American (Battle, 2009). Even in states that have more diverse overall populations and with large numbers of ELs and other linguistic minority students, the teaching force is predominantly White. In California, for example, 72% of teachers are identified as White, 16% Hispanic, 7% Asian American, 5% African American, 1% American Indian/Alaska Native, and 1% "multiple races" (Commission on Teacher Credentialing, 2008).

[3]Beyond the important relationship between early childhood literacy practices and school-based literacy, it is important to note that the most common country of birth among ELs is the United States, so ELs' development of literacy in both home languages and English is largely a product of their prior experiences in this country.

[4]It is possible that I am oversimplifying the notion of pedagogical content knowledge, certainly as it has been developed through the years since Shulman initially proposed it, and I would invite scholars of teacher development to weigh in on the matter. The point that I hope will stand up to scrutiny is that the language-related knowledge and skills necessary for mainstream teachers is of a different sort than the pedagogical content knowledge required for second language teachers or for teachers of traditional school subject areas.

[5]Contextualized science instruction was defined as the "systematic incorporation of sociocultural resources, existing prior knowledge from everyday life experiences, or funds of knowledge into science practice" (Stoddart et al., 2010, p. 157).

[6]I am grateful to an anonymous reviewer of an earlier draft for this particular articulation of my underlying argument.

REFERENCES

Achugar, M., Schleppegrell, M., & Oteíza, T. (2007). Engaging teachers in language analysis: A functional linguistic approach to reflective literacy. *English Teaching: Practice and Technique, 6*(2), 8–24.

Aguirre-Muñoz, Z., Park, J. E., Amabisca, A., & Boscardin, C. K. (2008). Developing teacher capacity for serving ELLs' writing instructional needs: A case for systematic functional linguistics. *Bilingual Research Journal, 31*, 295–322.

Alim, S. H. (2005). Critical language awareness in the United States: Revisiting issues and revisiting pedagogies in a resegregated society. *Educational Researcher, 34*(7), 24–31.

Andrews, S. (1999). Why do L2 teachers need to know about language? Teacher metalinguistic awareness and input for learning. *Language and Education, 13*, 161–177.

Andrews, S. (2003). Teaching language awareness and the professional knowledge base of the L2 teacher. *Language Awareness, 12*(2), 81–95.

Athanases, S. Z., & de Oliveira, L. C. (2011). Toward program-wide coherence in preparing teachers to teach and advocate for English language learners. In T. Lucas (Ed.), *Teacher preparation for linguistically diverse classrooms: A resource for teacher educators* (pp. 195–215). New York, NY: Routledge.

Atkinson, D. (2011). *Alternative approaches to second language acquisition.* New York, NY: Routledge.

August, D., & Calderón, M. (2006). Teacher beliefs and professional development. In D. August & T. Shanahan (Eds.), *Developing literacy in second-language learners: Report of the national literacy panel on language minority children and youth* (pp. 555–563). Mahwah, NJ: Lawrence Erlbaum.

August, D., & Shanahan, T. (2008). *Developing reading and writing in second-language learners: Lessons from the report of the national literacy panel on language-minority children and youth.* New York, NY: Routledge.

Baca, L., & Escamilla, K. (2002). Educating teachers about language. In C. T. Adger, C. E. Snow, & D. Christian (Eds.), *What teachers need to know about language* (pp. 71–84). McHenry, IL: Delta Systems.

Ball, A. F. (2009). Toward a theory of generative change in culturally and linguistically complex classrooms. *American Educational Research Journal, 46*, 45–72.

Ball, A. F., & Muhammad, R. J. (2003). Language diversity in teacher education and in the classroom. In G. Smitherman & V. Villanueva (Eds.), *Language diversity in the classroom: From intention to practice* (pp. 76–88). Carbondale: Southern Illinois University Press.

Ball, D. L. (2000). Bridging practices: Intertwining content and pedagogy in teaching and learning to teach. *Journal of Teacher Education, 51,* 241 -247.

Ball, D. L., & Cohen, D. K. (1999). Developing practice, developing practitioners: Toward a practice-based theory of professional development. In L. Darling-Hammond & G. Skyes (Eds.), *Teaching as the learning profession: Handbook of policy and practice* (pp. 3–32). San Francisco, CA: Jossey-Bass.

Barnes, D. (1992). *From communication to curriculum.* Portsmouth, NH: Boynton/Cook.

Battle, D. (2009). *Characteristics of public, private, and Bureau of Indian Education elementary and secondary school teachers in the United States: Results from the 2007–2008 Schools and Staffing Survey* (NCES 2009-323). Washington, DC: U.S. Department of Education, National Center for Educational Statistics, Institute of Education Sciences.

Baugh, J. (1999). *Out of the mouths of slaves: African American language and educational malpractice.* Austin: University of Texas Press.

Block, D. (2003). *The social turn in second language acquisition.* Washington, DC: Georgetown University Press.

Bos, J. M., Sanchez, R. C., Tseng, F., Rayyes, N., Ortiz, L., & Sinicrope, C. (2012). *Evaluation of quality teaching for English learners (QTEL) professional development* (NCEE 2012-4005). Washington, DC: National Center for Education and Regional Assistance, Institute of Education Sciences, U.S. Department of Education.

Bravo, M., Solís, J. L., & Mosqueda, E. (2011, April). *Pre-service teacher efficacy and practices with responsive science pedagogy for English learners.* Paper presented at the annual meeting of the National Association for Research in Science Teaching, Orlando, FL. http://education.ucsc.edu/estell/Bravo_et_al_2011_NARST.pdf

Bravo, M. A., Solís, J. L., Mosqueda, E., Collett, J. M., & Mckinney De Royston, J. M. (2011, April). *Integrating science and diversity education: Examining novice teacher practices and impact on student writing achievement.* Paper presented at the annual meeting of the American Educational Research Association, New Orleans, LA.

Brisk, M. E. (2008). Program and faculty transformation: Enhancing teacher preparation. In M. E. Brisk (Ed.), *Language, culture, and community in teacher education* (pp. 249–266). New York, NY: Lawrence Erlbaum.

Brisk, M. E., & Zisselsberger, M. (2011). "We've let them in on the secret": Using SFL theory to improve the teaching of writing to bilingual learners. In T. Lucas (Ed.), *Teacher preparation for linguistically diverse classrooms: A resource for teacher educators* (pp. 111–126). New York, NY: Routledge.

Bunch, G. C. (2006). "Academic English" in the 7th grade: Broadening the lens, expanding access. *Journal of English for Academic Purposes, 5,* 284–301.

Bunch, G. C. (2010). Preparing mainstream secondary content-area teachers to facilitate English language learners' development of academic language. In C. Faltis & G. Valdés (Eds.), *Education, immigrant students, refugee students, and English learners* (Yearbook of the National Society for the Study of Education; Volume 109, Issue 2, pp. 352–383). New York, NY: Columbia University Press.

Bunch, G. C., Aguirre, J. M., & Téllez, K. (2009). Beyond the scores: Using candidate responses on high stakes performance assessment to inform teacher preparation for English learners. *Issues in Teacher Education, 18,* 103–127.

Bunch, G. C., Kibler, A. K., & Pimentel, S. (2012). *Realizing opportunities for English learners in the common core English language arts and disciplinary literacy standards.* Paper presented at the Understanding Language Conference, Stanford, CA. Retrieved from http://ell.stanford.edu/papers

Calderón, T., & Marsh, D. (1988, Winter). Applying research on effective bilingual instruction in a multi-district inservice teacher training program. *NABE Journal, 12,* 133–152.

Carbone, P. M., & Orellana, M. F. (2010). Developing academic identities: Persuasive writing as a tool to strengthen emergent academic identities. *Research in the Teaching of English, 44,* 292–316.

Cazden, C. (2001). *Classroom discourse: The language of teaching and learning* (2nd ed.). Portsmouth, NH: Heinemann.

Chapin, S. H., Anderson, N. C., & O'Connor, M. C. (2003). *Classroom discussions: Using math talk to help students learn, grades 1–6.* Sausalito, CA: Math Solutions.

Commins, N. L., & Miramontes, O. B. (2006). Addressing linguistic diversity from the outset. *Journal of Teacher Education, 57,* 240–246.

Commission on Teacher Credentialing. (2008, January). *Racial and ethnic distribution of teachers.* Retrieved from http://www.ctc.ca.gov/educator-prep/statistics/2008-01-stat.pdf

Committee on Conceptual Framework for the New K–12 Science Education Standards. (2012). *A framework for K–12 science education: Practices, crosscutting concepts, and core ideas.* Washington, DC: National Research Council of the National Academies.

Cope, B., & Kalantzis, M. (Eds.). (1993). *The powers of literacy: A genre approach to teaching writing.* Pittsburgh, PA: University of Pittsburgh Press.

Cope, B., & Kalantzis, M. (2000). *Multiliteracies: Literacy learning and the design of social futures*. New York, NY: Routledge.

Costa, J., McPhail, G., Smith, J., & Brisk, M. E. (2005). Faculty first: The challenge of infusing the teacher education curriculum with scholarship on English language learners. *Journal of Teacher Education, 56*, 104–118.

Council of Chief State School Officers. (2012). *Framework for English language proficiency development standards corresponding to the Common Core State Standards and the Next Generation Science Standards*. Retrieved from http://www.cde.ca.gov/sp/el/er/documents/elpdframework.pdf

Crawford, J. (1992). *Language loyalties: A source book on the official English controversy*. Chicago, IL: University of Chicago Press.

Crawford, J. (1999). *Bilingual education: History, politics, theory, and practice* (4th ed.). Los Angeles, CA: Crane.

Cummins, J. (1981). *The role of primary language development in promoting educational success for language minority students. In Schooling and language minority students: A theoretical framework* (pp. 3-49). Los Angeles: California State University Press.

Cummins, J. (2000). *Language, power, and pedagogy: Bilingual children in the crossfire*. Clevedon, England: Multilingual Matters.

Cummins, J. (2008). BICS and CALP: Empirical and theoretical status of the distinction. In B. Street & N. H. Hornberger (Eds.), *Encyclopedia of language and education: Volume 2. Literacy* (2nd ed., pp. 71–83). New York, NY: Springer Science + Business Media.

Cummins, J. (2009). Foreword. In P. Gibbons (Ed.), *English learners, academic literacy and thinking: Learning in the challenge zone* (pp. ix-xii). Portsmouth, NH: Heinemann.

de Jong, E. J., & Harper, C. A. (2011). "Accommodating diversity": Pre-service teachers' views on effective practices for English language learners. In T. Lucas (Ed.), *Teacher preparation for linguistically diverse classrooms: A resource for teacher educators* (pp. 73–90). New York, NY: Routledge.

Dyson, A. H. (2008). Staying in the (curricular) lines: Practice, constraints, and possibilities in childhood writing. *Written Communication, 25*, 119–159.

Echevarria, J., Short, D., & Powers, K. (2006). School reform and standards-based education: An instructional model for English language learners. *Journal of Educational Research, 99*, 195–211.

Enright, K. A. (2011). Language and literacy for a new mainstream. *American Educational Research Journal, 48*, 80–118.

Enright, K. A., & Gilliland, B. (2011). Multilingual writing in an age of accountability: From policy to practice in U.S. high school classrooms. *Journal of Second Language Writing, 20*, 182–195.

Fairclough, N. (1989). *Language and power*. London, England: Longman.

Fairclough, N. (1992). *Discourse and social change*. Cambridge, England: Polity Press.

Fairclough, N. (1999). Global capitalism and critical awareness of language. *Language Awareness, 8*(2), 71–83.

Faltis, C., Arias, M. B., & Ramírez-Marín, F. (2010). Identifying relevant competencies for secondary teachers of English learners. *Bilingual Research Journal, 33*, 307–328.

Feiman-Nemser, S. (2008). Teacher learning: How do teachers learn to teach? In M. Cochran-Smith, S. Feiman-Nemser, J. McIntyre, & K. E. Demers (Eds.), *Handbook of research on teacher education: Enduring questions in changing contexts* (pp. 697–705). New York, NY: Routledge.

Fillmore, L. W., & Fillmore, C. J. (2012). *What does text complexity mean for English learners and language minority students?* Paper presented at the Understanding Language Conference, Stanford, CA. Retrieved from http://ell.stanford.edu/papers

Fillmore, L. W., & Snow, C. E. (2002). What teachers need to know about language. In C. T. Adger, C. E. Snow, & D. Christian (Eds.), *What teachers need to know about language* (pp. 7–54). Washington, DC: Center for Applied Linguistics and Delta Systems.

Finegan, E., & Rickford, J. R. (2004). *Language in the USA: Themes for the twenty-first century.* Cambridge, England: Cambridge University Press.

Fought, C. (2003). *Chicano English in context.* New York, NY: Palgrave Macmillan.

Freeman, D., & Johnson, K. E. (1998). Reconceptualizing the knowledge-base of language teacher education. *TESOL Quarterly, 32,* 397–417.

Freeman, D., & Johnson, K. E. (2005). Response to Tarone and Allwright. In D. J. Tedick (Ed.), *Second language teacher education: International perspectives* (pp. 25–32). Mahwah, NJ: Lawrence Erlbaum.

Galguera, T. (2011). Participant structures as professional learning tasks and the development of pedagogical language knowledge among preservice teachers. *Teacher Education Quarterly, 38,* 85–106.

Gándara, P., & Maxwell-Jolly, J. (2006). Critical issues in developing the teacher corps for English learners. In K. Tellez & H. C. Waxman (Eds.), *Preparing quality educators for English language learners: Research, policies, and practice* (pp. 99–119). Mahwah, NJ: Lawrence Erlbaum.

Gándara, P., Maxwell-Jolly, J., & Driscoll, A. (2005). *Listening to teachers of English language learners: A survey of California teachers' challenges, experiences, and professional development needs.* Santa Cruz, CA: Center for the Future of Teaching and Learning.

García, E., Arias, B. M., Harris Murri, N. J., & Serna, C. (2010). Developing responsive teachers: A challenge for a demographic reality. *Journal of Teacher Education, 61,* 132–142.

Garcia, O. (2009). *Bilingual education in the 21st century: A global perspective.* Malden, MA: Wiley-Blackwell.

Garcia, O., Flores, N., & Haiwen, C. (2011). Extending bilingualism in U.S secondary education: New variations. *International Multilingual Research Journal, 5*(1), 1–18.

Garcia, O., & Kleifgen, J. (2010). *Educating emergent bilinguals: Policies, programs and practices for English language learners.* New York, NY: Teachers College Press.

Gebhard, M. (2010). Teacher education in changing times: A systemic functional linguistics (SFL) perspective. *TESOL Quarterly, 44,* 797–803.

Gebhard, M., Demers, J., & Castillo-Rosenthal, Z. (2008). Teachers as critical text analysts: L2 literacies and teachers' work in the context of high-stakes school reform. *Journal of Second Language Writing, 17,* 274–291.

Gebhard, M., & Harman, R. (2011). Reconsidering genre theory in K–12 schools: A response to school reforms in the United States. *Journal of Second Language Writing, 20,* 45–55.

Gebhard, M., & Willett, J. (2008). Social to academic: University-school district partnership helps teachers broaden students' language skills. *Journal of Staff Development, 29*(1), 41–45.

Gebhard, M., Willett, J., Jiménez Caicedo, J. P., & Piedra, A. (2011). Systemic functional linguistics, teachers' professional development, and ELLs' academic literacy practices. In T. Lucas (Ed.), *Teacher preparation for linguistically diverse classrooms: A resource for teacher educators* (pp. 91–110). New York, NY: Routledge.

Godley, A. J., Sweetland, J., Wheeler, R. S., Minnici, A., & Carpenter, B. D. (2006). Preparing teachers for dialectically diverse classrooms. *Educational Researcher, 35*(30), 29–37.

Goldenberg, C., & Coleman, R. (2010). *Promoting academic achievement among English learners: A guide to the research.* Thousand Oaks, CA: Corwin.

Gollnick, D. M. (2002). Incorporating linguistic knowledge in standards for teacher performance. In C. T. Adger, C. E. Snow, & D. Christian (Eds.), *What teachers need to know about language* (pp. 103–112). McHenry, IL: Delta Systems.

Gort, M., Glenn, W. J., & Settlage, J. (2011). Toward culturally and linguistically responsive teacher education: The impact of a faculty learning community on two teacher educators.

In T. Lucas (Ed.), *Teacher preparation for linguistically diverse classrooms: A resource for teacher educators* (pp. 178–194). New York, NY: Routledge.

Grosjean, F. (1982). *Life with two languages.* Cambridge, MA: Harvard University Press.

Gutiérrez, K., & Orellana, M. F. (2006). The "problem" of English learners: Constructing genres of difference. *Research in the Teaching of English, 40,* 502–507, p. 6.

Halliday, M. A. K. (1993). Towards a language-based theory of learning. *Linguistics and Education, 5,* 93–116.

Halliday, M. A. K. (1994). *An introduction to functional grammar.* London, England: Edward Arnold.

Halliday, M. A. K., & Martin, J. R. (1993). *Writing science: Literacy and discursive power.* Pittsburgh, PA: University of Pittsburgh Press.

Hammerness, K., Darling-Hammond, L., & Bransford, J. (2005). How teachers learn and develop. In L. Darling-Hammond & J. Bransford (Eds.), *Preparing teachers for a changing world: What teachers should learn and be able to do* (pp. 358–389). San Francisco, CA: Jossey-Bass.

Harper, C., & de Jong, E. (2004). Misconceptions about teaching English-language learners. *Journal for Adolescent and Adult Literacy, 42,* 152–162.

Hawkins, M. R. (2004). Researching English language and literacy development in schools. *Educational Researcher, 33*(3), 14–25.

Hillocks, G. (2002). *The testing trap: How state writing assessments control learning.* New York, NY: Teachers College Press.

Hudley, A. H. C., & Mallinson, C. (2011). *Understanding English language variation in U.S. schools.* New York, NY: Teachers College Press.

Hull, G., & Moje, E. B. (2012). What is the development of literacy the development of? Paper presented at the Understanding Language Conference, Stanford, CA. Retrieved from http://ell.stanford.edu/papers

Hutchinson, M., & Hadjioannou, X. (2011). Better serving the needs of limited English proficient (LEP) students in the mainstream classroom: Examining the impact of an inquiry-based hybrid professional development program. *Teachers and Teaching, 17*(1), 91–113.

Ivanič, R. (2004). Discourses of writing and learning to write. *Language and Education, 18,* 220–226.

Johns, A. M. (Ed.). (2002). *Genre in the classroom: Multiple perspectives.* Mahwah, NJ: Lawrence Erlbaum.

Johnson, K. E. (2009). *Second language teacher education: A sociocultural perspective.* New York, NY: Routledge.

Korthagen, F. A. J., & Kessels, J. P. A. M. (1999). Linking theory and practice: Changing the pedagogy of teacher education. *Educational Researcher, 28*(4), 4–17.

Krashen, S. D. (2003). *Explorations in language acquisition and use.* Portsmouth, NH: Heinemann.

Lave, J. (1996). Teaching, as learning, in practice. *Mind, Culture, and Activity: An International Journal, 3,* 149–164.

Lave, J., & Wenger, E. (1991). *Situated learning: Legitimate peripheral participation.* Cambridge, England: Cambridge University Press.

Lee, C. D. (2007). *Culture, literacy, and learning: Taking bloom in the midst of the whirlwind.* New York, NY: Teachers College Press.

Leki, I., Cumming, A., & Silva, T. (2008). *A synthesis of research on second language writing in English.* New York, NY: Routledge.

Levine, T. H., & Howard, E. (2010). *Developing a faculty learning community to improve pre-service teachers' capacity to teach ELLs* (Unpublished paper). Retrieved from http://ncate.education.uconn.edu/schoolsasclinics/assets/File/pubs/Levine%20and%20Howard.pdf

Lightbown, P. M., & Spada, N. (2006). *How languages are learned.* New York, NY: Oxford University Press.

Lippi-Green, R. (1997). *English with an accent: Language, ideology, and discrimination in the United States.* New York, NY: Routledge.

Lucas, T. (2011). Language, schooling, and the preparation of teachers for linguistic diversity. In T. Lucas (Ed.), *Teacher preparation for linguistically diverse classrooms: A resource for teacher educators* (pp. 3–17). New York, NY: Routledge.

Lucas, T., & Grinberg, J. (2008). Responding to the linguistic reality of mainstream classrooms: Preparing all teachers to teach English language learners. In M. Cochran-Smith, S. Feiman-Nemser, J. McIntyre, & K. E. Demers (Eds.), *Handbook of research on teacher education: Enduring questions in changing contexts* (pp. 606–636). New York, NY: Routledge.

Lucas, T., & Villegas, A. M. (2011). A framework for preparing linguistically responsive teachers. In T. Lucas (Ed.), *Teacher preparation for linguistically diverse classrooms: A resource for teacher educators* (pp. 55–72). New York, NY: Routledge.

Lucas, T., Villegas, A. M., & Freedson-Gonzalez, M. F. (2008). Linguistically responsive teacher education: Preparing teachers to teach English language learners. *Journal of Teacher Education, 59*, 361–373.

Luke, A. (1996). Genres of power? Literacy education and the production of capital. In R. Hasan & G. Williams (Eds.), *Literacy in society* (pp. 308–338). New York, NY: Longman.

MacSwan, J. (2000). The threshold hypothesis, semilingualism, and other contributions to a deficit view of linguistic minorities. *Hispanic Journal of Behavioral Sciences, 22*, 3–45.

MacSwan, J., & Rolstad, K. (2003). Linguistic diversity, schooling, and social class: Rethinking our conception of language proficiency in language minority education. In C. B. Paulston & G. R. Tucker (Eds.), *Sociolinguistics: The essential readings* (pp. 329–340). Malden, MA: Blackwell.

Mehan, H. (1979). *Learning lessons: Social organization in the classroom.* Cambridge, MA: Harvard University Press.

Meskill, C. (2005). Infusing English language learner issues throughout professional educator curricula: The training all teachers project. *Teachers College Record, 107*, 739–756.

Michaels, S., & O'Connor, C. (2011, September). *Conceptualizing talk moves as tools: Leveraging professional development work with teachers to advance empirical studies of academically productive talk.* Paper presented at the AERA Research Conference, Pittsburgh, PA.

Michaels, S., O'Connor, C., Hall, M., & Resnick, L. (2002). *Accountable talk: Classroom conversation that works.* Pittsburgh, PA: University of Pittsburgh Press.

Moschkovich, J. (2007). Examining mathematical discourse practices. *For the Learning of Mathematics, 27*(1), 24–30.

Moschkovich, J. (2012). *Mathematics, the common core, and language: Recommendations for mathematics instruction for ELs aligned with the common core.* Paper presented at the Understanding Language Conference, Stanford, CA. Retrieved from http://ell.stanford.edu/papers

Nasir, N., & Saxe, G. (2003). Emerging tensions and their management in the lives of minority students. *Educational Researcher, 32*(5), 14–18.

National Governors Association Center for Best Practices and Council of Chief State School Officers. (2010a). *Common Core State Standards for English language arts and literacy in history/social studies, science, and technical subjects.* Washington, DC: Author.

National Governors Association Center for Best Practices and Council of Chief State School Officers. (2010b). *Common Core State Standards for mathematics.* Washington, DC: Author.

Nero, S. J. (2006). *Dialects, Englishes, creoles, and education.* Mahwah, NJ: Lawrence Erlbaum.

Nevárez-La Torre, A. A., Sanford-DeShields, J. S., Soundy, C., Leonard, J., & Woyshner, C. (2008). Faculty perspectives on integrating linguistic diversity issues into an urban teacher education program. In M. E. Brisk (Ed.), *Language, culture, and community in teacher education* (pp. 267–312). New York, NY: Lawrence Erlbaum.

New London Group. (1996). A pedagogy of multiliteracies: Designing social futures. *Harvard Educational Review, 66*, 60–92.

Okawa, G. Y. (2003). "Resurfacing roots": Developing a pedagogy of language awareness from two views. In G. Smitherman & V. Villanueva (Eds.), *Language diversity in the classroom: From intention to practice* (pp. 109–133). Carbondale: Southern Illinois University Press.

Olsen, L. (2010). *Reparable harm: Fulfilling the unkept promise of educational opportunity for California's long term English learners.* Long Beach, CA: Californians Together.

Orellana, M. F., & Gutiérrez, K. D. (2006). What's the problem? Constructing different genres for the study of English learners. *Research in the Teaching of English, 41,*118–123, p. 6.

Ortmeier-Hooper, C., & Enright, K. A. (2011). Mapping new territory: Toward an understanding of adolescent L2 writers and writing in US contexts. *Journal of Second Language Writing, 20*, 167–181.

Pawan, F., & Craig, D. A. (2011). ESL and content area teacher responses to discussions on English language learner instruction. *TESOL Journal, 2*, 293–311.

Pease-Alvarez, L., & Samway, K. D. (2012). *Teachers of English learners negotiating authoritarian policies.* New York, NY: Springer.

Pease-Alvarez, L., Samway, K. D., & Cifka-Herrera, C. (2010). Working with the system: Teachers of English learners negotiating a literacy instruction mandate. *Language Policy, 9*, 313–334.

Perry, T., & Delpit, L. (Eds.). (1998). *The real ebonics debate: Power, language, and the education of African American children.* Boston, MA: Beacon Press.

Pettit, S. K. (2011). Teachers' beliefs about English language learners in the mainstream classroom: A review of the literature. *International Multilingual Research Journal, 5*, 123–147.

Quinn, H., Lee, O., & Valdés, G. (2012). *Language demands and opportunities in relation to next generation science standards for English language learners: What teachers need to know.* Paper presented at the Understanding Language Conference, Stanford, CA. Retrieved from http://ell.stanford.edu/papers

Richardson, V. (2002). Teacher knowledge about language. In C. T. Adger, C. E. Snow, & D. Christian (Eds.), *What teachers need to know about language* (pp. 85–102). McHenry, IL: Delta Systems.

Rivera, C. (Ed.). (1984). *Language proficiency and academic achievement.* Clevedon, England: Multilingual Matters.

Rockman et al. (n.d.). *Report of a field study of Quality Teaching for English Language Learners (QTEL).* San Francisco, CA: Author. Retrieved from http://www.rockman.com/projects/projectDetail.php?id=127

Rogoff, A. S., & Wertsch, J. V. (1984). *Children's learning in the zone of proximal development.* San Francisco, CA: Jossey-Bass.

Rogoff, B. (1990). *Apprenticeship in thinking: Cognitive development in social context.* New York, NY: Oxford University Press.

Rogoff, B. (2003). *The cultural nature of human development.* Oxford: Oxford University Press.

Rosebery, A. S., Warren, B., & Conant, F. R. (1992). Appropriating scientific discourse: Findings from language minority classrooms. *Journal of Learning Sciences, 2*(1), 61–94.

Ruiz, N. T., Rueda, R., Figueroa, R. A., & Boothroyd, M. (1995). Bilingual special education teachers' shifting paradigms: Complex responses to educational reform. *Journal of Learning Disabilities, 28*, 622–635.

Sakash, K., & Rodriguez-Brown, F. (2011). Fostering collaboration between mainstream and bilingual teachers and teacher candidates. In T. Lucas (Ed.), *Teacher preparation for linguistically diverse classrooms: A resource for teacher educators* (pp. 143–159). New York, NY: Routledge.

Santos, M., Darling-Hammond, L., & Cheuk, T. (2012). Teacher development to support English language learners in the context of common core state standards. Paper presented at the Understanding Language Conference, Stanford, CA. Retrieved from http://ell. stanford.edu/papers

Schleppegrell, M. J. (2004). *The language of schooling: A functional linguistics approach.* Mahwah, NJ: Lawrence Erlbaum.

Schleppegrell, M. J., & Achugar, M. (2003). Learning language and learning history: A functional linguistics approach. *TESOL Journal, 12*(2), 21–27.

Schleppegrell, M. J., Achugar, M., & Oteíza, T. (2004). The grammar of history: Enhancing content-based instruction through a functional focus on language. *TESOL Quarterly, 38*(4), 67–93.

Schleppegrell, M. J., & Colombi, M. C. (Eds.). (2002). *Developing advanced literacy in first and second languages.* Mahwah, NJ: Lawrence Erlbaum.

Schleppegrell, M. J., & de Oliveira, L. (2006). An integrated language and content approach for history teachers. *Journal of English for Academic Purposes, 5,* 254–268.

Schleppegrell, M. J., & Go, A. L. (2007). Analyzing the writing of English learners: A functional approach. *Language Arts, 84,* 529–538.

Short, D. J., Fidelman, C. G., & Louguit, M. (2012). Developing academic language in English language learners through sheltered instruction. *TESOL Quarterly, 46,* 334–361.

Shulman, L. S. (1987). Knowledge and teaching: Foundations of the new reform. *Harvard Educational Review, 57,* 1–22.

Solís, J. L., Bravo, M. A., Mosqueda, E., Collett, J. M., & Mckinney De Royston, J. M. (2011, April). *Situating responsive science pedagogy with preservice teachers.* Paper presented at the annual meeting of the American Educational Research Association, New Orleans, LA.

Stoddart, T., Bravo, M., Solis, J., Mosqueda, E., & Rodriguez, A. (2011, April). *Effective science teaching for English language learners (ESTELL): Measuring pre-service teacher practices.* Paper presented at the annual meeting of the American Educational Research Association, New Orleans, LA. Retrieved from http://education.ucsc.edu/estell/Stoddart_et_al_2011_AERA.pdf

Stoddart, T., Pinal, A., Latzke, M., & Canaday, D. (2002). Integrating inquiry science and language development for English language learners. *Journal of Research in Science Teaching, 39,* 664–687.

Stoddart, T., Solis, J., Tolbert, S., & Bravo, M. (2010). A framework for the effective science teaching of English language learners in elementary schools. In D. W. Sunal, C. S. Sunal, & E. L. Wright (Eds.), *Teaching science with Hispanic ELLs in K-16 classrooms* (pp. 151–181). Albany, NY: Information Age.

Tarone, E., & Allwright, D. (2005). Second language teacher learning and student second language learning: Shaping the knowledge base. In D. J. Tedick (Ed.), *Second language teacher education: International perspectives* (pp. 5–24). Mahwah, NJ: Lawrence Erlbaum.

Teachers of English to Speakers of Other Languages. (2006). *PreK–12 English language proficiency standards.* Alexandria, VA: Author.

Téllez, K., & Waxman, H. C. (2006). Preparing quality educators for English language learners: An overview of the critical issues. In K. Téllez & H. C. Waxman (Eds.), *Preparing quality educators for English language learners: Research, policies, and practices* (pp. 1–22). Mahwah, NJ: Lawrence Erlbaum.

Tharp, R. G., & Gallimore, R. (1988). *Rousing minds to life: Teaching, learning, and schooling in social context.* New York, NY: Cambridge University Press.

Trappes-Lomax, H., & Ferguson, G. (2002). *Language learning & language teaching: Language in language teacher education.* Philadelphia, PA: John Benjamins.

Trumbull, E., & Farr, B. P. (2005). *Language and learning: What teachers need to know.* Norwood, MA: Christopher-Gordon.

Unsworth, L. (Ed.). (2000). *Researching language in schools and communities*. London, England: Cassell.

Valdés, G. (1992). Bilingual minorities and language issues in writing: Toward a profession-wide response to a new challenge. *Written Communication, 9*, 85–136.

Valdés, G. (1998). The world outside and inside schools: Language and immigrant children. *Educational Researcher, 27*(6), 4–18.

Valdés, G. (2001). *Learning and not learning English: Latino students in American schools*. New York, NY: Teachers College Press.

Valdés, G. (2003). *Expanding definitions of giftedness: The case of young interpreters from immigrant communities*. Mahwah, NJ: Lawrence Erlbaum.

Valdés, G. (2004). Between support and marginalisation: The development of academic language in linguistic minority children. *International Journal of Bilingual Education and Bilingualism, 7*(2&3), 102–132, p. 33.

Valdés, G., Bunch, G. C., Snow, C. E., & Lee, C. (2005). Enhancing the development of students' language(s). In L. Darling-Hammond, J. Bransford, P. LePage, K. Hammerness, & H. Duffy (Eds.), *Preparing teachers for a changing world: What teachers should learn and be able to do* (pp. 126–168). San Francisco, CA: Jossey-Bass.

Valdés, G., Capitelli, S., & Alvarez, L. (2011). Realistic expectations: English language learners and the acquisition of "academic" English. In G. Valdés, S. Capitelli, & L. Alvarez (Eds.), *Latino children learning English: Steps in the journey* (pp. 15–41). New York, NY: Teachers College Press.

Valdés, G., & Castellón, M. (2011). English language learners in American schools: Characteristics and challenges. In T. Lucas (Ed.), *Teacher preparation for linguistically diverse classrooms: A resource for teacher educators* (pp. 18–34). New York, NY: Routledge.

van Lier, L. (1995). *Introducing language awareness*. New York, NY: Penguin.

van Lier, L. (2004). *The ecology and semiotics of language learning*. Boston, MA: Kluwer.

van Lier, L., & Walqui, A. (2012). Language and the Common Core State Standards. Paper presented at the Understanding Language Conference, Stanford, CA. Retrieved from http://ell.stanford.edu/papers

van Patten, B., & Williams, J. (2007). *Theories in second language acquisition: An introduction*. Mahwah, NJ: Lawrence Erlbaum.

Varghese, M. M., & Stritikus, T. (2005). "Nadie me dijó" [nobody told me]: Language policy negotiation and implications for teacher education. *Journal of Teacher Education, 56*, 73–87.

Veel, R. (1997). Learning how to mean—Scientifically speaking: Apprenticeship into scientific discourse in the secondary school. In F. Christie & J. R. Martin (Eds.), *Genre and institutions: Social processes in the workplace and school* (pp. 160–195). London, England: Cassell.

Villegas, A. M., & Lucas, T. (2011). Preparing classroom teachers for English language learners: The policy context. In T. Lucas (Ed.), *Teacher preparation for linguistically diverse classrooms: A resource for teacher educators* (pp. 35–52). New York, NY: Routledge.

Vygotsky, L. (1978). *Mind in society*. Cambridge, MA: Harvard University Press.

Vygotsky, L. (1987a). *The collected works of L. S. Vygotsky: Volume 1. Problems of general psychology* (R. W. Rieber & A. S. Carton, Eds.). New York, NY: Plenum Press.

Vygotsky, L. (1987b). *Thought and language*. Cambridge: MIT Press.

Walker, C. L., Ranney, S., & Fortune, T. W. (2005). Preparing preservice teachers for English language learners: A content-based approach. In D. J. Tedick (Ed.), *Second language teacher education: International perspectives* (pp. 313–334). Mahwah, NJ: Lawrence Erlbaum.

Walker, C. L., & Stone, K. (2011). Preparing teachers to reach English language learners: Preservice and in-service initiatives. In T. Lucas (Ed.), *Teacher preparation for linguistically diverse classrooms: A resource for teacher educators* (pp. 127–142). New York, NY: Routledge.

Walqui, A. (2005). Who are our students? In P. A. Richard-Amato & M. A. Snow (Eds.), *Academic success for English language learners* (pp. 7–21). White Plains, NY: Longman.

Walqui, A. (2006). Scaffolding instruction for English language learners: A conceptual framework. *International Journal of Bilingual Education and Bilingualism, 9,* 159–180.

Walqui, A. (2008). The development of teacher expertise to work with adolescent English language learners: A model and a few priorities. In L. S. Verplaetse & N. Migliacci (Eds.), *Inclusive pedagogy for English language learners* (pp. 103–125). New York, NY: Lawrence Erlbaum.

Walqui, A. (2011). The growth of teacher expertise for teaching English language learners: A socio-culturally based professional development model. In T. Lucas (Ed.), *Teacher preparation for linguistically diverse classrooms: A resource for teacher educators* (pp. 160–177). New York, NY: Routledge.

Walqui, A., & Heritage, M. (2012). *Instruction for diverse groups of English language learners.* Paper presented at the Understanding Language Conference, Stanford, CA. Retrieved from http://ell.stanford.edu/papers

Walqui, A., & van Lier, L. (2010). *Scaffolding the academic success of adolescent English language learners: A pedagogy of promise.* San Francisco, CA: WestEd.

Wells, G. (1999). *Dialogic inquiry: Toward a sociocultural practice and theory of education.* Cambridge, England: Cambridge University Press.

Wertsch, J. V. (1991). *Voices of the mind: A sociocultural approach to mediated interaction.* Cambridge, MA: Harvard University Press.

Zentella, A. C. (1997). *Growing up bilingual: Puerto Rican children in New York.* Oxford, England: Blackwell.

Zwiers, J. (2008). *Building academic language: Essential practices for content classrooms, Grades 5–12.* San Francisco, CA: Jossey-Bass.

About the Editors

Jamal Abedi is a professor of education at the University of California, Davis. His research interests include studies in the areas of psychometrics and test and scale development. His recent works include studies on the validity of assessments, accommodations, and classification of English language learners. He is the author of many publications in the assessment of and accommodations for English language learners. He serves on assessment advisory boards for a number of states and assessment consortia as an expert on testing for English learners. He is the recipient of the 2003 National Professional Service Award in recognition of his "Outstanding Contribution Relating Research to Practice" by the American Educational Research Association and the 2008 Lifetime Achievement Award by the California Educational Research Association. He holds master's and PhD degrees from Vanderbilt University in psychometrics.

Christian Faltis is the Dolly and David Fiddyment Chair in Teacher Education, director of teacher education, and professor of language, literacy and culture in the School of Education at University of California, Davis. He received his PhD in bilingual cross-cultural education from Stanford University. His research interests are bilingual learning in academic contexts, immigrant education, and critical arts-based learning. Chris earned a Distinguished Scholar Award from AERA in 2001. His recent books are *Arts and Emergent Bilingual Youth* (with Chappell, 2013), *Implementing Language Policy in Arizona* (with Arias, 2012), and *Education, Immigrant Students, Refugee Students, and English Learners* (with Valdés, 2011). He also published "Art and Living Inquiry into Anti-immigration Discourse" in the *International Journal of Multicultural Education*, 2012. He serves as the editor of *Teacher Education Quarterly*. Chris is an oil painter whose work focuses on issues of Mexican immigrants and education.

Review of Research in Education
March 2013, Vol. 37, pp. 342
DOI: 10.3102/0091732X12464621
© 2013 AERA. http://rre.aera.net

About the Contributors

Rebecca Anne Alexander is an assistant professor of education studies at DePauw University in Greencastle, Indiana. She conducted her doctoral work at the University of California, Berkeley, with an emphasis on social and cultural studies in education. Her research interests include youth geographies, racial inequality in schools and communities, and critical pedagogies. Her ethnographic work focuses on how youth and adults "make sense out of" or theorize everyday racial inequality in a time when colorblind frameworks predominate. Her publications include *Marketing Whiteness: Geographies of Colorblind Liberalism* (2011) in the Working Paper Series of the Institute for the Study of Societal Issues, University of California, Berkeley.

Patricia Baquedano-López is an associate professor in language, literacy and culture (LLC), social and cultural studies (SCS), and in the leadership for educational equity program (LEEP) at the Graduate School of Education at the University of California, Berkeley. She examines practices of language and literacy socialization as they intersect with ideologies of language use, race, and class. Her research examines the complex ways educational policies structure practices of inclusion or exclusion. She writes on language practices in science classroom instruction in racially diverse classrooms, trajectories of language socialization, and Latino parent involvement approaches in schools. Her work has appeared in *Linguistics and Education*, the *Anthropology and Education Quarterly*, *Text and Talk*, the *Bilingual Research Journal*, the *Annual Review of Anthropology*, *Theory into Practice*, the *Journal of Mind, Culture, and Activity*, and in a variety of edited volumes.

George C. Bunch is an associate professor of education at the University of California, Santa Cruz. His research focuses on language and literacy challenges and opportunities for language minority students in K-12 and higher education and on policies and practices designed to serve such students. An experienced K-12 and adult education teacher and teacher educator, he holds a PhD in educational linguistics from Stanford University and an M.A. in bilingual education and teaching English to speakers of other languages (TESOL) from the University of Maryland, Baltimore. He was a 2010-2011 National

Review of Research in Education
March 2013, Vol. 37, pp. 343-348
DOI: 10.3102/0091732X12461476
© 2013 AERA. http://rre.aera.net

Academy of Education/Spencer Postdoctoral Fellow. He is a founding partner of the Understanding Language initiative (ell.stanford.edu), designed to heighten awareness of the role that language and literacy play in the Common Core State Standards and Next Generation Science Standards and to use the new standards to improve the education of English learners across grades and content areas.

Melisa "Misha" Cahnmann-Taylor is a professor of language and literacy education and program chair of TESOL and World Language Education at the University of Georgia. She is the winner of Dorothy Sargent Rosenberg Prizes and a Leeway Poetry Grant and has coauthored two books, *Teachers Act Up: Creating Multicultural Learning Communities Through Theatre* and *Arts-Based Research in Education*. Prior to working with bilingual youth and their families in Georgia, she was a researcher and teacher among Latin@ communities in Chicago, Los Angeles, Philadelphia, Boston, and Mexico City. She is the author of numerous articles and poetry about language learning and teacher education. She trains preservice TESOL and Foreign Language Teachers and offers courses on Spanish Children's Literature, Bilingualism and Bilingual Education, Theatre for Reflective Language Teachers, and Translingual Memoir. She has begun a series of travelling workshops titled "Spanish for Non-Spanish Speakers: What Every Educator Should Know." Follow her blog at www.teachersactup.com.

Vera Caine, RN, MN, PhD, is an assistant professor in the Faculty of Nursing at the University of Alberta. Her research interests focus on theoretical issues in narrative inquiry, visual methodologies, and narrative pedagogical approaches. She has worked alongside Aboriginal communities in Northern Canada, as well as urban Aboriginal women living with HIV/AIDS and their families, and most recently alongside youth who leave school early. She is coeditor, with Dr. J. D. Clandinin and Dr. P. Steeves, of a forthcoming book titled *Composing Lives in Transition. A Narrative Inquiry Into the Experiences of Early School Leavers* (Emerald, 2013). She is currently involved in a narrative inquiry alongside Aboriginal youth and their families inquiring into their schooling and educational experiences, as well as youth who are homeless and experience access to care issues. She also works alongside nurses and people living with HIV in exploring ways to address stigma and care issues.

Sharon Verner Chappell is an assistant professor in the Elementary and Bilingual Education Department at California State University Fullerton. She is an arts-based researcher interested in teacher education and youth art-making toward social justice. She holds an M.A. from the School of the Art Institute of Chicago and a PhD from Arizona State University. She taught K-8 multilingual, multicultural young people in Texas and California for 6 years before becoming a teacher educator. She has recently mounted the international bilingual arts exhibition at CSUF titled "Border Inspections: Arts-based Encounters with Language, Culture, Identity and Power." She learns how to live through social justice practices of care, creativity, and critique with her daughter Gillian and husband Drew.

Shaun R. Harper is on the faculty in the Graduate School of Education, Africana Studies, and Gender Studies at the University of Pennsylvania. He also serves as director of the Center for the Study of Race and Equity in Education and codirector of the Penn GSE Grad Prep Academy. He maintains an active research agenda that examines race and gender in higher education, Black male college access and achievement, and college student engagement. He has published nine books and more than 90 peer-reviewed journal articles and other academic publications. Harvard University Press is publishing his newest single-authored book, *Exceeding Expectations: Black Male Achievers and Insights into College Success*. He presently serves as associate editor of *Educational Researcher*, as well as editor-in-chief of the Routledge Book Series on Race and Racism in U.S. Higher Education.

Sera J. Hernandez is a Ph.D. candidate at the Graduate School of Education at the University of California, Berkeley, and a UC All Campus Consortium on Research for Diversity (UC/ACCORD) dissertation fellow. Her research focuses on language and educational politics in the United States and, in particular, how state and federal policies influence language and literacy practices in nondominant homes and schools. Her dissertation examines institutional discourses surrounding Latino education issues such as immigrant parent involvement, bilingual education, and high-stakes testing in English-only contexts. She has worked in public schools for more than 10 years as a teacher, counselor, professional developer, and teacher educator. Her research on language socialization and classroom discourse has been published in *A Companion to the Anthropology of Education* (edited by B. Levinson and M. Pollock) and in *Vygotsky in 21st Century Society: Advances in Cultural Historical Theory and Praxis in Non-Dominant Communities* (edited by P. Portes and S. Salas).

Tyrone C. Howard is currently a professor in the Urban Schooling Division in the Graduate School of Education & Information Studies at the University of California, Los Angeles. He is also the faculty director of Center X and the director of the Black Male Institute. He obtained his PhD in education from the University of Washington, Seattle, in 1998. His research interests include the achievement gap facing African American and other culturally diverse students and the salience of teachers' skills, knowledge, and behaviors in working with diverse student groups. He has also done research on the influence of culture on learning, critical race theory, urban education, and the experiences of Black males in schools. He is the past associate editor of *Theory of Research in Social Education*. His most recent book, *Why Race and Culture Matters in Schools: Closing the Achievement Gap in America's Classrooms* (Teachers College Press), was published in 2010.

Janice Huber is an associate professor in preservice and graduate teacher education at the University of Regina. She is a former elementary teacher and teacher researcher who, with Karen Keats Whelan, coauthored a relational, paper-formatted doctoral dissertation. Growing from doctoral and postdoctoral study, her relational narrative inquiries and coauthored publications, including *Composing Diverse Identities: Narrative Inquiries into the Interwoven Lives of Children and Teachers* (Routledge, 2006) and *Places of Curriculum Making: Children's Lives in Motion* (Emerald, 2011), continue to explore narrative understandings of identity in relation with the curriculum-, identity-, and assessment-making experiences of children, families, and teachers. With M. Young, L. Joe, J. Lamoureux, L. Marshall, D. Moore, J. L. Orr, B. M. Parisian, K. Paul, F. Paynter, she is a coauthor of *Warrior Women: Remaking Postsecondary Education Through Relational Narrative Inquiry*, which explores the experiences of diverse Aboriginal teachers in Canada as they navigate postsecondary, public, and First Nation school contexts (Emerald, 2012). In 2006, she was awarded the Early Career Award of the American Educational Research Association Narrative Research Special Interest Group.

Marilyn Huber currently works in policy research at the Ministry of Education in Alberta. As a secondary teacher, she worked with youth in junior and senior high schools, and their families, in rural and urban Alberta. She obtained her PhD in education from the University of Alberta in 2008 and is the recipient of the University of Alberta, Centre for Research for Teacher Education and Development Outstanding Dissertation Award and the American Educational Research Association, Narrative Research Special Interest Group Outstanding Dissertation Award. Her publications include the coauthored book *Composing Diverse Identities: Narrative Inquiries into the Interwoven Lives of Children and Teachers* (Routledge, 2006). Her research interests include narrative understandings of identity making as youths', families', and teachers' lives intersect on school landscapes.

Ramón Antonio Martínez is an assistant professor of language and literacy studies in the Department of Curriculum and Instruction at the University of Texas at Austin, where he teaches courses in sociolinguistics, literacy and social change, language acquisition, and community literacy. His research examines how the everyday language practices of Chicana/Chicano and Latina/Latino students overlap with the forms of academic language and literacy that are privileged in school settings. In addition, he explores how language ideologies inform policy and practice in urban schools and how students and teachers in those schools articulate, embody, and challenge such ideologies in their everyday interactions. Before earning his doctorate from the Division of Urban Schooling in the Graduate School of Education and Information Studies at the University of California, Los Angeles, he worked as a bilingual elementary school teacher and adult ESL teacher in the Los Angeles Unified School District.

H. Richard Milner IV is an associate professor of education in the Department of Teaching and Learning and a founding director of the graduate program Learning, Diversity and Urban Studies at Peabody College of Vanderbilt University. He is also a policy fellow of the National Education Policy Center. His research, teaching, and policy interests concern urban education, teacher education, African American literature, and the sociology of education. His work has appeared in several journals including the *Journal of Negro Education, Educational Researcher, Urban Education, Journal of Teacher Education, Journal of Black Studies, Teaching and Teacher Education*, and *Race, Ethnicity and Education*. His most recent book, published in 2010 by Harvard Education Press, is *Start Where You Are, But Don't Stay There: Understanding Diversity, Opportunity Gaps, and Teaching in Today's Classrooms*. It has been recognized with two awards: the 2012 American Association of Colleges for Teacher Education Outstanding Book Award and a 2011 American Educational Studies Association Critics' Choice Book Award. In 2006, he received an Early Career Award from the Committee on Scholars of Color in Education of the American Educational Research Association. Currently, he is editor-in-chief of *Urban Education*. He can be reached at rich.milner@vanderbilt.edu.

Deborah Palmer is an associate professor of bilingual/bicultural education in the Department of Curriculum and Instruction at the University of Texas at Austin. A former two-way dual language fourth/fifth grade teacher in California, she teaches courses in the foundations of bilingual education, teaching in bilingual settings, and second language acquisition. Her research interests include bilingual education policy and politics, two-way bilingual education, and teacher leadership in bilingual/ESL education. She is the director of the Proyecto Maestría Collaborative, a National Professional Development Project that aims to build teacher leadership and capacity in bilingual/ESL education in the Austin region. She works with teachers to define and build equitable learning spaces in diverse bilingual/multilingual classrooms.

Gloria M. Rodriguez is an associate professor in the School of Education at the University of California, Davis. She holds degrees from U.C. Santa Cruz (economics), Columbia University (public administration), and Stanford University (education—administration and policy analysis). Her research centers on educational resource allocation and leadership from a critical, social justice perspective and policy issues affecting Latina/o students and other minoritized populations. Her courses on diversity and leadership, social justice frameworks in education, and political economy of Chicana/o communities are strongly informed by the scholarship of teaching, with particular emphasis in critical pedagogy. Within her specialization areas, she recently coedited (with R. Anthony Rolle) *To What Ends and By What Means? The Social Justice Implications of Contemporary School Finance Theory and Policy* (Routledge, 2007) and coauthored (with Lisceth Cruz) *The Transitions to College of English Language Learners and Undocumented Immigrant Students: Resource and Policy Implications* (Teachers College Record, 2009).

María del Carmen Salazar is currently an assistant professor in the area of curriculum, instruction, and teacher education at the University of Denver Morgridge College of Education. She received her PhD from the University of Colorado at Boulder in 2004. Her research and teaching fields include transformative teacher education, linguistically diverse education, and college readiness for English language learners. She has published numerous academic journal articles in a range of leading educational journals, including *Equity and Excellence in Education, Bilingual Research Journal*, and *Multicultural Perspectives*. Additionally, she has published multiple book chapters including "A Journey Toward Humanization in Education," published in *Teaching as a Moral Practice*, edited by leading educational scholars Peter Murrell, Mary Diez, Sharon Feiman-Nemser, and Deborah Schussler. She has also served from 2009 to the present on the Interstate Teacher Assessment and Support Consortium (InTASC) to revise model content standards for beginning teacher licensing, assessment, and development.

Pam Steeves, PhD, is an adjunct professor in the Centre for Research for Teacher Education and Development at the University of Alberta. She has more than 25 years of diverse teaching experiences ranging from the primary classroom to graduate teacher education. Her research evolves from relational narrative inquiries where she continues to explore narrative understandings of identity and transition with self, diverse children, teachers, administrators and preservice teachers, youth who leave school early, and, most recently, alongside graduated teachers as they begin to compose their lives on new landscapes. She has coauthored numerous chapters and articles related to this work including the book *Composing Diverse Identities: Narrative Inquiries into the Interwoven Lives of Teachers and Children* (Routledge 2006). Currently, she is coediting the soon to be published book, *Composing Lives in Transition. A Narrative Inquiry into the Experiences of Early School Leavers* (Emerald, 2013).